Echoes in the Hallways

History and Recollections of 102 Closed Iowa High Schools

James Kenyon

Also by James Kenyon

Golden Rule Days: History and Recollections of 109 Closed Kansas High Schools
Meadowlark Books, Emporia, KS—April 2019
Winner of the 2019 Martin Kansas History Book Award

A Cow for College and Other Stories of 1950s Farm Life
Meadowlark Books, Emporia, KS—October 2017
Winner of the 2018 Martin Kansas History Book Award

The Art of Listening to the Heart
Ooly Booly Press, Chicago, IL—April 2017

Echoes in the Hallways

History and Recollections

of 102 Closed Iowa High Schools

To dear friend Margaret – supporter of the arts & a reader of great literature!

James Kenyon

The education received in the little hometown and high school molded countless Iowans in their pathway to becoming leaders in their communities. Whether a teacher, coach, janitor, cook, or bus driver – they all played significant roles in educating the masses.

Happy trails
James Kenyon

Meadowlark Press, LLC
Emporia, Kansas USA

Meadowlark Press, LLC
meadowlark-books.com
PO BOX 333
Emporia, KS 66801

Echoes in the Hallways: History and Recollections of 102 Closed Iowa High Schools

www.jamesrkenyon.com/

Cover art by Barbara Steward Kenyon

State maps attribution: David Benbennick [Public Domain]

Description: James Kenyon interviewed individuals from 102 Iowa communities, capturing the stories of those small towns, focusing on one closed high school per community. From the year of Iowa's statehood, 1846, to modern times, these profiles capture history, legend, and lore.

BISAC codes:
HIS036090 HISTORY / United States / State & Local / Midwest (IA, IL, IN, KS, MI, MN, MO, ND, NE, OH, SD, WI)
EDU016000 EDUCATION / History
HIS035000 HISTORY / Study & Teaching

ISBN: 978-1-7342477-9-4

Library of Congress Control Number: 9781734247794

To the nearly one thousand individuals from 102 small town communities who met with me to tell their stories on park benches, in libraries, community buildings, museums, cafes, and school buildings.

To the superintendents and principals who led and established the educational backbone of the schools.

To the tens of thousands of teachers, janitors, bus drivers, cooks, and board members who dedicated their lives to the nurture of hundreds of thousands of school children.

List of Schools

Counties

Introduction

I immigrated to Iowa some 42 years ago and my adult life has been immersed with its history, education, and small-town, rural life. I was a product of a farm family and a small high school in Kansas. With only six in my senior class, I never thought of myself as being disadvantaged to a proper educational opportunity.

This book is inspired by this identification with the villages and towns that dotted the countryside after Iowa became a state on December 28, 1846. After the first postmaster in a log cabin, the first school was established. Education was of paramount importance to these communities. Many of these towns eventually lost their schools due to dwindling enrollment, lost population, and economics. Yet, thousands of students thrived through their high school educations and experiences. For that reason, I am writing to try to preserve just a glimmer of this past and to tell their stories.

Iowa's place in American history is very recent compared to the eastern states. However, this "Land between Two Rivers" was explored centuries before by Louis Jolliet and Jacques Marquette in the 1600s on the Mississippi River to the east, and by Louis and Clark in 1804 on the Missouri River to the west. In the 250 miles between these rivers was an expanse leading from the forests of the east to the grasslands.

Black Hawk was a chief of the Sac and Fox Indians. He had seen the white man moving into Illinois, Wisconsin, and Iowa Indian lands. In 1832 he led an ill-fated retaliatory expedition into Illinois to drive these settlers out of his lands. For six weeks with 600 followers, including women and children, he was confronted by an army of soldiers and local militiamen. He escaped into Wisconsin territory and back across the Mississippi to the west before being captured. Many of his party were gunned down while trying to ford the river.

The Black Hawk Treaty of 1833 opened the Iowa Territory to white immigrants. The "Half-Breed" strip of land in the extreme southeast corner of the state was set aside for mixed race descendants of the Indians and Europeans from the Michigan, Illinois, Wisconsin, and Minnesota territories. Though this land was set aside for them, they were never allowed to own the land.

Indian stories are included in numerous histories of these Iowa counties and towns. The interactions and eventual resettlement to reservations and other states occurred for the next 70 years.

The Mormons leaving Nauvoo, Illinois, traveled east to west through the prairie of southern Iowa starting in 1846, the same year Iowa became a state. Some stayed and left their footprints in communities along the way.

The Civil War touched every community with volunteers leaving to fight for the Union. Abolitionist John Brown and his underground railroad visited Iowa before his raid on Harpers Ferry. Towns of Lewis, College Springs, and Lynnville all had ties to the underground railroad.

One-room country schools, which were placed approximately every two miles, dotted the landscapes of every county. The first town schools were often subscription schools where the parents paid a tuition to support the teacher and a building. Mill levies and bonding for schools provided for the school buildings. An explosion of school-age children made additions to these schools and constructions of new schools happen frequently.

Teacher education, state accreditation, and legislation for public education led to the advancement of curriculum and the eventual addition of a ninth, tenth, and finally a twelfth-grade diploma.

By the 1870s, the last county, number 99, was established, named, and recognized by the state government. The naming of these counties offers an historical perspective of the 19th century. Eleven counties were named after former presidents, from Washington to Buchannan. Fifteen were Indian names. Three counties were named for battles of the Mexican-American War, which was fought during the same year that Iowa became a state—1846: Buena Vista, Palo Alto, and Cerro Gordo. Three counties were named after Generals in that war: "Old Fuss and Feathers" Winfield Scott, Zachary Taylor, and Henry Clay.

County seat battles determined which towns would thrive and grow. Midnight raids to steal documents, fires, votes, and general thievery moved the seats of county governments to change in these counties from time to time.

The wellspring of consolidations came four decades apart. In the teens and especially after World War I, votes brought rural country schools and townships together to establish high schools. These high schools provided for the educational advancement in small towns.

Basketball, baseball, and football teams brought a hometown spirit to the citizens and high school students. Moving the basketball practice and games from an outside dirt court, then to the Opera House, and eventually to the newly built school gymnasiums was an advancement in the post-war era.

German, Norwegian, Danish, Czech, Swedish, and Dutch towns became part of the melting pots in the settlement of Iowa. These languages were spoken at home, and English was learned in the schools. A few schools still taught Norwegian and German as part of the curriculum. All schools dropped German teaching in 1918 with America joining in the European 'war to end all wars.' Latin was a requirement in many schools as it was believed essential to a meaningful and advanced education.

"Seventy-six trombones" of *The Music Man* of River City, Iowa, was reality for these high schools. The band instructor was as important as the athletic coach. They brought bands and music to the schools. Participation at local, district, and state contests for musicians gave an appreciation for music to thousands of rural students. These bands marched at parades, Memorial Day ceremonies, community celebrations, and traveled to Canada, Chicago, Minneapolis, Kansas City, and South Dakota. They played weeknights on many town squares for the community to gather and socialize while celebrating the music from the school band.

No Iowa high school story is complete without mentioning basketball. The coveted state tournament was played each March at the big arenas at Iowa University Field House, Drake Field House, and Veterans Memorial Auditorium in Des Moines. This tournament matched only sixteen schools from the largest to the smallest school districts. Both boys games and the storied girls six-on-six games brought a rallying focus and community pride to each school. The lore of the long jump shot at the buzzer, the missed free throw, the coach, and the love of a team is still being told at the local cafes, reunions, and town gathering spots to this day.

A second period of consolidation was spurred by the state legislation in 1958. This was led by the State Department of Education mandates for curriculum change and school size. This caused a tidal wave of closings between 1958-1968. The result was the closing and elimination of districts from nearly 2,500 (including the rural country schools) to 330 today in 2020. The remaining names of the schools have left little identity with a town as acronyms define them. Examples are AC/GC, BCLUW, MMRCU, AGWSR, WACO, OABCCIG, HSTW, PMC, MVAOCOU, and GMG. Others became directional schools with names of West, South, East, North, and Central. Still others added hyphens in trying to recognize parts of each town involved in the new school.

A law passed in 1983 provided for whole-grade sharing between adjacent districts. It put some school districts on the path to easing into mergers one step at a time. First, it was whole-grade sharing. Then sporting programs and busing brought the economic reality of consolidation and the closing of a high school. In some cases, two, three, four, and five schools closed at a time to form one.

Another law in the 1990s, intended to give students an opportunity take different curricular classes at adjoining districts, became the final straw of existence for struggling districts. These open-enrollment students took with them the property taxes and state aide for each student to the open-enrolled district, thus strangling the budgets of the districts they were leaving.

What was once hallmark of liberty is now but landmark to simpler time.

James Kenyon
November 2020

Echoes in the Hallways

History and Recollections

of 102 Closed Iowa High Schools

#1

Albion High School

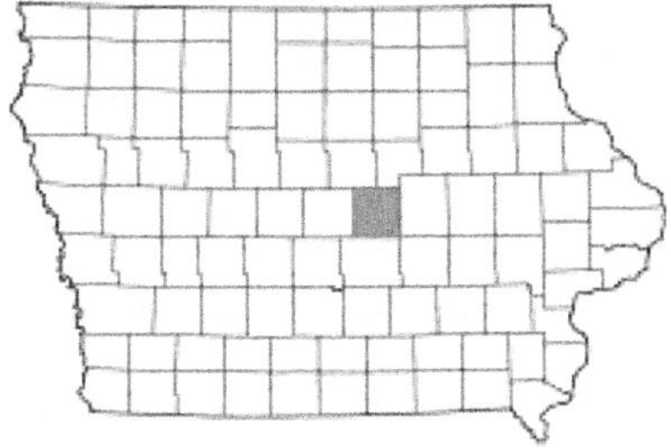

Mascot: Warriors/Warriorettes
Colors: Red and White
Closed: 1962
Location: North Central Marshall County

Early History—Lafayette was platted in 1852 by a surveyor from Iowa City. It became the first and thus the oldest town in Marshall County. The name was in honor of the great French patriot who was General George Washington's leading military advisor during the American Revolution. Marquis de Lafayette had recently (1826) made a reunion visit to the United States (from France) to commemorate the 50th anniversary of the Declaration of Independence. During the six-month reunion visit, Lafayette toured much of the United States. He was greeted by big crowds and veterans at every stop along the way. Naming towns, counties, townships, and colleges after Lafayette was very popular at this time. The only problem with the Marshall County Lafayette was that there was another town in Iowa at the time with the same name. In 1858, the name was changed to Albion. In that same year, Albion held the deciding votes in the quest for the county seat. Two other towns, Marshalltown and Marietta, were also in contention. Marshalltown eventually won the votes for the county seat.

The first newspaper in the county came to Albion by ox sled in 1858. The paper was called the *Central Iowa Press*.

The land that had been promised for the county high school in Albion changed hands several times. It was sold at a sheriff's sale to the Methodist Episcopal church. A college called the Albion Seminary was located on this site from 1872-1892. It was the first institution of higher education in Marshall County. For the next 32 years many men and women received an excellent education. The large, two-story building cost $14,000. A farmer in the area by the name of Swearingen was one of the promotors of the college and it is said that "not $100 in real money" ever changed hands. Workmen took their pay in swampland orders, trading them for goods in the DeShon store in Marietta. Albion citizens subscribed $5,000 toward the building but the subscriptions were paid in labor. Swearingen paid his in timber with all the lumber in the building coming from his farm. Adam Loucks of Albion burned the brick for the inside work, while bricks for the outside walls were burned in the city. After the school closed, the building was turned into a private school for three years and called Albion College.

The bell from the old seminary building was later placed on the new high school in 1915. It rang daily until the school closed in 1962. The bell had first been used on a Mississippi steamboat which later sank. It was then transferred to a plantation. Captain Gideon Wheeler heard its pleasant tones calling in the slaves while he was quartered on the plantation during the Civil War. Wheeler had attended Albion Seminary and he received permission to send the bell to his old seminary at Albion, Iowa.

Early Schools—In 1855, the children of Albion met in a log schoolhouse. The next year it was replaced by a frame building. This was replaced in 1865 by a brick school in the center of town. Ten years later, in 1875, a large frame building was constructed. There were three teachers in the grade 1 to 8 school with an average salary of $35 monthly.

In 1898, four rural schools were incorporated in Albion and a central high school was established. This was among the first consolidations in Iowa. The old seminary building was used until a new high school was built in 1915. In 1952, a large gymnasium and additional classrooms were added to the building.

Sports—The biggest rival was Liscomb, the town just seven miles north of Albion.

The 1952 yearbook, *The Arrow*, shows the Warriors playing Beaman, Union, Whitten, Liscomb, Green Mountain, Rhodes, Lamoille, Garwin, Le Grande, McCallsburg, Ferguson, and Dunbar. At one time there were fifteen high schools in Marshall County.

The boys basketball team won the 1931 Marshall County Tournament championship. Clarence Mann ('49) sported a great hook shot according to his son Merle Mann. "My dad (Clarence) told me one year that the Albion boys had lost all of their games going into the county tournament, and they won the tournament," said Merle Mann.

Dorothy I. Thomas Keeler ('50) remembered, "We played all of our games away because our gym was so small. As a sophomore, I was the tallest on the team and was a guard in the six-on-six game. I made the county all-tournament team. There were two Dorothy Thomases on the team, and I was called 'Big Dot' and Dorothy A. Thomas ('51) was called 'Little Dot.' Donne Nyce ('49) was small but she was quite a shooter and scorer."

Teachers—Avon Burt was the math and chemistry teacher in the 1950s. "She brought books and homework to me after I quit school and moved to Marshalltown so I could finish the semester," told Patricia Poling Western ('59). Janet Wilkining ('59) was another student that got married but was encouraged by Avon Burt to work at home and she graduated with the class of 1959. Avon Burt personally encouraged Diane Smith ('59) to go to college and she became a teacher.

Carol Berthrong was the principal and music instructor. She accompanied all of the band solos and directed all of the choirs and ensembles in the 1940s and '50s. She directed the operettas and had great participation from the student body.

Lura Kaldenberg was the innovative home economics teacher who introduced 18 boys to home economics in 1950. Albion became one of the first schools in the state to offer bachelors training or home economics to boys. A picture in the Marshalltown paper showed Wayne Christensen ('53), Corwin Keeler ('51), Ray McNeece ('51) and Eldon Loffgren making cheese rarebit. Under the study of meal planning and nutrition, the boys learned to plan and cook simple well-balanced meals and to choose foods that were nutritious.

Inez Black lost her husband and went back to college to get her teacher education degree. She was an elementary teacher who followed every student through high school with cards, letters, and was like a parent or grandparent to every student. Dorothy Thomas Keeler ('50) recalled, "She was very strict. She had long black hair that she put up in a bun. We all loved her and respected her."

Band—Complete with four majorettes with tall white hats, the band marched in every Memorial Day tribute at the cemetery. "I played the saxophone and we were invited to Waterloo to play in their city parade," remembered Dorothy Thomas Keeler ('50).

Notable Graduate—Donald Palmer ('25) returned to be the superintendent of the Albion Consolidated School in 1940. He provided leadership and guidance to many of his students. "Mr. Palmer is the one responsible for getting me my first job. I was a rather good typist and he recommended me to Lennox where I started working right out of high school. This typing speed and skill opened the door to me becoming a stenographer and eventually a supervisor," said Dorothy Thomas Keeler ('50).

Hot Lunch—The school lunches were served by the Methodist and Presbyterian church women on alternating weeks starting in the 1940s, and were served only one day each week. When the new gymnasium was built in 1952, the old gym became the lunchroom and hot lunch was served. The head cook was Etta Uhde. She held up the tan three-sectioned serving plate and told the students that "this plate will be clean after you eat." Merle Mann told, "She scared me so much, but I could not eat peas. I disguised them under my napkin. Somehow I managed to sneak them out without being caught by Mrs. Uhde." Janell Uhde Walker remembered, "I could not stomach the canned spinach and still can't to this day. She always caught her grandson and gave him a kiss which really embarrassed him."

School Newspaper—In 1943, the school newspaper's name was changed to the *Albion Arrow.*

On February 7, 1943, was this article:

> The government announced over the radio on Monday and Tuesday no shoes would be sold. People could then turn in coffee and sugar books to purchase one pair of shoes. Each person was limited to three pairs a year.
>
> Many schools dropped baseball for the duration of the war, and because of the shortage of farm help, school began one-half hour later. In November 1943, farm students stayed out of school to help harvest a bumper crop of corn. With the teachers' cooperation, they were able to keep up with their classmates.

Published in the *Albion Arrow* in February 1943:

> BIRTHDAY GREETINS TO DER FUEHRER
>
> by Keith Keoppel
>
> To the Fuehrer we all say, on this, your 54th birthday,
> We hope you're feeling pretty bad
> You sure have reason to be sad.
> You may be worshiped like a saint
> But you'd be better off with your pot of paint,
> 'Cause the Yanks are coming, Adolf, old chap.
> They'll wipe your Germany right off the map.
> Those Russian guys have called your bluff.
> They found out you ain't so tough.
> The British have turned on the heat
> They're nipping at Rommel in his retreat.
> Celebrate your birthday to the last degree;
> It's probably the last you'll see.
> So this to you and your "master race"
> Pooey—right in der Fuehrer's face!

Closing—The high school closed in May of 1962 following graduation. The next fall the high school students were bused to Marshalltown. In the 61 years from 1902-1962, there were 751 graduates from Albion High School The largest class was in 1929 with 25 seniors. The most numerous surnames of the graduates were: Collins-15, Arney-12, Hauser-11, Keeler-9, Smith-9, Hall-8, Fiscus-7, Springer-7, and Thomas-7. The last to receive a diploma from

Albion High School was Richard Whaley (alphabetically).

In 1981 with the decision of the Marshalltown School District to close the last grade school in Albion, a group called the SOS was formed. This stood for "Save Our School". The case was taken to the Iowa Supreme Court which chose in favor of closing the school. The $6,000 to fight this closing was all raised by the Albion community.

Few other communities in Iowa have lost their College (seminary), high school, and their elementary school.

Albion High School
Marshall County, IA

#2

Alleman High School

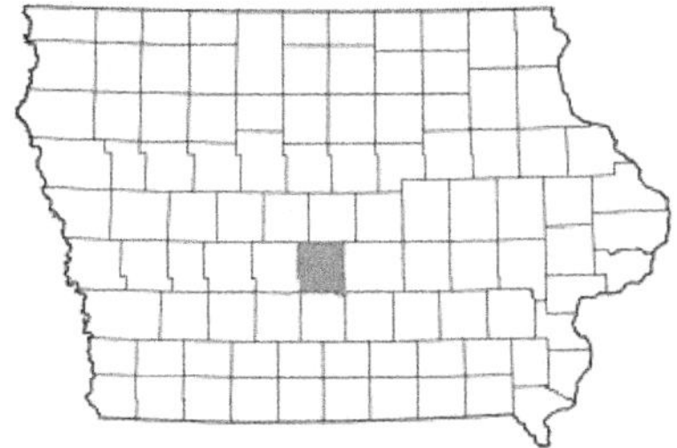

Mascot: Wildcats
Colors: Maroon and Gold
Closed: 1956
Location: North Central Polk County

Early History—The first land abstract in Lincoln Township of Polk County was on November 5, 1855. The land was sold from the United States to John H. Wise.

Peter Alleman and his three sons—George, John, and Daniel—arrived in Iowa from Switzerland via Sauk City, Wisconsin in 1865. John was twelve years old at the time. Other farmers that came to the area were predominantly Swiss and German. Some of these Swiss settlers joined the German Reformed Church. Others (the Allemans, Fauschs, Lehmanns, and Ringgenbergs) formed the Salem Reformed Church. It was organized in 1878. The congregation built a church in Alleman in 1926 to replace an 1885 church located in the country.

John Alleman accumulated land and ran a Hereford ranch on the land that later became the town of Alleman. In 1910, he donated some land for a new railroad, the Fort Dodge, Des Moines, and Southern Railroad. The right-of way ran directly through his land. The railroad named the station Alleman in his honor. John was also involved in establishing the Farmers Savings Bank and the Farmer's Elevator Company.

Early Schools—The first school in Alleman was built in 1914 and occupied in 1915.

The grade and high school were in the same building. This building continued as the elementary location for four more years after the closing of the high school in 1956. The high school at Alleman had many changes from 1946 through 1956. In 1946, the four-year high school was closed.

Third generation Alleman area farmer, Willard Lehmann, gave an account of the transitions during the next ten years:

> The high school closed in 1946 after my eighth-grade year at Alleman. The high school students then went to Ankeny where I graduated in 1951. The High School in Alleman started education again in 1950 with the junior class being the top class. The White Oak High School had burned down, and their students were sent to the restarted Alleman High School. The Alleman seniors received their schooling at Ankeny and graduated in the spring of 1951 from Ankeny. The White Oak seniors graduated from Huxley in the spring of 1951.

The first graduation class from the restarted, certified Alleman High School was in May 1952. By 1956, more changes came for the consolidation of high schools. Polk City and Elkhart High Schools closed and unified with Alleman High School to form the renamed North Polk High School which was held at the Alleman school. In 1957, Sheldahl joined the North Polk school. This newly formed North Polk school would now include the students from five towns: Alleman, White Oak, Elkhart, Polk City, and Sheldahl.

For the next four years the North Polk High School was held at the Alleman school building. In the fall of 1960, the new North Polk High School opened its new facility on the southwest edge of Alleman

Sports—There was no football played at Alleman High School. The boys played basketball and baseball. There were all-county Polk County Basketball Tournaments played into the 1950s. The 1953 boys team, led by Dave Longenecker, played in the county finals against West Des Moines Valley High School. Alleman lost the game but won the hearts of all the big Des Moines schools with their run for the title. The West Des Moines star that year went on to star at Drake University.

The girls played basketball. By the 1950s, Sheldahl was a basketball rival. Elkhart was the baseball rival.

With the consolidation of Sheldahl, Elkhart, White Oak, Polk City, and Alleman—to become North Polk Community Schools—they joined the Suburban Des Moines Conference with Ankeny, Urbandale, Altoona, Bondurant-Farrar, Saydel, Southeast Polk, and Johnston. Judy Bortz (NP '60) said, "That fall of 1956 was my freshman year at the new North Polk High School which was being held at the Alleman School Building. We had students from White Oak, Elkhart, Polk City, and Alleman all together in our school. The next year Sheldahl joined our school. Since Sheldahl had the best gymnasium, we played our basketball games on their court until the New North Polk High School was built southwest of town."

Football started for these Alleman boys with the formation of North Polk in the fall of 1956. Within three years, they tied in 1959 and 1960 for the Suburban League championship with Ankeny and Saydel.

Baseball was played for the next four years in Elkhart, and basketball played in Sheldahl until a new high school gymnasium and sports field could be built in Alleman for the North Polk High School.

Teacherage—The Alleman School Board purchased a building for the single teachers to live in through the early years of the school. By the 1950s the janitor and his family lived in the teacherage. Bill Haugland said, "My dad, Carl Haugland moved our family into the teacherage in 1953. I was 9 years old and my mother, Lela, was the cook for the Alleman school. Dad was the janitor but following a heart attack in 1956, he was not able to continue with the work. My idol at school was Frank Schill who was the girls basketball coach, baseball coach, and the Industrial Arts teacher. He and the industrial arts class constructed an indoor toilet for us in the teacherage. Until that time, all the teacherage had was an outhouse. We still had to pump our own water outside, but at least we had an indoor bathroom."

Notable Teachers—Dorothy Brazelton was the English and Social studies teacher at Alleman High School. She bridged the gap from the Alleman High School and taught at the new North Polk High School. Judy Bortz (NP '60) remembered, "I had Mrs. Brazelton in junior high and she was so influential in caring and melding all the students from the five towns."

"Mrs. Brazelton instilled my appreciation and love for writing and literature. I think often how she inspired me to my writing career. And how I envied her, because every spring she and her husband would take two weeks off to drive to Florida for baseball spring training," recalled Bill Haugland.

Frank Schill was the baseball coach, girls basketball, and industrial arts teacher. He continued to teach at the new North Polk school for three years. He instilled in many boys the love for baseball. During this time of semi-pro and town teams in all the towns of the Midwest, Frank had many boys that he coached who excelled at baseball.

Closing—Alleman High School closed following graduation in May 1956. The school building remained in use for four years and was called North Polk Community High School. The first graduation class was in 1957 with 21 graduates of which nine were from the former Alleman school.

Alleman High School
Polk County, IA

#3

Allerton High School

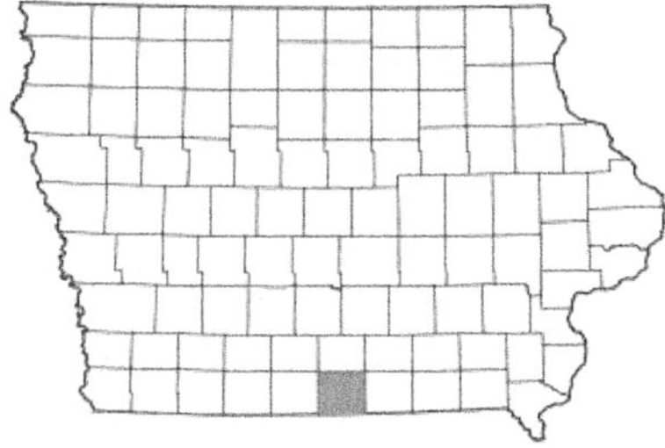

Mascot: Blue Devils
Colors: Blue and White
Closed: 1959; then ACL-1966
Location: Central Wayne County

Early History—Wayne County was organized on February 13, 1851. Judge Anderson was credited for naming Corydon after his home-town of Corydon, Indiana. Corydon became the county seat and is one of the few county seats in Iowa to only ever have one location in the county. There are some early 1850 accounts that Allerton may have also had some county records. Judge Anderson's decision became final to establish Corydon the county seat.

The Chicago and Southwestern Railway Construction Company (CSW) built a railway through Wayne County in 1870. This railroad ran through the towns of Seymour, Kniffen, Grainville (later Harvard), Allerton, and Corydon. The CSW purchased 160 acres about 12 miles northeast of Lineville which was to become the town of Allerton. The town was named after a secretary for the railroad, Judge H.M. Aller, who was a railroad magnate from Leavenworth, Kansas. The depot was built in the town named Aller-town. It was later changed to Allerton.

The railway became the Rock Island. The first train reached Allerton on March 29, 1871. A post office was established that same year.

Early Schools—A school was established in an upstairs room over a business on Main Street in 1873.

In 1876, the "Normal and Graded School" was organized with G.W. Cullison as the superintendent. A three-story brick school was built which was destroyed by fire on February 14, 1900.

Yearbooks—The 1922 *Allertonian* was produced with the leadership and direction of the principal, Miss Eva Burnett, and was dedicated to her. The Superintendent was O.G. Puckett who first established the high school orchestra.

Highlights from this 100-year-old yearbook:

- The band secured their instruments, there being some twenty-five members, and Mr. Puckett began training them one by one. It was a big task to undertake, twenty-five boys with only two or three in any way familiar with any instrument, but he worked and toiled night and day until at last he was rewarded by hearing a few harmonious tones instead of discords. Even with the coming of the summer months that band was not neglected and each night private lessons were given and once a week the entire band met to practice together . . . To show our appreciation and love to the faithful and worthy leader and instructor, Professor Puckett, the Band and Orchestra presented him with a beautiful ivory and gold inlaid baton. The Orchestra had 21 musicians.
- "A Faithful Friend" for the past twenty-one years. Mr. Walker (the janitor) has rendered inestimable services to this community . . . Probably the best evidence of the unfaltering confidence placed in him by everyone has been unconsciously though truly expressed by two of his little admirers: "Well, if the teachers don't know what to do, why don't they ask Mr. Walker!" "If I could have one more Grandpa, I would want him to be Mr. Walker."
- Girls basketball aroused interest this year in athletics and the girls organized a team under the supervision of Miss N. Ross. The team practiced each night and toiled long and hard . . . but the team progressed rapidly under the helpful coaching of Miss Ross, and although were so unfortunate and to lose all our games but one, the High School and town backed us loyally.
- Literary societies had great membership with the Phi Sigma Society and Philathean Society each with over 25 members.
- The Normal training club had 12 members.
- There were eight members on the debate team.
- Football was played though scoring was difficult. Allerton only scored two touchdowns all year in eight games. They played Corydon, Garden Grove, Humeston, Trenton, Chariton, Leon, and Seymour on the gridiron this year.
- The basketball teams played Lineville, Clio, Sewal, and Lucas.

The 1956 yearbook was named *The Devil's Tale*. It was dedicated to the home economics teacher Mrs. Irene Starry:

> In fond remembrance of her untiring efforts in helping guide us through High School that we the class of 1956, proudly dedicate our annual "The Devil's Tale" to her.

Notable Graduates—Bill Knapp ('44) was only 17 when he went into the Navy. He was on the beaches of Okinawa during the invasion of the island in 1945. He returned after the war to Allerton and married Irene Hill Knapp ('45). They had dated throughout high school and were nicknamed the "Hill-Billies." Together they farmed and ran a restaurant in Allerton. Bill attended the American Institute of Business and they together established Iowa Reality in Des Moines. Their business success has made the Knapp family a leader in philanthropy in Des Moines and Iowa.

Richard Henderson ('60) played on the great 1960 Allerton basketball team which reached the substates. He attended pharmacy school at Drake and was a pharmacist in Newton. He has been a principal contributor to the Allerton "Old Time Soda Fountain" and Museum project.

Notable Teachers—Mr. Sam Stites was the band leader in the 1950s. He started the high school dance band, "The Stardusters." Lorena Duncan Blount ('56) said, "He was excellent at what he did and the students responded. He started me on the string bass which he said just added more depth to the musical tone. We had over 45 students in our marching and concert band at the time. The dance band played for other schools' proms and dances." One such night, while playing the song "Smoke gets in your Eyes" at a dance in Ottumwa, smoke starting wafting across the band because of an electrical shortage in an amplifier.

Willie McClymonds started teaching in Allerton in 1951 and stayed until the school closed in 1966. He was a World War II veteran. He taught biology and the agriculture class. He coached girls basketball and track and some boys sports. Lorena Duncan Blount ('56) remembered, "In sports, he made everyone believe that they were special and that they were Olympic material. In Biology, he hammered into us that genetics are so important. A memorable statement he would make was, 'you can not just think about love, you have to know the person's background to make wise choices for your children.'" Richard Henderson ('60) told, "Every freshman boy had to take the course called Agriculture, whether you were a farm boy or a town kid. Mr. McClymonds loved to talk sports and of course we egged him on in class. He was my track coach and helped in getting me to the state track meet in three events. I even won a medal in 1960 in the low hurdles."

Sports—The boys played football, basketball, and baseball. The girls sport was basketball.

Allerton was a charter member of the Southern Iowa Conference in 1934 with Cincinnati, Seymour, Humeston, Moravia, Mystic, Corydon, Garden Grove, and Moulton. The biggest rival was Corydon.

The 1960 boys basketball team was special, posting a 22-2 record and advancing to sub-state only to lose to Moorhead. Richard Henderson ('60) remembered, "I was far from a star on that team. It was a great run and winning was not always our best at Allerton. My first three years in football we won a total of two games. By the time our senior year came around, we were respectable in football and, of course, that basketball team and our run in the tournaments was a highlight for all of us seniors."

Senior Trips—The 1927 seniors traveled in the back of a truck on chairs to Chariton. Thelma Hughes Fennell ('27) was remembered saying, "we were so excited. We had a picnic in Chariton and all of the 25 miles there was on a dirt road."

By 1956, the seniors were traveling in style in cars to the Lake of the Ozarks.

Polio—The polio epidemic left its marks on Allerton as well. Donald Watson ('55) was stricken when he was quite young, and the polio left him with one arm smaller than the other one.

Hal Greenlee ('48), another polio victim, had his throat muscles severely paralyzed. His mother took the thick rubber nipple from a lamb's bottle and cut a small hole in it for Hal to drink from it. He had to suck on it hard and thus strengthened his throat muscles for him to eventually regain the ability to swallow and talk. He became an Air Force weatherman after high school.

Pranks—'Spotlighting' pigeons with a flashlight became quite a sport for mischievous boys who know exactly where they perch at nights in farm buildings. Capturing them and putting them in a gunny sack for the ride to town was part of the midnight caper scene. Feeling the need to release the roosting birds in an open window at night at the Allerton High School was the final part of the scheme. Clell Bryan ('56) coyly completed the story, "I don't remember exactly who the ringleader was, but Joe Snodgrass ('55), HK Myers ('55), and I may have been involved. We were never caught, but poor Glen Houston, the janitor who had to clean up after the pigeons, probably had a good idea and could have picked us out of a lineup."

The Allerton Rexall Drug store was the hangout for every teenager in town. Chrissy Meyers was the druggist and wore a bowtie to work. He was meticulous and everything had to be in order. Occasionally pranks happened to get under his skin. Lorena Duncan Blount ('56) told about such pranks. "My sister Rebecca Duncan ('60) and Diane Hamm ('60) sat in a far back marble topped table and would slurp their malts intentionally loudly. Chrissy would come unglued. Hal Greenlee ('48) made a habit of coming into the drugstore and looking into the large mirror behind the soda fountain while he incessantly preening his hair with a comb. Chrissy would shout Out! Out! and chase Hall out the door."

Closing—Difficult times in the late '50s and early '60s led to discussions of mergers, consolidation, and grade sharing. In 1964 Allerton joined Clio and Lineville to form ACL or Allerton-Clio-Lineville High School. In 1966 the ACL High School in Lineville school was closed, and the students were bused to their one-time rival at Corydon.

Allerton High School
Wayne County, IA

#4

Alta Vista High School

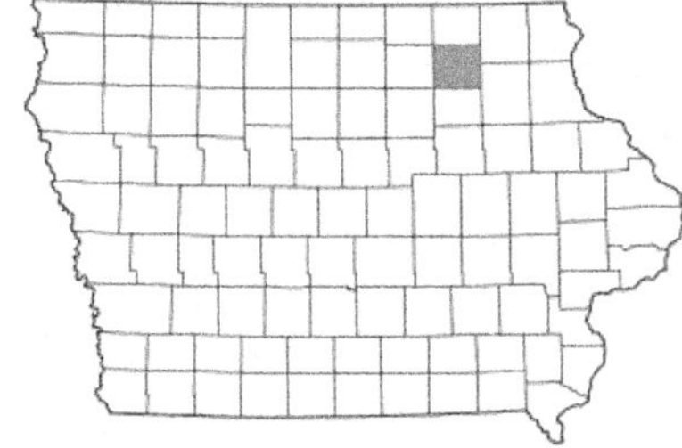

Mascot: Wildcats
Colors: Blue and White
Closed: 1957
Location: Chickasaw County

Early History—Alta Vista means "High View" in Spanish. The town was named by General George Wallace Jones who received a land warrant from the government for his service in the War of 1812 and the Mexican-American War. He was Iowa's first US Senator and credited for helping statehood in 1846. He lived in Dubuque where there is also an Alta Vista hill and street in his name. Jones never lived on his farm on the hill east of Alta Vista. A post office was established on the porch of a cabin of his tenant in 1873. It was called Alta Vista and W.P. Shannon was the first postmaster. The post office was moved from the farm to a village of Elk Creek, which then renamed Alta Vista.

The Chicago Great Western railroad was laid through the area in 1886. This railroad connected north to St. Paul, south to Kansas City, east to Oelwein and Chicago, and west to Omaha. There was much rejoicing in Chickasaw County and towns such as Alta Vista because it afforded shipping produce and greater facilities for travel.

The Cooperative Creamery was founded in 1890 which gave the farmers a market for their milk and was Alta Vista's largest enterprise.

Alta Vista was incorporated in 1894.

The first newspaper, *The Vidette,* started publication in 1899. Per that newspaper, the city council in Alta Vista had several unusual proceedings:

- A proposed "Blue Law" ordinance was passed. "It shall be unlawful for any person, partnership, or corporation, either by themselves, their agent, or servant to open or keep open their store, show, barbershop, saloon on the first day of the week, commonly known as Sunday, except cases of actual necessity." After the ordinance passed by 4 to 1, Mayor Otto Lorenz refused to sign it on grounds that it was unnecessary and unconstitutional.
- In 1895, George Witter resigned as marshal because there was no place to incarcerate prisoners. The council voted to build a "calaboose."
- October 1895, J.L. was paid $30 for building a calaboose set on stilts, and $13 for the fire engine shed.
- October 1895 a request of Tom Caugen and C. Erion to operate a saloon in town was rejected.
- March 1897, the Council voted to have Nichels and Klatt saloon operators pay the cost of hiring a marshal.
- March 1898, the Council paid Dick Tietjen and Bill Bauhaus $1 each to help take care of a "fighting intoxicated man."
- An unusual ordinance was passed by the council requiring the town marshal to take charge of the teams and horses that had been hitched on the streets for over four hours without being fed or watered and put them into a feed stable to have them fed at the owners expense.
- Anyone riding or driving through the streets faster than a "reasonable gait" was subject to a fine, according to another ordinance.

At one time in the early 1900s, Alta Vista had four saloons and in some circles was referred to as "Little Chicago."

Early Cars—Arnold and Theodore Piehn of Alta Vista built the second automobile ever to be operated in Chickasaw County. The brothers were known for their mechanical inclinations and their car made its debut in 1906. They had obtained a circular from REO. Their car was a crank start, two-cylinder, kerosene fueled, 32" diameter wheels, hard rubber tires, and could reach 25 miles per hour. The car proudly bore the Iowa license plate number 3, obtained from the state treasurer's office. The plate was handmade, the size of a silver dollar, and was placed in the front window.

Early Schools—The first school was in 1864 and held in the Gebel hardware building.

One of the first buildings in Alta Vista was a public school. It was sometimes used for a school, hall, and later livery stable.

In 1889, a new brick building was erected. This three-story schoolhouse remained the public school for all grades until the devastating fire of 1953.

Sports—When Alta Vista High School became a four-year high school in 1928, both boys and girls played basketball. There was no football at the school

In 1935 Alta Vista Wildcats competed in the Wapsie-Cedar Conference with Colwell, Floyd, Orchard, Plainfield, and Ionia. Elma joined in 1937.

Killed in Action—Two men, childhood friends, were killed in action. Lest we forget:

Jerome Nicholas Freidhof
Battle of the Bulge 12-25-1944

Paul Johann ('37)
Pearl Harbor 12-7-1941 on his 22nd birthday
(entombed with 1102 on the US Arizona)

Two High Schools and Closings—The Alta Vista school was expanded to a four-year high school and the first graduating class was in 1930; an incomplete list of the graduates has several classes missing. The available records show a total of 127 graduates for 1930-1957. The largest recorded class was eight graduates in 1941 and 1949. The last graduation was in May 1957 with Joyce Alt, Betty Buchholtz, and Bill Forster in the class. With the closing of the high school, the public-school students attended New Hampton High School in the fall of 1957.

St. William's was the parochial school in Alta Vista built in 1908. The Sister's quarters were on the north side of the building. There were two large dormitories on the third floor where the students boarded for the winter months. The first graduation class was in 1921. St. William's High School closed in 1966. A total of 291 graduated from 1921-1966. The largest class was 14 in 1959. The last graduate to receive a diploma was Rita Zweibohmer (alphabetically).

Alta Vista High School
Chickasaw County, IA

#5

Anthon High School

Mascot: Bombers/Bomberettes
Colors: Black and Red
Closed: 1959
Location: East Central Woodbury County

Early History—The town of Anthon was founded when the Illinois Central railroad built a branch from Cherokee west to Onawa in 1880. Many Indians roamed up and down the Little Sioux River, as hunting was good in this valley. Deer, quail, prairie chicken, and wild turkeys were in abundance. The Indians erected their teepees which were made of branches and skins or hides on the riverbanks.

Early Schools—A school in the area of Kedron Township (just north of Anthon) had already been established and named the Fox School, as Ada and Vivian Fox were among the first children to attend the school. This school also served as a place of worship. A cave was built in the hillside to serve as a protection in times of storms and a place to hide if Indians came too close. This school was moved into Anthon in 1890. (Information from the *Centennial Book of Anthon*.)

A larger two-story building was built 1890-91. This building was occupied until 1898 when the growing number of students required a new and larger schoolhouse. The next construction in 1898 was a fine four-room building built on the site of the present O'Neill town park.

Anthon school became an accredited high school in 1900. The graduation exercises were held at the Opera House and later the Methodist Church.

In 1909, the 12th grade was added to the high school. A Declamatory Club with twelve girls in white dresses and two boys in their suits was highlighted in a 1914 photograph.

A brick high school building was erected and dedicated in 1918. It was a classic castle, two-story building with two identical bell towers.

A combination gymnasium and auditorium were added in 1939 with partial funding from the Works Progress Administration (WPA). The cost to the district was $27,480.

Sports—A boys basketball team was organized in 1903. Regardless of weather, all games were played outdoors on a dirt court.

Baseball was the sport for Anthon. The boys played in nine state tournaments, winning the crown in 1949. The 1949 Bombers breezed through the championship game having entered the tournament with 17 wins without a loss that fall. Carrol Swain ('50) posted his eighth victory as he won all three game in the state tournament with two in starting roles and the third in relief. Earl Peterson ('50) blasted a single and a triple to lead the Bombers at the plate. The big blow came in the first inning with a bases loaded single by Bill Emery ('51).

The 1955 Bombers baseball team was undefeated before entering the state tournament. They had won the sectionals by defeating Quimby, Pierson, and Cushing. The team defeated Sloan and Pisgah in the districts but was upset by Remsen 2-0 in the sub-state.

Girls basketball started in the early 1900s. They also played and practiced on the outdoor dirt court. A photograph of the 1905 team shows twelve serious-faced girls with their bloomer type pants hung below the knee, sailor shirts, huge bow ties, and long stockings. Their hair was nicely pulled back with bows holding it in place on the back of their heads. High-top tennis shoes completed their outfits. Hazel Barto ('07) proudly holds a basketball with big number 05 painted in white.

Girls basketball was discontinued for a short time in the 1920s due to injuries, but a few years later the basketball program began again.

The Bomberettes made it one game shy of the state tournament in 1945. That year they were Woodbury County Champions. The girls' teams were Little Sioux Conference champions in 1946, 1948, 1952, and 1954. This was a dominant post-war decade of winning basketball.

A 1953 photograph shows the uniform comparison some fifty years later after the 1905 team photograph. The red shiny satin warm-ups, white tennis shoes, short hair, and beautiful smiles were quite a contrast to their 18-3 record and Little Sioux Champions printed below the picture. This team missed the state tournament by finishing with a 54-44 loss to Galva.

Busing—Bus transportation started in 1946. There were 13 buses used at the highest enrollment.

Cooks—The lunchroom was added, and the hot lunch program started in 1949. Katherine Reynolds was the first cook.

Music—The school band in 1937 had 50 members. Mr. Eitzen was the band and vocal music director in the 1950s. He had 42 in band, 35 in girls glee club, and 30 in boys glee club. This was great participation since there were only 100 students enrolled at this time in the high school.

Organizations—Future Homemakers of America was led by the home economics teacher. As a courtesy to the community, they sponsored a community potluck supper to meet the new teachers. Some of the other activities were Daddy Date Night, Grandmothers Tea, a senior breakfast, a Senior Citizen Help out, and the February Sweetheart festivities and dance.

Alumni Association—The alumni association was started in 1935. Several honored classes each year featured memories from those years. Alumni letters to the banquet were shared from graduates unable to attend.

Lucretia Ann Williams Osborne ('58) wrote, "I think of how very much we wanted to be non-conformists. I remember, when I was in the 10th or 11th grade, Elvis was our idol. I went downtown one day and had Eulis Lewis, the barber, cut my hair very short on top with long sides and formed a duck tail in the back. I remember how mad my mother got. Of course, we wore jeans with our dad's or older brother's long sleeve shirts with the sleeves rolled up (Elvis style). We were really cool and original. I think of the Jr-Sr banquets and the strapless formal—everyone came with sweaters or jackets (because we were hiding the bareness from our fathers) then when we got to school all you could see was snow-white shoulders—no tanning booths in Anthon!"

Gary Yockey ('58) wrote, "One I'll never forget was when right after I came to town from country school. I was giving "Big" Frank Hladik a bad time in the bathroom and he hung me up by my belt on a hook. I hung there until some one came along to let me down about a half hour later. I left Frank alone after that."

Wallace Parker ('42) wrote, "My best memory of my school days was that I admired Mr. Shedd (Superintendent from 1931-45). He was a brilliant man and he could substitute teach any class in school!"

Closing—Anthon High School district closed following graduation in May 1959. The school district unified with Oto, a district eight miles southwest, to become the Anthon-Oto or A-O school with the high school located in Anthon. The elementary school was located in Oto. The buses met halfway between Anthon and Oto and exchange drivers and the high school students from Oto would come to Anthon for school each day. Likewise, the Anthon elementary students on their bus would continue to Oto. A devastating fire in 1965 destroyed the high school. A new modern building was constructed in Anthon. A total of 892 graduated from Anthon High School in the 60 years from 1900-1959. The largest class was in 1940 with 36 graduates. The most numerous surnames of the graduates were: Petersen-24, Ashley-13, Walling-12, Yockey-11, Hansen-10, Thompson-9, and Paulsen-8. The last to receive a diploma from Anthon High school was Joyce Yockey (alphabetically).

Anthon High School
Woodbury County, IA

#6

Arnolds Park High School

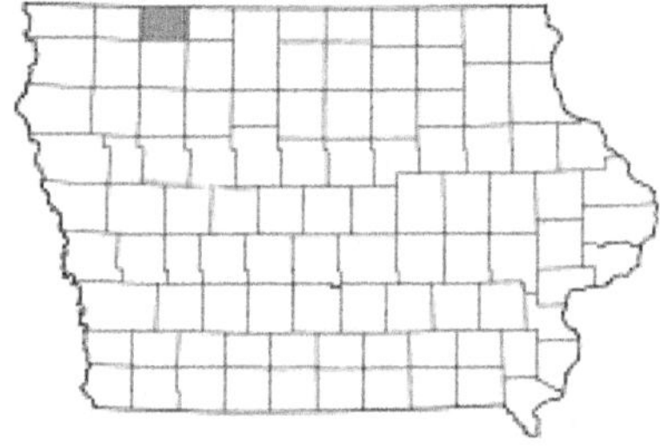

Mascot: Wildcats
Colors: Purple and White
Closed: 1988
Location: Central Dickinson County

Early History—The town of Arnolds Park was settled around the beautiful Okoboji lakes in the same year as the historic Spirit Lake massacre in 1857. This event was the last Indian revenge killings in Iowa. It came in the winter of that year when a band of Wahpekute Indians of the Santee Sioux were suffering through a hard winter. In revenge for the killing of his brother and families at Livermore by Henry Lott, they descended on the settlers in the Spirit Lake and Okoboji area and massacred between 35 and 40 people and took four girls captive. The youngest captive, Abbie Gardner, was kept for a few months before being ransomed in the early summer. Today there is a monument to commemorate the attack and the state maintains the park and the Abbie Gardner Sharp home site.

Arnolds Park, named after an early settler, became the mecca in Iowa for vacationing and the town thrived on tourism. From the first cabins, resorts, church camps, YMCA camps, and the Arnolds Park amusement park and Roof Garden, this town on the southeast corner of West Okoboji Lake became the destination for Iowa and midwestern tourists. One knew that you were a local if the name of Okoboji was pronounced properly. Don Gregerson ('50) smiles when he points out, "There is no 'gee' at the end of Okoboji and ends with 'a'."

Early Schools—Education in Arnolds Park could have been considered home-schooling. It started in the Roland Gardner cabin in 1857 (the same year as the Spirit Lake massacre). The next year, in 1858, Rev. J.S. Prescott conducted the first school in his new home, which was the former Gardner cabin. The school continued at this site until 1860.

The first public school was started in 1862 with Miss Myra Smith as the teacher. It was in the former cabin of Harvey Luce which was at the site of the New Roof Garden (2019).

The first structure built for a school was in 1865 from donations of money, labor, and materials. This 20' x 30' building was used for school, church, and community purposes. It was located at present day Pillsbury Point (2019).

In 1898, a new school was built at the cost of $1,850.00. This two-story building was only finished on the ground floor and the basement for a few years. When the upper level was finished it was divided into a 6th-8th grades side with the other side for the high school.

When Arnolds Park School combined with the outlying country districts, forming the Arnolds Park Consolidated School District, it became possible to pass a bond to build a new brick school building. This modern building, costing $40,000, had 14 classrooms, a small gym, dressing rooms, and restrooms.

The first graduating class was in 1914 with two members, Vivian Butler ('14) and Earl Miguel ('14). They were soon married and Vivian Butler Miguel ('14) came back to teach in the school.

Over the next 60 years, four more bond proposals passed for the community to add on to the building as increasing enrollment and expansion of the curriculum grew. These additions were:

- 1917: $4,000 for a pumping plant and purchased land next to the site to add an athletic field and an agricultural garden.
- 1938: $25,000 to match the $20,000 coming from the Works Progress Administration (WPA) for a larger gymnasium, additional classrooms, and a stage.
- 1955: $123,000 for an industrial arts room, five new classrooms, two restrooms, and a teacher's lounge.
- 1975: $471,000 for a new larger gymnasium with two team locker rooms, two new classrooms, and a combination elementary/public library.

Teachers—Claire Conkey was a business, typing, and bookkeeping teacher in the 1950s. She substitute-taught until she was 83 years old. Verne Eckman ('51) said, "Mrs. Conkey taught far beyond just the lesson for the day. She was shocked that we didn't know the states and capitals. So, right then in our typing class we all had to learn the states and their capitals and how to spell them." LaVonne Kilts Siemers ('55) recalls, "I went to Iowa State Teachers College (ISTC) to become a teacher and can still quote Mrs. Conkey today. One of her favorites was, 'the best way to stay young is to associate with young people—the fastest way to grow old is to try to keep up with them!' That is quite true these nearly 70 years later (2019)."

Everett Maas was the superintendent for 20 years from 1947-1967. He was known for being a disciplinarian sometimes to the extremes. His administrative abilities were known throughout the state. "He may have been the originator of the phrase, 'the buses will run where they can' as heard on KICD radio," said LaVonne Kilts Siemers ('55). School was never called off at Arnolds Park. Don Gregerson ('50) said, "He was such a great math teacher and the best administrator Arnolds Park ever had." Allen Smith ('65) recalled, "I had to bend over and grab my ankles a least once for Mr. Maas's swats. And no doubt I deserved it."

Rachel Forbes was the Home Economics teacher at Arnolds Park. She started an Annual Clothing Revue Program by the Home Economics class. A theme was chosen each year and some of these style show themes were: Living Mannequins; Sew Ahoy; Yesterday, Today, and Tomorrow; Adventures in Sewing; and Dealing with Fashion. Mrs. Forbes added a very popular Boys Home Economics class in 1965.

Sports – Arnolds Park had no boys football. In 1983, a sharing program with Milford High School started in football. That year, 19 Arnolds Park boys would start the first ever co-op sharing football program with Milford.

Basketball was played but there was no conference in the 1950s. The teams played were: Superior, Terrill, Lake Park, Harris, Spirit Lake, Greenville, Rosse, and Doliver. The school later joined the Clay Conference and were the Clay Conference Champions in 1973 and 1974.

Winning the Dickinson County basketball tournament was as important as going to the state tournament. The boys won the county tournament in 1927, 1930, 1932, 1942, 1951, 1953, 1954, 1958, 1959, and 1962.

Mr. Leonard 'Don' Gustafson was the coach for many years. "He loved Arnolds Park and his last years retired to Florida. I received a call from Coaches' wife announcing that he had died in Florida but wanted his ashes to be buried back home. So, when the ashes arrived, we all boarded the 'Queen' and we had a ceremony out on Okoboji and spread his ashes in the Lake," said Don Gregerson ('50) with a smile.

In 1965, the boys basketball team lost its first eight games. "Our coach at the time called the team aside and said we are going to change. Starting now we are going to insert a full court press and start fast breaking at every opportunity. We still played on our very small gym here at the Park. It was so small that every time you crossed half court you started thinking 'shoot.' We won our next 12 games and capped it with a 105-104 victory over who else, but our rival Milford," reminisced Allen Smith ('65).

The girls basketball teams started in 1918 when the high school was first built. A picture shows six girls in their white vee neck tops and dark skirts sporting a basketball with the lettering of A.P.H.S. The girls program was discontinued in the 1930s and revived in 1952. Patricia Ward Schuneman ('54) said, "I was the trainer and did all the bandaging of the girls' ankles and knees if needed. My dad was on the schoolboard and did all the school athletic physicals. I only sort of played because I was too short." LaVonne Kilts Siemers ('55) remembered, "I was probably not very good but we had a great time. Our excellent scorer during my years was Sharon Parks Hruby ('54)." Later girls teams would win Clay Conference Championships in 1970 and 1972. They were Dickinson County Tournament champions in 1958 and 1959.

Other sports were added as follows:

1951 Boys and Girls Golf
1967 Boys Wrestling
1970 Boys Track and Field
1972 Girls Track
1976 Boys and Girls Bowling
1980 Girls Volleyball (replacing softball)

Band and Music—In 1949, new band uniforms became the talk of the town. Judges at area contests would comment on their excellent appearance. Marching band was an extremely popular activity. The 1973 band consisted of 75 band members and ten twirlers.

The band would march in the Orange City Tulip festival in the spring each year.

In 1978, a Swing Choir and Jazz Band were added to the many music activities.

Notable Graduates—Don Orr ('24) was a machinist and had his shop in Arnolds Park. Verne Eckman ('51) said, "Mr. Orr was a very tall man in the six-foot-four range. He was able to build machines and equipment parts for many of the local factories and farmers. He designed and built a machine for Berkley's that made it possible for them to manufacture fishing rods efficiently. I used to go there with my dad to his machine shop which had dirt floors. He was very famous and in demand for his talents as a machinist."

Art Barron ('52) was the 1952 class president. Following his Navy duty, he became a Certified Public Accountant and worked for Desilu Studios in Los Angeles. When Desilu was bought out by Paramount Studious, he moved to New York and became the vice president of Paramount. He ended his career as the CEO of Time Warner. Verne

Eckman ('51) shared, "Art was here for a school reunion when he got a call from California that Lucille Ball had died. He immediately flew to California for the funeral."

Tom Smith ('63) became a Ph.D in geophysics and started Seismic Micro-Technology, a software company which was designed to help geologists and geophysicists in the oil and gas industry. The company grew to 150 employees with offices in Houston, England, Austria, and Singapore. He is a philanthropist and heads an Iowa State Foundation Campaign called 'For-ever True, for ISU.' Tom gives his wife, Evonne, much of the credit for his company's success. Though living in Austin, Texas, this poem he wrote told of his affection for his Arnolds Park upbringing:

> What is it?
> What is it,
> That stirs my soul so.
> Not just mine, but for so many now and so many in
> the past,
> It is special.
> That lake and that place we call the Park!
> We are drawn to it; we are part of it, we are of its waters.
> We are a part of the sunlight, the summer air, the joy,
> The children's laughter of the rides, the clack of the coaster,
> The Queen's lonely horn and the crunch of fresh snow.
> That lake we call West Lake Okoboji
> And that place we call Arnolds Park.

Patricia Ward Schuneman ('54) was instrumental with her husband in starting a business in their basement which evolved into a company with 50 employees. Based in New York, the company supported the entertainment business. With clients such as Bob Hope and the Judd's, the company received many awards at the New York Film Festival.

Allen Smith ('65) became a Vietnam-era pilot and had a distinguished military career. He became a Brigadier General and head of the Iowa Air National Guard. With 3800 flying hours, he was awarded many Military Honors. He returned to Arnolds Park to build and manage a manufactured housing business.

Senior Trips—The seniors of 1950 danced to the Jimmy Dorsey band when they traveled to Iowa State University to attend VEISHIA. They stayed all night in the famed Quonsets on Pamela Court. One student saw a bug in his bed and spent the rest of the night sleeping in a car.

The 1951 senior trip was to Des Moines. They met Governor Blue and stayed all night at the beautiful Savery Hotel.

The 1954, 1955, 1965, and 1969 classes traveled by bus to Minneapolis where they saw the Ice Follies, and performances at the Guthrie Theater.

Hot Lunch—In the early 1940s, farm ladies brought in their extra vegetables and garden produce and canned them in the school kitchen. These were used by the school cooks to supplement the groceries and government surplus that was served for the hot lunches.

A long-time, beloved head cook was Emma Hedrick. She was known for her cream pies. Don Gregerson ('50) said, "She had a heart for children. She knew the kids that may have not had enough food at home and would put an extra scoop of food on their plates. She was said to have been the one that taught the O'Farrell's (a renowned Okoboji restaurant) how to make their pies."

Pranks—Mr. Elston was the school janitor. He rang the bell each morning and at lunch two times about three minutes apart. The first one was to announce the starting of the period. The second one was the tardy bell. Patricia Ward Schumeman ('54), while not admitting her participation, remembered, "One night a bucket brigade was extended across the street and pouring water into the large bell on the roof. It froze solid and caused quite a scene when Mr. Elston tried to ring it the next morning. Upon finding the bell frozen solid, he tipped it over and this massive block of ice fell onto the roof. The next problem came when the consulting heads decided that the ice block may be so heavy that it could fall through the roof. Frantic attempts to melt some of the ice block proved successful and the 'ice block bell' was back in commission.

The school had purchased a new fire escape chute that was going to be initiated. Big Marv Mortensen ('56) went down first and was to catch everyone should they get going too fast and sail out the bottom. The second to go down was Superintendent Maas who hit his head. The third was the class president Jayne Keeler Grenvik ('53) who whizzed down the slide in her light tan colored slacks which were ruined because some prankster had greased the slide the night before. Mr. Maas yelled from below, "Stop No More!" The pranksters are still at large to this day (2019).

Killed in Action—The following were servicemen from Arnolds Park who were lost in the service for their country:

Hugh Allen, WWI
Walter Miguel, WWI
Howard Foss, WWII

Ralph Murray, WWII
Raymond Bean ('38), WWII
Francis Malloy ('36), WWII
Keith McKinney ('42), WWII
Terry Reed ('64), Vietnam

It had been nearly a quarter century since a casualty occurred to an Arnolds Park boy in a foreign war. When Terry Reed's death in Vietnam in 1966 was announced, it brought shock waves throughout the community and the high school. Sharon Kay Wilson Godfrey ('69) recalled, "I was just a freshman and the whole Vietnam thing was just beginning to get our attention and it was so confusing. When Terry Reed's funeral was held at the high school, there was such a gathering and it sunk into all of us that this war was a reality. He had been a photojournalist in Vietnam. Now over a half century later (2019), I remember the gymnasium being packed, the military flags and casket at the school. There was a lone jet flyover at the cemetery. Terry was raised on a dairy farm in our part of the township. He had married his sweetheart and classmate, Jeanne Elliott ('64) and they had a baby. They were considered a dream couple. That day had a lasting memory of sadness for me and our community."

Published in the 1945 issue of the *Snoop* under a title of *A Grim Reminder* in September 1945: "The Honor Roll in the front of our High School Assembly is a grim reminder that the war is not completely over. The 96 names represent the boys and girls who graduated from this school and answered the call of their country."

The Snoop—There was no yearbook printed for Arnolds Park. Instead, a school newspaper called *The Snoop* was published several times each year with gossip, school activities, sporting events, and class notes. A recurrent theme was included in many issues during the school years titled *Senior Ten Commandments for school*. These themes were:

1. Thou shalt not miss class—take the day off instead.
2. Thou shalt not copy someone else's homework—have them do it for you.
3. Thou shalt not run down the stairs—slide down instead.
4. Thou shalt not look at another person's test paper—have him hand it to you.
5. Thou shalt not push others in the hall—mow them down.
6. Thou shalt not whisper in class.
7. Thou shalt not talk back to the teachers—yell at them.
8. Thou shalt not write on the desks—write on the walls so everyone can see.
9. Thou shalt not borrow thy neighbor's articles—take them.
10. Thou shalt not chew gum in school—eat candy instead.

Alumni Association—An alumni association was organized and the first reunion was held in 1934. The association has been active and meets in July each year. Starting with a $450 contribution, an Arnolds Park Scholarship Foundation has grown to $68,000. Initially, a $500 scholarship was awarded to a senior from Arnolds Park each year. Now (2019) there are six scholarships awarded at $1,000 each, paid to the college of choice following one successfully completed semester of classes. These scholarships are given at the annual Alumni Banquet with the student and their parents present. Darlene Maranell ('51) was named the Outstanding Alumnus award winner in 1993 and was very instrumental in setting up the Arnolds Park Scholarship.

Closing—Following two unsuccessful votes, the referendum to close the Arnolds Park High School was passed by voters. The high school was closed following graduation in May 1988. The next fall the students were bused to Milford to attend the newly named Okoboji High School. In the 75 years from 1914 through 1988, there were 1,205 graduates from Arnolds Park High School. The largest class was 1965 with 35 graduates. The most numerous surnames were: Smith-25, Nelson-21, Hawn-14, Dyhrkopp-11, Orr-10, Wilson-10, Allen-9, Anderson-9, Elston-8, and O'Farrell-8. The last graduate to receive a diploma from Arnolds Park High School was Terri Small (alphabetically). A note of significance is that all Arnolds Park graduates are also college graduates of the renowned University of Okoboji. This mythical University is for all of the Iowa and surrounding states, young and old, who come to the Iowa Great Lakes each summer to broaden their education with fun in the sun.

Arnolds Park High School
Dickinson County, IA

#7

Aurelia High School

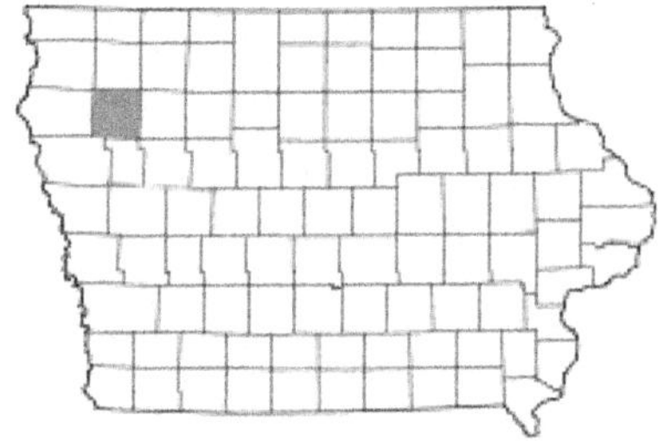

Mascot: Bulldogs (boys)
Atoms (girls)
Colors: Maroon and Gold
Closed: 2010
Location: East Central Cherokee County

Early History—Aurelia was named for the daughter of John I. Blair, the railroad builder. Railroad expansions meant new towns and John Blair is said to have laid out more than 80 town sites.

Aurelia is located in Pitcher Township which is named after the first permanent settler, Horatio Pitcher. He was a native of Maine and was educated in academies in Maine and Massachusetts. In 1869, the railroad was built through Pitcher Township and that year Horatio Pitcher was the first man to break soil in the township and plant 60 acres of corn.

The area around the town was settled by a true melting pot of ethnic backgrounds. It was the Germans north and south of town, and the Swedes predominated east and west of town.

National Attention on Aurelia—From the *Aurelia Sentinel,* May 11, 1916:

> The people of this community will be favored with a rare treat in the opportunity to hear William Jennings Bryan in a thirty minute speech in behalf of temperance and woman suffrage . . . "Bryan Day" dawned bright and cloudless this Thursday morning and as the fleeting minutes flew by it seemed apparent that the weatherman had in store for us an ideal day and such was the case. People began arriving on the streets soon after the noon hour and by the time the Bryan Special (train) arrived at 1:45 a large crowd had gathered . . . As had been announced, Mr. Bryan spoke on "Women's Suffrage and Temperance" . . . The speaker left a strong impression on the minds of those who heard him and without question his visit here won many to believe in the causes that he advocated.

The *Aurelia Sentinel* stated on March 30, 1930:

> The annual Fireman's Dance was held in the Community Hall Thursday night. An extremely large crowd attended and enjoyed the music furnished by Lawrence Welk and his orchestra.

Early Schools—The first school building in Aurelia was built in 1872, just three years after Pitcher first located in the area. It served the town until 1878 when the increased population led to the demand for a two-story, four-room building at the cost of $4,000. This building was destroyed by fire a decade later in 1889. It was replaced by a three-story building built on the same location, at the cost of $15,000. At this time, there were nine schools in Pitcher Township employing 11 teachers. The cost to educate each pupil was $1.75 annually.

The graduations were held at several churches in town. The curriculum was only through the 9th or 10th grade. Students wanting a four-year high school diploma would have to travel to the county seat town at Cherokee.

In 1916, Aurelia approved bonds for a new school, but because of the community's involvement in World War I, construction was not started until 1920. In January 1922, the students walked proudly with their teachers from their crowded classrooms of the old building to the new three-story Aurelia Consolidated School Building.

In 1938, the independent districts north of Aurelia transferred from Brooke to Aurelia. Under the Smith-Hughes Act, vocational agriculture and vocational homemaking became a part of the curriculum. Future Farmers of America and Future Homemakers of America were formed in the school.

Sports—The girls played basketball in the early years (1920s) until it was discontinued. "I was a sophomore when Joan Will, Ruth Renaud, and I went into see the Superintendent, Mr. Renaud. We asked him if he would be willing to let us start playing girls basketball. Without moving a muscle or looking up he emphatically said No!" remembered Norma Nelson Fox ('47). Some of the reasons for this refusal may have been that it was during the war years. The men were at war so there was a shortage of teachers and no available coaches.

Girls six-on-six basketball was started in 1949. That year the girls held a bake sale to buy equipment and suits. Pat Miller taught physical education and helped the girls that first season. They won their first game against Washta. "My dad, Gordon Fett, started teaching in the fall of 1953. The superintendent asked him when he was hired, 'What do you know about basketball?' Dad said, 'I don't know much.' To which the superintendent replied, 'well, you are the coach now,'" said Sue Fett Johnson ('75). The girls went on to win three sectional tournaments: 1955, 1961, and 1970. The girls team went to State in 1978, losing in the first round to Ames 73-67.

Girls volleyball was started in the 1970s.

Boys basketball started before gymnasiums were available. They practiced and played the games outside on the dirt. They went on to win the sectionals in 1940, 1962, 1963, 1972, and 1973. The boys' teams went to state in 1974 and 1978.

Boys baseball and track and field were started in the early years of the school. Aurelia was the District B winner in track in 1951, 1956, 1957, 1958, 1964, 1965, 1967, 1968, and 1969, and State B runner-up in 1956, 1961, and 1966.

The Cherokee County Basketball Tournament brought together area teams for the annual event. Winning the county tournament allowed bragging rights in later years for the area towns. Teams that competed were: Quimby, Marcus, Washta, Larrabee, Grand Meadow, Immaculate Conception-Cherokee, Cleghorn, Meriden, and Aurelia.

The Sioux Valley Conference during the last decades of the high school was recognized as the greatest small high school conference in the state. Teams in the conference were: Aurelia, Alta, Hartley, Sanborn, Sutherland, Milford, Paulina, and Primghar.

The athletic rival was Alta in all sports. Alta is located just seven miles east in Buena Vista County. In 1989, Aurelia and Alta schools started sharing football. The next year all sport teams were shared. Some classes were also shared. They changed their mascot to the Warriors. Students competed successfully until 1996, when the two districts went back to sponsoring their own individual teams. When the sharing agreement ended, the team mascot went back to the Bulldog and the football team started playing 8-man. In the fall of 1996, wrestling programs were shared with Galva Holstein and Schaller-Crestwood.

Music—An orchestra at the high school was led by the vocal instructor in the 1930s. In 1939 a full-time band teacher was hired and both a marching and contest band were organized, eventually replacing the orchestra.

In 1947, a girls vocal sextet of Norma Nelson Fox ('47), Harriet Ohlson ('48,) Ardyis Gustafson ('48), Beverly Ohlson ('47), Patty Clark ('48), and Phyliss Lenhardt ('49) won the district and state contests. They went on to the Nationals at St. Joseph, Missouri.

Aurelia was noted for its Jazz bands and won numerous state competitions. At one time the large vocal groups won fifteen #1's in a row. The band won sixteen #1's out of 17 years.

Pam Misner Allen ('72) and Barb Rath Huseman ('72) were the band librarians during their years in school. Pam shared, "This was a position that included gathering and organizing all of the music and special selections for the band and small groups. That was only a part of the job position. It gave the band instructor a backup as organizing the music for 60-plus students was a significant, time-consuming responsibility."

Speech—Aurelia's speech program was a leader in the state. A special speech teacher came for a few weeks of preparation before contests. This practice continued until WWII when gas and tire rationing made it necessary to add this curriculum to the English department. George Wharton, Jr. ('41) was Aurelia's first speaker to reach the state speech contest with the selection "The Flea Gangs' First Cigars." A generation later this same selection helped his nephew Paul Wharton ('71) receive an outstanding speaker award at the state contest in 1971. The contest work expanded from three declamation events to 13 individual events and four large group activities. For many years, Aurelia had state speech winners.

Notable Graduates—Tom Whitney ('57) received his doctorate in Electrical Engineering and is credited for the development of the calculator for Hewlett Packard.

Three notable sopranos from the class of 1969 were Sharon Allen Stevenson, Glenda Buenger, and Kay Dunkrieger. Under the direction of Tom Anderson, they took their music instructions and talents on to contribute locally, in the state, and nationally. Each, using their own talents in singing, instrumental, and church choirs, have impacted their communities. Sharon Allen Stevenson ('69) stated, "Mr. Anderson inspired us to succeed in music. He always chose very difficult selections for contests and performances. We worked so many long hours to perfect our numbers. The #1's at contests were always the reward, but this education in music led to our lifetime of enjoyment and contributions to others."

Teachers—When Gordon Fett took the math teaching job in Aurelia in 1953, he had a great influence on many students and particularly one prospective student teacher. Duane Kent shared, "I was a student from Buena Vista college. During second semester of my sophomore year, I observed Mr. Fett in the classroom, and he changed my life. I was planning on becoming an accountant. Mr. Fett's personality and teaching methods inspired me to become a mathematics teacher. How fortunate I was to student teach in Aurelia under Mr. Fett and take a math teaching assignment back in Aurelia."

Norma Nelson Fox ('47) returned to teach upper elementary school and was the high school drama instructor. "She recruited me out of the hallway for a play my sophomore year," relates Lynn Evans ('82). "She was strict and stern, but everyone looked up to her. She had high expectations and none of us ever wanted to disappoint her. She continued to substitute teach in Aurelia well into her eighties," Lynn Evans shared.

Duane Kent who had been so inspired by Gordon Fett, taught math for 15 years from 1964 through 1979. He also was the high school principal for six years from 1983-1988. He taught Algebra during that time. He took three years out to work as a banker. He also became a backup principal. Lynn Evans ('82) told of this teacher, "He was an exceptional teacher. He taught math concepts in multiple ways for the students who just had a difficult time understanding the first method. He never lost his cool and was so even-keeled. I would later become a teacher and so often tried to emulate Mr. Kent's delivery and mannerisms. Our students and community were so fortunate that he chose Aurelia to leave his mark on so many students here."

Both Duane Buttenob, who coached basketball from 1963-1987, and Myron Radke, who coached football, were named to the State Coaching Hall of Fame.

Lynn Evans ('82) was the superintendent of schools back in his hometown when the districts of Alta and Aurelia joined. Under his calm leadership, this unification was communicated to both communities in an excellent manner. Sharing teams together in the 1990s led to a mutual respect and success of the new Alta Aurelia High School.

Cooks—Imagine Parrot Galvin ('49) was loved by every student and teacher as the school cook for 30 years. Thursday's were a special chili and cinnamon roll lunch. Bread and butter sandwiches were always provided, and the boys dipped them into the chili to eat. The boys were allowed to come back into the kitchen and make their own bread and butter sandwiches if the supply ran short. Many mothers could not satisfy their children with their own chili served at home. "But your chili doesn't taste like Jeannie's" was the comment the mothers heard from their youngsters. Some fifty years later, in 2019 at a group meeting, Imagine Parrot Galvin ('49) smiled and shared her secrets, "The key to the chili is that I ground the beans and the kids didn't even know that the chili had beans in it." Duane Kent, a teacher reminisced, "On fried chicken day, there was always a chicken giblet pan. We could take as many of these fried morsels as we liked and they were so delicious."

Pranks—The mystery of the cow appearing on the third floor of the high school in 1948 went unsolved for nearly 70 years. The cow arrived on a Friday night after the janitor had gone home for the weekend. "Bossie" had free roam of the entire floor until Monday morning, when she was found early by the janitor. With the statutes of limitation long passed and in a true confessions moment, a very innocent-acting, Imagine Parrott Galvin ('49) confessed, "It was a dark and stormy night. Well, maybe not exactly like that, but there were six of us; Vernon Kaskey ('49), Don Mummert ('49), Dorothy Bengtson Fregen ('49), John Lockin ('49), Betty Spitzbarth Wieland ('49), and me. The cow led quite well going up the stairs in the dark. As I recall, she was not quite so willing to go back down the stairs on Monday morning. Miraculously, other than a few areas where she had relieved herself, there was very little damage done."

During the time of the late 1960s when long hair became the norm, Aurelia was not immune to the national trends. Early attempts at a dress and grooming code did not affect the "long hairs" of the time. Four boys who were not in compliance had been advised by the principal to get their hair cut. The next attempt was a scene at an away basketball game in the neighboring rival Alta's gymnasium. As the game was about to start, in walked Brad Johnson ('69), Drew Coombs, Tim Coombs ('68), and Mike Westphal ('69). Gone was the long hair, and it was modified into a perfect Mohawk. They had just reached the top of the bleachers when the principal, Roger Miller, caught them and motioned with his finger to come back down to the bottom. The new hair style gave each of them a three-day vacation from school.

Closing—The Aurelia High School closed after graduation in May 2010. In the 113 years from 1898 through 2010, there were 3,227 graduates from the high school. The most numerous surnames of the graduates were: Nelson-97, Johnson-90, Peterson-77, Anderson-70, Coombs-34, Mummert-32, Ohlson-28, Gustafson-27, Miller-2, Winterhof-25, Bruce-23, Galvin-23, Kolpin-23, Carlson-2, Bengston-21, Otto-21, Parrot-21, and Allen-20. The last to receive a diploma from Aurelia High School was Hilary Elizabeth Zarr (alphabetically). In the fall of 2010, the students were bused to Alta to begin the year as the new Alta Aurelia High School.

Aurelia High School
Cherokee County, IA

#8

Batavia High School

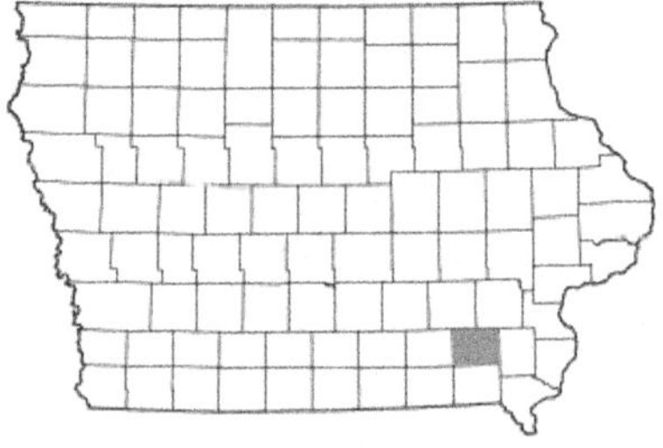

Mascot: Warriors/Warriorettes
Colors: Blue and White
Closed: 1958
Location: West Jefferson County

Early history—Batavia is on the western border of Jefferson county in Locust Township. The Wapello county line is only one mile west of Batavia. Early documented accounts say that there were close to 2,000 settlers and families camped in this area waiting for the push into Wapello county when government opened that land for settlement in 1843. This spot was referred at the time as "Hominy Town" because of a large, black hominy pot which was passed from family to family.

On May 1, 1843, when the shot was fired that marked the opening of Wapello county to settlement, most of the families rushed to claim their new land. Among those who remained in Hominy Town were three men who had bought there on July 6, 1838 when Locust Township land sold for $1.25 an acre. These three men were Elijah O'Bannon, William McKee, and Henry Creese. They conceived of the idea of founding a town and they hired the county surveyor David Switzer. Switzer laid out the town of Creeseville on August 26, 1846. The plat was recorded on September 26, 1846.

The first Justice of the Peace was John Sloan, whose "courts" were held in an old log hut without a window. It later became a schoolhouse. William McKee was the first postmaster and held the office under appointment from President James K. Polk.

In 1853, the Iowa legislature authorized changing of the name from the original Creeseville to Botavia. The common usage made the spelling become 'Batavia' by the time the town was incorporated in 1853.

The Mississippi and Missouri Railroad (M&M) was built through the south edge of town in 1859. Track was laid to Ottumwa, ten miles west of Batavia, when the Civil War halted construction. The M&M became the Chicago, Burlington, and

Quincy Railroad (CB&Q). An addition to the south part of town was called Whitwood's Addition. It was on forty acres and bounded by the line of the CB&Q. Whitwood was an agent of a Boston company who purchased eighty acres of land lying south of the original town site which was divided into equal parts by the railroad.

The westbound morning train and the east-bound morning train took workers to Ottumwa and provided mail delivery twice daily to Batavia. The train also brought lumber and sand to Batavia by rail. The loaded car was pulled off to a sidetrack and was unloaded in 24 hours. Local youth were hired to unload the cars.

Early Schools—The first school held in Batavia was in a little log cabin in a field. The next school was described as the pride of the town and located at the north end. It was a large one-room building built in 1855.

The Independent School District of Batavia was organized in 1862. In 1866, the schoolhouse was moved along with the rest of the town toward the railroad. It was placed just northwest of where the community center building is today (2020).

The third schoolhouse in Batavia was built in 1870 at the location of the present building (2020). This large three-room building had two rooms below and one large room above. Later, two more rooms were added on the south side. When digging the foundation, a human skeleton was unearthed. Scary tales were told to youngsters if they were not good in school. Very few were brave enough to go near the area alone after dark.

This school lasted until March 16, 1914, when, at 8:00 AM, the cry of fire resounded through the streets of Batavia. The fire started inside the large hall and shut off all the ways to get to the upper rooms where the records were kept. Lost in the fire were the first 50 years of the school's history and graduation information. School was held for the next two months in the Methodist Church, the IOOF Hall, Copeland's Hall, and the Masonic Hall.

Built within six months, the new brick three-story school building was occupied on September 14, 1914. The entire building cost $20,450.

A gymnasium was dedicated on December 27, 1927, with doubleheader games against Lockridge. The girls won 29-9 and the boys completed the sweep 30-16.

Sports—The girls basketball team was organized in 1903 and boys basketball started in 1912. The 1953 girls team was the Jefferson County Tournament champions.

The basketball teams played in the Je-Wa-Ke (Jefferson, Wapello, and Keokuk) Conference organized in 1952 with Ollie, Agency, Hedrick,

Packwood, Farson, and Batavia. In the final season in 1958, the schools which Batavia played were Farson, Ollie, Douds, Agency, Pleasant Plain, Libertyville, Packwood, Lockridge, Hedrick, Birmingham, Eldon, Fairfield, and Blakesburg.

Yearbook—The yearbook was called *Chieftain*.

Notable teacher—Lloyd Ruby was the band and music teacher in Batavia in the 1950s. His bands had community concerts and provided the music for the basketball games. They traveled to parades in Ottumwa and the Drake Relays. When the high school closed in 1958, Mr. Ruby continued teaching music at the new Cardinal High School. Brother and sister, Randy and Judy Major, started playing the trombone and drums while at Batavia grade school and continued with Mr. Ruby at the new Cardinal High School band.

Aileen Emry was the home economics and typing teacher through the 1950s until the high school closed. Mary Dunne Campbell ('58) remembered, "Mrs. Emry was wheelchair bound. She cared about everybody. Two years of typing were required and did she ever put us through the drills."

School General Rules—The General Rules of the school were prominently posted:

Attendance

a. There are two kinds of absence excused and unexcused.
b. Unexcused absences will result in F's for all classes missed and double time for all missed must be made up.
c. The sole judge of the excuse being unexcused or excused will be the administrative official.
d. Repeated unexcused absence will result in dismissal.
e. Excused absences are as follows:
    1. Illness.
    2. Death in the immediate family.
    3. Seasonal work when requested by the parents in advance.
    4. School sponsored activities.
    5. Exceptional excused left to the administrator.
f. Excuses must be in the hands of the administrator and passed by him before the student will be allowed in classes after absence or tardiness. Failure of this results in absence or tardiness being unexcused. Excuses must be written and signed by the parent.
g. All schoolwork for the time missed on excused absence must be made up before a grade will be allowed.
h. Unexcused and excused tardiness will be treated the same as absence except that each unexcused tardiness will require at least one hour make up time.
i. No parental telephone call for excuses except in emergency cases. Leaving school for a part of the day requires a written excuse in the hands of the administrator before leaving. Violations of this rule means unexcused absence.
j. Tardiness during class changes in school will be treated as unexcused tardiness.
k. Study Hall periods are to be regarded as classes. Absence or tardiness from them will be treated as any other class.

Janitor—Leo Reid was a longtime janitor. Randy Major (Cardinal '67) recalled, "He seemed to like the girls and was hard on the boys." Judy Major Dovico (Cardinal '66) smiled as she remembered, "Mr. Reid pulled most of my teeth. I did not loose my teeth early like most kids my age. Every morning Mr. Reid saw me and asked if I had lost any teeth overnight. They would be wiggling, and he always assisted in their removal."

Killed in Action—Locust Township lost two men in service to the country:

William Harness, WWII
Marvin Weigler, WWII

Cooks—The hot lunch program was started in 1945. The cooks were Mildred Reid, Martha Salts, and Herma Park. "They made all of the bread and the homemade buns, the smell started permeating the classrooms each morning. Another specialty was sauerkraut. That smell in the morning was so distinct," remembered Randy Major (Cardinal '67).

Closing—Forced by the state legislature due to financial concerns, Batavia High School closed after graduation in May 1958. From 1917-1958 there were 438 graduates from Batavia High School. The largest class was 25 seniors in 1932. The most numerous surnames of the graduates were: Curtis-13, Gorman-13, Whitmore-12, Frescoln-9, Harris-9, Walker-9, and Davis-7. (Records destroyed in the fire of 1914, and several missing graduation lists for 1915, 1916, and 1937, are not included in these numbers.)

The last to receive a diploma from Batavia High School was True Wheeldon (alphabetically). Some discrepancy exists whether the class of 1957 or 1958 was the last class that had the diploma naming Batavia. Betty Wood ('57), the superintendent's daughter, was the last graduate in the class of 1957 (alphabetically).

A new consolidated school was built north of Eldon called Cardinal High School. In the fall of 1957, the Batavia students were allowed to take classes at Eldon and Agency but were still at the Batavia building. In the fall of 1960, all high school students were bused to Cardinal High School, which had been completed north of Eldon. This school had students from four counties of Wapello, Jefferson, Davis, and Van Buren. The schools that joined at Cardinal were Eldon, Selma, Agency, and Batavia.

Batavia High School
Jefferson County, IA

#9

Beaman High School

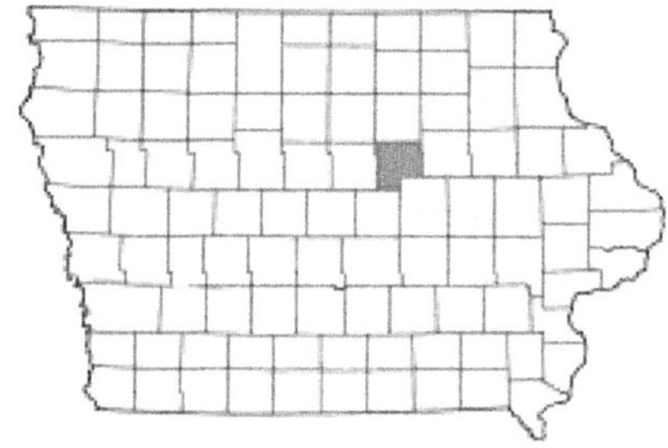

Mascot: Wildcats
Colors: Black and Gold
Closed: 1958
Location: South Grundy County

Early History—The town name of Beaman comes from Henry and Sarah Beaman. Henry's father, S.S. Beaman, and two sons, Harrison and Horace, came to Clay township and Grundy County. By 1860, the Beaman's owned 1,165 acres. Their land was situated partly along Wolf Creek and the remaining three miles north on the Grundy prairies. The products of this immense tract of land were 4,500 bushels of wheat, 1,000 bushels of oats, and 125 acres of corn, which proved only a tolerable crop.

Horace went into the Union Army at the age of 18, and made a noble record there. Noble record may seem like an understatement as Nedra Fitzgerald Vint wrote for the *Beaman Centennial* in 1976:

> Horace S. Beaman was in the Co. II 8th Regiment of the Iowa Cavalry during the Civil War. He was a prisoner and placed in the infamous Andersonville Prison Camp in August 1864. While there he suffered from swamp fever, diarrhea, stomach and liver disease, scurvy, and rheumatism . . . He applied for a pension for his incapacities in 1891 and was sent a voucher for $36.20 with a request for his signature. He replied "Dear sirs, on the day I received the certificate and voucher for the magnificent fortune, I sent them with my compliments to Green R. Baun at Washington D.C. No sir, not since I left Andersonville have I been hungry enough to accept a pension of $2.00 per month. You can do whatever you think best with the fortune. Yours very respectively, H.S. Beaman."

It was his brother, H.H. Beaman, who gave the town site to the community. The town was first called Wadeloupe but became Beaman upon the donation of the land by Beaman.

Railroads—The town of Beaman came into existence when the old narrow-gauge road from Liscomb made its terminus. From the Marshalltown paper in March 1913:

> And the railroad was built from Liscomb to Beaman a distance of 12 miles with Liscomb as the headquarters. The official name of the railroad was the Farmers Union but more popularly it was termed Tripp's Basswood railroad. The rails sawed out of basswood trees were made by John Tripp at his sawmill one mile west of Liscomb. The rails were laid to a narrow gauge and steam trains were operated over the line for a period of six months. If J.B. Grinnell had lived the basswood rails would have been supplanted by steel, it is said but this dream was never realized. The little locomotives and rolling track passed into the hands of the narrow gauge road that later ran from Ames to Des Moines

The first train rolled into Beaman on Christmas Eve 1875. The railroad suspended business in 1876. The railroad was built by the Farmers Union and for six months the trains were transported by steam engine. These were abandoned as too expensive and horses were substituted. The town was incorporated in 1884. The population ranged around 200. With the advent of the extension of the Chicago and Northwestern Railroad through the county, Beaman took a spurt of growth and population grew to near 400. As many as four passenger trains passed through town until 1941 when they were pulled.

Early Schools—In the first year of consolidation in 1917, the Civil War prisoner, H.S. Beaman, gave five acres of land for a new school location. This consolidation included three districts in Grundy and one in Marshall Counties. At the all-school reunion for 1971, Jennie Rowe Stull ('06) reported:

> I graduated with the class of 1906, with eight in my class. School days and school ways have changed since my days, but we all share one thing in common and that is our love and loyalty to dear old Beaman High. I entered the Beaman school in 1895 . . . the seventh, eighth, ninth, and tenth grades were on the second story in one room and German and Electricity were taught in a second one. The high school subjects taught were Algebra, Latin, Ancient and Medieval History, Physical Geography, Rhetoric, and Civics.

When the school added the 11th and 12th grades, Physics, Geometry, Biology, and Political Economy were added to the curriculum.

Hattie Foster Miller wrote about her memories of the school:

> The first school was held on the WW Brooks farm in 1857. The school had no desks and we put our books on the benches behind us. In the winter of 1858-59, school was held in a log house just south of Wolf Creek on a farm owned by Simon Clay. Clay Township is named for him . . . The old Beaman school house was built east of town on the ground which is presently Oakland Cemetery. I had schooling at Albion Academy. My first position was teaching school where I taught all six terms. I taught the spring term in the old Beaman school. It was then called Sub-District No. 1 Clay Township. That was the spring of 1866. I remember it especially as I finished the term before I was 16 years old . . . The Wolfs Grove school was located Northeast of Beaman Cemetery and in 1881 was moved into Beaman. The building was later torn down and replaced with a two story, four room building. This building remained in use until the first consolidation in 1917 when it was torn down and the new school was erected.

This account was recorded in the *Beamans "First 100 years"* centennial in 1976 by Elizabeth Vint Boss ('32).

Band—Beaman was known for its bands. As early as 1892, the Beaman Band uniforms were well known in the vicinity for their music. They played concerts on Saturday evenings each week.

Dorothy Stull McMartin ('19) wrote in the *Beamans "First 100 years"* book:

My mother graduated from high school in 1889, Grace Evans Stull ('89). She married Guy H. Stull in June of 1897. Since he was a farmer and it was a busy season, they had no honeymoon. The Beaman Band was invited to Holland, Iowa (12 miles north) that summer for the Fourth of July celebration. My father (Guy) was the drummer for the band. Mother reported they were treated like kings and queens. Everything was free to the band and their families. Mother always said they went to Holland for their honeymoon. Transportation was by horse and buggy.

When news of the end of World War I was flashed over the telegraph wires on November 11, 1918, the happy news spread by word of mouth and then by telephone to the entire town. Bells rang and whistles blew.

Nedra Fitzgerald Vint ('25) wrote:

A delegation came from Conrad inviting the Band and town to come to Conrad that night to attend their celebration. That afternoon young people met in homes and made confetti out of newspapers to take with them that evening. At 7:00, led by the Beaman Band, we marched up Conrad's Main Street where a huge German flag had been spread in the street, then on to the school grounds . . . A large stand had been built where various people gave talks and groups sang . . . free coffee and hotdogs . . . An Effigy of Kaiser Bill was hung and later consigned to a huge bonfire. The Beaman band played all during the evening. We all sang the World War I songs, "K-K-K-Katy, There's a Long Long Trail, Long Boy, Goodbye Broadway-Hello France, Keep the Home Fires Burning, and Over There." We were a tired but happy group that wended our way back to home to Beaman after the celebration.

High School Band—It was after a lapse of some 25 years in the Beaman community, but in 1948 a modern day "Music Man" came to teach and start a band at the high school. Sherman Botts inspired the students, and the fledgling band made a community relive its previous love of a band. The students' mothers served dinners of fried chicken in the city park to crowds of over 350 to raise money for the band uniforms. For a quarter, the community bought the chicken dinner of two pieces and another piece for ten cents along with the menu of mashed and French potatoes and gravy, potato salad, kidney bean salad, Waldorf salad, hot rolls, coffee, milk, Kool-Aid, ice cream cones, ice cream sandwiches, assorted pies and cakes, plus a culinary masterpiece of green custard topped with whipped cream. Enough money was raised to make the new uniforms a reality.

"Oh, he was renowned to having a temper as he would often break the baton on the music stand as he directed his startup musicians," told Barb Kospa Ream ('56). Before long most of the student body had an instrument in their hands.

The next band director to come to the high school was Marlyn Ridout. Sharon Cain Ziesman ('58) shared, "He had played with the John Philip Sousa Band. We went to the music contests and won #1s every year with the band and small groups. Every year in our selections we would have at least one Sousa march. The one year we did not play a Sousa march we got a second, so we did not make that mistake again. I played the clarinet as did Pat Ashton Reuter ('59-Beaman Conrad) and Barb Kospa Ream ('56). My classmate, Richard Stewart ('58) played the cornet." Leon Webb ('54) remembered, "Mr. Ridout always teased me about my cornet playing and practicing. My dad played in a band and also the church organ at the Methodist church. Dad insisted that I play the piano and I had to practice three a hours a day. Mr Ridout would say, 'Webb you'd be a surprisingly good cornet player if you'd practice it the way you do the piano.'"

Richard Stewart ('58) elaborated, "It is true that I played the cornet, but the cornet trio of Leon Webb ('54), Larry Zink ('56), and Roger Hertema ('57) was the most outstanding and won many honors at contests."

"We wore black pants and white shirt and were always so proud of our band marching in parades," recalled Leon Webb ('54). "We played at the Beaman bandshell in the park, designed by my father Leon Sr. It still stands and is the center of the annual Memorial Day celebration which brings hundreds of visitors from miles around."

Notable Teachers—John Sackett came to Beaman after the Korean War. He had been a freshman in high school from Van Meter when hall-of-famer Bob Feller was a senior. He taught world history, arithmetic, science, coached all sports, and was the principal. Pat Ashton Reuter (BC '59) shared, "Mr. Sackett taught us so many activities in P.E. Can you believe we learned archery? Not that it ever came in handy in life, but it sure exposed us to other things and teachings." Every year he took the teams to the state basketball tournament to experience the event. Barb Kopsa Ream ('56) said, "We all loved him. On these trips to the tournament, he taught us how to dress appropriately and be respectful. I can still remember standing in lines for a long time waiting for a snow cone. We sure didn't have that in Beaman."

Gus Selzer taught social studies. "He taught us to think bigger thoughts and be innovative. He let us know that there were larger things out there in the world than just the farms that most of us lived on. One field trip was to the Independence State Mental Hospital which was over 75 miles away on two-lane roads. The memory that is so vivid was of a frail little lady psychiatrist with a perfect bun hairdo telling us 'be careful what you say because there are people in here that only takes a few words to put them over the edge.' Those are some of the remarkable things that Mr. Selzer exposed us too," shared Sharon Cain Ziesman ('58). "Mr. Selzer made history and geography so interesting. I can still remember him saying that hundreds of years ago and the years after the ice age that the earth had become warmer and that once warmer areas would eventually cool down," shared Barbara Kopsa Ream ('56).

Notable Graduates—Leon Webb ('54) became an aerospace engineer in the Air Force, for Hughes Aircraft, TRW, and Ball Aerospace. He helped repair the Hubble Telescope in 1993 while it was in a space orbit. He designed many satellites and space cameras that were still in space in 2020, including Kepler, which discovered over a thousand possible life exponents and the "next-gen infrared Hubble", called the Webb telescope (no relation).

Ardis Walter McMechan ('47) became a noted home economist. She hosted a radio program on WOI Radio called the Home Economics Homemaker Show.

Senior Trips—The 1954 class of seven journeyed to Chicago. "With the principal, Mr. Perry, and the English teacher, Mrs. English, as our chaperones. That's right, her name really was English. They had a great time introducing us to the city. We always said that we still have neck aches from looking up at all of the skyscrapers. We stayed at the Sherman House and saw a live show at the Shubert Theatre. Coming from 'Mayberry' it opened our eyes to another world. What an educational experience," remembered Leon Webb ('54).

The senior trip for one day to Chicago by train was usually taken each year. Knowing that the school was to close after their senior year in 1958, the class went before the school board to get permission for a three-day trip to the Lake of the Ozarks. They raised money by picking up the stray ears of corn in the fields and selling them to fund the trip. Six seniors, along with their sponsors Superintendent Max Mabie and his wife Bev, and Homer ('30) and Mildred Zink Anderson ('34) made the trip. Homer's sweet little innocent daughter Marsha was a senior and one of the two girls on the trip. Checking out of the motel to make the trip back to Iowa, he had volunteered to carry her suitcase to the car. "As we left the parking lot and for some miles up the road, we heard all kinds of honking and people waving to us. We just thought these Missouri people sure were nice and friendly. It was sometime later that we stopped for gas only to find one of Marsha's bras had been tied to the car aerial antennae of the car. Some chaperones!" laughed Sharon Cain Ziesman ('58).

The class of 1956 traveled to Chicago for the Museums. The girls all loved going to Marshall Fields.

Sports—No football was played at the high school. The sports offered were boys and girls basketball, and spring and fall baseball. Other teams they played in the area were Conrad, Gladbrook, Garwin, Whitten, Green Mountain, Albion, Dinsdale, and Reinbeck. The strongest rivalries were against Conrad and Gladbrook. When playing Conrad, whose colors were also Black and Gold, the teams alternated tops and bottoms, so the jersey colors were different. Pat Ashton Reuter (BC '59) remembered, "the rivalries were so significant with Conrad that some parents even discouraged dating anyone from Conrad. When the school closed in 1958, of course, it was Conrad who we unified with. At least we didn't have to change our colors."

Closing—Beaman High School closed after graduation in May 1958. There were 462 graduates in the 54 years from 1905 -1958. The most numerous surnames of the graduates were: Rowe-12, Lynch-9, Vint-8, Sanderson-7, Meyers-6, Simms-6, Eberhardt-5, Hertema-5, and Stull-5. The last to receive a diploma from Beaman High School was Larry Westcott (alphabetically).

Beaman High School
Grundy County, IA

#10

Beaver High School

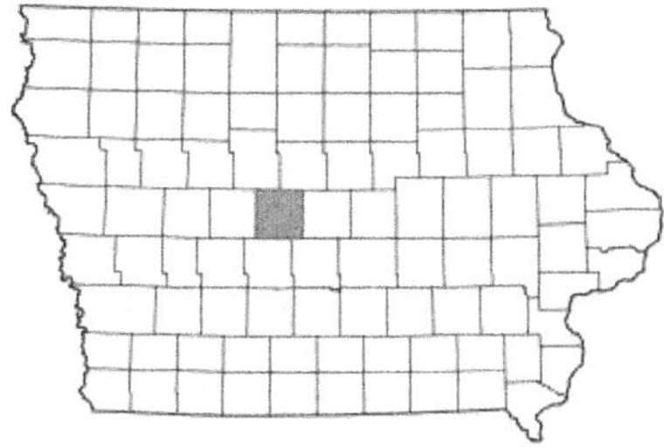

Mascot: Beaver
Colors: Green and White
Closed: 1946
Location: Extreme western Boone County

Early History—Beaver is in Amaqua Township in Boone County. Amaqua is the Indian name of the beautiful little creek that runs from north to south through the township. Beaver Township, which is south of Amaqua Township, received the English name of the creek. The town of Beaver was laid out on June 30, 1879. This platting was a few years before Angus, the neighboring town to the south, was at the height of its boom and was considered the greatest mining town in all of Iowa. Angus had a population of 3500.

From the *1902 Biographical Records,* fifteen men and families were recognized. The following few political sentences tell of these individuals. They are representative of the beliefs and views of those who farmed, went to church together, and were leaders in the townships and schools:

- like his father, a staunch Republican-socially connected with Good Templars of Beaver.
- a Democrat, having continuously supported the Party since attaining his majority.
- a Republican and earnestly supports the Party.
- always given a loyal support to the Republican Party—member of Ancient Order of Woodmen.
- his political support has been given the Democracy—from Germany—German Lutheran.
- crossed the Atlantic in 1872 from Germany—farmer—290 acres has never wavered in the allegiance to the Republican Party-believing that its principles are best calculated to conserve the general good and promote national progress and the welfare of the country.
- a Democrat in his political views, strongly endorsing the principles of the Party—classed among the progressive farmers of the county.
- a staunch Republican.

- his right of franchise in supporting the men and measures of the Republican Party, believing firmly in its principles.
- in politics he at first supported the Republican party, but now is a Prohibitionist.
- votes with the Republican Party.
- identified through membership relations with the Methodist Episcopal church of Beaver, and in his political views, Mr. Rinker is a Democrat.
- bade adieu to home Alsace, Germany, at 21 . . . purchased farm . . . a Republican unwavering through all the period during which he has had the rights of a native born American citizen. German Evangelical Church . . . no native son of this country is more loyal to the interests and welfare of the United States than Phillip Walter.

In the history of *Boone County Iowa 1914, Volume I,* is an account of the community at that time:

> . . . in the midst of a rich farming section it is a trading point of considerable importance . . . two churches, a Methodist Episcopal church . . . the other society is of the Dunkards.
>
> . . . Beaver Cooperative Association does a very extensive business in shipping grain and livestock . . . it is owned by 90 farmers. It has one school building with two departments. It has a consolidated district of eight sections, four of which are in Amaqua and four in Beaver Township. The name of the District is Dewey, so called in honor of the hero of Manilla Bay. The school has 65 scholars enrolled.

Early Schools—The people of Amaqua township educated their children in nine country school districts. The Beaver Consolidated School District was formed in 1916 out of the "Dewey" District No. 4 of Amaqua Township and Pleasant View District of Beaver Township.

Contracts for a new brick building were let in the spring of 1920 with the total costs of the construction around $60,000. The three-story building was adjacent to the two-story wooden grade school.

Sports—Football was not played at Beaver.

Basketball was played in the small gymnasium with the stage on the east side and the out-of-bounds lines against the walls with a beam across the court. "It did not allow for much arch on the shots to the basket. I was not the greatest basketball player but did play on the team," Bob Powers ('45) remembered with a smile.

The boys teams of 1924 and 1925 had some incredible records with only 31 enrolled at the high school at that time. Out of 70 games played in these two years, they lost only 13. Forty-seven of these games were basketball and 23 were baseball. In 1924, with a new coach and Superintendent, Mr. Robb, the team won 20 out of 25, playing in the finals of the county and sectionals. With four starters graduating in 1924, the 1925 team continued this streak with 30 games in baseball and basketball, losing only one in baseball and three in basketball.

The boys basketball team in 1941 won the Boone County Tournament and Sectionals by defeating Bagley, Boxholm, Dawson, and Pilot Mound.

Notable Teacher—Bond Romans was a science teacher in the 1930s. Harold McCombs ('39), at the age of 99 in 2020, remembered, "Our science room had folding doors that were a perfect target for the chalk thrown across the room as the racket and noise it made invariably got us in trouble with Mr. Romans. He was a great teacher and helped in coaching. I had been a starter on the basketball team in my 9th, 10th, and 11th grade years, but a new superintendent moved the practice times to after school, and I had to help at home on the farm. Mr. Romans was sure sympathetic to my cause but could not change the superintendent's new practice times."

Pauline Lamb taught at Beaver from the 1930s into the 1950s. Myron Rinker said, "Mrs. Lamb was a nice gal and we all had great respect for her. She demanded excellence in our English and grammar. We were drilled in sentence structure and her direction has been a great influence on my life." Bob Powers ('45) added, "Mrs. Lamb was hard for me to get along with in Algebra, but she was a good teacher."

Pranks—Watermelons at Tony Boe's watermelon patch came under siege in the fall of 1944. Bob Powers ('45) confessed, at the age of 95 years old in 2020, "Henry Rinker ('46) had a hot 1935 Plymouth four-door. The two other accomplices were George Stotts ('45) and Jack Schall ('45). The four of us marauded the watermelon patch and had so many melons which we hid under culverts throughout the countryside. We were so proud when we climbed the stairs above the bank building to present a huge melon to Superintendent W.W. Delmege. I'm sure he knew it was a hot melon, but he just smiled and thanked us."

Unique community business—At the age of 17, Russell Smalley's 'beeing' came quite naturally. For more than a century, every generation on his mother's side who came from England had bees in their families. Starting with a single hive in 1919, he built up his beekeeping sidelines to 250 hives by 1932. He quit farming to concentrate on honey production. Ninety-five percent of his bees were killed in the extreme cold of 1934. By 1939, he moved 400 colonies to Beaver. During WWII, Russell increased his bee business to over 1,000 colonies. Eventually, the numbers increased to 1,500 colonies, giving him a workforce of eight employees and five million worker bees, producing 170,000 pounds of honey a year. In 1957, Iowa ranked third in the nation in honey production, with Russell producing over 219,000 pounds. Many high schoolers found part-jobs at the bee farm.

Notable Graduate—Jim Doran ('45) did a short stint in the Navy at the close of WWII before entering Buena Vista College in Storm Lake. He never played high school football as it was not offered as a sport at Beaver High School. After Jim was told he was too slow to be a football player, he played on the defensive line on the "B" team weighing 175 pounds and standing 5 foot 10 inches. The next year he transferred to Iowa State University where he earned a bachelor's degree in agriculture. He competed on the men's track and football teams. He lettered in both sports. In 1949 and 1950, he received first team All-American honors and was an All-Big Seven Conference selection as an end. Doran set a national collegiate record against Oklahoma by catching eight passes for 203 yards—a mark that remains unbroken in the Iowa State record books. He was drafted by the Detroit Lions where he played for nine years. While a Lion, Doran was on three world championship teams and was named the most valuable player as a rookie on the 1952 world championship team. In his last two years, he played for the start-up Dallas Cowboys and was the first Cowboy to be named to the NFL All Pro team and played in the Pro Bowl. Many honors were awarded following his retirement from football, including being named a member of the *Des Moines Register's* Hall of Fame, and the Football Writers Association selection as its all-time Big Eight end.

Notable Student—Pam Slock graduated from the eighth grade in Beaver 11 years after the closing of the high school. She went to high school at East Green in Grand Junction. She was named to the *Des Moines Registers* First All-State basketball team in 1961. She was runner-up in the State Free Throw contest in 1961. She set a state record (at that time) with 51 points per game in 23 games with a total of 1,173 points. Pam also held six of the seven conference records in scoring. She was named to the girls Iowa Basketball Hall of Fame.

Killed in Action—The following boys from Beaver were killed in action:

Jon Murray ('38), WWII
Glenn Murray ('40), WWII
Dwight Gilbert, WWII

Bus Driver—Hartcliff Murray was **a** bus driver for many years. Bob Powers ('45) remembered, "On our bus there were two boys, Arnold Bosch (41) and Melvin Litchlighter, that were continually fighting. I swear to God, I thought they were going to kill each other. Mr. Murray was afraid to break them up because these boys were mean. All the McCombs kids rode on our bus, too. We would have to wait for them often, as they were taking the milk from the barn to the house and changed their clothes for school."

Closing—The Beaver High School closed after graduation in May 1946. In the 25 years from 1922-1946, there were 146 graduates from Beaver High School The most numerous surnames of the graduates were: Doran-13, Powers-8, Rinker-7, and Van Pelt-5. In the fall of 1946, the high school students were bused to the Ogden school district.

Beaver High School
Boone County, IA

#11

Benton High School

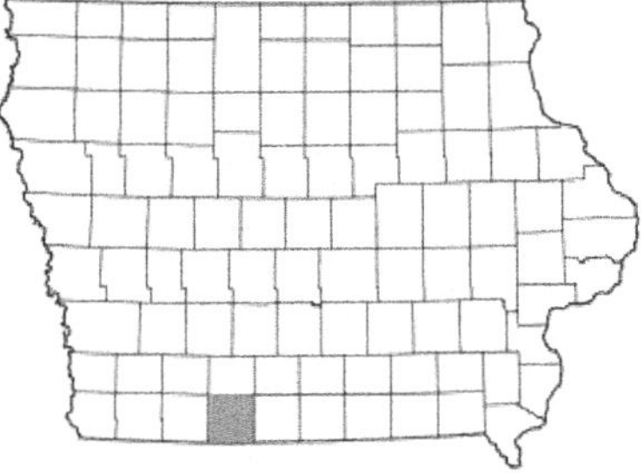

Mascot: Bearcats
Colors: Red and White
Closed: 1958
Location: West Central Ringgold County

Early History—The Chicago Great Western railroad was built in 1887. It ran diagonally through western Ringgold county. Three new towns were established along the railway. They were Knowlton, Maloy, and Benton. The name of Benton is thought to have originated from Thomas Hart Benton who was a United States Senator from Missouri. Benton was platted in 1889 and was originally in a larger township. When the town was a little more than a few years old, the county board of supervisors made two townships out of the larger area. Benton ended up located in both new townships of Benton and Rice with the Main Street being exactly on the dividing line. Benton was incorporated in 1894. The 1895 population was 200.

Early Schools—The first-two room school was built by the IOOF (Independent Order of Odd Fellows). Previously, the children east of the main road running through Benton were in Rice township and attended what was called the old Enterprise School. Those living west of the main road were in Benton township and attended Buffalo School. The school boards got together and decided to budget enough money for a school to be built in Benton. This private IOOF building was used for several years. The citizens of Benton were determined to have a school district of their own. They marked a territory of approximately two square miles of land from the two townships.

A two-room school was built just a few feet from the eventual long-standing Benton School. This school only went through the sixth grade. Miss Etta Rans was the teacher in 1898 and 1899. She received a salary of $25 per month. In her certificate statement at the end of the term she wrote, "the average cost of the tuition each month for each pupil was 96 cents."

The 37th General Assembly noted the need for higher education in the state in rural communities. They passed a law known as the Consolidated School District legislation. This law provided that rural communities, including towns and villages, could incorporate into a Consolidated School District of not less than 16 sections of contiguous territory if a majority of the voters authorized consolidation. The law was for a 12-year school and the children were to be transported to and from school. In 1914, the people of Benton decided there was a definite need and voted on the consolidation in March of that year. However, the vote did not carry so nothing was done at that time.

In 1916, S.S. Hall and W.T. Haley became interested and conceived a plan of voting on an enlarged Independent School District. This plan was presented to the voters and it carried. The territory involved 11 sections of land. Hall was elected president of the new school board. The others on the board with Haley were C.D. Nichols, Frank Rychnovsky, and Dora Vaughn. (Rychnovsky's son, Lewis, was in the first graduating class of 1919 and became a dentist.) They located four more sections to bring the total area to 15 sections and 240 acres.

The new brick three-story building was finally built in 1916. There was a new barn built on the north side of the road for the children to house their horses when they rode them to school. There were two floors in this building for use as classrooms and a gymnasium.

Benton Milestones—One of the first automobiles in Benton was owned by Asa Bains. It was a Huppmobile and purchased in 1911. He lived north of town and was still driving it in 1942. It had been registered 32 times. Mr. Rains refused offers from the Huppmobile Company to buy back the car.

In November 1961, Benton became the first town in Iowa to be governed totally by women. The mayor, town clerk, treasurer, and five council positions were filled by women.

Dial telephones came to Benton in 1966. Before this the only telephone system was manned by one person, Vantia Butler. The phone system was in her home. If anyone wanted to contact someone, they called the switch board, and she would tell them where they were. After her death, the switch board was moved to the home of Iona Groves who was the operator when the dial phones came.

Sports—There was no football played at Benton. The boys and girls played basketball. They played against all of the schools in the county except for the largest town, Mt. Ayr. They played Kellerton, Delphos, Ellston, Redding, Beaconsville, Tingley, Grand River, Blockton, Diagonal, Sharpsburg, and Gravity. (Author's Note: All of these towns had closed their high schools by 2020, except Diagonal.)

Louise Groves Frost ('49) and Shirley Graham Klejch ('58) were both guards on their basketball teams. Louise said, "I remember Blockton's gym. It was all concrete and when you fell it was really hard on the knees." Shirley remembered, "Kellerton had the newest gym in the county. We played all of the county tournaments there on that court." Mary Matthews Gepner commented, "Our gymnasium had no bleachers, and everyone had to sit on the stage. It was really a 'cracker box'. I was a really short forward. If you arched your shot too much you would hit the ceiling."

Band—Benton did not have a band. Mrs. Imogene Roberts was the vocal music teacher. She started a Recorder band and taught history. Mary Matthews Gepner (Mt. Ayr '60) added, "She wasn't the greatest teacher. It became difficult to attract the best teachers to our little school." Due to it's small size, classes such as drivers education were never taught at Benton.

Senior Trips—The 1958 class went to Osage Beach, Missouri. Superintendent Loring Forrest Snooks drove the car and took all five class members. Shirley Graham Klejch ('58) laughed as she shared this story. "Larry Blunck ('58) took a bicycle boat out on the lake and couldn't get it back to the dock because of the wind. Snooks and us four girls had to rent a boat and go to the rescue."

Mary Matthews Gepner (Mt. Ayr '60) said, "Mr. Snooks was a character and came back many years to our alumni banquets. Joe Bowen was mischievous. He did graduate from Mt. Ayr after Benton was closed. He became a schoolteacher and a long-time administrator in Ft. Madison, Iowa schools. Snooks always said, 'I only had one failure in all my years as a superintendent, and that was Joe Bowen. I tried everything to keep him out of Ft. Madison (Ft. Madison is the location of the Federal Penitentiary and is often identified with the town of Ft. Madison).

In 1947 and 1948, the entire high school went to Kansas City and Omaha in the back of a stock farm truck.

Notable Teachers—Loring Forrest Snooks was the superintendent, science teacher, and basketball coach. He helped arrange for the Coca Cola truck to come each April and every student received a small seven-and-a-half-ounce cold Coke.

Hot Lunch—Ruth Herrington was a great cook. Shirley Graham Klejch ('58) remembered, "She made everything from scratch. Her homemade rolls were smelled throughout the school. It was just like mother's home cooking."

Don Burch ('48) remarked, "Floy Watts was the cook in my days. She always made me eat the sauerkraut. It is taste that I never learned to like."

Prisoner of War—The Butler brothers, Merle ('41) and Hollis, were both prisoners of war at the same time in Europe during World War II.

Closing—The Benton High School closed following graduation in May 1958. There were 236 graduates in the 40 years from 1919-1958. The largest classes were ten graduates in 1921, 1931, and 1948. The most numerous surnames of the graduates were: Schlapie-11, Campbell-7, Blunk-5, Cole-5, Fertig-5, Groves-5, and Vaughn-5. The last graduate from Benton High School was Daisy Wilson (alphabetically). In the fall of 1958, the students from the junior and senior high school from Benton were bused to Mt. Ayr.

Benton High School
Ringgold County, IA

#12

Bonaparte High School

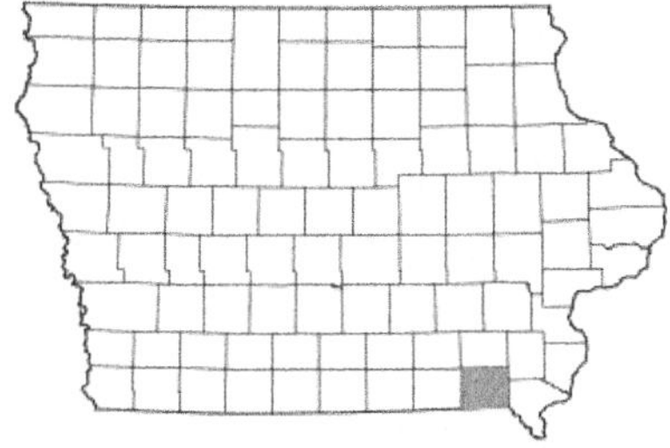

Mascot: Indians
Colors: Black and Red
Closed: 1959
Location: Southeast Van Buren County

Early History—Van Buren County was formed from a part of Des Moines County. The courthouse in the county seat at Keosauqua was built in 1843 in a Greek Revival style. It is the oldest continuous courthouse in Iowa and the second oldest in the United States.

William Meeks came to this area along the Des Moines River in 1836. He was from Michigan and built a wing dam, flour mill, and a sawmill. The dam area was designated as Meeks Mills, Wisconsin Territory, USA. A hotel was soon built called The Tavern. The first steamship up the Des Moines River arrived in 1839. William McBride, the surveyor, laid out the town and changed the name to Bonaparte to honor Napoleon. A small settlement across the river named Napoleon had failed.

Here are a few highlights from the early years of Bonaparte:

1844 Meeks Flour Mill and Aunty Green Hotel were built.

1846 The Mormons spent the winter two miles east at Reed's Creek encampment. They had left Nauvoo, Illinois, in March 1846.

1847 A state road was built from West Point to Bonaparte (dirt surface).

1853 William Meeks and Sons built the Woolen Factory.

1854 The Des Moines River between Keokuk and Des Moines carried heavy steamboat traffic.

1858 The Keokuk, Ft. Des Moines, and Minnesota Railroad was completed, and trains arrived in Bonaparte.

1875 The population of Bonaparte was 1,339 with 668 males and 671 females.

An account about the Mormons was written by Marion Flake from Bonaparte. This was printed in the booklet *History of Bonaparte* and compiled by The Van Buren Historical Society:

The Mormon pioneers marked the first great route from the Mississippi to the Missouri, opening a thoroughfare which later guided thousands of home seekers to the great West. From the city of Nauvoo, the largest city in Illinois, with a population of 20,000, refugees streamed across Iowa. In July of 1846, 15,000 people with 3000 wagons and 30,000 head of livestock were camped along the Iowa trails. Over 150 companies made the trek over a period of eight years . . .

The first train consisted of 500 wagons, which approached Farmington (four miles east of Bonaparte) March 3, 1846, from camp 4 miles below, near the present site of Croton. One party camped ¾ mile north of Farmington . . . A burial ground for this camp remains on a bluff north of Reeds Creek . . . Grain of the pioneers was ground at the Bonaparte Mill (Meek's Mill) . . . crossed the Des Moines River. Brigham Young writes that they crossed just below Bonaparte Mills where the water was 2 feet deep . . . There were countless smaller groups, branching out from the main companies, which camped, often for several months . . . The "Brass Band" which accompanied the first company, to ease the discouragement of the travelers, played concerts for the Iowa citizens also . . . Farmington on March 4th, and at Keosauqua on March 8, 10, 11, and 17, on the Main Street and on "Court House Hill."

The Historians of Iowa remind us that "in the persecution the Mormons endured in their early years, Iowa never joined. The people of Iowa seem to have enjoyed their music, made use of and paid fairly for, their labor and skills, and in general, conducted themselves in marked contrast with the officials and citizens of Missouri and Illinois, for which the struggling thousands of those pioneers years, must have been very grateful."

Early Schools—Following the end of the Civil War in 1865, the Bonaparte Academy Association was incorporated by a group of community leaders who were seeking to provide a formal educational opportunity. They established the Academy which was built in 1865-1867 for $20,000. It became known as Howe's Academy named for its principal, E.P. Howe.

In 1870, the Bonaparte School District became independent and bought Howe's Academy for $12,000.

This report of the schools is from the *Bonaparte Journal* in 1887, reported by the editor:

Bonaparte schools are now in a most flourishing condition, and nothing can better substantiate this than to note the goodly number of pupils enrolled, the general average attendance, the punctuality and deportment. The course of study requires 12 years to complete it and in addition to common branches it takes in algebra, philosophy, physiology, zoology, botany, bookkeeping, civil government, and rhetoric . . . enrollment 38 of whom are tuition pupils, 40 in primary, and 53 intermediate.

The first graduation was held in 1891 with two graduates. Nelle Jones Brown Price ('91) gave the oration at the ceremony titled, "The Blessing of Poverty."

On January 23, 1915, the schoolhouse burned to the ground. There was $8,000 of insurance money collected. School for the rest of the year was held in the Meek Pants Factory. By June 1915, work commenced on the new school. This new school had all 12 grades. This building still stands (2020) on a hill on the north side of town overlooking Bonaparte and the Des Moines River Valley.

The new school opened on January 3, 1916. Here are some highlights recorded of the Bonaparte High School:

- Each room was connected by phone to the principal.
- A fuel famine in 1919 closed the school for two weeks.
- School became accredited by the State of Iowa in 1920.
- There were 79 high school students with tuition of $7.50 a month for non-residents.
- The building was wired for electric lights in 1924.
- Basketball was played at Rees Hall.
- In 1926, the *Cauldrin,* the school newspaper was first published.
- Graduation was held at the Whitely Opera House in 1930.
- The first typing class was offered. Students had to provide their own typewriter.
- The girls advanced to the State Basketball Tournament in 1934.
- On the year of the Bonaparte's centennial in 1937, a new gymnasium was constructed and dedicated on October 8, 1937.
- In 1937, enrollment in the high school was 108 students.
- In 1944, the school published the *Pow Pow*. The first yearbook, *The Aloha,* was released.
- A new 42-passenger school bus was purchased in 1945 for $1,085. The bus driver was William Ollman.

Killed in Action—Four area men were killed in World War II:

Albert Mills, WWII
Claire Osweiler, WWII
Donnie Tate, WWII
Alden Watts, WWII

Sports:—No football was played at Bonaparte. The boys played basketball and ran track. The girls played basketball. The 1934 team went to the state tournament. This team featured four girls that made All-State teams that year. They were Jane Warner (1st team), Elaine Cummings (2nd team), Eloise Cummings (3rd team), and Dorothy Troutman (3rd team).

This team won their first two games at the tournament defeating Cumberland 24-20 and Dana 23-11. They lost in the semifinals to Aplington and to Johnston in the consolation game to garner the fourth-place trophy for the state of Iowa.

Several school songs were part of the pep squads' cheers.

(To the tune of On, Wisconsin)
Onward Bonaparte, Onward Bonaparte
March right down that floor.
Ever ready, firm and steady
Fight forever more.
Rah! Rah! Rah!
On Victorious, ever glorious
To the very end.
Fight comrades, fight
And we will win this game.

(To the Notre Dame Victory Song)
Beer, Beer for Bonaparte High
Shake up the cocktails, bring on the rye
Send some Freshman out for gin
Don't let a sober person in
We never stagger, we never fall
We sober up on wood alcohol
While our royal sons are
Marching back to the bar for more.
Rah! Rah! Rah!

(Author's Note: The PTA, WCTU, and Superintendent may have not appreciated the second song, but the students surely loved it.)

Closing—The Bonaparte High School closed after graduation in May 1960. The new Harmony High School was built four miles northeast of Bonaparte. The consolidation of the Bonaparte, Farmington, and Hillsborough school districts became the Harmony Community School District.

Bonaparte High School
Van Buren County, IA

#13

Bussey High School

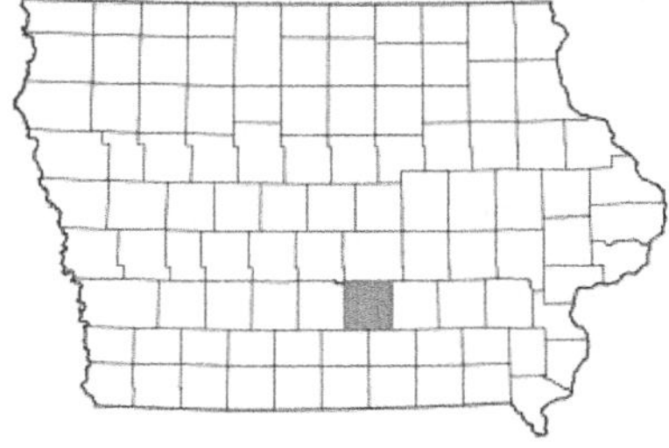

Mascot: Yellowjackets
Colors: Purple and Gold
Closed: 1960
Location: Southeast corner Marion County

Early History—Jesse Bussey "The Father of Bussey" was born in 1820 in Green County, Pennsylvania. He came to Iowa to buy livestock and ship it back east. In 1864, he bought the land where the town of Bussey is now located. In 1867, Bussey moved his wife Isabelle and family to Iowa. They came on a freight train, a one day and two night journey, riding in the caboose with their goods. They were met by their brother-in-law, Alf Jemison, at Eddyville which was 15 miles south from their new home. They loaded their goods into wagons and ferried across the Des Moines River. They drove their wagon teams over what they called 'the terrible clay hills' between Eddyville to their new, double log cabin at their farm.

One of the first post offices in Marion County had been homed in this log cabin by its previous owner.

In the year 1875, Jesse Bussey gave 50 acres of land and, in partnership with former Governor Samuel Merrill, platted the town. Jesse also gave the right-of-way across his land and half interest in the town plat to the railroad company to locate a depot there. Its location was ideal because of the heavy grade to the north between Bussey and Cedar Creek. The depot was located at the head of the grade.

The Albia, Knoxville, and Des Moines (AK&D), later the Burlington, finished laying track in 1875. Because of the long uphill grade north between Tracy and Bussey, it was necessary to divide the train in half to "double the hill." The engine brought the first half of the train over the hill, turned around at Bussey and went back for the other half of the train. The Chicago, Burlington and Quincy (CB&Q) or just the Q, built a track paralleling the AK&D and built another depot in Bussey. These two railroads joined and dismantled the AD&K depot.

With meager equipment, Sam Sherman started a newspaper in 1894 called the *Bussey Banner*. In 1897, the name was changed to *the Tri-County Press* (Marion, Mahaska, and Monroe). In 1902, the paper had a circulation of 2,500 and the subscription was 50 cents a year.

Coal mining in this area started in the 1890s. By 1902, there were three coal companies operating in the vicinity of Bussey. The Cedar Creek Coal Company employed 30 men, Columbian Coal Company employed 100 men, and the O.K. Coal Company employed 300 men. Daily output between the three companies was 120 tons. Coal mining continued through the centennial year in 1975. Strip mining had replaced the deep shaft mines. The countryside surface was never restored. Strip mining left hundreds of acres northwest of Bussey useless for farming.

The *Tri County Press* reported on January 11, 1906:

> Bussey's location is the envy of all Iowa for it is midway among splendid county seats of Oskaloosa, Knoxville, and Albia while Des Moines is easily reached, and one of these days as we believe we shall be hitched up not only with Oskaloosa but with Des Moines and Ottumwa by Inter-Urban road. To this end we should be organized and lookout for developments and should strive to turn something up. Factories are attracted, railroads are located, new enterprise through just such means. The farmers on Long Lane, the mining in Everest, Durfee, and Buxton are saying to us: Keep up the Inter-Urban agitation. We need 'em and must have an outlet.

Early Schools – Liberty township is in the farthest southeast corner of Marion County. It had rural country schools nearly two miles apart and two districts in Bussey. The pupils from north Bussey attended the Lickskillet school. The pupils in south Bussey attended Pack school between Bussey and Hamilton.

In 1885, the Bussey Independent School District was formed. The first school in Bussey was located on Merrill Street. Dr. Sanders was the teacher in this one-room school in 1891 for $32 a month. The school was soon overcrowded.

One acre of land was purchased from J.A. Bussey for $450. A four-room brick building was built for $4,000 on the southeast corner of Bussey.

The first commencement from this school was on March 22, 1903 with two graduates. Their oration subjects were "Preparation" by Fredrick Newman and "Improve Thyself" by Nora Olive Johnson.

February 6, 1906 in the *Tri County Press* showed enrollments at the school: Primary-41, Secondary-33, Intermediate-42, and Grammar-34.

The Bussey High School was built in 1916. This was a two-story brick structure with a half basement. The Bussey District consolidated with a small part of Mahaska County and surrounding Marion County.

Sports—The small gymnasium at the high school was in the basement. It was a great facility when the school was built in 1916 but became a place that some visiting teams refused to play in. A *Herald* newspaper article on March 22, 1946 reported:

> The Bussey boys record is particularly outstanding in view of the fact that they are forced to play at home and play in a 'ban box' gym which is so small that baskets are only nine feet from the floor instead of the regulation 10 feet and roof supports make it impossible to play the type of game they must play on foreign courts.

Ray Dunkin ('44) once said that "the key to making baskets was to shoot underhanded and it really became our home court advantage."

Despite all these handicaps, the 1946 boys team made it through the districts and sectionals to advance to the Boys State Basketball Tournament. With only 30 boys in high school that year, Bussey had an exceptionally tall starting line-up with the starters at 6'5", 6'2", 6'2", 6'2", and 6'1". They lost in the first round to a powerhouse Crawfordsville team.

The new gymnasium and auditorium were dedicated in 1949. The measures to finance the construction of the new gym had been defeated in the district prior to the bond election in 1948 for $35,000. Principal Clarence Villont led the final effort by advocating that a new gymnasium would help keep the high school open. Orville Dunkin ('49) shared, "My Dad had become ill and our family was extremely poor. I was the youngest of nine in my family and I was allowed out of class one day a week to help work on the construction of the new gym. It was really a shame that I was never able to play ball on that court as it was not finished until after I graduated."

The boys were playing 6-man football in the 1930s and early 40s. Bussey won the Mar-Mon Six Conference championship in 1938. They were the Keomah League Champs in 1939, 1940, and 1947.

Football was dropped during the war years. It returned as a sport at Bussey in 1946. They played 6-man. Orville "Junior" Dunkin ('49) played quarter-back on that team. He said, "By the next year in 1947, Coach Lapitz scheduled both 6-man and 8-man games. We went undefeated and played five 8-man and four 6-man games that year. There were only five schools in the state of Iowa playing 8-man football. We defeated Hedrick twice, New Sharon, What Cheer, and Delta. At the end of the season, he bought us an emblem that said, State Champions 1947."

More football success followed with Bussey being the undefeated Keomah Conference Champions in 1954 and 1955 and Co-Champions in 1957.

The girls team in 1955 advanced to the Girls State Basketball Tournament with a 23-2 record. They were led by junior Beverly Mick ('56) and Judy Duffy ('54). They lost in the first round to Monona. Mick was named to the all-state team in both 1955 and 1956.

Janitor—The school bell and John Hooten became almost synonymous. He was the janitor for 31 years from 1921-1951. He only had one eye. His hand bell began on the first year of his employment as he rang it to start the classes in the morning and at the end of the day. For many years, students were allowed to ring the bell on their birthday. He was so associated with the bell that on one occasion, the young Vance twins were being pressed as to who the 'John' was they were talking about, and they replied, "You know, John ring-the-bell." His services required firing the furnaces both day and night during the winter months. He was a good disciplinarian who showed both great care and concern for all students. When John retired, the hand bell was replaced by an electric buzzer bell.

Hot Lunch—Sherrill Peters Spaur ('62 Twin Cedars) remembered, "As a freshman we could be helpers in the kitchen. The money earned for our efforts were in exchange for our lunches. I loved helping the cooks prepare the meals and set the tables." The first cooks who started after the war years were: Ruth Comer, Maggie Heaton, Mary Frost, and Verla Spaur. Teddy "Sonny" Spaur ('56) replayed the aroma still wafting through the room, "the steamed burgers and lemon white sauce cakes were everyone's favorite meal. Verla Spaur was known for her wonderfully thin noodles served with mashed potatoes."

Notable Teachers—Glen Chance taught industrial education. "He was known for his patience, kindness, and was always pleasant," remembered Orville Dunkin ('49). "It was unusual that I had Mr. Chance as a first grader in country school and my senior year he became the football coach and physical education teacher."

William Bean was the history teacher and coach in the 1950s. He was an American Indian and graduated from Northeastern Oklahoma College. He was the coach that took the girls to state in 1955. He was the coach of the two undefeated football teams of 1954 and 1955. "We had a crazy year in 1956 when we played one 6-man game against Mingo, an 11-man game against Lovilia, and the rest were 8-man games. Talk about preparation and knowing all of the assignments with the different formation," recalled Teddy "Sonny" Spaur ('56). Mr. Bean later became the State Indian Affairs Director.

Notable Graduates—Harold "Mick" McConnell ('40) stood 5'1" but always said he was a vital part of the basketball team. That being the ball boy. He enlisted in the army during World War II and took pilots training. He was discharged on a Friday and bought the café in Bussey the next day, on Saturday, with no restaurant experience. In 1950, he started the McConnel's Wholesale and bought the Knoxville Beverage Company and Bottling Works. He added to his businesses with the A&W Franchise in Indianola and two more in Des Moines. His voice as the barker at the "Old Time Soda Fountain" at the Iowa State Fair was legendary. He was named Iowan of the Day at the State Fair in 1999. As a lifelong writer, he was the editor and publisher of the A&W newsletter for 40 years. His book of memories sold over 600 copies with proceeds going to charity. The list of his accomplishments is long, and he lived by a motto of his: "I lived a big life for a Little Guy. Live a Big Life".

Beverly Mick ('56) was on the high school all-state first team in 1955 and 1956. She graduated from Central College in mathematics in 1960. She earned a masters from San Diego State University when there were only two women in the mathematics department. She taught school in Gowrie and California for over 40 years. She was awarded the Women in Education Award by Cuesta College in California. She was a collector of fine art which she later donated to Cuesta College. She returned to live in Albia after her teaching career. In those ten years in Albia, she bought and renovated an old church and restored it to its architectural beauty. It is used for various community functions. Beverly was on the Chamber of Commerce board of directors and belonged to the DAR, and the Bussey United Methodist Church. Beverly Mick tutored students in math and French until her final days.

Yearbooks—The printing of a yearbook was discontinued from 1947 through 1955. The yearbook was again issued in 1956, named *Vespa,* which means yellow jackets in Latin. That annual was dedicated to Kay Joann Trinkle who was stricken by leukemia and died in February of her senior year in 1956.

Pranks—The typical outhouse on Halloween story became quite a humorous one in 1950. Carl Voorhees had the general variety store on main street. He was known as an extraordinarily strong Republican. An outhouse was deposited on the front steps of the store on Halloween night with a sign that read "Republican Headquarters." Not to be outdone, Mr. Voorhees placed another painted sign on the side of the outhouse that read "Democrats meet in the basement."

The plan was laid for a great night watermelon heist. Deb Ford ('56), Alvin Heaton ('56), Sonny Spaur ('56), and Hymie Bonnett ('57) carefully parked their car at the outskirts of Acie Van's watermelon patch about three miles outside of town. After crossing the creek and brush to get to the patch, they were unbelievably pleased to find a pile of watermelons already picked and laying at the edge of the field. As they reached down to lift their first armfuls of the green bounty came the "Boom! Boom! of a shot gun." Terrified, they dropped the melons and ran. This time not taking time to walk across the creek on the logs, they swam through the creek to the safe refuge of their cars and fled the scene. They retreated to Sonny Spaur's ('56) house to find Sonny's dad, Ted Spaur, and Uncle Rex Spaur grinning from ear to ear. It seems the men had overheard of the watermelon stealing plan and had gone first to pick the melons, place them by the edge of the field, and laid in ambush with their 12-gauge shotguns. Some laughter ensued but it made an even better story than all the watermelons these boys could ever eat in a lifetime.

Killed in Action—The Bussey community lost eight men in service to their country. Lest we forget:

Frank Bonnett, WWII Germany
Kenneth Cecil Bunch, WWII Pacific
James A. Bussey ('40), WWII Germany
Kenneth F. Dunkin, WWII Philippines
Orra Eugene Gilbert, WWII New Guinea
John W. Harrison, WWII Germany
Merle E. Vanderhorst, WWII Austria
Francis Glazebrook, Jr, Vietnam

Closing—The Bussey High School closed after graduation in May 1960. The students continued to attend high school at Bussey until the new Twin Cedars school was completed three miles west of Bussey. In January 1962, the Twin Cedars building was completed and all high school students were moved into the new school. In the 43 years from 1918-1960 there were 615 graduates from Bussey High School. The largest class was 25 seniors in 1938. The most numerous surnames of the graduates were: Smith-13, Bonnett-12, Spaur-12, Hugen-10, Wales-10, Jones-9, Parker-9, Davis-8, Mick-8, McConnell-7, Amsberry-6, Plum-6, Vanderhorst-6, Bussey-5, and Dillon-5. The last to receive a diploma from Bussey High School was Toni Watkins (alphabetically).

*A special note is needed about the combined class from Attica, Tracy, and Bussey which attended and graduated from the Bussey High School building in 1961. They were often referred to the

Twin Cedar students and had Twin Cedars on their diplomas. Fifty-four seniors graduated in the spring of 1961 and are not counted in the numbers of Bussey only graduates.

Bussey High School
Marion County, IA

#14

Casey High School

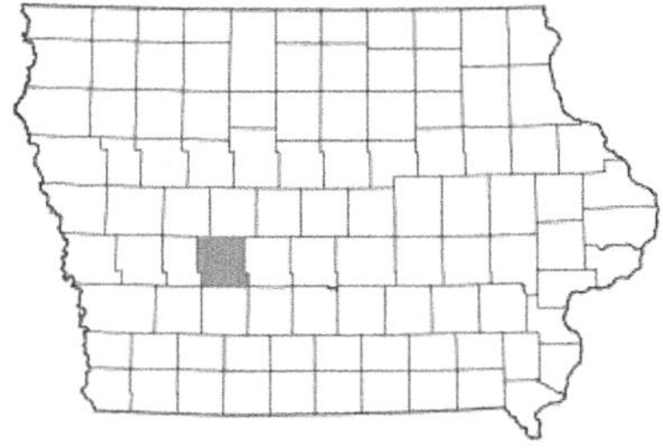

Mascot: Rams/Ramettes
Colors: Blue and White
Closed: 1957
Location: Guthrie County

Early History—Casey is in Thompson Township on the southern border of Guthrie County. It was named after the Casey brothers, John and James. These brothers were born in Cork, Ireland, and their families were relocated to Canada by the British government in 1825 as part of a resolution of the poverty and famine crisis in Ireland. The brothers brought their contracting firm to Iowa and were awarded the contract to build the railroad from Kellogg to Council Bluffs in September 1866. They oversaw 2,000 laborers and 1,000 teams of horses as they laid track across Iowa at one mile per day. The average pay was $2 per day and $4 per day for a team. On July 23, 1868, the track was laid 40 miles west of Des Moines in the approximate location of Casey. The site defined as the "Grand Divide" was the summit cut one mile in length and sixty feet deep. East of the summit the waters flowed east to the Mississippi and west of the divide the waters flowed west toward the Missouri River. By mid July 1868, the new town of Casey was laid out on a 90-acre site on the line between Adair and Guthrie counties. Effort was made to establish a rail station there.

Early Schools—The first school in Thompson Township was a subscription school in the NW quarter section 35. Another school was erected at the Quaker settlement along Middle River. The first school in Casey was a two-story public school built in 1870. Another new school was built on the hill in 1881.

In 1915, the Casey school district voted to build a new three-story brick structure for $35,000. In *Casey 150 History,* Carrie Mowery Kading ('08) was quoted. "When I was eight, two more rooms were added to the school. Then around 1916, the high school was built. In the early days, the school yard was fenced due to many people keeping cows and a single driving horse in town. Most of the yards were fenced in, too."

Notable Graduates—Dale Eichor ('56) took his love for music and forged it into a career in entertainment and broadcasting. He played in the high school band and taught himself the guitar and bass. He played in country bands. He worked for 40 years in broadcasting and in county radio. He was inducted into the Country Music DJ Hall of Fame. He worked for stations in Iowa, Texas, and Illinois. He was the DJ and Music Director at KWMT in Fort Dodge, Iowa. He was involved in promoting bus trips to Nashville and Branson for the community to enjoy country music.

Thomas Duncan ('22) spent the summers of 1924 and 1925 working with a Chautauqua theatrical troupe. He was a student at Drake and the editor of the school newspaper, debate team, and involved in politics. He enrolled for his junior year at Harvard and received his degree in 1928, graduating cum laude in poetry. He wrote for the *Des Moines Register* and *Des Moines Tribune*. His first book, published in 1935, *O Chautauqua,* was the first of many books that he wrote. His greatest success was his renowned book *Gus the Great* which took him ten years to write. It was about a midwestern defunct circus and it won national acclaim. It was sold for movie purposes but, to date, the movie has not been filmed. He was honored in Casey with *Tom Duncan Day* in 1947, the same year that *Gus the Great* was released. His former teacher at Casey High School, Ruth Henderson, mused, "It would present such a study combined with one of Hemmingway's books . . . Chapter One of *Gus the Great* is almost worthy of *O. Henry*."

John Buchanan ('36) graduated from the University of Colorado in 1940. He worked as a reporter, photographer, sports editor, and editorial writer for the *Boulder Camera*. He covered city hall for the *Denver Post* for 15 years and wrote a weekly column in city government affairs. He became the assistant editor for the *Empire* Magazine, a weekly supplement to the *Denver Post,* and wrote a weekly column for the *Empire*. His over 200 columns and cartoon drawing were often linked to his hometown of Casey. In the *125th History Book of Casey* he wrote:

> Casey? Oh, those were the great days! Those days of crossing the railroad dam barefooted, of swimming in Middle River on hot summer days, of catching bullheads, of gathering walnuts in Johnson's Timber, of listening to Jess Burkey play in the band, of watching Harry Evans dribble a ball down the basketball court, of holding a Jack-O-Lantern up to Doc Maulsby's window on Halloween, of seeing Wally Blackmer wheel his paint cart through town, of watching the Rocky Mountain Limited roar through town and of flying kites—those days of a small town Iowa boyhood.

Notable Teachers—Vernie Van Duzer taught English in the 1950s. Colleen Stolk Ruppert ('53) said, "Mrs. Van Duzer was my favorite teacher. She was very, very attractive and strict in English. She inspired us to read good literature and was so particular with our performances in plays. She was a perfectionist and instilled in us the desire to attain our best in writing, performance, and in our readings." Vernie Van Duzer later became a school principal in Colorado.

Eugene Andrews was the very respected Superintendent and teacher in the commerce department teaching typing and bookkeeping from 1951-1957. He led the district in successfully consolidating with Adair and the passing of a bond to construct the new Adair-Casey High School. He was the senior class sponsor and accompanied most of the senior trips in his six years at Casey. Verdel Nelson ('51) remembered, "Mr. Andrew kept all the boys after morning assembly and carefully addressed the quiet group. 'It appears that some of you are really proud of your penmanship and artwork on the bathroom stall walls. If you are so proud of your work and words, why don't you put it on paper and let others see your talent.' That's all he had to say, and the graffiti stopped immediately. I will never forget his dressing down and that was 70 years ago, and he did it so calmly with such effect."

Sports—The tremendous football teams of 1953 and 1954 were both undefeated ending with an 18-game winning streak. The 1954 team outscored their opponents 238-12. After starting the season with a 0-0 tie with Earlham, they went on to defeat Anita 25-0; Bagley 20-0; Adair 40-6; Orient 34-6; Exira 46-0; Dexter 54-0; and Fontanelle 19-0.

Polio—Handsome Bill Van Duzer ('38) was injured in a football game and later came down with polio. Following law school, he became an attorney in Casey and was on crutches for the rest of his life.

Killed in Action—The following Casey boys lost their lives in the world wars:

Jesse Wise
William Seeley
James Stammer
Donald Rutt

Janitor—There were only two janitors in the years from 1915 through 1967 at the schools in Casey. Earl Bassett was there for the last 37 years of the school. He started working at the school when the steam furnace was only a year old. For ten years, he hand-fired the furnace making his day start at 4:00 A.M. With the many night activities, his day ended at nearly 10:00 to 11:00 P.M. The first summer Bassett was employed at the school, he and a W.P.A. worker sanded every room floor. The process of taking off the dark oil restored the floors to the white pine finish that remained on the floors until the time a fire destroyed the building in 1977. Each year the state inspector credited Earl for having one of the neatest and cleanest buildings in the state. Tom Cline said, "He was always available when a student needed a friend to talk to or if repairs were needed. He kept the school in pristine condition." Kay Hamilton Faga ('58) added, "Mr. Bassett was my best friend." He had his office in the basement of the school. "More than one of us free sprits would sneak down to his den and suck on a cigarette with him," shared Verdel Nelson ('51).

Bus Driver—Marian "Shorty" Boblett drove the south bus for many years. He had a clean driving record though the steep hill south of town often scared his student riders. "I don't think he did it on purpose but with the grade and a muddy road, the bus would just barely slide to a stop before it had to turn the corner at the bottom of that hill," remembered William Kading (AC-'66).

Snow Day Card Game—On March 25, 1956, a late spring snowstorm blanketed Casey. It happened to be the superintendent's birthday, though that is not the reason Mr. Andrews called off school. The foot-deep, heavy, wet snow continued to fall throughout the day. By late morning, Mr. Andrews walked up town to join some businessmen at Vernon Joint's ('21) clothing store to play a few hands of cards. They could see the bus barn out the back window of the store with the heavy snow accumulating on the roof. As they periodically gazed out to assess the steady buildup of snow, the bus barn roof started to sag and bow to the middle. An alarmed posse of four men slogged through the deep snow, entered the bus barn with the superintendent's key and backed all of the buses out before the roof collapsed. 'Knowing when to fold 'em and knowing when to run' saved the Casey bus fleet that day.

Senior Trips—The 1946 seniors traveled in their parents' cars to Lincoln, Nebraska. They toured the University. Earl Joint ('46) remembered, "We made it to a museum in Omaha and had a real thrill at the airport. Most of the class rode on a ten-passenger airplane, but Dick Mains ('46) and I got to ride in a private plane. Dick asked, 'What is a Wing Over?' Wow, after experiencing the complete 360 rollovers, we didn't ask any more questions."

Collen Stolk Ruppert ('53) told, "In May of 1953, our class headed out in three cars for the Ozarks. Mr. Andrews, Vernie Van Duzer, and Martha Snitler were the adults in each of the cars."

Band and Music—The school owned most of the instruments played in the band. A full-page advertisement in the *Casey Vindicator* announced the first day of classes for the fall of 1936. In the advertisement was: Free Band Instruction—Casey school is one of the very few schools in the State that offer free band instruction to all the students, High School and grades. Students may receive private music lessons on any instrument once a week during the school day. Free of Charge.

Closing—The Casey High School closed following graduation in May 1957. In the 43 years from 1915-1957 there were 843 graduates from the school. The names and numbers in the 1924 class are missing. The most numerous surnames of the graduates were: Kading-41, Smith-26, Whetstone-20, Williams-20, Thompson-10, Betts-9, Hubbard-8, Jensen-7, and Ludwig-7. The last to receive a diploma from Casey High School was Donald Dean Williams (alphabetically). In the fall of 1957 Casey students were bused to the new consolidated Adair Casey High School.

Casey High School
Guthrie County, IA

#15

Clearfield High School

Mascot: Orioles/Oriolettes
Colors: Orange and Black
Closed: 1986
Location: Extreme East Taylor County

Early History—In 1881, the Burlington railway came to Clearfield as track was laid from Humeston to Shenandoah. It entered from the east into Taylor County and into the northeast section of Grant Township. A town was platted close to the Ringgold County line. This marked the new town of Clearfield. It was named by John and Miles Green from Clearfield City in Clearfield County,

Pennsylvania. They had worked for the Town and Lot Company. Clearfield was incorporated in 1882 and had a population at that time of around 200.

From *1910 History of Taylor County*: "The land around Clearfield is productive and there are many wealthy farmers and stock raisers in the vicinity. At first land sold for $12 acre, but now sells for $27 after two years."

The railroad station at Clearfield was the scene of around-the-clock activity as four passenger trains and two freight trains stopped daily.

A newspaper, *The Clearfield Enterprise,* was formed in 1882.

Early Schools—Grant No. 1 was the first school in the township located in the northwest corner, one mile west of the south end of Main Street. It was also known as the Jones school. It became too small for all the students and a larger school was needed. When the railroad came in 1881, and the birth of the town of Clearfield, a school district was organized in 1882. The first white-wooden, two-story school building was constructed for $2,200. When a high school was added it created an L-shaped structure. The first graduating class from Clearfield Public School was in 1895.

A community disagreement on the location of a new and larger school building raged for several years. Patrons living north of the railroad wanted the new school built on the north side of the tracks. The school board appealed to the County Superintendent who agreed with the school board. The decision was appealed to the State Education Superintendent who also sided with the school board's decision. The case made it all the way to the Iowa Supreme court which ruled that the Superintendents had no jurisdiction and the decision where to build the school was up to the School Board. After the ruling by the Supreme Court, the preparations for the new school building started again. In 1908, a new building was built at a cost of $20,000. It was constructed of pressed brick. It had 11 rooms and was a very modern building in every respect. The high school course of study provided for the full four years of work and the school was accredited.

From an article in the *Clearfield Enterprise* dated May 4, 1911:

> The new school boasted of a larger number of tuition pupils than any other school in two counties. In 1910-11, a total enrollment of 218 incudes 64 being non-residents. The high school enrollment is 73 with 43 of those being non-residents.
>
> Athletics have a given place in the school. Even earlier than this, basketball, football, and track provided the opportunity for physical achievement through competition with neighboring towns.

In 1924, a $30,000 addition of a gymnasium, stage, library, and two classrooms were added to the main structure. The interest rate was 4%.

The alumni banquet was first held in 1924. It has been held every year since (2020).

On Easter Sunday April 24, 1940, the entire community was saddened and shocked when a fire destroyed most of the school. Some equipment and school records were saved. With the insurance money and bonds for $25,000 at an interest rate of 2 1/8%, a new building was constructed the following year.

School Highlights

1927 *The Magnet* was the first yearbook printed. It recorded that the first 20 minutes of the school day were set aside for recreation. Monday and Friday had a study period. Tuesday and Thursday-singing; Wednesday was Chapel day. The 11-man football team went 8-2.

1937 The first *Oriole* yearbook was printed.

1938 Manual training and Normal Training (teacher preparation) was taught.

1939 An electric scoreboard was made by Coach Rood, and the boys in shop installed it in the gym. Chapel was held in the mornings. Six-man football was played.

1941 The first school hot lunches were served. Classes were held in the Methodist church until the new school was finished (following the fire). First undefeated football team.

1942 State required all girls participate in Physical Education.

1943 No Alumni banquet as food was rationed (WWII).

1945 Football team finished with record of 7-1 and ranked No. 2 in the state of Iowa. All six starters named to the All-State teams. The girls basketball team carried a 22-caliber rifle shell for good luck.

1946 Flu epidemic.

1947 Students were X-rayed for tuberculosis.

1948 40 students were in the band, 30 students in girls glee club.

1949 The entire school was bused to Blockton for X-rays for tuberculosis.

1951 Teacher's salaries ranged from $1,412.60-$1,952.72. The janitor was paid $2,011.70.

1952 FFA organized with 20 boys enrolled. 300 attend the first PTA meeting.

1958 The school switched to 8-man football. There were 82 students total in high school.

1959 The girls basketball team was undefeated in regular season with a record of 18-0. It was Coach Jim Rood's first year as the girls' coach.

1960 The football team was undefeated. Taylor County Sheriff asked the school board to place all automobile keys on board in the office. Students who drove had to place their keys on the board when they arrived and the keys stayed there until the student went home.

1965 CHS won the trophy from Pi Beta Kappa of State University of Iowa. It was presented to the high school in recognition of outstanding scholastic achievement by students from the high school in their first year in college.

Sports—Clearfield played in several sports conference affiliations. In 1955, teams competed in the Waubonsie Conference. Conference members were Prescott, Nodaway, Sharpsburg, Conway, Gravity, Blockton, and Clearfield.

In 1957, a new conference was formed called the IAMO (Iowa-Missouri). This was the only conference in Iowa to include teams from two adjoining states. Conference members were: Coin, Clearfield, College Springs, Emerson, Stanton, New Market, Hopkins (Missouri), and Westboro (Missouri).

In 1967, Clearfield joined the South Seven Conference. The 1974, 1975, and 1976 football teams were conference champions.

The last conference affiliation was the South Central Eight. Schools in the conference were: Diagonal, Van Meter, Lineville, Corydon, Wayne, Prescott, Grand Valley, and Clearfield.

The 1964 girls basketball team finished the year at 25-2. They made it to State, losing in a thriller 66-64 game to New Market. They were behind in the game 61-49 with four minutes to go and rallied to tie before losing in the final seconds. The whole town formed a caravan of cars to travel to Des Moines.

Not all teams were victorious. Carroll Baker ('53) recalled, "My sophomore year we got beat by Coin 86-6 in football."

Doug Boyer ('65) did not have the greatest eye for the ball. He said, "Jim Rood was our baseball coach. He informed me that I had struck out 17 times in a row. After this reminder, I swung so hard that the catcher missed the ball and I sat on first base with a big smile back at Coach."

Markeeta Beggs Baker ('70) remembered that in the 1969-70 basketball year there was a new boys basketball coach. "I was a cheerleader. The new coach and the players did not see eye to eye. There had been a mutiny of the upperclassmen and the year was played mostly by freshman. We lost most games with the opposition scoring over 100 points against us. In one game against Grand Valley, our team did not cross half court in the first half. The final score was 153-19. The coach asked the cheerleaders why they weren't cheering, and I said that we couldn't think of any cheers as all of our cheers had the word 'victory' in them." That same year (1970), the boys baseball team was the conference champion.

In 1971, under the direction of a new coach, the basketball team ended a 32-game losing streak with a victory over Lineville.

Notable Graduates—Jim Duncan ('26) graduated when he was 14 years old. He had been home-schooled until the age of nine and entered high school at that time. In order to play sports, he had to focus on running. He excelled in track. He entered Drake University and won the Missouri Valley Conference 440-yard dash. He became a member of the prestigious American Scholastic Honorary, Phi Beta Kappa. He graduated from Drake with a degree in Philosophy. He became a coach and principal at Milburn before returning as a professor at Drake for 31 years in journalism and mass communications. He was the voice of the Drake Relays from his student days until his death. A coach, writer, and broadcaster, Jim Duncan was beloved by everyone. He touched many lives.

Elmo Nelson ('28) was Clearfield's greatest athlete according the Jim Duncan ('26) in one of his presentations. Nelson started catching for the high school team when he was in the sixth grade. As a freshman at the first track meet of the season with Cromwell and Lenox, he picked up the javelin and threw it 156′ 6″. This throw beat the Cromwell javelin thrower that had finished second in the state the year before. At the University of Iowa, Nelson won three letters in football, played baseball, and ran track. In one meet, the University of Iowa chartered a plane to fly him after the baseball game to a track meet, so that he could compete in both sports on the same day. He played baseball professionally, reaching the high minor leagues with the Texas League.

Donald McRae ('24) received a PhD and taught in college. He published a fiction book titled *Dwight Craig* which was based on Clearfield and the Evans Hotels.

Jim Rood ('49) attended Simpson College and Northwest Missouri State. After a two-year hitch in the Army, he returned to Kellerton to teach and coach. He came Clearfield to teach in the fall of 1958. His first girls team in 1958-59 was undefeated in the regular season. He became the Superintendent at Pekin. At the age of 90 (in 2020) he remembered, "I loved teaching. Kids even signed up ahead of time for my courses. I had to be the luckiest superintendent of schools at Pekin. There were five schools that I advised and consulted in their closing in a 300 square mile area and they still didn't run me out of town."

John Thomson ('60), following graduation from Iowa State College of Veterinary Medicine, came back to Clearfield to join his father in the Clearfield Veterinary practice. He became the head of the South Dakota Veterinary Diagnostic Laboratory in Brookings, South Dakota. He then became the Dean of the Veterinary College at Mississippi State University. He was chosen to become the Dean of his alma mater at Iowa State University College of Veterinary Medicine. Under his leadership, he lobbied the State Legislature and Agriculture Association to help raise and build an addition to the veterinary teaching hospital and diagnostic labs during a time in the early 2000s when the college had lost its accreditation and the state was out of money. His coach and teacher, Jim Rood ('49) said in 2020, "John was not the best athlete that I ever coached. But he worked so hard at everything. He became a great rebounder. We have stayed in contact over the years and we have such a mutual admiration of each other.

(Authors Note: As a veterinarian myself, I share that John is the most modest man that I have ever known. He is a quiet and effective leader).

Notable Teachers—Nadine Madsen taught English and French. Marvin Baker ('79) said, "Mrs. Madsen would often put me in detention saying that I could do better at my schoolwork. She organized a memorable class trip to France that I will always remember. She invited us to her home for French dinners and even was known to serve us wine. In fact, some of us students 'drank the hell' out of the wine at her dinners. She had a mischievous spirit and may have been credited for spiking the punch at the prom. She was one heck of a teacher and always had our attention and we so respected her."

Grace Rood was the English teacher in the 1950s. Leanne Porter Baker ('53) smiled as she shared, "Mrs. Rood had really long feet. She was stern and could make you melt. She always wore a suit and tie shoes with the small heal. The suits would alternate from the blue, gray, brown, black, and burgundy colors. It would be a new one for each day of the week. I sat in the second row. Junior Parker ('53) and John Borland ('53) started pulling my desk when Mrs. Rood was not watching and I would end up at the back of the room. Then, they would start pushing the desk and me forward until I was back on the second row again. Somehow, I don't think she ever caught on, or more likely she did not want to overreact to such chicanery. Now, I can appreciate that she was not as clueless to our stunts as I thought back then."

Killed in Action

Ernest William Bye, WWII

Ivan C. Dowell, WWII
John. B. Hannow, WWII
Robert Larson ('40), WWII
Arthur Woodrow Pine, WWII
Charles Francis Reynolds, WWII
Lloyd Whipp, WWII Iwo Jima
(word reached back to Clearfield the same day that President Roosevelt died)
William Leonard Witter, WWII
Darrel Woodside ('37), WWII

Speech—Clearfield was known for its outstanding speech program. The students received two #1 ratings at State in 1970. This was followed with three students to State in 1972, four in 1975, four in 1976, and two in 1977.

Band—In the 1960s, the marching band had over 50 members every year. The director was Bob Danner. Markeeta Beggs Baker ('70) was in the drill team and told, "Mr. Danner was our director and his demands and perfection drew students in to play in the band. He made it fun and traveling to contests made us realize how fortunate we were to have him for our instructor."

By 1972, the band was made up of all girls. There were 81 students in high school that year. The brass quintet (five horns) received a #1 rating at the state contest.

Marvin Baker ('79) shared, "I played #2 saxophone, but it was all by ear. When my cousin, Sherri Baker Dogget ('77) graduated, my music abilities were exposed. Since I did not know music, I was encouraged to take my talents elsewhere. Mr. Mason was our instructor but had an unusual habit of knitting with the needles. He knitted on the bus going to band festivals and particularly at regional and state contests. We were embarrassed so we taped paper over the windows to the practice rooms so that other schools could not see our director sitting on the floor knitting."

In 1981, 80% of the students in school were either in band or chorus.

Cooks—Marietta Abaar started cooking at the school in 1945. Her husband had left her with seven small children to raise alone. Her first year, she was paid $12.50 per week. She was noted for making most everything from scratch. She carried the dough home in five-gallon buckets so she could knead it at home. This dough then became her famous cinnamon rolls to be served with chili.

She was honored during National Hot Lunch Week with "Marietta Abaar Day" when she retired after 23 years in 1975. She remembered at that time in her first years as the cook that the chickens were brought to her alive. She had to kill them, pluck and cut up the chicken, and cook the meal.

Senior Trips—The class of 1953 went to Kansas City by cars. They saw the Harlem Globetrotters play. They rode their first escalator for what seemed like hours. The girls all missed their next tour because they went into a bridal shop and tried on wedding dresses and lost track of the time. They toured a car plant. Carroll Baker ('53) chuckled as he remembered, "On the road going and coming home, the kids would be hanging out of the cars as we pulled into gas stations. Even though there was a parent riding in each car, some of the gas stations saw us coming and closed down the station."

Closing—In a *Des Moines Register* article on October 11, 1981, biased opinions against small schools were exposed by the paper. Since there were not enough boys to play football that year in Clearfield, the school decided not to let the freshman play against the other teams in the league. Max Morrison from the Department of Public Instruction was quoted, "Clearfield's been over the hill for a long time. I talked to them quite strongly about reorganization back in the early 1960s. But that's all water under the dam. No one wants to do it voluntarily. Some of these schools simply shouldn't be saved."

During this time, the State University of Iowa had awarded Clearfield High School with the Phi Beta Kappa for outstanding academic achievement for freshman students in school that year.

Dick Stephens, a teacher of 24 years at Clearfield shared, "It has long been that the state prefers to remain out of forcible school reorganizations, but instead to apply enough pressure to the district that patrons eventually destroy the district themselves. It appears to me that the Clearfield district provided a classic success to that theory."

The school closed following graduation in May 1986. In the 92 years from 1895-1986, there were 1,387 graduates from Clearfield High School. The largest graduating class was 33 in 1969. The most numerous surnames of the graduates were: Baily-30, Brown-23, Baker-14, Larsen-14, Wilson-14, Nelson-13, England-11, Gaule-10, Smith-9, and Benett-8. The last graduate from Clearfield High School was Marcia Wurster (alphabetically). The next year the students were bused to Lenox.

Clearfield High School
Taylor County, IA

#16

Clutier High School

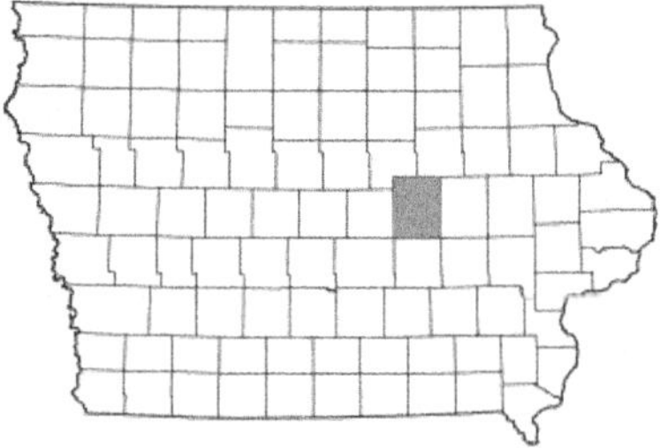

Mascot: Charging Czecks
Colors: Orange and Black
Closed: 1961
Location: East Central Tama County

Early History—Early settlers arrived in Tama County in 1848. By the spring of 1853 there were neighborhoods in various parts of the county and the population was considerably over 200.

Townships were organized in 1853. One of these was Howard Township, which includes the territory now comprising Oneida and Carroll Townships. The first settlers in these townships came in 1853 and 1854. There were a few Irish and other nationalities among these settlers, but most of them were Czechs and Germans. The Czechs chose the hilly sections rather than the open prairie because of the abundance of timber and brush which covered the hillsides. Fuel in their native country had been scarce, so they were attracted to sections where wood was plentiful. Neither Oneida or Carroll Townships had an inland town or a railroad. The nearest railroad in those early settlement years was Iowa City.

In 1899, William Brice was the principal capitalist and promoter for a railroad that ran from Belle Plaine on the southeast to the northwest to Blue Earth, Minnesota. Brice was raised in Tama and had run a general merchandize business before moving to Mason City. He had been the primary investor in two other railroad ventures. The new Iowa, Minnesota, and Northwestern Railroad started grading in 1899. Brice soon sold his interests in the railroad to the Chicago Northwestern Railroad, but retained the rights to develop the town sites along the track.

Clutier was founded in 1900. It was named for William Brice's sister and brother-in-law, Maude Brice Clutier and Bertram L. Clutier. They never lived in the town. Bertram Clutier was a bank employee in Tama and later in Chicago. Other townsites along this 200-mile railroad were named for Brice's friends and railroad employees. Some of these were Zaneta, Voorhies, Dike, Hanlontown, Wheelerwood, Doughery, Carterville, Eleanor, Bricelyn, and Keiserin, Minnesota.

Brice bought an 80-acre site for the depot and laid out lots for sale. Lots sold for $300 to $500 with the top sale of $600 in the spring of 1900. By November 24, 1900, a newspaper had been established called the *Clutier Record*. The following is an editorial from the first issue:

> By a proper effort of the part of those who are fortunate to be pioneers in this new town of Clutier, it can be made one of the prettiest towns in the state. Lying on a tract of land sloping gently to the south, is an ideal location for a town.

Early Schools—The Oneida No. 4 country school was located one-half mile east of the new townsite. The school district bought a two-acre tract for the new school building. The town constructed a new two room school in Clutier for $2,500 in 1902. The first year there were 67 students enrolled.

The Clutier school operated six days a week, eight months a year. At a special meeting in March 1905, it was decided to hold no more school on Saturdays. In 1910, the school year was extended from eight to nine months. In 1915, an additional room was built on the back of the school building. Three grades were taught in each of the three rooms.

In 1925, the new modern school building was erected. The voters had authorized a $35,000 bond issue and a tax levy to pay the bonds. The new three-story brick building cost $40,000. With the completion of the new building, the Clutier school became a 12-grade school. The first graduation class from the new four-year high school was the class of 1928.

Notable Graduates—Marie K. Caloud Vileta ('31) was a fifth grade teacher for 16 years. She was born in 1914 and often said she "grew up when the town was new" and did not know it. She wrote columns for the *Tama News Herald* titled "From out of the Past." She wrote over 1,250 columns and was still writing at the age of 86 in 2000.

Hurbert Caloud graduated from the eighth grade in Clutier in 1968 and later from North Tama High School. "The Clutier High School had been closed by this time. He had been an outstanding product of the Clutier grade school and of our town and its heritage," said Hurbert's brother, Delbert Caloud (eighth grade graduate from Clutier in 1965). Hurbert became a Sergeant Major in the Marines and in 2002-2003 led 4,500 Marines in the invasion of Iraq. He is a leader of the American Battlement Monuments Commission.

Clarence Hach was born on a farm east of Clutier. His parents were Czech farmers. He graduated from nearby Dysart High School and received his BA from the ISTC (Iowa State Teachers College), an MA from the University of Iowa and graduate work at Wisconsin, Minnesota, Columbia, and Rutgers. Hach was awarded the Ford Foundation Fellowship, the Pioneer Award, The Distinguished Service Award, and twice recognized as the Illinois Journalism teacher of the Year in 1947 and 1974. He wrote textbooks and a math book which were used at Clutier High School. His fame was shared with the students in the last year of the school by Mr. Schoenferder. "Next year you will be going to Traer to High School. The math book that you just have used is written by Clarence Hach. When those kids at Traer try to call you "Dumb Boehmies" you just show them that you are not so dumb as one of your own wrote the math book that they are now using. And that you have already had the whole text as eight graders in Clutier," chuckled Delbert Caloud.

Dorothy Hadacek Haack Hayek ('43) played on three state tournament teams for the Charging Czechs in 1941, 1942, and 1943. She received her teaching certificate from Iowa State Teachers College in Cedar Falls. She taught in a country school at Oneida No. 6 for 11 years which was the school she had attended as a student. She moved to Elberon and, with her husband, raised four children. At the untimely death of her husband in 1974, she became the bookkeeper at the elevator and substitute taught in Elberon.

Notable Teachers—John Schoenfelder was the superintendent and girls basketball coach. He left and then returned to the school and coached the boys basketball team and taught math, social studies, and shop. In his years at Clutier he taught three generations of families. Richard Wiebbecke remembered, "Mr. Schoenfelder wore crepe soled shoes and would carry an eraser and his books under his arms. He would throw that eraser at a disruptive or inattentive student even if they were not in his class." Dorothy Hadacek Haack Hayek ('43) at the age of 95 (2020) shared, "Mr. Schoenfelder made basketball players out of every girl in the school. He was strict and maybe a better coach than teacher."

"He was nicknamed 'Schonnie' and in my times at school he had returned to Clutier and was a teacher and not the girls coach. I remember him saying from the spectator chairs at a game, 'If you girls are going to foul them, scratch their eyes out,'" said Carol Novotony Vokoun.

Mr. Schoenfelder was the typing, bookkeeping, business training, and sociology teacher in the 1940s and '50s. "He had a nice personality and was easy to talk too. He really encouraged me to become a teacher," recalled Dorothy Hadecek Haack Hayek ('43).

Sports—Football was not played at Clutier High School.

The boys played basketball and baseball. Asked if the boys had the same skills in basketball as the girls, George Hayek ('61) said, "We weren't worth a damn! We had such a beautiful new gymnasium but with so few boys out for basketball, we just had a tough time competing with other schools."

The game in Clutier was girls basketball, and did they ever light it up. From 1938 through 1948 the girls teams won 201 and lost 18 games, seldom losing more than two games in a season. They made it to the state tournament six times: 1941, '42, '43, '46, '47, and '48. This was the most by any school in the state during the six-on-six basketball era. The name Clutier was synonymous with girls basketball throughout Iowa. They were coached all those years by John Schoenfelder.

The "Queens of 1942" won the first place state tournament trophy defeating Centerville, Ankeny, Havelock, and Wiota. They were led by Verna Mae Vorba ('42). The "Charging Czechs" were the only undefeated team in the state that year. Dorothy Hadecek Haack Hayek ('43), the last surviving member of the team at the age of 95 (2020), vividly remembered. "I was a forward. Verna Mae Vorba Hartwig ('42) and I would feed the ball into our tall six-foot pivot Delona Zmolek Severein ('43) who was a prolific scorer. Our biggest rivals were not really close to our school. Elberon was the nearest town and we once scored 100 points against them. We really had some battles with Steamboat Rock, Wiota, and Wellsburg."

Marie K. Caloud Vielta ('31), columnist for the *Tama News Herald,* wrote 58 years later (2000):

> When the returning team arrived at the Tama County line six miles south of Tama, they were met by fans and escorted to Tama where they were treated to a luncheon at a café by the Tama Commercial Club. When they reached Toledo, a car with a siren led a parade through the business district. At the Clutier city limits, the town band on a flat-bed truck met them and escorted them to the schoolhouse where 500 people, almost twice the town's population had gathered into the gymnasium. It was 3:30 p.m. by this time! . . . Mary Caloud, president of the school board addressed the crowd assuring the team their championship would long be remembered . . . Clutier will long be remembered for the glorious achievement of producing a state championship basketball team. In 2000 the Charging Czechs will still be welcomed as the Queens of 1942.

Verna Mae Vorba Hartwig ('42) and Ardella Knoop ('49) were elected to the State Girls Basketball Hall of Fame.

The 1942 team was led by three elementary school boy cheerleaders: Paul Babor ('49), Leroy

Bata ('49), and Wayne Novotny ('49). They received state-wide recognition when they cheered the girls to the state title. Dressed in their cute striking orange and black bell hop suits, they were coached from the third grade on by their teacher Mrs. Diel. They had black caps with an orange 'C' on the front.

Band—The band heritage in Clutier dates back to the great Bohemian bands from as early as 1902. The Czech and German waltzes were played every Saturday night at the renowned Z.C.B.J. Hall (Zapdne, Ceska, Bratska, Jednota Lodge—Cesti Bratra No. 104). Big bands entertained, and the festivities brought hundreds to Clutier for the dances. Clutier was named the Kolache Capital of Iowa for their Kolache Day held on the grounds surrounding the bowery and the baseball diamond.

The high school band played at the Waterloo Cattle Congress parade and at the Cedar Rapids Band Festival. Richard Wiebbecke remembered, "I played the coronet. I started in the band in the third grade. It was really fun. Going out of town to parades and festivals was a great day out of school."

Bus Drivers—Jim and Ralph Sienknecht were bus drivers. Ralph drove for 55 years. George Hayek ('61) shared, "When he looked up at you in the big rearview mirror, he did not have to say a word and you immediately straightened up and shut up. One time when plowing through the winter roads when school had not been called off, Jim got onto the superintendent. He told him to just ride with him that day and he would see the conditions. After that experience, the superintendent always took Jim's advice on closing the school during bad weather."

Senior Trips—The 1941 senior trip used personal cars and left early in the morning on an educational journey. The eleven seniors with sponsors John Schoenfelder and Mrs. Harry Rambow, traveled east through Vinton and had breakfast at Independence. In Dubuque, they ascended the high hill to Eagle Point Park where they could see portions of three states. Crossing the "Father of Waters" to Dickeyville, they visited the world-famous Grotto. In Lancaster, Wisconsin, they traveled on the first one-way street that they had ever seen in their lives. Of course, they were traveling the wrong way. In Prairie du Chen they crossed the river to Marquette. They rode speed boats on the River and scaled the heights of Pike's Peak in the middle of town. At Elkadar, the students saw the famous school constructed out of glass bricks. Then to Backbone State Park and the state fish hatchery where Mr. Schoenfelder and Victor Knoop ('41) unraveled their lines and tried to hook a trout in the stream passing through the park. It was supper back in Manchester at the Coffee Den and these road weary seniors passed up skating at Waterloo to seek their beds back in "Dear Old Clutier." This great day together with their classmates capped off a senior memory that lasted for a lifetime.

The 1943 senior trip was called off because of the rationing in World War II.

The last year of the high school, the class of 1961 chartered a bus to Chicago. George Hayek ('61) shared, "We raised money by picking up field corn and other fund raisers through the school year. We thought we were quite the stuff by going on a chartered bus. The chaperones were Mr. Kenny Freeman and his wife and Miss Schaeffer (social studies teacher). We went to the Science and History Museum and other attractions and spent two nights on the town. Being such great kids, we did not get into any trouble," said George Hayek ('61) with a wink.

Killed in Action—Clutier boys killed in action were:

Joseph A. Hora, WWI
Louie Machacek, WWI
Edward Husak, Korea

In 1986, sixty-eight years after World War I, Charles Cizek received the Purple Heart.

Closing—Clutier High School closed following graduation in May 1961. In the 34 years from 1928-1961 there were 337 graduates from the school. The largest class was 1943 with 17 seniors. The most numerous surnames of the graduates were: Yuska-11, Dvorak-10, Konicek-10, Caslavka-9, Sienknecht-7, Novotny-7, Krezek-7, Hach-6, and Hora-6. The last to receive a diploma from Clutier High School was Stanley Svoboda (alphabetically). In the fall of 1961, the high school students were bused to the newly named Traer Clutier High School in Traer. One of the conditions on the agreement to merge with Traer was that the new school would start girls basketball. The name of the new high school was changed in 1965 to North Tama High School when Dinsdale joined the district.

Students in front of new brick school building, school year 1926-27.

Clutier High School
Tama County, IA

#17

College Springs High School

(Amity High School)
(South Page High school)

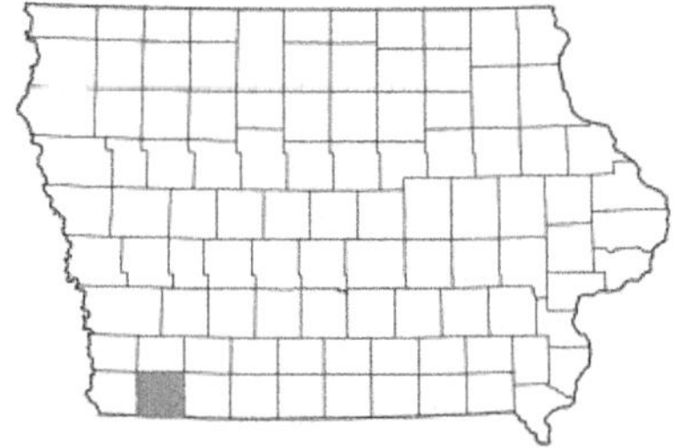

Mascot: Amhawks
Colors: Red and White
Closed: 1959 College Springs
2020 South Page
Location: South Central Page County

Early History—College Springs was once called Amity. It was settled by non-denominational Christians who were advocates of temperance and anti-slavery. They came to establish Amity College. The community flourished around the college. With the spirit of the anti-slavery movement, the town played an active role in the Underground Railroad. Evidence was found in homes that had secret rooms to hide African Americans fleeing from the South.

Settlers came from Illinois and bought 7,000 acres in southern Page County and across the border in Missouri. The plan was conceived at the Western Industrial and Scientific Association in Galesburg, Illinois. The group led by Rev. F. Kaskins saw the good that Knox College was achieving. Forward thinking men with full confidence in education organized the association to form a colony in the west for education which would be "Christian", co-educational, and strictly anti-slavery in its beliefs. The expeditionary group was sent to western Iowa and Missouri to purchase land after selling shares for $100 each. In 1855, the "Association" was incorporated in Iowa and its name changed to Amity College when the group decided unanimously on the site in Page County. According to the founding articles, some of the land was to be sold after the college laid out town grounds. The funds went partially toward buildings and the balance of the funds were invested to draw interest to pay faculty salaries. Land owned today (2020) by John and Elaine Christensen and Gene Ripley has the wording stating that alcohol is not to be made or sold on the deeded land. The first year, in 1857, there were 30 students enrolled. The peak enrollment was 422 students in 1892. The Amity College thrived from 1857-1914.

Amity was nicknamed 'Little Jerusalem' because of a code that no alcohol could be made or served in the town. The name Amity was changed to College Springs because there was another Amity post office in Iowa. The new name was based upon Amity College, Amity Township, and the ample springs located in the area. On January 19, 1875, the town incorporated with a vote of 41 to 30, and the name changed to College Springs in Amity Township of Page County, Iowa.

The spring fed Crystal Lake was named and developed by Albert Arendsee. It operated as a resort beginning in the early 1900s. Ice was harvested from the lake for the homes in College Springs.

Early Schools – At least for the first two years of the high school, it was also located at the Amity College and academy. Normal training was taught to enable the students to obtain a certificate to teach in the one-room country schools in Iowa with a two-year high school education. This preparatory course was the equivalent of a high school education.

Elementary schools in College Springs and the nine one-room country schools in Amity Township may have existed, but there is little documentation of their history.

The community school offering expanded to a four-year high school with the first class of six graduating in May 1913. There were three boys and three girls. The boys all had the last name of Williams.

By a vote of over five to one, College Springs passed a bond to build a new three-story brick school that was constructed in 1917. The building featured a clock tower at the peak facing east. The building stands majestically in its regal beauty over a century later (2020). It was built for the elementary and high school grades. In 2020 it still has 22 students that are part of South Page High School.

The school district was called College Springs. All the sports uniforms had Amity on the fronts and the names of College Springs and Amity High School were used interchangeably.

Sports – Football was started in 1913. The boys and girls basketball teams played in the new gymnasium starting in 1917.

From the 1917 *Amitonion* yearbook, the boys defeated the following schools that year: Farragut, Ellston, Elmo, Westboro, Sharpsburg, Clarinda, Blanchard, and Shenandoah.

The 1920 *Amitonion* reported that the boys basketball team outscored its opponents 487-179, ending with an 11-1 record. A popular cheer from the pep club that year was:

First in War, First in Peace
First in the hands of the chief of police
Ruff and tuff, tuff and ruff
Always ready, never get enough
Oh! Yes we'll never die
We're the students of Amity High

Literary Societies—The Athenian and Theonian Societies each had 54 students and were important in development of the intellectual scope of each student. Later literary society groups were called Adelphian and Philomathean.

Yearbooks—The 1915 *Amitonian* had advertisements from Tarkio College, Monmouth College in Illinois, Simpson College, and Cornell College. (This may have been because of the closing of the Amity College that year and hoping to attract prospective students to these colleges.)

The 1920 *Amitonian* featured a picture of an orchestra with 19 members and their instruments. Also, pictured in 1920 were 28 seniors, 39 juniors, 32 sophomores, and 35 freshmen. The Junior class presented Shakespeare's "*Merchant of Venice.*" The yearbook featured poetry sprinkled throughout its pages.

In 1917, the German class and the German club were dropped with the outbreak of World War I. The Latin club that year prospered with 45 members. The Ukulele Club had six participants.

The 1947 yearbook was named *The Scoop.* Highlights included:

- Under the leadership of principal Bess Anderson ('14), the school had a very active Declamatory Club.
- The Y-Teens with 34 members performed three one-act plays.
- The homecoming game was against Thurman. Lloyd Cavner ('47) was crowned the King and Corrine Christensen ('49) became the Queen.
- The FFA organization had 26 members.
- The girls track team, which had started in 1944, defeated Blanchard at the Clarinda Cardinal Field by a score of 27 $^1/_2$ to 24 to win the Little Seven Track meet.
- The boys football team in 1946 was undefeated with an 11-0 record with wins over Westboro, Clearfield, Coin, Randolph, Malvern, Tabor, Thurman, Farragut, and Stanton. Four of the wins were by shutouts. They won the first championship of the newly formed Iowa Six Man Conference.

March 1st Moving—In Iowa, the first day in March was when farm renters moved from one farm to the next. They were never called sharecroppers, but they rented land and houses from the landowners. Gene Ripley ('57) said, "In my years at school about one-third of the class would leave on March 1. This was very normal, but we seemed to always recoup and get a new one-third, new students that moved into the district on March 1.

Notable Graduates—Bess Anderson ('14) graduated from Monmouth College in Monmouth, Illinois. She returned to College Springs to teach and became the principal. John Christensen ('51) shared, "She was always addressed as Miss Anderson to her face but 'Bess or Aunt Bess' otherwise. A niece and nephew, Reva Anderson ('46) and Reid Anderson ('47), were in high school a few years ahead of me and perhaps that's where the 'aunt' comes from. She first taught at Amity in the early 1920s and, after a ten-year stint at Sidney, Iowa, returned in the early '30s and retired in 1959. Three generations of a single family remember her. Bess was very even-tempered, and I do not recall her ever laughing out-loud. In her giddiest moment, she might display a smile equal to da Vinci's "Mona Lisa" and when she became irritated, the smile would lessen a bit and she would turn a little grey in the face. Whether you were the banker's daughter or the street cleaner's, you were treated the same. We all thought she worked hard to help us attain the best education possible."

Lenore L Johnson Miller ('28) married her classmate Robert Miller ('28). She became the class and school historian for the College Springs "Amity" High School Alumni. Her beautiful cursive writing listing all 881 graduates, from A to Z, is a treasure for the annals of history. At the fortieth reunion of their graduating class, she recorded the accomplishments from some her class of 24 graduates of 1928. They became:

- Consulting Engineer
- Farmer Angus breeder
- Bookkeeper at Implement dealer
- Homemaker visitor to Ireland to grandparents' roots
- Professor at Oklahoma State in Agriculture Journalism
- Farmer (four)
- Purchasing Agent for ABEX
- Five housewives, one a private music teacher
- Henry Field Seed Company worker
- Funeral home worker
- Teacher
- Superintendent of schools at Page County
- Frock shop owner
- Meat Cutter
- Real Estate Salesman

Pranks—A cow mysteriously ended up in the school library on Halloween in 1956. Gene Ripley ('57) shared, "It took me 25-30 years to figure out who did it. I was a senior and had to help clean up the mess the next day. Superintendent J.C. Green was furious, but Principal Bess Anderson was quietly smiling. I can still see the stains on some of those books." Even though the statute of limitations surely has past these 65 years later, Gene Ripley would not reveal who the pranksters were.

Another prank in the 1950s involved the new Mayor Lucile Bast Simpson and her appointed lady marshal for College Springs. Even though there had not been much juvenile chicanery, the new mayor decided she was going to restore order. The kids divided up in four groups and located one in each corner of town. They set off cherry bombs in one part of town and listened for the 1950 straight-eight Hydrostatic Pontiac to start up in pursuit to find the culprits. Upon stopping the car, a new sound of cherry bombs echoed from another area. The pranksters had great fun and the new Mayor and Marshal eventually stepped back their rigid surveillance. They may have been packing pistols, but they had met their match with the kids of College Springs.

FFA and Y-Teens—FFA (for boys) started in the 1930s. Kenneth Ripley ('37) was in FFA the first year it was offered. His son, Gene Ripley ("57) told, "My first project was two Jersey heifers. I guess it must have taught me something because I later milked cows for 40 years."

Y-Teens was the girls leadership organization. Each year they would send a representative to leadership camp at Lake Geneva, Wisconsin.

Hot Lunch Program—School lunches began in the 1940s. The cooks were Ina Black and Ruth Perry. "Mrs. Perry always knew what we liked. I hated diced beets. She would try to put them on my tray. I'd say 'Mrs. Perry, you know I don't like beets' and she would put a small square on my plate and say 'now Gene, you've got to eat at least one,'" remembered Gene Ripley ('57).

Closing—In the 1950s the Department of Education mandated the elimination of small high schools and forced consolidation. The College Springs High School closed after graduation in May 1959. Five towns and districts united in establishing South Page High School with the attendance at the majestic College Springs building. These towns were: Blanchard, Braddyville, Coin, Shambaugh, and College Springs. The district stretched from the Taylor County line on the east, the Missouri border on the south, and four miles west of Coin including three townships. The first class of the new South

Page High school had 60 graduates in 1960. In the 47 years from 1913-1959 there were 881 graduates from Amity-College Springs High School. The most numerous names of the graduates were: Hill-18, Kenagy-18, Faquhar-17, VanFosson-16, Griffith-13, Dugan-12, Whipp-12, Anderson-11, McCullough-10, Stanton-10, Blair-9, Andersee-8, and Christensen-8. The last graduate from College Springs High School was Mary Yaple (alphabetically).

Amity—College Springs High School
Page County, IA

#18

Dayton High School

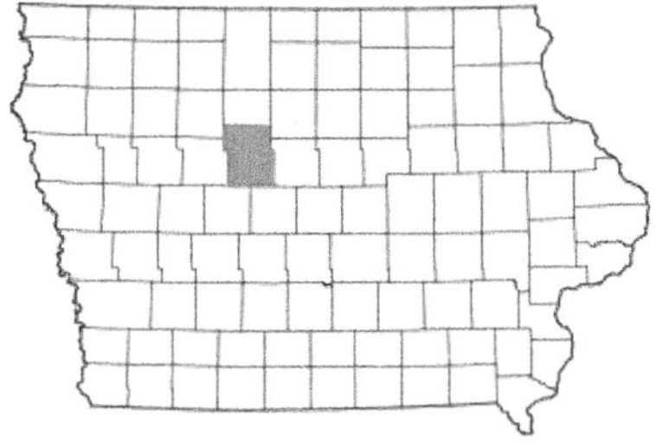

Mascot: Tigers
Colors: Scarlet and Black
Closed: 1986
Location: Southeast Webster County

Early History—In 1857, this town was first called West Dayton and settled by many Swedish immigrants. It was renamed Dayton in 1877. At one time lore was that there were 750 Swedes and 75 others who made up the population. They were mostly farmers or small landowners from Sweden who came to Iowa with the purpose to become independent landowners. They were settlers called "prairie chickens" because they turned to the open prairie for their land. They were distinguished from the "timber coons" who were mixed immigrants from other nations who settled in the timber along the Des Moines River. These "timber coons" were mainly from European cities, mining areas, and industrial cities, and preferred the woods to the open spaces.

Railroads arrived in 1881 with the north-south railroad called the Minneapolis-St. Paul and the east-west railroad called the Great Western (later the Chicago-Northwestern).

Early Schools—The Independent School District was organized in 1872. The first schoolteacher's salary was $30 month. By 1876, the school building was not large enough, so a new frame building was constructed for $1,200. Less than ten years later in 1885, a new two-room building with one room above the other was constructed. The room on the ground floor was for the school. An identical two-room building was added in 1889. Tuition was $1.50 for high school and $1 for the lower grades.

A beautiful two-story brick grade school with a belfry was built in 1901. It was hit by a tornado in 1918. The roof and belfry were destroyed. The roof was repaired; the belfry was not replaced.

The high school was completed in 1920 and the auditorium was added in 1932.

Community Stories—The United Brethren Church in Yell Township was presided over by Bishop Milton Wright. He was the father of Orville and Wilbur Wright, the noted aviation pioneers. This church was originally called the McGuire Bend Church.

The *Dayton Review* newspaper reported in October 1886:

> Professor Carr brought a skull of some unfortunate man down to school on Tuesday for the A and B Physiology class to examine.

From the *Dayton Review* in October 1896:

> The flag has been floating over the schoolhouse since last Thursday in honor of the 50th anniversary of Iowa as a state, which is being celebrated in Burlington, the former capital of Iowa.

Boys did not wear "jeans" to school as they considered them work clothes. After consolidation, the town fellows got the idea of wearing jeans to school. Their jeans did not sit well with the faculty and the boys were dismissed for the day.

Killed in Action—The following were lost in action in service to their county:

Duane H. Peterson, WWI
Charlie Peterson, WWI
Benny Petersen, WWI
Ruben Petersen, WWI
Dale R. Anderson, WWII

Oscar W. Oberg ('26), WWII
Ronald L. Schwendemann, WWII
Fredrick W. Thomas Jr., WWII
Wallace Wise Jr., WWII
Clayton Helms ('49), Korea

Sports—Dayton High School was one of 16 high schools in Webster County. With an average enrollment of 90 in the 1920s, it was the third largest in the county. During that time there were 850 smaller high schools than Dayton in the state of Iowa.

In February 1924, Dayton High School had the dubious honor of being the first high school in Iowa banned from playing high school sports by the fledgling Iowa High School Athletic Association. The facts were recorded and shared by Earl R. Shostrom ('39):

> In 1920, the new high school was constructed. Dayton had two athletes Carl "Hughie" Nelson ('25) and Lawrence Commer ('25) who were the greatest athletes to ever attend high school together at the time. They both starred in all sports as freshman (football, basketball, and track). Their senior year, DHS was invited to a four state 54 team tournament at Morningside College in Sioux City (23 teams Class A & B and 31 teams Class C). As a young grade school student, I was always enthralled by the large silver basketball prominently displayed in the entrance to the high school. It was explained to me that it was the first-place trophy for the 1925 Morningside College Invitational basketball tournament. When I asked whether Dayton won the State Tournament that year (1925), all I usually got were grumbles about 'dumb superintendent and coach'.

Playing eleven-man football at the time with limited face protection, soft helmet design, and less padding caused many injuries. In the final game of the 1923 season, Rockwell City (who had three weeks before postponed their game with Dayton because of injuries) was to be the opponent. Dayton, who had played two more games, had itself racked up many injuries and needed to cancel playing the rescheduled game at Rockwell City. The Rockwell Superintendent wanted to play in the worst way and stating that he did not want to make refunds to season ticketholders. Dayton sources claimed that the Rockwell Superintendent urged them to fill in their squad with alumni players. Dayton finally did so and lost the football game despite the alumni filling in the roster.

It was not until February 24, 1924, that Dayton was notified, they were banned from basketball tournaments, track and field, and from football the fall of 1924. The IHSAA had difficulty enforcing rules and there were no full-time employees.

It was this silver basketball at the entrance to the school which was for the Championship for the Morningside tournament that seemed to tell the story of the great teams that had been suspended the year before. In that tournament DHS defeated Randolph, Nebraska, Burke, South Dakota, Laurens, Pocahontas, and Milford in the finals to bring home the trophy.

"In the 1940s the sports rivals were Boxholm, Pilot Mound, Stratford, Lehigh, Burnside, and Gowrie," shared Gordon Lundberg ('49). "It always seemed no matter what sport, we always came down to having to play Gowrie."

The 1942 boys team won the Webster County Basketball Tournament. These tournaments were always played in Dayton because Dayton, along with Callender, had the best gymnasiums.

The 1960s had great baseball teams and finished second to Keystone in the state finals led by the Rankin twins, Robert ('65) and William ('65), Denny Jensen ('66), and the Lambert twins, Bill ('65) and Bruce ('65). The coach was Jim Reiter who had been a pitcher for the New York Mets until he was injured.

The 1974 girls basketball team went to the state six-on-six basketball tournament losing to Woodbine in the opening round. The small community of Manilla won the tournament that year.

The 1985 boys team was the state basketball tournament runners-up in Class B.

Drivers Education—Drivers education was started in the spring of 1949 for six weeks. Phyllis Sandholm Kinsey ('49) smiled as she remembered. "We started at 7:00 AM with three students in the car, each driving for one-half hour. Rosemary Hall was the first instructor. Miss Hall was the principal, girls basketball coach, and taught sociology and bookkeeping. Talk about wearing many hats. The car was a white Chevy from the local car dealer. The shift was on the column and a clutch was needed with many grindings of the gears and tense moments for some of us first time drivers."

Music—The early bands were led by Howard Nelson. Larry Hansen conducted the bands from the late 1960s through the 1980s. The marching band was the featured band for the renowned Dayton Rodeo and parade on every Labor Day weekend. This Rodeo takes place in the natural amphitheater in the valley on the southern border of town. The Rodeo weekend attracts well over 10,000 each year and draws cowboys who compete for money. They earn points that impact their standings in the National Rodeo competition. Gordon

Lundberg ('49), Phyllis Sandholm Kinsey ('49) and Lynne Richardson Schlief ('63) have been parade marshal's. Gordon shared, "I was at the first one in 1937 and have not missed one since in 82 years (2019)."

Music education and development of talents were evidenced by four students who used their music abilities to provide enjoyment to thousands in the Midwest. Don Myers ('69), Joe LeValley('71), Roger Peterson ('72), and Mark Phaln ('72) grew up together in Dayton. During their high school years, they formed the Morning Glory Rock Band. They played consistently for three years to crowds throughout Iowa and three bordering states. When they were in college, they played 169 nights in one year. The band and all four members were inducted into the Iowa Rock 'n Roll Hall of Fame in 2016. Their first performance outside of Dayton was made possible because their principal, Norman Kolberg, recommended them to another high school.

Yearbook—The first yearbook was printed in 1923. There are pictures of some of the activities in the school at the time including the Ukulele Club, glee club, Declamatory, domestic sciences, Parent Teachers Association, and Normal School. There were 68 enrolled in Normal Training which was the largest one in the state of Iowa.

Bus Drivers—Nellie Munson, single with a very short haircut, was a no-nonsense driver.

Joe LeValley ('71) shared, "I've heard the story that my great-grandfather, Dan Lavelle, was a tobacco chewing, swearing driver who really enjoyed the job. He was called before the school board and warned that he would need to stop chewing tobacco and swearing in front of the kids. He told the board, 'I can give up the tobacco chewing, but I can't give up the cussing.' He was fired."

Teachers—Howard Rankin was the Superintendent from 1957-1982. He was an excellent administrator and teacher. Lynne Richardson Schlief ('63) remembered, "He taught math or whatever needed taught. He managed budgets well and had an enormous and intimidating voice that rattled the windows when he yelled at the end of the day 'BUS RIDERS!' He was such a calm person when things got tense. One morning at 3:00 AM, he was found with a hose in hand washing the outside of his house. When asked by a neighbor what he was doing, he replied, 'Silly kids egged the house and I am just getting it off before it dries.' He put boxing gloves on the boys who may be having a spat and they settled their disagreement with the gloves." Phyliss Sandborn Kinsey ('49) continued, "One night there was a knock at Mr. Rankin's back door, and he opened it to find boys, one with a gun in his hand. He calmly said 'Oh boys, why don't you come back in the morning. You are drunk."

As the years passed, Mr. Rankin became quite a legend in Dayton. John Hambleton ('52) said, "I called the sidewalk up to the door of the grade school the 'Rankin Freeway.' Rankin raced each day to the post office to get the mail and sped back to school and just drove right up the sidewalk to the door to deliver the mail, so to not miss a beat of the activity."

Janitor—John Hambleton ('52) became the janitor right out of high school. He cleaned the school while wearing roller skates. When the superintendent asked "What do you think you are doing?" John said, "I'm going to clean."

Notable Graduates—Dale Nelson ('37) was the CEO of Iowa Farm Bureau. He ran both the insurance and service sides of the company.

Robert "Bob" Williams ('42) was a radio announcer for WHO radio in Des Moines. He came from a family of ten and got his first start at KVFD radio in Fort Dodge.

Earl Shostrom ('39) was a successful Des Moines attorney and well-known referee at the state sports tournaments.

Joe LeValley ('71) became the Senior Vice President of Mercy Medical Centers. He was inducted into the Iowa Rock 'n Roll Hall of Fame. He is an author and an award-winning novelist and public speaker in Iowa.

Senior Trips—Superintendent Harold Schmickley wanted to start senior trips in 1949. The seniors that year chartered a bus and went to Chicago. Gordon Sundberg ('49) recalled, "We went to the Lamar Ballroom, Marshall Fields, stayed at Stevens Hotel on Lake Michigan, ate at a Swedish restaurant in our dress up clothes, and went to a baseball game. Each of us paid our own way. All we needed was $75 for the trip."

This tradition continued with later trips to the Lake of the Ozarks, Colorado, St. Louis, and Chicago. Lynn Richardson Schlief ('63) remembered, "I was horrified in Chicago to see a man eating from a garbage can!" These trips extended the learning for students which could not be given in a classroom.

Closing—The high school closed after graduation in May 1986. In the 97 years from 1890-1986, there were 1,694 graduates from Dayton High School. The largest class was 37 graduates in 1978. The most numerous surnames of the graduates were: Johnson-61, Peterson-60, Anderson-40, Hanson-9, Carlson-

28, Swanson-28, LeValley-23, Nelson-21, Olson-19 Tell-12, Erickson-11, Richardson-11, Magnuson-10, and Strandberg-10. The last graduate from Dayton High School was Angela Troutwine (alphabetically).

(Author's Note: Notice all of the surnames of the graduates from DHS with the Swedish ending of 'son'.)

Dayton High School
Webster County, IA

#19

DeSoto High School

Mascot: Whirlwinds
Colors: Orange and Black
Closed: 1961
Location: Extr. South Central Dallas County

Early History—The town of DeSoto was named in honor of a Rock Island Railroad officer. The land for the town site was donated to the railroad by Thomas Hemphill. The direct line to Chicago was by the Rock Island and it made a good market for the surrounding countryside. The railroad bought 160 acres of land adjoining the original town platting and laid it out in plots of three to five acres each. These were the most desirable sites for residences. The railroad company built a large well that furnished the depot. The water in the tank serving the trains was supplied by a spring from nearby Bulger Creek. During these years the town was a division point. It grew rapidly and business was humming. Saloons and gambling flourished and much disorder prevailed. The population rose to 600 when the town was incorporated on January 1, 1875.

Some town events and activities were:

1878 The first telephones in town were installed.

1878 A movement began under the leadership of John W. Harden of Des Moines. The DeSoto Temperance Reform Club was organized on March 17, 1878 with a membership roll of 500. Desoto was very firm on temperance and was one of six towns in the county that had no saloons.

1918 On November 11, 1918, a big bonfire celebrating the end of WWI featured the hanging of the Kaiser in effigy.

1920 Vote to consolidate the DeSoto Independent School with surrounding rural schools passed on October 26, 1920. A separate tally for women showed that 75 women in town voted with 72 yes and 3 no votes. The women's tally outside the district or in the rural school districts was 31 yes and 29 no votes. The rural vote to consolidate squeaked by. This vote may have showed there was fear in losing the close sense of community they enjoyed because of the country school. (This desire to preserve the community was again experienced with the closing of the DeSoto High school some 41 years later).

1922 DeSoto Day at the Iowa State Fair on August 25, 1922, featured three concerts in the pavilion. T. Fred Henry was the bandmaster. N.N. Blackman was the organizer.

1924 The DeSoto High School orchestra broadcast from WHO Broadcasting Station from 7:30-9:00.

1927 The bank in town failed and depositors lost $10,000.

1928 DeSoto population was listed as 261.

1940 Bea Boots was elected mayor, the first women mayor in Iowa.

Early Schools—Soon after the town was established, a frame building was constructed near the park. It served a double purpose as a school and church.

In 1870, the DeSoto Independent School District built a two-story brick school building. It was 30′ x 60′ and had four large rooms. It cost $5,000 to construct. The first floor was used for the primary and intermediate departments. The second floor was occupied by the high school. There were nearly 200 students in attendance.

The first graduating class from the high school was in 1882 with Principal C.M. Pinkerton presenting diplomas to seven graduates.

In 1882, an addition was built onto the schoolhouse. The educational advances in this prosperous community were made possible with many excellent teachers in the school system.

A bond election for $18,000 for a new schoolhouse was defeated by the voters in the spring of 1915. In 1920, the DeSoto Independent School District voted for school consolidation. The details for consolidation were drawn up by the State Department of Instruction, the county board, and the local school board. The district annexed the rural county schools and became the DeSoto Consolidated School.

In January 1922, J.G. Riley was paid $6,750 for ten acres of land to be used as a school site. Bids were taken for the construction of a beautiful new three-story school building in March 1922. The low bid for $68,057 for the general construction work was submitted by John A. Benson from Des Moines. The low bid of $14,348 for the plumbing, heating, and ventilation work was submitted by Benge and Robinson of Winterset. The school district purchased the brick at $28 per thousand from Twin City.

In January 1923, the entire school body, led by the faculty, marched from the old school building to the new one. The school board now met at the new school building. Before this time, they had always met in the home of the Secretary.

School Colors—J.G. Riley was born and raised in Illinois in a Republican family who named him after the president, James Garfield. When J.G. and Ethyl Smith Riley moved to the DeSoto area to farm, he was one of the few Democrats in the area. The Riley's were proponents of education and J.G. Riley was a member of the school board. It may have been from his admiration for President Woodrow Wilson and his leadership at Princeton as an education leader that the school colors of Princeton were to also to become the Orange and Black colors for DeSoto High School.

Busing—For several years after consolidation in 1923, the country children were brought to school in horse-drawn school buses. The district did not have enough buses. For a time after consolidation, school board member J.G. Riley drove children to school in his seven-passenger Luxury Packard car which had a jump seat.

Notable Teachers—Ruth McCorkle Wenger ('24) wrote in her book, *My Dear Grandchildren*, "With the new school came good teachers . . . George Wallace and Mary Guthrie . . . taught Latin and English . . . missionaries in India . . . told of Oberammergau Passion Play in the Bavarian Alps . . . saw many years later . . . such a good influence of good teachers is priceless . . . taught art . . . ordinary kids showed remarkable talent (Paul-my brother too.) . . . new school teachers clothes, their beaux, coming and going had to bear the scrutiny of the town folk. They had few secrets." (When George died suddenly in April 1923, Mary became the Superintendent of the school.)

Jack Boots ('46) told of Ruth Jennings, "She had a wooden prosthetic thumb. When there was misbehavior in her classroom, she would thump the student with this thumb, and it hurt!" Ruth Jennings taught for 22 years, from 1922-1943, as an elementary teacher.

Bessie Crowe taught from 1922-1958 in the upper elementary. Records for both Miss Jennings and Miss Crowe only date back to 1922 with the new school opening. They may have been in the district prior to 1922. Both were single and chose to teach rather than marry. (At those times, only single women could teach school). The Chaplin parents worried about their son Glenn, but a community member said, "just wait until Miss Jennings gets him, he'll learn something!"

LaVonne Jennings (niece of Ruth Jennings) came home from the Women's Marine Corps during WWII. She taught English and literature, debate, and drama. Jack Boots ('46) edited the *Whirlwind,* the first school yearbook in 1945, under the direction of Lavonne Jennings. John Jensen ('45) said, "She was a very tough and effective teacher."

Kermit Chase and his wife, Ardith, came to De Soto in 1948 as superintendent and principal. By direction of the school board they were to emphasize the sciences, college preparedness, and to provide a well-disciplined school. Mr. Chase taught physics and chemistry in alternating years and advanced math. He directed the band and coached girls basketball. His many responsibilities were typical of many superintendents of the small schools of Iowa. Kermit and Ardith opened the door for a number of students to go to college including several women who became nurses. As the band director, Mr. Chase was insistent that his band members not tap their feet. "I did not have him for an instructor as he had left by my time. I was aware of his dislike for foot tapping and made a point of standing up to make sure we were not tapping our feet when he was a judge at our regional music contests," said Jim Riley ('58).

Harold Miller was the superintendent in the late 1950s and taught math. Richard Fleming ('56) shared, "My first love was history. Superintendent

Harold Miller taught four of us boys—Willard Van Buren ('56), Seth Riegle ('56), Walter Eierman ('56), and Richard Fleming ('56)—an extra class of advanced algebra and trigonometry in a broom closet after hours. He would say, 'It is not like history which is changing all of the time. Two plus two will always be four.'"

Music—Roger Chrysler was an excellent teacher in band and chorus in the 1950s. He had some of his own arrangements for popular music written for the glee club to sing along with the band. Jim Riley ('58) remembered, "I especially remember the song 'Sugartime' which he arranged for the glee club. We went on to contest and received a first."

Sports—Football was not played at DeSoto High School. The boys played basketball and baseball. There were never any outstanding team records though they did have some success in upsetting area teams.

Robert Donnell started boys track in the early 1950s. There was a quarter-mile area marked around the grassy area near the school. In the schools' first ever dual meet, they handily defeated Earlham.

Girls basketball had several outstanding teams in 1930 and 1940. Coach and Superintendent S.C. Highbarger led the 1940 team to the Iowa State Girls Basketball Tournament. They won their first game at State against Farmington 43-42, and blasted College Springs 44-19 in their second game They lost to Hansell (the eventual state champions) in the semifinals and in the consolation game to Numa. They finished fourth place and the trophy was proudly displayed in the trophy case at the high school. Members of the 1940 team were: Peggy Brower ('41), Madelyn Dunbar ('40), Ruby Maricle ('40), Evelyn Rater ('40), Delores Martens ('42), Mary Olive Elder ('40), Ida Jurgensen ('40), Doris Palmer ('42), Ruth Petty, Hilda Rinard ('41), Gladys Cade ('42), and Virginia Olmstead ('40). Some controversy was always exchanged about which team was better. Madelyn Dunbar Bratton ('40) said, "the 1930 team only had one loss to Perry which went on to win state that year, but we brought home the trophy in 1940."

Another great team that did not make it to state was in 1958, but they were "giant killers." As told by Patsy Jurgensen ('58), "The De Soto girls team in 1958 had a very successful season with a 15-1 record. The game of basketball was huge in our lives that senior year. I will always remember my white jersey #44 and the black #23. Sandra Sediwy ('58), Eunice Burgett ('58), and I have been close friends since the second and third grades. We practiced diligently with one another whenever we got a chance ... Now it was tournament time—1958.

We had a string of 22 wins and only two defeats. Our pre-season loss was a county game to Perry. I remember setting a block on a sturdy Perry forward and her charging through me, and I went rolling down on the floor. We headed on to sectional play. We Whirlwinds defeated Van Meter 46-22 and Norwalk 43-31. Now we were to go up against a much larger team of Valley of West Des Moines. I believe that Valley had about 400 students in their high school to our 55. Eunice Burgett ('58) was averaging about 20 points per game. The Valley girls were very confident of a win, and they invited us to their victory party BEFORE the game. They didn't know that they caused the spark that lit the fire in us! We DeSoto girls were very 'pumped' and we outplayed the Valley girls every quarter but the first with a final score of 57-48. The Dallas County News headline was: 'De Soto Girls Blast Valley: In District now.' This hard-fought win was, I felt, the high point of many of our girls basketball season, especially mine. Traveling back to DeSoto after the Valley game, our bus had several cars following it. There was great excitement in the gym and in our little town . . . now in the District play . . . we were deflated and defeated in the first game by the Huxley girls."

Killed in Action—The following men were killed in action while serving the country:

Max Stump ('40)
Wayne Martins ('49)
Virgil Lienemann ('50)
John McClurg, Vietnam
Steve Edwards, Vietnam

Notable Graduates—Willard 'Van' Van Buren ('56) became an executive at IBM. He became an executive in Hospital Systems in Texas. He said, "We were pretty naïve when we graduated from high school. Yet, our educational culture had honed our intelligence to think we could accomplish some things before we knew what we were doing."

Richard Fleming ('56) became a PhD in math. He taught at the universities of Missouri, Memphis, and Central Michigan. He published 40 technical articles and two research-level books.

Gail Reigle ('52) had a doctorate in Endocrinology and physiology and taught at Iowa State University. He later was an administrator at the College of Osteopathic Medicine and a Dean at Michigan State University.

Elaine Riegle ('60) became a specialist in Pediatrics and anesthesiology. She remains in active practice today (2020) in a St. Louis, Missouri, hospital.

James C. Riley ('58) became a minister after receiving his degree at Garrett Theological Seminary at Evanston, Illinois. He became a pastor at Atlantic, Ida Grove, Albion and Beaman, Northwood, Council Bluffs, and Corydon. His book, *Who Made Your World Bigger,* is one of the best chronicled histories of a family's contribution to a community and the De Soto High School. (Some of the excerpts for this story of the De Soto High School have come from his research and collections).

Betty Tracy Gustafson ('61) received her Master's from the University of Iowa. She worked with children and families as a licensed clinical social worker at the Atascadero State Hospital in California. The hospital is a forensic mental hospital for male criminals. She says "So who made my world bigger? Lots of people—my dad started the process. His interest as a farmer in reading and nature got me curious about my world." For nine years she has been a legislative clerk in the state legislature for her husband Stan Gustafson.

Closing. The DeSoto High school closed following graduation in May 1961. That fall the high school students were bused to the new district in Adel called Adel-DeSoto. In the 67 years from 1895-1961 there were 571 graduates from DeSoto High School. The largest class was in 1927 with 27 graduates. The most numerous surnames of the graduates were: Lienemann-11, Stump-10, Jensen-8, Jurgensen-8, Riley-8, Johnson-7, Ganoe-6, Merical-6, and Smith-6. The last graduate from DeSoto High School was Betty Tracy (alphabetically).

DeSoto High School
Dallas County, IA

#20

Donnellson High School

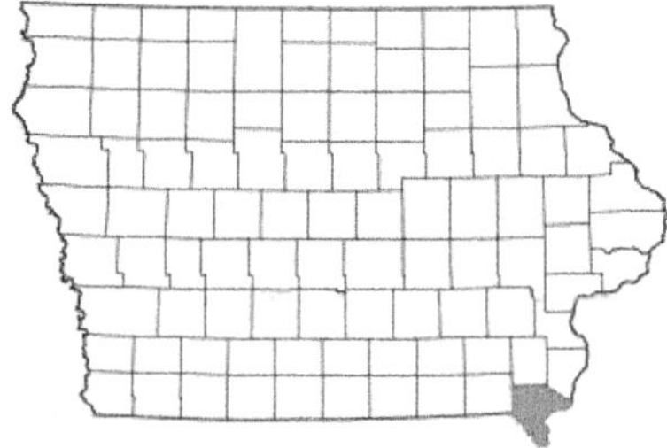

Mascot: Tigers/Tigerettes
Colors: Orange and Black
Closed: 1961
Location: Central Lee County

Early History—Donnellson is in the most southeast county in the state. The southern half of what was to be named Lee County was set aside in 1825 by the United States Government and designated as Half Breed Tract. This was for an area where the descendants of Indian and European-American mixed-race people were to settle. The government drew a line extending along a line of 40° 23′N latitude (the length of the Missouri-Iowa border) across Lee County to the Mississippi River for this mixed blood population from the Great Lakes regions.

The relationship between the mixed-bloods and their ancestral tribes particularly affected the descendants when the tribes ceded lands to the United States Government in exchange for payment. The rights of the mixed-blood descendants to payment or a part in decision making was not acknowledged. In 1830, the United States arranged by the Fourth Treaty of Prairie du Chien, to set aside a tract of land for mixed-blood people related to the Oto, Ioway, Omaha, Sac and Fox, and Santee Indians. The treaty granted these Half-Breed Tracts as sections of land in the form of "Indian Reservations."

A treaty in 1824—between the Sac People, the Fox Tribe, and the United States—designated 119,000 acres between the Des Moines River and the Mississippi River as area the mixed-bloods had the right to occupy, but not to buy or sell. Land sales from the government started in 1837.

Ft. Madison, in the northeast corner of the county, had been established in 1810 as a fort and one of the three westernmost forts along the Mississippi River. Keokuk, on the furthest southern tip of the county and state, was a fur trading center and became a settlement in the late 1820s. Both towns would later become the county seats and the only county in Iowa with two county seats.

The town of Donnell, later Donnellson, was established in 1871. It was named for two brothers and their sons who settled in Franklin Township. The Donnellson Cemetery is located on land donated from the brothers and the final resting place for their families.

Early Schools—The first school was a log and stone cabin school south of town called Donnell School. The school was located on Donnell property in the Waverly School district in Charleston Township. A contentious vote held in 1889 in Donnellson about building a school in town found the town progressives losing the election for a new town school. As reported in the *Evening Democrat* of Ft. Madison on March 25, 1889:

> The contest at the school election last Monday was equated in excitement only by the presidential election. The cause of it was a proposition to vote a tax sufficient to build a schoolhouse in town, or rather, to complete a fund for that purpose a subscription having been raised for over $800. The measure was defeated by a small majority. The district is a very large one and to a great extent composed of a non-progressive element that came to the polls in full force and consigned the cherished measure of our citizens to "innocuous destitude"
>
> . . . the rising generation will be forced to grope in darkness or travel a long muddy road to a small house for light.

After 1888, the town children attended school in the stone schoolhouse known as District No. 2 of Franklin Township north of town. In 1892, the citizens of Donnellson Public School district voted for a school board and decided to build a two-story brick structure in town.

In 1904, there were forty students in the two, four-grade rooms. The Professor, or man who taught the upper grades, received a higher salary than the unmarried lady who taught primary. By 1911, they received $65 and $50 a month, but with the minimum wage of 1914, the salaries increased to $116 and $59.

The eighth-grade graduates in 1903 were the first class to attend Donnellson Public School all eight years. In 1913, the Donnellson school board went to Danville to inspect their newly built high school. They returned and two months later held a meeting with the boards from Charleston (Waverly school) and Franklin Townships. Several more votes ensued before the townships and town agreed to build a new high school.

On March 8, 1915, there was a vote for a proposed bond issue for $18,000 for the erection and equipment of a new school building. Women were allowed to vote for the first time. The women's vote carried by 66% compared to 59% for the men. In May 1915, the bonds were sold, and work started on the new school. Five months later the new high school was completed with 110 students attending seventh through tenth grades.

The 1927, an addition to the high school was built to alleviate overcrowding. This time the bond for $45,000 was passed 310 to 76. The addition was also for a new gymnasium, home economics, sewing, and agriculture rooms.

Academic Curriculum—With the new high school came advancements:

1915 Nine students begin their freshman year with an approved state curriculum.

1916 The state granted approval for two years of high school work.

1917 The school began four classes of high school.

1918 Three graduates were in the first class. French was offered as foreign language.

1921 Reading a portion of the Bible was made part of the daily program.

1923 The school joined the State Declamatory Association and State Debating League.

1928 The school and a malted milk company made special arrangements to treat underweight students with two glasses of chocolate malted milk for twelve weeks.

1920s and 1930s Latin was offered for foreign language.

1931 The first intelligence tests were administered to students and repeated in 1934 to verify reliability. Of 106 students, 20 were superior, 22 were dull or on the border, and 64 were normal.

1932 On February 22, the entire high school body listened to the radio address of President Hoover officially opening the bicentennial George Washington celebration.

1937 A schoolbook rental plan was begun.

1942 No school was held May 4 and 5 while compulsory registration for sugar rationing was held. New courses were added in geography, hygiene, sociology, and two more vocational homemaking courses.

1943 Free dental examinations were given to all students.

1948 Spanish and Music Theory and Appreciation were new subjects offered.

1955 Drivers Education was offered.

Notable Graduates—John "Johnny" Johnson ('60) was the only African American to graduate from Donnellson High School. He was raised in an extremely poor family in a very marginal rundown home. He became an orthopedic surgeon and practiced forty years in Davenport. He had an incredible following and gave of himself and his resources to the poor and less fortunate in the Quad Cities.

Bert Vandenberg ('56) was honored to be awarded with the "American Farmer Degree." This is only given to a select few high school students every year.

Dorothy Krebill ('47) was an opera singer and sang all over the world. She graduated from the University of Iowa and resided in New York City. Roberta Leisy Krehbiel ('55) said, "My mother, Alice Leisy, played the piano for her at our church and Dorothy's vibrato rattled the windows and caused them to vibrate.

Wendell Sander ('52) PhD was the sixteenth employee at Apple Computer. In 1986, he invented the Apple III computer.

Daryl Smith ('56) PhD was a professor of biology and science education at the University of Northern Iowa for over 40 years. He taught more than 40 classes in science and science-education. Dr. Smith founded and directed the UNI-Tallgrass Prairie Center from 1999-2014. He was the executive director and co-producer of the PBS documentary film "America's Lost Landscape: The Tallgrass Prairie."

Bus Drivers—Roy Bauter owned an old bus and drove for the district. The district bought a new bus and, as it turned in front of Bauter on Franklin Road, Roy revved the old bus and passed the new bus on the gravel road to the surprise of everyone.

Don Schweer ('58) recalled, "I got on the bus at 7:15 in the morning. We only lived six miles from Donnellson, but I had to ride for 46 miles to get to school. Our driver was Roy Lowenberg and he never let a snow drift across the road keep him from going on the route. He would yell back, 'Hang on!' and we plowed through any drift. One time, he hit a drift so hard that the door flew open and the bus filled with snow. Roy calmly barked, 'Get the snow off the little kids.'"

Erma Trabert DeRosear ('37) wrote about the Otto Rasch School Bus: "I graduated from the eighth grade at Primrose in the spring of 1933. The Depression was on and very few people had cars; roads were poor. There were five Primrose kids for high school. Otto Rasch ran the service station and was also the dealer of Dodge cars. He wanted his daughter to continue her education, so he did a little work on his car, placing two small seats in the back parallel to the regular seat. He could then haul five students. Wayne Benjamin ('37) rode in front and Violet Rasch ('37), Florence Proenneke ('37), Doris Benjamin ('36), and Erma Trabert ('37) occupied the back. He charged $1 per week. Times were hard and it was a hardship some weeks for my parents to pay for my transportation. Otto ran his bus until the spring of 1937 when his daughter graduated."

Notable Teachers—Miss Jewell Berger taught Home Economics and English for twenty years from 1929-1948. She was very strict and was known to throw erasers at students to get their attention. "She was a stickler on grammar, sentence structure, and enunciation. She taught me to say the word 'interesting' the proper way instead of 'inter-resting'," remembered Vi Young Wilson ('54) with a smile.

Elbert Groendyke taught math, science, and trigonometry as well as being the principal from 1946-1953. Roberta Leisy Kreibiel ('55) said, "Mr. Groendyke was a very good teacher." Her twin brother Bob Leisy ('55) mentioned, "Mr. Groendyke was very regimented. If we didn't read the chapter in science before class, he made us copy the whole chapter by hand. You didn't forget to read the chapter very often."

Donald Finney not only was a very successful girls basketball coach but also taught social sciences and history. Lillian Kirschner Schweer ('60) grinned as she shared, "We played our hearts out for him in basketball. He was a very popular teacher and we were able to have great fun with him. His little 1937 Chevy called 'Leaping Lena' ended up on top of the school on more than one occasion. Another time, his car was found out by our farm on a road south of town."

Sports—In the early 1920s boys football was offered. It was discontinued in the 1930s and 1940s. The girls basketball team went to the state tournament three straight years in 1953, 1954, and 1955 with Donald Finney as the coach. One of the stars on those teams was Judy Hodson Finney ('58) who went on the play five-on-five basketball at Iowa Wesleyan. In 1959 she was a member of the USA team that toured in the country playing the Soviet Union National team. In 1961, she toured the Soviet Union with the US team. She later married her high school coach, Donald Finney.

Deloris Kaltefleiter ('53) was named first team all-state in 1953.

Athletic rivals were Argyle, Denmark, Montrose, and Farmington. Argyle and Montrose later joined Donnellson to form the Central Lee High School in 1962.

The most heated competition and contests for bragging rights were the Lee County Little Four Basketball Tournaments (Donnellson, Denmark, Argyle, and Montrose) held in February each year.

Polio—Few small towns in the state had as many polio victims as Donnellson. Howard Hohl, Ann Krehbiel, and infant Sherry Schau died of the disease. Bob Hodson, David Kirchner, Harvey Seyb, Melvin Frueh, and John Sander contracted the virus but recovered.

1955 was the peak of the polio epidemic. The whole country was in the prevention stage. The Ft. Madison swimming pool was off limits and the Lee County Fair was canceled due to the close congregation of people. Don Schweer ('58) said, "I was just 15 years old but had grown a great beard for the centennial celebration held at the Fair. When it was called off, I would have won the teenage beard category. By 1956, the contest found me winning the teenage beard first place at the Lee County Fair."

"Until the polio vaccine became available, the only preventative was a shot giving ten milliliters of gamma globulin in the arm," remembered Lillian Kirschner Schweer ('60)." Late in 1955, the polio vaccine was released, and each pupil received the vaccination. The long-suffering epidemic soon came to an end.

Hot Lunch—The hot lunch program started in the fall of 1955. Mrs. Mullin was known for her bread and butter sandwiches. The boys could take as many as six of them. By the second year of the lunch program, they were limited to three of the bread and butter sandwiches.

Pranks—In 1946, two senior boys decided to showcase their artistic abilities at Halloween and used chalk to mark up the side of the school wall. Either by interrogation or by their spelling on the wall, the culprits were called on the carpet by Superintendent Leonard Haase. They were expelled from school. In sympathy the entire student body except for two students went on strike. "I remember a large sheet hanging from the schoolhouse window with the red letters painted on it 'ON Strike!'" told Bob Leisy ('55). The strike took the students on a walk downtown where they met with townspeople who were not sympathetic to their cause. One lady even threw a bucket of paint at the strikers. No one can remember the outcome of the strike, or if the expelled ever returned to school, but the fact that there was a strike still lives in people's memories.

Lamar Carpenter was the vocational agriculture and manual arts instructor. While overhauling a two-cylinder tractor in the auto mechanics class an incident of explosive nature occurred. Don Schweer ('58) chuckled as he shared, "The tractor overhaul was almost completed when one of the boys poured a thimble of gas in the carburetor. Someone cranked the wheel and the tractor backfired, shooting a hole in the roof of the shop. Mr. Carpenter was the one called on the carpet by the Superintendent for not controlling the classroom." Don Schweer ('58) continued the story. "Superintendent Brian Starr called each individually into the office to question who had caused the tractor to backfire and cause the hole in the roof. All I remember saying, 'No I did not do it.' To which he asked me if I would swear on it in court? I said most certainly I would. We did not rat out on anyone and in a few days the roof was patched, but the fun of hearing that explosion has lasted for sixty-five years."

Closing—The Donnellson High School closed following graduation in May 1961. In the 44 years from 1918 through 1961 there were 997 graduates from the school. The largest graduating classes were 33 graduates in 1935 and 1961. The most numerous surnames of the graduates were: Krebill-33, Lowenberg-31, Schlicher-23, Krehbiel-21, Seyb-16, Bentzinger-14, Kirchner-14, Wagner-12, Frueh-11, Young-10, Wirsig-8, Wolfe-8, Schmitt-7, and Smith-7. The last graduate from Donnellson High School was Douglas Wolfe (alphabetically). In the fall of 1961, the students were bused to the new Central Lee High School which consolidated the five schools of Argyle, Denmark, Farmington, Montrose, and Donnellson.

#21

Doon High School

Mascot: Dragons
Colors: Royal Blue and Gold
Closed: 1959
Location: Extr. South Central Lyon County

Early History—The town of Doon was named after the Scottish tune, *Bonnie Doon*, written by Robert Burns.

One illustrious pioneer, H.D. Rice of Clay County from the town of Petersen, Iowa, heard of wonderful tales of Lyon County and came to explore the Rock River region in 1868. Rice and L.F. Knight reached the forks of the Little Rock, Big Rock, and West Branch streams and built a cabin in Lyon

County. Rice returned with his family and while he was gone, Knight penned his thoughts in the following lines: "Sitting in solitude on the banks of this beautiful stream, far removed from all humanity, with naught but the song of the wild birds or the soft murmur of the waterfall to break the silence of this green, glad, solitude, I cannot help but recall the touching words of Robert Burns beginning:"

"Ye band and braes O'Bonnie Doon,
How can ye bloom sae fresh and fair?
How can ye chant ye little birds?
And I sae weary, fu' o'care!

And thus, the town received the name, Bonnie Doon.

Railroads played a big part in the development of the town. Doon was the southern terminal of the Chicago, St. Paul, Minneapolis, and Omaha (CSPMO) Railroad. The Northwestern Line was built in 1879 and came through Doon. The CSPMO was later extended to Sioux City. The Great Northwestern, or Sioux City and Northern, reached Doon in 1889. "Bonnie Doon" prospered with activity.

Doon was incorporated 24 years later, in 1892. Rice developed and built a hotel in 1871. His second and much larger hotel was erected in the business district of Doon. It became one of the finest and largest in Northwest Iowa. It was called the Bonnie Doon and had 54 rooms. For many years the Bonnie Doon was the overnight stop for agents, salesman, and adventurers.

The local Temperance Union was organized in the 1880s. The saloons, however, flourished despite this feminine opposition.

Early Schools—A school was one of the first seven buildings in the town by 1889. In 1896, a permanent wooden building was built and used until it was condemned in 1939.

A bond issue was floated in 1940, and with the help of the WPA (Works Progress Administration), a fine school was started and completed in 1941. This school was one of the finest in the county. The first county basketball tournament was played in the new gym in 1942.

Newspapers—The *Lyon County Press* was the first newspaper in the county. The name was changed several times to the *Doon Press*, *The Doon Bargain Counter*, *Doon Reminder*, and then back to *The Doon Press*.

Sports—The boys played basketball and baseball. Eugene Schroeder was the last coach for the Dragons coming to Doon in the Fall of 1958. He was principal and also the drivers education teacher. He had told his wife they were only staying one year and to not unpack their bags. This one year turned into 61 years and counting (2019). The high school did close after just one year of his coming, but he stayed on to become a teacher, principal, mayor of Doon, and a beloved member of the community and greater Lyon County.

Football was never played in Doon.

The school yearbook of 1955 notes that the basketball team played the following towns: Newkirk, Lester, Larchwood, Little Rock, Ireton, Inwood, Rock Valley, and Alvord.

The Lyon County Basketball Tournament in 1955 was played in Doon with the following schools competing: Larchwood, Inwood, Rock Rapids, Alvord, Little Rock, George, Lester, and Doon.

Louie Koupas ('49) told of his family and his father's love of the game of basketball: "My Dad was a Greek who came to Doon with the railroad. He and my mother, Caroline, raised ten children. When at the ball games, he could be heard yelling encouragement to his sons during the game. His voice could be heard above the crowd bellowing out to my brother Gust ('56), 'kill 'em Gussie, kill 'em'. That maybe is not too correct now, but dad would get so caught up in the action his emotions would just spill out."

Louis Sneller ('55) holds the Iowa state record for scoring in a boys basketball game in the modern era of records. On January 18, 1955 he scored 71 points in a 83-75 win over rival Larchwood.

Notable Graduates—Harold Aardema ('48) did all of the fun things a young boy does in the 1930s. However, at the age of 11 he was stricken with the dreaded disease polio and confined to a wheelchair the rest of his life. (Polio took the lives of two other Doon citizens.) He took classes by a Twin-Phone and graduated in 1948. During his junior year, at the age of 17, he purchased a mimeograph shopping guide called "The Bargain Counter" and renamed it "Doon Reminder." This led to offset printing and was upgraded to a small newspaper called the *Doon Press*. As the editor of the paper, he traveled widely to Europe five times and throughout the United States. A regular at the Philosophy Club meetings in Rock Rapids, he became a long-time friend of Doon native novelist Frederick Feikema Manfred. Harold loved country journalism and had a nose for news. He wrote a weekly column called 'Ink Spots.' With his own sweet concoction of humor and nostalgia, including a twist of curmudgeon, his works were widely read about the Siouxland and "the darned beauty that God of this Dutch Calvinist gave us right here in the Siouxland."

Rich Ricke ('14) was a performing artist and composer. A pianist and promoter for "The Korn Kings," he played for events and was a contemporary of Lawrence Welk. He played the piano without looking at the piano or music. He composed dozens of songs. Some of the most famous were "You Tickle Me Pink," "Legionnaires on Parade," and "Universal Draft." He was a veteran of World War I.

Though a graduate of the Christian high school in Doon in 1930, Frederick Feike Feikema VII was a renowned regionalist author. He was six-feet-nine-inches tall and a third generation Frisian American. A prolific writer under the name of Frederick F. Manfred, he wrote this of the area he coined "the Siouxland":

> Doon was a magical place for me. I've learned such manhood as I have in the good old town: going to school on horseback when it was thirty below, picking corn on a cold wet freezing morning, scooping out the road for miles, thawing out a frozen car, pitching straw onto a rack from an old strawbutt in freezing driving snow, fixing my old tin lizzy with some bailing wire and fresh water for the radiator . . . I've raided watermelon patches when just a lad; I've gone on long hikes through the back-country pastures and 'wildlands'; I've cut my name on the boulder north of town; I've gone swimming down various lover's lanes.

Notable Teachers—Charles Siebsen was a history, science, and math teacher. Darrell Vande Vegte ('59) remembered, "Mr. Siebsen had such a special way of connecting history with our classes. In 1958, he made all of us write down something that we thought would happen ten years in the future. Some of us wrote wild ideas like there would be no hand labor and we would only have one eye. I remember distinctly that he wrote that in ten years, man would walk on the moon. How prophetic he was because it was just 11 years later that Neil Armstrong did walk on the moon. He was a wonderful teacher."

Mr. Charles Yestness was the government teacher and music director. He was remembered as the superintendent who wore the same suit to school every day. Louie Kopsas ('49) shared,"Mr. Yestness was instrumental in getting us a pop machine for the school. It was that type that when you put a nickel in the slot, you could slide the bottle along the track and get it to come up through the wedged opening. The price eventually went up to ten cents." Darrell Vande Vegte ('59) said, "I had lost my dime in the pop machine, only to find out that a guy had somehow rigged the machine and had taken my orange pop. I did tell Mr. Yestness and he walked into the room and asked Frank 'is that your orange pop.' To which he admitted that it was not and said he didn't know why he did it. Mr. Yestness picked him up by the collar and started shaking him. There was my pop spraying all over the room and onto Mr. Yestnesses only suit. He often asked the class, has anyone seen my glasses. And there they would be on top of his head!"

Closing—The last graduating class from Doon High School was in May 1962. The next year the high school students were bused north to Rock Rapids and the new high school called Central Lyon. The largest graduating class was 17 in 1914. The last graduating class had 12 graduates. The last to receive a diploma from Doon High School was Elaine Ver Beek (alphabetically). By 1961, the junior high students were attending school at Rock Rapids. All the grades were moved to Rock Rapids in 1985. The school building was purchased by the city of Doon. It currently houses a pre-school, library, and a community center.

Doon High School
Lyon County, IA

#22

Dow City High School

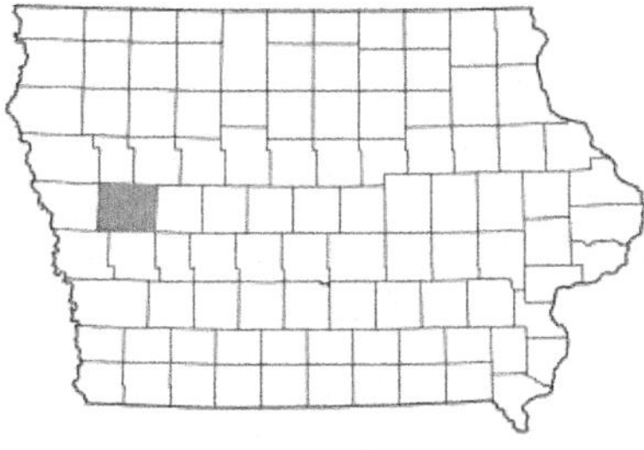

Mascot: Greyhound
Colors: Orange and Black
Closed: 1989
Location: Southwest Crawford County

Early History—Dowsville or Dow City was named in the honor of the first mayor and later Judge S.E. Dow, who owned the original town property. The area was settled by many German Methodists.

Early Schools—A log cabin on the north side of the Boyer River became a school in 1858. When a flood washed out the bridge, a father on the south side of the river rowed his boat back and forth morning and night taking his children to the log cabin school. A later school in Dow City near the cemetery, called the Cemetery school served the rural area from 1867-1871. In 1871, a 26′ x 36′ frame school was built.

The frame school was replaced in 1878 by a four-room school, but only two rooms were used at the beginning for the two teachers. By 1887, this school became a graded school having all eight grades. The high school four-year course was started in 1890 with Latin and solid Geometry being taught. German was taught up until WW I.

In 1897, a two-room, two-story addition was added to the schoolhouse.

The town newspaper published on August 28, 1895 reported, "School begins next Monday. Boys go and stick to it, for now is your golden opportunity. Don't waste your time on the street with cigars and tobacco."

The Dow City High School alumni association and alumni banquet started in 1907 when it was proposed by Superintendent Harry D. Kies. With school spirit and loyalty being so great, he wished to have each new graduating class participate in the alumni banquet celebration. Orange and Black were chosen as the school colors.

In 1916, the country schools were consolidated to form the Dow City Consolidated School. It was the first to consolidate in Crawford County. The district was one of the largest in the state with 26,720 acres, including all of Union township and six sections of Paradise township. There were 15 teachers and six buses to transport the children to school.

A bond issue for $75,000 passed and a beautiful three-story high school was dedicated on March 5, 1918. The high school was complete with a basement and gymnasium. More science and domestic science classrooms were added. Basketball was played for the first time indoors.

Bus Drivers—Gene Harre drove a school bus for 45 years. His wife Mary Ellen Putnam ('52) Harre recalled, "I often rode the activities bus with Gene as the driver. We went to ball games, and many of the senior trips usually acting as chaperones. He sang to the students on the bus. One that always got a rise out of Kathy (Kathryn) Kahl TenEyck ('70) was when he greeted her in his beautiful baritone voice with 'K K K Katie, beautiful Katie, you're the only g g g girl that I adore!' It was always good for a crimson faced blush from Kathy."

Charles (Plato) Gorden was remembered for always waiting for farm children who were late for the bus. "My first day in kindergarten, my collie dog Rex, followed me on the bus. My mother had to come on the bus and drag a very protesting Rex back up the aisle and off the bus. I was so embarrassed and almost cried. Mr. Gorden was so patient and acted like this happens all the time," told Jeri Nelson ('74) Vogt. She continued, "Plato had a very full bus when I was in junior high and there were no seats open when I got on the bus. He said, 'just go find a good looking boy to sit on his lap.' So, I did, and he immediately pushed me off. Plato just laughed as he drove off."

Senior Trips—The senior trips were greatly anticipated by the graduating seniors. In 1952, the seniors went to Omaha and Lincoln, Nebraska, for the day. "We rode an airplane, and toured the state Capitol and some museums. It was topped off by roller skating before we returned home," said Mary Ellen Putnam ('52) Harre.

Not all the seniors were able to afford these trips and others did not go because of other circumstances. "My parents had moved from Dow City before my senior year. I wanted to stay and graduate with my class, so I lived with a family and paid $5 per week for board and room. I did not believe that I could afford to go on the senior trip, and I was needed at my waitress job at the café. I had worked that entire year from 4:00-9:00 PM every night that year," remembered Linda Christiansen McCutcheon ('63).

The seniors of 1964 went to Des Moines by bus for the day. In 1974, the seniors went to South Dakota and the Black Hills. Jeri Nelson Vogt ('74) recalled, "What a trip! It started off a little rocky as many of the seniors had attended a 'kegger' the night before at the Arion Tap. When we got on the bus that morning, Kevin Garrett ('74) really looked green. With all the bumpy roads and the bouncing up and down he looked even worse. Plato just said, 'just put a waste bucket back there for him and we are going to keep going.'"

Mary Ellen Putnam ('52) Harre remembered, "When getting to accompany the seniors on the bus as a sponsor we went to a great variety of places over the years. We went to Branson, Colorado, the Arch in St. Louis, and Kansas City. I was so embarrassed at the Swope Park Zoo in Kansas City as we had to hold the bus because my own son Ray Harre ('74) was late in getting to the bus. These trips were so educational for these kids. There were seldom any disruptions and the memories for all of them are retold often at our alumni reunions."

Polio—Dow City was not immune to the polio epidemic from the 1930s, 40s, and 50s. Kathy Lambert ('62) and Connie Basel ('79) were wheelchair bound. Joan Keairnes ('64) was slowed with the disease but could drive and played the trumpet in the band.

Hot Lunch—The hot lunch program was started in 1944. Cinnamon rolls and chili together were always the favorite menu. This combination was so prevalent at the time that it should be called the 'Iowa traditional' lunch of choice.

Notable Graduates—Raymond Harre ('76) was a National Merit Scholar Finalist. He became a medical doctor and Radiologist.

Tom Ahart ('43) was a recognized education leader in Iowa. He became the Superintendent of the Des Moines schools.

Linda Christiansen ('63) McCutcheon received some unexpected notoriety. With a two-year-old at home, she was told three weeks before the delivery of her next child that there would be triplets. Jenna, Julie, and Jolene became celebrities with their mother in magazines, and a national commercial for Maytag. Linda became a valuable bank vice president in Dow City for many years. Jenna, Julie, and Jolene McCutcheon graduated together from Dow City High School in 1987.

Lyle Bresmer ('34) had a byline that will live forever in the Nebraska sports history. "Every man, woman, and child" could be heard on the radio. He was the long-time beloved announcer for Nebraska football and basketball games.

God be with us till we meet again—This final song is sung every year at the end of the Alumni reunion for the Dow City Alumni banquet. This tradition has continued annually since the first reunion in 1907.

Killed in Action—The following were killed in service for their country:

Louis Miller, WWI
Gary Spence, WWI
George Richard Houston, WWII
Lyle W. Stapanek, WWII
John Elburn Mathys, WWII
Vernon Walter Schnoor, WWII
Carl W. Peterson, WWII
Harold Scott Sharp ('39), WWII
Walter Peter Henry Thomson, WWII
George F. Taylor, WWII
James L. Houston, Korea
Charles Jasper Cook ('49), Korea
Michael Heller ('68), Vietman

Teachers—Al Ordal retired in 1973 as the long-time leader of the Dow City music program. Nancy Stepanek ('64) Rosburg told, "When we went to contest, we always got #1's or #1-plus. If we ever failed to get a #1 we were devastated. Linda Christiansen McCutcheon ('63) remembered, "Mr. Ordal also was the band director but gave that up in his later years. The honor to sing in his choir was so popular that each year there had to be auditions just to make the choir."

Arnold Faltinson taught science, Physics, and drivers education from 1955-1988. Linda Christiansen McCutcheon ('63) smiled as she shared, "He taught all of us and our children, too. He had a passion for science. His name always comes up when we are reminiscing in town. I think of him every time I am in my car and driving. In drivers education, he would sit a glass of water on the dash and if it spilled when we started, stopped, or shifted our grade may show it. This was even driving a stick shift. The car was provided by M and S Chevrolet in Dunlap." Jeri Nelson ('74) Vogt said, "He was so intelligent. He should have taught in college, but I am sure glad he did not. I learned to change a tire with a bunch of other girls." Nancy Stepnek Rosburg ('64) added, "Mr. Faltinson was known to occasionally take a nap or two while we were learning to drive. Of course, we always quietly snickered as he would doze off."

Sports—There was no football played at Dow City until 1956 when the 11-man game was started. The first coach was Vernon Shotwell from 1956-1961. He was also the business teacher. At an Alumni reunion nearly 50 years later, Coach Shotwell recalled, "When I came here, I had 27-28 kids who had never played football." Some of his players remembered, "Coach even had to show us how to put on our pads. At half time of the first game when Coach had given his pep talk, he asked if there were any questions. A hand went up and a (unnamed) player asked innocently 'Coach what is a first and ten?'" In the following years, Dow City became a football school. The 1964 team went undefeated at 9-0. They knew they were going to be good that year, and had a motto "9-0, Let's Go."

The 1960 schedule included games against Woodbine, Menlo, Charter Oak, Dunlap, Riverside, Irwin, Ar-We-Va, Schleswig, and Logan.

Girls basketball started in 1910 and was played every year until the school closed in 1989. Several teams made it to the sectional finals in the 1950s and 1980s, but there was never a trip to the coveted state girls basketball tournament.

Mascot—The Greyhound became the school mascot in the 1940s when a group of students were seeking a donation from Art Wilson at his 120 acre Greyhound Farm outside of Dow City. This unique Greyhound business was one of a kind in Iowa. These dogs raced in Florida and New York and some of the greatest breeding stock originated from the Wilson Greyhound Farm. For his donation, Mr. Wilson suggested that the mascot for the school should be the Greyhound. As history unfolded, the name for the school mascot for Dow City High School became the Greyhound.

Closing—The Dow City High School closed following graduation in May 1989. Whole grade sharing with Dunlap started in the fall of 1989, and the districts officially consolidated in 1994 to form Boyer Valley Community School. In the 106 years from 1884-1989 there were 1,754 graduates from Dow City High School. The most numerous surnames of the graduates were: Beam-30, Sharp-30, Ahart-27, Smith-25, Brasel-21, Muff-19, Cross-18, Garrett-18, Houston-18, Brink-17, Thomsen-17, Butterworth-16, Argotsinger-15, Gorden-15, Malone-15, Thomas-15, Keairnes-14, Laubscher-14, Riddle-14, Ettleman-13, Clark-12, Gibson-12, Lambert-12, and Wood-12. The last to receive a diploma from Dow City High School in 1989 was Susan Wright (alphabetically).

Dow City School Building
1918 - 2004

Dow City High School
Crawford County, IA

#23

Earlville High School

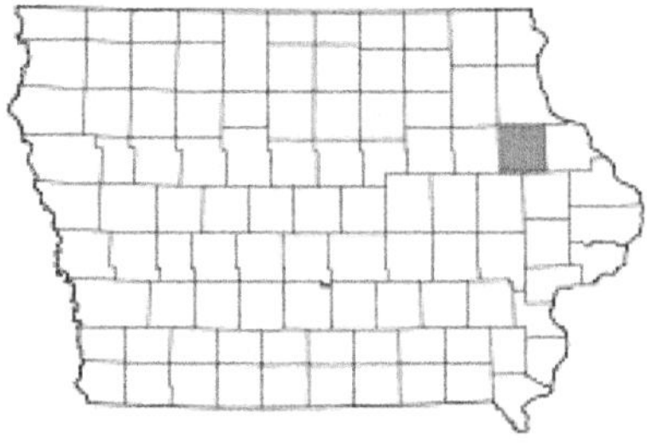

Mascot: Eagles
Colors: Purple and Gold
Closed: 1959
Location: Eastern Delaware County

Early History—The population for Delaware County in 1840 was 168. By 1850, the population was 1,759. During this time period Iowa became a state. An account of the value of goods at the time was printed in the Earlville history . . . "Bear skins brought $10, deer hides 50 cents, cows sold for $10, a mare cost $60, hogs sold for $1.00, and sheep sold for 50 cents with the lamb thrown in." In 1847, there were five townships divisions in the county: Delhi, Eads Grove, North Fork, Colony, and Buchanan.

George Earl and his partner, Henry Bentley, came to Delaware County in 1851 to purchase land. They chose a mile square of land with deep cool springs and a heavy timbered section near where they found a trapper's cabin. Earl was a Quaker whose ancestors had come to America in the late 1680s with the Penn Colonies. These early Quaker families were given original land grants in the new world by the British Crown. In 1827, The Friends (Quakers) split into two main groups—the Orthodox and Dissenters. The younger members of this sect migrated westward into the Ohio and Indiana settlements, and George Earl became prosperous in the South Bend, Indiana, settlement. He was married there to Sarah Ann Bugher, and his children Harriet, John, Mark, Sarah, Ann, Mary, and Isabell were born in Indiana. Saddened by the death of young Isabell and alarmed at the feelings of unrest among eastern settlements after the publishing of *Uncle Ben's Cabin* by Harriet Beecher Stowe, the Earl family decided to move westward in the vain hope of preventing their sons from taking up arms which was against religious beliefs. The Earl boys, however, were in the first group to enlist in the Civil War from Delaware County.

Early Schools—In 1853, Joel Seger, an expert carpenter made plans to build a log cabin school for the children. The parents in the area were settlers who enjoyed fine educational facilities in the eastern states. They understood the necessity for early and proper schooling. Families bore the expense of the school and the teacher's salary was assessed with each family paying $25.

The Dubuque and Pacific Railroad arrived in 1856 and a little depot was erected. It had the letters "Nottingham" on the building, named after a large stockholder in the railroad.

By 1859, the little log cabin school on the hill was outgrown and a large frame building on 6 ½ acres was set aside as school land. It remained classed as Subdistrict #9 until 1865 when Nottingham became an independent school district.

In 1860, the court petitioned to change the name of Nottingham to Earlville. However, in 1861, Judge Baily made a definitive refusal to the petition and mail continued to wander to the other Nottingham, Iowa, also. That spring Abraham Lincoln was inaugurated. Ft. Sumter was the scene of the first clash between the North and the South and Iowa was plunged into a Civil War. Delaware County pointed with pride to their record of sending many men during the war years, 1861-1865. One of the most tragic mistakes of the Civil War was in the recruiting of whole companies of young men from the same locality. In Hopkinton, just 13 miles southeast of Earlville, 24 young men from the Lennox College in Hopkinton lost their lives in battle or from starvation in prisons. In total, Hopkinton listed 44 men as casualties of the war.

The need for a more modern school building came in the 1890s. At the cost of $10,000, a large brick building was erected in 1894 and completed in 1895. In 1896, Miss Mattie Murley began teaching her "chart class" which was a kindergarten held during the months of April and May to help little ones transition to first grade in the fall. She continued to teach in Earlville for fifty years and was one of the most beloved residents in all of Earlville.

The Earlville school district was consolidated. A fine new school building was erected in 1915 and the school became a four-year high school.

A new gymnasium and auditorium was added in 1948. At the commencement program that May, Dr. Marcus Bach from the School of Religion at the University of Iowa was the guest speaker. On that occasion he admitted he had "never addressed an audience before in an uncompleted gymnasium," as the floor had not been laid at that time. He returned in 1955 to again address the graduates as the commencement speaker.

Notable Teachers—Leola Ham taught American literature and vocal music for many years at Earlville High School. She judged music contests throughout the state. Lucille Gibbs Holtz ('56) recalled, "She was a wonderful teacher. Every year we read a Shakespeare story as well as *Chaucer's Canterbury Tales*. She got everyone to participate in chorus. We had to memorize and stand before the class to recite poems and literature selections."

One of Leola Ham's trios of Vivian Hackbarth Ham ('55), Joann Clute Bishop ('55), and Carol Gibbs Rathel ('55) won the state of Iowa music contest in the spring of 1954. This qualified them to go to New York City to appear on the Ted Mack Amateur Hour on television. They were pictured in the Des Moines paper mapping out their trip to New York.

Eldon (Pete) Sassen ('55) shared, "Mrs. Ham got the best out of everyone. She insisted on having an operetta every year. My senior year there were 22 of us in the operetta, "The Soldiers of Our Queen." That same year, we won the state one-act play competition with "Playgoers" held at Iowa City. We were blessed to have Jeanlee Mathey ('55) performing in our cast. She was so led and inspired by Mrs. Ham's directing that she continued at the University of Iowa as a theater major."

Maud Clifton taught history and government and was also the principal. She never married and

Lucille Gibbs Holtz ('56) claimed, "She always seemed to favor the boys. However, she was a buddy to all of the students. She had never married, and we were just her family." "Every year we celebrated with Miss Clifton's birthday which just happened to be St. Patrick's Day, March 17. She was born in 1900 and uniquely died on her birthday in 1973," remembered her nephew Jim Clifton ('56).

Pranks—Jim Clifton ('56) shared, "Aunt Maud, (Maud Clifton) the principal, was my dad's sister. She was a fabulous teacher. One day in class Jerry Wilson ('56) broke a pencil in half and stuck the two ends in his ears. Of course, somehow, I am the one who got in trouble from Miss Clifton. Asking why I was the one that got in trouble, she replied, 'because you snickered at such a dumb stunt.'"

Every town had its usual Halloween pranks, but Earlville's featured only the senior boys. A nearby farmer, Gene Wendt, had all his feed neatly stacked in tepee-like stacks to dry for the fall harvest. Each year, only the senior boys would sneak into his field and knock over and scatter his shocks. As usual, Mr. Wendt would call the school and report the hoodlumism, and the principal, Miss Maude, would send the senior boys out of class to reconstruct the vandal's acts from the night before. Gene Wellman ('58) carries a three-inch scar to this day as a memory of that night in 1957. "We were running across the field at Mr. Wendt's, doing our mischief, when we thought he had spotted us. In escaping, I jumped the barbed wire fence thinking I was on the top wire. However, I was not, and I flipped, cutting my leg, and I should have gone to the doctor for treatment from the old rusty wire cut. Instead, I limped home and actually burned my jeans because they were torn and had blood all over them. I wanted to destroy all of the evidence so my mom would not kill me. She did not find out, but I carry the scar as a memory. I guess I got my punishment after all."

Sports—Earlville played mostly the other county high schools and the big event of the year was the Delaware County Basketball Tournament with teams from Colesburg, Oneida, Greeley, Hopkinton, Dundee, and Delhi. The fiercest rival was Delhi. The boys basketball team of 1955 was an outstanding team. Three from this team were chosen for the all-conference team: Eldon Sassen ('55), Dave Whittmore ('56), and Delmar Thibadeau ('55). Earlville won the coveted Delaware County Tournament. Football was never played at Earlville. Spring and fall baseball was played. Boys track started in 1955.

Girls basketball was the only girls sport. Lucille Gibbs Holtz ('56) remembered, "It seemed that the only training I recall was running around the gymnasium court." Connie Clifton (from Delhi) distinctly recalled playing against Earlville and being overshadowed by an opposing player, a very tall Bettey Werner Herman ('57), "I was just a small sophomore and she seemed like a giant to me. Of course, it was over 60 years ago, but she was really tall."

Killed in Action—World War II took the lives of two men from Earlville:

Forrest Diesch ('37)
Donald Carpenter

Francis Pierce ('41), the son of Frank Pierce of Earlville was awarded the Congressional Medal of Honor for bravery and achievement in WW II.

Polio—Larry Slick ('57) was stricken by polio in the epidemic of the early 1950s while he was in junior high. He was in an iron lung which saved him from the paralyzing virus. He recovered with only a slight paralysis to his arm and leg and graduated with his class in 1957.

Notable Graduates—Jeanlee Mathey Poggi ('55) graduated in drama from the University of Iowa. She earned multiple master's degrees and used her creative talents in directing teaching of writing and working with neighborhood youth groups and organizations. She was one of the founders of the West 181st Street beautification projects and helped create a playground in Park for little children in New York City. Jean shared, "The community garden has been the delight of many people in the neighborhood for many years. I had two great opportunities in my work life: one in teaching writing at the college level and the other in teaching young people from grade school to adulthood with learning disabilities."

Gene Wellman ('58) became a school superintendent and reflected on the inspiring guidance and mentor Mrs. Leola Ham from Earlville High, "She was so instrumental in getting me to go into teaching and encouraged me to go to college. Under her direction in speech and English, I chose these along with theater for my major in college. I taught in nearby Manchester for 11 years, often meeting with Mrs. Ham as she would continue to encourage me, and when I became a principal she lamented, 'I guess I'll have to look up to you now'. On the contrary, everyone looked up to Mrs. Ham. I later became a school superintendent and I honestly believe I would not have done this without her leadership." Gene further shared that during his educational career, special education became part of each school's curriculum. Special classes were held for the disabled, disadvantaged, and special needs students. After several years of this mandatory secluded teaching, mainstreaming gained favor as the best method for educating the special needs students. It was a novel approach, however Earlville and all the small schools across the state had been mainstreaming for 60 years before the word pedagogy was conjured.

Yearbook—The school annual was called *The Eagle*. The 1955 annual shows an enrollment of 67 in the high school. A remarkable percentage of the student body are pictured in the boys and girls choirs led by Mrs. Ham. There were 28 boys and 24 girls pictured in the choirs. The marching band with instructor Joe Craig had 25 band members with four majorettes. Jim Clifton ('56) grinned as he recalled, "I played the snare drums. What fun we had and I learned so much about music."

Closing—Earlville High School closed after graduation in May 1959. After five votes, the Earlville schools consolidated with Delhi, Hopkinton, Oneida, and Buck Creek to become Maquoketa Valley with the high school located in Delhi. In the 75 years from 1884-1959 there were 827 graduates from Earlville High School. The largest class was 25 seniors in 1925. The most numerous surnames of the graduates were: Hunt-38, Laxson-16, Gibbs-17, Robinson-11, Schaller-11, Klaus-10, Clifton-9, and Rogers-7. The last to receive a diploma from Earlville High School was Larry Walters (alphabetically).

Earlville High School
Delaware County, IA

#24

Eldon High School

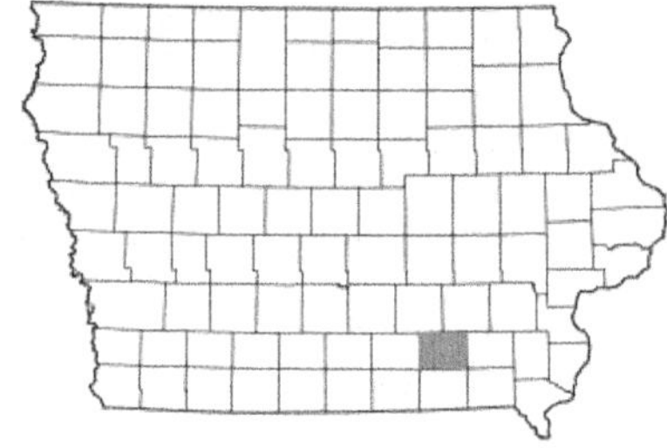

Mascot: Pirates
Colors: Red and White
Closed: 1958
Location: Extr. Southeast Wapello County

Early History—Eldon is on the banks of the meandering Des Moines River at a bend in the river often referred to as "Around the Gentle Bend." The town's history with the Indians, the river, and the settlement of Iowa date to before Iowa became a state.

The Sac and Fox Indians lived in this area following the Black Hawk War in 1832. Black Hawk, then 65 years old, led a small number of Sac and Fox across the Mississippi to re-occupy their homes in Illinois in defiance of the American settlers. Conflict with the settlers was inevitable. Thus began the "Black Hawk War." The Indians were doomed from the start. Most of the Sac and Fox opposed Black Hawk's actions and, under the leadership of Chief Keokuk, stayed in their villages along the Iowa River.

For 15 weeks the Indians led their pursuers around northern Illinois and southern Wisconsin. They were slowed as they had their families with them. Black Hawk realized that their only safety lay on the western bank of the Mississippi. On August 2, 1832, Black Hawk and his band were caught trying to cross at the mouth of Bad Axe River. Most of his warriors were killed by US troops supported by a gunboat. Families were slaughtered by the Americans' Sioux allies as they tried to swim the Mississippi. Black Hawk escaped for a time but was finally captured and imprisoned at St. Louis.

In 1838, Black Hawk moved to a new home along the Des Moines River just below Eldon. The Sac and Fox agency was then under construction at Agency (ten miles northwest of Eldon). The agent, Joseph M. Street, took a special interest in the aging warrior and made him the gift of a cow. In September 1938, Black Hawk fell ill with a fever which lasted for two weeks. In accordance with his last wishes, Black

Hawk was buried in his finest regalia near his home above Iowaville (downstream from Eldon) on the northeast side of the Des Moines River. Black Hawk was not given any peace, even in the grave. Grave robbers stole his bones and sold them to a physician who planned to exhibit them for profit. Through the intervention of Governor Robert Lucas, they were recovered from a shop in Illinois where they had been sent to be articulated. They were eventually transferred to the museum of Geological and Historical Society in Burlington. His bones were destroyed when the building burned in 1855.

The Des Moines River in the 1850s was active with steamships traversing the locks and delivering freight and passengers from Keokuk to Des Moines.

The early settlement of Washington Township dates to the pre-treaty days. John B. Grover, a German, settled on the site of Eldon before the treaty of 1842. He built a cabin but was driven off by the government troops in compliance with the law. After the first of May 1843 (when the land was opened to settlement), he returned and lived on his claim about three years. The township of Washington was among the first in the county organized in 1844.

Eldon became a railroad town and its origin was due to the construction of the Keokuk and Des Moines road. A flag station was located on the site of the town shortly after the road was opened and was named Ashland Crossing. Subsequently, the little town was called Williamsburg and a post office was established with Bert Loftis as post-master.

The prospects of the area improved when the Chicago Rock Island and Pacific Railroad pushed its southwest division to that point.

In 1870, the town of Eldon was laid out by Judge L.M. Love, Col. George Gillaspy, Hon. Edward Johnston, Col. Willis Leighton, and George Williams. In 1873 the town was incorporated.

An English nobleman named Lord Eldon came to this territory and wanted to live the rest of his life here since he thought it was so beautiful. On December 16, 1879, James Love as trustee, made and filed his plat of the town and gave it the name of Eldon in honor of the admirer of the land. For a while, the town had three names. The railroad called it Ashland Crossing, the post office was Williamsburg, and the people called it Eldon. The peoples' will was recorded and the chosen name was finally adopted.

Eldon Historical Highlights

- In 1890, the Big 4 Fair (Wapello, Davis, Van Buren, and Keokuk counties) was first held. It has been held annually for 130 years.
- In 1899, the little city's population was 2,000.

- According to local historians, the area one mile from Eldon was referred as "Pull Tail." A law required the railroad transporting animals had to provide them with water after a certain distance and time. The animals were taken off the train and watered, their tails were pulled to get them back on the railroad cars—hence the name "Pull Tail."
- Former President Teddy Roosevelt visited on August 12, 1912. He was running again for president on the Progressive ticket that year.
- The American Gothic painting by Grant Wood was of the house one mile southeast of Eldon. American Gothic hangs at the Art Institute of Chicago. It has become one of the most recognized paintings in the world.

Early Schools—A brick two-story Lincoln school was built in 1888. It included all 12 grades. In 1903, a second modern brick school building was built to serve all the grades through high school for the pupils on the east side of town. Lincoln became the school for grades 1 through 6 who lived on the west side of town The first graduation class was in 1886 with three graduates.

Notable Graduate—John Sharp ('28) was accepted at Grant Wood's Artist Colony at Stone City, Iowa, after three semesters at the State University of Iowa. Sharp's paintings in the 1930s were awarded commissions by the Treasury Department. He painted a mural titled "Autumn in Iowa" in 1939 for the Bloomfield, Iowa, post office. "Summer" was the 1940 mural for the Rockwell City post office, and "Hunters" was painted for the Hawarden post office in 1942. Two of his best known canvases are "Nantucket" and "Old South Wharf." These works were produced while he lived and taught in Nantucket.

Yearbook—The yearbook in 1952 was named the *Pirates Roundup*. The 1957 yearbook was the *Eldonian*. That year, the band was pictured with 34 members. There were 31 in Girls Glee Club and 15 in Boys Glee Club. The Homecoming Queen was Linda Hamilton ('57). The King was Loren Fligg ('58). There were 127 students enrolled in 1957 at Eldon High School.

Sports—No football was played at Eldon. The girls played basketball and the boys played basketball and baseball.

The development of broadcast media in the 1950s made every boy believe they would someday make it to the major leagues in baseball. One dream was almost fulfilled in 1960 when Eldon's Bill Campbell ('58) was a minor leaguer with the Athletics and Cardinals. As a third baseman, he competed with some of the later major league stars at Lubbock and Keokuk such as Jack Hamilton from Lost Nation and Juan Marichal.

Killed in Action—The following men were killed in service to their country. Lest they be forgotten.

George F. Canny, WWI
Walter F. Reno, WWI
Francis Carl Canny, WWII
Roy Dewey Cox, WWII
Curtis Dickens, WWII
Carl Edwin Finney, WWII
Don Hart, WWII
Rex Leo Hibbert, WWII
Robert L. Hodson, WWII
Walter McCoy, WWII
Leland C. McDonald, WWII
David Murray, WWII
Thomas William Noviock, WWII
Victor Charles Saltzgaver, WWII
Durward Lee Van Dever, WWII
Charles Wilburn, WWII
Lloyd Wilkenson, WWII

Closing—The Eldon High School closed after graduation in May 1958. The Eldon students in the fall of 1958 attended the new Cardinal Community School three miles north of Eldon. Cardinal was the unification of 19 school districts, three of them with high schools from the four-county area of Van Buren, Davis, Jefferson, and Wapello counties.

In the 63 years from 1888-1958 there were 1,261 graduates from Eldon High School. The largest class was 51 seniors in 1928. The most numerous surnames of the graduates were: Thomas-23, Moore -19, Finney-15, Carter-14, Jones-13, Sloan-13, Hancock-12, Stephenson-10, Walker-10, and Hart-9. The last to receive a diploma from Eldon High School was Carl Wolf (alphabetically).

*Beginning in the fall of 1958, high school classes were still being held at the old Eldon High School as well as at Batavia and Agency. Students from these three former high schools were taking some classes at each of the locations. They were under the name of Cardinal High School until the new school complex was finished three miles north of Eldon. The first class to graduate at the new building of Cardinal High School was in 1961.

1903 - 1953
Eldon High School
Wapello County, IA

#25

Emerson High School

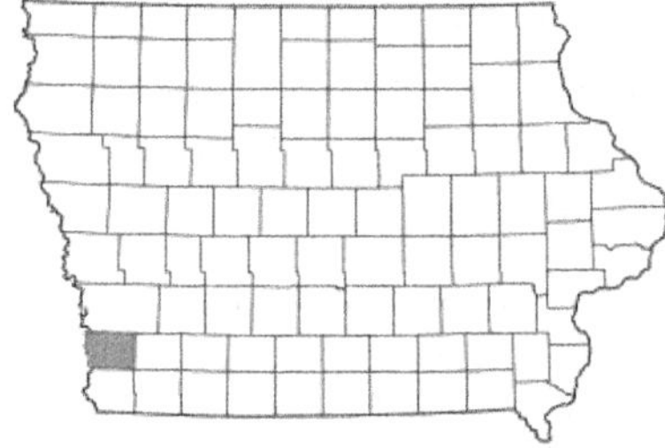

Mascot: Eagles/Eaglettes
Colors: Maroon and White
Closed: 1960
Location: East Central Mills County

Early History—Mills County was organized in 1851. In 1853, it was divided into five townships and in 1857 into 11 townships. The territory where Emerson was later plotted was named Indian Creek Township because of an Indian village that was in the area. The creek running east to west and emptying into the Nishnabotna River at Hastings was called Indian Creek. The Pottawattamie Indians occupied this part of the state until 1846-47 when they were moved to Kansas by the government.

Settlers came from Canada and New York to the area and bought land for $1.25 per acre. Some land was sold as a soldier's grant (Mexican-American War veterans). In 1860, a plague of black fever hit the country and settlers paid dearly with deaths in their families. One burial lot in North Grove Cemetery shows four deaths in one family all within a few days of each other. (Black fever was caused by the bite of an infected female phlebotomine, also known as a sand-fly. The bite transmits the potentially fatal protozoa leishmania, which results in black fever or the hemolysis of the red blood cells.)

In the 1860s, settlers came from Germany, Nova Scotia, Vermont, and points east. Civil War veterans purchased land on a soldier's grant.

Judge Lewis Tubbs and family moved to Malvern (13 miles southwest of Emerson) in 1854. He was a miller by trade. He organized the 1st Cavalry Company in Mills County known as the Mills County Minutemen to fight in the Civil War. He owned 3,200 acres of land in Mills County and 1,280 acres in Texas. He donated the land in Emerson for the three churches and the city park.

Judge Tubbs, acting as a land agent for the Chicago Burlington and Quincy Railroad (CB&Q) purchased land for a new railroad to go through the area. Originally the town was platted one mile west. The site was changed to the present location of the town of Emerson when it was determined that a large hill was going to pose a problem in laying the railroad track. A.B. Smith, an official of the railroad, named the new town after the philosopher and writer Ralph Waldo Emerson. All towns from Red Oak to Glenwood were named for noted authors or poets such as Hawthorne, Hastings, and Malvern.

Notable First Settlers—A railroad depot was the first structure to be built in Emerson. In 1874, Willis Patrick said, "It was all prairie as far as you could see. Emerson had about four houses, a hotel, café, and three little stores." Patrick later married the first graduate from Emerson High School, Eurana Cheney.

R.M. Shipman and his wife came to Emerson in 1875. She died shortly after arrival and was the first burial in the Emerson cemetery. Mr. Shipman was a musician of some stature having played the drums at Abraham Lincoln's inauguration. He ran a drugstore and sold it to start the Farmers State Bank with partner M.L. Evans. They later bought the Exchange Bank which became known as the Emerson State Bank.

In 1878, Charles E. Lakin came to Iowa at the age of 18 from Illinois. He picked corn for one dollar per day and worked as a hired man for $18.50 per month plus board and room. By the time of his death he owned 1,000 acres of Mills County.

Early Schools—In 1871, the first schoolhouse was built. This school opened on the subscription plan (families paying money for each student to attend school). The pupils numbered 17. The teacher was an Englishman by the name of Reece or Rice. The teacher's compensation was $25 a month.

In 1873, a larger school was built north across the street from the first school. The cost of the building was $3,500. There were soon 85 students and three teachers. Within ten years, in 1881, there were 81 boys and 75 girls between the ages of five and twelve years old. The male teacher was paid $50 per month and the female was paid $31.50 per month.

Emerson Chronicle—The first newspaper was called the *Emerson Chronicle*. Excerpts of the April 18, 1890 edition show, "The streets were nearly blocked with teams and wagons Saturday bringing customers who were busy purchasing merchandise from the Emerson's business places."

Advertisements in the issue of the *Chronicle* were:

W.J Crawford City Meat Market
25 lbs. boiling beef........$1
16 lbs. roast beef $1
15 lbs. steak $1
High prices paid for hides and tallow!

Taylor Bros.
Tonsorial Artists and practical barbers
The only first-class barber shop in the city

KKK—The Ku Klux Klan was organized in Emerson on September 24, 1926. It was incorporated under the Great Imperial Seal of the Invisible Empire by His Lordship the Imperial Wizard, in the Imperial Palace in the Imperial City of Atlanta, Georgia, United States of America. The Emerson Klan was no. 88 *(Author's Note: it is not known if this was the 88th Klan formed in Iowa. See the Ocheyedan story).*

Sports—Boys football was started in 1950. The senior boys were not allowed to go out for the team because they were considered too big to practice against underclassman. They played six-man football until 1956 when the team changed to eight-man. In 1959, in the last year of the high school, Emerson started playing eleven-man football.

The sport at Emerson High School was girls basketball. The 1958 team lost only two games all year to finish with a 20-2 record. They lost their first and last game that year. They made it to the state tournament, losing in the finals to West Central-Maynard 59-51 and taking second place. The star player and scorer on the team was Vivian Fleming Seipold ('58). She reminisced, "I was the only senior on the starting team with one junior and four sophomores. It was a great honor to be the oldest on the team as we were young and small. We were all short, and I was barely 5′ 6″ tall in my shoes. Our Coach, Marlin Mercer, was tough and challenged us. We always practiced with music blaring. Our trademark was to race out of the locker room at full speed and take a lap before starting our pregame drills. That trip to the state will be replayed in our minds forever. Here I am 62 years later remembering that we got a bye the first round. We then played Blakesburg, the tallest team in the state averaging over six feet tall. At the time it was the highest scoring game ever in the state tournament and we beat them 98-86. Next up was an undefeated States Center team, which we outlasted 73-71. In the championship game against West Central-Maynard, we bowed to them as they won back-to-back state tournaments." Vivian modestly said that her teammates were her inspiration, but she scored 200 points in those three state tournament games. Her jersey number 22 was imprinted in the memories of Emerson fans. The 32-game winning streak in 1955-58 is tied for second as the most consecutive wins in the state of Iowa girls basketball.

Gary Elkins ('59) remembered that tournament. "It so happens that there was a high school at Wales which was seven miles from Emerson. It has a post office address of Emerson. So, when we got to the state tournament, somehow the school at Wales was represented in the program as being from Emerson, too. So people were asking just how big Emerson was because we had two high schools."

Notable Graduates—Kenneth A. Evans graduated from the University of Illinois. He was veteran of World War I. He was a member of Phi Kappa Psi. Kenneth was also a member of the Iowa Senate for eight years, and the Lt. Governor of the state of Iowa from 1946-1952.

Notable Teacher—Marlin Mercer was a science teacher and the coach of the girls teams in the 1950s until the school closed in 1960. Kirk Hascall ('58) remembered, "Mr. Mercer was very strict. He was so thorough in his science presentations that everyone wanted to take his classes. The girls loved his discipline, and did they ever play their hearts out for him."

Senior Trips—The class of 1958 took four cars and were the first class from Emerson to go to the Lake of the Ozarks. Kirk Hascall ('58) drove his family's car and three mothers drove the other cars. Kirk recalled, "That place was hopping. There were kids everywhere. Everyone had such a great time in the sun and the water. Every other class before us had to go to Chicago by train. There were sure a lot of girls and they really were having a great time with boys from all over the Midwest."

Closing—The Emerson High School closed following graduation in May 1960. In the 73 years from 1888-1960 there were 772 graduates from Emerson High School. The largest class was 25 seniors in 1954. The most numerous surnames of the graduates were: Smith-19, Cheney-14, Davis-12, Edie-12, Honeyman-12, Hascall-12, Taylor-10, Carson-9, Salmons-9, Johnson-8, and Thorson-7. The last to receive a diploma from Emerson High School was V. Neil White (alphabetically).

The Emerson students continued attending high school at the Nishna Valley High School held at the former Emerson High School building. They joined the students from Hastings, Henderson and Strahan to form the Nishna Valley School District. This arrangement lasted for three more years until the new Nishna Valley Consolidated High School north of town located on Highway 34 was completed for the opening in September 1963.

Emerson High School
Mills County, IA

#26

Everly High School

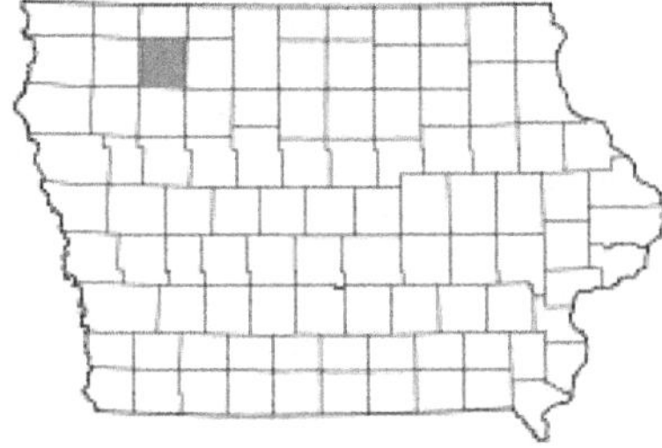

Mascot: Cattlefeeders/Mavericks
Colors: Red and White /Red and Gold
Closed: 2019
Location: Northwest Clay County

Early History—Clay County was not named after the renowned orator and Senator from Kentucky, but after his son, Henry Clay Jr. Clay was a Lieutenant Colonel, leading his company of Kentucky volunteers when he was killed at the Battle of Buena Vista in the Mexican-American War in 1847. Ironically, Buena Vista County immediately southeast of Clay County is named after that battle.

From the *Everly Centennial* history book:

> In the spring of 1884 . . . 24 families arrived by immigrant train to settle the prairie site of what was to become Everly. The men bought land here the previous year and now were bringing the women and children from Benton County Iowa to their new home. Only two of the men were still living in 1944 or sixty years later. They were John Krambeck and Lewis Scharnberg.
>
> Scharnberg, in telling of the track, said that the train came in on the main line from Keystone as far as Spencer and then shunted on a side-track which had been built on west.
>
> The families settled into houses dug into the hills and heated with buffalo chips gathered from the prairie. It was open country and there was no timber. Scharnberg and his brothers stayed for a while with a man named 'Clark' who lived southeast of the Everly site in a shack. He 'ran a herd' of about 3000 cattle.

The town of Everly was first called Clark until it was discovered that there was another Clark, Iowa. The town was incorporated in 1902.

Lone Tree Township was named for one large tree which stood near the government fording, where people could get across the Ocheyedan River.

Early Schools—The first school in Everly was a small one-story building in 1888. In 1889, a two-story building with one room on each floor was constructed. More classrooms were needed so another school was built in the east part of town where the school buildings stands now (2019).

Residents from seven Lone Tree Township schools and nine Waterford Township schools voted to consolidate with Everly in 1915. The seventh and eighth grade students attended school in Everly and the first six grades continued to attend the one-room country schools. There were six one-room country schools at the time. This arrangement was unparalleled in the state at that time. The name of the district was "The Consolidated Independent Everly School."

In the early 1900s, only a three-year high school course was offered. It was necessary for students to attend high school elsewhere, such as Spencer, for the fourth year or to attend summer school sessions in Everly to attain a four-year high school diploma.

The school became accredited under the leadership of Superintendent Ira. R. Baker in 1913 when it became a four-year high school.

As the community grew, the need for larger facilities became apparent. In 1926, a $80,000 bond was approved for a new building and was completed in 1927. The 1928 class of ten seniors was the first to graduate from this school building.

Busing—By late 1925, some of the rural schools were closed and a bus was purchased to transport the children. The bus, costing $504.55, was purchased from Ketelsen Implement Company with the lettering "Everly Consolidated School." The bus driver was Otto Koehnk. The route extended east and picked up children from the Spring Creek School and farther east into Clay Township. The next year another bus was purchased for a route southeast of Everly.

Notorious Bank Robbery—The infamous gang of Bonnie and Clyde made a visit to Everly on a Thursday, May 3, 1934 driving a car with Calhoun County license plates. After stopping at the South Ocheyedan street station for oil and gas, two men and two women entered the Everly Bank asking for change for a $5.00 bill and announcing, "This is a stickup." An automatic gun was rammed into the side of H.C. Clark, who was a customer in the bank at the time. He was ordered into the vault along with Bertha Holst and Owen Goodspeed, the cashier. At the onset, the bandits ordered their captives to make no noise, and the whole robbery worked with clock-like precision. The gang left the bank with $700 and met their fate four weeks later in east Texas under a barrage of bullets. They were still driving the same car with the Iowa Calhoun license plate.

Mascots—The name Everly Cattlefeeders and Cattle-feederetes occurred in the 1930s during a community fund drive to raise money to buy baseball uniforms. A large number of farmers fed out cattle for decades in the surrounding areas. John Jelden was approached to donate funds, and he was quoted as saying that he would give $50 if the team name was "Everly Cattlefeeders," and the name stuck.

This same "Cattlefeeder" baseball team soon won the state baseball championship in 1939. John Jelden was also a baseball man and had challenged the team if they won the state championship, he would take them to the Chicago stockyards. Following the winning game, the team headed for Chicago on the train. Pictures of the boys with their show canes directing livestock was the crowning reward for winning the state in baseball.

The high school joined Moneta in 1959 with the Moneta district dividing between Hartley in O'Brien County to the northwest and Everly in Clay County to the northeast.

The mascot remained for the Every High School until consolidating with Clay Central in 1989 to become Clay Central-Everly. The mascot then was changed to the Mavericks. No known wild horses were currently in the area.

Sports—Football was first played in Everly in 1962. The rival in all sports was Hartley in the 1950s and 60s. In the 1970s, the rival became Clay Central-Royal.

The "only" game in town became girls basketball. The fans started lining up outside the gymnasium at 3:00 PM on game days for the night contest. The players' parents were escorted in through the side entrance. The girls made trips to the state basketball tournament eight straight years from 1961-1968, 1971, and 1972. They won the state championship in 1966. Chlea Wilkin Follon Rafdal ('65) played on four straight state tournament teams that won three trophies from 1962-1965.

Chlea shared, "There have been many excellent basketball players from Everly, but Jeanette Olson was outstanding. The four years that she was in high school, the girls basketball team made the trip to the state tournament and brought a 1st, 2nd, and 3rd place trophy back to Everly. Her senior year was 1968 and Everly played Union-Whitten in the finals. The final score was 113-107 in overtime, Everly losing. To this day, that game is considered by locals to be the best 6-on-6 girls basketball game ever played. Jeanette scored 76 points that game. She was picked to be on the All-Tournament Team and the *Des Moines Register* All-State Team and is in the Iowa Girls High School Basketball Hall of Fame. She accomplished this and remained humble, always giving credit to her teammates."

The coach for the first five tournament teams was Coach Bill Haines. He was succeeded by his assistant coach Larry Johnson who also became the principal. "We just listened in the huddle and Coach would tell us what we were to do. Then we just went out and did it. They were such great leaders and mentors that we believed them and carried out the plan," said Chlea Wilkin Follon Rafdal ('65).

Teachers—Nancy Patrick came to Everly in 1990 as the music and band teacher. "I had a principal that said 'music is an experience' and he never gave me a budget," said Nancy in 2019. "We had a school musical every year in the spring with the talents of many students performing." Two classes were added as electives to the curriculum: music theory and music theatre. Patrick continued, "Ben LeClair ('97) and Scott Kruse ('09) both have beautiful voices and perform on stage and in operas around the country and internationally."

Edith Sackett was the English teacher in the 1960s and 1970s. Chlea Wilkin Follon Rafdal ('65) glowed when she said, "She brought 'class' to class. I would greet her with a 'Good morning, Mrs. Sackett' and she would respond with 'Salutations.' She was such a great teacher on vocabulary." Under her direction, the Everly speech and debate programs were among the leaders in the state of Iowa. There were so many students in her courses that there had to be weed-outs in Declam (declamation) before going to contests. Each year Mrs. Sackett took a group of students to the Guthrie Theater in Minneapolis for live performances to expose them to the theater and arts.

Another English teacher in the 1970s was Margaret Jordon. She and her husband Lee Jordan, the math teacher, were exceptional instructors. "She was barely five-foot tall in stature, but when she stood on her stool she was in command with her ruler. She could snap that ruler with precision and had no discipline problems," said VerDon Schmidt ('73).

Marilyn Meyer was the first-grade teacher for 37 years. She became a friend of every one of her students and followed them throughout their school days. She had truly a genuine interest in their education and their continued success after high school. Her former students often came to see her, bringing a new spouse for her loving approval.

Bus Driver—A most colorful bus driver in Everly was "Tommy the Cop" Lowell Thomas. He was also the town cop. All the kids called him affectionately by his nickname. VerDon Schimdt ('73) said, "I was raised about five miles out and was the first on the bus in the morning. During a blizzard, Tommy made the entire route in the morning and bucked drifts and whiteouts to get the bus full of students.

As he was stopped at the railroad tracks coming into town, he heard on the radio, "School has been called off today!" His only response was Dammit! And he backtracked in the blizzard to take us all home safely."

"Our family was notoriously late for everything. Tommy would drive by to pick us up and honk. He would then go around the section to pick up the others and return to pick up the Wilkins. My senior year, he would stop halfway to school to let me off so that I would get in with my boyfriend, Bill Follon ('65), and I would go with him to school in his car," reminisced Chlea Wilkin Follon Rafdal ('65).

Another character bus driver was Pat Engel who ran a gas station in Moneta. He carried a shotgun on the bus during pheasant season. The last boy in the bus on the way home was Rodney Thompson. Mr. Engle let Rodney drive the bus while he did the cleanup and sweeping so that the bus was ready to go when it arrived back in Everly for the next day's run.

KIA—Everly had many service men die in foreign wars. Mr. Del Thayer was a high school teacher at the outbreak of World War II. He went into the service and died in the war. The following are those from Everly and the high school that died in military service:

Everett Boyles ('40), WWII
William Busing, WWII
Fred Dehrkoop ('19), WWII
Doyle Klett, WWII
Howard Robert, WWII
Russell Scharnberg ('39), WWII
Del Thayer, WWII
Wyatt Wood ('27), WWII
William Follon ('65), Vietnam
Arnold Lohse ('64), Vietnam

William Follon ('65) was killed in Vietnam in February 1970 on the day he was to return to the United States. He left his wife and high school sweetheart, Chlea Wilkin Follon ('65) with two little girls in Everly. Stan Blair ('65), his best friend from high school, was the military escort to bring his remains home. The memorial service was held at the Everly United Methodist Church. Chlea's great friend and basketball coach called on her in her home to express his condolences. Chlea related this story: "When I asked him (Coach Haines) 'Will I ever be happy again?' . . . Coach said yes. Decades later Coach Haines had relocated in retirement to Arkansas. I had heard that he was failing. With my new husband, we went to Arkansas to see him. He was unable to speak, but the look in our eyes conveyed that 'yes I truly was happy again.' Two weeks later, back in the classroom in Everly, the superintendent knocked on my classroom door to inform me that Coach Haines had died." A teacher, a coach, and a friend had left a lesson in life and education to his student.

Closing—The Everly High School, which became Clay Central-Everly, closed following graduation in May 2019. With this closing the high school students were given the choice of three schools to attend: Hartley-Sandborn-Melvin (HSM), Sioux Central, or Spencer starting in the fall of 2019. In the 118 years from 1902-2019, a total of 2,613 graduated from the school. The largest class was 51 seniors in 1969. The last graduating class had 21 seniors. The most numerous surnames were: Schoelerman-28, Roskins-28, Scharnberg-27, Thiessen-25, Johnson-21, Petersen-21, Winterboer-20, Schmidt 19, Meyer-18, Stueben-18, Fell-17, Holst-17, Schoenewe-14, Klett-13, Geerdes-12, Hartmann-12, and Thompson-12. Gale Stoneking III was the last to receive a diploma from Everly High School (alphabetically).

Everly High School
Clay County, IA

#27

Farragut High School

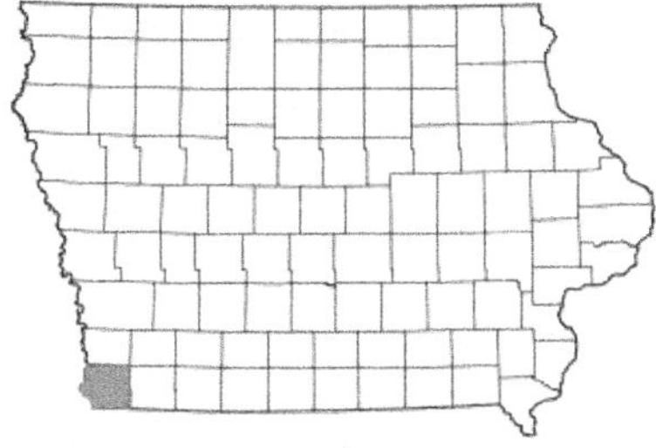

Mascot: Admirals/Admiralettes
Colors: Royal Blue and White
Closed: 2016
Location: East Central Fremont County

Early History—Following the Civil War, veterans came to the Nishnabotna (Nishna) River Valley to settle. They were able to buy this productive land at an economical price in Fisher Township. The townsite was started when the Burlington and Missouri Railroad was completed from Red Oak to Hamburg in the summer of 1870. This railroad later became the Chicago, Burlington, and Quincy (CB&Q). When the first train ran through the area on

August 1, 1870, the railroad called it Lowland. It was soon changed to Lawrence. Mayor U.D. Coy was a veteran of the Black Hawk War, the Mexican-American War, and the Civil War. He suggested the name Farragut, from one of his Civil War heroes, Admiral David Farragut. Farragut led 17 ships into Mobile Bay in 1864 to capture the port for the North. His famed quote, "Damn the torpedoes, full steam ahead," is a renowned American battle cry.

Fisher Township is on the edge of the Loess Hills of Iowa. These hills are a result of the wind-blown deposits of the post glaciated flats of the alluvial plains west of the Missouri River. This unique geological formation has led to a terracing affect from these hills. The region also features manmade push type terraces that allow for a conservation process for farming of the rolling hillsides.

The name was officially changed to Farragut in 1872. The town was incorporated in 1878.

Early Schools—The first one-room frame school building was erected in 1873. By 1880, the Independent District of Farragut was established. Fisher Township gave the town the old No. 6 schoolhouse and a dower of $1,500, and the district took steps to erect a new school building. This brick 30′ x 50′ building was built for $4,700 and described as the "very best school building around."

The first graduating class was in 1889 with three graduates. For the next 35 years, the graduations were held in the open-air city park pavilion. The Seniors presented their class play there in early May with the graduation afterward. The class of 1928 was the last class to sing their class song (to the tune of "The End of a Perfect Day") before the tin-shaped footlights on a cool, rainy spring evening. The next graduations moved to the spacious new auditorium.

In 1909, an addition was built to accommodate the increasing number of students. It contained a larger assembly room, recitation rooms, and grade school rooms.

In 1916, the school board furnished caps and gowns for commencement and required the class to wear them.

The consolidation of the school district occurred in 1928. A vote was held on a proposition for bonds in the amount of $75,000 for purchasing a site and the construction of a new school building. The election carried 225 to 170.

Sports—The sports conference was the Corner Conference. Other schools were: Hamburg, Sidney, Nishna Valley, Malvern, Coin, and Fremont Mills.

The first girls basketball team was formed in 1923. The first basketball court was in the A.C. Coleman Drugstore. This became one of the states most frequent girls teams to ever participate in the state girls tournament. From 1931 through 1971, the Farragut girls went to state 15 times. They won the state tournament in 1971.

Football was introduced in the 1950s. The first teams were six-man. It became 11-man in the mid-1950s. By 2000, an eight-man game was played. The 1952 team was undefeated with nine wins and no losses. The 1953 team was named number one in the state of Iowa.

Wrestling became a sport in 1962. Larry Hausman was the first coach and 29 boys participated.

The biggest rival schools depended on the decade. Lenox girls were always a big rival. In football it was Hamburg and Essex. In the 1950s, the Oakland girls were the team to beat. Sidney was a bitter rival in the 1960s.

Music—The first orchestra was established in 1916. The orchestra was under the direction of Randall Ross and featured a piano, cornets, saxophones, clarinets, tuba, alto, piccolo, drums, violins, and a banjo.

Another first was uniforms for the girls and boys glee clubs and orchestra in 1930. Girls' uniforms were white sweaters with navy treble cleft insignia and white skirts. The boys wore white sweaters with navy bass cleft insignia and dark trousers.

Using the tune to "Anchors Aweigh," a new school song was composed by Mr. Ted Reith who was the principal and girls basketball coach.

Yearbook—The high school yearbook was called the *Green and White*. It was changed to the *Admiral* in 1926.

Notable Teachers—Harold Penwell came to Farragut in 1945. He was the first vocational agriculture teacher. The Stoney Point Chapter (F.F.A.) was organized with 40 members in 1947. The name was taken from the hill north of Farragut. A new vocational agriculture building was constructed from the prisoner of war buildings at Clarinda for a district cost of $6. Disassembling the building, it was moved west of the main school building and reassembled. The total cost of the new facilities was $48,000. Mr. Penwell later became the principal.

Leon Plummer started teaching in Farragut in 1959. He was the girls basketball coach and took them to the state tournament his first year and 12 more times. He started coaching the girls in the fourth grade. His junior high teams had a record of 305 wins and six loses. Fellow teacher Harold Dinsmore said, "Mr. Plumber coached discipline and strategy like no one else. He could see other teams' weaknesses and coached against it." Penny

Hamilton Bredensteiner ('66) recalled, "He made all of his forwards become shooters and not just one main shooter."

Joe Jack taught science, drivers education, and track. He took four boys to the state track meet and won the state title that year.

Merrill Howery was the band director. He always got the most out of his bands at regional contests. He arranged to take the band to Rapid City, South Dakota to a band event. At the Clarinda Band Festival, the Farragut band was selected in the top two bands with only 25 students in the band.

Harold Dinsmore came to Farragut in 1958. He became the first drivers education teacher in 1963. He later taught at the high school for a total of seven decades from 1958-2016.

Helen Limbacher taught English, History, and French from 1950 until 1988. She died during a trip to California. Five teachers and a pilot attended her funeral in Los Angeles. Jeff McQueen ('75) said, "She was respected by all the students and had a lot of class. She always drank the small bottles of Coca Cola."

Bus Drivers—Harold Dinsmore, a teacher, drove the activities bus for many away games and school activities. He was paid $2 when he drove the bus to a girls state tournament game, but got into the game at no charge. The girls lost their game and Harold drove back to Farragut that night. The boys bus arrived at Farragut at 3:00 AM. The next day in his class lecture, most of the boys fell asleep. It was very quiet in the room, when those still awake noticed that Harold, too, had dozed off.

Senior Trips—Lake of the Ozarks was always the destination for the seniors for a last fling together as a class. Harold Dinsmore remembered, "These senior trips did not start until Superintendent Herring came in 1966. What an education for our students. I firmly believe that a big school is not always better." Jeff McQueen ('75) remembered, "We were allowed to smoke and even smoked on the bus because we were 18 years old."

Notable Graduates—Donald Vance Cos ('38) graduated from Wentworth Military Academy in Lexington, Missouri. He became a Rear Admiral in the Navy service in World War II, Korea, and Vietnam. He was twice deployed to Vietnam and the Tonkin Gulf and Sea of Japan. In 1964, in honor of the 100th anniversary of the Admiral Farragut capture of Mobile Bay, he was able to organize a Navy band to come to Farragut for the celebration. A Navy jet landed on the highway north of town and paraded up main street.

Ira Eugene Livingston ('57) graduated from the Naval Academy and was with three nuclear missile submarines. He became a Lt. Commander in the

Navy with a post graduate degree from the Kennedy School of Government at Harvard.

Andy Klein ('86) graduated from Macalester College with B.A. in Geography and Environmental Sciences. After receiving his PhD from Cornell University, he joined the faculty at Texas A&M University where he still teaches in the Geography Department (2020). He has made 18 trips to Antarctica doing scientific environmental research. He has synthesized a 15-year record of localized anthropogenic impacts at McCurdo Station and Palmer Station, Antarctica.

School Facts—The Imogene District consolidated with Farragut in 1959 with the high school students coming to Farragut. Riverton was consolidated into Farragut in 1964.

In 1962, the French club and Future Teachers club were organized with 13 students in each group and Helen Limbacher the sponsor. Mrs. Limbacher also formed the Thespian club that year with nine student members.

Killed in Action—Farragut soldiers killed in action were:

Leslie Burrows, WWI
Ernst Harshorn, WWI
Joe Norris, WWI
Otto Poulsom, WWI
Harry Roberts ('11), WWI
Hubert Shafer, WWI
J. Harvey Scott, WWI
Arthur Simmerman, WWI
Glen Smith, WWI
Howard Turnbull, WWI
Carlie Walters, WWI
Jack Brown, WWII
Amos Butts, WWII
Fred Crawford, WWII
Herman Engel, WWII
Delbert Foster, WWII
Jack Hazelton, WWII
Fred Lorimor, WWII
Warren Pease ('39), WWII
Carl Walters, WWII
Dwight McMahon ('47), Korea
James A Davis ('48), Korea
Donald Scott ('48), Korea
Durward A Limbacher, Vietnam

Pranks—A new press box for Farragut was constructed in 1965. It did not get painted. One night some enterprising youths decided to have some fun. Some tasteful red graffiti was added to the clean wooden sides of the press box. The next day at school, Superintendent Lyle Latimer did not have to use fingerprints to identify the culprits. He had all of the upperclassman boys hold out their hands and the stained fingers and hands gave away the juveniles. The Class of 1966 got the honor of repainting the whole building the next weekend with a beautiful red paint.

Closing—The high school closed abruptly in 2016 with demands from the Department of Education and the State School Board. Red flag warnings and suggestions had been made to the superintendents as early as 2013 about mismanagement of the district's finances. For the first time in the state of Iowa, a district was split up with parts of the district going to Sidney, Fremont Mills (Tabor), Hamburg, and Shenandoah. The state board did such a unique job in redrawing the district lines that parts of the Farragut city limits were in two districts (Hamburg and Sidney).

Farragut High School
Fremont County, IA

#28

Fertile High School

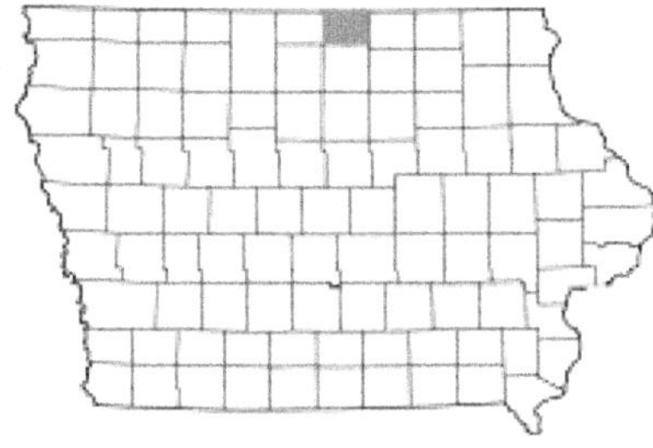

Mascot: Indians
Colors: Black and Gold
Closed: 1962
Location: Southwest corner Worth County

Early History—A common scenario for the location of town sites was the availability of running water. This was to form a mill, which led the first settlers to this area along Lime Creek. William Rhodes was the first settler in Fertile Township, arriving here from Charles City in 1856. Through careful measurement, he could back water around the curve three-quarters of a mile to create a ten-foot dam. Rhodes encountered Indians while camping along Lime Creek, though it did not deter him from the prospects of the location. He returned to Charles City to make arrangements, purchase tools and supplies, and loaded up a wagon drawn by oxen. He traveled 70 miles across the prairie with no roads and reached this spot along Lime Creek on August 6, 1856. On this very date 100 years later, the town of Fertile celebrated its centennial.

Rhodes built a cabin and a grind stone to sharpen the scythe for cutting grass for the oxen. He constructed a dam and then the extension of the dam by 50 feet in 1859. This dam lasted 70 years until high waters in 1929 washed it out. At that time, a new concrete dam was constructed, and the mill modernized. The Rhodes mill became a fixture well into the 1900s and operated as W.M. Rhodes and Son Fertile Roller Mill.

William Rhodes was the first man to answer the call of duty from Fertile to the Civil War. He enlisted on August 22, 1862 in Co. B., 32nd Iowa Volunteers and served the full term of the enlistment with the regiment. He was on detached service with Sherman's Expedition from Memphis, Tennessee, to Meridian, Mississippi. On his return to Memphis, he was ordered to join Major General Banks in the Red River Expedition and participated in all the battles of that disastrous campaign. He was also in the battles of Pleasant Hill, Louisiana, on April 9, 1865. He was discharged at Clinton, Iowa, on August 24, 1865 and returned to Fertile. He had left his wife and son with his in-laws at the beginning of the enlistment.

The first persons in the Worth County to be naturalized and receive their citizenship were Ole Knudson, Aaron Robinson, and Soren Banson in 1860.

William Rhodes became the first postmaster when the post office was established in 1868.

During the fall of 1871, Scandinavian settlers held their first religious service at the house of A. Halvorsen. The service was led by Rev. T.A. Torgensen. The town was first called Rhodes Mill and then called by the nickname of Putsy for many years. When a name was to be officially adopted, Fontanelle and Blaine were both considered, but Fertile became the official name. The village of Fertile was platted in 1877 and the first lot sold that year. Thomas Emsley of Mason City owned this town site.

Andrew A. Elthon came to Fertile in 1893 and started a business with $36 of merchandise. He was highly successful and soon started a general store. When he retired, his son, Thelan, continued on with the business. The name Elthon became very significant in Fertile and then later for the state of Iowa.

Unusual Businesses—Hans Johnson did a large live turtle business for many years, shipping to many parts of the United States.

In 1925, Harley Ouverson started custom hatching with a capacity of 3,340 eggs in the basement of his home south of town. In 1934, he built a large, modern brick hatchery. In 1946, an addition to the hatchery expanded it to a 132,000-egg capacity. His daughter and her husband, Jean ('42) and Wayne ('43) VanDenBosch, became partners and they constructed a broiler plant that produced 5,000 broilers every 10-12 weeks.

Call to Arms and Killed in Action—The state of Iowa had more soldiers enlisted in the Civil War per capita than any state in the Union. Fertile and Fertile Township stand out for the large number of soldiers during each of the wartime conflicts. The following is a list of the numbers involved in those wars:

Civil War-7
Spanish American-1
World War I-54
World War II-142
Korean War-73

Thirteen men lost their lives in these conflicts:
Wayne Wescott, France WWI
Guy Roath, France WWI
Carlos Robinson, France WWI
Ire Myhre, France WWI
Earl Humphrey ('26), WWII
Fred Kirk ('24), WWII
Edwin Johnson, WWII
Roy Highsmith, WWII
James Frankell, WWII
Eldon Stuerwald, WWII
Donald Nissen, WWII

Early Schools—The first school was a summer term in 1860 taught by Phoebe Dennis. She had five scholars. The first Norwegian school was taught by Betty Resta during the summer of 1873.

The first large school was a wooden frame two-story building with eight grades. In 1917, a fine brick building was built. The first graduation from this 12-year high school was in 1917.

In 1939, a WPA built limestone gymnasium and classrooms were added. In 1955, another brick building was added to the south making room for a new kitchen, dining room, and more classrooms.

Community Heritage—Fertile was a very conservative Norwegian community. Dancing, drinking and card playing was not condoned. Howard and Beverly Drevs were the shop and home economics teachers at the high school. They had a party at their home and did have a folk dance one evening for their students. Subsequently, they were called before the school board and were almost fired for allowing such dancing.

Notable Graduate—Leo Elthon ('17) was the son of A.A. and Olena Elthon, the merchant who came to Fertile in 1893. After graduation from high school in 1917, he attended Augsburg Seminary in Minneapolis, Iowa State Teachers College in Cedar Falls, and Hamilton University of Commerce in Mason City. He taught manual training and athletics in Clear Lake and later was principal in the high school at Fertile. He was engaged in farming and quarrying. He married his classmate Synneva Hjelmeland ('17) in 1922. He served in the Iowa State Senate from 1936 until 1952 when he was elected Lieutenant Governor. In 1954, he was sworn in as Governor of Iowa on the death of Governor Beardsley. Mr. Elthon was widely known throughout Iowa and was a distinguished son to the Fertile community. His residence was in Fertile and he continued to be active in affairs of business, community, and church.

Donald Roberts ('55) was born blind, the son of Forrest and Viola Miller ('33) Roberts. He attended the Vinton Iowa School for the blind through his sophomore year and returned to the Fertile High School his last two years to graduate in 1955. At 105 years of age, his mother Viola Miller Roberts ('33) (the oldest living Fertile High School graduate in 2019) in an interview shared, "Donald was a near genius. He never once complained. He married Peggy Oliver, another blind lady and had four delightful children. He distinguished himself as a musician and played the piano much like Liberace." Donald Roberts ('55) once wrote, "I want to be remembered as the only student that Gib Kruse ever drove with who never even took the drivers training test!" Donald was the only student who took typing on a braille typewriter. Harriet Stokke Winden ('55) shared, "Mr. Kruse was a great typing teacher. I still have my 60-word-per-minute pin. I believe that Donald Roberts was just as fast and as accurate. He was an unbelievably talented man."

Drivers Education—Drivers education became part of the curriculum in 1953. The instructor was Gilbert Kruse, a single teacher who also taught typing and geometry. Betty Tuttle Waddington ('56) said, "He understood kids. At first he used his own car. I had never driven before but he just said, 'get in and drive. Let's go downtown first.' I took the course two years because it was an easy course. He was an excellent teacher and married another teacher from Fertile."

Notable Teacher—Mrs. Sylvia Evans was the English and speech teacher. "She was everyone's favorite," remarked Gwen Johnson Scott ('59). Mrs.

Evans could not drive and lived in Joice about eight miles away. She hired high school boys to drive her to and from her home each day.

Sports—The boys 1953 basketball team was the first to go the state tournament and lost their initial game to runner up Ottumwa. They finished the year with a record of 29-2. They were coached by Paul Bruns. The 1954 boys team repeated going to the state tournament. They lost in the opening round to Hull. They finished the year with a record of 32-3. They were coached by Edward Colbert

The girls basketball team made it to the state tournament in 1920. They had a male coach, Kenneth Prescott. Interestingly, all the officials in the Des Moines tournament were women.

There was never a football team at Fertile High School. The boys played spring and fall baseball.

Pranks—Vivian Foster was the home economics and biology teacher in the 1950s. At one of the all-school reunions she once asked, "Who put the snake in my desk drawer?" From the back of the room a sheepish Paul Thovson ('53) raised his hand.

Closing—The high school closed following graduation in May 1962. The students were bused to Forest City the next fall. A total of 629 graduated from Fertile High Schools in the 46 years from 1917-1962. The most numerous surnames of the graduates were: Ouverson-34, Humphrey-16, Purcell-16, Suby-12, Haugen-10, Miller-9, and Hjelmeland-7. The largest class was 23 seniors in 1924. The last to receive a diploma from Fertile High School was Rose Marie Vaage (alphabetically).

Fertile High School
Worth County, IA

#29

Floyd High School

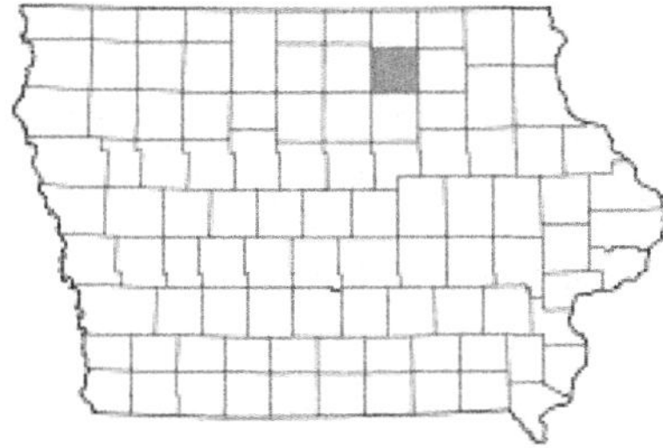

Mascot: Pioneers-later Hawks
Colors: Purple and Gold
Closed: 1958
Location: Central Floyd County

Early History—Floyd was named after Sgt. Charles Floyd who was the only man to perish in 1803 on the Lewis and Clark expedition. He is remembered in Iowa at Sergeant's Bluff, overlooking the Missouri River.

Reported in the 1975 *History of Floyd County*:

> In July of 1855, the town of Floyd was laid out by James Griffith and Henry C. Tatum. The first bridge to be erected in the county over the Cedar River was built here but was carried away by a flood in the summer of 1858. The town is handsomely located on the west side of the Cedar River six miles above Charles City. The Illinois Central Depot is on the east side of the river and is easily accessible by means of a substantial bridge. The Depot of the Milwaukee and St. Paul Railroad is some distance south of Floyd . . . the Independent District of Floyd has a fine graded school edifice, erected at a cost of $10,000 . . .

Another account in the *Brief Outline of Floyd, Iowa* in 1872 by Ed. Wright, Sec. of State reads:

> On the street called Church Street are three Churches and a fine public school building arranged in a direct line . . . all in line of battle we trust for the advancement of knowledge, truth, and righteousness. The Methodist Episcopal cost $5,500; The Adventist, $4,000; The School House $12,000 all built since 1864.

With the early settlement of Floyd came the establishment of the county seat. A vote to move the courthouse site from St. Charles (Charles City) to the geographical center was taken on April 5, 1858. There were 453 voting to remove and 432 against removing. The total was a 19 majority for moving.

Soon after the vote, Judge Ripley ordered the county records to be moved to Floyd since there were no buildings at this time at the center of the county. It became proper for the county judge to designate a place for a temporary courthouse. An injunction was filed on the county judge, to not remove any more books to Floyd, and commanding him to return those already there. The injunction was squashed, but by some "hook or crook," the matter was carried to the State Supreme Court. The court house remained in St. Charles City.

Larry Stewart ('49) remembered, "My grandpa, George Stewart always told the story of the day that Charles City stole the county seat from Floyd."

Early Schools—The old stone schoolhouse served the town of Floyd until 1917. The building was torn down and stone from the school was used to build the double-stone building on Main Street. At a cost of $45,000, this new brick building replaced the stone school. It was two stories plus a basement for the Consolidated School of Floyd Township. The surrounding territory in the township sent pupils there by means of six horse-drawn wagons. The school had 19 rooms and a fuel room. There were three male teachers and five female teachers. Its departments included manual training, domestic science, and agriculture. A teacher with a state certificate in ag education was employed specifically to teach this important subject.

A $50,000 gymnasium was added to the Floyd School in 1949.

Student Memories—Sid's Saddle Shop in Floyd was the hangout for all the high school boys before and after school. This store repaired saddles, harnesses, canvas, and shoes. "This is where the stories flew and the yarn was spun," said Larry Stewart ('49). "Oh, and they even kept our cigarettes under the counter for us so that we had them when school was out in the afternoon," he chuckled. Chuck Thorson ('57) remembered, "My dad would give me a five-dollar bill in August to buy a new pair of Levi's for school. I would go to Sid's and pay $4.74 for a pair of Levi's and have 26 cents left over for a huge chocolate malt."

Chuck Thorson ('57) shared, "During the 50s there were about 100 enrolled at Floyd High School. My freshman year in 1953, we had 22 in my class. By the time we graduated in 1957 there were just 11 seniors. This was what happened in those years when the manufacturing jobs in Charles City were having layoffs. Great job cuts at Oliver made our bedroom community lose population and students. Every Wednesday and Saturday evenings the stores would stay open late and everyone came to town to shop and socialize. The band played in the park and it was followed by a movie."

Sports—The girls played basketball and softball. The boys played spring and fall baseball and basketball. There was never a football team in the high school. The big-time rival was Orchard, but Rockford and Marble Rock were close seconds. The highlight for both girls and boys was the Floyd County Basketball Tournament. Larry Stewart ('49) grinned as he shared, "Since we did not play football, the first basketball games each November were always against Riceville and Nora Springs. Those guys had just come off the football season and were rough and fouled us a lot." Eleanor Mills Waid ('54) smiled as she said, "We had some great basketball teams in the early 50s. We lost a heartbreaker to Hansell in 1953 in the sectionals at Mason City which kept us from going to the state tournament."

Baseball was the other big sport in Floyd. Bob Picken ('49) played professional baseball for five years. He played town team ball and helped Floyd to the Northeast Iowa Championship sponsored by the Waterloo Courier. Bob's uncle, Jim Picken, was a carpenter and came to Floyd from Scotland. He helped build the high school in 1917. He was credited for hanging the doors on the outside entrances to the school which never sagged and stayed perfectly balanced to the last days of the building.

Veterans and the Wars—Jess Sherman ('38) enlisted early for the war. Larry Stewart ('49) stated, "So many predicted that he would never return from the war as he was always a number one gung ho! This marine gave his life on the rocky hills of Iwo Jima in 1945.

Another Floyd man, Lynn Davidson, was an air force pilot and was killed in World War II.

At the beginning of the Korean conflict many young men and women volunteered for the service. Larry Stewart ('49) recalled, "Having just finished the fall term at ISTC in Cedar Falls, we were playing Huckle Be Buck around a card table at Slim's Café. Maybe it was the beverages being consumed or just outright patriotism, but the idea was sprung that we should all volunteer for the Navy. With courage, Bob Picken ('49), Jim Lindsay ('49), Willard "Bud" Hennick ('48), Harold O'Rourke ('48) (whose parents owned and ran Slim's), and I decided to drive to Mason City the next morning and enlist in the Navy. Upon arriving at the recruiting office, we were told the Navy did not need any more enlistees. So, we walked down the street and signed up for the Air Force. Two weeks later, on January 10, 1951, we were on a train headed for Lackland AFB in San Antonio. When we arrived, the Air Force had no uniforms for us so we had to wear our street clothes for the next 30 days."

Notable Teachers—Drivers Education was started in the early 1950s. Eleanor Mills Waid ('54) beamed as she reminisced, "We had a manual transmission with a shift stick on the steering column. Mr. Dewy Breish, our teacher, would take us to Charles City and have us down shift as we drove up the steep hill south on Jackson Street. If that wasn't hard enough for a fourteen-year-old freshman, we then had to learn to parallel park going up that same hill. The farm kids always seemed to take to it like ducks to water, but the learning curve was greater for us town kids."

In 1956, the English teacher, Mrs. Brown, was late getting to school. This had never happened. When she did arrive, a mischievous crime had taken place in her classroom. A can containing a fire cracker had been propped in a window. An explosion ensued. Not quite as famous as the Chicago Seven, but the Floyd Seven were assumed guilty without a trial. They had all been signed out of their class that morning. Chuck Thorson ('57) smiled and winked as he shared, "I was innocent but went down on my sword with the others. My dad was on the school board so there was double jeopardy for a crime I did not commit."

A renowned music teacher at Floyd who was also known at other schools all over northern Iowa was Mr. Donald Whitcomb. He touched many lives with his trumpet playing and music teaching abilities. He and his wife farmed north of town. Floyd students were always so prepared and won mostly #1s at music contests. He came back for school alumni reunions and led the alumni group bands well after the age of 100. Eleanor Mills Waid ('56) played the French horn and Nancy Brownly Norby ('58) played the trumpet for Mr. Whitcomb. At the age of 101, he was the Grand Marshal at the Mason City Parade. Scores of his former students and admirers poured into the streets along the parade route to greet, touch, and say hello to Mr. Whitcomb. He amazingly was able to name everyone along this crowd of admirers. Eleanor Mills Waid ('56) said, "Mrs. Whitcomb accompanied the Floyd students on the piano at contests. She stood at the back of the room and was able to pick out which instruments were flat and sharp. It was told that she was able to milk cows and drive a tractor right alongside her husband. What a wonderful couple to mentor and educate each of us and gave us such an appreciation for music and performance to this day."

Another all-star teacher was Alan "Deke" Fowler who taught history, drivers education, and coached both boys and girls basketball. He was very respected and beloved by all the students. "One day in practice a kid who was shirking running wind sprints grabbed my shirt to hold me back. Later in the locker room I called him out on it, and somehow it led to me clocking him with my fist. Deke caught wind of the incident and called me out and reprimanded me in front of all the whole team. Later in class that day, he admonished me to stay after class. I thought, oh boy here it comes. When everyone had left the room, he said to me, 'Thorson, the next time give him a second punch,' and he winked at me," Chuck Thorson ('57) recalled.

Busing—The six Field sisters, Deloris, Darlene, Donna, Diane, Dixie, and Debbie rode the school bus with Chuck Thorson ('57). Chuck shared, "It was a short bus that only had room for 24 students. I was little so I always got to sit on pretty Darlene's lap. This was always a treat for this little farm boy."

Closing of the School—The high school closed after graduation in May 1958 with the remaining students bused to Charles City to high school that fall. A total of 733 had graduated from Floyd High School in the 41 years from 1918 through 1958. The most numerous surnames of the graduates were: Stewart-16, Anderson-9, Brown-9, Jacobson-9, Rademacher-6, Becker-5, Schmidt-5, and Thomas-5. The last graduate from Floyd High School was Patricia Townsend (alphabetically).

Floyd High School
Floyd County, IA

#30

Fontanelle (BF) High School

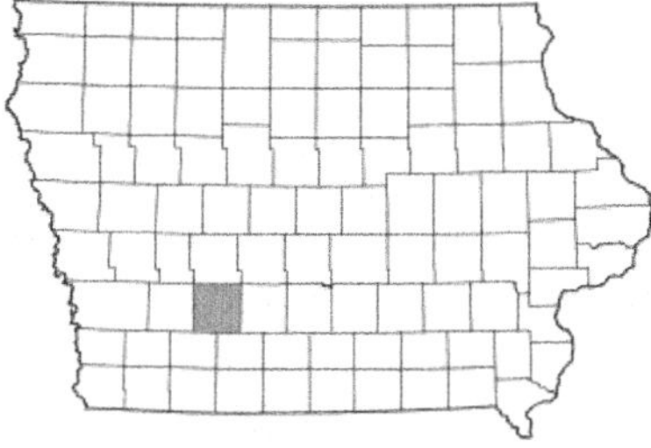

Mascot: Wolves/Panthers
Colors: Black and White/Black and Red
Closed: 1994
Location: Adair County

Early History—Fontanelle was named after Chief Logan Fontanelle. The Mayor of Fontanelle, R. Scott Homan signed a proclamation on February 14, 2005 (150 years after the naming of the town) which describes the naming and its historic significance:

> Whereas the town was born on January 15, 1855 and given the name of Summerset and made the county seat of Adair County on April 24, 1855. Whereas the

name of the town was changed to Fontanelle by an act of the Sixth General Assembly of the State of Iowa on December 22, 1855 and

Whereas the name Fontanelle originates from Chief Logan Fontanelle, son of Lucien Fontanelle, a native of New Orleans born of French parentage and Omaha tribe and

Whereas Chief Fontanelle was effective as a mediator between the two races and wielded much influence with the Omaha tribe of which he was Chief from 1851 to 1855 and

Whereas Chief Fontanelle, well known to the white people at the time in connection with negotiation of the Omaha Tribal Treaty of 1854, when seven chiefs of the Omaha Tribe went to Washington to make the treaty of cession of their lands to the United States and

Whereas Chief Fontanelle was unfortunately killed by a rival tribe in a hunting party. The exact location of his burial site remains under dispute

Whereas the spirit, will and determination of citizens of Fontanelle, no unlike the City's namesake have kept the city a viable community for 150 years and continue to do . . .

Fontanelle was the county seat for only 30 years. After three elections in the county, it was moved to Greenfield in the center of Adair County. 250 men and 75 wagons from Greenfield came on March 22, 1875 to forcibly remove the county records and take them back to Greenfield and relocate the county seat.

Early Schools—The first school in the county was held in the courthouse in Fontanelle in 1857.

The first high school in Adair county was built in Fontanelle in 1882 for $10,000. It was a majestic two-story brick building with a large bell tower. Though described as a high school, it was not a 12-year school. The twelfth year of high school classes was added in 1903. The primary classes were on the first floor and the higher grades were the second floor.

In 1902, a proposition by the school board was submitted to the community to build another building for the primary grades. Women were allowed to vote in the election. Results of the elections showed: For (73 men, 8 women); Against (41 men, 1 woman). With the passing of the bond, the school was built and called the "Little Red Schoolhouse." It had two rooms, a large hall, and a vestibule. There was a basement, furnace, store-room, and a large playroom. Statistics from the 1915 *Adair County History* book show that in the Little Red Schoolhouse in 1903 there were one male and eight female teachers for Fontanelle schools. There were 227 students enrolled with the average attendance of 187. P.P Sullivan was the Superintendent. He later served as the principal at Fontanelle for many years until 1951.

Railroads and Markets—This same P.P. Sullivan wrote an article about *Markets and Trading Places* in

1952 about the railroads coming to Fontanelle and Adair County. Highlights of the article were:

- In the early days of Adair County most of the fat cattle were driven to Ottumwa. As the Chicago, Burlington, and Quincy Railroad (CB&Q) was built across southern Iowa, the towns of Chariton and Afton became marketing places.
- When a battle for the roundhouse between Afton and Prescott ensued, the railroad chose the area on a rise to place its terminal and the town on the crest became Creston.
- Creston became the great railroad center. The CB&Q built a branch to towns in Adair County.

According to Sullivan, "It might be interesting to the later inhabitants to know that at about this time a railroad from St. Louis to Minneapolis promoted a line via Greenfield, so the CB&Q, in order to hold the territory, began a road into the territory to the north. The race became quite exciting and for some time grading crews were working both roads between Creston and Greenfield. The St. Louis project was finally dropped. The Burlington had reached Greenfield, but almost out of breath, so it stopped there for a season of rest."

After recuperating awhile, the road was continued to Fontanelle where it took another long rest for about six years. In 1884, the road was continued westward and three more towns were established, Bridgewater in Adair County and Massena and Cumberland in Cass County.

This branch was 46 miles long and rated by the railroad officials as the best paying 46 miles of their system as it tapped one of the richest livestock areas in the country.

New High School—The events of 1915 unfolded with urgency for a new modern and enlarged schoolhouse.

- April 1, 1915, election for a $25,000 bond defeated 128-191.
- April 29, 1915, state inspector declared present building unsafe.
- May 6, 1915, school lost accreditation.
- June 3, 1915, $35,000 bond approved.
- August 5, 1915, contract let for new school.
- October 7, 1915, cornerstone set by Grand Lodge of Iowa in a ceremony.

In 1915, the beautiful three-story brick high school was constructed for $35,000. This building served the district for the next 80 years. Additions in 1951 were made for a new gymnasium, stage, and vocational farm shop with the design allowing for addition of more classrooms in case of eventual consolidation or reorganization. This foresight came to fruition in less than ten years with the consolidation in 1958 with nearby Bridgewater.

From the *Fontanelle Observer* on February 7, 1957:

> The Bridgewater-Fontanelle communities have enjoyed friendly and cordial relations and have many common interests. A community school system would not only benefit our children but would do much to further develop the friendly relations which have always existed. The adoption of the school plan as presented could well result in a community school district of which all students, parents and citizens of the area could be proud to be a part.

The final remodeling came in 1962 when a new wing was added on the southwest corner. The remodeled rooms provided: a boys shower and two locker rooms, girls locker and shower, hot lunch kitchen, and home economics room. Additional new rooms included: band, vocal music, industrial arts, vocational agriculture, typing, commercial and superintendent's office-work room.

Normal Training—A benefit of the new high school was the beginning of the teaching of the Normal Training High School. It was another focus area in selling to the voters in 1915 for the new high school. The state would pay the school $750 annually for teaching normal training. In the appeal to the community, it was promoted as: We want this, not only for the money, but so that we may offer our young people the same advantage as Greenfield, Adair, and Anita, which are Normal Training High Schools.

Sports—Six-man football was played at Fontanelle in the early years. The 1939 six-man team was the Champion of Western Iowa with an undefeated season.

In 1940, Fontanelle started playing the 11-man game. The 1941 football team only had one blemish on their record of a 7-1 season. That was the opening game loss to Clearfield. It was followed by wins against Bagley, Prescott, Massena, Cumberland, Afton, Bridgewater and Stanton.

The 1963 Bridgewater-Fontanelle football team was undefeated with a 9-0 record. There were 42 boys on the team.

The girls played basketball. The 1958 girls team went to the state tournament losing in the first round to Cedar Valley 66-58.

After the consolidation to become Bridgewater-Fontanelle in the fall of 1958, two more outstanding girls teams played. The Bridgewater-Fontanelle girls team of 1965 had a record of 20-1, losing in the finals of the districts to prevent them from going to state. The 1981 team finished with a record of 20-4, losing in the first round of the state tournament.

Hot Lunch—Following the depression years, government programs were made available for schools to receive surplus commodities. Such items as hominy, figs, and prunes had never before made many dinner tables in Iowa. These and other bulk canned goods became available to schools. On November 5, 1941, with food ordered from Des Moines, the first hot lunches were served at Fontanelle.

Yearbook—The name of the 1946 yearbook was *The Summit.* There were 84 students in high school. Even though this senor class had been in high school through the war, there was no reference made to any hardships or events of the world. There were 12 seniors, 25 juniors, 25 sophomores, and 22 freshmen that year. There were 28 in the band and a 13-member team of baton twirlers and cheerleaders.

There were 11 faculty members in K-12 in 1946. Of those faculty, they had degrees or had pursued education from a wide variety of colleges such as Drake, Des Moines University, University of California, University of Iowa, University of Boston, Iowa State College, College of St. Scholastica, Grinnell, Iowa State Teachers College, University of Nebraska, Missouri Teachers College and William Penn.

A quote from this yearbook that was relevant for all years: "The school annual is a great invention. The school gets all the fame, the printer all the money, and the staff all the blame."

The 1956 yearbook was named *Wolf Tails.* There were 28 senior graduates. The football team gave up only 26 points in compiling an undefeated season with a record of 8-0-1. The only blemish was a season opening 6-6 tie with rival Adair. The girls basketball team won the Adair County Tournament by defeating Zion, Orient, and Richland Township. The girls lost to Beaconsville, 50-53, in the district competition. The boys basketball team won the county tournament by beating Adair, Zion, and Bridgewater.

Notable Teachers—Jan Wollenhaupt taught typing and was the sponsor for the National Honor Society in the 1970s. Deb Miller Gevock ('76) shared, "Mrs. Wollenhaupt was amazing and so professional. She had a dignified demeanor and dressed so well. She walked to school every day. Her husband was a banker in town. After I graduated and went to college, I came back to teach in Fontanelle. Mrs. Wollenhaupt was still such a role model and had such respect from the students. She once told me, 'You can call me Jan.' There was just no way that I could ever bring myself to do that, even to this day (2020). She once called my mother, Ethelmarie Martin Miller ('50). and told her, 'You need to have Deb stop talking so much in typing class, she would do much better.' Talk about a phone call that made me a better student, and I realized that someone cared and was watching out for me."

Erma Golz was the French and English teacher in the 1960s and 1970s. When Deb Miller Gevock ('76) asked, "Could we just go to some Island that speaks French? Mrs. Golz said, 'Why don't we just go to France?'" That next spring she led a group of 11 students for two weeks to France. Each student stayed in a French home for a week and were immersed in the language. Deb continued, "The next week Mrs. Golz led us on a phenomenal sight-seeing tour of France. It has really changed my life and it was because of Mrs. Golz that I went into teaching."

Consolidation—One of the more harmonious consolidations was with the joining of the high schools of Bridgewater and Fontanelle in the fall of 1958. With the towns only six miles apart, the traveling and busing was a short distance. The first Bridgewater-Fontanelle graduation class of 1959 had 39 graduates.

Closing—The high school closed after 108 years, 1887-1994. Seventy-two of those years it was called Fontanelle High School. The last 36 years it was called Bridgewater-Fontanelle. A total of 2,244 graduated from the high school. The most frequent surnames of the graduates with the total and the Fontanelle/Bridgewater-Fontanelle in parenthesis were: Jensen-51 (28/23), Miller-44 (22/22), Queck-27 (14/13), Martin-26 (12/14), Purdy-21 (14/17), Brown-24 (8/16), Westphal-19 (8/11), Goetz-12 (6/6), Johnson-12 (6/6), Lowery-11 (6/5), and Williams-11 (4/7). The largest class from Fontanelle High School was 39 in 1942. The largest graduation class from Bridgewater Fontanelle High School was 60 graduates in 1979. The last to receive a diploma from the high school was Todd Westphal (alphabetically) in 1994.

In the fall of 1994, all the Bridgewater-Fontanelle students were bused to Greenfield where they attended the new school district school called Nodaway Valley High School.

Fontanelle High School
Adair County, IA

#31

Frederika High School

Mascot: Trojans
Colors: Purple and Gold
Closed: 1958
Location: North Central Bremer County

Early History—Bremer County was named after Frederika Bremer of Swedish nobility. She was the mother of women's emancipation in Sweden and published the novel, *Sketches of Everyday*, in 1828. In 1849, she toured the United States, where she traveled to Washington D.C., down the Mississippi to meet slave owners, north to the Indians, stayed with Quakers and Shakers, and heard sermons in all kinds of churches. The Governor of Iowa was a great admirer of Frederika and urged the county to be named Bremer. Thus, the town of Frederika also took on this Swedish noble's name.

This location along the Wapsipinicon River was the site of the first sawmill started by Loren Rima in 1855. The sawmill was run by waterpower from the Wapsipinicon. In 1854, Norton Henry built a powered grist mill on the banks of the Wapsipinicon. It operated in connection with Rima's sawmill.

Norton Henry's land was surveyed and platted for a town in 1868. In 1873, the first village was called Henry's town and Henry's Mill.

An oil well was drilled near town in 1902 by the Prospecting Oil Company. Shares were sold to fund the endeavor in the amount of $9,400. There was no oil found and to this date (2020) there have not been any producing oil wells in the state of Iowa.

The Farmers Savings Bank opened its doors in 1926 in Frederika. It survived the bank closings during the banking crisis in the 1930s depression. It remains in the Rewoldt banking family's name today, nearly 100 years later. Frederic Rewoldt ('46) started working at the bank as a young boy doing cleaning duties. He worked himself up through all the positions to become the president of the bank.

Early Schools—As early as 1850, there was a schoolhouse built in Frederika Township. A log farmhouse became the next established school. In these schools, there was not a grading system, and everyone studied from the same textbook. The most difficult textbook was McGuffey's fourth grade reader. Following the Civil War, more children in the area meant a larger school was needed. A new school called "The Little Red Schoolhouse" was built. The building was 36′ x 36′ with attendance of about eighty-five students. This Little Red Schoolhouse was moved several times and joined the Frederika School District with its eleven grades. With so many classrooms needed, the Methodist Church was also used for schooling.

A 1920s newspaper clipping found in a scrapbook of Ladonna Bravener Bergmann ('48) had an account of Miriam French: "There was an epidemic of chicken pox in the community. She encouraged the students to come to school anyway, because they couldn't expose anyone else, anyhow."

By 1923, a new high school building was proposed. In 1926, the first high school graduation was held with five graduates.

Sports—The boys sports were baseball and basketball. There was no football played at Frederika. The girls sports were basketball and softball.

The Tripoli newspaper reported:

> The girls basketball squad from Frederika accompanied by Coach Earl O. Berge, Mrs. Earl Lease as chaperones are headed for Des Moines to compete in the State Girls Basketball Tournament at Drake Fieldhouse floor. They are the first team from Bremer County to ever get there. They will play Callender.

The 1945-46 girls team was coached by Superintendent Earl O. Berge, who returned after four years' service in the armed forces. He coached at Frederika from 1940-42 and produced teams that, combined with this year's group, had a four-year record of 80 wins and seven losses. The 1946-47 record was 20-1 with the only loss to Steamboat Rock, another state qualifier. Arlene Rewoldt ('47) was not with the team for the Steamboat Rock game. Gloria Alcock was named second team All-State.

The Tripoli newspaper story stated:

> Indications now are that somewhere around 150 Frederikians will follow the lasses to Des Moines . . . they've chartered two buses and are looking for two more . . . Early March will be moving time for more than farmers . . . or individual town dwellers, for that matter . . . especially if that town happens to have a basketball team in the state tournament . . . That rabbit foot that Marilyn Moeller carries into battle may make a difference. The Trojan girls believe in it!

From the *Des Moines Register* and *Tribune*: "The Trojans battled valiantly against greater size and their own 'coldness' at the basket but lost 46-31."

The Tripoli paper in 1948 reported:

> Fame is so fleeting-You'll hear from them again later. Just two short seasons ago, 1945-46, the Frederika girls basketball team were playing in the Iowa Girls State Basketball Tournament. They had won the Bremer County Tournament, too. FOUR SUCCESSIVE YEARS and were perennial winners in the county conference and sectional tournaments. Then, in 1946-47 with a record of 23-1 they lost only to Waterville by two points when colds and illness riddled the team. Now less than two years later there are not enough mature girls to play this year.

Whether it was coaching, development, tenacity, or a combination of all, this same girls basketball team regrouped the next year in 1951-52. They did not play the year before and struggled and won no games all year in the conference round-robin schedule. Then came the Bremer County Girls Tournament. Frederika not only won a game, they swept Readlyn by 41-26, then Denver by 47-43, and won the County Tournament in dramatic fashion trimming Janesville 35-28. Darlene Bergmann Andrews ('52) remembered, "I was on that team. The tournament was in Plainfield and the excitement carried back to Frederika for weeks. I was a senior and it was devastating the year before in my junior year that we had to disband the team because we did not have enough girls in high school to have a team. We may not have made it to state but winning that County Tournament in the fashion we did has given us bragging rights in Bremer County all of our lives."

Notable Teachers—Florence Lease was a teacher and became the principal. She was a widow and the school was her life. "She kept in touch with us and followed our progress well into her 90s," told Helen O'Connell Schumacher ('56).

Mary Rewoldt taught business classes for one year at Frederika. "Our principal was Mrs. Lease. She was so likeable and was so good to the students. I was one of Principal Lease's teachers in the business department," said Mary Rewoldt.

Notable Graduates—The class of 1957, with 11 graduates, produced three members with doctorate degrees: Bill Heffernan ('57), Kenneth Stumme ('57), and Berth Ann Bockhaus Werderitsch ('57).

Cooks—The M and M ladies, Marion Bahlmann and Mrytle Rausch were the long-time beloved cooks for the hot lunch program. "They were both just good home cooks and the meals were so good, " said Mary Rewoldt. "I came as a teacher in 1954 and their use of the commodities and the state nutrition guidelines made them special."

"It takes everyone in a school to educate. My greatest counseling came from my dear cooks. My sisters and I all worked in the kitchen to pay for our meals. Mrs. Bahlmann and Mrs. Rausch were 'our counselors' and gave us such great advice as teenagers," said Helen O'Connell Schumacher ('56).

Polio—Frederika was stunned when Maxine Richmond was stricken with polio at 17 years of age and died.

Virginia Mueller Fowler ('56) contracted polio her senior year. "That year seemed to be the most memorable to me with the polio epidemic. It was the year before the Salk vaccine was introduced and the fear of contracting the disease was ever-present. It seemed to really change our social life. No swimming and congregating at fairs and all events were discouraged," said Helen O'Connell Schumacher ('56).

Killed in Action—Though fate and life have no lottery, there were four from this small Frederika High School killed in WW II:

Lester Bremer ('37)
Junior Carroll ('37) Germany
Charles Henniger ('38)
Elwin Alcock ('43) Iwo Jima.

Closing—The Frederika High School closed after graduation in May 1958. The remaining students were bused seven miles south to Tripoli. The rival school, Tripoli had never had a girls basketball team, but subsequently benefited with the Frederika students. A total of 288 graduated from Frederika High School in the 33 years from 1926-1958. The most numerous surnames of the graduates were Bergmann-9; Bockhaus-8; Bremer-8; and Mowatt-5.

Fredrika High School
Bremer County, IA

#32

Fremont High School

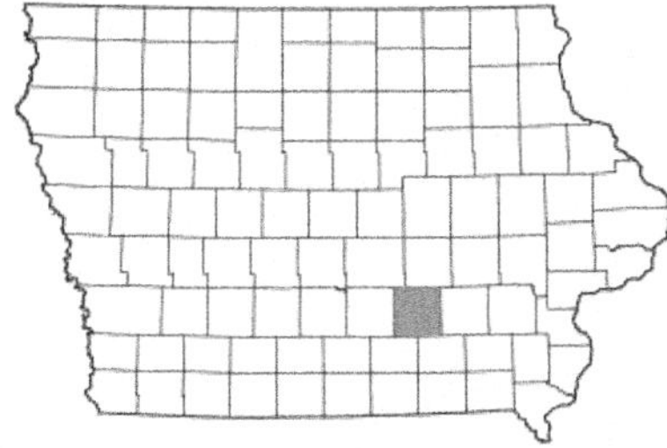

Mascot: Wildcats/Wildkittens
Colors: Maroon and White
Closed: 1988
Location: Southeast Mahaska County

Early History—Mahaska County was one of the original lands formed with the "New Purchase," the lands that were opened to white settlers. The county was established by the territorial legislature in 1842. It is four counties away from the Mississippi River and in the third tier up from the southern border of Iowa and Missouri. Immediately on May 1, 1843, with a gun shot fired, the land claims became available to the settlers.

Big Grove was a 300-acre wooded area north of the later town of Fremont. A letter from Germany came addressed to the writer's acquaintance at Big Grove, Mahaska County, North America.

The township was named Cedar. The first post office in Cedar Township was in the home of William Morrow at Big Grove. Morrow was also the Justice of Peace and is credited for naming Fremont after the "pathfinder" John C. Fremont, who had traveled through southern Iowa in the 1840s as an Army scout heading west. A grist mill and sawmill were constructed on the Skunk River. The town was platted in 1847.

There were two railroads with the CB&Q (Chicago, Burlington, and Quincy) running east-west on the southern edge of town. The Iowa Central Railroad, which later became the Missouri and St. Louis track, was on the north edge of town and ran next to the school grounds.

Early Schools—The first school in Cedar Township was held as a subscription school one mile north of Fremont in 1846. It had a rather primitive look with logs, greased paper windows for light, a clay chimney outside, puncheon floors, and desks.

The first school in Fremont was a log structure built in 1849. The first teacher, E.H. Bobbit, helped build the school. The school year was three terms: fall, winter, and spring. The winter term had the largest attendance.

In 1856, another 50′ x 25′ school was built that had as many as 125 pupils in the winter term.

In 1871, there were demands for a larger building. A 24′ x 60′ x 12′ structure was built on the site of the present school grounds (2020). It had two rooms for the primary and advanced students. It cost $1,600 with an additional $450 for the lot and furniture. It seated 150 pupils. The school year was seven months and the teachers' pay was between $35 and $40 each month.

In 1890, an imposing three-story school was completed with a beautiful brick exterior and white bell tower.

Building a gymnasium in Fremont met resistance from the community. In 1889, a proposal to the electors to add a $500 gymnasium and equipment was defeated, 125 yes to 151 no. Forty-two years later, in 1931, a bond to build a gymnasium for $12,000 passed 168-92. After construction had started, another vote was necessary because the first election was ruled illegal. The second vote passed 72-34. The gymnasium was finished in three months construction time and dedicated on September 18, 1931.

This 1931 gym was small, and the floor was well-maintained by the janitors. However, Fremont had to hear the ridicule from their archrival, Hedrick, when they visited. Jackie Sieren Perkins ('69) said, "The Hedrick students (and a few adults) would chant '1-2-3 CRACKER BOX!' We were the Wildcats (maroon and white) and we didn't care if our gym was small—it was home!" Finally, in 1973, a bond for $290,000 passed and the gymnasium named Raymond H. Byers (after the superintendent) was finished for commencement in May of 1975.

A fire on August 11, 1945 delayed the start of school for one week. For the next year, the teachers and students had to endure the rebuilding and remodeling of the school.

Sports—No football was played at Fremont after an injury in 1916. The boys played basketball, baseball, and cross country. The girls game was six-on-six basketball. The teams competed in the Empire Conference with other charter members Blakesburg, Fox Valley, Hedrick, and Moulton-Udell. Other schools joining the conference during its years were Russell, Tri-County, and Deep River-Millersburg.

The girls won the Mahaska County Tournament in 1938. The Fremont team had to deal with an end of the high school and lack of girls out for basketball in 1987. A new girls coach, Sue Decker, had arrived at Fremont that fall and found only eight girls out for six-on-six basketball. Practice and demands on playing both offense and defense took its toll on the team. With grades, flu, and injuries hitting the team, they found themselves playing with only five girls against Hedrick. The teams did not win a game in the final year of the Fremont High School

Hot Lunches—The Fremont school served lunches starting in 1935. Ora Newell was in charge and it is not known if the lunches were every day or the cost to the student.

Later cooks, Ruth Towns (baker), Della Barker, and Bernice Gordon cooked for many years together. Jackie Sieren Perkins ('69) remembered, "Mrs. Gordon's goulash was a famous favorite of all. Years later, in trying to find a recipe, she shared this memorable dishes ingredients with me. They were macaroni, tomato paste with equal parts water and chili powder, with some sugar and onion. Ruth's gooey cinnamon rolls seemed the size of a plate to young admirers." Milk was always on tap at Fremont for any student at any time of the day. And it was free.

Polio—Though no students are remembered who may have suffered from polio, one teacher had been afflicted. Mrs. Ardyce Prather had to wear braces and used crutches. The school adapted the restroom with bars for her use. Jackie Sieren Perkins ('69) said, "It was such an honor to get to carry Mrs. Prather's lunch tray for her."

Janitor—Lyle Bales was a caretaker of the schools in the 60s. The Rose Hill students who had come to Fremont after their school closed had to pay tuition. Some of the Rose Hill pupils helped sweep the floors and helped Mr. Bales with the janitor duties to help pay their tuition. Greg Perkins ('69) grinned as he shared, "Lyle was such a nice guy and so easy going. We were always willing to help him, and of course, we often went down to the furnace room to smoke with him."

School Events—Not unique to Fremont school, but these are some of the special activities that created school memories for all:

- All-school carnivals on a Friday night in the fall. Tickets were twenty-five cents. The Carnival King and Queen crowns were determined by voting with a penny for each vote.
- Nearly half of each class attended school together all 13 years.
- Skating parties four times each year with each class taking turns in sponsoring to sell tickets as a fundraiser. Skating was at the US Naval Base used during WWII between Fremont and Ottumwa called Skateland. Everyone learned to skate and even skate backwards.
- Soup suppers in the winters were for fund-raisers. Donations of hamburger, home grown onions, canned tomato soup, pickles, and PIES! The mothers prepared the chili. Planning, organization, and volunteering were important learning times together.
- Christmas programs with a real tree lighted, standing over the entrance to the gym. The

Christmas songs, an operetta, and ringing of bells with the surprise visitor arriving . . . "It's Santa."

- A tea and style show was presented by the home economics class. They baked cookies and prepared punch for the mothers and teachers. All high school girls and female teachers were invited guests. And in the believe it or not category; senior boys supervised the elementary classes during the event.
- Class rings were something that everyone had to have. The class voted on the design and teens could pick the color and stone they wanted.

Notable Graduate—Steve Bales ('60) earned his engineering degree from Iowa State in May 1964. One month later, he was working for NASA. He was at Mission Control on July 20, 1969 when Apollo 11 was circling the moon with Michael Collins piloting the command module. It was time for the lunar module to split from the command ship and a power-descent to the moon surface. As it drifted toward the surface, bad things happened. The space craft moved faster than it should, and it approached its abort limits. Bales told the *Des Moines Register* 45 years later, "It lasted about 13 minutes. The entire 13 minutes passed so fast, and yet I think every flight controller on duty that day could tell you about every second of the experience." Bales stayed glued to the data, kept his eyes on the control panel screen, and remained cool. On his recommendation, the mission was deemed still doable. Still a go. More trouble came in the last few minutes before touchdown as the guidance computer alarms flashed. The computers seemed overloaded. Now it was the 11th hour, 59th-minute decision. Abort or proceed?

Bales sorted out the problem and made a decision, which took about 15 seconds, during the powered descent and "Flight we are GO" on that alarm. A co-worker had instantly heard and recognized the alarm and said the warning was passable."

A car caravan from Fremont was organized to travel to the Iowa State Fair to honor the Apollo astronauts and Steve Bales in 1969.

Pranks—The music teacher, Mrs. Mary Lou Abernathy, also directed the junior and senior plays. More than once when ornery thespians would show up backstage with a goat she would yell, "I quit! I quit!" Somehow, with promises to never do this again, the show went on. At least until the next class play was being practiced.

The coaches room also doubled as a sickroom with a cot for students who were ill to lay down for recovery. On an escape from study hall, John Carter ('69) and Jerry Van Palen ('69) were playing cards with coach Erwin Schoppenhorst. Two girls just happened to be in the sickbay that day also. The ever-vigilant superintendent happened upon the scene and was flabbergasted as he shouted, "Schoppenhorst! What in the hell are you thinking?" The experience may have paved the way for John Carter, as he later served on the school board and was sure to hear other nuisances to come before the board.

Killed in Action—Eight men from the Fremont area lost their lives in service to their country.

Jesse Burch, WWII
Denzil Hibler, WWII
Albert Systna, WWII
Arthur McGarvern, WWII
Ames McGhghy, WWII
David Moore, WWII
Warren Newman, WWII
Ivan Smith, WWII
James Robins ('65), Vietnam

Student Protest—A student petition and walkout in the spring of 1988 was held to get the schoolboard to listen to the students' concerns about the closing of the high school. The 15 students were expelled and a hearing with the schoolboard did not change the board's decision to close the high school and unify with Eddyville, 14 miles southwest of Fremont.

In 1987 and 1988, Fremont shared boys sports with Hedrick, their archrival to the east.

Closing—The Fremont High School closed following graduation in May 1988. In the 95 years from 1894-1988 there were 1,358 graduates from the school. The largest class was 28 seniors in 1966. The most numerous surnames of the graduates were: Lee-25, Brown-21, Williams-20, Dinsmore-16, Steele-16, Phillippe-14, Triplett-14, Thoads-13, Fuller-11, Miller-11, Davis-10, Martin-10, and Perkins-10. The last to receive a diploma from Fremont High School was Melissa Wyngarden (alphabetically).

Fremont High School
Mahaska County, IA

#33

Galva High School

Mascot: Blue Devils/Devilettes
Colors: Blue and Gold
Closed: 1980
Location: Northeast Ida County

Early History—The town was named after Galva, Illinois. The only other Galva in America is in Kansas. The early settlers in the area were Germans, Swedes, and Irish.

Early Schools—A country school building was moved into Galva in 1885. It was used until a new two-story school building was occupied in 1895. The first graduate from this school was in 1895. A manual training room was added to this structure the following year.

In the Spring of 1916, groundbreaking for the Galva Consolidated School began. This was one of the first consolidated districts in the state to incorporate rural country school districts. The bond for $55,000 at 4½% interest was passed, and 12 acres were purchased three blocks east of Main Street. This new school was for grades 1 through 12. A sunken gymnasium was on the bottom level. The plan was to use it later for a swimming pool.

The subjects offered at the new high school to fulfill requirements were:

Advanced Math	Algebra	Geometry
Domestic Science	History	Physics
Manual Training	Music	Pennmanship
American and English Literature	Latin	Physiology
Agriculture (boys and girls)	English	Economics
American Government	Speech	Drawing

German was discontinued as a subject on April 26, 1918, when war against Germany was declared and America entered World War I. German as a foreign language was again taught in 1962 for two years. The subject was discontinued because Stan Nading ('63) was the only student taking German for those two years.

In 1938, the United States Government offered to finance a new gymnasium using WPA workers for 45% of the cost of the gymnasium. The community vote was unanimous, and the project was completed in 1940 at a cost of $31,000. This new gymnasium was the largest and most modern in the surrounding area.

Buses—The first buses used were called hacks. They were wooden coaches pulled by horses. Soap stones heated at the school furnace were placed in the buses during the winter to help keep the children warm. In 1932, the first motorized buses designed by Jim Fleetwood ('32) were used to transport the students.

By 1954, the Galva Community School District had expanded to 72 sections of land and used seven 24-passenger buses. The drivers each owned their buses and the district paid them mileage.

With declining rural enrollment in the late 1970s, the district used three 48-passenger buses.

Music—In 1932, there was a school orchestra with 14 students.

A picture of the 1939 Girls Glee Club showed 24 girls dressed in identical dresses. These dresses had been purchased from Younkers in Sioux City for $1.50 each.

In 1962, a new band and music instructor came to Galva. Mr. Jim Inman led the band and music department for the next 18 years, until the high school closed. The school purchased new band uniforms in 1965. The dark blue and gold uniforms with Galva printed diagonally across them became known throughout the state. They were even seen in Winnipeg, Canada, as the entire marching band traveled across the border to perform at the Winnipeg Band Festival and Parade. Between 90 to 95% of the student body was involved in some performance position including twirlers, flags, majorettes, and instrumentalists. Galva set an Iowa State record in Small Group (Class) contests with 50 Division #1s in instrument solos and ensembles.

Sports—Football was played for the first time in 1906. For the next three years all the team's games had to be played away as Galva had no field. The teams they played were Ida Grove, Correctionville, and Early.

Boys basketball became a school sport in 1912. All the practices were outside on a dirt court as the school had no indoor practice facility. The team's first game was at Holstein which sported the indoor Turner Hall. The Holstein team was dressed in uniforms, but Galva only had cut-off overalls. With the indoor surroundings and the awe of the uniforms, Galva lost the game handily.

An early athletic league was chartered in 1931 with the following schools being members of the Maple Valley Athletic Conference: Galva, Battle Creek, Correctionville, Danbury, Holstein, Ida Grove, Mapleton, and Odebolt.

The track season of 1938 was remembered by France Wanberg ('38). "We had a great relay team. I was nipped at the tape by a team from Sac City which kept us from the state track meet. I can still see that race yet today these 81 years later (2019) at my age (98). I was also on the basketball team and, even with my speed, I was really great at sitting on the bench to keep it warm."

In the 1940s there was another league affiliation called the Popcorn Loop. The schools in this affiliation were: Arthur, Galva, Nemaha, Schaller, and Sulfur Springs.

The Bo-Coon Conference (Boyer and Coon Rivers) was formed in 1950 and continued until the school closed in 1980. The initial members of the conference were: Galva, Battle Creek, Crestland (Early), Lakeview-Auburn, Lohrville, Lytton, Newell, Schaller, Wall Lake, and Pomeroy.

The first Homecoming royalty was chosen in 1948 with Jean Sears ('49) selected as the queen by the students. Her attendants were Marlys Rydberg ('49), Betty Rusch ('50), Helen Frank ('52), and Donna Sorensen ('51).

The 1955 football team was undefeated and won the Bo-Coon Conference title.

All home games had to be played in the daytime until lights were installed at the football field in 1956. By 1958, with less boys out for football, Galva started playing eight-man football. They joined the Little Sioux eight-man conference. By 1960, the football team was the undefeated league champion with Delaine Koch as the coach.

The boys made it to the state basketball tournament in 1948. They won the first-round game against Hudson 36-27, but lost to the eventual state champion, Manning, in the semifinals. The girls basketball team made it to state in 1949 and lost in the first round to Guthrie Center 38-37. The 1953 girls basketball team went to the state tournament. They won their first-round game but then lost to New Sharon, the eventual state champion.

Events and Activities – With the outbreak of World War I, the students were involved in rolling bandages for the Red Cross.

In 1920, the Malloy house provided room and board for many of the teachers at the school. This arrangement continued for the next 30 years. The teachers staying at the Malloy house could get their lunch meal at noon. A student from school walked to the boarding house to get the hot lunch for the teacher, who was staying back at the school to supervise over the noon hour.

In 1942, the grading system was changed to drop the letter grade E, between D and F.

Kindergarten was started on March 6, 1944 on a part-time basis due to the large class that was anticipated for the first grade the next fall. Kindergarten became all day in 1950.

An honor roll was prepared by the high school students to commemorate and recognize the 105 Galva graduates that were serving in World War II.

The first school annual yearbook was printed in 1953 and called the *Galvacade* (named based on the popular radio show called Cavalacade of America).

On November 22, 1963, Kathy Wanberg Breyfogle ('67) was going to home economics class when she passed by the superintendent's office and heard that President Kennedy had been shot. "I hurried into the home economics room and announced that the President had been shot. At first, nobody wanted to believe this freshman, but with my horrified look it finally set in," she remembered.

Hot Lunch—Hot lunch was first prepared by the Domestic Science class for lunches at Galva starting in the late 1940s. The hot lunches were later prepared in the lunchroom kitchen. "Georgia Malloy was a cook nearly forever," said Stanley Nading (63). "One of her specialties was called 'Taverns' which was like todays Maid-rites as a loose meat sandwich. On one occasion, she fed us something like a biscuit and gravy and I told her, 'I wouldn't feed that to my dog.' Our family couldn't afford the hot lunch for me all of the time, but when Georgia told my parents about my refusal to eat the biscuit and gravy and my statement, I ended up having to apologize to her."

Another lunch story emerged regarding the government surplus food and the canned spinach served by Georgia Malloy. Keith Adams ('66) said, "None of us could stomach that canned spinach and I can't eat it to this day. But Lynette Kreutz Fey ('67) thought it was wonderful, and she loved the soggy spinach. We all were required to finish our plates at noon and Lynette always helped us out. Those light brown plastic plates with the three sections seemed to always have that green spinach in one of the dividers."

Killed in Action—The following were Galva area residents and graduates who either were killed or died while in the service to the country:

Arnold Niemeier

Thomas Irwin

Bloyce Bruns ('39)

Everett Boyce

Edward Bush
Stanley Bush
Paul Kind
Donald Kistenmacher
Walter Dibbenn

Notable Teachers—Jeanie Holm taught math. As a reward in class for successfully completing a problem or answering a question, she was known to hand out 'sen sen.' Randy Hustedt ('76) remembered sen sen tasting like charcoal and turning tongues black. He shared, "She would say 'Okay children, it is time for your treat,' and you would take it. She had a big bee-hive hair doo and she was a tough teacher, but man did we get a great education from her."

Marvin Ziesmer was the superintendent from 1950-1957. He had a B.S. from Drake and an M.A. from the University of Minnesota. He taught government, economics, and civics.

Ellen Wanberg was the principal from 1946-1957. She had a B.A. from the University of Iowa and took classes from Colorado State. She also taught sociology and directed every class play.

Jim Inman came to Galva in the fall of 1962 to teach music and direct the band. The results of his efforts were 17 Division #1 ratings in a row at the state band contests. His marching and concert bands were a pride of all the student body and the town. Mr. Inman thrived on perfection and brought his own performing background with him to Galva. He played with the Carl King and Legion bands.

Ab "Hap" Hafener had a B.S. from Morningside and taught woodworking, civics, and science. He was the coach of the boys basketball teams in the 1940s and 50s. He led three teams to the state tournament in 1948, 1949, and 1953.

John Doversberger was a principal and the Drivers Education instructor. He was a renowned hunter and allowed the boys to take their guns from their car trunks and put them in the car trunk while they were doing their morning drivers training in the countryside around Galva. "During my year in drivers education, there were 34 in my class. So the class was split in half based on our birthday ages. The oldest half got to drive in the first semester and the other half in the spring semester. In-between Mr. D's hourly cigarette breaks, we would often get to go hunting before school," remembered Gary Wanberg ('72).

Pranks—A very spry character, France Wanberg ('38) at the age of 98 told about incidents from his acting past, "I was in the school play titled 'I Was the Butler.' After the play was over, there was a play cast refreshment time. Someone slipped a pint of whiskey in the punch. The director and drama coach was my cousin Miss Ellen Wanberg. She couldn't understand why we were all so happy."

Another character, Virdene Otto ('55), not to be outdone in story telling recalled an incident when he was late for typing class. When he arrived at class, Miss Wanberg asked for his slip. Virdene quipped, "Miss Wanberg, I don't wear a slip. She didn't think it was funny and I got sent to Mr. Ziesmer's office for reprimand. He only said to me, 'straighten up.' For some reason Miss Wanberg never selected me for another school play."

Closing—Due to the State of Iowa education requirements, declining enrollment, and financial concerns, Galva High School closed after graduation in May 1980. The Galva Community School District was reorganized and joined their rival school district to the west. The new district became the Galva Holstein School District. In the fall of 1980, the high school students were bused to Holstein. In the 95 years from 1895-1980 there were 1,295 graduates from Galva High School. The largest class was 34 seniors in 1972. The most numerous surnames of the graduates were: Peterson-21, Wanberg-18, Johnson-17, Radke-16, Young-16, Anderson-12, Carlberg-12, Schmidt-12, Nielsen-11, and Hansen-10. The last to receive a diploma from Galva High School was Mark Volt (alphabetically).

Galva High School
Ida County, IA

#34

Garnavillo High School

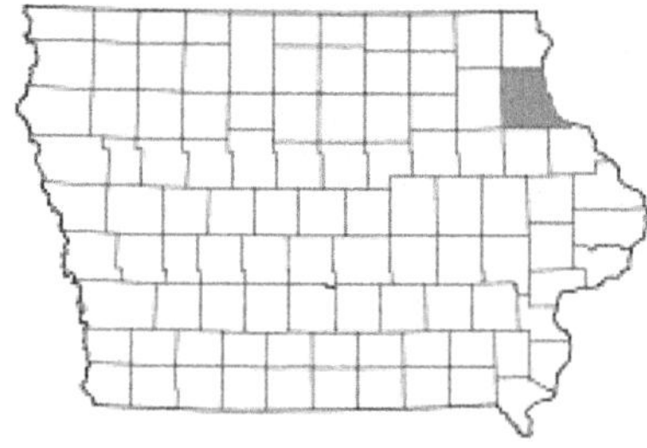

Mascot: Hawks
Colors: Red and White
Closed: 2001
Location: East Central Clayton County

Early Schools—Garnavillo was described in a 1988 publication by the Clayton County Historical Society as the "Gem of the Prairie."

The first schoolhouse was in a frame structure built as a Congressional Church in 1844. It was situated in the western part of the town, near the cemetery. According to the historical society, the first teacher in Garnavillo was Helmuth Brandt, an immigrant from Germany. He taught German-Lutheran pupils until their confirmation.

This news item appeared in a June 1855 issue of the *Clayton County Herald* published in Garnavillo: "At a School Meeting held on Monday evening, one thousand dollars were voted to build a Schoolhouse in our village." This Stone Schoolhouse would serve as the Clayton County courthouse in 1859 when Garnavillo was the county seat. The official site for the County Courthouse would change at least three times between Garnavillo, Guttenberg and finally Elkader, where it is located today (2019).

A debate about a county high school occurred as early as 1859, which was 100 years earlier than the actual consolidation of high schools into more regional county high schools. In 1858 it was proposed to erect a county high school building in Garnavillo. The citizens of Garnavillo subscribed $2,000, together with two blocks of land, and the county promised $18,000 toward the building. The low bid proposed was an estimate of $19,764. This included $1,175 for the woodhouse and privy. Work began quickly and soon the 67½′ x 51½′ foundation was complete. The foundation was laid and all of the building supplies had been shipped to town when a second bid was received. A district judge ruled the work on the high school was to stop. The county judge ordered the funds be withheld. Then defense, led by Alonzo Brown, prepared a six-page rebuttal which was signed by thirty teachers of the county. However, their plea was rejected, and the community lost this school.

A 1859 report by the county superintendent of schools, Alonzo Brown, detailed:

Persons of School Age—6,859
Attending School—3,695
No. of Schools in County—108

Male teachers were paid $4 to $9.50 per week. Female teachers were paid $2.08 to $5.00 per week.

In 1860, the Old Stone School was under the direction of Prof. Johnathan Briggs, and called the Briggs Academy. Prof. Briggs taught there until 1874. Students attending this academy were from the town and country. Those from the country came on horseback and kept their horses in a barn across the street. A quote from Cecil A. Carters' book *The History of Education In Clayton County, Iowa states:* "One gentleman, W.A. Kroegel, described the country pupils coming into town 'like a troop of cavalry.'"

In 1873-1874, a new brick two-story, four-room school was built at a cost of $3,000. It had two large rooms upstairs, the grammar room, and the high school assembly room. The first-floor rooms were for the intermediate and primary grades. The high school classes went to the eleventh grade until the fall of 1920 when twelfth grade was added.

March 27, 1876, Garnavillo was made an Independent School District with an increased enrollment of 134 students.

A news item in the *Garnavillo Tribune* on March 7, 1901 stated: "a meeting was scheduled to get the feeling of the districts surrounding Garnavillo regarding a consolidation of the district."

It was 46 years before the consolidation of these districts occurred. In 1901, town enrollment was: 21 enrolled in the primary school, 20 in the intermediate grade school, and 37 in the high school.

In 1906, the school closed for a time because of a diphtheria epidemic.

Electric lights were installed in the brick school in October 1917. In 1922, a movement started for the building of a new school after the state fire marshal reported the school was in dangerous structural condition. On May 23, 1922, a bond issue of $37,000 was voted on and passed by a two-to-one margin. Work was started immediately to raze the old building and start on the new one. The new school was finished in 1923 with an enrollment of 34 high school and 42 elementary students.

A new gymnasium was completed in 1949. The enrollment increased and this freed up space in the existing building. The adjacent Congregational

Church building was used for typing classes, a library, and study hall. At times classes were also held at St. Peter's Lutheran Church, in the Lodge Hall, and in buildings along Main Street.

Busing—In the early 1940s, a private bus was operated by Don Stoeffler, who took the students to both the public and parochial schools. In September 1945, the public school acquired their own bus. The first year one bus was used with two routes. One route arrived at school an hour early and left an hour before dismissal. Every six weeks the routes would exchange times. The next year the district purchased a second bus. During the peak enrolment there were as many as nine bus routes.

Carolyn Kainz Koopman ('63) remembered, "Dwight (Bubbie) Dickman ('57) was our bus driver. When he came to our house, he always said he could fill the bus as we had eight girls and one boy. Mommy had died when I was seven, so my sister had to learn to cook for the family." Marjorie Kainz Jensen ('54) shared, "I had to help milk as I was older. I learned to yodel while milking. I was always the one who got that job or running the cream separator."

Sports—The boys played basketball and spring and fall baseball. Tennis was added in 1958. Track and cross country emerged in the 1960s. Golf was added in 1974.

Girls basketball put Garnavillo on the map, with back to back girls basketball state championships in 1953 and 1954 (the first and only time in state history). The 1953 team was coached by Superintendent L.E Daily and the 1954 team by Bob Allen.

A late roster change in 1953 was done by Coach Daily, supposedly because he wanted the team to be recognized as having no seniors on the roster. By promoting freshman Janet Kainz ('56) in place of her sister Iola Kainz ('53), the state tournament team would show there were no seniors on the team. Another sister, Marjorie Kainz ('54) also was on this state tournament team. Garnavillo defeated New Sharon 67-60 in the state finals of the 16-team tournament at Drake Fieldhouse in Des Moines.

The 1954 girls basketball champions defeated Oakland 48-45 to bring home their second state title.

Tait Cummins, the broadcaster for WMT radio from Cedar Rapids, nicknamed the Garnavillo girls basketball team "Candy Kids" after their striped red and white satin skirts. They would go on to win 60 straight games without a loss over three seasons. Coach Daily claimed, "We lacked height and speed but we were intelligent and industrious and they did their best to do everything asked of them."

A star on both championship teams was Sandra Fiete ('55). To show that a team is not only one player, Sandra was not able to lead the team to a repeat performance during her senior year in 1955. In many circles, Sandra Fiete was considered the best girls basketball player to ever play in the six-on-six game. She was elected to the Iowa Girls Basketball Hall of Fame in 1961. She played on the USA team that toured the Soviet Union in 1958, was a member of the AAU All-American team in 1959, and played in the Pan American Games in Sao Paulo, Brazil.

Twenty years later, in 1973, Garnavillo girls basketball team returned to the state tournament but lost in the first round. They returned in 1987 and 1988 but were not able to bring the state title home.

The school's rivals were Guttenberg, Monona, and McGregor. The girls also played tennis, softball, and track.

In 1971, first year teacher and coach, Bob Lee, was coordinating the use of the gymnasium practice time. The boys practiced after the girls and did not finish until after 6:00 pm on most nights. He was called in front of the school board and asked why the boys were getting home so late from practice. The questioning board member said his son did not get home most nights until after 9:00 pm. Coach Lee asked the board member, "Sir, what is your son's name?" Hearing the name of the boy from the board member, Coach Lee calmly said, "Sir, your son is not out for basketball." Busted!

Garnavillo played in the Upper Mississippi Conference. Other members of this conference were: Guttenberg, McGregor, Luana, Marquette, and Monona. Later other northeast Iowa schools joined. The conference disbanded in 1990.

The girls softball team coached by Steve Schlafke, made five trips to the state softball tournament in 1980, 1981, 1984, 1987, and 1988. They were never able to win the championship. The 1988 team was rated first in the state throughout the entire season. Three girls were inducted into the Iowa High School Athletic Hall of Fame for pitching 100 winning games: LuAnn Campbell Schlafke ('83), Tracie Helle Schmelzer ('88), and Tracy Hamann Nemecheck ('88). During her high school career, Luann Campbell Schlafke ('83) had 18 no-hitters.

In July 1986, the Garnavillo Girls Softball team played a 31 inning game against Waterloo West, the longest inning game in the state's history. The game lasted five hours and 35 minutes. Top ranked Garnavillo was beaten 2-1 by Waterloo West. There were 186 outs, 47 hits, 11 walks, 10 errors, and over 600 pitches. Garnavillo's All-State pitcher, Tracie Helle Schmelzer ('88) pitched the entire 31 innings.

Girls volleyball was added as a school sport in 1988.

The boys cross country teams won multiple state championships. In 1970 they were coached by James Fiete. In 1972, 1973, and 1978, the boys were coached by Bob Lee. Looking back, Andy Reimer ('93) was glad he attended a small school, "I think we had more opportunities than students in larger school, such as playing basketball, or just dressing for varsity, even though I didn't play much, and being involved with cross country and track."

Band and Music—Mr. Joseph Hrecz was a well-remembered band and music teacher at the high school. He was an ex-Marine and was a perfectionist whose ire would occasionally come to the surface. Breaking batons was a regular occurrence when whacking it on the music stand. His watch often went flying as he directed the band. "Mr. Hrecz was my choir director. During rehearsal, one of the boys was cutting up. As Mr. Hrecz was scolding him, his partial plate flew out of his mouth. He quickly picked it up and ran out of the room. He came back and thankfully saw the humor in it," Jane Meyer Thein ('71) remembered some fifty years later. Mr. Hercz's bands received #1 ratings at contests 11 straight years. "Riding home on that bus the year that the streak ended with us getting a #2 was not fun as Mr. Hrecz was mad with our performance. He always stressed excellence," remarked Ron Kaiser ('66). "Band was my favorite class. What a perfect way to start each morning as band was our first class. I wanted to be in the band after watching them march down Main Street each Halloween," said Carol Goedken DeSotel ('60).

The band traveled extensively performing at Veteran's Day parades, the Cedar Rapids Band Festival, Franklin Park in Waterloo, and at high school and college homecomings in Wisconsin and Iowa.

Troy Thein ('83) stated, "I only took about a month of baritone horn lessons my senior year. Not because I was a superior player but because the new band director was my sister-in-law, Peg Thein. We spent the whole time talking about my family so we decided to suspend the lessons."

Andy Reimer ('93) remembered, "Pep band was easily the most fun activity I was involved with in school. It was the only time Mrs. Thein let us 'blast' and play as loud as possible."

During the 50s and 60s the high school choir presented the entire Handel's Christmas Messiah. After band concerts were discontinued, it became a tradition for the choir to sing Handel's "Hallelujah Chorus" at the winter concert until the school closed.

Sharon Kuehl Stade ('57) said, "We lived south of town just outside of the district lines. My dad drove me every day to meet the bus just so I could attend school in Garnavillo. We had to pay tuition, but our family thought the schools were superior in Garnavillo."

Notable Teachers—The drivers education program started in 1957. Mr. Whiting, the history teacher was given this teaching assignment. Carol Goedken DeSotel ('60) commented, "We had to learn to drive a stick shift and I did not like it." A later drivers education teacher, Dick Bangs, taught a Nicaraguan-born adult student to drive using sign language as she only knew Spanish.

Other memorable teachers with long tenure who taught parents and then their children were: Miss Lucia Roggman, Mrs. Marge Wright, Miss Florence Tayek, and Jan Wood.

Activities—The school newspaper had many names throughout the years: *The Headlignt, Cosmocrat, Exhaust, Go Hawk Gazette, and the Hawk Tales.*

The school yearbook was called *The Hawk* and was first published in 1949. The 1957 edition had pictures of the Speech class with 24 students, Band with 45, FFA with 26, and Commerce Club with 26 students. By 1971, the band had grown to 79 members.

Senior trips started in 1947 with day trips to Cedar Rapids. Later classes went to Chicago in 1959, 1966, and 1969 on the train for the one-day trip. In 1971, the Chicago senior trips became overnight stays by bus when the train service discontinued at the Dubuque departure site.

Pranks—A note on a relocated outhouse placed on the steps of the high school on Halloween read: "Please Leave Or Pee." "This may have been directed at the principal but the superintendent at the time did not find this funny as a number of us were reprimanded," remembered Ron Kaiser ('66).

"Bruce Tischauser ('48) brought a mouse to school with a string tied around it's neck. He would carefully let it crawl on the floor until Dixie Coffman Zehr ('49) screamed so loud, then he pulled it back into his pocket," laughed Don Koss ('47).

"I took the screws out of a desk so that when the teacher touched it the whole thing collapsed. She directed me to go straight to the office to see the superintendent. I slowly walked out of class and up the steps to the superintendent's office. I could see him in there working through the glassed entrance and I walked around on the outside for several minutes daring not to go in and confess my sins. Soon, I went back to class, and the teacher asked me if I had seen the superintendent. I could honestly reply that, yes, I had seen the superintendent. As I recall there was never any other punishment for my chicanery," remembered Don Koss ('47), 70 years later (2019).

Notable Graduates—"Lloyd Kaiser ('27) and Gertrude Kaiser ('27) were on the Judging Team that won the County, State, and National Dairy Judging contest. They were honored by meeting President Hoover and traveling to Europe to meet the Queen of England and traveling to Austria and Switzerland," Lloyd's daughter, Gwen Kaiser Gunderson, ('53) proudly shared.

Killed in Action—Garnavillo men that lost their lives in foreign wars were:

Richard Henry Eulberg ('35) -
Pearl Harbor December 7, 1941

James L. Matt ('39) - Italy April 17, 1945

Reed Rowland ('35) - December 1943,
buried at sea Hawaii

David Harold Mueller ('63) - Vietnam 1966

Consolidation and Buildings—After consolidation of some of the rural country school districts, the name of the district became Garnavillo Community School District in 1956.

Enrollment continued to grow following World War II with the baby boomers entering school. In April 1959, voters overwhelmingly defeated a bond issue for $360,000 to construct a new junior-senior high building. Some indicated that a lower cost building should be built on the site next to the school. After a month of changing the approach and the site plan, a second vote defeated the bond by an even larger margin in May 1959. In December 1959, the state fire marshal found that the overcrowded conditions at the school were "extremely serious." The voters went to the ballot box three more times in 1960 in February, April, and December before the bond issue was approved.

Groundbreaking started in May 1962, three years after the need was presented to the community. When challenges such as these with a growing enrollment and insufficient facilities arose, the position of school superintendent became most difficult. New superintendents were to come in 1954, 1960, and 1965, each faced with building insufficiencies.

Clayton Independent District joined Garnavillo in 1961. Due to the overcrowding conditions, the grade school was kept open at Clayton for their pupils.

With the state requiring greater consolidation of the small schools to provide a more efficient delivery of public school funding, the decreased number of schools in existence changed rapidly in the late 1950s and 60s. The last year a Clayton County Basketball Tournament was held was 1962. This was because of the dwindling number of high schools in the county. The Garnavillo girls won the county title by defeating the MFL (consolidated Monona-Farmersburg-Luana) team by the score of

35-34. The boys won their title by defeating the Elkader team by 89-63.

With the completion of the new school in 1963, advanced subjects were added in math, science, and foreign language. Special Education classes began with an exchange program with the Guttenberg school system.

Janitor—A notable janitor was Hermie Hamann who kept the school clean and orderly for 25 years. Upon his retirement, a big assembly was held in the gymnasium in the late 1950s. Gwen Kaiser Gunderson ('53) stated, "Hermie was so pleasant, fun to talk too, and really helpful. We went to him first when we needed something. He would meet us each morning and always greet us as we came into the school."

Closing—When the school board voted to close the high school there were several options available. Central-Elkader and Guttenberg were both under consideration, with Guttenberg being the final choice. The consolidation went very smoothly considering the schools had been fierce rivals. The new school district was renamed Clayton Ridge. The school mascot was changed to the Eagles with the new colors of green, silver, and black.

The high school closed after graduation in May 2001. The students were bused the next year to Guttenberg to attend the newly named Clayton Ridge High School. Nearly 2,000 students graduated from the high school from 1894 through 2001. Several years of missing records make the actual count unknown. The most frequent surnames of the graduates were: Berns-93, Schmelzer-35, Brandt-31, Kregel-30, Meyer-30, Kann-30, Matt-29, Mueller-29, Reimer-28, Kuehl-26, Stickfort-23, Kruse-20, and Schroeder-20. The largest classes were 47 seniors in 1965, 1976, and 1977. The last to receive a diploma from Garnavillo High School was Melinda Zittergruen (alphabetically).

Garnavillo High School
Clayton County, IA

#35

Garrison High School

Mascot: Rockets/Rockettes
Colors: Red and White
Closed: 1969
Location: Northwest Benton County

Early History—Many towns are named Garrison because of a nearby military post. However, this Garrison was named after Nelson Garrison, an early postmaster in the area. The Rock Island Railroad spur ran through the town as it continued from Vinton to the northwest through Garrison, Reinbeck, Iowa Falls, and Estherville on to Watertown, South Dakota. A passenger train ran daily into the 1950s.

Early Schools—In a story written in *The Garrison Ad Lib,* Ilene Kreider reported in 1994:

> Garrison Independent School District, called Locust Hill was organized in 1880 . . . The wooden building was built at a cost of $1290 and had two rooms added in 1893 . . . Alumni banquets began on June 1, 1901 and then discontinued and reactivated some 50 years later and have met annually since . . . Citizens of the community voted to build a new school house in 1910 . . . The bond issue that passed was for $10,000 and later one for $3500 with the schoolhouse being completed in 1912. It had no gymnasium so basketball as well as baseball were played outside. The first girls basketball team was in 1919 . . . The "go-getter" team of 1922-23 won 15 of their 19 games against opposing teams from LaPorte City, Newhall, Shellsburg, and Keystone . . . A school orchestra was organized in 1927 and a band in 1928 ... In 1936 a gymnasium and two classrooms were built. Journalism was added and the school paper *"The Blazer"* began publication.

In 1946, the school district consolidated with the surrounding country school districts and these country children came to Garrison to school. This brought the need for buses. Personal cars were still driven for out-of-town ballgames until 1949.

Depression Years—Millie Armstrong Kalish's ('40) bestselling book *Little Heathens,* depicts this area during the 1930s depression years. These years are remembered by farm foreclosures, poverty, unemployment, and desperate people needing the basics of existence.

Paul Schellhase ('60) said, "My parents Oran and Lucille Kirkwood Schellhase ran a restaurant and bar in town. Lucille was in the class of 1937. On some of the passenger trains, unfortunate men would get off the train and knock at doors of several houses asking for food. Word had been passed down that a person would help them and allow them to sleep in their barn. Many of these men who were called 'dandy dancers' would come from Chicago and were dressed more like hobos or gypsies."

Band and Music—The band marched at the Cedar Rapids Festival each year. Dick Grimm ('52) was asked to participate after he had graduated because a first trumpet was needed for the marching band to perform.

Music played a great part in the school's education. The 1960 school yearbook, *The Rocket,* pictured 37 in the marching band with four majorettes. The enrollment that year was 68 students.

Drivers Education—Drivers Education became part of the curriculum in 1953. The instructor, Mr. Keith Shadduck, also taught industrial arts. He was remembered for not following all the safety rules he taught in shop. An accident with the circular saw cost him the loss of a finger. His motto in drivers education resonated to the students, "Do as I say, not as I do!"

Sports—The boys sports were basketball and baseball. They traveled to away baseball games loaded into Coach Ben Corbett's car. For the out-of-town games, they were allowed to sit in the trunk of his coupe with the lid held open using a baseball bat. Coach Corbett was the principal, math teacher, guidance counselor, bus driver, and coached both the boys and girls basketball teams as well as boys baseball and girls softball. He had been an officer in World War II and had a company of German soldiers (over 100) surrender to him in mass. He was a great leader in the school, too.

Ben Corbett stories are still told over 60 years later. He took both the 1957 girls and boys teams to the state basketball tournament. The 1957 girls team won state with a season record of 31-1. The girls defeated Maynard (West Central) by 47-46 for the championship. Ironically, they had started the first game of the regular season in November beating Maynard 52-51.

The boys record that year was 23-5. They lost in the first game at state to Roland 46-51. The Roland team's star player was the legendary Gary Thompson.

Zelda Kirchner Sackett ('60) remembered, "We all had a passion for basketball. 'Let's go and shoot hoops' was always the pastime. My dad called Garrison a 'one horse town,' so I guess we just thought basketball all of the time."

Coach Corbett's girls teams dominated basketball for years. They won the Benton County championship 18 of the 20 years that he coached until the school closed. They won state in 1957, were the runners-up in 1956, and took third in 1959. Zelda Kirschner Sackett ('60) recalled, "Mr. Corbett would not even allow us to drink pop."

Harold and Evelyn Pennell had three daughters: Nancy ('56), Bonnie ('61), Karleen ('49), and one son Robert ('58). All the Pennell children were basketball players. They had two goals in their back yard. They had basketballs on their closed-in back porch. The Pennell's welcomed all of the town's kids to reach inside the backdoor to the house and turn on the lights to the dirt court when the family was not home. The only condition was that they turn the lights off when they left. The door was never locked. Both the girls and boys of the town spent endless hours dribbling and shooting at the rims, often with no nets. It is no wonder that Garrison was known for basketball.

Garrison's rival in sports was Keystone for the boys. Van Horne was the girls' big rival. They played in the Benton County League with Newhall, Keystone, Blairstown, Atkins, Urbana, Norway, and Shellsburg.

The cheerleaders were allowed to ride on the boys and girls team buses to away basketball games. The girls played the first game of the evening followed by the boys. Elsie Neve ('54) and Dick Grimm ('52) would entertain the team as they sang duets to the bus riders. They later married and sang for many weddings and community events for decades. Elsie graduated from Iowa State Teachers College (ISTC) and came back to teach second grade at Garrison. Steve Young ('67) said, "I was in her first class at Garrison. She was beautiful and my secret love."

Notable Teachers—"It takes a village to raise a child," reflected Zelda Kirchner Sackett ('60). "We were all poor, or at least in the same boat for family resources. We received a wonderful education there. Everyone—the bus drivers, cooks, janitors, students, principals, superintendents, schoolboard and volunteers—helped shape us into productive adults and citizens. A great home economics teacher, Mrs. Sue Johannes, had a unit on upholstering. We were to buy the material for the class and bring in a chair to reupholster. I went to the principal and told him that my family could not afford to buy the materials. His secretary, Mrs. Ruth Ridenour, overheard our conversation. She privately offered that she had an old chair which needed recovering, and if she bought the material, would I be willing to reupholster it for her."

Dorothy Sturtz Readnour ('61) smiled as she said, "Mrs. Johannes would never eat anything we cooked." Zelda Kirchner Sackett ('60) remembered, "She made me tear out a zipper three times, as she taught us to be perfectionists."

The 1965 Yearbook was dedicated to Lucille Pollack. She was the English and Literature instructtor. Bruce Gardner (Vinton '68) reminiscenced, "She was a tiny wisp, but not to be challenged. I watched her command some of the huge farm boys who were up to mischief. They accepted her chastisement. She taught me of the world, such as Shakespeare, and to have such an appreciation for those things of which we probably would never have heard. She had been an instructor at the Iowa Braille School in Vinton. Her stories of students there were inspiring."

Pranks—R. L. Holliday was the superintendent for nearly 20 years until the school closed in 1969. He was remembered as a very firm leader and respected by all the students and townspeople. Paul Schellhase ('60) reported a prank in one of Mr. Holliday's classes. His face gleamed as he told, "we all agreed to duck on cue as if there was something flying low over our heads. After doing this stunt a second time, Mr. Holliday looked up and pointed a finger at me to come forward. He demanded, 'Schellhase, what's going on here?' I tried to explain to him that there was something buzzing through the air at us. At about this very moment, I gave the cue again, and everyone ducked-even Mr. Holliday!"

Senior Trips—Senior trips were held annually after graduation. Chicago seemed to be the favorite destination. Students travelled by various modes of transportation from 1950 until the school closed, included cars, trains, and planes (1960). The length of stay in the Windy City was from three to seven days. Experiencing the museums, Navy Pier, and Michigan Avenue together was the culmination for these high school graduates. There was some chicanery accompanying these outings, but harm did not come to these country kids. The stories surely get bigger each year. Diana Henkle ('54) was known to have painted a dark black mustache on Bob Grimm ('54) so that he would look older as he was sent into a store to buy some adult beverages.

Notable Graduates—Fred Lund ('47), 'or Freddy', as most would call him, was a prime example for all the Garrison students and community of a hard-working and dedicated worker. He became a janitor for the Garrison school after the Green Giant canning factory closed and he lost his job. He also drove a school bus for away basketball games. When the industrial arts teacher had an accident with a saw and lost some fingers, Freddy was asked to teach the class until Mr. Shadduck could return. Being a mentor to many in this educational setting, inspired him to go back to college to become a teacher. With all of his other duties he decided to attend Iowa State Teachers College in Cedar Falls. He opened the school, started the furnaces, hand shoveled three blocks of sidewalks when it snowed, and drove 50 miles one way to attend morning classes. Freddy then came back to school in the afternoon to finish the school chores. Along with all of this, he raised a family of five children. He received math degree in four years and went on to teach math for 32 years.

Harold Noe ('28) was a farm boy. He is remembered by his daughter, Ilene Noe Krieder ('68), "On graduation day that year, there had been several days of heavy rainfall. The muddy country roads became impossible to travel by vehicle. Harold walked 3½ miles from home to attend his graduation. He was the only one in his family in attendance."

Pilot Lt. Dean Gillaitt ('38) lost his life in the South Pacific in World War II in 1944. Cpl. Edward Fry was killed in Italy in 1943.

Hot Lunch—Renowned mentor and beloved cook, Tina Koutney, provided the hot lunches for Garrison. "She was of Czech heritage and her food was to die for," remembered Steve Young ('67). "And boy, she loved to drink and fish. We were told that we could go into the lunchroom after basketball practice and it was okay to help ourselves to left-overs, as long as we cleaned up after ourselves." Dorothy Sturtz Readnour ('61) added, "Her kolaches were the best ever." The class of 1958 dedicated their yearbook to Tina Koutney: "To whom all students and graduates of Garrison Consolidated school are greatly endeared. Tina has been a cook at the school for seventeen years. Each year, Tina's faithfulness and her love for children becomes more and more evident to all. It is because of these human qualities and because everyone knows and loves Tina Koutney, that we dedicate this annual to her."

Closing—A vote was held in March 1969, in Garrison and Vinton, to consider the consolidation of the two school districts. The plan was that

Garrison would close their high school, but that the elementary was to remain open. By a vote of 216-121 in Garrison and 315-80 in Vinton, the districts were consolidated. Garrison's district was debt free, but Vinton's district still had outstanding bonding to pay by the district's tax payers. The cost of educating the high school students at that time was $803 per student in Garrison and $586 in Vinton. At the time there were 128 students in the elementary school and 48 students in the high school in Garrison. This plan worked for four years until 1973 when the new Vinton District closed the elementary school in Garrison as well. The *Vinton Times* on June 14, 1983, reported:

> Preliminary public hearings brought out suggestions of closing East Elementary in Vinton and allowing the Garrison school to remain open with Garrison and Vinton students in attendance. The idea was opposed by Vinton parents. Dr. Robert Jacobsen, the Vinton Superintendent of schools, conceded that some parts of the Garrison school were in better shape than some of the Vinton schools. But the cost of the heater replacement was just too high.
>
> Finally, at a meeting on October 28, 1973, which was described as a "shocker" by the Times then, the school board voted to close the Garrison school and ship its students to Vinton schools. The lone dissenter in the 4-1 vote was Garrison's representative, Merlin Christy.
>
> Cries of "sell-out" and unfairness ran rampant in the Garrison community. The Times quoted one disgruntled resident saying, "They (the school board members) failed to go along with the wishes of the Garrison people."

The Creamery was one of the towns businesses that flourished and always supported the school. The business community purchased ads in each team program, yearbook, and sponsored many school activities. It was a "double whammy" when the Creamery closed its doors. Farmers brought in their milk in ten gallon cans. It was made into butter. A Garrison graduate told of a time while he was stationed in Okinawa, that he saw a wrapper for Garrison Creamery Butter.

The high school closed after graduation in May of 1969. An account of that day was written by the last graduate from Garrison High School.

> I entered Garrison High School as a freshman and as it seemed TROUBLE was never a real problem for me to fall into, and in my opinion, not always my fault. However, for one of the officials in charge, my opinion was not what he wanted to believe. That official being R.L. Holliday, high school superintendent who always would tell me that "It would be easier to just close the school than deal with me."
>
> For the next four years whenever something went wrong it seemed I would hear "It would be easier to close the school that deal with me."
>
> Come graduation time for the class of 1969, which I was a member, Mr. R.L. Holliday was the official to hand each graduating senior their diploma. It was always . . .

Congratulations on your achievements and good luck in the future . . .

Now remember in this year of 1969 . . . This was the last graduating class to ever graduate from Garrison High and it was tradition for seniors to receive their diplomas in alphabetical order . . . I, Roger Witt was the last one to cross the stage to get my diploma. And what I was told by R.L. Holliday was . . . "I told you we would close this damn school when you left."

With that I have had the honor of being in the last class to graduate from Garrison and also the last individual to get a signed diploma from Garrison High.

A total of 714 graduated from the school in the 70 years from 1900-1969. The largest class was 26 seniors in 1956. The most numerous surnames of the graduates were: Merchant-23, Noe-23, Flickinger-17, Henkle-15, Barkdoll-9, Wilson-9, Fry-8, Harwood-8, Bryant-6, Wolfe-6, and Young-6. The last graduate of Garrison High School was Roger Witt.

Garrison High School
Benton County, IA

#36

Hansell Consolidated High School

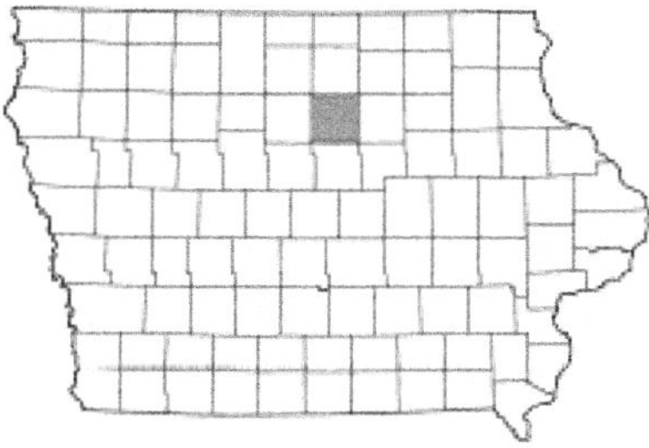

Mascot: Huskies
Colors: Red and White
Closed: 1961
Location: East Central Franklin County

Early History—The town of Hansell was incorporated in 1918. It was named after Geroge and Laura Hansell who sold the land for 25 cents an acre to establish lots in 1881. The land had high grass and was thought to be worthless for farming. The Dubuque and Dakota Railway completed a 41-mile line between Hampton and Waverly in 1881. This railroad later became the Minnesota and Northwestern Railroad. The rail was extended to Sumner and on east into Illinois. The railroad thrived in this location in the heart of a very fertile agricultural countryside. The grain, livestock, and produce from the surrounding area were transported and marketed east primarily to Chicago. Four passenger trains passed through Hansell daily. During this time, the stockyards and this shipping point were the largest railhead in Iowa.

Early Schools—Land for the first school was purchased from the Hansell family in 1884. George Hansell died of measles only four years later and did not see the development of the school and town.

At the time of World War I, the state of Iowa experienced great interest in higher education for all students, both city and rural. Hansell was one of the leading areas in exploring how to have a high school. Some residents proposed centralizing all the small country school districts. There were nine rural one-room schools serving the communities in Ingram Township and part of Geneva Township. These residents wrote letters to the State Department of Education. The citizens of Hansell and vicinity were invited to a lecture by Mr. Woodruff from the state board on March 18, 1914. Local citizens were impressed, and these country school districts consolidated in 1914. This led to a construction contract being awarded for the first consolidated school building in Franklin County.

A new, three-story, 14-room school was built in 1915 for a cost of $25,549. In the fall of 1915, nine handsome horse-drawn spring wagons were purchased to bring all the children to school.

From the *Des Moines Register,* October 4, 1914:

> **"School on Every Hill" Soon to be a Reality in Progressive County.**
>
> Hampton, IA Oct 3 Special: A schoolhouse on every hilltop and no saloon in the valley is an axiom that has been largely quoted in this state during the last few years. The later part of the quotation is more and more coming to be a certainty as the days go by and the facilities for education and training of the young and daily growing greater and the latter statement need not go better . . . The people of Ingham Township with the exception of one district, Allen's Grove, (near Aredale) voted a few weeks ago to join efforts for a new plan of a consolidated independent district, the first in this county . . . as a site for the new building, the board purchased four acres of land . . . just opposite the site of George Hansell homestead . . . ideal location for the school to furnish a large campus.

From the Ottumwa Tri-Weekly Courier September 14, 1915:

> **Hansell Children to their schools**
>
> Hampton, Sept 11: Nine good looking spring "Kid Wagons" were received here the first of the week. . . will seat 16 to 20 students, have padded seats and backs . . . covered and can be entirely enclosed when the weather necessitates.

The covered vehicles had a rear entrance for passengers. The cushioned seats were arranged along the sides. The wagons cost $175 each. The boys and girls basketball players drove their horse and buggy to Hansell and then boarded the bus to go to games out of town. They often rode the train home because there was no heat in the wagon bus. A large barn 50′ x 64′ in size was built to cover nine or more teams and wagons that were used for transportation. It also provided shelter for the hay and grain for the teams.

From the *Evening Times-Republican* Marshalltown January 6, 1916:

> **Hansell Jan 6, Clarke to Dedicate School**
>
> Governor to speak at opening of new school building at Hansell. School officials of the Hansell Consolidated District have waited long for the opening exercises of the new schoolhouse . . . Governor George W. Clarke and Albert M. Deyoe state superintendent of public instruction due for the headliners on the program . . .

The Hansell school was looked upon as a model and one of the stronger school districts in the state of Iowa. There were only 187 consolidated school districts in the state at this time. The first class to graduate from Hansell Consolidated High School was in 1918.

An event occurred in December after opening the new school which represented the public health concern of the times at the school.

Des Moines Tribune (Des Moines, IA) December 26, 1916:

Fever Closes School

Hampton IA Dec. 26—The Consolidated school of Hansell . . . is closed on account of scarlet fever breaking out among the pupils . . .

A devastating fire in 1923 completely gutted and destroyed the stately red brick school. It occurred after the end of school in May. A baseball tournament was held on the school grounds and members of the teams used the locker rooms for dressing purposes. When the fire was first discovered, citizens rushed to the structure but found the water had been shut off the day before and the fire extinguishers had been locked up. The fire spread rapidly and was soon out of control. Many fire causes were discussed, but the one recorded for history in local papers was the fire started in one of the locker rooms between ten and eleven P.M. on May 24, 1923. (from *Railroading Through the Century*—written for the Hansell Centennial June 1981). After the fire, school classes for 1923-24 were held in the church and local businesses.

The Hansell Savings Bank was the only bank in Franklin County that did not close during the 1933 banking crisis and depression. The bank charter was later moved to Sheffield and renamed the Sheffield Savings Bank.

Curriculum—Vocational agriculture was taught in the school and the Future Farmers of America organization was established in the 1930s. Domestic Science and Homemaking was taught in the first curriculums for the school.

Band—A band was organized in 1930 with 21 members. Miss Campbell, the band instructor in 1942 had 25 students in the band. By the 1950s, Mr. Hanawalt and William Zabika led the band. This band participated in the Mason City Band Parade and, combined with Geneva's band, marched at the Iowa State Fair. Kenny Armstrong ('56) winked as he said, "I played the tuba in band. We all had separate, private lessons during the day with Mr. Zabika. He made it fun and I have remembered the experience to this day."

"Oh, yes you better believe we had a band. We had nice wool uniforms and we loved marching in parades and playing at school recitals. I played the French horn. I may be nearly blind as I am now 90 years old, but I have a vivid memory," a very spry smiling Doris Schulz ('47) shared. There were 35 in the band when there were only 49 enrolled in high school when the school closed in 1961.

Notable Teacher—Miss Holmes was the typing and business teacher. Doris Handorf Crandall ('46) recalled, "I was raised on a farm just southeast of Hansell and rode the bus. I was the first on and therefore was the last off at night. Being in junior high and high school during the war, we all lived a much different life. We would walk the ditches collecting milkweed pods to be used for life jackets for the Navy. I recall Miss Holmes, my typing and business teacher. She was short and rather stumpy and not too attractive, but she inspired me to go on to college at ISTC in Cedar Falls where as a junior I decided that I, too, would like to be a business education teacher. The teachers during the war years seemed to come and go rather quickly, but I have told my children that I received a better education in this little school than they did in Cedar Falls public schools."

Sports—Girls basketball at Hansell was known throughout Iowa. Hansell won the state championship in 1940 and 1951, and also played in the 1945 state tournament. Since there was only one class division for all schools, this sport was six-on-six basketball against all of the high schools in Iowa. Two girls, Helen Van Houten ('41) and Alberta Van Dyke Speedy ('51) became members of the Iowa Girls Basketball Hall of Fame.

A great town celebration was held after each state tournament championship. Photographs of the cars lining the parade route in 1940 show Hansell's pride and recognition for the girls accomplishments.

Pretty Virginia Harris ('40) from the state championship team was featured in *Life* magazine April 18, 1940. Candid classic photographs of the girls in the Des Moines tournament and at the state capital building showcased the significance of Iowa girls basketball. This was at a time when there was a national movement to eliminate girls' participation in athletics. So-called medical experts opined that girls' bodies should not be exposed to the exercise of sports. Another belief was that such physical activity could harm the girls' reproduction systems. However, Iowa did not succumb to this movement. The surrounding states of Nebraska and Minnesota, and even the larger high schools in Iowa, did eliminate girls sports at this time.

The girls sports in Hansell were basketball and softball. The boys played basketball and spring and fall baseball. Football was never played at Hansell. Sheffield was a big rival in basketball, and Geneva a rival in all sports. By 1951, there were eight high schools in the county in addition to the larger county seat high school at Hampton. Ron Schulz ('51) smiled as he shared, "Hampton would not play Hansell or the other small schools because they had some early defeats in the 1920s and 30s. All of the other schools would play in the Franklin County league and Franklin County Tournament."

The whole town packed up and supported the girls at the state tournament. Ron Schulz ('51) chuckled and said, "There were four of us boys, Bill Folbrecht ('50), Gene Harper ('51), Gene Behrens ('52), and myself who set out for Des Moines in a 1939 Dodge coupe. We were going over the viaduct in Iowa Falls when we came up on a six-car pileup at the south end of the bridge. Our brakes failed and we piled into the wreck, too. Our radiator was punctured and we had no money to fix it. We all hitched a ride to Des Moines to the old Drake fieldhouse. None of us had any money but somehow we got into the game. We bummed rides back to Hansell and did all of this with absolutely no money. Wow, did we have a great time, and to top it off, we won the state!"

The mixed chorus in 1947 listed 37 members in the choir. This was over half of the student body at the time.

A new gym was added to the school in 1953. The old gym was in the lower level of the school with a balcony on each end. For the next eight years, many capacity crowds cheered on the Huskies. The last boys team in 1960-61 had a record of 18-3. These three losses came at the hands of Thornton. The final game at sectionals against Thornton kept the boys from making their only trip to the state tournament. There were three Harper boys on the starting five of this team.

Senior Trips—Senior trips were an annual event. The class of 1961 made their own history with a four day trip to Chicago highlighted by a visit to the Chicago Natural History Museum. They toured other Chicago landmarks and shopped along the famous Michigan Avenue.

Killed in Action—Two boys, Dean Fredricks ('44), a pilot in the Korean War and Orval Burnam ('43) lost their lives in combat.

100 Years of Alumni Gatherings—The alumni organization, formed in 1919, met on the third Saturday of June for the next 100 years. The centennial banquet in 2018 was to be the last meeting for these proud alumni from Hansell High School.

Closing—The school closed after graduation on May 18, 1961. The remaining students attended Hampton High School in the fall of 1961. A total of 578 graduated from Hansell Consolidated High

School. The largest class was 23 seniors in 1945. The smallest class was three in 1920. The most numerous surnames of the graduates were: Hannah-14, Harper-14, Allen-13, Davis-13, Woodley-13, Krukow-12, Savidge-11, McKinney-9, Morgan-8, VanWert-8, Kelley-7, Schulz-7, Pyle-6, Schwab-6, and Tucker-6. The last class in 1961 had nine seniors with Janna Towel the last to receive a diploma (alphabetically) from Hansell High School.

Parade and town celebration following the 1940 Girls State Basketball Championship.

Hansell High School
Franklin County, IA

#37

Hawkeye High School

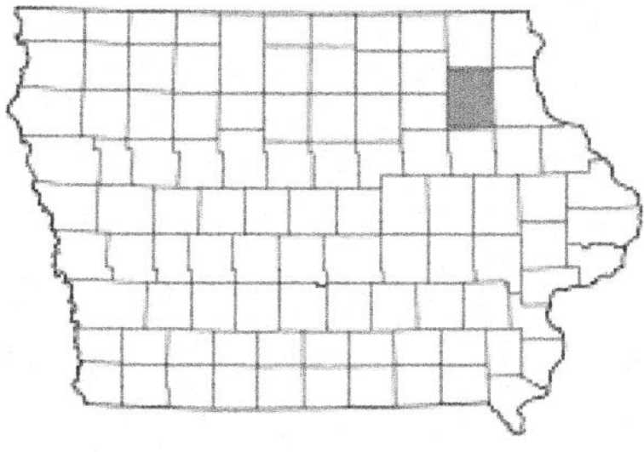

Mascot: Go Hawks
Colors: Black and Gold
Closed: 1957
Location: North Central Fayette County

Early History—Hawkeye is located in southern Windsor Township. Early settlers arrived in 1855 to break up the low rolling sod. Mail service to West Union, brought letters from relatives in Germany and the eastern states. By 1868, there were enough settlers to request a closer postal service.

D.D. Hull applied for a post office to be established in his home in Section 20. His sister, Jane Place, suggested the name Hawk Eye which may have been a familiar Indian name. Mr. Hull suggested the name of Hawk Eye or Ridgeway to the West Union Postmaster, who then asked his brother to choose the name. On March 5, 1889 Hull received the appointment and mail was delivered to his door at Hawk Eye once a week by horseback rider on his route to Wilson's Grove.

When the Davenport and St. Paul Railroad started building a line across southern Windsor Township in 1872, the town evolved. The money panic in 1872 ceased the activity after the roadbed was completed to Calmar. The Chicago, Milwaukee, and St. Paul took over the project, laid the rails, and built a depot in March 1880 in Hawk Eye, Iowa.

Highlights in Hawkeye history:

- 1892, the official spelling was changed to Hawkeye.
- Town incorporated April 9, 1895 by vote, 63 yes to 62 no.
- 1898 Hawkeye Free Public Library started with a generous donation from Charles W. Boop (It is the oldest continuous library in the county.)
- 1904 town water works installed.
- 1913 electrical service installed.
- 1918 the first sewer installed.

Early Schools—Two one-room country schools were established nearby. The Wilbur school was one mile south of Hawkeye and the other school north of Hawkeye. These small buildings became inadequate for the needs of the students. As Hawkeye became progressive, several attempts were made to establish a Hawkeye Independent District. Bitter fights with the districts north and south carried the contest to the State Superintendent of Schools. The Hawkeye petitioners won. [Information from Lillian Gieske Parker ('03).]

In 1894, a brick building was constructed and remained part of the school until its closing in 1957. This structure contained four rooms: primary, intermediate, grammar, and high school. Each room, except the primary, contained three grades. This was a two-year high school which existed until 1909 when a third year was added to the curriculum. Hawkeye High School became accredited by the State of Iowa when the fourth year of school was added. These four rooms were heated by large oak heaters. After several years, a furnace was installed. The school day began with ten minutes of singing songs in rounds, followed by ten minutes of physical culture exercise directed by the Superintendent. Arbor Day was a holiday when the students raked, cleaned the yard, and set out some trees. [Information from Lillian Gieske Parker ('03).]

The first graduation was held in 1897. The school term ended in the middle of June. Each graduate was required to write an oration of not less than 1,000 words to be memorized and delivered before the public on graduation night. The ceremony was held at the Merchants Opera House.

A bond was issued for $15,000 to build the front addition to the school in 1915. This expanded the high school with manual training, domestic science, a library, laboratories, and drinking fountains. New playground equipment was added. The sidewalks were laid, the grounds graded, and trees and shrubs planted.

The 1923 yearbook recorded pictures of the orchestra and music performances.

The new gymnasium was completed in 1926. The opening play, "Safety First," was presented for two nights by the local community people. The proceeds were used to buy velvet curtains for the stage.

The Great Depression and the war years were times of few improvements in the education and school structure. Following WWII, the new superintendent Harold Lincoln began a campaign for improvement of school facilities. Bus transportation was started for the rural students. A hot lunch program was inaugurated. The Parent Teachers Association was started. Visual aids became an important part of instruction. Girls basketball and boys football were added. Band became an extracurricular activity. The curriculum was strengthened, and courses added to benefit the students. In Mr. Lincoln's five years, the culture of the school changed dramatically. Known to the students as "Old Abe," he coached both the boys and girls teams.

Sports—The boys sports were baseball, basketball, and six-man football. The girls played basketball in the 1910s and it was restarted in 1946. An article in the West Union paper on November 4, 1943 described:

> The Hawkeye football team remained undefeated for the season by winning the final game from Elgin by the score 44 to 6. They won the championship in the northeastern Iowa League for 6-man teams. The game featured long runs by Paul Lentz and Bob Jordon. Only two days after the last game had been played, Paul Lentz met an accidental death.

The 1947 football team finished the year at 2-3-2. They had the notoriety of not scoring in five of these games. The final scores of two of the games ended in a 0-0 tie.

Basketball was played in the Fayette County League with Randalia, Alpha, Clermont, Maynard, Stanley, and Waucoma. Shirley Hughes Gibbs ('50) was pictured with the girls team that won the county championship in 1949. Shirley commented, "Alpha was the closest school to Hawkeye but Randalia was our most fierce rival. They had a little 'cracker box' gym. Every time you took the ball out of bounds you were under the balcony and could not throw the ball up without hitting the bottom of the balcony. Mr. Lincoln was a great Coach. He was in his first year at Hawkeye my freshman year and he had us winning the state sectional title over Stanley. Winning the Fayette County League in 1949 was thrilling."

In the early years, baseball was the primary sport for the boys. Four graduates played baseball for the University of Iowa Hawkeyes: Ed Heiserman ('23), Lloyd Parker ('23), Louis Hauth ('26), and Robert Carmichael ('37).

Drivers Education was started in 1949. Shirley Hughes Gibbs ('50) proudly remembered, "It was such a fun addition and one of the first schools in our area to offer this program. Our car had a manual transmission and we were all so excited. Once again it came under Mr. Lincoln's guidance and leadership."

Notable Graduates—This small high school had 627 graduates in its 61 years from 1897-1957 (which included the 11 years of two-and three-year high schools). A graduation year listing of many of the graduates highlighted their significant contributions:

1909 Kingsley Palmer was head of the Iowa Department of Social Services.

1919 Newell Rogers managed his father's printing business as a youth, later a journalist in New York and London.

1919 W.E. Walsh was a local MD in Hawkeye and West Union.

1922 Leland "Bill" Hurd owned Ben Franklin Stores and endowed the Hawkeye Museum with $300K to help finance operations in the building which his father had once run a department store.

1924 Lucius B. Libby was Iowa Secretary of Agriculture.

1946 Lois McIntyre Schutte, genealogist, author of column, "Hearts," and pilot.

1953 Millicent Lentz Gibson was Professor at SUNY and author, also member of Who's Who, Mensa.

1953 Dorothy E. McIntyre, Minnesota educator and administrator, pioneer advocate for girls and women's sports, historian, author.

Notable Teachers—Superintendent Fred Prusha, 1950-1955, brought great distinction to Hawkeye. He required every student to write poetry. Within a short time, Hawkeye became the Poetry Town of Iowa.

Teacher Bernice Halverson taught English, Biology, and music. She made a significant contribution to these writing initiatives. "She was so bubbly and happy-go-lucky. She made us all want to learn," said Evelyn Schultz ('53). Dorothy McIntyre ('53) said, "The whole town became involved as the townspeople were required to write a poem, also. I was in typing class and we had to retype the poems before sending them to the sponsoring group." Is it any coincidence that from 1946 through 1953, there would become three authors who graduated from Hawkeye? Hawkeye was certainly the poetry town of Iowa.

Activities—The school newspaper was titled the *Black and Gold.* A weekly publication was printed and the writing displayed the abilities of the students during this activity.

The yearbook was the *Hawkeye*. Many contributed to its publication. An opportunity to be on the Annual staff was another extracurricular activity this small high school offered.

Senior Trips—The senior trip in 1950 was to Chicago with two cars and eight graduates spending a week in the Windy City. The museums, a boat ride, Michigan Avenue, and the camaraderie during the learning experience were shared for a lifetime. Again, Mr. Lincoln was the sponsor and made this opportunity possible.

The Junior-Senior Banquet in 1953 was held at the Hotel Mealy in Oelwein. The senior trip that year was after graduation to the Wisconsin Dells. Riding on the "Ducks" was the excitement.

Pranks—Pranks at Hawkeye were very harmless but provided lasting memories for those involved. Kate Wiedeman ('54) would leave the room and later return to study hall and find her books on the floor under her desk. No one knew how this happened.

Kenneth Schultz ('42) (94-years old relating the incident) remembered clearly, with a glint in his eye, "A high school lady teacher was afraid of mice. One day a student placed three live baby mice in her study hall desk drawers. She was in charge of first period study hall. When the bell rang for the students to go to their classes, she opened the drawer and her screams could be heard in all the rooms on the second floor. The principal did make remarks to suspected students but of course no one confessed." Kenneth still claimed innocence well after the statute of limitations had passed.

Possibly it was the Senior Class of 1957, excited for the last year of high school, or simply mischievous members in the class, but chicanery was rampant that year. James Kocher ('57) described a few stunts that were popular that year and remembered fondly in 2019. "As seniors we had taken up chewing tobacco as a skill that could be done without the teacher seeing us. Our desks had a slot for the ink well opening, so we would put a can in the opening to spit into. One boy had a poor aim and the girl sitting in front of him 'lost her lunch!' Another favorite trick was filling your mouth full of BBs and slowing spitting them out so they would roll down between the desks in study hall. We thought we were clever, so we filled up the chalk board erasers with chalk dust to bombard the juniors as they came into the room. The door opened and an avalanche of erasers flew, but directly into the superintendent's face. Busted!"

Closing—The high school closed in May 1957 and was consolidated with West Union. The new name became North Union High School with the high school located in West Union. Of the 627 total graduates from Hawkeye High School, the most numerous surnames were: Burkhart-13, Schlatter-12, Miller-11, Ungerer-11, Smith-9, Wendland-9, Rogers-8, Hurd-7, McIntyre-7, and Sorg-7. The last to receive a diploma from Hawkeye High School was Judith Ann Weidermann. (alphabetically).

Hawkeye High School
Fayette County, IA

#38

Hedrick High School

Mascot: Foxes
Colors: Red and White
Closed: 1991
Location: Southwest corner Keokuk County

Early History – John Morrow Hedrick was a farmer, businessman, and postmaster from nearby Ottumwa. At the onset of the Civil War, he enlisted a company of men from Wapello county. He became a First Lieutenant in Company D, 15th Iowa Infantry in September 1861. He was made a quarter-master of a regiment and promoted to Captain as they entered the field. Hedrick was wounded at Shiloh, discharged, and then rejoined the regiment in 1863 in Tennessee. In the Battle of Atlanta in July 1864, he was severely injured in his leg and arm. Hedrick was promoted to Colonel in August 1864 and was detailed for special duty in Washington D.C. on March 13, 1865. During this time, he was promoted to Brigadier General. When he returned to Ottumwa, he became the editor of the *Ottumwa Courier*. He helped secure the Chicago Milwaukee and St. Paul Railroad (CMSP) through Ottumwa. This railroad extended north bound into Keokuk County where a depot was built in 1882 and named after the Ottumwa General Hedrick who died four years later at the age of 54.

Hedrick became a crossroads of three railroads with two east west and the CMSP, a north south train. Today, this depot in Hedrick provides a history of the railroads. On one day in 1904, there were 50 trains pass through Hedrick. By 1906, there were 22 passenger trains through town.

The decade of the 1890s was a time with great promotions and dreams in Hedrick. In 1890, plans for a college were drawn. The proposed four-story Normal School, led by Professor W.O. Mullin, bordered the land between the timber and hills on the one side and the prairie on the other.

In 1892, 80 acres were secured southeast of the Union Depot by W.H. Williams and Lon Cremer. The plan was to develop a horse track and to offer large purses and induce the best horses in the country for the races. Known as the Kite Mile Track, the kitelike "figure eight" pattern was constructed. The whole track was thoroughly drained and tiled for $2,700. The driveway was 70′ wide and as level as a marble floor. An amphitheater 150′ x 40′ was built on the west side of the track. The shape of the track made the horses change leads when turning the loop of the track. The band and reporter's gallery were situated in the center of the amphitheater. The stables were the finest in Iowa.

Papers were received on September 24, 1892 making the Hedrick Mile Kite Track Association a member of the American Trotter Association. The racing program on the new track was held October 4, 5, & 6, 1892. Trains brought racing spectators from Peoria, Des Moines, Davenport, and Cedar Rapids. The decade of existence of the track may not have been the financial success of its owners' dreams. On one four-day race from August 8-11, 1899, 422 trotters and pacers competed in 13 races each with $1,000 purses. Admission was 25 cents. Horses came from South Dakota, Kansas, Nebraska, Illinois, Colorado, Minnesota, Delaware, Wisconsin, Montana, Arizona, California, Missouri, Pennsylvania, and all throughout Iowa. All of these racing sulkies and horses came to Hedrick by train. Four hotels and many private homes were used to house the participants and spectators.

The Fox was the small train which ran on the little 80-mile track from Burlington to Oskaloosa. The speculation about the name came because the train moved so fast it could slip up on one at road crossings. The Fox went to Burlington in the morning and back to Oskaloosa at night. The Fox operated for nearly 20 years. When the CB&Q track was widened in 1902, the Fox was placed on a siding. It laid idle for the Hedrick youngsters to play on for hours with the bell and make-believe train robbers and hobos hiding out under the cars. The Fox was loaded onto a flat car and moved to Colorado where it again was used on the narrow-gauge railroad in the Rocky Mountains.

Early Schools—The first school in the town of Hedrick was a two-story wooden building. In 1883 a brick structure was built for $3,500.

The Normal School, which had been proposed by W.O. Mulllin, was downsized to a one-story structure of 52′ x 54′ for $3,500. Carved above the front door entrance was "Normal School A.D. 1890." The first year there were 50 students from five states enrolled. Classes started at 9:00 AM through the last recitation at 7:40 PM. The first commencement was in August 1891 with 15 graduates from different courses. Three were from the Teachers Course, three from the Commercial Course, and nine from the Preparatory Course. By 1893, every department was well supplied with apparatus, globes, maps, charts, musical instruments, mathematic blocks, skeletons, microscopes, and libraries. The instructors were all graduates of Normal Schools, Universities, Business Colleges, and Musical Conservatories. The Normal School was sold at auction in 1902.

In 1901, a new schoolhouse proposition was put to the voters and women were entitled to vote. The three-story brick structure was built in 1903 for $7,000. This building burned in 1918. The last Hedrick school was built following the fire in 1918 for $90,000.

Highlights for the Hedrick High School were:

1895 W.O. Mullin (Normal School Professor) became the Superintendent.

1902 School Board resolution to order vaccinations from contagious disease for all school children.

1902 Bonds sold for $7,000 at 4½ percent.

1903 January 7, the new school opened.

1905 School enrollment was 328.

1919 Following the fire, $7,000 bond was passed by the voters.

1919 Bus drivers under strict contract and under more stringent legal restrictions than the teachers.

1933 The Hedrick School faculty was the same as the previous year, except at a 25 percent reduction of salary.

1940 The floor in the gym was removed and new floor purchased.

1942 County schools were facing a great shortage of teachers. Request that all former teachers validate their expired certificates and contact the school.

1948 Martinsburg school closed, students came to Hedrick for high school.

1961 Twenty-five became the magic number, as every class from K-12 at the opening of school had an unbelievable 25 students in each of the 13 grades.

1962 Paul Johnson, State Department of Publication Instruction, met with the school board with warnings to terminate Hedrick High School in two years if no improvements in the physical plant and courses were made.

Sports—The boys played football, basketball, and track. In 1938, with a reduced football squad, the school chose between playing six-man or quitting football. They played Brighton in the first six-man game by either school. In 1943, no football was played because of a shortage of coaches and players. Hedrick joined the Keomah Conference to become the first conference in the state to try eight-man football in 1947.

Coach Paul Reberry considered starting a baseball team in the spring season and dropping track as a school sport. Several boys convinced him that they much preferred track over baseball. Track and field and cross-country teams had many champions. The following became state individual champions:

1953 Bob Toomire, pole vault 10′6″
1957 Harlan Millikin, mile run
1957 Medley Relay 3:49.2 (Lloyd Woodward, Gerald Bradley, Ralph Pilkington, Harlan Millikin)
1959 Duane Handy, pole vault 11′ 6″
1958 Arvene Bradley, cross country 9:48.0
1970 Art Millikin, cross country 10:55.2
1979 Nan Doak, 800m 2:15.56
1979 Nan Doak, 1500 m 4:46.00
1980 Nan Doak, 1500 m 4:43.24
1979 Nan Doak, #1 cross country

Notable Teachers—Louise Doak came to Hedrick in 1928 as a math teacher. Due to the depression and reduction of teachers, she went to Webster in 1932 as a teacher and principal. She returned to Hedrick to marry Donald Doak ('27), thus ending her teaching career. In 1945 she was asked to return to Hedrick High School as the principal and math teacher. Her method of discipline as a principal was to have a student give her time. She ate her sack lunch while that student was eating and doing class work during lunch time. She did not tell them how many lunch times they would have to spend with her. She just told them she was watching their behavior.

Miss Verna Foster taught English and geography. She directed all the plays. Harlan Millikin ('57) shared, "Oh, she was stern and mighty straight-faced. Every once in a while, you could get her to laugh. I occasionally wrote essays at 50 cents a page for classmates to turn in as their work. She may have caught on, but never said anything."

Alice and Paul Reberry taught shorthand and business and social studies. They were both very respected because of their concern for their students. Mary Doak Spears ('60) said, "Mr. Reberry taught many different subjects. One term, he had to teach geometry as the teacher had either left or was ill. He admitted to the class 'this is not my thing' and went occasionally to Mrs. Doak for help in the lessons preparations."

Notable Graduates—Nanette Doak Davis ('80) became a record setting runner at the University of Iowa. At Hedrick High School she won six state of Iowa individual track and cross-country championships in the 800 meters, 1500 meters, and the two-mile indoor and outdoor championships. She qualified for the Drake relays and was an All-American High School Athlete. She set records at the Big 10 and University of Iowa in the 5000 meters and the three-mile run.

Sandra Lanz Moore ('61) received a teacher's certificate from Drake and taught in public school for a few years and gave private lessons. She played flute in the Des Moines Symphony for 20 years. She founded the "Odyssey Trio" made up of a flute, harp, and cello in 1996. The trio played for weddings and many other groups and made four CDs.

In 1972 Sue Berry ('73) was selected to participate in "America's Youth in Concert" European Tour.

Jerry Rice ('62) and wife Georgia went to Nepal in November 1967 as Agricultural Missionaries. Jerry worked with local farmers in agronomy, animal science, and horticulture.

Janitor—Carl Craft was the janitor at the school for nearly 50 years. Harlan Millikin (57) remembered, "He was so particular and we all respected him so much. He was strict and so protective of our beautiful new gymnasium floor. He placed tarps over it for any event held in the gym. When the school closed, it was only natural that the community named the remaining gymnasium after him. It became the Carl Craft Civic Center."

Yearbooks—The 1940 yearbook was named *The Echo*. It pictured a band with 30 members.

The yearbook became *Fox Tales* in 1961. The yearbook was dedicated to retiring janitor Carl Craft. It read:

> We, the members of the graduating class of 1961, do hereby dedicate this annual to Mr. Carl Craft, our school custodian. With a friendly smile, Mr. Craft had done his utmost to render service to every member of the student body. To him, we owe every measure of gratitude. The innumerable hours he has devoted in maintaining the building, in which we have spent so much time, has been immensely appreciated by students and friends alike.

Pranks—A perfect crime, or at least a perfect act occurred 65 years ago at the Hedrick High School. The scene happened during the senior play practice. The set had Miss Verna Foster diligently coaching the committed thespians while a trio of actor's backstage were up to a pigeon heist. The setting was the study hall. The props were some innocent pigeons, already gone to roost for the evening, captured from their perch. The fowls were bird-napped and needed to be released. Study hall seemed an appropriate resting place. The actors promised each other to never say a word about the stunt to anyone. All that remained after an early morning cleanup by janitor Craft was one fluttering feather found in a corner of the room. Let it be known that the crime has been uncovered, the birds have flown away, but Harlan Millikin ('57), Ralph

Pilkington ('58), and Glen Miller ('57) now need to report to the Principal Doak's office immediately.

Band—During the most difficult year of the Depression, in 1933, 38 band members from Hedrick went to Chicago by train to play in the biggest band in the world at the Century of Progress exposition.

The Music Boosters Club considered new band uniforms in 1954. A representative from Kansas City was on hand as the proposal was presented and samples were examined. The colors chosen were dark green with gray trousers trimmed in gold. These gorgeous uniforms were purchased for 60 band members at a cost of $48 each.

Buglers Holiday was heard at nearly every concert and community program and event in the mid 1950s. The trumpeters were Leonard Bull ('57), Janet Watts ('57), and Harlan Millikin ('57).

Senior Trips—Charter buses took Hedrick seniors for their end-of-year trip to Chicago in 1957, 1958, and 1960. They enjoyed the elegance of the Conrad Hilton and Palmer House hotels. Plays, the Science and History Museum, and the Magnificent Mile were memories still shared among these classes 60 plus years later (2020).

Closing—Over 30 years later, after Paul Johnson at the State Board of Instruction served the warning that Hedrick High School needed to close and reorganize, the school closed after graduation in May 1991. In the Fall of 1991, the high school students were bused to Pekin. In the 92 years from 1900-1991 there were 1,732 graduates from Hedrick High School. The largest class was 35 seniors in 1973. The most numerous surnames of the graduates were: Davis-30, Smith-18, Watts-17, Baker-16, Doak-16, Miller-16, Wilson-14, Johnson-13, Morgan-13, Porter-13, Schwartz-11, Brown-10, Lanz-10, Bottoroff-9, Hornback-9, Messerschmidt-9, Moore-9, Utterback-9, Dickey-8, and Westercamp-8. The last to receive a diploma from Hedrick High school was Connie Louise Van Zante (alphabetically).

Hedrick High School
Keokuk County, IA

#39

Kalona High School

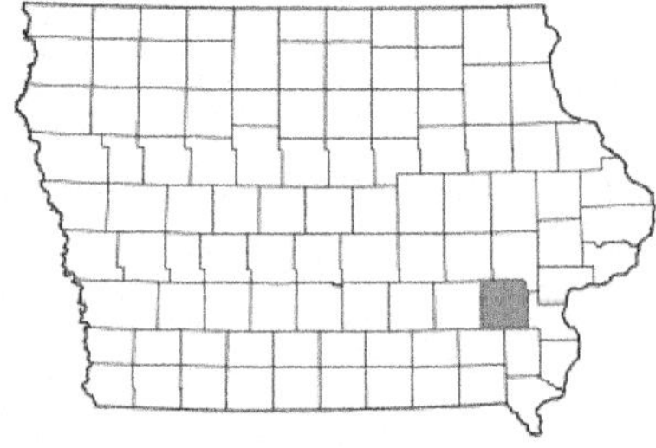

Mascot: Kubs
Colors: Purple and Gold
Closed: 1961
Location: North Central Washington County

Early History—Kalona may be the only town in the world to also have the distinction to be called Bull Town. Among the earliest settlers in this northern Washington County area were John Myers and his wife Eliza Saylor from Des Moines. They settled along the banks of the North English River in 1851. They had 12 children and accumulated 700 acres of land. Myers raised pedigreed Shorthorn cattle and registered hogs.

The Muscatine branch of the Burlington, Chicago, and Rock Island Railroad chose to build a line through the English Valley 1879. It cut across some of Myers's land. When asked to name the depot station, John Myers suggested Myersville. The railroad officials refused. Myers, with some humor and wit, offered the name Kalona. This may have sounded like it had something to do with Indians and it suited the officials. What they did not know was that Kalona was the name of his prize sire bull, thus the name of Bull Town.

Platted on John Myers's pastureland on August 6, 1879, Kalona was a difficult place to reach. There were no roads leading to this area. In 1880, "Bull Town" was only reached by crossing Myers's pasture. That spring, Myers gave notice that he was closing his eastern fences, an action that came after the town constable was thrown over the fence by one of the Shorthorn bulls. The road into the town from the south was impassable as it ran across marshy places.

Like its champion namesake, the town of Kalona proved its strength and endurance. It weathered the decline of the railroads, the demise of small rural communities, and presently is a growing community in the twenty-first century.

Kalona has a unique identity with the largest Amish and Mennonite population west of the Mississippi. It is a place where British Novelist Angus Wilson once said, "You can meet the 19th century coming over the hill in a horse and buggy." In the 140 years since its beginning, there are still over 1,000 Old Order Amish who are prosperous and hardworking farmers living mostly north of Kalona. These people, as well as their one-time Brethren, the Mennonites, have drawn tourists and foreign visitors to Kalona.

Early Schools—The country school called Buzzard Roost was two miles northeast of the new town of Kalona. There were no other private schools in the area at the time.

The first school in Kalona was held on the first floor of a two-story building which was also used for church and Sunday School services.

In 1887 a two-room frame building was built with Miss Ross and Miss Ray as the teachers. This frame building was moved to the site of the next school building in 1894. A brick two-story building was built in 1894 and divided four rooms. Three of these rooms were used for elementary education while the fourth room and the old frame building were later used for high school classes.

In 1897, the Kalona High School was organized. The course consisted of two years at the time. The subjects offered were: First year: literature, US history, English composition, algebra, and civil government. Second year: algebra, physics, book-keeping, general science, rhetoric, and physical geography.

The first graduation from Kalona High School was held on May 27, 1898 with two graduates. The course was changed to three years in 1901.

An election held on May 11, 1914, to build a new high school carried 157-33. This new two-story brick school with gymnasium in the sub-basement was estimated to cost $12,000. The new high school was built in six months and ready for occupancy on November 30, 1914.

In 1936, with the help of $45,000 from the Works Progress Administration (WPA), a new gymnasium and classrooms were added to the high school.

An account in the mid-1930s recorded:

> The normal enrollment of Kalona High School is about eighty-five. The present course of study is much more efficient and extensive than that of previous years. It consists of three years of mathematics, four years of English, two years of Latin, home economics, manual training, economic geography, physics, business arithmetic, biology, government, bookkeeping, shorthand, economics, general science, biology, vocations, two years of typing, and two years of history.

Sports—The biggest athletic rivals were the Wellman Wildcats, a town just seven miles west.

The boys played basketball, football, and track. The girls played basketball, but the sport was dropped in the 1940s.

In 1929, Kalona High School started playing sports in the Ke-Wash Conference (Keokuk-Washington counties). Other original members of the conference were Wellman, Richland, Brighton, and Keota. West Chester joined in 1931. North English joined in 1942, and Williamsburg in 1946.

The 1939 boys basketball team went to the state tournament. They were led by brothers Delmar ('40) and Floyd ('40) Yoder. That year in one game, there were reported five Yoders on the court at the same time.

Boys track became the leading sport in the 1950s. Some of the milestones reached were:

1957 state record setting 440 relay: Tom Hofer ('58), Gary Rhodes ('57), David Dayton ('57), Marlin Brennaman ('57)

Ned Miller ('55) State records in the 440 dash in indoor and outdoor

William Reif ('58) State Class C Shotput record

1957 boys won the Ke-Wash football championship

Notable Graduates—Allen Haberman ('60) was a significant part of the 1969 Apollo 11 moon landing. He was the leading engineer for the takeoff of the lunar capsule to bring Neil Armstrong and Buzz Aldrin from the moon's surface back to dock with the orbiting craft and Mike Collins. Alan always said there was a backup plan for nearly every maneuver except for the takeoff of the lunar capsule.

Gary Kallous ('55) never met a person he did not like. When entering the Army following high school, he was stationed at Ft. Leonard Wood. His typing skills and organization of files was immediately recognized. He was admired by all the officer staff and even babysat for the commander's children. Gary advanced to an E-5 in just his two years of active duty. He worked in the banking business and returned to the Farmers Saving Bank at Kalona. Gary's organizational skills and love for his hometown are displayed in the Kalona High School Alumni room at the Kalona Historical Museum. This memorabilia exhibit is not equaled anywhere in the State of Iowa. "Gary has the talent of always including everyone in projects and a great love and appreciation for his Amish friends," said his sister Angela Kallous Hofer ('58).

Notable Teachers—When Dick Oyer came to Kalona, he immediately became involved with the community and a church. Tom Hofer ('58) recalled, "Mr. Oyer had been in the military and had a wonderful way of relating with people. He made math interesting and even for the students who may have not cared for the subject." Steve Reif ('60) shared, "Mr. Oyer was a tremendous instructor and so active and involved in the community."

Mrs. Sara Back was the English teacher at Kalona in the 1950s. Louise Kallous Sattler ('52) reminisced, "Mrs. Beck was an outstanding teacher. Maybe not my favorite, but she was so good. She never played favorites and made us appreciate language and being exact in our diction and descriptions. I have no idea if it influenced me, but she had been a graduate of Mt. Mercy in Iowa City, and 'low an behold' I went there too for my nursing degree. I thought of that often while I was there and using my language skills."

Janitor—Wes Burrows was the janitor in the 1940s and 50s. Larry Kern ('55) commented, "He was a really nice guy. He really cared about the school and was proud of his work." Steve Reif ('60) added, "When my dad was on the school board, he always said that finding a good janitor was harder than finding a good teacher. They had to be an electrician, plumber, carpenter, mechanic, and a meticulous custodian of the building. Wes surely filled all of these roles."

Band—Kalona had an outstanding music program. A 1935 picture of the marching band showed the marching band in a parade with their white tops and white slacks and a cape. Their instructor was Gerald Boshart.

The band always marched on Memorial Day at the cemeteries and played on Saturday Night performance in the bandstand. Steve Reif ('60) recalled, "I played the drums. I always thought the band couldn't march with out me keeping the beat. When we played on Saturday nights, we were given a silver dollar."

Senior Trips—Most of the senior trips were taken to Chicago by train out of Iowa City. Angela Kallous Hofer (58) shared, "We had 17 in my class. We stayed at the elegant Palmer House Hotel. We saw the Broadway play, 'My Fair Lady,' at the Shubert Theatre. It was the first time to Chicago for most of us and did it ever open our eyes. Somehow, I got coerced into buying beer for the boys. I was getting married that summer to a fellow classmate and the trip was a great ending to our wonderful class of friends."

Pranks—Miss Plum was the principal in the 1950s. A dead skunk somehow mysteriously ended up on the back seat of her car. Feeling rather chagrined over the act, Tom Hofer ('58) tried to relocate the black and white carcass to the school steps. This good deed earned him a two-game suspension from the football team.

On another occasion over a lengthy Christmas vacation, a door was found unlocked by Jim Batterson ('58) and Mike Niffenegger ('59). Upon entering the school, they distributed moth balls throughout the building, and on every radiator and heating register. The janitor found this break-in and fumigation project. Wes Burrows was able to locate most of the stink and get the school aerated before classes started in January. There was no record of any sentencing of the two culprits or if they were still out on probation.

Closing—In 1945, the Iowa Mennonite school opened a few miles north of Kalona and took many of the students that would have attended Kalona public schools. With the decreased enrollment in the 1950s and the State Department of Instruction mandated small schools to consolidate. Kalona High School closed after graduation in May 1960. In the fall of 1960, the high school students were bused to the new Mid-Prairie High school at Wellman. They joined the communities of Wellman, West Chester, and Sharon No. 2 at the Mid Prairie School. In the 64 years from 1898-1960, there were 881 graduates from Kalona High School. The largest class was 28 seniors in 1946. The most numerous surnames of the graduates were: Miller-36, Yoder-36, Gingerich-20, Grady-14, Fry-12, Hershberger-12, Hockstetler-12, Kern-12, Schleichter-12, Schwartendruber-9, Shalla-9, Stumpf-9, Kallous-8, Snider-8, Strabala-8, and Rhodes-8.

Kalona High School
Washington County, IA

#40

Kimballton High School

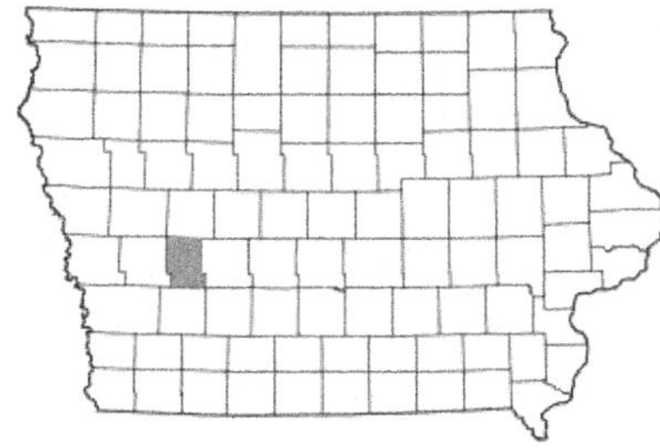

Mascot: None
Colors: Blue and White
Closed: 1944
Location: Southwest Audubon County

Early History—In 1882, Hans J. Jorgensen, as a young man, traveled from Denmark to America and settled in the area now known as Kimballton. He bought 240 acres of prairieland for eight dollars an acre. There were no roads in the area when he proceeded to carve out a living. As a farmer he was a very particular man. He was the only one to plant the corn. The rows had to be straight as this was the mark of a good farmer. Indians, gypsies, peddlers, and other wanderers stopped by and received a warm welcome, food, and shelter. He greeted them, knowing the Indians and Gypsies camped on the outskirts of town and milked the cows while they grazed.

As more people moved into the area, Jorgensen recognized the importance of church and school. He donated land to erect both and served on the boards. The Immanuel Lutheran Church still stands as a monument to Hans Jorgensen. In a book called *Our town Kimballton*, 1922, a poem by Sam Walter Foss honored Jorgensen.

Let me live in my house by the side of the road
Where the race of men go by—
They are good, they are bad, they are weak, they
are strong
Wise, foolish—so am I.
Then why should I sit in the scorner's seat
Or hurl the cynic's ben?
Let me live in my house by the side of the road.
And be a friend of man.

The town was named for Edward Kimball, an official of the Atlantic Northern Railroad. He suggested the name of Kimballtown for the village. It was later trimmed to Kimballton.

Martin N. Esbeck was a gold miner from the west who opened a hardware store in Kimballton. For many years he worked to bring a railroad to Kimballton. On New Year's Day 1908, the first train steamed into Kimballton and Esbeck and his co-workers were justly honored. Shortly after Esbeck's store opened, a flour mill was built by Jorgen Miller. It was fashioned after the old Danish mills with a huge wheel that became a landmark.

Saloon in Kimballton—The saloon in Kimballton was a popular and profitable business. One source termed the saloonkeeper as "rather an original—Jorgensen was his name, and he and his two small sons tended the joint which also served them as a home."

On December 29, 1886, the Elk Horn Lutheran Church congregation (three miles south in the town of Elk Horn) decided to "do what it could" to close the saloon. A committee of Knud Petersen, George Bruhn, and Fred Petersen used its "influence" in doing away with the evil existing so close to Elk Horn.

The influence of the church committee was apparently considerable. The means was not recorded, but the Elk Horn church noted on April 2, 1887, "Committee for closing the Kimballton saloon reported that the saloon was closed, and the owner arrested. Committee was thanked."

In a 2019 interview Annette Overgaard Anderson chuckled and said, "This just may have been the start of the long-standing schism between the two Danish churches in 1894. The Kimballton Danes were the 'happy Danes' and the Elk Horn Danes were the 'holy Danes.'"

Early School—The first school was south of Kimballton on top of Creamery Hill. It was known as District #9 and opened in 1895.

In 1908, land for the school in Kimballton was donated by Hans. J Jorgensen, the founder of the town. Construction started that year and was completed in 1910. Early records list 29 students in the first three grades. The 9th and 10th grades were added in 1919. Annette Overgaard Andersen told, "The school had four rooms and one small room at the back that the superintendent used for an office. Mr. Garlock could hardly turn around in this small office. He was one tough 'old bird' to all of the students." For many students this completed their education. Some continued their education at near-by Audubon and Elk Horn High Schools. When the high school classes were discontinued in 1944, the students were tuitioned-out to the school of their choice.

Community Features—A unique swimming pool was built in 1925 and was the first of its kind in this part of the country. This pool had a sand bottom and concrete sides. It was 70′ x 225′ and filled by large wells pumping water by electric motors. The park on the south side was lined with spacious shade trees. A bathhouse and refreshment stand served the many visitors and community people. The 1936 National Danish Lutheran Church Conference was held at the large covered shed. Concert bands, folk dancing, speeches from religious leaders and politicians used the park. Later concrete bottom pools, state regulations, and lack of chemicals during the war years caused the closing of the Kimballton swimming pool.

School Activities—The tenth grade graduation ceremony was held at the church and followed by an end of year picnic. School plays, carnivals, Christmas programs, Freshman-Sophomore banquets, gym classes, Home Economics classes, and class picnics at Elk Horn and Gasnick's Grove were activities at the Kimballton school.

Notable Graduates—Clark R. Rasmussen ran for governor of Iowa in 1974. He represented Polk county as a state representative in 1964. He became the chairman of the state Democratic Party.

Eivand Lillehoj attended all grades at Kimballton School. He graduated from Iowa State college. He became a microbiologist with the USDA and worked in the states and abroad for many years.

Notable Leader—T.G. Muller organized packages to be sent to the Danes in Denmark. He also organized tour boats back to Denmark to vote in their elections.

Notable Teacher—Nadjeschda Lynge Overgaard was born in Siberia as her first name is representative of the Russian influence. Her father and mother were sent to Siberia from Denmark in 1884 by the Danish government to help establish dairies and creameries. She was six years old when the family moved back to Denmark fearing the political instability in Russia at the time. The family later emigrated, arriving in America via Ellis Island. They came to Iowa by train to the Danish settlements of Kimballton and Elk Horn. Miss Nad taught at the Kimballton school from 1929-33. She had learned to speak and write in English and shared, first-hand, her European experiences with her students. Annette Overgaard Anderson remembered, "Even though my mother was a teacher, I was raised speaking Danish at home. I didn't know English until I went to school in 1935, as well as all of the other children at that time." Nadjeschda taught for many years while raising her family of seven. In 1998, Nadjeschda Overgaard received "The National Heritage Fellowship" award from the National Endowment of the Arts in Washington,

DC. This award honored her tireless effort to keep artistic traditions alive in her community.

Music—Robert Mortensen was a vocal baritone soloist. As a freshman, he won a two rating in the National Music Contest in Kansas City. As a sophomore, he received a superior rating at the district contest and at the national regionals in St. Paul, Minnesota.

Sports—In 1936, Superintendent A.O. Garlock set up a comprehensive athletic program. His goal was to interest farm boys and girls in sports and thus to continue their education in Kimballton. Ground was graded for a basketball court and the manual training class constructed the backboards for the poles. This was an outdoor court. Practice was outdoors if weather permitted. Occasionally the boys ran drills in the Elk Horn High gym (three miles away). Mr. Garlock furnished transportation in his brown Pontiac to Audubon for practice. The Audubon coach, Dwight Hoover, drove them back home. The boys played on the Audubon football, baseball and basketball teams.

Kimballton was the only two-year high school to hold membership in the Iowa High School Athletic Association (IHSAA). All games had to be played at other school courts because the school had no gymnasium. The team competed in sectional tournaments. Their uniforms were white satin trimmed in blue. The numerals were blue and KIMBALLTON was printed on the fronts of the shirts.

Boys tennis was offered as a sport and the practice area was also a dirt court. In 1939, Eddie Faaborg and Herluf Jensen won 14th place in the Iowa State High School Tennis Tournament competing with over 900 high schools. This feat, considering that both boys were just sophomores, underscored their achievement.

Closing—The high school closed following graduation in 1944. The two-year high school was the last of this unique nature to close in Iowa. In the fall of 1944, the high school students chose between going to school in either Audubon or Elkhorn to attend school.

Kimballton High School
Audubon County, IA

#41

Klemme High School

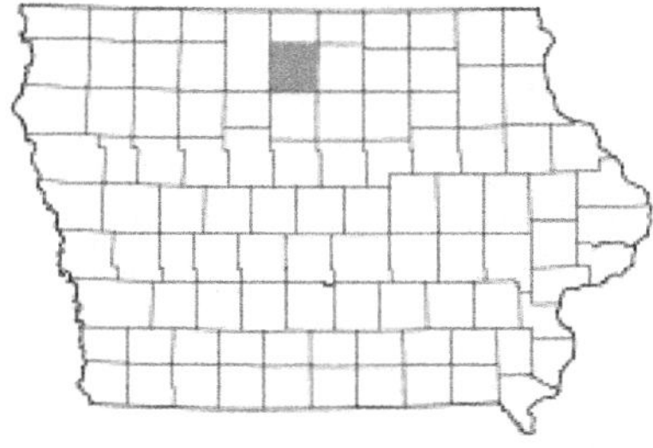

Mascot: Shamrocks
Colors: Kelly Green and White
Closed: 1990
Location: Southeast Hancock County

Early History—Klemme was founded in 1889 by Harmon Johanas and Effie Klemme. They bought a 160-acre farm in Avery Township in 1878. The next year, Avery Township was divided into several smaller townships. Ell Township and the Klemme farm was in section 31. Harmon Klemme was able to persuade the Burlington, Cedar Rapids, and Northern Railroad to run a north-south track through the area in 1896 and build a depot at Klemme. As reported in the *Garner Democrat* on January 9, 1890:

> A new town of Klemme seven miles south of Garner is doing a large business having shipped over 100 car loads of grain in the past two weeks. The new town consists of two grain and coal dealers, a lumber yard, a grocery store, and a restaurant in being built. The town well is almost completed. Abdon Schafer was appointed postmaster and 100 farmers have signified their intention of getting their mail at Klemme. All this for a town that is two months old.

Klemme moved his house to the center of the town to become the first house in town. The town was incorporated in 1899.

Early Schools—In 1892, the first one-room school was built in the village. It opened with seven students. Enrollment grew rapidly and a handsome four-room school was built in 1895 for $2,445. By 1899, three teachers were hired, and a new four-room school was built. It was the pride of the community. In less than two years, it burned to the ground with only the desks, books, and a few furnishings not destroyed. Another four-room school was built that served the district until 1939.

Three graduated in 1902 from the two-year high school. A third year was added in 1918 and a fourth year in 1923.

A bond issue for $45,000 was defeated in 1923 for a new school building. It was later voted to remodel the existing four-room school and add a gym, domestic science room, assembly room, manual arts, and a new classroom.

The bond for $30,000 to build a new school passed in 1938. With the addition of $10,000 from the district operating fund, and a grant for $32,715 from the WPA (Work Progress Administration) a new two-story brick building opened in the fall of 1939 with kindergarten offered for the first time. A newspaper account proclaimed: ". . . it is one of the most modern and up to date schools in Iowa."

A final bond in February 1957, for $375,000, was passed for a new 11-room grade school, vocal music room, and central library.

Though the official population of the town never reached more than 600 (1980) the school enrollment peaked at over 400 in the early 1970s.

Yearbook—The first yearbook published in 1938 was named *The Shamrock*. The second yearbook was published in 1953.

Sports—The athletic conference called Seven Eagles was formed in 1932. The following schools were members of the conference: Crystal Lake, Corwith, Wooden, Kanawha, Goodell, Hayfield, and Klemme.

The team nickname and school mascot were the Shamrocks, first mentioned in a November 1923 newspaper report on the boys basketball game between Klemme and Goodell (Klemme won, 20-16). Prior to that mention of the name, Shamrocks, the Klemme teams were on some occasions referred to as the "Green Devils."

A new conference alignment formed in 1953 and was called the North Star Conference. Klemme was a member until the school closed in 1989. Other members of the conference were Dows, Fertile, Franklin Consolidated, Sheffield, Rockwell, and Ventura.

The big rivalries in the early years were with Goodell and Kanawha. In the North Star conference, the big rivals were Sheffield, Messervy-Thornton, Blue Valley, and Ventura.

There was no football offered in 1941, as noted in the school annual. In 1962, with encouragement and help from the local veterinarian, Dr. John Baker, football was restarted at Klemme. Doc Baker had an amputated leg and was quite an advocate for football as a sport in the high school.

The 1941 boys basketball team lost to Mason City in the state tournament. Mason City had four players on the All-State team that year.

Girls basketball was restarted in 1950. It was later discontinued in the 1960s, but had another recovery and play started again in 1975.

Killed in Action—Many casualties in the world wars would come from the surrounding area. Two of them were graduates of the high school. Those killed in action were:

Ben Schaifer, WWI
Verner Bredlow, WWI
Frank Addam, WWI
Leanard Burrows, WWI
Elmer Hartbeck, WWI
Marvin Bredlow, WWII
Doarrance Grange ('40), WWII
Duane Ridder, WWII
Lyle Schoenwetter, WWII
Harold Wicks ('44), WWII

Notable Teachers—Among the educators that made a lasting impact on Klemme was the principal and superintendent, Henry Galbrith. At the age of 96 (2019), John Schwichtenberg ('41) shared, "Mr. Galbrith taught math and formed a calculus class which he taught after hours to three of my classmates. He handpicked them as he could see their aptitude and knew they needed the calculus for their college endeavors. These boys were Melvin Coobs ('42), Bruce Arnold ('42), and Bill Zabilka. Since the class was not approved to be taught by the school board during the regular school hours, he gave freely of his time to help these boys. Melvin later excelled in electrical engineering at the University of Iowa and at Johnson Controls."

A long-time music teacher was Gracka Quandt Gerardi ('32) who returned to Klemme after the war with her husband. They owned and operated the Gerardi's Restaurant. "My dad and I would go often to Gerardi's to have their hot roast beef sandwich. We would sit there on those stools and the warmth of the place left an indelible mark on my life and such a love for my hometown," recalled Rick Hartzel ('70). Gracka graduated from the University of Iowa in 1936 with a B.A. in Music Education. Gracka taught piano and was the organist at the Lutheran Church. Her husband Ernest taught accordion lessons. A picture in the *Klemme Centennial* book shows Gracka and Ernest in 1952 with 29 students and their accordion choir. The students are dressed in white shirts and bow ties and their Sunday-best clothes, holding accordions. Gracka taught music in the Klemme schools from 1965-1982. Her love of music and passion for teaching made her a community treasure. At the time of her passing in May 2018 she was the oldest living University of Iowa Alumni at the age of 103. The class of 1932 was noted for their longevity with four members living into 2016 as centurions.

Marlin Nielsen was the physical education and science teacher, and a coach in the 1960s. Rick Hartzell ('70) admired him and shared, "He thought bigger than others. He was such a handsome guy and we all looked up to him. He seemed much older than us but was probably only about 30 years old when he came to Klemme. He was a singer and sang at school activities. We all thought his yellow sweater was so cool and that it must have cost a lot of money. He would say to me 'you could be really good' and made us feel like we could be something special."

Band—The music teachers in Klemme were noted for their bands. From 1938 until 1989, the band performed annually in the North Iowa Band Festival in Mason City. Most years the bands nominated a band queen to represent Klemme at the festival. Sheila Henschen ('87) was selected the overall Queen at the North Iowa Band Festival. Charles Whitford was the band director for 11 years, from 1951-1961. His bands, complete with twirlers and pom pom girls, proudly marched at parades. LaVern Velau ('67) played the trumpet in the band as a freshman in the fall of 1963.

Notable Graduates—Luverne Schmidt ('51) was noted for community service and contributions in the field of agriculture. He was the center on the great basketball teams in 1948 thru 1951. In 1948 and 1949, these undefeated teams ended their seasons losing in the last game both years against Messervy by one point at the Belmond gymnasium in the sectionals. Luverne served on the school board for 21 years and was a "no" vote when it came to closing the high school in 1989.

Novella Bredbenner ('34) returned to teach in the country schools in Hancock County for three years after receiving her certificate from Iowa State Teachers College (ISTC). She later received a B.A. and M.A. from ISTC and taught for over 35 years in the Des Moines public schools. At her retirement, Governor Bob Ray attended her recognition party at the school where she taught his children. She was the only child of Anna Marie and Clark Bredbenner. Her father ran the livery business and died when she was in the seventh grade. She graduated as the class valedictorian in 1934 from Klemme and put herself through college. As an unmarried teacher, she returned to Klemme on weekends, holidays, and each summer to live in her home. Novella willed the city all her many collections from around the world and her home. She made a gift to the foundation to support the establishment of the Klemme Homestead Museum. She traveled to all 50 states and the world with more than five inter-continental trips.

Virgil Goodrich ('62) graduated from State College of Iowa (SCI) and returned to Klemme to teach mathematics and coach for seven years. He had never played football since it was not started at

Klemme until the year after he graduated in 1962. He became the new football coach and upon his arrival found Klemme had not won a football game in three years. The first game in 1967, Klemme won with a score of 7-6. Virgil's coaching philosophy was teaching attitude and fundamentals. He became the first girls basketball coach when the program was restarted in 1971. The first year the girls were struggling through an 0-17 season but pulled off a miracle win over Garner-Hayfield in the first game of the sectional. Young coach Goodrich was thrown into the showers by the girls. Virgil later quipped, "I was the first coach in history ever to be thrown into the shower having just won a game whose team just two games before lost by over 100 points." Through his Klemme education and teaching experience, he became an outstanding superintendent of schools and leader at Aplington-Parkersburg.

Rick Hartzell ('70) became an English teacher after his football playing days at University of Northern Iowa. Two degrees later and a renowned college basketball official and college athletic director, he penned the book *Whistle in the Hay Stack*. He gives much credit to his parents, farm upbringing, teachers, church, and Klemme as being the bedrock for his later endeavors.

Polio—Two students, Bob Hagen and Doug Schoop ('53) contracted polio in the 1950s.

Closing—Klemme High School closed in May 1990. In the 67 years from 1924-1990 there were 1,367 graduates. The largest class was 36 seniors in 1973. The most numerous surnames of the graduates were: Lemke-23, Anderson-22, Johnson-18, Barz-16, Stille-15, Schoenwetter-14, Lau-13, Schmidt-11, Neuberger-10, Gibbs-9, and Pringnitz-9. The last to receive a diploma from Klemme High School was Misty VanderWolde (alphabetically).

**Local historian, LaVern Verlau has preserved the Klemme history at the Homestead Museum. Some of this information has been used in this story.*

Klemme High School
Hancock County, IA

#42

Ladora High School

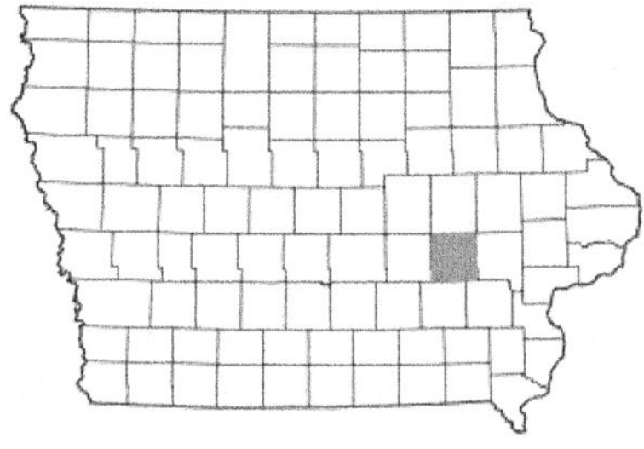

Mascot: Panthers
Colors: Red and White
Closed: 1958
Location: West Central Iowa County

Early History—The first post office was located in the home of William Doward, two miles east of present day Ladora. In 1865, a post office was officially established on the Wilson farm about one mile west of town. When the application was formally made, there was some difficulty in choosing a name for the office. Grace Schofield, a music teacher living at Wilson's farm conceived of the idea of combining the syllables La—Do—Ra (which is usually spelled Re) to name the post office. The town became LaDora on the postal records due to a clerical error. The capital D appeared when a clerk in the post office department in Washington mis-took the name as French and capitalized the D. The post office was moved into the town of Ladora in 1868.

The Chicago Rock Island and Pacific Railroad (CRI&P) extended east to west through Iowa County and Ladora. US Highway 6 traverses from Chicago through Illinois, Iowa, Nebraska, Colorado, and west to California. Traveling through Ladora was bumper to bumper traffic on Iowa Hawkeye football game days. When the new four lane Interstate 80 was built through Iowa county, it was four miles south of Ladora and game day traffic ceased. This occurred in the early 1960s. Lack of traffic, closing of the high school in 1958, and declining population led to business erosion in Ladora.

Early Schools—In 1873, the first school building consisted of two rooms in one long building laying east and west. Later, a third room was built to the north from the center of the building. This facilitated the use of a center entrance from the south into a hall which led to each room.

In 1881, there were two teachers and attendance of nearly 60 pupils This first building was replaced in 1903 with a two-story brick structure that was used through the 1937 graduating year. A new school was built and a gymnasium added in 1951. It was funded by a bond, donated labor, and financial donations.

Ladora Fun Facts—In 1863, there was a report of frost every month of the year.

A picture of Troop A, 1st Iowa Cavalry, depicts 27 soldiers from Ladora mounted on horses and called to duty at Camp Young, North Liberty. In July 1916, they were mustered into Federal service.

From the Marengo *Pioneer Republican,* June 1902:

> Ladora boasts of a high school of 10 grades, at the present three teachers.
>
> This school is under fine organization and is doing excellent work along educational lines.
>
> Ladora has an excellent livestock market and for its population is said to be the very best on the great Rock Island system.

There is a story told about Ladora's last "Old Day's Saloon." It seems a group of customers got the Saloon keeper intoxicated and drank up the available liquor on hand. The next morning the walls were covered with charge slips for the drinks. Some were charged to the President of the United States, etc. One wonders if a few drinks were charged to Sam Whitlock for he bought the ground and building and had Dan Graff destroy the remaining liquors.

1919 Iowa County Medical fees:

Office calls $1.00
Day visits in town $2.00
Day visits in country $2.00
Normal charge for obstetrics $22.00

The Ladora Café had an illegal slot machine in the 1950s. Vera Primley York ('44) and Nancy Slaymaker Weisskopf ('53) recalled working for one dollar a day plus tips at the café. Lois Morgan Kovar (HLV '74) remembered, "By my days the pay was up to one dollar an hour."

Sports—There was no football played at Ladora.

The biggest rival was Marengo. Ardillo Fay ('53) recalled, "In basketball, Marengo always tried to run up the score. They also stole all of our girls and ran our boys out of town."

The boys and girls played basketball. The 1953 girls made it deep into the district competition, losing to Kinross in the finals and thus missed a trip to state. This team had the distinction of beating Marengo four times that year. They won the 1953 Iowa County Tournament at Conroy. "They had a new gymnasium and we were good. I was a guard and my sister Kay Mead Betz ('54) was a forward and led the team in scoring. Our first year coach was M.D. Geraghty and he was new to coaching. He said, 'you girls have hips, use them,'" laughed Bernna Deane Mead Hawkins ('53). "After we won the county tournament, we came all the way back two cars abreast from Ladora to Victor and back on Highway 6!" Bernna Deane ('53) must have used those hips as she led the team with 87 fouls in 1952-53.

Vera Primley York ('44) (age 94 in 2019) remembered with a grin, "We had just started playing basketball in 1942. Conroy, Deep River, and Hartwick all had crackerbox gyms. In one game against Marengo, every one of Marengo's players fouled out but two. And they still beat us."

Band—Dick Davidson was the band director. Vera Primley York ('44) shared, "I played the saxophone. We never left town with the band but did play for community events. We probably weren't very good, but we learned a lot of music."

Yearbooks—The 1950 yearbook was called the *Round Up*. The following eight years, until the school closed, it was called the *Panther*.

The 1953 *Panther* recorded:

- Psychology class took a field trip to the State Mental Hospital in Independence.
- General business class took a field trip to the Public Library in Marengo.
- The following subjects were taught in high school: geometry, American government, typing, algebra, agriculture, English, general science, psychology, shop, general business, sociology, home economics, clerical office practice, and business arithmetic.
- The PTA paid off the debt of $2,258 on the gymnasium. A total of $4,615 was raised during the year.
- There were 15,365 lunches served and 13,045 half pints of milk served.
- Music groups made 17 public performances and participated in the Williamsburg Music Festival.

Buses—As a senior, Ardillo Fay ('53) drove one of the buses on the day route and to the away basketball games. "We were trusted. Of course, all the roads were two-lane and country roads. My dad was a minister, that's maybe why I had so much fun."

Ed Kuhnle drove another bus. Nancy Slaymaker Weisskopf ('53) recalled, "We did not dare act up or the culprits had to sit on the step up by Mr. Kuhnle. He always let his daughter and me off downtown so we could get a donut and coffee before school."

Pranks—Larry Rathjen ('52) was a real prankster. He took a wad of chew and placed it in a new book. Some of his friends retaliated and took some horse manure and put it in his notebook.

Bill Hollopeter ('51) climbed out a window and slid down the drain pipe and was not missed the rest of the day.

Janitor—Frank Lutz was the loyal janitor for 30 years. Ardillo Fay ('53) said, "He was a peach of a guy. After evening church, he and my father (the preacher) would talk for an hour about the Bible. One day he was climbing the light pole on a ladder. I was watching out the window as the ladder slipped and he fell to the ground. I was one of the first out there, but he was unhurt. So much for needing spotters."

Killed in Action—Ladora boys who lost their lives in service to the country were:

Clyde Albert, WWI
John Kious, WWI
Lawrence Smith ('40), WWII
Mervaille Rinehart, WWII
Harry Slaymaker, WWII
Lloyd Junior Heller, WWII
Francis Kochuyt, WWII

Notable Graduates—Mildred Augustine Benson ('22) wrote 23 of the first 30 Nancy Drew books. She was the first ever female graduate in Journalism from the University of Iowa. She authored as many as 41 books. Mildred was a pilot and was married and widowed twice. She died at the age of 98 while she was at work at the *Toledo Blade* newspaper.

Billy Maschmann ('39) was an Air Force Pilot. He flew the helicopter for presidents Kennedy and Johnson.

Closing—The high school closed in May 1958. In the 58 years from 1901-1958 there were 392 graduates (including the two-year high school). The next year the high school students were bused to Victor in the new HLV school district. The most numerous surnames of the graduates were: Shaull-16, York-12, Smith-10, Davis-8, Thompson-7, and Maudlin-6. The last to receive a diploma from Ladora High School was Shirley Tuttle Shaull (alphabetically).

The elementary school remained opened until 1985 and held grades K-6. Upon closing the remaining students were bused to HLV in Victor.

Ladora High School
Iowa County, IA

#43

Lakota High School

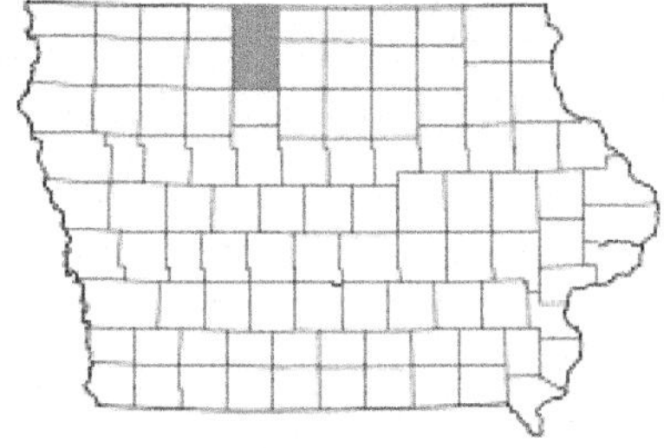

Mascot: Eagles
Colors: Purple and White
Closed: 1987
Location: Northeast Kossuth County

Early History—Kossuth County was created by the legislature in 1851. Originally it was platted the same size as the counties on the east (Hancock) and west (Palo Alto). Each county had 24 square miles. Kossuth was 17 miles from the Minnesota line and bounded on the north by Bancroft County. In 1855, Bancroft County was blotted out of existence and added to Kossuth. This was often referred to as "the 1855 freak legislation." The new Kossuth county is the only double-county in the state.

Located in Ledyard Township, the town of Germania was one of three towns in the township along with Ledyard and Gerled. Parts of the township did not settle rapidly because much of the land was owned by land companies and speculators. In 1892, the Burlington, Cedar Rapids, and Northern Railroad started extending track from Dows and Forest City on a branch west to Estherville.

All Germania's boxcars were loaded with hay for the return trip to feed the huge population of horses in eastern cities. The land was covered by native grasses, at least eight-foot tall. When it was cut, dried, and baled, it made excellent feed. As the land was plowed and the many ponds and sloughs were drained, the freight changed to corn, wheat, and oats. Cattle and hogs were shipped to packing points in Chicago and St. Paul.

An article published in the *Fairmont Sentinel* by Nadine Jorgensen revealed the story of the town name change from Germania to Lakota:

> Names have their ins and outs and that's how it happens that Lakota is more than a quarter of a century older than its name. Back in 1892, when the town was surveyed, Indians were "out" as some people were still around to give eye-witness accounts of bloody massacres and other atrocities inflicted on early settlers.
>
> So, the German immigrants who settled in the area appropriately named the town Germania, little

dreaming that some years later the shoe would be on the other foot. In 1918, the hysteria of World War I was sweeping the country and the Germans—even those resettled in this county—were "out."

Residents could not change their origin to protect themselves from the slings and arrows of the popular hatred of the time, but they could take the stigma of all things German from the town by wiping its name off the map. So, they did.

They renamed the town Lakota, as the Indians were entirely subdued and largely forgotten, and Indian lore was now just a pretty piece of background. In other words, the Indians were "in" again and they've held the last "inning" ever since.

Lakota, as Germania, began to grow when the Rock Island Railroad built a branch from Lakota to Albert Lea in 1892. At the time there were 45 men employed at the roundhouse in Lakota. Today (2020) there is but one man employed part-time.

Early Schools—The first schoolhouse was built in Germania in the summer of 1893. A few years later another one-story building was erected near the schoolhouse to form a T-shape. The school was in the northeastern part of town and had two rooms and three teachers.

The Independent School District of Germania was organized in 1897. The minutes of the school board meeting in March 1897 recorded 48 votes in favor and 16 against the formation of an independent school district. A contract for a new building went to Julius Bork for the sum of $5,975 to erect a new schoolhouse in the winter of 1902-1903.

A school annual was published by the senior class of 1912. This was called *The Mite,* and dedicated to their teacher and principal, B.L. Troup.

A four-year high school was established in 1914 following the new accreditation standards set by the state of Iowa. The class of 1916 was the first group to have 12 years of schooling.

Kindergarten was started in 1954 with Mrs. Dime as the first teacher. She drove every day from Swea City. Bruce Meurer ('67) smiled as he said, "I was in that first kindergarten class. We liked to call her Mrs. Penny for fun."

Sports—Basketball was a great sport from the early years of the school. The 1926-27 teams traveled seven miles to practice in the Ledyard school gym. This was very much appreciated according to an article from the school notes of the time.

One game ended with the score 21-15 in favor of Lakota. Teams from Elmore, Bancroft, Wesley, Buffalo Center, and Lone Rock were competitors. When new high school students came in from the country schools, more patience and practice were needed. When the new school was completed, the practice sessions were held in their own gym. Lakota had one of the largest gyms in the county.

Girls basketball was organized when the new building was constructed. Grades eight through 12 were included in playing. They practiced between classes. A group of ladies from town formed a team and played against the girls team to help them practice. The girls' mothers made their first shorts and blouse outfits. In 1933-34, the team started playing competitively against teams from other schools.

In 1946, the Lakota girls basketball team went to the state tournament. The team was coached by John Cook and had an outstanding record. They won four trophies that year by winning the county, sectional, district, and State Line Conference tournaments. They won the first round at state by defeating Braddyville but were eliminated by New Providence in the second round. "My sister, Wanda Hietland Bloome ('46), was on that team," recalled Joan Heitland Mabus ('44). "I was a basketball player, too, and we had great teams as good as the 1946 team, but we always seemed to lose in the finals of the regionals."

Ledyard, Titonka, and Burt became the fiercest rivals in sports.

The sports athletic conference was the State Line Conference. Other schools in the league were Woden, Titonka, Burt, Swea City, Thompson, Lincoln Central, and Sentral.

With Coach Don "Pete" Peterson as the coach, girls track was a special program in the 1960s. Bobbie Jo Price Wolfe ('87) wrote, "When I think back to high school I think of Pete, our coach. He coached all the girls sports programs from seventh grade until 12th grade. I remember my sophomore year I was considering not going out for track. I told Pete. He asked why. I said I don't want to run all the time. I won't go out for track unless I start to get chubby. So, the next day he told me I looked a little bit chubby. I was baffled and remembered our conversation from the previous day. And yes, of course, I did go out for track—for Pete."

Sharon Erdahl Price ('57) remembered, "I did not go home on the bus one night after a basketball game at Titonka. I rode home in Bob Price's car and we stopped at his grandmother's house after returning to Lakota. Each morning, all four grades would have assembly in the gymnasium for announcements and a general school meeting. I got called out of assembly because someone had seen me going into Bob Price's grandmother's house the night before. Once in the office, I was informed that I did not have permission to stay in town and not ride the bus. I eventually did marry that same Bob Price ('56)." Sharon added, "From the graduation classes of 1955, '56, and '57, there were 16 couples that married, and they all stayed married."

Busing—The first bus for the Lakota School District was owned by Albert Krosch. He started the route in 1932 and continued until 1939 when he sold out to Alvin Boettcher. The bus was a Model A Ford chassis with a wooden frame structured body. In 1940, Alvin purchased a chassis from Ley Motor Company, and they sent it to Indiana to have the body mounted. During these times, the chassis was privately owned, and the school owned the body of the bus.

Hot Lunch—The hot lunch program started in 1949 in the basement of the Methodist Church. When hot lunch started in the school kitchen, Emma Bierstedt became the cook for nearly a quarter of a century. Royce Janssen ('74) quipped, "We always would butter up Mrs. B. and then could come in later after basketball practice for extra chicken and her wonderful cinnamon rolls."

Mildred Berhow Heiderscheidt ('56) wrote, "We had the best hot lunch program any public school ever had."

Notable Graduates—Ester Johnson Steele ('29) went all through her school days without ever being absent. This is a record that was never topped. She graduated in 1929.

Notable Teachers—Mr. John Cook became the superintendent in 1943 and coached both boys and girls basketball. That year a school annual was printed and the school paper was again published after an absence of many years. The Band Mothers' Group was organized for the first time. A school bus was purchased. The bus had been used by the Navy and was painted the traditional orange. All of these firsts came under the leadership of Mr. Cook. "He was an incredible construction engineer. His supervision of the school additions in 1951, 1953, and the new gymnasium in 1959 left a legacy of great planning and oversight," boasted Royce Janssen ('74). Royce later bought the old high school and converted it into condominiums. After visiting the old school condominium complex, this author believes the remodel is the best example of restoration of any former high school in the state, if not the Midwest.

Joyce Leonard Paulsen ('69) recalled, "It was amazing everything John Cook was able to do. He taught geometry, algebra, and physics, and coached girls basketball." Mr. Cook started the Future Teachers of America group in the 1950s. "Not that we didn't test all of the school policies. The girls were all instructed to assembly in the gymnasium and told to get down on our knees. If our skirts did not touch the floor, we were not allowed to wear them. We thought we were smart when we rolled them up at our waists to make them shorter. The boys were to always wear a belt. So, they would cut off their belt loops."

"My brother was a brain in math. When I got to Mr. Cook's class he said, 'Are you sure you are Gerald Bierstedt's sister?' He was able to get me through math. What a wonderful man. Everyone had such respect for him when he walked into the room," reminisced Gwen Bierstedt Good ('56).

A renowned home economics teacher was Mrs. Beulah Mae Budlong. She also taught biology, art, and was the cheerleading sponsor. Sharon Erdahl Price ('57) remembered, "I was a cheerleader and we all wanted to get sweaters for our outfits. We approached Mrs. Budlong with the idea, and she said, 'No way, because you cannot begin to fill them out!' as she stood there with her arms crossed across her own quite large bosoms."

Polio—When polio stuck in the 1950s, Lakota suffered casualties. Albert Becker ('62), Jon Smith ('52), and George Weringa ('64) came down with the paralysis. Linda Koppen Nydegger ('61) told, "I was a first grader that year and school started late that year because of the epidemic. There was no vaccine yet available."

Band—The band program was conducted by Virgil Barrett in the 1950s and 1960s. He developed a very disciplined band. "The marching part was not his strong point as he was slightly overweight and did not march along and instruct. We did participate in the Mason City Band festival and always played at the Algona Band Festival," shared Linda Koppen Nydegger ('61).

"Every Saturday evening the town came to life," wrote Bruce Meurer ('67). "During the week Lakota was a quiet little farm community intent on going about the normal everyday activities . . . but on Saturday evening it became a bustling little city . . . the high school band was a big attraction for many families . . . Virgil Barret would conduct the weekly music for the community to enjoy. The band members would bring chairs and their instruments out of the city hall and perform the music which included the likes of John Philip Sousa marches. Listeners would park their cars by the city hall and others sat on the lawn on blankets and chairs clapping and honking their horns after each selection. Upon completion of the evening's concert, each band member got a 25-cent ticket for ice cream or a soda."

Janitor—Mr. Hank Mitchel was the janitor and he was a meticulous custodian. "We all had to take our shoes off to go into the gymnasium and onto the beautiful shiny floor. We were not allowed to chew gum, therefore none of the desks or tables had any gum pressed underneath. He did not allow us to run up the stairs. What a disciplinarian, but we all were so proud when visiting teams would come to our gymnasium and marvel at our beautiful court," remembered Gwen Bierstedt Good ('56).

Senior Trips—The 1956 seniors took a day trip to Arnold's Park. The 1967 seniors went to Minneapolis for the day and toured the Betty Crocker factory, the Ford factory, and went to the Cinema. The 1970 class was the first to go overnight, as they ventured to Chicago. Rumors spread that several adventurous seniors snuck out to see the Broadway presentation of *Hair*.

Siobhan Chambers Wood ('80) wrote about this memory, "Cheer, cheer for Lakota High . . . I still hear the school song playing in my head, and as a former cheerleader, I think I can still remember the actions that go with the song! My family had moved to Lakota from New York during my sophomore year . . . We soon adjusted to this farming community where everyone knew your name, literally! I found myself taking a Hunter Safety course, complete with handling a gun in school! The guys in my class tried to teach me to play cards, but I had no idea that the clovers were actually called spades or was it clubs! Not having an athletic bone in my body, I was on the cheerleading squad for basketball. It didn't matter that I could not do a cartwheel . . . We also took a weeklong, school-sponsored senior trip. This shy New York girl had learned many things from these 16 classmates who still hold a special place in my heart."

Closing—The high school closed after graduation in May 1987. However, the baseball team played that summer. Doug De Boer remembered, "It was my wife, JoAnn, and my first teaching job. Between the two of us, we coached just about every extra-circular at the high school. While we had many successes in speech, drama, and athletics, it is actually a loss I want to expand on. It was that summer of 1987 and our baseball team was about to play its last game ever as the high school was going to start whole-grade sharing with Buffalo Center-Rake in the fall. We had won our first two tournament games and were now in the sectional championship. Our opponent was the two-time state champion Bancroft-St. John Johnnies and we had to play them on their home field. It was a close contest throughout, but our last inning rally was stopped short and we lost the game 5-4. Although everyone was bitterly disappointed with the final outcome, we all agreed that if it had to end this was a more than respectable way to finish it off. This just goes to show the great character of the young people I was so privileged to work with and the families who raised and supported them."

Earlier that March of 1987, Amy Larson Kahler ('87) wrote, "We were undefeated in basketball . . . we were playing in the regional championship game against Terrill High School . . . a win would have landed us in the state basketball tournament . . . but we lost . . . we had a dream, which was to play in 'The Barn' especially since our school was closing in a few months. Unfortunately, our dream was cut short by a few points . . ."

A total of 1,058 graduated from Lakota High School. The largest classes were 32 seniors in 1960 and 1965. The most numerous surnames of the graduates were: Christ-27, Meyer-21, Koppen-20, Johnson-18, Thompson-14, Heitland-13, Rippentrop-11, Kollash-10, Olson-10, Lewis-9, Boettcher-8, Smith-8, Hippen-8, Peterson-8, and Schroeder-8. The last to receive a diploma from Lakota High School was Tina Spear (alphabetically).

Lakota High School
Kossuth County, IA

#44

Laurens Marathon High School

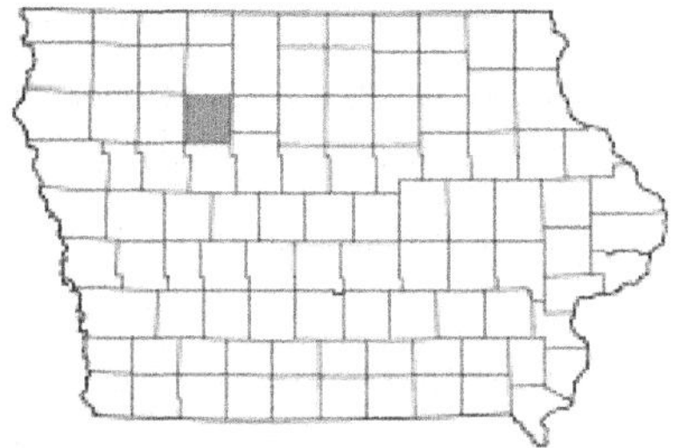

Mascot: Elk-Elkettes
1976 became Chargers
Colors: Scarlet and Black
1976 became Blue and Gold
Closed: 2017
Location: Northwest Pocahontas County

Early History—This town was named in honor of Henry and John Laurens, father and son. They were French Huguenots who became residents of Charleston, South Carolina, and distinguished themselves by their patriotism and loyalty to the colonialist cause during the revolution. Henry (1724-92) was a member of the first provincial Congress in 1775 from South Carolina and he was president of the Continental Congress in 1777-1778. John (1756-82) was an aide to George Washington in all his battles during the Revolution and was killed in a skirmish at its close.

In the book by R.E. Flickinger, *The Pioneer History of Pocahontas County Iowa,* it reports the time of the county's earliest settlement up to the present time of 1904.

> Laurens, one of the largest and most important towns in the county, is located in the northwest part of the county . . . the site of the town is upon a high rolling prairie and one mile south of Swan Lake . . . the population primarily American and the people cultured, refined and educated.
>
> It has two railways, the Chicago & Northwestern and Chicago Rock Island, and Pacific that afford excellent shipping facilities in every direction.
>
> A fire on Main Street in 1883 completely burned one block of buildings on the west side.

Early Schools—The first school building had only one room and was built in 1883. The independent school district of Laurens was established on February 14, 1891. In 1889, a four-room frame building was built at a cost of $3,000. The school building was not completed until the new district was established in 1891. It was expanded in 1900 for $7,000. By 1902, there were 300 pupils and seven teachers in this schoolhouse.

Flickinger's history book relates:

> The course of study is equal to any of the public schools of Northwest Iowa and parents find here the facilities for giving their children a fine education.

School Board Notes—A collection written by the Laurens Historical Preservation Commission in June 2007 is a chronological review of the school board minutes from 1882 through 2007. It outlined some of the board minutes and highlights for the Laurens schools. This collection is noteworthy because of the year-by-year accounting of the 125-year existence of the school. These highlights give an insight and perspective of the issues of the times and decisions that provided the backbone of a school's operations. For example:

- The first school in Laurens was held in the second story of J.P. Shoemaker's Hardware Store in 1882. L.M. Starr instructed six pupils.
- The next year a one-room building was erected on the present school grounds. The original building, a four-room building, was erected in 1889. The town now had a school with five rooms.
- In 1891, Laurens formed the Laurens School District, by a vote of 29 to 3. The average teacher earned $50 a month. The principal earned $60 a month, but he had to do the janitor work for his

part of the building. Students did not pay to attend school unless they were non-resident pupils, in which case they paid $1 a month.

- In 1892, the Board of Education asked the voters to pass a bond issue for $500 to operate for one full year. The figure decreased to $300 for a few years, but the cost of operating a school for one school year climbed rapidly. Coal was one of the biggest expenses.
- In 1896, a boy was suspended for refusing to sit where the teacher placed him. For several months, board members agonized over what to do about a teacher who disagreed with them publicly and took her vacations when she wished. You can almost hear the sigh of relief when she resigned to care for her ailing mother.
- In 1885, the first class graduated from the Laurens school. They held the exercises at the First Christian Church, and the school paid a bill of less than $25 for the ceremony.
- In 1898, high school students could develop their knowledge of the language arts by taking rhetoric, English grammar, Latin or English literature; business skills (a choice of commercial arithmetic or bookkeeping); social studies included general history, civics, geography, and US history; sciences (physiology, botany, physics, and chemistry; and mathematics (algebra or geometry).
- In 1900, a library consisting of a few volumes was added at one end of a classroom. In 1907 voters agreed to provide students with free textbooks.
- The graduates of 1914 were the first students to wear uniforms to these exercises.

A federal law in 1913 added agriculture, manual training, and home economics departments to the school. These programs were originally funded by state aid. The additions shifted some of the emphasis from the three R's and college preparatory classes to courses for students who went straight from high school to work. The school board began looking at the ever expanding territory that the school served. The first consolidation took place and all buildings inside the new boundaries were sold.

In 1916, the dream became a reality when the new school was completed, and the students and teachers were able to occupy it. It was the largest construction project the Laurens school system had undertaken, and it had problems. The construction company failed to complete its tasks, and lawsuits were threatened. The construction company left some of its equipment on the site. A creditor of the company tried to claim the items, but the Laurens Board of Education legally won the right to keep the machines. A lesser problem, although it must have caused some dissension, was the installation of the first water closets. Nobody could agree on where to put them.

In 1917, the board refused to consider a demand made by a grade school teacher so long as "it was couched in the present language." The minutes were silent as to what the demand was. The next year the board moved to not hire teachers who did not reside in the district. One wonders if this decision was the result of the unpopular demand of the previous year. This policy did not last long. By the 1920s, non-district residents were again teaching. Grade school teachers were making $75 a month in 1918. The same year the board brought to public attention the matter of bus drivers failing to stop before railroad tracks. Early buses were horse driven, and stalls for the horses were present in the bus barn.

In 1918, the board demanded that every student be vaccinated for influenza. In March of that year, the school was closed for a week due to an outbreak. This happened again in 1921 due to a scarlet fever outbreak.

In 1923, the board voted to add a normal training course to the curriculum. Designed for future teachers, the course did not receive a wide following and it disappeared from the subject offerings a few years later.

Other year-by-year highlights and board actions:

1930: Board allotted $50 to build bleachers.

1934: Board added typing to the curriculum, renting 12 typewriters for $11.25 a year.

1936: Worst blizzard in Iowa history caused school to cancel for three weeks.

1937: Decision was made to fire a teacher who was married after she had signed her contract.

1939: The class of 1939 donated money to help light the football field.

1930s End of the decade, it was agreed to share cost of instruments and an instructor for a community band. Also had an orchestra for many years.

1941: Added an instructor for a civilian ground school.

1941: Board passed resolution allowing Juniors to hold their Prom in the schoolhouse.

1948: All employees received free tuberculosis tests.

1950: Voters approved construction of a new high school building.

1951: Girls basketball was added to the athletic program.

1952: Board ruled that a pupil must be five years old on or before September 1st before being admitted to kindergarten.

1952 The Board ruled that teachers must retire at the age of 65.

1950s: In the 1950s, the board ruled that students could not drive to school except in cases of hardship, handicap, or necessity.

1957 Remedial reading became a part of the curriculum.

1958: Driver Education added to the curriculum.

1960: Ware students in ninth grade began attending school at Laurens.

1961: A guidance counselor and school nurse were shared with the Pocahontas School.

1965: Golf added to the extracurricular program.

1968: Reduced price meals for students who could not afford the full price became available.

1972: The first female physical education teacher; volleyball added to the girls athletic program.

1974: New school and agriculture facilities approved; Board agreed to sell all the orchestra music in files to Storm Lake High School; Students who met all the requirements of the school won the right to graduate mid-year.

1975-76: At the end of the term, the Laurens school system ended and the new school became Laurens-Marathon.

1980s: Ayrshire reorganized and joined Laurens-Marathon.

1987: 40 credits were required to graduate: English-8, Social Sciences-6, Math-4, Science-4, P.E. and Health-1 credit each.

1994: $35,562 was appropriated for purchasing computers.

1998: A new gym, wrestling room, and band and music wing completed; Baccalaureate was held separately as a non-school function.

In 2014, the Laurens School Board appeared before the State School Budget Review Board to inform the body of the financial changes the district would make to correct the spending authority issue since the district was $139,000 overspent. Meetings were initiated with the Pocahontas Area School Board to discuss partial-day sharing. Further agreements with the Pocahontas District eventually led to the dissolving of the Laurens-Marathon School district and the high school was closed and consolidated with Pocahontas in the fall of 2017.

Sports—In 1962, a magical boys basketball team won the conference (first time in 15 years), won the Palo Alto County Tournament (first time in 10 years), won the sectionals, district, and sub-state to progress to the state tournament. Since there was only one class in boys basketball, this team joined at the state tournament with schools with much larger enrollment. Led by Floyd Winter, a 25-year-old coach in his fourth year, they headed to Iowa City with a record of 25-1. Coach Winter once said, "Half of my team had never been to Des Moines in their lifetimes, much less Iowa City." With lopsided wins over Sac City and Waverly, they met Iowa City Regis in the state championship game. Falling behind by double digits in both halves, the boys came back to tie the game. However, the Elks lost their bid for a state championship. The leading scorer, Bob Ziegler ('62), made the all-state team and later returned to Laurens to teach and coach.

The 1963 boys team would again make it past a great Mason City team in the finals of substate to win by 23 points and once again advance to the state tournament. This time they fell in the opening game to a Council Bluffs team that had an enrollment five times larger than Laurens.

Girls volleyball became a sport in 1978 and was coached by a 22-year-old rookie head coach, Leslie Hardie. In the second year of the sport, this team progressed to number 20 in the state which included all the state's schools (only one class division). They were upset at Ft. Dodge by Manson, a team they had defeated twice before that year, which denied them reaching the state tournament in just the second year of the program. Leslie Hardie Stewart remembered, "We had a really good gym. Going to Havelock was an adventure with a cracker box gym with a stage at one end and overhanging balcony. The bathrooms left something to be desired."

Other state tournament teams were the 1958 girls softball team and the 1969 girls basketball team.

The rivals were Twin Lakes in the 1950s and Manson in the 1990s. Pocahontas was always included as the chief rival through the decades.

The athletic conference had the following schools: Pocahontas, Rolfe, Plover, Manson, Rockwell City, Prairie-Gowrie, and Lake City.

Teachers—Dick Mosbach ('62) stated, "Outside of my father, Floyd Winter was the most influential person in my life. He was a great teacher, coach, and leader. He came to Laurens right after graduation from Luther College. He saw something in this tall green skinny sophomore to start me at center in basketball. We had a group of guys that played every sport together since elementary school. He molded us into a powerhouse making it to the state two years in a row when there was only one class or division in the whole state. This opportunity made it possible for Everett Barr, a referee from Algona who officiated many Laurens game to see me. Something he saw must have impressed him to recommend me for the Air Force Academy. This enabled me to make a career in the Air Force. Floyd took a chance on me. Had he not, I may not have been seen by Everett Barr. Floyd

Winter was named the most outstanding coach in the state of Iowa at the age of 25. A teacher, coach, gentleman, and friend to this day."

Driver Education—Mr. Ziegler ('62) was a noted instructor behind the dual controls of the driver education car. Kelly Snow Tate ('99) added, "Mr. Ziegler would occasionally doze off as we drove around the countryside."

Another instructor was Dick Hawes. Connie Hopkins ('82) once asked Mr. Hawes, while passing a car on the highway, "Am I by that car yet?" Mr. Hawes asked, "Well, can't you tell?" Connie gasped, "I don't know because I have my eyes closed." This story was shared by her sister-in-law Jerlynn Nagel Svuba ('82) who was in the back seat as a star witness.

Pranks—Wayne Snow ('77) once shot firecrackers in the gymnasium. Fleeing the scene, he would later tell his mother of the incident. She asked, "And what did you do?" Wayne coyly said, "Well, I just ran." A very wise mother stated, "We're going back to school and you are going to tell them you did it." The next day, Wayne apologized for this 'accidental' use of fireworks at school and got detention for his deed.

Ed Devereaux ('56), Ron Cowan ('56), and Scott Wasson ('56) dismantled an antique car and reconstructed it on top of the gym roof.

Music—Mary Svuba Wright ('55) remembered, "I played the E Flat Mellophone in band. I owned the instrument and later donated it to the school." The band was so big in the school that there were two sessions so that all those interested could participate. Don Kunkel was a noted band instructor. Jerilyn Nagel Svuba ('82) said, "We had instrument lessons at school and over the summer. I played the flute and even practiced at home."

Speech—No other elective courses made an impact on so many students as the Laurens speech program. From the 1990s through 2005, this department excelled in the districts and state competitions against the "big boys" (very few high schools this size had speech departments). LMHS made it to state in 1998 with "Voices that Care." This told of declaration of war, sacrifices endured during the fighting, and names missing in action. Performers wore uniforms belonging to relatives and Laurens citizens. There were 20 groups that performed at All State and Laurens Marathon received the "Critics Choice Banner," which was displayed at the high school for a year. The coach was Rose Davis.

In 2002, Tiffany Dallenbach Hill ('02) became a four-time individual All State performer. Very few receive this honor in the state.

Closing—The high school closed in May 2017. In the 125 years from 1895-2017, there were 4,122 graduates from Laurens (Laurens-Marathon) High School. The largest class was 80 seniors in 1978. The most numerous surnames of the graduates were: Johnson-59, Anderson-54, Peterson-50, Richardson-41, Olson-34, Ferguson-28, Larson-24, Hanisch-23, Hakes-22, Siddall-22, Carlson-20, Oleson-19, Dahlberg-18, Dubbert-16, Smith-15, Schmidt-14, White-13, and Gulbranson-11. The last graduate from Laurens was Ricky Unger (alphabetically).

#45

Le Claire High School

Mascot: Hornets
Colors: Green and White
Closed: 1960
Location: East Scott County *(along Mississippi River)*

Early History—The town of Le Claire is situated on "the point," where the Mississippi River makes a sharp turn to the right and flows in a west-southwesterly direction for 15 miles.

The Indians around the Le Claire and Scott County areas and adjacent land in Illinois were members of the Sac and Fox tribes. The Black Hawk

War in 1832 was fought in Illinois and Wisconsin. After the war, the west side of the river was lost as indemnity. Veterans of the War were awarded land grants. A section of land at the Upper Rapids or the Rock Island Rapids was given to Antoine Le Claire by the Indians. The Black Hawk Treaty allowed the Indians to stay on this land until June 1, 1833. Le Claire was part French Canadian and Indian, and traded on the river. Because of the Upper Rapids, river pilots were needed to navigate the rapids for the steam ships. Many pilots lived in Le Claire and the town flourished.

In January 1846, the county commissioners from the election precinct of Parkhurst named the township "Fairview." Three months later, in April 1846, the name was changed to Le Claire as people protested. They wanted to honor the founder of the area.

The town was incorporated in 1855. A historical account reads, "At the crest of Le Claire's prosperity wave in 1856 there were located in the town 18 dry goods, clothing, and grocery stores . . . plow factory, coal and lumber yards, two ferries to cross the river."

Le Claire once had ten saloons. The saloon in northernmost Le Claire was called "The First Chance." At the South end of town was one called "The Last Chance."

Historical Events and Activities

- Billboards leading into town read: Birthplace of Buffalo Bill and the famous Green Tree.
- The famous Green Tree was a huge elm tree along the Mississippi which had extended branches reaching the ground in all directions. It provided shade for river captains, towns people, and travelers.
- A school in a log structure was taught by one "Daddy" Lincoln, a cousin of Abraham Lincoln.
- William Frederick Cody was born here February 28, 1846.
- An older brother and sister of William Cody attended Le Claire schools.
- October 23, 1942, the Le Claire Public School collected 23 tons of scrap metal for the war effort. Superintendent A. B. Long stated he believed this was a record for a school with 270 students.

Early Schools—A school was held in the Philip Suiter home in the winter of 1837 with his five children as the pupils. The Suiter name was the most numerous of all the graduates through the years from Le Claire High School.

In 1846, the Baptist built a small brick church. The basement was used as a school for many years.

The first brick school in Le Claire Township was built in 1851.

Several private schools, subscription schools, and academies were held in homes named after the homeowner. Stone School, Scharf School, Coe School, Argo School, Indiana School, Quarry School, and Skakerag School were some of those schools named either by their homeowner or their early connections to their founders.

In 1855, the new state constitution required for six months of school be held each year and requirements for teachers were upgraded.

A great number of German settlers came in the 1850s. They established their own German school which existed for twenty years. This two-story building is still standing (2020) on Ewing Street and is presently an apartment building.

In 1870, the town built a two-story stone school for $13,000. This building replaced the old "black" and "white" schools. It made room for the later high school grades. The "white" school had been painted, and the "black" school was the old Presbyterian church which had never been painted and was dark from weathering. The first graduation class with four students was in 1878. This school was destroyed by fire on November 24, 1924.

Following the fire, the Albert Gross School was built. Albert Gross had been a grubstake prospector looking for silver in the West. His sister donated heavily to the building and his name remained on the front of the building until it was replaced in 1965.

Buffalo Bill's last autobiography was published in 1917. He said, "At Le Claire I was sent to a school where by diligence and fairly good conduct I managed to familiarize myself with the alphabet, but further progress was arrested by a sudden developed love of skiffriding on the Mississippi."

Sports—There was no football played at Le Claire. The boys played basketball, baseball, and track. The girls played basketball.

In 1939, the school played Weldon, Andover, Buffalo, St. Ambrose, Gooselake, Woodhull, Durant, and Bennett.

The biggest rival for all sports was Buffalo, another river town south in Scott County.

Yearbooks—The first yearbook in 1939 was titled *Our Green Tree.* Noted in the yearbook was the boys cross-country team which won the state meet at State University of Iowa in Iowa City. The runner's placings were Paul Hammill-19, John Moffet-21, Leon Hammill-22, Harvey Phillips-27, and Henry Clark-28.

The 1942 yearbook was named the *Broadcaster.*

The last yearbook in 1960 was titled the *Hilltopper* because the school was located at the top of the hill on the bluff overlooking the Mississippi River. That year the school played sports against Durant, Elvira, Gooselake, St. Joseph, Hayes, Miles, Wilton

Junction, Wheatland, Charlotte, Andrew, Weldon, and West Branch.

Notable Teachers—Inez Hulet was born in 1898 and was a teacher at the high school when it burned in 1924. She continued to teach until the high school closed in 1960. She taught business classes and was the principal of both the elementary and high schools. Marie Brand Spinsby ('48) related, "Mrs. Hulet was the one responsible for me being able to get a job and my career for the rest of my life. I took her bookkeeping class and it enabled me to get my first job with Alcoa. I had graduated at 16 years of age. Alcoa hired me and after three months came to me and were starstruck that I was not 18 years old. The superintendent and principal had to sign off on the fact that, even though I was a minor, I had graduated from high school. Mrs. Hulet also taught music and played the piano for all of the groups."

Dick Wales ('48) added, "Mrs. Inez Hulet always showed up on Monday mornings with a different color of hair. Sometimes it would be dark, the next time it was a greenish color, and another time it was orangish. We all snickered and tried to guess on Mondays what color it was going to be. It was sort of a game, though we never let on to her."

A.J. Jones came as the Superintendent for Le Claire in 1944. He taught in most every class as needed and was the basketball coach for both the girls and boys. He stayed at Le Claire for ten years. "He was like a father to me," remembered Dick Wales ('48). "There were others that looked up to him because they had no father. He made such a difference in so many lives. He let us into school to play basketball after hours and weekends with the only rule that it had to be picked up and cleaned or it would be the last time we could stay late at school," continued Dick Wales ('48). "When called into his office for discipline his renowned retort was to say, 'You fathead,'" remembered Marie Brand Spinsby ('48) over 72 years later.

Notable Graduate—Rodger Weismann ('30) was musically talented. He wrote the first school song. His mother helped start the school orchestra in the 1920s. Rodger started the first high school band. He graduated from the State University of Iowa and was called into the army in 1941. He accepted a three-year fellowship in general surgery at the Mayo Clinic in Rochester, Minnesota. He practiced in Minnesota, California, Arizona, and New Hampshire.

Keith Jacob Rynott ('47) joined the Army after college in 1954. He served for the next 28 years and became a Master Army Aviator serving in Germany, Okinawa, Thailand, and Vietnam. He retired as a full Colonel. He and his unit outfitted and operated the first American armed helicopters during the Vietnam conflict. He was a great athlete and loved music.

James J. Ryan II ('20) graduated from Iowa State University and accepted a teaching position at the University of Minnesota. He was a national advocate for automobile safety and invented and patented several safety improvements, including the first automobile retractable seat belt. He earned the nickname of "CRASH" by using himself and his graduates as subjects testing the seat belts by crashing into walls. He was responsible for improving the shock absorbing bumpers, recessed dashboards, and collapsible steering columns. His biggest achievement was design and patenting of the aircraft "BlackBox" flight recorder which is now required on all aircraft.

Killed in Action—The following lost their lives in service to the country:

William J. Steel, Civil War
Raymond J. Reiter, WWI France
Joe Lawrence, WWI Germany
Glen Lester Holden, WWII Pacific
Donald G. Manning, WWII
Albert Earl Moore, WWII Pacific
Laverne Oscar Kruse, WWII
Gary Keith Rath, Vietnam
Patrick Loyal Fricke, Vietnam

Closing—The Le Claire High School closed following graduation in 1960. There were 889 graduates in the 83 years from 1878-1960. The largest class was 31 seniors in 1958. The most numerous surnames of the graduates were: Suiter-22, Brown-12, Clark-12, Johnson-11, Thompson-10, Long-7, Moore-7, and Speer-7. The last to receive a diploma from Le Claire High School was Judy Walsh (alphabetically).

In the fall of 1960, the high school students attended the Pleasant Valley High School.

Le Claire High School
Scott County, IA

#46

Lewis High School

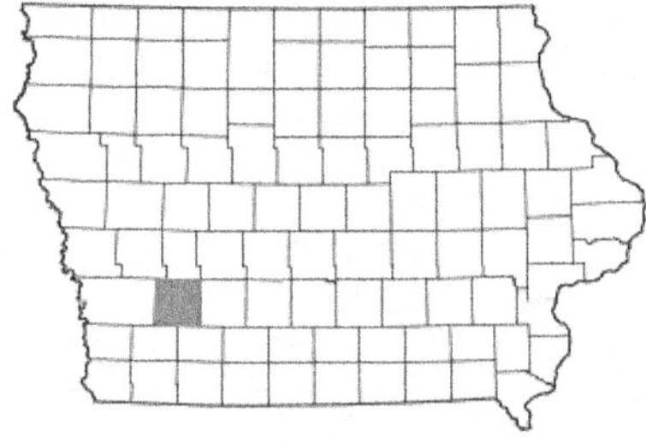

Mascot: Cardinals
Colors: Red and White
Closed: 1960
Location: West Central Cass County

Early History—In 1846, more than twenty Mormon families began their trek west and settled along the Nishnabotna River and along Indian Creek west of present day Lewis at Indiantown. They built cabins and dugouts and stayed in the area for five to six years. The last families left Cass County in 1852.

In 1851, the land known as Cass County received its name after Lewis Cass, a United States senator from Michigan. That year a settler, Jerimiah Bradshaw established a store a short distance from the old Indian village. Indiantown grew and the first school was held with six pupils. Mr. Hazen was the school master.

Lewis was established in 1853, approximately one mile east of Indiantown on the east side of the Nishnabotna River. It was at the crossroads of two stage lines. Lewis was named the county seat on March 1, 1853. The court house was built on the south side of present-day Pioneer Park. The town was a stock trading center. Cattle and hogs were driven to Iowa City (200 miles east across rivers and streams) and shipped to Chicago by rail from there. In 1879, a branch of the Rock Island was built to Lewis from Atlantic.

Lewis was on a direct route from the south to Canada that followed a much-used cattle trail. With the ferry just below the mill dam on the Nishnabotna, it became quite famous during the days of the underground railroad. Reverend George Hitchcock of the Congregational Church was among the friends of the slaves. Abolitionist John Brown arrived in Lewis in 1857. He may have been in Lewis several more times. When the Civil War became a reality, a surprisingly long list from Lewis answered the muster call. It is unknown if any of the men who accompanied John Brown on the raid of Harper's Ferry in 1859 were from Lewis. Men from nearby Tabor were part of the raiding party.

Early Schools—In 1855, the first school opened in a building west of the court house. The next school was in the court house. In 1859, a one-room brick building was constructed. This building was soon too small and primary pupils were transferred to a small blue frame house.

In 1869, the district bonded for $10,000 to pay for a new building. This two-story brick building was completed for $9,200 and stood until 1917. The high school had its first graduation class in 1892. The graduating class of 1894 organized the Alumni Association which still meets to this day (2020).

The beautiful two-story consolidated grade and high school was built in 1917 for $72,246.

Lewis Standard—Interesting stories were reported in the *Lewis Standard* newspaper:

1907 OBITUARY: The honorable Oliver Mills was one of the prominent pioneer residents of Cass County. He brought the first pedigreed shorthorn cattle to the county. He engaged with John Brown in the Underground Railway—Lewis at the time was the county seat and an important station. Mr. Mills kept the station and John Brown with other abolitionist were prominent in assisting refugees to get out of the country.

1909 ADVERTISEMENTS:

- Very latest in hipless Corset—Woodward and Elston
- All bonnets go on sale for 10c. Straw hats 15c. Okell and Weaver
- Chautauqua in Atlantic—order your tent at once and be among the campers.

Notable Graduates—Roderick Kunze ('43) was a flight officer and navigator in the Army Air Corps in World War II. He was assigned to the squadron which included the Enola Gay which flew the nuclear bomb to Hiroshima. Shortly before he was to leave, he was reassigned to a radar navigation school.

Randall Breckerbaumer ('56) returned to Lewis after service in the Army. He joined Clarence Hancock in the insurance business for several years. He became an outstanding insurance businessman in Atlantic. Accompanied by his beautiful wife, Sharon Cassidy Breckerbaumer ('57), he sang for over 1,000 weddings and funerals.

Roy Marshall ('58) attended Iowa State University. After a hitch in the Army, he worked for more than thirty years for the Iowa Department of Public Safety. He graduated from the Iowa Law Enforcement Academy, the FBI National Academy, and the Hazardous Devices Technicians Certification Program. He was appointed by Governor Branstad as the State Fire Marshal. He was a founding member and officer of the Iowa Chapter of the International Association of Arson Investigators and served on board of the National Association of State Fire Marshals.

Dorsey Lee Anderson Dinkla ('54) was a pretty, rugged, and hustling member of the Red Heads basketball team. At six-feet-tall, she played on a team that beat 134 consecutive men's teams from 1953-54. From 1936, the Red Heads played before 4,500,000 spectators.

Notable Teachers—Helen DeLean ('19) returned to teach at her high school alma mater. She taught nearly every subject. Randall Breckerbaumer ('56) remembered, "She was a legend. She wore a big, blue oblong ring that she would use to hit students as she walked down the aisle. The first day of school one year she knocked a kid out of his seat. She never had any problems with discipline." Robert Jobe ('55) added, "I learned more from Miss DeLean than any teacher I ever had." Roy Marshall ('58) stated, "She was a big woman and wore her hair tied back in a bun. It was fear when you saw her coming." Lila Mundorf Kunze ('44) related, "She was here forever. She always seemed to like the boys better."

Ruth Slocum was the wife of Superintendent Darrell Slocum. Emily Blakely Jobe ('59) remembered, "Mrs. Slocum was a remarkable teacher. She was extremely attractive and was able to understand young people. She would announce, 'okay now get your newspapers out and bring me your current events.'" Emily continued, "Mr. Slocum was a great leader. He was involved in all the sports and activities. He even organized ping pong intramurals and made the school environment special. He had a habit of jingling his change in his pockets as he came down the hall. It was our warning to straighten up before he reached the study hall. 'Here comes Slocum' was the warning signal."

School District Policy—The following 1915 Rules for Teachers were expected by the School Board:

1. You will not marry during the year of your contract.
2. You are not to keep company with men.
3. You must be home between the hours of 8 PM and 6 AM unless attending a school function.
4. You may not loiter downtown in ice cream stores.
5. You may not travel beyond the city limits unless you have the permission of the Chairman of the Board.
6. Your dresses must not be any shorter than two inches above the ankle.
7. You may not ride in a carriage or automobile with any man unless he is your father or brother.
8. You may not smoke cigarettes.
9. You may not wear bright colors.
10. You may under no circumstances dye your hair.

11. You must wear at least two petticoats.
12. To keep the school room neat and clean you must: sweep the floor at least once daily, scrub the floor at least once an week with hot, soapy water, clean the blackboards at least once a day, and start the fire at 7 AM so the room with be warm by 8 AM.

Sports—Football was discontinued following a player breaking a limb in 1947.

The biggest sports rival was Griswold. "You aren't just kidding," remarked Lila Mundorf Kunze ('44) at the age of 94 (2020).

Pranks—A small gag gift given to a teacher by Norman Fulton ('44) and Don McCaskey ('44) landed the boys in the superintendent's office. With expulsion on the line, the student body decided to have a strike. The plan was to stay seated after the morning assembly and not stand to go to classes. "So, when the bells rang, the students just stayed in their seats. I feel badly that I did not stick it out all day like some of the other braver kids. The strike must have had some small results, because both boys remained in school the next day," smiled Lila Mundorf Kunze ('44).

Killed in Action—Three men from Lewis lost their lives in World War II.

Bernard Kaiser ('37)
Kenneth Lawton ('38)
Harry Potter ('42)

Mother's Day 1960—The beginning of the end for Lewis High School started with an early morning fire on Mother's Day 1960. An account of that day was written by Roy Marshall ('58) in 1993 after this tragic fire that changed Lewis forever:

> Thirty-five years have passed since I graduated from high school. Last spring, with a few classmates and others during the Memorial Day/Alumni banquet weekend, there were the usual discussions about the fire and what we remembered of the Mother's Day in 1960.
>
> Someone recalled that Dwight Eisenhower was in the White House. The Cold War had school children practicing 'Duck and Cover' drills to insure a proper reaction in the event of nuclear attack. There were fallout shelters on main streets everywhere, each equipped with battery-operated radio, food and water, with the route marked by signs bearing the familiar FCDA (Federal Civil Defense Administration) symbol. A concern that shelters might be needed increased when, on May 1, Francis Gary Powers and his U-2 spy plane were shot down over Russia.

Several military 'advisors' went to Vietnam in 1960. Dimmer switches were still on the floorboard (of cars). "Cathy's Clown" was a hit. That spring, Marty Robbins went to #1 with "El Paso" and Fats Domino was "Walkin' to New Orleans."

A freshman at Iowa State, I was home to see a girl and pay respects to mom.

Early Sunday morning I joined a crowd to watch the school burn. I did so from a vantage point of deep left field, a place where I once chased a baseball that was hit as far as any I'd seen. Delmar Martins ('57) did it. Delmar, a burly farm boy and a rank pull hitter, tried his best during batting practice to hit the ball through a second-floor assembly room window. He succeeded from time to time-a truly majestic and unforgettable sight.

The flight of a long fly ball and the musical tinkle of breaking glass left a deeper impression on me than did the burning of the school three years later. This was because I was nineteen years old and had only the slightest concept of what was taking place.

I had a vague awareness that school reorganization was an issue, that some were for and some against, that rumors had the fire connected—although I didn't know how—and that it had been set. None of this mattered much to me. I was struggling with college-level calculus, my love life was not good, and my draft number was coming up . . . Despite doing a hitch in the Army and working for more than thirty years for the Iowa Department of Public Safety I knew next to nothing about a fire I'd witnessed, and one that had a profound effect on my home town.

Marshal ('58) went on to research the records, the circumstances of the school board, interviewing the fire marshal, and the events on the weekend leading up to the early morning blaze. He agreed with the conclusion that the fire may have started in the wiring above the kitchen area and that arson was not the cause.

Closing—With the burning of the school building, Lewis High School came to an end. In the fall of 1960, the students were split between two school districts. Those living east of town went to Atlantic. Those living west of town were bused to Griswold. The last event for Lewis High School was graduation in 1960 with ten seniors. In the 79 years from 1892 to 1960 there were 872 graduates from the school. The most numerous surnames were: Kunze-20, Smith-18, Marshall-13, Jahnke-12, Albright-11, Woodward-10, Baker-9, Blakely-9, Breckerbaumer-9, and Johnson-9. The last to receive a diploma from

Lewis High School was Charlotte Schnomier (alphabetically).

Lewis High School
Cass County, IA

#47

Livermore High School

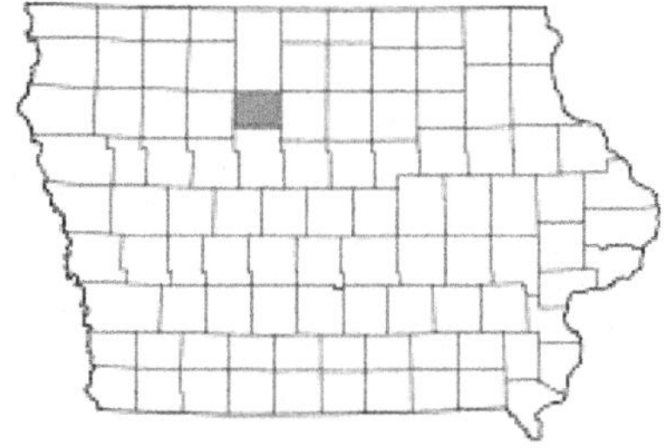

Mascot: Bulldogs
Colors: Purple and Gold
Closed: 1956
Location: Northern Humboldt County

Early History—Humboldt Township was founded in 1857 at the point where three waterways converged. They are the East Branch of the Des Moines River, Bloody Run, and Lotts Creek (named after the first settler).

The town of Livermore was established in 1879 at the junction of the Minneapolis-St. Louis Railroad and the Burlington, Cedar Rapids, and Northern Railroad along the banks of the East Des Moines River.

Livermore had the distinction of having the first and only liquor store in Humboldt County. It was occasionally referred to as "Liquormore" by locals and out of town people.

First Schools—A two-story school was built in 1882 for $2,000. It educated elementary students and eventually added a high school course on the second floor. This building was used for the next 32 years. On June 19, 1913, a vote to build a new school passed 161-19. A second vote held the following spring passed a bond of $6,000 for the new school. Construction started September 7, 1914, and in just five months, the new school was dedicated on February 11, 1915.

The first graduating class was in 1893. It is not known if the first graduating classes were two, three, or four-year courses.

A vote on August 5, 1937 to bond for a new gymnasium for $11,996 was proposed. The gymnasium was to be as large as Renwick's which was the envy of neighboring schools. The bond vote passed 67-17.

Sports—The Little Nine Tournament was organized in 1917 with Livermore, Bode, Humboldt, Dows, Goldfield, West Bend, Clarion, Renwick, and Lu Verne as member schools. This annual boys basketball tournament was held every February for the next 25 years. Dows dropped out in 1930. Clarion dropped out in 1940 and Corwith was added. Humboldt dropped out in 1944 and Vernon was added. The boys also played in the Boone Valley Conference.

Orlean J. "Lefty" Cayou was hired as a teacher and coach in 1928. He taught manual arts, algebra, and geometry. He stepped down in 1935 to own and operate K.O. Hardware on Main Street in Livermore. The next coach was released by the school the first week of school on September 2, 1937 for a new job at Waterloo West. Lefty agreed to come back to coach for a temporary assignment until another coach could be found. This temporary job lasted for the next 18 years. The boys basketball teams brought excitement to Livermore. They advanced to the state tournament in 1932, 1942, 1946, and 1948. The 1932 team challenged the big Iowa City High School and beat them but lost in the semifinals to Central High from Sioux City. Dennis Behounek ('42), at 95 years old (2019), remembered, "We went down to Iowa City for the state tournament. It was such a huge court and we got tripped up in the first round. We were the only class B team in the tournament." The 1946 team went undefeated at 22-0 until losing to Iowa City in the first game at state. The 1947 team won 27 straight and the 1949 team won 26 straight games.

Coach Cayou's teams won many honors include-ing 87% of their games over his tenure. Some of these honors were:

- 8 Boone Valley Conference titles
- 10 Humboldt County Championships
- 12 Little Nine Tournament Championships
- 10 Sectional Trophies

Winning ways began with Coach Cayou when he won the heart of Ethyl Welter ('29) who was a senior during his first year at Livermore. They sold the hardware business and retired to Tucson in 1955.

Coach Lefty Cayou was inducted into the Iowa Coach's Hall of Fame in 1971. His record for three sports (baseball, basketball, and football), all at Livermore, was 568 wins and 109 losses in 27 years.

Senior Trip—The 1937 class of 16 "dignified seniors" along with their principal, Mr. Solar and his wife journeyed to Olson Park in Ft. Dodge for a class picnic.

Notable Graduates—Paul McKibban ('54) played on the offensive and defensive lines and reminisces, "My junior year we played Ventura at their field. They had all white uniforms. When we saw them doing warmups they looked huge and we thought there was no way we could beat them. Size must not have been everything as we thumped them 61-0." The 1953 team went on to become the fifth rated team in the State of Iowa. The last game of that year found Livermore beating Thompson 46-0.

Kenneth Underberg ('45) shared, "I was consi-dered big at six foot tall. We played man to man in basketball which gave us the distinction of having a very stingy defense. Holding the other team down from scoring led us to win many games." Kenneth winked as he continued, "I went into the Navy weeks after graduation in 1945, even though the war was over in Europe. I was sent to Okinawa as part of the occupying force. I must have done such a good job because they asked me to come back for the Korean War for active duty in Korea."

Killed in Action—Harold Smith ('42) was killed in World War II.

Large Families—Large families were common in the Livermore area. The Fox family had 11 children and nine graduated from Livermore High School. Each of the older siblings helped the younger ones further their education after high school. They were: Donald ('23), Curtis ('26), Emma ('27), Elvin ('29), Victor ('33), John ('35), Mary ('37), Edith ('39), and Albert ('43). Among the Fox graduates were three college professors, two nurses, a career Naval, and conservation technician.

The Raymond and Pauline Wilson Family had the distinction of having ten daughters. They lived a short distance from Livermore. The first six graduated from Livermore before the high school closed: Norma Wilson Barret ('48), Marilyn Wilson Hansen ('50), Shirley Wilson Cook ('51), Phyllis Wilson Burk ('52), Lois Wilson Moore ('54) and Sue Wilson Berthay ('55). The younger four graduated from Twin Rivers High School (the consolidated Livermore-Bode High School to the west): Sheryl Wilson Fox ('58), Carol Wilson Cox ('59), Linda Wilson Mlandy ('61), and Cynthia Wilson Borodkin ('69). Seven of the girls worked professionally for the FBI.

Band and Music—Music was first offered in 1912. An announcement in the Livermore newspaper on August 24, 1914 reported:

> The progressive course of music which is an entirely new idea regarding the teaching of music is the course which will be used . . . in addition to regular courses home economics is offered to all girls. Miss Ina Salyers will teach music and home economics.

The band was started in 1941 with 27 students in the first band. Band became a very active extra-curricular activity. All sports and activities met during school hours. The marching band performed at the Mason City Music Festival each year. Janine Baker Berte ('56) and Geraldine Haack Smith ('56) were both twirlers in the marching band.

The band had a distinction of having a Band Queen from 1949-56. They were elected by the band members. These queens of Music and the Band were:

1949 Gertrude Larson ('50)
1950 Kay Cayou Sawyer ('52)
1951 Dolores Stiltz Beardsley ('52)
1952 Beverly Blumer Wilcox ('53)
1953 Jean Larson
1954 Sue Wilson Berthay ('55)
1955 Linda Butler Bahr ('55)
1956 Pat Hefty Schultz ('56)

Notable Teachers—The *Livermore Star* headline on August 25, 1949 reported:

> **Livermore School to Open Monday**
> 75 High School students and 168 elementary students will start the school year. The teachers are Superintendent Lowell Cockrill—science, history, and social sciences; Orlean Joseph Cayou—Coach, math and shop; Bob Shaw—music, science, and social sciences; Henrietta Squires—English . . . new lunch room will open with seating of 200 . . . it is state approved and state planned . . . The Federal Government will furnish much of the equipment.

Coach Orlean Cayou was notorious for entering the room each class period and kicking the edge of the leg on the first desk in the room. No one ever knew why but it was noted by all the students. With the help of another teacher, Maurice Olson, a plan was devised to remove the screws and support bolts on this desk. When Mr. Cayou arrived at class that day and kicked the first desk, a crashing calamity ensued, and the desk collapsed. This was the last time a desk was kicked during his tenure at Livermore.

Pranks—When the south sun shone brightly into the second floor of the school, a magnifying glass came out of the pocket of Paul McKibban ('54). He accidently focused this sunlight onto a page of a book and in no time at all the little scientist had smoke curling up from his desk. Paul confessed, "I had to go to Mr. Cockrill's office only once for a disciplinary matter that I can't tell to this day (2019). The magnifying trick just got a few laughs and some quick blowing to extinguish the combustion."

Closing—The high school was closed after graduation in May 1956. In the fall the remaining students were bused to Bode to form the new Consolidated Twin Rivers High School. Bode was the most bitter rival of Livermore for many years. As is often the result, the students quickly assimilated, but the parents came around to the unification more gradually.

There were 622 graduates from Livermore High School in the 64 years from 1893-1956. The largest classes were 32 seniors in 1938 and 1953. The most numerous surnames of the graduates were: Wilson-18, Davis-15, Larson-12, Fox-10, Haack-8, Smith-8, Baker-7, Hewitt-7, McKenna-7, and Nelson-7.

Livermore High School
Humbolt County, IA

#48

Lohrville High School

Mascot: Blackhawks/Hawkettes
Colors: Red and Black
Closed: 1988
Location: South Central Calhoun County

Early History—Lohrville was named after Jacob Lohr. The Western Plat Company purchased land from his farm for the purpose of selling lots. The railroad was coming through the area in 1881. Lohrville became a railroad town with three railroads crossing here and each had their own depot. They were the Toledo and Northern Railroad (later became the Chicago Northwestern), the Des Moines and Northwestern (later the Chicago, Milwaukee, and St. Paul), and the Chicago Great Western. A watchtower east of town controlled the rail traffic. Lohrville and Rockwell City were the leading rail centers in Calhoun County.

Lohrville and the settlement of Union Township was a melting pot beginning with Civil War military veterans who took advantage of government land available for purchase. Farm families started arriving in 1871. They came from Germany, Ireland, Switzerland, Quebec, and many states east of Iowa. The New England states of Vermont and New York were also represented. Though not any separate ethnic areas were settled, the area south of town found many Irish and German catholic families. The Irish were heavily represented by the surnames of McClure, McDonald, McCrea, McDermott, McKreigh, McCloud, McGee, McGrath, McCullough, McGowan, McCreedy, McGraile and McCormick as listed among the surnames of the graduates from Lohrville High School.

Early Schools—Rural one-room country schools were scattered throughout Union Township. Schools called Union 1, 2, 3, 4, and 5 were built from 1885-1889. The first public school in Lohrville met on the second floor of Safley Hall in 1882. A frame school was built in 1883 and a new brick building was constructed in 1890-91. This school was also used for the eleven-grade high school. The twelfth grade was added in 1906. A new brick building was constructed in 1914 for the high school and new grade school.

Following the consolidation of the township one-room schools, transportation was needed to bring the students into Lohrville. A 1920 photo depicts five new Reo buses with lettering on the side, "Lohrville Consolidated Schools." Another horse-drawn bus was driven by a student Ramer Ressler ('23).

Notable Town Events

From the *Lohrville Enterprise* newspaper:

> Lohrville celebrated July 4, 1890, and a great crowd of people came to Lohrville from every direction to witness and participate in the celebration. It is estimated that between 2000 and 3000 were in attendance and a more pleasant and orderly celebration the writer has never witnessed.
>
> October 8, 1908 Governor A.B. Cummings spoke in town trying to show why William Jennings Bryan "was an unsafe man to elect to the presidency and why William Taft should be elected."
>
> July 1911 William Jennings Bryan gave an address in Lohrville
>
> On September 9, 1937, The Postmaster General of the United States, James Farley stopped in Lohrville during a noon hour on the Chicago Great Western to greet and meet people from the community.
>
> Governor George Wilson was the guest speaker at a meeting in Lohrville in the early 1940s.

Pulitzer Prize Winner—Pulitzer prize winner Clark Mollenhoff, in the forward of the 1991 *Lohrville Centennial Book,* wrote:

> Lohrville in the 1920s and 1930s was a special place . . . it was the center of the universe for my childhood memories through grade school and the first years of high school . . . the formative years . . . touched by men and women who had come to Iowa at the juncture of three railroads. We saw the forerunners of the air age when the open cockpit biplanes barn-stormed from a makeshift landing field in Winkelman's south pasture . . . went from muddy streets with horse drawn buggies and wagons to the paved streets of the automobile age. We were so proud of our new paved streets while Gowrie, Farnhamville, and Lake City had only gravel or mud . . . the twenties with the turbulent excesses of fast cars, bootleg liquor and slot machines . . . followed by the Great Depression of the Thirties and humbling and enlightening experiences of the poverty that touched almost everyone in that small prairie town.

Bus Drivers—Harold Brown was not only a bus driver, but also the secretary of the school board, the school business manager, the town's fire chief, pilot, worked at the Brown Funeral Home, and ran an appliance and furniture store. Tim Blair ('69) maintained, "He ran the school." Lois Earwood Irwin ('71) remembered, "He loved the school. He was always dressed up and was here for over forty years."

Janitor—There is a plaque commemorating Earl Luhman for his dedication and service to the Lohrville schools. Lois Earwood Irwin ('71) said, "He was right above the principal. He was so protective of everything." Lynne Kail Gentry ('65) remembered, "I stayed all night at Jill Luhman Brozeks's ('65) house and got to stay after school and clean erasers-what an honor!"

Sports—The biggest school rivals in sports were Cedar Valley, Battle Creek, and Paton-Churdan. The sports conference in the 1950s was the Bo-Coon Conference (Boyer and Racoon Rivers). The other schools in the conference were Schaller, Lakeview-Auburn, Battle Creek, Wall Lake, Newell, Galva, Crestland (Early), Lytton, and Cedar Valley (after 1954 Farnhamville-Rinard-Somers).

Girls basketball was discontinued at one time but restarted in 1956. In the 1960s summer girls softball and boys baseball became school sports.

The great football team in 1968 had an undefeated season. The 1969 team lost just one game against Galva. Tim Blair ('69) told, "I had my foot broken in that game when one of the big heavy Hendrick boys fell on my foot." Tim Blair was a star athlete on those teams. He also was an outstanding track athlete and participated at the state track meet in the shot put and the dashes. Blair's abilities in both running and field events were unique in high school athletes.

Drivers Education—Drivers education was started in 1957. "The first car provided by the local dealer was a 1957 Chevy. It was a classic car model and we thought it was quite the deal to have as our drivers ed car," recalled John Anderson ('60). Mr. Fisher was the first instructor and was amazed how many kids had already been driving. Darlene Johnson Latoris ('60) was one who had never driven. Darlene remembered, "I was so nervous and worried. Of course, I still have visions of the time I was learning to parallel park. The car ended up crosswise in front of the Catholic church. I still think of that experience every time that I try to parallel park to this day."

The next instructor was the football coach and history teacher, Bill Shuey. Lynn Kail Gentry ('65) chuckled when she told of driving with student driver, Jonalyn Kunce ('65). "She tried to take a corner at 30 miles an hour. Mr. Shuey sat on the brakes and we came to squealing stop."

Band—Roger Chrysler was the band instructor in the 1960s. He drove a little Volkswagen Karmann Giha two seat convertible. He could barely be seen when he was in the car because it sat so low to the road. He took the marching band to the Dayton Rodeo and Carroll Band Days. They played in the park at Lohrville in the summers. Lynn Kail Gentry ('65) shared, "I was in grade school and still had braces on my teeth. Mr. Chrysler decided that I needed to play the tuba. I think it was not so much for my musical talent, but because Russell Stanburg ('61) graduated, he needed a tuba recruit for the next year."

Notable Teachers—Frank Walter taught math, algebra, analytical geometry, and trigonometry in the 1960s. Carol Johnson ('69) was so inspired by his leadership and skills in education that she became a math teacher and taught for over 35 years in the Davenport schools.

R.W. Fewson was the principal in the 1960s and taught analytical geometry classes. Jon Johnson ('66) recalled, "Mr. Fewson was a remarkable administrator. He could put the fear of God in the bad kids and inspire the good kids. I always admired his leadership and mentoring as a classroom teacher and friend."

Pranks—Two renowned imps, Stan McClure ('64) and Vernon 'Butch' Stephenson ('65), were credited for crawling up the fire escape and releasing eight pigeons into the school on a weekend night. They borrowed the innocent birds from the pens of homing pigeons belonging to Enoch Rasmussen the Vo-Ag teacher, across the street from the school. There was quite a mess on Monday morning and at least one dictionary was soiled from the frantic bird droppings.

History class was a scene of more mischief. There was a time when the sound of dropping BBs onto the floor would ping and resonate through the class period lectures. Mr. Howard Ortheyer, while trying to stop the interruptions, was in mid-sentence attempting to say, "If I hear one more BB drop, I am going to . . ." when three more BB's went bing-bing-bing from the back of the room. John Anderson ('60) laughed, "He was so mad that he flipped the top of Susan Seeck's ('60) desk and the wads of sunflower seeds that she had been innocently eating went flying all over the room. He even had to laugh at the scene of the calamity."

A generation later, John Anderson's ('60) son was involved in another interesting event. Bob Anderson ('85) brought a bucket of hog manure into the school on a weekend and set it under a teacher's desk. On Monday morning, Superintendent Roger Baskerville called the boys together and threatened them until Bob confessed. The word spread around town of the mischief and Bob Anderson's penalty for bringing such a stink to school. Hearing of this at Red's Café, where she worked, Mrs. Toms immediately nabbed her son, Gary Toms ('85). She cajoled him to confess because the boys were always together. She marched Gary to school to Mr. Baskerville's office, and he admitted to the foul bucket escapade, as well.

Notable Graduates—Bill Winkelman ('50) served 12 years in the Iowa House of Representatives and eight years in the Senate. With his father, they had the largest pony herd in the country in the early 1950s. They initiated the chariot races at the Iowa State Fair and entertained the crowds with their four pony chariot races. Bill Sr. had four white Shetland stallions and Bill Jr. drove four black Shetland stallions. Pictures of them in their authentic, Roman-style dress, racing around the arena, depict a special time at the Iowa State Fair.

Closing—The high school closed in May of 1988. The next year the students were bused to Lake City. In the 90 years from 1899 through 1988, a total of 1,799 graduated from Lohrville High School. The largest class was 38 seniors in 1940. The most common surnames of the graduates were: Johnson-23, Brown-21, Cavanaugh-19, Lohr-19, Morris-18, Anderson-17, Miller-17, Kavanaugh-17, Christensen-15, Winkelman-14, and McClure-13. The last to receive a diploma from Lohrville High School was Diane Vogel (alphabetically).

Lohrville High School
Calhoun County, IA

#49

Lorimor High School

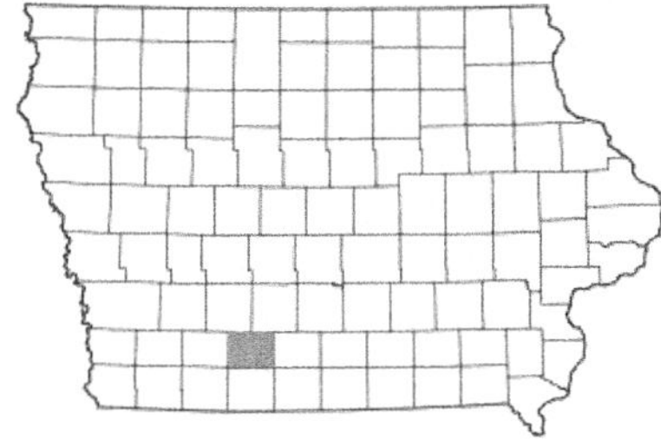

Mascot: Indians
Colors: Black and Gold
Closed: 1959
Location: Union County

Early History—New Hope Township is in the northeast corner of Union County and is on the great divide that drains east to the Mississippi, and west to the Missouri River. The earliest settlers were Mormons who left Nauvoo, Illinois and headed west in 1847 and 1848. They built cabins along the east branch of the Grand River. Some Mormons stayed in this township for a few years. They began heading west for Utah in 1850. By 1852, most had sold or abandoned their cabins. In 1856, four men; J.S. Lorimor, William and Henry Groesbeck, and Henry Jeter were instrumental in organizing and naming the township. Local legend maintains when they saw the land, they declared, "This is it! This is our New Hope."

J. S. Lorimor arrived and settled in Union Township in 1854. He purchased 1,200 acres from the government and began to break sod and develop a new farm. He was from Ohio where he completed two years of schooling at Muskingum College. For several years after his arrival, he taught school through the winter months. He was one of the pioneers in public education of Union County. He did much to promote the early intellectual advancement of the community.

In 1886, news came that the Chicago, St. Paul, and Kansas Railroad was building a railroad through the township. J.S. Lorimor offered a right-of-way through his land. It was accepted. In 1887, Lorimor materialized as a boom town and the first train passed over the newly laid tracks that same year. The railroad had many names. It was first known as the Hook and Eye. Later names were the Cornbelt, Chicago Great Western, and finally Chicago Northwestern.

The next year, in 1887, Josiah Lorimor laid out the town of Lorimor and gave the railroad the right-of-way and 24 acres of land. He subdivided the town plat into 16 blocks and lot sales began in May of the year.

Early Schools—The schools in Lorimor had many highlights.

- The first school was held in the back room of a store building.
- In 1890, a new frame schoolhouse was built with two rooms for the grades on the first floor. The second floor had the high school assembly and classrooms.
- 1912, a new brick building of mat-faced brick with concrete floors surfaced with wood was constructed. It was a 50′ x 80′, built for $19,000.
- The first graduation class from the new school was 11 students in 1915.
- There were 50 students in high school. Boys and girls basketball was played.
- In 1926, a petition to the Board of Education was to call a special meeting for the purpose of voting on the proposition of erecting an addition to the present building.
- Superintendent A.M. Weyrouch was killed in a car-train accident in Ames in 1929.
- Senior Normal Training for girls had practice-teaching in rural schools in New Hope Township in 1929.
- In 1940 *The Echo* was the first yearbook to be published.
- The boys basketball team of 1941 went to the state tournament
- The high school closed as Lorimor High School in 1959. The consolidated school name became East Union with Thayer students coming to attend school in the former Lorimor building. The towns in this new East Union School District were Afton, Shannon City, Thayer, Arispe, and Lorimor.
- In 1965, all students attended the new high school built at Afton called East Union High School.

Band—The marching band, under the direction of Mr. Graham, was started as school opened in the fall of 1939. The band placed first in their division in the state marching contest in Red Oak. As a result, Lorimor High represented Iowa in the Regional Contest in Kansas City on May 9, 1940. They also went to Minneapolis in 1941 and Chicago in 1958.

Hot Lunch—The school hot lunch was started in the early 1940s.

A January report in the 1950s tallied the 21 school days that month:

- 4,322 lunches served at the high school (included grades K-8)

- average of 216 students and adults
- 4,620 bottles of milk
- 202 loaves of bread plus cornbread
- 140 round buns
- 400 biscuits
- 1,054 baked rolls

Normal Training—In 1915, the Iowa legislature established the normal training program for Iowa teacher education. Its purpose was to give training within the high school for students (primarily girls) to allow them to teach in the country schools at that time. To maintain a normal training course in a high school, the local school had to meet certain qualifications. Among these qualifications were (a) the enrollment of a least ten in the junior and senior classes taking this course, (b) a teacher who is interested in rural teaching and who meets certain requirements to supervise this work, (c) teachers in grades who are able to meet certain requirements, and (d) have a professional library and texts used in the rural schools.

The Lorimor School Board approved starting the Normal training course. It allowed for students to get their start in teaching. An additional expense for a teacher to provide a classroom and the costs was incurred. This educational opportunity was a start into teaching for many as they would get a certificate. Many then received a two-year college degree to become teachers.

Girl Reserves—In 1939, a Girl Reserves unit was organized at the high school. They met at the schoolhouse after school hours. Each year a teacher was chosen to be the sponsor and attended all the meetings.

The Girl Reserves Code: I will try to be—
Gracious in manner
Impartial in judgement
Ready for service
Loyal to friends
Reaching toward the best
Eager for knowledge
Seeing the beautiful
Earnest in purpose
Reverent to God
Victorious over self
Ever dependable
Sincere at all times.

Community Events—The Lorimor "Little Worlds Fair" was held every year from 1919 until 1956. It was the grand county fair and celebration of the year for 4-H clubs and all the agricultural and domestic clubs and organizations. It was discontinued when the county fair was moved to the Afton Fair grounds.

In 1971, a Lorimor girl, Caren Corsbie McNaught, won first place in the state in the area of consumer education. She then competed in Chicago at an international competition with her 4-H work and won an award of $700.

Notable Teachers—A long time teacher at Lorimor was Daisy Del King. Wayne Tucker ('63) recalled, "She just had a way of reaching each student. She told our class that this class was the best she had ever had. It was only later that I heard that she told every class the same thing."

Pranks—The word "Brewery" was spray painted on the outside brick of the high school building. The culprits were not apprehended at the time. Decades later, in a "tell all session," Paul Tucker ('61) and Jay Allender ('61) were named and credited for this misdeed, but the statute of limitations had long run out.

The freshman shop class got the honor of using a wire brush to clear up the graffiti. Bob Tuttle ('60) stood up in assembly to proclaim his innocence in announcing, "It can't be me 'cause I don't even know how to spell the word "brewery."

Wayne Tucker ('63) left school one day an hour early for a new job. As he arrived at school the next morning, he was met by Principal Clair Henderson. Wayne said, "I had to go back with my mother to get back in school. Mr. Henderson decided that I should give him the keys each morning when I arrived at school. As far as I know, those keys are still hanging in his office because I could start that old '49 Ford with a screwdriver."

Senior Trips—John Tucker ('57) shared, "Our class in 1957 took our senior trip to the Ozarks. I was driving Butch Macumber's ('57) car when the rear end of his '56 Mercury went out somewhere in Missouri. The rest of the caravan went on without us. We went to a junk yard and found a new rear end, put it in and maybe sped a little and caught up with the other cars."

Lee Decker ('63) recalled, "The class of 1963 went to Kansas City by bus. We stayed at the Muehlebach Hotel. We ate at the Golden Buffet which was owned by Alvin Meyers from Winterset. All I remember is that it wasn't in the best part of town."

Bus Driver—Owen Dudney drove the school bus for 25 years. Wayne Tucker ('63) related, "He started driving the very first day when I was starting my first day of kindergarten. Christmas was always special because he gave each of us a ten-cent candy bar. He and his wife had no kids, so each of us were his kids and family. Owen got in trouble with the school one time when he let an older kid off the bus for misbehaving and made him walk to school. The next time this happened to the same kid, he made him get off the bus and had him walk in front of the bus to school."

Closing—The school closed in May 1959. For the next six years, the school was called East Union. Classes were held in the former Lorimor High School building. A total of 827 graduated from Lorimor High School in the 65 years from 1895-1959. The largest class was 30 seniors in 1937. The most numerous surnames of the graduates were: Thompson-16, Edwards-14, Hammans-13, Grandfield-12, Berry-10, Davis-9, and Emerson-9. The last to receive a diploma from Lorimor High School was Blanche Tuttle (alphabetically). An additional 160 graduated from East Union at Lorimor from 1960-1965.

Lorimor High School
Union County, IA

#50

Lost Nation High School

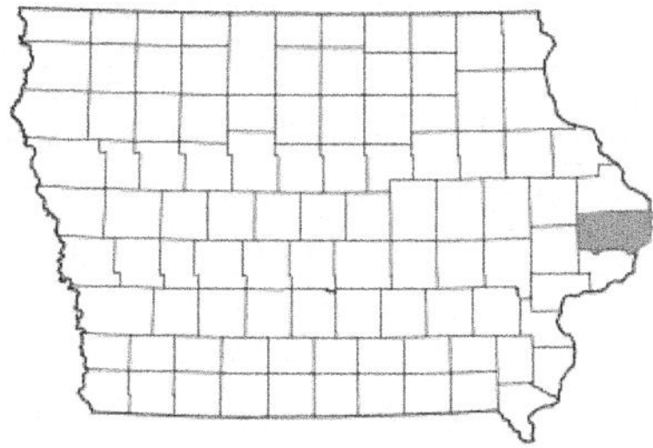

Mascot: Bobcats
Colors: Purple and Gold
Closed: 1988
Location: Northwest Clinton County

Early History—Lost Nation is a quaint name for a town, and there is no other post office with this name in the United States. The question, "How did it come by its name?" has had many answers through the years. Some of those conjectures are:

- A German named Balm was looking for relatives near this point. The land all about him was unbroken prairie and the grass was man and horse high. When asked where he was going, he said he was looking for the "lost nation."

- The Longs came to the area in 1850s and platted the town. They told the story that years before many people had settled in this country, two men were traveling on foot. They lost their way and saw a light and went to the house of Abrum Balm. When they were ready to leave, Mr. Balm remarked that he certainly lived in a lost nation.
- Folks came to the area from the Nation River or a town of that name in Canada, looking for relatives. When they found them here, they said they had found the "lost nation."
- A later tale maintained that a relative of Carrie Nation was lost in this area.
- Another version is that H.V. Cook came into the locality to buy stock from Balm. He had searched for him one day and the part of the next before locating his cabin and thus called it "lost nation."
- A final version is that a hunting party was lost here, remained for some time in the area and named their camp "Lost Man's Camp."

Lost Nation is in Sharon Township, which was organized on April 5, 1852. The first permanent white settlers purchased land from the government in the late 1840s and 1850s at a cost of $1.25 an acre for good land and $1 an acre for swampy land. These settlers came from Canada, England, Ireland, Germany, and eastern states. The land which became Lost Nation was owned by John Culbertson. He sold it to Abrum Balm. After two more land sales, Jacob and Elizabeth Long platted the original town and began selling lots.

In September 1871, a strip of land was purchased by the Sabula, Dakota, and Adley Railroad for a right of way. The contract for the railroad from Delmar to Marion was let to A.K Davis in 1871, and work was pushed forward immediately. The railroad was built onto Oxford Junction in 1872.

Early Schools—On November 13, 1880, Lawsen Daniels deeded a plot of ground in Block 10 to the Lost Nation Independent School District. A two-room school building was erected, and it became the first graded school in Lost Nation.

Because of property constraints and growing numbers, a controversy arose about whether to continue to use the two-room school and part of the Dunkard church or build on a new location.

By September 1899, there were 100 pupils for the two-room school, and it was anticipated that another 25-50 students would be attending in the winter months. In April 1899, the school board met and adopted a resolution to borrow $6,000 to purchase land and build another school on a larger plot of land. A.H. Gish and his wife deeded the land to the Lost Nation Independent School district for this building. It became the site of the present school building (2020). The first graduating class from this high school was in 1903.

On September 1, 1914, bonds for $7,500 were sold for a new addition to establish an accredited 12-year high school. This building was opened in September 1915. That year, domestic science was added to the curriculum. Under the direction of Bernice Shick, the three girls in the class made their graduation dresses.

The Opera House on Main Street was used for basketball for the boys and girls. In 1937, 13 bonds of $1,000 each bearing 2½% interest were issued to build a new gymnasium.

In 1946, the school district consolidated with all or parts of 14 rural districts to become the Lost Nation Consolidated School District. A bus barn was constructed for the five buses that transported the rural children. Between 1950 and 1952, the Burr Oak and Excelsior districts consolidated with Lost Nation.

Music—*Lost Nation Press* reported on August 14, 1934, that the Lost Nation school concert band was organized in 1927 with Harley Booth as the director. By 1932, Superintendent R.J. Farris helped form a marching band. He agreed to drill the marching band if Mr. Booth would teach the music.

The next director of the band was Mr. O.H. Story. He had a military background. Under his direction the band featured marching while playing their instruments. This band became well known throughout the state and won 25 'firsts' in contests. National championships were earned in 1934 and 1939. The 1939 band was invited to New York to perform. Due to the costs of travel, the school had to decline the invitation.

Jean Machande Scott ('44) said, "I played the clarinet and still play it at my home, even today (2020). We had maroon and white pants and wore black shoes. We played at the Nationals in Minneapolis, many parades, Labor Day events, and other town celebrations." Nancy Dake Hertner ('62) exclaimed, "I played that same clarinet when I was in the band from grade school through high school." The band always had a piccolo which was owned by the school. "I played the piccolo because we could not afford an instrument, but I can't say I liked it very much," remembered Phyliss Carraher Schneden ('57).

In 1950, Bona Rutenbeck ('51) was chosen Miss Eastern Iowa band queen at the Eastern Iowa Band Festival at Cedar Rapids.

Lost Nation had several excellent piano teachers. Pamela Myatt Crawford ('68) shared, "There were only three contestants allowed from each school to enter the state piano contests. We often had contests at our own school just to finalize which three would move on to the state competition."

Sports—Football was not played at Lost Nation.

The biggest rival was Elwood (later to become Delwood) a town just five miles to the northeast.

Boys baseball was played in both fall and spring. A star pitcher, Jim McAndrew ('61), went to the major leagues and won a World Series ring with the "Marvelous Mets" in 1969.

The 1988 boys team made it to the state basketball tournament in the last year of the high school. Members of the team were Cary Greenwood ('88), Chad Snyder ('88), Gary Brady ('88), Monte Kann ('88), Mark Schmidt, Greg Rickels, Alan Brown, Chuck Brown, Brent Willmark, Shane Muhl, Toby Mullins, and Wayne Berner. They were coached by Bryce Smeins.

The girls basketball teams of 1953, 1960, and 1961 made it to the 16-team girls state tournament. The girls did not bring home the championship trophy. The team lost in the finals to Valley of Elgin in 1961 and earned the second-place trophy.

Town Newspaper—The *Lost Nation Press* reported highlights in the community.

April 1973 — The general public was invited to discuss a proposal to issue $275,000 in bonds to build a new gymnasium.

May 1973 — The school bond passed with 61% of the voters' approval.

March 1974 — The school board began reorganization talks.

October 1974 — The public was invited to an Open House to inspect the new gymnasium.

Notable Teachers—Ralph Holmes was a music instructor from after WWII until the 1960s. Pamela Myatt Crawford ('68) remembered, "Mr. Holmes established a dance orchestra that played for many groups and even other schools' proms." Wayne Dvorak continued that group as the jazz band during his tenure as band director from 1964-1970. He led the marching band to second place in the Eastern Iowa Band Festival.

Georgia Watt-Scott was a beautiful black teacher who came from Canton, Mississippi. She got the music job because the previous music teacher broke her contract in late summer to teach in Illinois. Though she was to teach only two years at Lost Nation, her social conscience would impact the students for their lifetimes. Pam Myatt Crawford ('68) shared,"Mrs. Watt-Scott was such a beautiful person and extraordinary vocalist. After a small groups piano clinic near Cedar Rapids, the group stopped to eat and had to sit in the back of the restaurant because of the color of her skin. At a contest in Clarence, an audience person sitting near the judges panel overheard a judge mumble that 'blacks should not be teaching our white children.' Mrs. Watt-Scott also sang in our Presbyterian church choir."

Senior Trips—Senior trips were started to Washington D.C in the 1950s. Phyliss Carraher Schneden ('57) remembered, "None of us had ever been to Washington and it opened our eyes to our country. We toured the Library of Congress, the Capital, and Smithsonian. What an education!" The 1968 seniors arrived in Washington just one month after the assassination of Martin Luther King. They felt the tension and saw the burned out neighborhoods just a few blocks from their nation's Capital.

Drivers Education—Ray Kennedy was the drivers education instructor during the early years it was offered at Lost Nation High School. He also taught Vo-Ag. All students were taught to parallel park out in front of the school. He placed cones in the street to back around. Connie Browne ('58) shared, "If you hit one of the cones, the student had to get out and run around the car three times before they were allowed another chance to parallel park the car. It always provided quite the entertainment for those in the science room looking out at the parking attempts and changing of the tires on the drivers ed car."

Pranks—A memorable cow was placed in the bell tower of the school one Halloween night. This deed was done by none other than the school superintendent's son, David Dake ('37).

Though not listed as a prank, the tubes used for the fire escape were always a scene for amusement by ornery boys. During fire drills, they had to race to be the first down the chute. The boys then had a front row view of the girls sliding down the tubes wearing their mandatory dresses.

Bus Drivers—David Dake ('37) drove the kindergarten bus and became a friend of every five-year-old that ever rode his bus. To this day, he is remembered as the kind farmer friend who one time stopped the bus so that a turtle could make its way across the road unharmed.

Yearbook—Using the Greek words for the cover to name the yearbook and using the L and N of the town name, the first editors named the yearbook *Lambda Nu*.

Curriculum—The term "special education" did not come into pedagogy for several decades after it was already in practice in Lost Nation. Laura Ann Myatt Schultz ('42) became wheelchair bound with polio in the fall of 1940. She had marched in the National Champion band in 1939. The school hooked up a special wireless radio so she could be taught her classes at home. She was named an honorary valedictorian in 1942.

In the 1960s, Lost Nation offered a curriculum that was substantial in subject depth for a Class C (now termed 1A) school. The offerings were two years of foreign languages, four years of science including both physics and chemistry, four years of math including trigonometry and analytical geometry, four years of English including British Literature, plus electives of psychology, commercial secretary courses, industrial arts, drivers ed, band, and vocal music. These were critical as the first round of recommended school reorganizations were pro-posed by state superintendent Paul Johnson. Pink slips were issued for deficient curriculum and lack of certified staff to many small Iowa high schools.

Along with this strong curriculum, in the mid-60s the high school Iowa Basic Skill scores were high in the state rankings. Lost Nation was in the top 1% statewide and the top ½% in the nation.

Notable Graduates – JoAnna McAndrew Lund ('62) was the author of over 40 cookbooks and promoted the Healthy Exchange. She hosted two National PBS Television series. She was a frequent guest on QVC, a national shopping network from Philadelphia. Her books sold over 2,000,000 copies.

Michael Seng ('60) became a corporate attorney. He was a talented pianist and performed extensively in college. He served on the US District court and was a professor at the John Marshal Law School where for 40 years he focused on discrimi-nation in housing. He was twice recognized by the Fulbright program with teaching posts in Nigeria and the Czech Republic. He inspired Chicago students and many abroad to devote their carriers to public service and the highest ideals of the profession.

Joe Seng ('64) was a noted musician playing the trumpet in the Iowa State Marching Band and the accordion at many opportunities around the state. He became a veterinarian and served three terms in the Iowa Senate.

Glen Myatt ('43) graduated from high school having just turned 16 years old. He played on the Iowa state basketball team that made it to the National Final Four tournament in the winter of 1944, becoming one of the youngest NCAA Tour-nament team members. This entire team disbanded after the tournament and was called to active service in the Army and Navy. Glen served for two years in the Pacific in the Navy. He returned to his community to become a farmer, cattle feeder, and member of the school board.

Gary Mohl ('56) was the president of the FFA, prom king (the queen was his future sister-in law), and broke the basketball scoring record for Lost Nation. He was a star basketball and baseball athlete at Lost Nation and ISTC. He was an outstanding musician in both band and vocal. He returned to Lost Nation High School as a science teacher, principal, administrator, coach, farmer, husband, and father. Gary Mohl ('56) was the epitome of the "all-American boy." Reached for comment, Gary in 2019 said, "I truly enjoyed every student I had, and given the choices of life to make again—I would have chosen as I did to come home to Lost Nation to teach again." He proudly has the carved "Bobcat" mascot for Lost Nation on his front steps at his home. At the final Lost Nation alumni reunion to be held in the school gym (2010), this carved Bobcat was presented for auction, cries from the crowd went out for Gary to buy the Bobcat, for he deserved it more that anyone. No one gave more to his community than Gary Mohl.

Hot Lunch—The hot lunch program was started in 1944. At the beginning there were only two cooks to make all the meals. This lasted three weeks until additional help and cooks were added. Rica Rutenbeck cooked into the 1970s. Pamela Myatt Crawford ('68) remembered, "She was a jovial lady. Her husband had played with the John Philip Sousa band so there was always music in her life. We had band rehearsal just as the lunch was being served, so band members got to eat last. The boys thought this was a great deal because they got to heap extras onto their plates."

Military Service and Killed in Action—The Civil War took a heavy toll of the young men from Sharon Township. The roster from the Iowa Roster of Civil War veterans shows that at least 44 men of the township served and 17 of them died of their wounds or disease.

Fifty-eight local men served in the Army and Navy in WWI.

Thirteen men from Lost Nation gave their lives in service to the country:

Edward L. Busch ('07), WWI
Raymond Corkery, WWI
William McAndrew, WWI
Menso Widle, WWI
Laverne P. Busch, WWII
Onie Butt, WWII
Milton Durkop, WWII
Irwin Ehlers, WWII
Charles Edwin Leffingwell, WWII
Raymond B. McAndrew ('34), WWII
Sydney Story, WWII
Charles O'Hara, Vietnam
John Stradovskis, Vietnam

Closing—Following the wave of reorganizations in the late 1980s, which included special education and post-secondary options, Lost Nation entered the Midland District with a "black budget" that supplemented the Midland red budget. Lost Nation High School closed following graduation in May 1988. The next year the students were bused to attend high school at Midland High School at Wyoming. There were 1,551 graduates in the 86 years from 1903-1988. The largest class was 42 in 1964. The most numerous surnames of the graduates were: Busch-34, Burmeister-23, Ales-21, Feuss-18, Wulf-18, Eldeman-17, McAndrew-17, Mohr-17, Wolfe-17, Gilroy-16, McAndrews-15, Smith-15, Schroeder-14, Christensen-13, White-12, Brown-9, Myatt-9, and Snyder-9. The last to receive a diploma from Lost Nation High School was Stacy Zeller (alphabetically).

#51

Lovilia High School

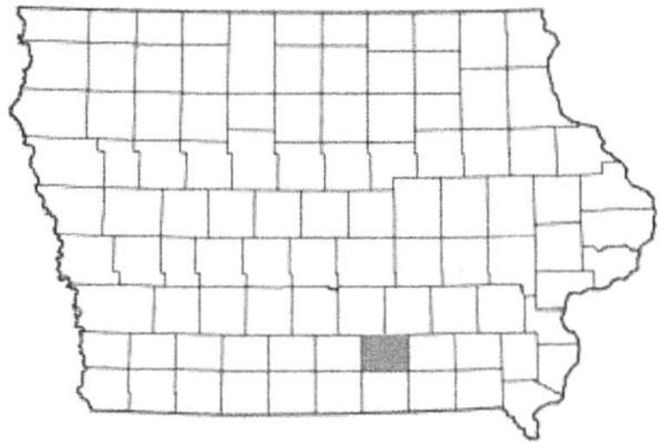

Mascot: Lions/Purplettes
Colors: Purple and Gold
Closed: 1962
Location: North Monroe County

Early History—A wagon train of 25 families came to this area of Monroe County in 1843. Land was offered for $1.25 an acre by the government. Much of the land was claimed on land warrants for prior military service. Anyone with $150 to buy 120 acres was considered "well-to-do."

In 1844, the population of Monroe County was 384. Six years later in 1850 it had grown to 3,000.

Several small gatherings of cabins were scattered throughout Monroe County. A location five miles south of present day Lovilia missed being the county seat by four votes in the 1846 election.

David Dixon was the founder of this area. He and his wife Bernice moved from nearby Hamilton. He bought portions of property with the last ½ acre costing $170 to get enough land to plat a town. It became named Bremen. Legend and lore are all part of the origin of the name of Bremen. At least three different theories have surfaced about the name. A logical one handed down to Luella Jones Plum through her grandmother who came to Monroe County in the wagon train was that it centered around a man in the wagon train named Bremen who opened a "sort of" combination grocery store and "beer joint." Whenever people were looking for something to do on Saturday night someone would say, "Let's go down to Bremen's place."

The most controversial name change occurred when the town's name went from Bremen to Lovilia. Legend and lore maintain at least six possibilities for the name of Lovilia. Several of these were because of daughters' in the area named Lovilla. When the Albia, Knoxville, and Des Moines Company Railroad came in 1867, there was another town in Iowa called Bremen. When the new line was connected with the main line of the Chicago Burlington Railroad in 1871, the little red depot was built to mark its path through the prairie. The Lovilia depot was completed in 1875 and was officially named. At this time, could a careless sign painter have dotted an "L" changing Lovilla to Lovilia?

During the Civil War there were over 200 men in Union Township eligible for the Union Army. The town had more than 48 casualties of wounded, missing, and killed. Celebrations and reunions for the veterans were large community events. The 1898 Southern Iowa Old Soldiers and Settlers Association celebration brought over 10,000 on a single day to Lovilia. Governor Leslie M. Shaw addressed the crowd. From the podium he advised that he had no prepared speech and commenced to give a 30-minute talk. As reported in the *Albia Union* newspaper, "In summary, advising you sons of farmers to stick to rudimentary education, acquire a nest egg—and then go to college for a time to brush up against the world."

In 1903, the Old Soldiers and Settlers celebration drew an even larger crowd of 12,000.

In the 1910s, coal prospectors and miners brought their families with children who enrolled in the Lovilia school. Quoting from the *Bremen to Lovilia 125th Anniversary* book, "Lovilia was riding the crest of the wave. With the end of World War I, it ushered the most prosperous time that Lovilia had ever known. While it lasted, the young and old, the rich and poor romped in a carnival atmosphere as though the bubble would never burst. With the Depression came John L. Lewis's edict to hold up King Coal's year and silently steal away. It was not until federally secured banks and social security that most of Lovilia's people would ever have it so good again."

Signs leading into the town on the north and south read: Lovilia "Coal Center of Iowa". Miners came from the eastern states. Others came directly from many European counties to work in the many mines in the area.

The Blackstone mine was one of the largest in Iowa from 1935-1948. By 1938, it was producing 500 tons of coal each day. There were nine docks on the railroad siding which extended between the railroad and the highway for the Burlington and Wabash trains.

The cinch bug invasion in 1933 devastated the crops. During the Great Depression, the government ordered five million pigs from 30-100 lbs. to be killed and made into grease and tankage. An additional one-million sows were slaughtered to help reduce the oversupply of unneeded pork.

By far the worst mine disaster came on March 31, 1953 at the Oberlin Mine. Five miners lost their lives when a gas formation and explosion occurred. Two miners, Harold Barnes, age 36, and Ben Nichols, age 47, had remained to set off explosive charges to loosen coal for the next day's production. When they failed to surface, fellow workers tried to reach them but because of gas fumes were unsuccessful. It was more than two hours before the bodies could be removed. A short time later an "unauthorized inspection" was planned and three more men were killed because of the gas fumes.

Early Schools—A 1902 smallpox epidemic closed the school for several weeks. A sign marked SMALLPOX was nailed to houses—no one was allowed to leave during the quarantine. The *Lovilia Press* reported:

> The Lovilia school which has been closed because of the smallpox scare the past two weeks will open next Monday. The smallpox is subsiding and those who are unfortunate enough to have an occasional pimple on their face are no longer quarantined.

In 1903, the *Lovilia Press* printed a Progress Report:

> The school complete cost something over $6,000 and in every respect is an ideal structure. In speaking of our school, it is but natural to hope the time may not be far distant when the grounds will extend over the entire block.

The program for the commencement on May 17, 1907, listed three graduates. Each graduate had 30 minutes to present their memorized oration. Topics were: Americas Position Among Nations, by Inez

Mae Amber; Abraham Lincoln, by Ralph Harrison Armstrong; Achievements of Science, by Emma Mae Cobb.

In 1919, with the war over and the coal mines booming, the schools were overcrowded. There were 45 students paying $100 a year to attend school in Lovilia. The voters were asked for another bond to take care of the overflow. On January 2, 1920, by a vote of 178-32, the citizens approved $42,000 for a new schoolhouse. Classes were being held in five different buildings in the community. The new three-story modern brick building was completed in the fall of 1920. This 60′ x 90′ structure with a full basement cost $50,000 and the levy was increased from 52 to 125 mills.

Notable Teachers—T.J. Barnes was the track coach and taught many different subjects. Goldie Walter Kraber ('55) said, "I loaned Gary Slay ('55) my math paper to copy. Mr. Barnes spotted my deed and said in class, 'there goes your grade!' And he really did drop my grade that six-weeks term."

Killed in Action—At least 14 men from Union Township and Lovilia lost their lives for their country. Lest we forget:

Bruno Avon, WWII
Frank Ballalatak, WWII
William Gail Barnes, WWII
Donald Brown, WWII
Kenneth Dunkin, WWII
Francis Hutchinson, WWII
Dallas Johnson, WWII
Lewis Robinson, WWII
Russell Robinson, WWII
Paul Schoolen, WWII
Thomas Slofkosky, WWII
George Soltis, WWII
Marvin Gordon, Vietnam
James Comstock, Vietnam

Janitor—Tommy Ballard was the janitor at the Lovilia school from the early part of the century. He loved the children. A former student recalled, "Tommy let us help him ring the bell with the rope hanging from the belfry to the second floor. During the school year in 1929, Tommy died, and the entire school went to his home in Lovilia to tearfully file past his casket."

Sports—The girls played basketball. They were known as the "Purplettes." They won the Chariton Valley Conference Tournament for 12 straight years from 1947-1959. In 1958, after having started the season with 19 consecutive wins without a loss, they were denied a trip to the state tournament losing to Pella in the sectionals. They settled for the consolation trophy by beating Knoxville. Their coach was Pat Porter. The leading scorers were Rosetta Bryson ('58) with 598 points and Beverly Dunkin ('58) with 338 points.

Helen Corrick Baker ('49) was chosen for the first team all-state in 1949. She was the all-time school scoring leader with 3,271 points. She had 1,323 in her senor year. At the age of 15 she scored 101 points in a single game. In 1978, Helen was elected to the Iowa Girls Basketball Hall of Fame.

The boys played basketball, baseball, and track. Football was started in 1954.

The boys basketball teams defeated a much larger Chariton High School in 1938 and won the Coal Valley Conference Tournament. Bob Jones was selected to the All-Southeast Iowa first team.

The boys made it to the sectionals in 1939 and 1947. They advanced to the sub states in 1949.

Boys track in the 1950s became a popular sport. Coach T.J. Barnes became a prominent name around the state for his track teams' performances. In 1951, Les Stevens ('52) became known as Lovilia's "One Man Track Team." That year he garnered 18 medals and 'Lanky' Les broke many records in the high jump, high hurdles, and relay teams. He was pictured with the great Jesse Owens in a newspaper sports page photo.

Comet—The school newspaper was called the *Comet*. From the February 17, 1916, issue:

The Literary Society of Lovilia High School was first begun in 1914 with H.L. Amber the organizer. Before this time there has been no social side whatsoever to the school life and a school certainly needs something to break the studious monotony. . .

The six seniors were asked about their favorite expression. They said: For the love of Mike; Criminy! O Man; Kingdom Come; Gee Whiz!; and Aw Shucks.

The practice in the art of debating both in the Literary Society and by means of inter-high school debates was started . . . In competition against Hiteman High School the debate topics for the three debates were: "Resolved, that the Panama Canal ought to be fortified," "Resolved, that further immigration is undesirable," "Resolved, that a minimum wage scale should be adopted."

Music—A marching band was started in 1950 by I.O. White. There were nearly 40 musicians, five twirlers, and a drum majorette that performed at all the home football games. Fred Kraber ('54) played the drums and remembered, "We played at the Pella Tulip Festival parade each spring." Judy Church Geno ('59) played the cornet at the Centerville Pancake Days. Bill Barnes ('63 Albia) recalled, "Mr. White came down to the grade school to recruit a dozen of the bigger kids to help do the halftime designs for the marching band programs at the football games. We even had matching band uniforms and thought it was big stuff. The football field sat down in a lower area and the spectators were able to sit up higher and could enjoy our halftime band maneuvers."

Pranks—Halloween was no time to be an elected official in Lovilia. The city council and mayor were hung one year in effigy. Mayor Don Major saw no humor in the act and resigned as mayor.

A stray stick of dynamite for the mining operations was once placed against a post at Sofranko's Garage by Carroll Dorman ('51). Upon lighting the dynamite, a loud bang was heard but no damage was done to the garage because the dynamite was not self-contained.

Bus Drivers—Charles "Hardrock" Slay drove the north and west bus routes to Hamilton and Marysville. Bill Barnes ('63 Albia) remembered, "He was quite a baseball player and worked at Slay's Furniture and hardware store. He used to keep the bus in the old 50-50 garage because it just cleared the roof most of the time. Occasionally, it would scrape the top, and the bus got the name of 'old silver top.'"

George Williams drove for Lovilia and later Albia after the consolidation. Goldie Walter Kraber ('55) recalled, "At times George was known to have a short fuse. He took no guff. When Gary Kindle and Richard Plum carried milkweeds onto the bus and were blowing the flying pods through the bus he screamed, 'enough is enough.' On another occasion while driving to Albia, he had the kids get out and walk the rest of the way to school."

Closing—In 1955, rumblings were heard about school reorganization which could lead to the loss of the high school. At the time, the school enrollment was 305 students with 132 in the high school. For 14 years, since the beginning of World War II, as many as 48 Marysville, Hamilton, and outlying districts students in Marion County had been attending Lovilia High School as tuition students. They were happy to be part of the school system. When the first phase of the reorganization plan came, the mandate that Marion County school boards made these students attend school in Marion County, mostly at the new Twin Cedars school at Bussey. Lovilia's enrollment dropped overnight. Attempts to organize a community district with Melrose failed.

The Lovilia High School closed after graduation in May 1962. In the fall of 1962, the high school students were bused to Albia. In the 57 years from 1906-1962 there were 894 graduates from Lovilia High School. The largest senior class was 32 in 1956. The most numerous surnames of the graduates were: Barnes-29, Beary-13, Dunkin-13, Davis-12, Henderson-11, Clark-9, Cobb-9, Nedderman-9, Slay-9, and Jones-7 The last to receive a diploma from Lovilia High School was Armadine Walters (alphabetically).

Lovilia High School
Monroe County, IA

#52

Lucas High School

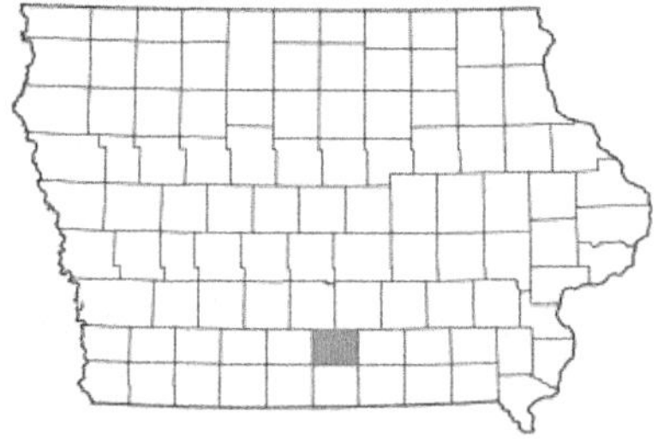

Mascot: None
Colors: Red and Gold
Closed: 1959
Location: West Central Lucas County

Early History—Lucas was named after the Iowa Territorial Governor Robert Lucas. When the Burlington and Missouri Railroad was constructed across southern Iowa in 1867, the station was named Lucas Station. It was platted in 1867 and incorporated in 1868. When an application was sent to Washington to the Postal Department for a post office, the Lucas Station people received their mail from the Tallahoma Post Office. In granting this new post office, a clerk in Washington dropped "Station" making the official name Lucas.

H.S. Russell started platting the town in March 1868. The original town consisted of 12 blocks separated by streets and contained 108 lots.

Lucas became the shipping point for the railroad and attracted farm commodities from the north into Warren County.

When coal was discovered along Whitebreast Creek (one mile east of Lucas) in 1873, the town and surrounding Jackson Township population boomed to over 3,000. For the next 50 years, as many as twelve mines in a two and a half mile radius of Lucas were operated.

The first was Whitebreast (Cleveland No. 1 or Whitebreast Coal and Fuel No. 1) and it was the largest and deepest in Iowa. In 1874, a five-foot shaft was sunk to 250 feet. A 5′ 4″ vein of coal was discovered. This mine produced the greatest tonnage in the shortest time of any in Iowa. Electricity was installed in the mine which was the first light bulb in the state. When the mine inspector visited the mine in 1880, he found 405 men and 52 mules employed raising up 640 tons each day from the mine.

In that same year of 1880, John Llewellyn Lewis was born in Cleveland to Thomas and Louisa Lewis. His father, Thomas was a coal miner and the family lived in the camp called Cleveland. The family spoke Welch, and English was their second guage. The family moved to Des. Moines where John L. attended school. The family returned to Lucas where John L. worked as a mule driver in the Big Hill Mine. He joined the United Mine Workers of America (UMWA) 799 in 1900. John L. Lewis married the local doctor's daughter and moved to Illinois where he became a traveling representative for the UMWA and became the International President of the UMWA in 1920. With the advent of television in the 1950s, John L. became a very visible and powerful leader in the International Labor Union. With his heavy, bushy eyebrows and dark suits his figure was known throughout America.

The town grew rapidly in the 1880s, reaching a population of 3,450, of which 2,000 were miners. The additions to the town differed as to the width of the streets and alleys and size of the lots. These were done at the whims of the developer. One result is that the east-west streets of West Lucas joined the east-west alleys of East Lucas.

Significant historical facts about Lucas are:

- John P. White's boyhood home was Lucas. He rose to become the president of the UMWA. He appointed John L. Lewis as the vice president and Lewis succeeded him as the President of the UMWA.
- The first electric light bulb in Iowa was used at Cleveland No. 1.

- In 1914, Jack Larsen was paid two cents for each hundred weight for hauling coal to the schoolhouse.
- In the 1917 military draft in Washington, Herbert Spencer's name from Lucas was the first name drawn from the 'fishbowl'.
- The first lady postmaster in the State of Iowa was at Lucas.

Early Schools—The first school in Lucas was built in 1869 and was a log cabin. School was later held in the Presbyterian church.

A frame one-story, one-room school was built in 1879. A second story was added and the outside stairway to the second floor was used by the Miner's Union.

The 1878 history states there were three schools in Lucas District. Two of them in the town of Lucas and one in a room furnished for the purpose in Cleveland (one mile east of Lucas).

The *Lucas Leader* on July 13, 1882 reported, "No longer cry down the Educational facilities of Lucas, at present we have four select schools conducted respectively by Miss Katie Morrison, Miss Eva Maxwell, Miss Bertha Sheridan, and Mr. Molesworth.

In 1884, a two-story four-room school was built on the site of the present school building (2020-today is apartments).

The old Cleveland mines closed in 1891, and the school there was moved to Lucas. It sat on the north side of the Lucas school building making it a T shaped structure. The first graduation was held in Knotts Opera House on June 19, 1886.

The west side school was sold in 1907 for $325, but the school board reserved the outhouses for use at the East School.

School improvements that were added throughout the years of the Lucas School were:

- Trees planted in 1905.
- Cement sidewalks laid in 1910.
- Exterior plastered and pebble dashed in 1924 for a cost of $1650.60
- 1926 a stage added, and PTA got the Board to buy a roll curtain and a wood scene and parlor set.
- Gymnasium built in 1930 for $1940.
- Professor M.F. Warnstaff was injured on floor of gym. He died a few days later in 1931.
- December 12, 1932 a fire in the furnace room destroyed the school.
- A two-week vacation after the fire and school resumed in the Presbyterian church basement, IOOF, and the gym. All sporting events were canceled.
- A new two-story '54' x 62' school was built for $18,000. $10,000 worth of bonds were sold at 5% interest to Dan Ferry, $1,000 to Lee Hooker, and $8,000 to Norm Baker.

The new school building was dedicated on November 24, 1933. Though the mines had been closed more than ten years before the dedication ceremonies, the influence of the town's mining past are noticed in the program. Some on the program were John P. White—Dedication Address (International Rep of UMWA), Greetings by W.A. Dunlavy—Inspector of Mining Camp School, Remarks by Mrs. J.S. Cramer—Pres. of Daughters of Unions Veterans (DUV), Flag Presentation by Effie Peterson—Patriot Instructor of DUV.

Pranks—The typing room had previously been the industrial arts classroom. It had a side storage room where the typewriters and papers were stored. This room was called the "tool room or Cave." "My dad was on the school board and my mother was a schoolteacher," said Roger Allen ('57). "My classmate, Robert 'Bob' James ('57) and I, on unwise impulses, locked the door to the 'Cave' with high-spirited Elizabeth 'Tootie' Dixson ('57) inside the 'Cave.' The bell rang and we sauntered off to our next class. "Tootie" became claustrophobic and kicked the door down and called her mother on the school phone. It was not long before Superintendent B.W. Burnison fingered me to come out of class and I casually asked, 'what's this all about?' He blurted 'You know damn good and well what it's about!' I had to apologize to "Tootie" and even bought her a corsage some 40 years later as we rode on a float together with our class. Finally, all was forgiven," smiled Roger Allen ('57). Willard Allen ('40), Roger's cousin, was known to have said he didn't think Roger was a true Allen until he heard of this prank.

Yearbook—The 1923 yearbook was called *Lucasian*. The last yearbook in 1959 was called *Golden Memories*. This 1959 yearbook was dedicated to William Merle Fierce ('59). It read:

> He has always been a grand fellow . . . Early in this his senior year, an unfortunate physical development made necessary the removal of his right eye followed by an emergency surgery.
>
> He hopes to return home in the near future and back to school with his classmates. We are dedicating Golden Memories to him and using this method to boost his moral, and ours, and telling him that we expect him to be with us in all our senior activities and that it is our sincere desire that complete recovery may be very soon and permanent.

(Author's Note: William Fierce died from cancer and never returned to graduate)

Sports—There was no football played at Lucas. The boys played basketball and track.

The girls played basketball. Nearby Woodburn was one of the school rivals. Janice Israel Heston (59) grinned as she recalled, "I was a forward on a rather poor basketball team. When we played Woodburn, we always said we should be playing the Woodburn boys team because neither of us were worth two cents nor could never win."

Buses—Jim Blizzard drove the Lucas bus in the 1940s and 1950s. Mike Goben (Chariton '68) remembered, "I always thought he was mean. Maybe it was because he ran a tight ship or bus as it would be. He kicked me off the bus on the top of Narber Hill and said you can just walk the rest of the way home. I happened to get a ride back to Lucas and beat the bus back to town that afternoon." Becky Patterson Allen (Chariton '69) remembered him more fondly telling, "Mr. Blizzard made the boys act like gentlemen. One night I was staying overnight with Victoria Kent and he had me put my suitcase up in the front of the bus. When he let us off at Victoria's lane, he instructed her brother Danny to carry my suitcase. Danny was not happy but complied. As soon as the bus was out of sight, Danny dropped the suitcase and ran. So much for being a gentleman. I believe that the bus drivers are just an extension of the school as they are the first and last to interact with many of the children every day."

Notable Teacher—A teacher that had nearly every student as they came through Lucas schools was Frances Marker. "We all had Miss Marker and I even had her for three years," said Roger Allen ('57). "She was my favorite teacher. She taught us to recite and we had so many poems to tell by memory. Unfortunately, I remember one such story to this day some 70 years later. It was about 'Frances the Flying Horse.' For some reason, I was feeling somewhat tired of the story and wrote on a piece of paper, 'I hate Francis the Flying Jackass!' I dropped it in the trash can on the way out of class and someone took it to the teacher, and I got into trouble with Mrs. Marker. It resulted in my spending several recesses making amend with Miss Marker."

Notable Graduate—Ronald Roberts ('57) graduated from Graceland and Louisiana State University. He was a Sociology professor at the University of Northern Iowa. He was a writer and wrote extensively about John L. Lewis. He was a benefactor to the John L. Lewis Museum in Lucas and gave items and extensive monetary gifts to the exhibit.

Janitor—Albert Baker was a longtime Lucas school janitor. Becky Patterson Allen (Chariton '69) shared, "He was not my grandpa, but he and his wife Irene who helped him were such sweet people. They kept the school spotless. He could fix anything even a wooden sled." Roger Allen ('57) remembered, "My classmate Robert James ('57) and I were waiting our turns to be starters on the boys basketball team, and we were team managers for both the boys and girls teams. More than once on a game day we requested to be let out of class to go down to polish the basketballs, mainly so that we could go down to the furnace room to visit with Albert."

Senior Trips—The seniors of 1957 must have either needed some additional education or their sponsor was trying to make a point. They traveled to visit the Eldora Boys Reform school and to the Ft. Madison Penitentiary on a same day trip.

The schools last graduating class of 1959 traveled to the Ozarks in three cars. Janice Israel Heston ('59) reflected, "In our class, as in all small towns, we knew each other and were so close. No one was left out and we helped each other to be successful and leaders in all endeavors and activities."

Closing—Lucas High School closed after graduation in 1959. In the fall the remaining students were bused to their new school at Chariton nine miles to the east. The last to receive a diploma from Lucas High School was Dale Edward Tuffs (alphabetically).

Lucas High School
Lucas County, IA

#53

Lynnville High School

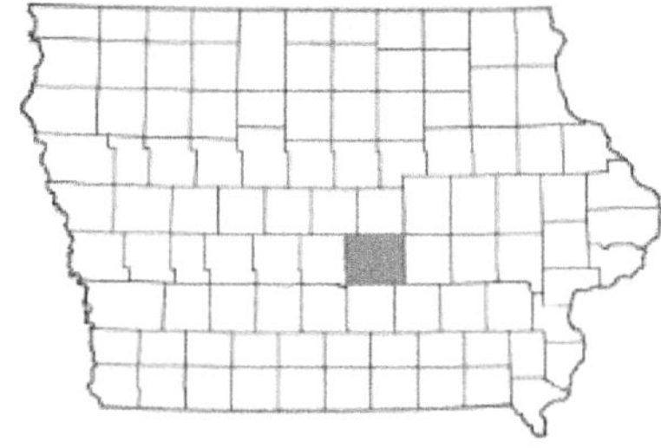

Mascot: Lynnx
Colors: Purple and White
Closed: 1956
Location: Southeast Jasper County

Early History—In the spring of 1844, Wesley Stallings and his sons, William and David Campbell, arrived in the Lynn Grove Township by oxen to establish a home. They then traveled back to Illinois. Stallings returned with his wife and five children with seventy-five cents in his pocket.

John R. Sparks was a veteran of the Black Hawk War. In 1845, he and his wife and eight children arrived in Lynn Grove Township from Lee County, Iowa. He possessed $25 in cash, a team of horses, a team of oxen, and a team of oxen steers. Sparks first endeavor was the construction of a small paddle wheel sawmill. Power for the mill originated from a mill pond, the resultant backwater of a large wooden dam constructed across the North Skunk River.

The mill was greatly prized by the people of the county, saving as it did three days conveyance to Oskaloosa over uncertain streams and roads. The buhrstones of the Sparks mill were said to have been the best, French-made.

This started 175 years of a mill operating on the North Skunk River at Lynnville. Today (2020) the history of this mill is preserved at the Wagaman Mill Museum at the original site.

The underground railroad for runaway slaves was a significant part of the Lynnville community in the 1850s. From time to time, John Sparks employed several fugitive slaves about the sawmill.

One night, Jervis Johnson received a cargo of fugitive slaves. It was the custom to keep such a transaction a secret even from the family. On this occasion Jervis suspicioned that his son, Charles, had caught on. So, in a very impressive manner he pointed a finger at him and said, "Don't thee tell this, it will be the risk of thee life," "Tell what father?" asked Charles. "None of thy business," said his father, determined that if he did not know he should remain in ignorance. These negro slaves were moved at night northward to Grinnell and eventually to Canada.

The town was named after the Linden trees in the nearby grove. It was incorporated in 1875 for the purpose of controlling the liquor traffic.

Early Schools—In 1847, the first school was in a log cabin with paper windows and a pine puncheon floor. The desks and seats were made at the sawmill.

The Society of Friends was organized in 1851. The Friends (Quakers) established their school across the river from the mill. They built the Friends Academy in 1866. After a few years, this Academy failed, and the building was moved to Lynnville across the North Skunk River in the winter when the river was frozen. In 1870, the Lynnville Independent School District was created. An arrangement was made with the Lynnville school to rent the second floor of the Friends building for a school. The Friends used the first floor for their church services.

When a disagreement ensued over the use of a church facility arose, the community passed a $2,000 bond for a two-story school which served until 1913. In 1913, the new brick schoolhouse was built. A gymnasium was added in 1928 for $28,000.

The first graduation from the two-year high school was in 1886. The first graduation from the three-year high school was in 1900.

When the new school was built, the fourth year was added to the curriculum and the graduation in 1913 was the first of the newly accredited high school. At this same time, the Sully District broke away and built their own high school.

Notable Graduates—Dwight Davis ('37) became an educator and was the Superintendent of the Des Moines school system.

Laurence Gertsma ('50) received his BS from the University of Iowa and MS from Case Institute in Aeronautical Engineering. He worked at NASA at the Lewis Flight Propulsion Laboratory which is now the John Glenn Research Center.

Alice Terpstra LaRosa ('40) returned to Lynnville in 1948 to teach and was the principal of the high school for two years. She moved to St. Louis where she taught and was an administrator in the St. Louis schools. She was elected to the Iowa Girls High School Basketball Hall of Fame in 1970. Living in St. Louis, she asked her brother if the Hall of Fame honor was a worth the trip back to Iowa. To which Albert Terpstra ('44) replied, "Well, they wouldn't want to give it to me."

Richard Sparks ('48) received his medical degree from the University of Iowa. He returned to Lynnville to practice in 1958. He lived in the former home of Dr. Charles Quire. Quire had lived in the home when he practiced medicine in Lynnville for

40 years. Dr. Richard Sparks died young at the age of 36 in 1966.

Sports—Football was played in the early days of the school but was discontinued. On September 27, 1933, after eleven years of no football, a game was played against New Sharon.

In the 1930s, the teams were transported to out of town games in Clifford Shaffer's truck. Straw was laid down with blankets over the top. Eight girls who made the traveling team, the chaperone, their basketballs and uniforms, and Coach Howard Macy all crawled into the truck. Upon returning to Lynnville, Coach Macy treated them all at the Lynnville Hartstock Café. The cafe was always open and waiting for them. Mr. Macy then delivered all the girls to their homes.

Girls basketball excelled at Lynnville. They went to the state tournament in 1937, 1939, and 1940. Berdene Gause ('37) made the second all-tournament team in 1937.

The 1939 team only had one loss going into the state tournament. They were led by a 6'0" forward, Ruth Petersma ('40), and Alice Terpstra LaRosa ('40) who made the all-tournament first team. Betty Ratcliff was chosen the Princess of the Tournament. This team won the third-place trophy with a win over Wellsburg in the consolation bracket.

In 1940, Alice Terpstra LaRosa ('40) repeated on the first team all-tournament team. Wanda Terpstra Dunsberger ('42) at the age of 95 in 2020 said, "I played guard on that 1940 team. When Alice got into foul trouble, I became a forward. I made 29 points in one of those games." She continued, "That was such a special year because the boys team went to state in 1940 also. It seemed the whole month of March, we were away from school playing basketball. It was the thrill of a lifetime. The boys' team was from the smallest enrollment school in their tournament."

The 1953 and 1954 boys teams had a special run. They were 52-2 over that two-year period. Wilbur Terpstra ('54) recalled, "Those were my junior and senior years. I can still replay that final game in my mind with Winfield. We lost in the finals of the Sub State 49-51. The 1954 team won the Jasper County Tournament and the Rock Lake Conference crown."

Standing at 5' 6" Joan VanManen Eysink ('56) was a guard on the basketball team. She made the honor roll (honorable mention all-state team) in her senior year. Joan shared, "I had that Dutch height and it sure was used to my advantage in basketball. Being a guard there were many jump balls at my end of the court and we sure took advantage of my jumping ability."

The biggest sports rivals were Deep River and Keswick.

Notable Teachers—Mrs. Audry Kuening taught English in the 1950s. Gary Needham ('56) remembered, "Mrs. Kuening gave me so much confidence in my studies. Her husband had been a farmer and suffered a stroke and was wheelchair bound. I broke my arm with a compound fracture at the ice-skating rink. Since the rink was on the school property, I was so fortunate that the little amount of insurance I had paid at the beginning of the school year helped cover the cost of the plate and the casting. Mrs. Kuening helped me get through that mishap. I later became a teacher and, with her example, I always tried to understand and give my students confidence." Joan VanManen Eysink ('56) added, "Mrs. Kuening set me on to reading. I had never liked to read, and she inspired me in that direction. The bookmobile visits were all part of her emphasis."

Pranks—It was a top priority to be the first one out of the schoolhouse to the playground. The first on the football field got to make up the rules for the game that day and divided the teams. The direct path down the stairs and out the front doors was a mad rush of pushing and elbowing to be the first to the field. A short cut seemed logical, which was jumping out of the second-floor window. Wilbur Terpstra ('54) grinned but seemed remorseful about his leap without a parachute. "I still feel the cramp in my hand, and that is not from the jump. I had to write 1,000 times 'I will not jump out of the schoolhouse window anymore.'"

It may not be considered a prank, but a story from the Case Country school may have been the harbinger of things to come. Five-year-old Wilbur Terpstra ('54) was visiting in the spring before he was to enter the first grade. His deed was not remembered, but he ended up standing in the corner before he was ever enrolled in school. Several years later, while in the third grade, his mischievous character arose again, and he was caught smoking in the pony barn. The disciplinary action required him to stay after school each day for a half hour and hand write 1,000 times, "I will not smoke in the pony barn, again." After the half-hour detention, young Wilbur would jump on his horse Patsy, and run hard to catch up with his sister Ila Mae on her horse Topsy. His goal was to beat her home.

Senior Trips—Two carloads of seniors headed for St. Louis for their senior trip in 1951. Ila Mae Terpstra Sprouse ('51) vividly recalled, "We were the first class to go out of town for our senior trip. We stayed overnight and the highlight was going to the baseball game with the St. Louis Browns and the visiting Cleveland Indians. Van Meter's Bob Feller was not pitching that day, but we hung around the dugout to catch him after the game. I asked for his autograph and he brushed us off saying he wasn't signing autographs today. We pleaded, 'Not even for us kids from Iowa?' He stopped short and asked us where we were from and said he would autograph a baseball or score card. That autographed scorecard is at the Wagaman Museum on display these 70 years later."

The 1954 seniors were back for a three-day trip to St. Louis. Wilbur Terpstra ('54) remembered, "The highlight for me was the doubleheader at Sportsman's Park and seeing Stan Musial of the Cardinals hit five home runs out in our seating area in right field in the doubleheader."

The school's last senior trip in 1956 was to the Lake of the Ozarks. Seventeen seniors traveled in three cars and stayed in a boys' cabin and a girls' cabin. Laverne Jones ('35) was the teacher-sponsor. He later became the Superintendent for Lynnville Sully.

Killed in Action—Several men from the Lynnville area lost their lives while in service for their country.

Leland Max Pothoven, WWII
Jean Alan Morris, WWII
Earl VerSteegt, WWII
Howard Devere Stanley, WWII

A great number of men served in the military conflicts and previous wars. John R. Sparks served in the Black Hawk War. Seven Sparks boys served in the Civil War (unknown if they were all sons of John Sparks). A total of 81 from the township and nearby Lynnville area served in the Union Army in the Civil War. There were thirty-two in the First World War and 136 men and women in World War II who served in the military.

Closing—In the 1950s, conversations were started between the communities and school boards of Searsboro (four miles east in Poweshiek County), Sully (four miles west of Lynnville), and Lynnville, about the consolidation of their schools. Searsboro wanted no part in sending their students to Lynnville at that time. Lynnville High School closed after graduation in May 1956. They combined with Sully in the fall of 1956 to become the Lynnville Sully School District. For the next two years, the former Lynnville High School building was used until the new Lynnville Sully High School was constructed in Sully. Searsboro joined in 1960. In the 71 years from 1886-1956, there were 519 graduates from Lynnville High School. The largest class was 17 seniors in 1956. The most numerous surnames of the graduates were: Sparks-26, Meridith-24, Macy-22, Gause-20, Renaud-17, Ratcliff-12, Quire-11, Williams-11, Johnson-9, and Terpstra-9. The last to receive a diploma from Lynnville High school was Larry Willemsen (alphabetically).

Lynnville High School
Jasper County, IA

#54

Macedonia High School

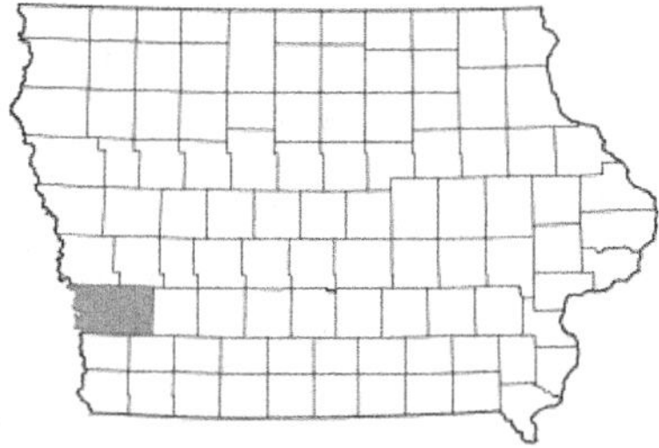

Mascot: Trojans
Colors: Purple and Gold
Closed: 1958
Location: South Central Pottawattamie County

Early History—The Mormons, John Brown (known as the Harper's Ferry Abolitionist), melting pot, and railroad—all had their influence on this little town in the rolling hills along the Nishnabotna River.

When Lewis and Clark forged their way up the Missouri River in 1804, they met the Pottawattamie Indians in southwest Iowa. Lewis and Clark held council with the Indians as they flocked in from every direction to examine their boats and equipment.

The Pottawattamie had originally been in Indiana, the southern part of Michigan, and the eastern part of Illinois before coming to Iowa. During the French and Indian War in 1755, General Braddock (English) had been sent to drive the Pottawattamie further west. They lived in southwest Iowa until the 1840s when they sold their possessions to the government as a result of a treaty signed on June 5, 1846—the same year of Iowa's statehood—and moved to Kansas.

The native relocation left the area open to the Mormons. They were leaving Nauvoo, Illinois (along the Mississippi River), following the shooting of their founder, Joseph Smith, at Carthage, Illinois. He had been jailed by vigilantes in 1844. Brigham Young's vision in 1846 was to lead the Mormons west. Brigham Young and several hundred of his followers left Nauvoo in February, crossed the Mississippi, and blazed a "Mormon Trail" across southern Iowa. This trail followed Indian paths and was from grove to grove of trees where firewood was available. They did not follow the Indian trails exactly since the oxen-pulled wagons were not able to stay on the same trail that Indians used on their horses. Many more Mormon settlers followed and camped along the way at Garden Grove in Decatur County, at "Indian Town" (between Griswold and Elliott), and in Pottawattamie County at Kanesville (today Council Bluff). A cemetery just east of Macedonia, called the Mormon Cemetery, is an indication that some Mormons settled and stayed there for a time. At the winter quarters, Kanesville, some Mormons defected after learning of Brigham Young's polygamy practices.

The trail crossed the Nishnabotna River just west of the future Macedonia site where a rock bottom made the crossing safe and easy. The name Macedonia was taken from the Bible's New Testament, the book of Acts, Chapter 16 v. 9, ". . . and a vision appeared to Paul in the night: There stood a man of Macedonia . . ." This was part of a sermon that a Mormon elder gave at a mill site along the river. After the sermon, a petition was prepared and sent to Washington D.C. asking for a post office to be established. On May 11, 1850, because of the petition, a post office was established at this site (Stutsman Mill) with Elder Beebe named the first postmaster at his log cabin.

In 1853, the first sale of public land in Pottawattamie county took place. Speculators came from all parts of the country. With removal of the Indians and the departure of the Mormons, the county was open for settlement.

No history of Macedonia would be complete without adding John Brown's underground railway, which crossed the river at Old Macedonia and traversed Macedonia Township. John Brown, the radical anti-slavery leader, came up from Kansas through Missouri to Tabor, Iowa in the spring of 1859. He crossed the river at Macedonia with three six-mule teams laden with former slaves. They were seated in covered wagons and dressed in women's clothing to help disguise them. Brown himself rode a roan colored horse. That fall in 1859, aided by recruits from the Tabor area, Brown led the ill-fated attack on the Federal Armory at Harper's Ferry, Pennsylvania.

Railroads—A north-south railway, the Chicago, Burlington, and Quincy Railroad, was laid in 1880. The first steam locomotive invaded the quiet countryside east of old Macedonia on July 4, 1880. The town of "old Macedonia" was moved away from the river one mile east to the railroad and platted as a new Macedonia. This history is well documented in the book *Macedonia, Iowa History* published September 2005 by the Macedonia Historical Preservation Society.

Early Schools—The first school was constructed near old Macedonia. The building was a frame 25′ x 40′ and built for a cost of $1,000. It was used until 1881 when the town was moved one mile east with the arrival of the railroad. Located on a hill overlooking the valley, new Macedonia created a need for a new school.

The Independent District of Macedonia was carved out of the township district and received 21% of the township funds or $1,840. With this money in hand, the school board proceeded to purchase nearly six acres of land at a cost of $65 an acre or $275. A new two-story brick schoolhouse was built for $5,210. This building stood for 54 years until replaced in 1936. It was a graded system and added three grades for a total of eleven. This constituted a complete course of study for a high school diploma. The first graduation was held in 1893.

Excerpts from the 1906 Macedonia yearbook:

- New slate blackboards replaced the old painted ones.
- A new organ ordered months before and thought never to be coming, surprised everyone as it had been installed Halloween morning.

Community Involvement—In 1928, John Hamilton gave $8,000 for the development of an athletic field and stadium in memory of his only child, John G. Hamilton, who died in 1903 at the age of 22. It remains today with a plaque that reads, "This park is dedicated to the children of Macedonia in memory of my son." It is one of two such grandstands in the state of Iowa.

Sports—Boys basketball was started in 1910 by Superintendent T.O. Tacy. The first game was with

Carson (a town six miles north). They were coached by E.E. Coe. Before the first basket could be made, a dispute arose over a decision by Coe to have refereeing. The two schools immediately became fierce foes until they were merged into a unified high school in 1958.

Girls basketball was started soon after the boys. In 1926, a picture of the team depicts nine girls with their coach, Miss Gladys Hooker. They had Donia printed on their midis (shirts), bloomers, long knee-high socks, and matching two-toned ankle high shoes.

"I didn't get to play basketball, because my dad said 'no girl of his was going to get out there and straddle around without no clothes on,'" remembered Dale Stevens Bolton ('22).

Games were held in the Opera House which had a beautiful maple floor. The building burned to the ground in 1936. "When the fire broke out, it was debated that the best way to fight the fire was to cut a hole in the middle of the floor. But most of the fire fighters opposed this because of the integrity of the beautiful maple floor. So, the building burned to the ground instead," shared Emest Carley ('42) in an interview in 2019.

With a gift of $25,000 which was bestowed to the school board and matching funds from the WPA (45% of the construction costs), a new gymnasium and grade school were constructed and completed in 1937. A large crowd attended the laying of the cornerstone by the Masons. The new addition cost $101,000. "The new gymnasium was the envy of every school in the area. It was a work of art and many tournaments and sectionals were played on its gym floor," told Joan Scott whose husband Richard Scott ('44) played basketball for Donia.

In the eyes of a little kindergarten student in the fall of 1953, this gymnasium had an unusual feature. Gary Forristall ('67 Carson-Macedonia) remembered, "There was a spittoon on the east wall of the gymnasium. This thing looked awfully high to me. When I first saw it, I thought it was to be used for a urinal."

Janitor—Bill Pope and his family lived in the basement of the school. He had been a farmer in the area suffering with poor health. He was appointed the school janitor in the summer of 1953. He died in the arms of his son, James, who was trying to get a nitroglycerin tablet under his tongue. The Macedonia school board decided to have 15-year-old James continue as the school janitor for the rest of the year. Mrs. Pope and James continued to live in the basement of the school. This remarkable story can be read in *Post Hole Digger,* written by James Pope, which chronicles this experience of living in the school while being the janitors for the buildings.

Pranks—Bill Pope had a watermelon patch which often was raided by some of the high school boys. James Braden ('53) who had gone to the movie theater that night gave an accounting of one such raid, "Robert Braden ('49), Don Kash, George Kash ('49), Martin Herbert ('49), Leo Herbert ('51) and I were filling the trunk of my dad's car with sweet green contraband when Leo yelled 'Hey, there is someone with a gun!' A distant voice bellowed, 'What are you boys up too?' A gunshot was fired as the car made haste out of the watermelon patch. The next day, we took the car to Albert Kash's station, where a hole through the tire and inner tube and back fender was found. We didn't tell our dad until his later years how the hole got into his car."

Buses—The first school bus in 1917 was a G.W.W. Model 10. It had no glass windows and held 24 students. Bret Bisbee, who ran a trucking business in town, was a bus driver from the 1920s into the 1940s. "My twin Laurane and I rode the bus for my twelve years to school starting in 1928. His son Max Bisbee ('47) and Catherine Keast Lett ('46) drove the buses during their senior years. Mr. Bisbee always gave us ice cream on the last day of school. My brother, Marian Plumb ('34), was one of many who rode their horses to school so they could play football and stay for practice," shared Lavonne Plumb Pilling ('40) at the age of 97 in 2019.

Notable Graduates—Gertrude Carley Brown Ensign ('38) worked at the Department of Defense. "She took the call from President Harry Truman to drop the atomic bomb on Japan and passed it on to the Generals in the Defense Department," shared her brother, Emest Carley ('42), choking up as he recalled the tragic phone call to his sister.

Marion Coons ('33) developed the accounting system used by Hy-Vee. He was one of the three who founded the Hy-Vee grocery store chain.

Lowell Smith ('39) played baseball at the University of Iowa. He became a medical doctor and was the team doctor for several California colleges.

Closing—Macedonia High School closed in May 1958. The next fall the students were bused to Carson to the new high school called Carson-Macedonia Community Schools. In the 66 years from 1893 through 1958, there were 516 graduates from Macedonia High School. The largest class was 26 seniors in 1935. The most numerous surnames of the graduates were: Smith-23, Miller-18, Peterson-14, Dye-13, Lewis-12, Plumb-11, Braden-11, Clayton-10, Coons-10, Clark-9, and Hobson-9. The last graduate from Macedonia High school was Midge White (alphabetically).

Macedonia High School
Pottawattamie County, IA

#55

Malcom High School

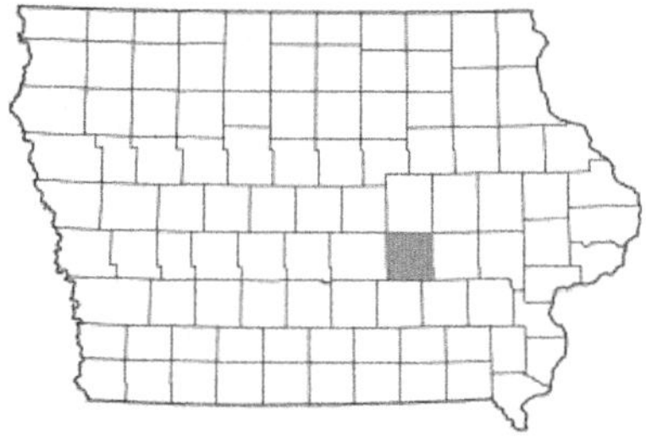

Mascot: Eagles
Colors: Blue and White
Closed: 1960
Location: Central Poweshiek County

Early History—Malcom Township is in the geographical center of Poweshiek County. The county was named for a Chief of the Sac and Fox Indian tribes. The last treaty which opened the land containing Poweshiek County to the white settlers was signed in 1843. The first settlers migrated to the area from Vermont. The area became known as Yankee Settlement because of all the New England settlers. There were Germans that came directly from Germany starting in 1858. Scottish families settled south of the town of Malcom. While it is unknown the origin of the name Malcom, L.E. Cardwell from Vermont is given credit for naming the township. Cardwell was one of the first three Vermont families to settle in the area.

Another Vermonter, Church Meigs, built a sawmill on Little Bear Creek where much of the lumber was cut for the settlers. A grist mill on Little Bear Creek soon followed for farmers to bring their grain to be made into flour.

The stagecoach line between Iowa City and Des Moines came directly through Yankee Settlement and a stage station was completed for the changing of horses. The stage station included a tavern that was called "The Halfway House" since it was halfway from Iowa City to Des Moines. This stage trail later became Old Highway 6.

The Chicago, Rock Island, and Pacific Railroad came through the township in 1863. The village of Malcom was laid out along Little Bear Creek in 1866 by Wigton. The town was platted in 1872.

Rarely mentioned in any other town or area were former confederates that relocated in Iowa following the Civil War. The Heishman, Richman, and Lineweaver families were a few of those resettling to start a new life.

The stockyards at Malcom were such a shipping point for livestock to the packing houses that the town was dubbed "Little Chicago." As many as 500 car loads of cattle were shipped each year from the Malcom stockyards to the Chicago packing houses.

Early Schools—The first school in Yankee Settlement was held in 1855 at the home of Church Meigs with six students. This school was taught by his daughter, Patience Meigs Wallace. In 1858, a country school two miles north of Malcom, called Malcom No. 2, became the first school building.

In 1872, after platting the village of Malcom, a wooden two-story school was constructed in town. By 1880, there were 136 students enrolled through the eighth grade. This building lasted for 20 years and was large enough to accommodate up to 300 students.

In 1885, a high school was established in a frame building and offered three years of classes. Graduations were held in the town auditorium. The first graduating class was in 1888 and included Ada Royce Gross, who became the mother of a long time US Congressman from Iowa, Representative H.R. Gross. For a 12-year diploma, students had to travel 12 miles west to the Grinnell Academy.

By 1902 a newer building was needed. The district had accumulated a building fund and cash that paid for labor and materials of $11,000 for a brick school. It became the cornerstone for the east side of the Malcom community schoolhouse. When it was completed it had no debt. The twelfth grade was added in 1904. The last addition for the west part of the school was added in 1924 at the cost of $38,000 and included the gymnasium, classrooms, and assembly hall.

Besides the independent Malcom school, there were nine rural one-room country schools in the area. Students attending an eight-year "country school" were required to pass state examinations before going to high school. Rural families had to pay tuition for their children to attend high school in town.

Notable Graduates – Merrill Church Meigs finished his schooling at Malcom with eleven grades in the school. His interests in mechanical devices led him to his first job in 1901 with the J.I. Case Threshing Machine Company in Racine, Wisconsin. Within a year he oversaw sales in South America. He enrolled at the University of Chicago without graduating from a 12-year high school. He played football under Alonzo Stagg and was the starting left guard on the University of Chicago national championship team in 1905. While at college, he was also the campus correspondent for the *Chicago Herald and Examiner*. He later became the publisher of the paper. Inspired to become a pilot by Charles Lindbergh's solo flight across the Atlantic Ocean, Meigs became a booster of Chicago as a world center for aviation. He gave flying lessons to President Harry S. Truman. He became a senior vice president of the Hearst Corporation, publisher of the *Chicago American*, and headed the Chicago Aero Commission. Merrill Meigs insisted that in addition to Midway Airport and O'Hare Field, the city needed an airfield within ten minutes of the Loop. It opened in December 1948 and was named Meigs Field in his honor.

Frederick C. Eisele ('38) received his PhD at the University of Iowa. He was a professor of Business Administration at North Dakota State University (NDSU) where he established the College of Business Administration. An award is presented to members of the teaching staff at NDSU who demonstrate the characteristics, and model established by Dr. Frederick Eisele.

Keith Alan Barnes ('58) received a degree from Parsons College and an MBA from Syracuse University in 1963. While in the United States Coast Guard, he stood in the honor guard at the United States Capitol rotunda while John F. Kennedy was lying in state. He became an executive and CEO in the food industry at Proliant Inc. in Ames. His talents were shared on numerous boards in Ames and the state ranging from chairing the United Way, the Iowa Planning and Zoning Commission, and the Board of Directors of the Iowa State Research Park.

He was an ardent fisherman from his first catch as a boy in Malcom to his fishing clubs in Ames. He is noted for saying, however, "the greatest catch of my life was in landing Karen" to be his wife.

Notable Teachers—Iness Straight Raffety came to teach music in Malcom in 1924. She attended Bedford High School and graduated from the State University of Iowa in 1903 with a Bachelor of Arts in Music. Her first job was teaching music, English, and dramatics in Guernsey. On her journey there by train, she came to Carnsforth where, according to the maps, there was a train to Guernsey. To her dismay, she learned that the railroad to Guernsey was for freight only! She rented a horse and wagon to travel there. The following year, Iness took the job just nine miles to the west at Malcom where she became involved with the girls basketball program. As a music teacher at the school she used a tuning fork for a pure musical tone for teaching. It was used to give a starting pitch for a soloist or a group singing without accompaniment. At Malcom, the visiting boys basketball team dressed in the music room on the second floor of the school. After the Brooklyn boys basketball team visited, the tuning fork came up missing. Iness had to contact the Brooklyn coach with a note asking for the return of the tuning fork. His name was LaVerne Raffety. He was not only the coach of the basketball team, but was also the Principal of Brooklyn High School. When LaVerne received the note, he investigated the problem and indeed did retrieve the tuning fork. He brought it over to Malcom to return. They met and were married a short time later.

Arthur L. Converse was the superintendent and science teacher from 1951-56. He wrote a two-page letter questionnaire to Albert Einstein requesting his reply to an experiment. Einstein wrote back on a single page with his response to the questions:

The Institute of Advanced Study
Princeton, New Jersey

September 4, 1953
Dear sir: there is no difficulty to explain your present experiment on the basis of electrostatic theory . . . complete with drawings explaining the theory . . . If the mentioned body is an open electroscope it behaves as if it would be situated near the floor and charged to the potential (-p).

Sincerely,
A Einstein
Albert Einstein

This letter would be sold later at auction for $53,500.

Sports—The first football game played was about 1900. In 1905, they only lost once. Football playing did not last many years. The boys played basketball, track, and spring and fall baseball. Dick Puls ('59) remembered, "I was the tallest in school at 6'2" but not worth much in basketball. We sometimes scrimmaged the girls. I know they would have beaten us in a real game. My 'claim to fame' was that I was the tallest catcher around and had a great arm. No one ever stole second on me during my senior year."

The girls organized a basketball team in 1905 and played on an outside dirt court. The first game was played in Malcom against Montezuma before a boys football game. Malcom won the game. The girls resumed playing basketball when the new gymnasium was built. In 1945 and 1955, they were Poweshiek County champions and sectional champions in 1939, 1957, and 1958.

Mr. Logan was the girls basketball coach and superintendent from 1956-61 when the school closed. "I was a starting guard on our team. We made it to the district finals game in 1958 but had to play a great State Center team. They defeated us to keep us from going to state. They went on to finish third place in the state tournament," remembered Janet Longnecker McNaul ('58). Jane Barnes Sherwood ('59) added, "With Coach Logan being the superintendent also, we always seemed to be able to get extra practices before big games. Our gymnasium was one of the best in the English Valley Conference."

The biggest sports rivals were Guernsey, Montezuma, Hartwick, and Brooklyn.

Activities—Malcom High School students sold more War Bonds than similar sized schools in the state. They were rewarded when a leader of the WAC came to Malcom to give them the honor. "We all had a chance to ride around town in her Jeep. My sister, Barbara Sherwood, and Mildred Porter got to go to Des Moines and appeared on WHO with the great interview with Jack Shelly," remembered Marcia Sherwood Braley ('46). "On VE Day on May 9, 1945 we all got out of school and went to Grinnell for a picnic to celebrate. Three of my classmates were already in the service, Wayne and Eugene Dayton, and Xen Stoner. The Dayton boys did receive their diplomas later and are both pictured with us in our class of 1946 composite. Due to those war times, we had started with 17 as freshman and only nine of us graduated."

Band—A band was organized in 1940. There were not any out-of-town parades or contests for the Malcom band. Students in band remember marching and playing from the school to the cemetery for the Memorial Day ceremonies. "I played the drums as we marched every Memorial Day to the cemetery. When approaching the cemetery, the instruments would stop playing and I would be the only one playing on the rims of the drum with the sticks. It was a dramatic scene and we all were so proud to be a part of the program. We only had capes for uniforms, but we still had such camaraderie," told Janet Longnecker McNaul ('58). Lucy Lu Schneekloth Axmear ('59) recalled, "I had an ear for music and was often asked to play different instruments if we did not have a specific player because of graduations. I played the trumpet, drums, and even the tuba. That march on Memorial Day from the high school to the cemetery was special."

Polio—"My dad, Fred Story, came down with polio when he was a teenager. He was able to make a full recovery," shared Sharon Story Robinson. "When the vaccine came out in 1955, we all received the first shot of the vaccine."

Killed in Action—The following from Malcom area were killed in wars:

Guy Early, WWI
Dewey Gruhn, WWI
Iver Davis Jr., WWII
Don Story, Korea

Senior Trips—In 1948, the seniors were loaded into the back of a stock and grain truck and traveled out of town to a lake for a day-long picnic.

By 1956, the transportation was by car for the day to Omaha. Arlene Hautekeete Reimers ('56) told, "There were nine in my class. We squeezed into two cars with two teacher sponsors and headed west. A lifelong memory is our tour at a packing house. Why we went there is beyond me, but our eyes were opened. I guess that is what education is all about because none of us ever wanted to work in a packing house after that day."

In 1958 and 1959, the seniors traveled to the Lake of the Ozarks and Branson, Missouri for a four-day trip. Traveling by cars, they were greeted by hundreds of other high school seniors from a five-state region, there to frolic in the spring sun at the beach. New friendships and acquaintances and lifelong memories of boating, swimming, and dances were established. Dick Puls, ('59) reflected, "We went into Springfield to see the Ozark Jubilee with Red Foley. He was quite a showman. My mother, Evelyn, was one of the chaperones, so I was on my best behavior. The senior boys drove the three cars for the trip. We squeezed into the small cabins and what an education we received with all of the other schools and kids at the Ozarks." Jeanne Barnes Sherwood ('59) recalled, "We all went on a plane ride over Bagnall Dam. It was three at a time with the pilot. I had never been in a plane before and I wonder if it was ever required to get permission from home to fly in a plane on a senior getaway."

Drivers Education—Lyle Oswood was a new graduate and a first-year teacher from Iowa State Teachers College (ISTC) who taught the business classes and drivers education. "I was driving in a time that we wore big skirts and double can-cans underneath. Mr. Oswood was trying to teach us to know where the different buttons and controls were on the dash. I reached down blindly and touched the wrong button and immediately a blast of air blew open the outlet and my skirt with the cancans lifted like a sail. Poor Mr. Oswood was embarrassed and sputtering as he quickly reached over and turned off the fan. The boys in the back seat couldn't control themselves with laughter," remembered Sharon Story Robinson. "Mr. Oswood was young, and we loved him. He was just one of us. We were all part of each other." Lyle Osgood transferred to BGM when the high school closed and continueed there as a teacher until his retirement.

Bus Driver—In the 1950s there was only one bus driven by the janitor, Ray Dayton. He drove south on the first route to deliver the pupils to school and then head off for the second route north of town to do the same. He drove to all the away ball games and out of town activities. Dick Puls ('59) remarked, "Not only did he drive the bus morning and night-he was the only custodian for the whole school. That had to be a full day's work."

Pranks—Morgan Hicks was the city marshal. He and his family came to Malcom in the 1930s. He was the father of five daughters and one son. The middle daughter, Nedra Hicks Neville ('48) shared, "There were always boys that reveled in teasing and pulling shenanigans on the town marshal. I recall of an outhouse that would be dragged out in the street shortly after my dad would pass in his car. Another time, while his car was parked, they jacked it up on blocks so that the tires were not in contact with the street. These boys then sped by in their cars and when the marshal attempted to chase them in his car, the car engine would roar but the tires just spun a 'hundred miles an hour'."

Extra baby chicks from the town hatchery sometimes were given away. Jeanne Barnes Sherwood ('59) smiled as she remembered, "Every spring the hatchery downtown gave away baby chicks. We were able to leave the school grounds during the lunch hour. So, some others in my class went downtown and asked for some chicks. They put them in little boxes and four of us brought them back to school and put them in the cloak room behind the coats. Everything was so quiet until it started getting warm for the chicks in the boxes and a chorus of cheeping started in the hallway. Our young first-year teacher, Mr. Gerald Johnson exclaimed, 'Whose chicks are those?' I was one who had to confess. All Mr. Johnson said was, 'I would have appreciated if you would have asked.'"

Norman Schroeder ('49) grinned as he told, "I was involved in a snipe hunt. We coaxed a boy to go along. He had never caught a snipe before. We drove a few miles out in the country. We encouraged him to get down in the grader ditch and be quiet and we would go out and chase the snipes back to him. All he had to do was throw the gunny sack over it and quickly close the end. Poor kid. He never did catch a snipe and may have never graduated from school either."

Closing—In the 57 years from 1904 through 1960, there were 480 graduates from Malcom High School. The largest classes were 18 seniors in 1929, and 1931. The most common surnames of the graduates were: Davis-16, Eisele-9, Vogel-9, Beck-8, Stephen-8, Carpenter-7, Wolfe-7, Smith-7, and Meigs-6. The last to receive a diploma from Malcom High School was Garry Story (alphabetically). In the fall of 1960, the high school students were bused to the new BGM (Brooklyn Guernsey Malcom) high school in Brooklyn.

Malcom High School
Poweshiek County, IA

#56

Mallard High School

Mascot: Ducks
Colors: Black and Gold
Closed: 1991
Location: Southern Palo Alto County

Early History—The town of Mallard was named by Charles E. Whitehead, the president of the Des Moines Ft. Dodge Railway. He was a great hunter and had hunted in this area several years before the railway arrived. His railroad track was laid as far north as Mallard in September 1882. The railway station was the first building on the town plat. Whitehead had a good sense of humor and after naming the station to the south "Plover," he named this station "Mallard" because of the great quantities of ducks inhabiting the sloughs and ponds. The railroad continued to the northwest, where the next town and station was identified. This town was named Curlew by Whitehead after yet another bird in the area. A road built along this diagonal was never constructed. The town names of Plover, Mallard, and Curlew, all in a row, are unique, and not found elsewhere in the world.

School Building—The high school had two entrances. One was for the boys and the other for girls.

A sharing arrangement with St. Mary's catholic school started the hot lunch program for all the students. Meals were prepared at St. Mary's and brought to the lunchroom at the lower level of the Mallard school.

Sports—Basketball was the girls sport at Mallard. They entered the state tournament in 1950. An account in the *Des Moines Tribune* paper during that March read:

> This week is a big one for Mallard. The Mallard High School girls basketball team will begin making its eighth bid for the state championship in the Drake Fieldhouse . . . Seven times Mallard has accomplished the great feat of qualifying for the state tournament, but never have the Ducks won a championship. Back in 1941, they played in the final game and lost 43 to 39 to

> Numa . . . This time, Coach Darold Enderson and his girls are hoping for a title, but they know how rough and tough is the road ahead of them in Des Moines . . . the Mallard coeds have chalked up their usual record and have notched 23 victories, suffered 2 defeats, and had to accept one tie . . . with such menacing clubs as Hartly, whom the Ducks defeated in the District tournament at Estherville . . . with the top 16 contenders for the 25th annual girls meet at Des Moines . . . the Ducks play their first tournament game against Luana, one of the toughest teams to meet.

Other teams in that 1950 sweet 16 state tournament and their records were: Centerville 13-9, Slater 28-4, Messervy 25-5, Meriden 20-2, Deep Rock 23-2, Winterset 19-3, Charter Oak 27-2, Runnels 25-2, Wiota 26-1, Coggon 21-3, Kamrar 24-2, Sperry 22-0, Oakland 26-2, and Luana 17-7. The flight of the Ducks ended in the semifinals game with a loss to Kamrar 55-49. Mallard returned to the state tournament in 1952, but lost this time to Monona in the quarterfinals, 59-51.

Dorothy Stafford Lyon ('52) played on three state tournament teams in 1948, 1950, and 1952. Dorothy at the age of 85 (2019) remembered, "I played in the first state tournament year as an eighth grader. We played a powerful Seymour team which returned four starters from their state championship team from 1947. We beat them in the opening round 31-25. Just being an eighth grader, I did not play often and was so nervous that someone would get into foul trouble because coach would put me in. We never were able to come home with a championship trophy, but what a time we had, and I loved the game so much."

The boys basketball teams had some great years.

The 1946 annual named, the *Black and Gold,* lists the Palo Alto County Tournament brackets. The Mallard Ducks were 15-0 going into the Tournament. The other teams in the tournament were: Ruthven, West Bend, Curlew, Graettinger, Cylinder, Ayrshire, and Rodman. Mallard defeated Ruthven and Curlew to reach the finals. They beat Cylinder for the county championship.

The sports rivals were Havelock and Curlew. Kenneth Lyon ('51) stated, "Even though others were our bitter rivals, we could never beat Rodman."

Boys track started in 1961. The principal Robert Hoogeveen was the coach. John Hartman ('63) was in his first year at Mallard, transferring from Rodman which had closed after his sophomore year. John recalled, "I had never run track before, and Mr. Hoogeveen told us all to line up and run the quarter mile. Completing the run and still trying to recover my breath, he said five minutes later 'okay, now let's run that quarter mile again.' After that second run, he says to me, 'you are my half-miler!'"

Mr. Hoogeveen was also the football coach. In his first year at Mallard in 1961, there were 12 boys out for football. That October a historic event occurred, never to be equaled in high school football. The

Mallard football team would play in two homecoming games away on the same night. The principal before Mr. Hoogeveen somehow had scheduled two games on the same night. Neither of the opposing schools released Mallard from the commitment. So, the Mighty Ducks split their squad in half. They had to recruit from the rest of the boys in school who had never played football before to get enough players for two teams. They traveled to Marathon and Pomeroy on two different buses on the same night to play both schools in their homecoming game. John Hartman ('63) shook his head and remembered, "Both of our teams lost badly, really badly."

The boys basketball team won the last Palo Alto Tournament in 1962. The teams in the tournament were: Mallard, Ayrshire, West Bend, Cylinder, Graettinger, and Ruthven. Mallard won in the finals against West Bend.

Judy Goodchild ('65) had a pet mallard duck and brought it to all home football games for a live mascot.

Drivers Education—Judy Fosnot Miller ('68) lived in the country and reflected, "We lived down a long narrow lane. Our teacher was George Kruger who also was a basketball coach. He left from the school with the car and picked up each of the students from our homes along the way. If we could drive down our narrow lane, we knew we were going to make it. Driving that black Chevrolet with a stick shift and learning to change a tire was a challenge."

Notable Teachers—Joy Gehrt ('42) returned to teach in Mallard. She had taught in the county school. She first taught kindergarten and then upper elementary. One year she had 60 kindergarten pupils and she was the only teacher. She was nearly five feet tall, and had bundles of energy, and played the violin and piano by ear. Though she was not one of the high school teachers, she is remembered by every Mallard student to have made a significant impact on their lives.

Robert Hoogeveen was the principal and taught social studies. He was also the guidance counselor. He had come from Sheldon and made an impact on every student. John Hartman ('63) remembered, "Mr. Hoogeveen was the best teacher that I ever had. He called me into his office on one day during my senior year. He asked what my plans were. I told him that I was thinking about going to Estherville Junior College for a start. He suggested that he thought I would be a great teacher and encouraged me to think about it and directed me to SCI (State College of Iowa). Another time he called me into his office and asked if I would go down to the fifth-grade classroom to sit-in for the teacher who needed to be away from the school for a short time. I did go on to SCI and become a teacher and coach for 40 years. I use some of Mr. Hoogeveen's quotes to this day. One was, 'experience is the best teacher, but it charges like a specialist.'" *(Author's Note: John Hartman was an excellent science teacher, coach, and mentor who left an indelible impression on my three children at Cedar Falls.)*

Another student (name withheld) was called into the guidance office and Mr. Hoogeveen asked her what she was planning on doing after graduation. He had observed her and knew she was an excellent student. She said that she was thinking about beauty school but didn't know how she was going to pay for it. He asked her if she had considered college and she again replied that she couldn't see how her family could afford it. He replied, "If I could get you a scholarship, would you consider it?" A few weeks later, he called her back into his office and told her that he had nearly a full scholarship to Northwestern in Orange City and that it would only cost her $200 for the year. She replied, "But Mr. Hoogeveen, where would I ever get $200?" This girl went on to Northwestern and became a teacher for the next 40 years.

Pranks—The town cop in the 1950s and '60s was Charlie Prochaska. Judy Fosnot Miller ('68) told, "He was a dear soul, but the kids played tricks on him. He was always so naïve and gullible. Darla Larson told the story that one night they made a call to report a car squealing and burning rubber around corners, but they had the license plate number. Poor Charlie carefully wrote down the number and drove around town looking for the car with the license plate number. He finally figured out the number was his own personal car."

Music—The marching band played during halftime at the football games. They also traveled annually to the Algona Days parade. Peggy Heldt Kenyon ('72) shared, "We did not have many times to play out of town. I played the snare drums faithfully for four years."

Killed in Action—Two men from Mallard were killed in action:

Richard Echert, WWII
George Hersom, WWII

Bus Drivers—Many of the school bus drivers were senior boys with their new drivers licenses. "The district had seven or eight buses. I drove a bus my senior year. Johnny Vaugh ('51) also drove a bus that year. He took the bus home each night and then reversed the route to come back to school the next morning. Every night at his house he had to drain the oil in the winter time, take it inside for the night, and put it back in the next morning because the bus motor was so stiff that it would not start with cold oil," remembered Kenneth Lyon ('51).

Senior Trip—John Hartman ('63) said, "As a senior myself, I drove the bus for our senior class trip to Minneapolis in 1963. We went to the Ford plant and the cinema with three screens to see *How the West Was Won*."

Closing—Mallard High School closed in May 1991. The next fall, the high school students were bused to their once bitter rival, West Bend. In the 65 years from 1926-1991, there were 1,447 graduates. The largest class was 36 seniors in 1975. The most numerous surnames of the graduates were: Johnson-41, Schuller-36, Goodchild-22, Gretchen-19, Hersom-17, Reinders-17, Schultz-16, Schumacher-16, Kacmarynski-16, Smith-16, Thompson-16, Larson-15, Baxter-11, Hurley-11, and Kunz-11. The last to receive a diploma from Mallard High school was Jeffery Wickman (alphabetically).

Special Note—The journalist, Chuck Offenburger, from the *Des Moines Register*, was the commencement speaker for the last graduation. The title of his speech was, "The Last Flight of the Ducks." In his column in the *Register*, he had recognized Mallard on two different occasions. One was the column about the worst Iowa high school mascots—The Ducks. In another article about the worst cheers, Mallard was again recognized. As he closed the graduation address, he led the crowd in that cheer:

Black and Gold
Gold and Black
Mallard Ducks
Quack, Quack, Quack!

Mallard High School
Palo Alto County, IA

#57

Marathon High School

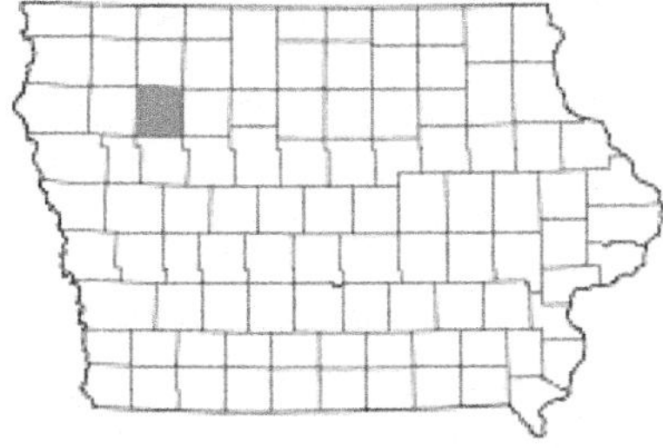

Mascot: Minuteman/Minuettes
Colors: Maroon and White
Closed: 1976
Location: Northeast Buena Vista County

Early History—In 1869, several citizens in the southern half of Buena Vista county desired to build schools. They went to the county seat at Sioux Rapids to consult the supervisors and petition for the establishment of new townships in the south part of the county. A map was prepared dividing the county into seven townships.

In 1881, a narrow-gauge railroad was planned to connect the Chicago, Milwaukee, and St. Paul Railroad with the Illinois Central. The railroad was to pass west of Poland and Lee Townships. A town was needed at this location. Immediately, Richard H. Olney endorsed the company a six-percent tax to change the town site to the center of Poland Township. The township had been named after the Olney's old hometown of Poland, Ohio. With this leverage, Chicago Northwestern built a road and put a town right where it was requested. They called the town May View. The name was later changed to Marathon after an old Greek battlefield. It was given this name by the daughter of the Chicago and Milwaukee Railroad president. The town of Marathon was in the center of Poland Township. This daughter also helped name the streets in town. The streets were named after Greek gods and places, with names like Neptune, Piraeus, Athens, Agora, Illissus, Attica, Bernice, Scott, Minerva, Morea, and Hawk.

Early Schools—The first school was a one-room township school. After the town was incorporated in 1893, another one-room school was erected. This proved to be inadequate and two more rooms were added the next year.

In 1903, five of the rural one-room school districts, numbers 2, 3, 4, 5, and 8 of Poland

Township, were added to the Marathon Independent District. A fine new pressed-brick building was erected, and the school became a fully qualified 12 graded school. The erected value was $20,000. In 1916, this building was remodeled. The high school was moved from the first floor to the second and the lower grades were moved to the first floor. The basement was remodeled to provide for a gymnasium, manual training, and home economics. The pupils living in the country were brought to school every day in horse drawn hacks on six bus routes. The drivers were paid $293.33 per year, varying from $33 to $45 a month according to the length of the route. The high school offered four-year courses and was fully accredited.

In 1927, a new high school building was erected. An agriculture building and farm shop were added in 1950. The new addition completed in 1968 included a new gymnasium, a music department, a cafeteria, and ample classrooms.

School Activities—The biggest sports rivals were the 'Swedes' from Albert City.

The school newspaper was called the *Monocle* and the yearbook was called the *Reflector*. In the 1954 yearbook, the following groups are pictured: FFA with 30 members, Madrigal Choir-14 members, band-33 members, choir-38 members, and boys glee-36 members. The homecoming queen was Eloise Anderson ('54).

The band played every Wednesday night on a flat rack in the town center. On Saturday there was a free movie in town.

Notable Teachers—Mrs. Helen Danielson taught typing, bookkeeping, and was the yearbook sponsor. Darel Burns ('49) remembered, "She was the best teacher I ever had. She was very motherly to all of us. She had no children of her own and treated us all like we were her own children." Carol Bahde Schulz ('57) shared, "After graduation, those who ever came back to Marathon to visit, always wanted to call on Mrs. Danielson."

Rex Trafton was the superintendent at Marathon from 1931 until 1966. Darel Burns ('49) said of him, "He believed in corporal punishment. I got the rubber hose from him on occasion. I was a little mischievous. In shop, we were to make paddles for Mr. Trafton. So, I cut one of the paddles down the middle and filled it with saw dust. The first time he used it, of course, it broke right down the middle. I was directed back to shop to make a new and sturdier one."

Victor Bunge was the junior high principal and then moved to the high school. He taught civics, government, and history. He only had one arm. Darel Burns ('49) said, "Between Victor and Mr. Trafton was probably why I went to college. If you were willing to work for him, he would always help."

Hot Lunches—The hot lunch program was started in the 1950s.

Pranks—Gus Cox ('49) and Darel Burns ('49) had girl friends in Laurens. They put papers over the windows so that no one could look out to see them leaving. They crawled out a window and went to Laurens (eight miles to the east) to see the girls over the noon hour. Upon arriving at the Laurens school, the Laurens superintendent caught them and sent them back to Marathon. Of course, there was detention handed down from Mr. Trafton.

Alumni—In the summer of 2019, the Marathon Alumni celebrated their 114th annual meeting.

Closing—The Marathon High School closed in May 1976. The next year the students would be bused to Laurens to the new Laurens-Marathon High School. There were 1083 graduates from Marathon from 1884 through 1976. The largest class was 40 seniors in 1940. The most numerous surnames were: Anderson-52, Johnson-31, Peterson-28, Erickson-22, Carlson-22, Smith-15, Wilson-13, Wells-13, Lindgren-11, and, Okerberg-10. The last graduate from Marathon High School was Bruce Stone (alphabetically).

#58

Maurice High School

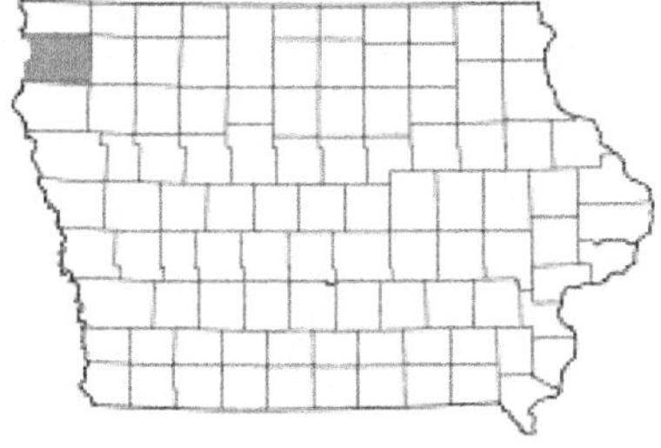

Mascot: Monarch (Lion)
Colors: Blue and Orange
Closed: 1959
Location: South Central Sioux County

Early History—Maurice was a railroad town. The signs leading into town on Highway 75 from the north and south feature a hot air balloon and say, "Small in Size but on the Rise." The town was located at the crossroads of the Great Northern and Union Pacific railroads. The nearby west branch of the Floyd River and the rolling, beautiful Loess Hills (a geologic formation only seen in western

Iowa and one location in China) make it a most picturesque setting.

There was a nighttime raid in the 1860s by some men from the neighboring town of Hawarden. A safe was stolen in an attempt to relocate the county seat to Hawarden. Orange City eventually became the county seat.

Dutch families settled most of Sioux County. They immigrated through Ellis Island. These families migrated to Pella in south central Iowa and then to northwest Iowa. They came to the countryside to farm.

Maurice had three churches—St. Mary's Catholic, American Reformed (English speaking), and the First Reformed Church (Dutch speaking). Only the First Reformed exists today (2020).

Four loud city whistles blare in Maurice every day and have for years. They blow at 7:00 AM, 12:00 noon, 1:00 PM, and 6:00 PM to alert workers to start work at seven in the morning, to break for the noon hour, to return to work, and the final whistle for the end of the work day.

A devastating flood occurred on the Floyd River in 1926. At the crossroads of Highways 10 and 75 north of town, several lives were swept away as the four small railroad bridges and the main bridge over Highway 75 were washed out. In a project the locals call the "million-dollar corner", the government relocated the main channel of the river to the east side of the highway. The railroad put in a small bridge to the north, and a large one to the south. Two new bridges were constructed for the east-west Highway 10 and for the north-south Highway 75. This project has lasted nearly 100 years and the million spent in 1926 would be quite inflated in today's dollars (2020).

Early Schools—In 1900, H.A. McCormick, the editor of *The Maurice Review*, printed "Maurice believes in education." The first nearby country school was held at the Van Horssen schoolhouse three miles east of Maurice. This building was constructed with square nails and rough sawed boards. Other classes were held in the H.M. Mensink granary one mile east of Maurice.

A small one-room school was set up in an old building on Elm street in 1884. Another one-room building was erected on the site of the present school. Traditional academic subjects were taught, and every morning began with a Bible reading.

In June 1890, the Independent School District of Maurice was officially formed. The upper grade teacher and lower grade teacher were paid $40 and $35 each month, respectively.

This one-room school soon became difficult to support financially because the district was so small. Annexing Sherman Township created an enlargeed district. In November 1895, a new two-room schoolhouse was completed at the cost of $3,000 following a unanimous vote to issue bonds.

Additions to the curriculum and school events included:

1898 Vocal music added.

1899 The school hired a janitor.

1900 Problems in the school room: "Unclean and lousy" students were sent home with a note to parents saying they could return when presentable.

1905 Ninth, tenth, and eleventh grades added.

1912 Eva Henrietta Mensink and Tillie Duven became the first two Maurice girls to go to college, though their parents opposed it. Eva earned her own way and later returned to Maurice as a teacher.

1917-18 The school closed for four weeks because of a smallpox epidemic and for four months because of Spanish influenza.

Sports—Football was not played at Maurice. The boys basketball team went to the state basketball tournament two times when there was only one tournament for all the teams in the state. The first time was in 1940, led by the 6′ 9″ center Alb Jager. The second time was in 1953. With only 52 students in school that year, this team journeyed to Des Moines to take on the 15 other schools in the tournament. It was reported that the seedings were drawn out of a hat. The draw of the Maurice Monarchs just happened to be Sioux Center. Sioux Center was a school just eight miles north of Maurice and a team they had defeated in the county tournament. Unfortunately, Sioux Center edged Maurice in the opening round of the state tournament.

This 1953 team featured three brothers, Don ('54), Stan ('53), and Norm ('56) Van Ommeren, and two other brothers, Lewis ('54) and Martin ('53) Weirda. This team was very tall for a school this size. The team's starters were Don at 6′7″; Stan 6′2″; Lewis 6′3″; Martin 6′1″; and De Jager 6′1″. The third brother, Norman Ommeren, was the first substitute. Other team members were Roger Harnelink ('54), Eugene Van Roekel ('54), Richard Moir ('55), Gary Dale Korver ('54), Peter Ver Mulm, and Paul Dekker ('54).

Boys baseball was played in the fall and spring. Maurice played in the state tournament in 1956. In the quarter finals matchup, it was again neighboring Sioux Center as the opponent. Maurice won 1-0 on a home run by Don Van Horssen ('56). In the semifinals, they lost to Grandville 3-2, a team that featured a set of twins who were the pitcher and catcher. One was left-handed and the other right-handed. They would change positions during the game to match up with the best arm on the mound meeting the other teams' batters.

Winning the county tournament was almost as big as going to the state tournament. Maurice won the Lyon County Basketball Tournament in 1953 and 1955. The other teams in the County Tournament were Orange City, Rock Valley, Hull, Hawarden, Boyden, Newkirk, and Alton.

Girls basketball was played only one year in 1950. Evelyn Van Horssen DeVries ('51) smiled as she remembered, "We made our shorts in home economics class. We had some 'natty' tops that we wore with numbers cut out of felt and sewed onto our backs of the shirts."

School Activities—Hot lunch was started in 1954. In the years before this was offered, a Friday hot lunch was prepared by the home economics class.

Each morning the school day convened with assembly. It began with a Bible reading, a prayer, and the Pledge of Allegiance. When a student was not in a class, they were expected to be in their seats in the assembly room.

A wonderful sledding hill was located just south of the school. During the noon hour, students ran to the hill with their sleds to race down the two-and-a-half block slope. There was only time for two runs by every student which allowed time to get back the assembly room before the bell rang. Only one student could get three runs and still make it back. Don Horssen ('56) reported, "Allen Wichers ('56) had long legs and was a fast runner. He could race down the hill a third time and be back at school just as the bell rang. I don't remember the consequences for being late, but it must have been significant because we never wanted to be late."

Pranks—In 1928, a fire escape was purchased to cover the chute that came out of the fifth and sixth grade room. This was used in fire drills. It was a scary chute for young children and sometimes girls would get so scared they "piddled their pants" coming down the chute. Pranksters often poured water on the slide making others that followed them down think that the moisture was an accident of some frightened youngster (shared by several alumni).

Janitor—"Abe Levering was a super guy. All of us loved him. The last day of school he allowed us to climb the fire escape slide from the bottom. We doctored the slide down with wax paper from our lunches and it made it almost impossible to climb backwards," recalled Eileen Vogelaar Wichers ('57). Abe often sat by the coal furnace and built doll houses out of sucker sticks and later sold them.

Bus Driver—Bill Korver ran a gas delivery service in town and drove the school bus for years. He was a character. He did not allow water pistols on the bus except for the last day of school. Every boy waited anxiously for that day. They brought a gallon of water to resupply their guns for this water-soaked celebration for the end of the school year.

Senior Trips—The seniors from the class of 1951 went to Storm Lake for the day. They went to a movie and a boat ride on the lake. Each of them received a navy sailor hat for the memory.

The class of 1956 traveled 150 miles to Lincoln, Nebraska. Their class sponsor for all four years was Betty Pippet. Motoring in three cars, they toured the college, the state capital building, rode rented horses in the hills, and toured a museum. They loaded up at the end of the day and arrived back late in Maurice with educational memories to last a lifetime.

Killed in Action—Six Maurice men were lost in war. They were:

Jake Levering, WWI
Herman Vander Laan, WWII
Clarence Vore, WWII
Gerald Bosch, WWII
Nick Stellingwerf, WWII
William Leusink, Iraq

Closing—Maurice High School closed in May 1959. The ending was a bitter finish to the merging of the district with Orange City, the larger county seat town to the east. Negotiations on the closing finally won the support of the town, but only if the new high school and district would be named with the Maurice name coming first. Thus, Maurice Orange City, or MOC, became the district name. When absorbing Floyd Valley of Alton a year later, the district name was changed to MOCFV. The last graduation was in 1959 with Leon Wichers receiving the final diploma from Maurice High School (alphabetically).

Maurice High School
Sioux County, IA

#59

Mechanicsville High School

Mascot: Bullets
Colors: Maroon and Gold
Closed: 1961
Location: Northwest Cedar County

Early History—Settlers came from the eastern states and settled among the timber and along a stream one and one-half miles northwest of present-day Mechanicsville. A post office was established in 1846, the same year of Iowa's statehood. The settlement was called Pioneers Grove. Tracts of land were cleared to the south by 1850. Another tract to the east of the village was purchased and named the Iroquois tract. The railroad located its depot on the south side of this land, which brought another plot of land on which a village was built. The site was plotted by John Onstott. The town was named to reflect the workers' jobs of carpenters, masons, and wheelwrights. Thus, the name Mechanicsville seemed to be appropriate.

Written in the *Mechanicsville Town History* booklet published in 1991:

> During the winter of 1858, Jacob Onstott, then 14 years old, made five trips to Muscatine helping drive hogs to the market. As many as 250 heads were taken at one time. A team and wagon lead the way to break down the snow, and hogs followed on foot. If a hog became exhausted it was put in the wagon and hauled. The trip took many days, so the travelers stayed overnight at a tavern and homes along the way. There surely was no excess fat on those hogs when they reached the market.

The first ordinance passed by the city council of this new town was on April 6, 1868. This ordinance prohibited letting horses, mules, and hogs roam the streets. The hogs wallowed in mud in the streets and were hard on lawns and gardens. It was difficult to enforce, and two different town marshals quit because it was too much pressure to enforce the ordinance. Livestock on the streets were quite prominent during this time but nothing compared to the sight on July 29, 1870. A drove of 2,500 sheep passed through Mechanicsville on their way from Wisconsin to Colorado territory. No wonder fences and ordinances were needed to protect lawns and gardens.

Early Schools—John Onstott built the first schoolhouse for Mechanicsville. This one-room school had six windows and one door. The window glass and finishing lumber used for building the desks were hauled on a one-horse wagon from Muscatine. The expense of running the school and paying the teacher for the first term (three months) was obtained through subscription from the pupils attending.

In 1866, an independent school district was formed. There was some opposition to such a move and it required a lawsuit with a decision from the Supreme Court to settle. There was no instruction above the eighth grade.

By 1875, a larger and more permanent school building was necessary because of an increasing population. The community erected a three-story brick building at a cost of $10,000. The bell from this school is still mounted to a frame in the town (2020).

In March 1908, the voters cast their ballots for a new building to replace the 1875 structure. There were 341 votes cast; 204 by men and 137 by women. The election authorized the district to bond for $20,000 for the new building. The new school was designed for the elementary grades and high school. Primary grades were housed on the first floor and the high school on the second floor.

Several notes in the school board minutes during these years included:

1867	44 for and 5 against having school terms. Winter term—1st Monday in January, Summer term—1st Monday in May, Fall term—3rd Monday in September. Salaries: Male teachers—$50 per month, Female teachers—$35 per month, Secretary and Treasurer—$15 per annum.
1872	Number of school months reduced to 9 from 10.
1885	Principal salary raised to $100 per month.
1885	Moved to pay Mr. Morse $2.05—cleaning the privy and hanging door.
1879	"After cool and deliberate thought on the subject by the board," Latin was a standard course.
1887	Admission fee of 10 cents charged at graduation exercises.

The graduates from 1886-1889 completed the first two years of high school. From 1891-1906, the graduates completed eleven years of school work. In 1907, the twelfth year was added to the high school curriculum.

Athletic Activities—Track was the earliest form of competitive sports at Mechanicsville. David Ferguson ('44) told, "My dad, Everett Ferguson ('11) and Clement Wilson ('08) both attended the National Meet in Chicago in 1907. Clement placed first in the 220-yard dash and Everett third in the mile run (he was just 15 years old at the time). Clement Wilson was chosen for the Olympic team to represent the United States in the 1912 Olympics in Stockholm, Sweden." Their track coach was the Superintendent Mr. E.L. McConkie.

His relay team of Jack Kohl, Clement Wilson ('08), Leo Miller, and Carl Thomas ('08) was the best in this section of the state. Track was on dirt at the Mechanicsville school.

The Mechanicsville relays, or the "M" relays, were founded by Don Gemberling ('22) and were one of the outstanding relays in eastern Iowa. The M Relays were discontinued during the war in 1942.

Don Gemberling coached and taught at Mechanicsville from 1931 until 1945. In the spring of 1943, Betty Ferguson Emrich ('44), Florence Gleason ('44), Elizabeth Kress ('44), and Lois Boots ('44) were bored in study hall. A spirited Betty Ferguson ('44), at the age of 93 (2020), with a gleam in her eyes, recalled, "We asked Mr. Gemberling if we could go out for track. He said yes, but we would have to do all of the same events that the boys did in practice. So, that is just what we did. And I recall that the boys actually got better showing off for us or at least not being shown up by us girls!" She continued, "I was a cheerleader for the boys and played guard on the basketball team. We girls got the bright idea to order t-shirts with two bullets on the front to represent our mascot. Of course, they came with the bullets across the front where our boobs were. Boys being boys, snickered at us. We only wore them once!"

The baseball team of 1912-13 won the Iowa State Baseball Championship.

Competitive girls basketball was shown in a 1930 picture. The girls posed with their new uniforms and a basketball.

The fiercest rivalries were against Morley, Stanwood, and Lisbon.

The 1958 boys basketball team finished with a 15-3 record and were the Cedar County Champions. That year they played Olin, Lowden, Oxford Junction, Stanwood, Clarence, Morley, Wyoming, Lisbon, Solon, Tiffin, St. Marys, and Durant.

Football was not played at Mechanicsville.

Yearbook—The last school annual in 1961 had pictures of clubs and activities: FFA with 22 students, FHA-28 students, Librarians-8, Speech-15, Girls Basketball-12, Newspaper-29, Boys Choir-12, Annual Staff-26, Girls Softball-14, Boys Baseball-15 (County Champions), and Concert Band-30 (each decked out in their white shoes). The homecoming King and Queen were James Hoffman ('61) and Edith Oldorf ('61).

Notable Teachers—A popular teacher, mentor, and counselor of many was Eloise Martinez. She taught English in Mechanicsville from 1941 until the closing in 1961. Dorothy Ferguson Herring ('44) simply said, "She was an outstanding teacher."

Mr. Hammer was the principal in the 1940s. Betty Ferguson Emrich ('44) told of a study hall in the early 1940s when a salesman stopped into the school to meet with the principal. "I believe there were like 78 students in the study hall when he poked his head in the door. We were all sitting like cherubs hard at work with our books open. He was amazed how quiet and well behaved we were displayed studying quietly. He would later ask Mr. Hammer, 'just how do you keep them so quiet?' Hammer answered back, 'because I am a mean old bastard!'"

Betty Ferguson Emrich ('44) added, "Mr. Hammer announced in assembly that we would be having school on a Saturday. I stood up and said that was impossible, because I had a business and it was impossible for me to attend. He was stern but listened that I had two paper routes and Saturdays were the collection days and the customers depended on me to come and collect. Somehow he backed down on the Saturday class idea and I was quite popular with my classmates."

A Mechanicsville alumni, Bernice Koppenhaver Kern ('31), returned to teach at MHS and knew how to discipline and control the rowdies. An innocent looking Janet Maher Ford ('58) told, "Mrs. Kern had long fingernails and she would stab the boys on the top of their heads with her fingernails. Of course, I was good and never received any of her wrath."

Killed in Action—Five Mechanicsville graduates were casualties in World War II:

William Koppenhaver ('28), POW Germany 1945
Wayne Bordern ('35), Germany 1945
Everett Kline ('35), France 1944
Lyle Wagman ('39), Iwo Jima 1945
William Zenishek ('41), Germany 1945

Band—Each spring the band performed annually at the Eastern Iowa Band Festival in Cedar Rapids. Janet Maher Ford ('58) played the drums. "These band trips were always highlighted by a stop on the way home at the Butterfly Café," Janet longingly remembered.

"I was in the band, too, and we played at the boys basketball games. I was a guard on the girls team. I couldn't shoot worth a damn, but boy could I guard," Betty Fergeson Emrich ('44) remembered.

Teacher Contracts—The teacher contracts from the 1920s through the 1940s were worded to recommend the teacher stay in town on weekends and only travel out of town one weekend each month.

The teachers were to attend a church and had to get permission to wear slacks. Smoking was to be done only in the boiler room at the school.

Closing—The Mechanicsville High School closed in May 1961. A total of 911 had graduated from the school in the 75 years from 1886-1961. The most numerous surnames of the graduates were Ferguson-20, Jackson-20, Johnson-14, Hatcher-11, Boyles-10, Brown-10, Koppenhaver-10, Young-10, Miller-9, and Rhoads-8. The largest graduating class was 33 in 1941. The last to receive a diploma from Mechanicsville High School was Milton Zimmerman (alphabetically).

Mechanicsville High School
Cedar County, IA

#60

Melvin High School

Mascot: Comets
Colors: Blue and Gold
Closed: 1980
Location: South Central Osceola County

Early History—Osceola County was organized on October 3, 1871. Baker and Goewey Townships are the middle two townships on the south border of the county. In 1878, an Iowa Synod Lutheran church was organized in Baker Township south of the township cemetery. A roving post office, by the name of Gopher, was the address for area settlers from 1872-1896. It was located on the property of the individual serving as current postmaster. It served Goewey and Baker Township, and this location could be quite inconvenient for some patrons.

Newspapers in Sanborn (12 miles south in O'Brien County) reported the formation of a new town called Eden City. Mail was delivered three times a week from Sanborn. The new village name vanished quickly when it was discovered that there was another Eden and the founders needed a new name. They agreed on "Melvin" honoring brothers Henry and Edward Melvin who were early 1870s settlers. The Melvin brothers owned the adjacent land to the village. A schoolhouse already existed at the site and was joined by a store, blacksmith shop, creamery, town hall, wagon works, and hotel and boarding house.

Rumors of a planned railroad circulated. In 1900, the Rock Island Railroad built an extension in Iowa from Gowrie to Sibley. The plan depicted tracks crossing one mile south of Melvin. Meetings with area residents were held. All attempts to convince the railroad officials to alter their plan to go through the existing Melvin were in vain. The village moved south to its present location and expansion occurred rapidly. The new Melvin was incorporated in 1901.

Early Schools—Children attended rural schools located about every two miles in each direction. The children living north of town went to the school one mile north, and the children living south of Main Street attended the school one mile south of town. In 1903, a two-story frame structure was built to house all eight grades. This structure was adequate until 1914 when a new four-room brick building with a furnace and indoor plumbing replaced the wooden one. Ninth grade was added, and during the next few years the remaining grades were progressively added until all twelve grades were included. In 1920, a class of five graduated from Melvin High school with 12 years of credit.

In 1919, the first school bus came. It was a Studebaker with 12-foot-long wooden planks along each long side serving as seats. In the winter, a bob sled was used.

Following World War I, more room was needed. A consolidation program to incorporate a 24 square mile area surrounding the town was adopted. A board of five men was elected to visit each farm home to persuade the families to send their children to the consolidated school and to close the country schools.

In 1922, a new and larger brick addition was added to the four-room school, including a gymnasium, auditorium with a stage, home economics room, manual training shop, science room, and additional classrooms. The first athletic events were played in the theater building downtown. With the new gymnasium, this was no longer necessary.

The school board agreed to have a two-week corn picking vacation every October so the farm boys could help with harvest without missing school.

In 1925, the school paid for diphtheria vaccinations for all children. In 1933, the school was closed for two weeks because of a scarlet fever epidemic.

Teachers were forced to take a pay cut during the depression years of the 1930s.

Graduate Stories—Bob "Lefty" Benz's ('43) twin brother drove over Bob's leg with a tractor when he was a boy. "I had to lay in bed while it healed so I missed a whole year of school. To top it off, I got erysipelas and later missed another six weeks of school. Baseball was our main sport in the early 40s. Being a lefthander, I was a fair pitcher. It seems like only yesterday that I pitched a no hitter against Little Rock," Bob fondly recalled.

The Frank Knapp family had 16 children. Two mothers would die in childbirth. The third wife, who had immigrated and come through Ellis Island, was 25 years younger than Frank and would bear six of his children. Phyllis was the youngest of the 16 children. Phyllis Knapp Benz ('41) was nicknamed "Flash" and while telling of the girls basketball in those early 40s, the name still fits her today (2019). She quickly noted, "My dad had the dairy just south of town called Frank Knapp Grade A Guernsey Dairy. I ran on foot the entire milk delivery route. On Saturdays, I collected for the week's milk deliveries. Our coach tried to schedule an emergency basketball practice, but I told him I had a business and could not make it. He countered 'how could you have a business'. I shot back that it was collection day and that unless I collected, we could not pay the bills. He had met his match and I was excused from the Saturday practice."

Music—The 1915 yearbook has a picture of the band with 30 members dressed in their white trousers and bow ties. The band in the 1940s had no uniforms, so the mothers found some used uniforms. They later found a second set of uniforms for the band. Phyllis Knapp Benz ('41) remembered, "I played the clarinet and our marching band had a great time in going to parades. In later years, the band paraded in Storm Lake at Buena Vista's homecoming, and to Orange City for the Tulip Festival. The big trip was all the way to Sioux City (72 miles) to the Morningside College parade."

"Oh, I remember those band days. We played every Memorial Day at the Baker Township Cemetery. The taps echoing and the band marching was such a part of the 'Decoration Day' recognition. Those wool uniforms were either stifling hot or freezing cold," a smiling Fay Schmidt Schall ('71) said.

Hot Lunch and Building Additions—The hot lunch program began in 1946 for those students that lived more than a mile from the school. Following World War II, more room was needed for the music and shop departments, and for the hot lunch program. The old farm shop room was remodeled into a kitchen and the gym was used for the lunch tables. A barracks building from Ft. Leonard Wood (Missouri) was purchased from the Army, and moved onto a concrete foundation just east of the brick building. It was remodeled to accommodate the music and shop departments.

A corporation of twelve organizations which included three churches was formed to raise money to build a Community Building to avoid asking for another tax increase. The building was completed in 1949 and a contract was negotiated between the school and the community Building Board whereby the expenses, responsibilities, and privileges of use were shared. Musical programs, class plays, sports events, and community events were held in the Community Building.

In order to accommodate the post-World War II baby boom, a $245,000 bond was approved to build a new elementary building. It was completed in 1958 and included a multipurpose room, superintendent's and secretaries' offices, teachers' lounge, music and supply rooms, kitchen, lunchroom, and twelve rooms for lower grades. With extra space in the new 1958 addition, school lunches became available for all students.

Bus Accident—A tragic bus accident occurred in 1966. The rural bus was carrying 27 kids; some of the girls were dressed as boys and the boys dressed as girls for Sadie Hawkins Day at the school. The new bus with only 1,800 miles on it was turning by Annie Hook's house southwest of Melvin on Highway 59. Traveling north, the bus was preparing to turn left. It was hit by a cattle truck. The bus rolled completely over with a 360-rotation coming to rest against a row of trees. Fay Schmidt Schall ('71) recalled, "I was just an 8th grader. I woke up on the floor of the bus after the rolling, and there was such an eerie silence. I had lost my glasses. Then there was horrible wailing coming from all directions. I started picking glass from the hair of my younger sister Paula Schmidt ('73). My dad happened to be coming down the road about a mile away and saw the accident. He said that it seemed like the longest ten minutes of his life passed in racing the one mile driving to get to the accident scene. We were all taken to the Sheldon Hospital wearing our Sadie Hawkins crossdressing. It had to be quite a scene. There were three students injured and two had to be hospitalized."

The *Melvin Shopper* reported on October 13, 1966:

> Pictures indicate the damage clearly to a Melvin school bus struck Friday morning by a semi-trailer cattle truck. Though badly wrecked, students and driver Dick Stellingwerf escaped miraculously without severe injuries . . . Nineteen of the passengers on the bus were taken to Sheldon and Hartley hospitals. All were released except Steve Nielsen, 14, and Mary and Paula Noelthe, 14 and 12-year old sisters . . . They were hospitalized and were released two days later.

Notable Teachers—Mr. Victor Burge was a one-armed teacher with a way of getting the students attention. He made an impression with his discipline as he walked down the classroom aisle. He backhanded the student on the left side and then the one on the right side as he strolled toward the front of the room. One day Mr. Burge threw a book at a disrupting (and probably deserving) Russell Benz. This incident was still shared at reunions many years later.

Mr. Wayne Remme was the shop teacher and later became the principal. The students all respected him. He carried a 'big stick'. He had been a marine stationed at Subic Bay in the Philippines and made a great impact on all the students at Melvin High School.

Sports—The Game! If not the game of all times, this one has no comparison in the annuals of Iowa girls basketball. The location was Sheldon, and the date was February 21, 1979. The occasion was the district tournament semifinals and the game pitted the Melvin girls against Sibley. The fans' expectations were of a high scoring contest. Both squads had solid offenses and liked to put the ball in the air. Melvin Coach, Roger Tassler, was uneasy. Questioning his team's chances in a shootout, he opted instead to hold down the scoring.

Melvin controlled the opening tip and went into a passing rotation. The Sibley defenders, refusing to be drawn out, hung back in a zone. Minutes passed without a shot being attempted. Fans expressed displeasure, but this was six-on-six girls basketball, and the chess game was on.

The first quarter ended with the score 0-0. The half time score was still 0-0. The intense mind game was interrupted by occasional bursts of frantic action. As the third quarter ended, Sibley swung into its offense. The basketball clanged off the rim and spectators, some rubbing their damp palms on their knees, settled back to wait for the fourth quarter, still tied at 0-0. The fourth quarter ticked away, and Sibley played for the last shot. Regulation ended at 0-0. Following FOUR overtimes, the Melvin girls with Debra Mow ('79) scoring all the teams' points, prevailed 4-2. Pandemonium ensued.

Closing—The district reached its peak enrollment in 1965 with 365 pupils and then decreased to 101 in 1980. According to the State Department of

Education requirements, a district of Melvin's size could no longer comply. A vote was conducted in 1980 to close the school and consolidate with Hartley, 15 miles to the southeast.

There were 957 graduates of Melvin High School in the 61 years from 1920-1980. The most numerous surnames of the graduates were Benz-22, Graves-17, Nonneman-14, Jobes-13, Steinmetz-12, Brandt-11, Knapp-10, Dvorak-9, Keller-9, Schroeder-9, Schultz-9, Sorensen-8, Kleaver-7, Lorenzen-7, Schaffer-7, Schmidt-7, and Strubbe-7. The largest classes were 33 in 1970 and 1972. The last to receive a diploma from Melvin High School was Marsha Vander Lee (alphabetically).

#61

Merrill High School

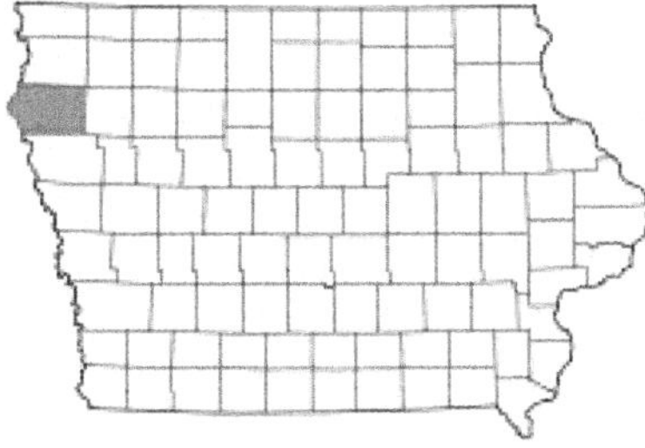

Mascot: **Warriors**
Colors: **Purple and Gold**
Closed: **1959**
Location: **Central Plymouth County**

Early History—Merrill is located along the Floyd River in the center of the fourth largest county by area in the state. It was named by a great railroad tycoon of that time, John I. Blair, after the seventh Governor of Iowa, Samuel Merrill. Blair used his name in over twenty towns in the area including Blairsburg, Iowa; Blair, Nebraska; and Blairsburg, New Jersey. Merrill was incorporated in 1890.

There were four railroads that passed through Merrill. These railroads were the Illinois Central, CSTMO (Chicago, St. Paul, Minneapolis, and Omaha), Great Northern, and Chicago Northwestern. A switch tower south of town controlled over sixty trains which went through Merrill every day. Daily commutes to Sioux City for shopping and work were common by many of the area residents.

Early Schools—The first schoolhouse in Merrill was built in 1889. The building was 32′ x 44′ and built for $1,450. Over the next 12 years, fifteen more lots were purchased for the school at a total cost of $951.

In 1898, a tenth grade was added to the school. Before this time, most students traveled to LeMars to finish high school. The building was in the southeast corner of the block where the main building was later built. The money for the school bell was raised by a home talent play. The north part of the main building was built in 1912. The first graduation class from the four-year high school was in 1914.

The first superintendent of schools in Merrill was Mr. W.A. Julian. He also published the first newspaper. This was a bold venture for him since the population of Merrill was 200, hardly an inviting field for a newspaper. With the type set by hand, it was published weekly and became a success.

Sports—Basketball was played by the boys and girls, with girls basketball being discontinued in 1933 during the Depression and restarted in 1948.

The boys basketball team of 1922 was the greatest team that played at Merrill. There was not a state tournament in Iowa in 1922. After a 23-2 record, they were among the elite teams in the state. The town chartered a bus to Cherokee to play in the equivalent of a regional state competition tournament, but lost to Newel in the finals 39-16. At a ceremony at the Kale Hotel and Restaurant, the businessmen encouraged the colors for the school to be changed from red and white to purple and gold. A star on the team was Dwight Hauff ('22). Hauff went to Morningside College and played basketball and baseball. He was All Conference in basketball in 1926.

A new gymnasium and four classrooms were added in 1925. This gymnasium was the newest and nicest in this part of the state. Many tournaments and district competitions were played in Merrill because of this great gymnasium.

Viola Hauff Todd ('25) played basketball in this gymnasium. Her niece, Sara Jane Hauff ('56), remembered her sharing, "We jumped at center court after every made basket."

The boys basketball team narrowly missed its best chance for state tournament berth in 1951, losing to Hull in the finals of the sectionals. The school's all-time points leader, Richard Strub ('52), starred on this team. He was awarded second team all-state that year. After graduation, he played in college at the Iowa State Teachers College.

The basketball teams played in the Little 8 League with Lawton, Sergeant Bluff, Hinton, Bronson, Hornick, Sloan, and Liberty.

The Plymouth County Tournaments were always for bragging rights. The teams competing in the tournament were Merrill, Liberty, Kingsley, Akron, Hinton, Union, and Remsen.

The chief rival was Hinton, eight miles south of Merrill on Highway 75. "We always said, 'to Hinton or Hell,'" said George Kale with a smile ('50). "I only missed one half day of school in four years and that was because I was an altar boy at a funeral. I hated school and sitting in class. If it had not been for sports, I would have never graduated. When I was in the Army, I quickly learned that I did have a good educational background and did very well on the Army tests," said George Kale ('50).

Six-man football was played only one year in 1936.

Notable Teachers—Joseph Kissinger became the superintendent following the war in 1945. He stayed as the superintendent until the high school closed and remained as the elementary principal until 1972. The elementary school is named after him because of his great contributions to the school and community. Sara Jane Hauff ('56) related, "He was kind and understood the kids were young and sometimes dumb in their development." Maurice Blum ('50) said, "He had a paddle with holes in it and warned that he would use it often."

"Ellen Oliver was the class sponsor for our class all four years," remembered Sara Jane Hauff ('56). "She always seemed to love the boys the best. She was the only math teacher I would have from fifth grade through my senior year. When I enrolled in college at Westmar in LeMars, I'll be darned if I didn't have her there, too."

Coach Don Coome taught world history and social studies, and coached both the girls and boys basketball teams. Sara Jane Hauff ('56) remembered, "He was so keyed up that he would vomit before most of our games." Margaret Olund Marienau ('57) smiled as she remembered, "If we could get him talking about the game from the night before, he did not get to the lesson. For some reason, the day's information would always be on the tests even though we had not talked about it in class."

Notable Graduates—Dwight Hauff ('22) lived to the age 104½ and never retired from his business, Hauff's Sporting Goods Store, in Sioux City. He was an over the road salesman for A.G. Spaulding. He purchased the business and expanded it to six locations, selling athletic equipment and clothing to high schools and colleges. He was a guest on the Tonight Show with Jay Leno at the age of 100 and recognized in a group of the oldest working people. He told Leno that they sold three types of chin straps. There was a small and a regular chin strap. He then reached into his pocket and pulled out an extra wide strap for people with double chins and gave it to Leno. This brought down the house with laughter and applause.

Band—Several good band instructors taught at the high school. One noted instructor in the mid-1950s was Jay Wandscheer. Over half of the students were in the band. They played at homecomings for other school parades and annually at the Orange City Tulip Festival. "Occasionally, the marching and playing at the same time was a challenge, so the band was put between two other bands in the parades for our marching talent to be seen. I just held the trombone, as I really couldn't play," told Al Fagan ('49). Margaret Olund Marienau ('57) shared, "I loved band. I played the trumpet. I still take it out and play it even to this day. We had lessons in school and it really made me appreciate and love music."

Polio—Jeanette Mattas Engle finished high school at LeMars. She had contracted polio in the early '50s and had big braces to help her walk. Maurice Blum ('50) shared, "She was a beautiful person. It is said she even danced at our proms in a wheelchair. She later married and had a family. We just accepted her handicap and she was just one of the great family of students in our high school."

Killed in Action—These Merrill men lost their lives in service to their country.

John Halweg, WWI
Leonard Oleson, WWI
Casey Lawrence, WWII
Francis Crowe ('41), WWII

Pranks—The teacher is not supposed to get the upper hand in a prank. Sara Jane Hauff ('56) and Nancy Ruedy Riley ('56) hurried to eat their hot lunch at school and ran downtown to the drug store every day before the bell rang for afternoon classes. One day, they found a garter snake and coaxed it into a cup. They brought it back to school and for the first class that afternoon they put it into Mrs. Edna Danner's top desk drawer. Angst and wondering just where the snake had gone was brought to a head when the bell rang at the end of the period. "I had zipped up my school binder and Mrs. Danner suggested that I should open my zippered binder and place my papers in it. Wow, was I ever surprised to unzip it and out crawled a garter snake. Busted!"

Closing—Merrill High School closed in May 1959. The next year the students were bused to LeMars. A total of 592 graduated from Merrill High School in the 46 years from 1914-1959. The largest class was 20 in 1940. The most numerous surnames of the graduates were Dennler-10, Strub-8, Brown-6, Vanderloo-6, Kale-5, and Mertes-5. The last graduate from Merrill High School was Gaylen Vermilyea (alphabetically).

Merrill High School
Plymouth County, IA

#62

Milo High School

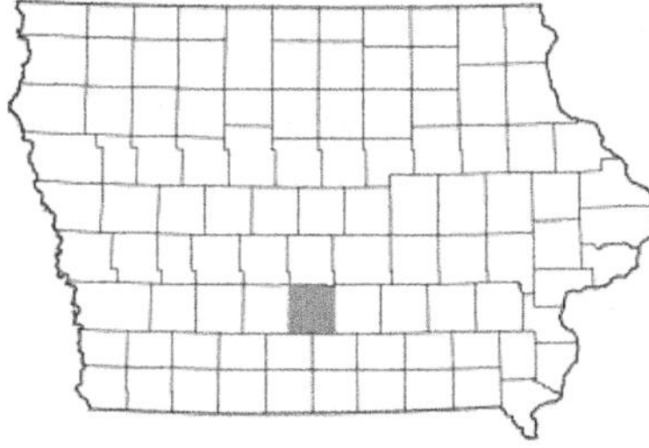

Mascot: Mustangs
Colors: Orange and Black in 1956 changed to Blue and White
Closed: 1959
Location: Southeast Warren County

Early History—The Nutting family from Massachusetts came to Missouri and then to Otter Township in 1855. They were seeking relief from the growing troubles over slavery. Mrs. Nutting was a graduate of Amherst College and immediately began teaching her sons since there were no schools in the area. Public schools were organized when more settlers came into the township. The Nutting's son, David H. Nutting, served in the Union Army during the Civil War, and his letters home reflected his language skills and writing ability. The Nutting family name is still very prominent in the Milo area today (2020).

Smith Henderson Mallory was born in 1835 in central New York. He relocated to Illinois when he was 15 years old. By the time he was 25, he was a construction engineer for the Chicago, Burlington, and Quincy Railroad (CB &Q). The CB & Q Railroad had a contract to build bridges from Ottumwa to Chariton. Mallory moved to Chariton and became the president of First National Bank in Chariton. He was elected to the legislature in 1877. Through his association with the railroad, he launched the railroad branch named the Chariton, Des Moines, and Southern line (CDMS). He was able to secure land using eminent domain and some bidding from the towns along the way. The track was laid along the Otter and Belmont Township line. A depot was built at the spot named Milo by Mallory.

Early Schools—Upon the arrival of the CDMS railroad and the establishment of the town of Milo in 1879, citizens organized a school. A framed public school was finished in 1882. High school students gathered on the first floor. The first high school graduation was on March 23, 1887 with four girls in the class. The ceremonies were held at the Methodist Church. They had completed the three-year course. The next year two more girls graduated. Professor Eli Beard left in 1888, and no more high school classes graduated even though classes were still offered.

In 1895, a bond issue for $6,000 was approved to build a two-story, seven-room, red brick building in the northeast corner of Milo. Mr. Beard was again employed as soon as the school was ready in 1898. High school graduation was again held with the new school. There were three rooms on the first floor and a general assembly room on the second floor with individual desks nailed to the floor. Acetylene gas lamps were installed, and slate blackboards lined the walls. A large bell in the belfry was rung by the janitor to indicate time for classes, recess, and dismissal. There was a grassy playground and a shallow well for drinking water with a standard tin drinking cup firmly wired to the pump. Two wooden outhouses (one for girls and one for boys) were stationed on opposite ends of the school grounds. Commencements were held at the Opera House located on Main Street which was built in 1899.

A third school building in Milo was constructed in the northwest part of town and the first graduation was held in the gymnasium in 1925.

Newspaper Stories from the *Milo Motor*:

- From 1908-1913, agriculture was added to the curriculum.
- In 1917, manual training was added to the curriculum. Rural students continued to pay tuition to attend the high school.
- Basketball was introduced in 1923 for both boys and girls. There was no gymnasium, so practice was held on the outside dirt court. When inclement weather occurred, practice and games were held indoors at the Opera House.
- In 1923, an orchestra was introduced by Principal Blythe Clayton Mitchell. She was a graduate from Milo in 1916 and played the cello with the orchestra. The orchestra played frequently for public gatherings.

Sports—A death related to a football injury in the 1920s resulted in permanently discontinuing football at Milo High School.

The school was in the Little Six Conference with Beech, Lacona, New Virginia, Spring Hill, and Liberty Center.

Bob Lyle Davey ('42) recalled, "I had a heart condition and could not play an instrument in the band. Baseball was the sport most popular in the 1940s. My heart condition did not keep me from playing baseball. After one year at Central College, I enlisted into the Air Force."

In 1936, the boys basketball team made it to the District Finals. They lost by one point to Ottumwa and were denied a chance to go to the state tournament.

With a record of 22-2, the final 1959 boys basketball team from Milo lost to Central Dallas in the District Tournament.

In 1952, the girls basketball team was in need of new uniforms. Carol Barnes Kaldenberg ('56) remembered, "The Van Ginkel's sporting goods store in Des Moines which supplied many of the sports teams with uniforms, gave the Milo school a deal at a huge discount. It seems they were already in their stock at the store and they wanted to find a home for them. The tops were a white satin material trimmed with orange and the white skirts had black on the inside pleat. I cannot say we ever liked the satiny skirts, but they were indeed better than the old ones they replaced."

There were many high school teams in the area with the orange and black colors. Milo High school adopted new school colors of blue and white in 1956. The old uniforms were discarded, and new ones were purchased. To help pay for the new uniforms, students picked up dropped corn in the fields and had a scrap metal drive.

Music—In 1926, instrumental music was introduced into the Milo Schools with J. Worth Miller as the instructor. An orchestra was soon reorganized with 12 violins, cello, string bass, and the proper balance of wind instruments. By 1928, a band was ready to perform public programs. For three successive years the band gave concerts on Main Street and at the Warren County Fair. During the depression in the 1930s, music was discontinued at the Milo schools.

Notable Graduates—Joe Graham ('36) was a veterinarian and came back to his hometown to establish a veterinary clinic. He was recognized in the state as a leader in his community and his profession. He served many years on the State Board of Veterinary Examiners.

Ardelle Michener Keeney ('37) when reached at her home in Milo at the age of 99 (in 2019), gave an insight into her high school days and life. Ardelle said, "I graduated at the age of sixteen. We had a nice gym and basketball was my life. I once made 10 straight free throws in a game. We won the county tournament in 1937. The boys were good too. My husband-to-be, Bill Keeney ('36) was a good basketball player too. We played Beech, Lacona, Liberty Center, Hartford, and St. Marys. Our big rival was Lacona. We had music but I preferred taking the agriculture, math, English, and history classes. Doyle Carpenter was our superintendent (1932-1945) and a very good coach. All these years later (90 years plus), I can still remember seeing that flag flying to the east, high above the trees, as I watched it out of my elementary school window."

Rashal Stanger Harmison ('17) graduated from Park College. With advanced degrees from Drake and University of Iowa, she taught mathematics and became an administrator and principal at Milo High School. Her teaching career spanned 47 years at country schools in Jasper County, North Dakota, Missouri, and 21 years in Churdan where she was the high school principal. She returned to the Milo High School faculty in 1946 to teach math and later became the principal. When the high school closed in 1959, she taught another five years in the Southeast Warren district. She was instrumental in organizing services for senior citizens in the area and active in community and church activities.

Sallie Smith ('87) not only graduated in the first class from Milo High School, she taught school for 60 years. She was the first-grade teacher in Milo for 54 of those years, and she referred to her pupils as 'her babies'. Many former students, parents, and grandparents learned to read very quickly and to respect and honor her influence. She was honored at the 50th High School Reunion in 1949 for her outstanding teaching career and her gift of education to the community. Sallie Smith is also commemorated at the Salisbury House in Des Moines for an incredible life in education and service.

Notable Teachers—J. Worth Miller became the music and band instructor and baseball coach in the 1920s. He left and returned to Milo High school in the 1950s. He was a patient and beloved teacher who had the respect of all the students.

Coach Jarold Lister was the all-sports coach in the 1950s. He was inducted into the Iowa Sports Coaching Hall of Fame.

Doyle Carpenter came to Milo High School following graduation from Simpson College in 1931. He coached both the boys and girls athletic teams. Within two years he became the superintendent. His leadership and business acumen led the district through the Depression and war years.

Yearbooks—The yearbook, *MI-HI-DAYS,* was last published in 1953. The editorial staff picture shows 24 students gathered around a typewriter. The girls are dressed in long skirts, bobby socks, saddle oxfords, and neck scarves with short curled hair. The boys are in jeans with the cuffs rolled up. One student has a camera in his hands. The editor-in-chief was Carolyn Arnold Lundberg ('54). The senior class history illustrates the student body at the time:

> The Class of 1953 has the unique distinction of having three members, Raymond (Jeep) Kendall, Charles Howe, and Marlene Jacobs finishing twelve years of schoolwork in Milo. Only two of our fourteen members, John Endres and Edna Mae Coffman entered in the ninth grade to spend four years with us . . .

There were 12 girls posed in a picture with their new black and orange satin basketball uniforms with the two colored short pleated skirts.

The band picture has 44 musicians with their Director, Mr. J. Worth Miller, who had returned to Milo High School to teach.

Other yearbook highlights include:

- A new arc welder was purchased for the shop and agriculture classes so they could learn to weld metal from 1/16th to ½ inch thickness.
- The English Club, with nine girls, organized to study and enjoy English.
- Leather craft class with leather ordered from California.
- Drivers training, with 18 boys and girls, was offered for the first time in the fall of 1952.
- Homemaking under the direction of Mrs. Lewis Nichols learned to make tomato and grape juice, canned apples for pies, apricot preserve, strawberry-pineapple jam . . .

The 1950 yearbook reported an activity by the students in the Fall of 1949:

> Those strong winds which prevailed over the countryside last fall made corn picking difficult for the farmers. Some corn fell to the ground and had to be picked up by hand. This gave the high school pupils an

opportunity to raise some funds for the athletic and educational equipment for our school.

On the afternoon of September 30, 1949, there were many ambitious pupils anticipating the thrill of getting away from "books" for a while and getting out into the fresh country air. We went to the corn fields in one of the buses. The first farm was Shoemakers, then Risinger, Amsberry, DeHoet, Younker, and Wilkinson farms . . . Tractors and wagons were furnished by Bob Alexander, Bill DeHoet, Rolla Streeter, Gordon Wilkinson, Bob Dollison, Tom Spaur, and Gene Howe . . . Approximately 1,200 bushels averaging 45 cents a bushel were harvested . . . $518.97 went for new basketball suits, the boys sweat jackets, and pads for under the baskets in the gymnasium, and a slide projector and screen for the school.

Pranks—The gymnasium was located on a lower level and there was a walkway on the north side of the school. Joe Kuhn ('54), not involved in the school plays, told, "During play practice, the windows were opened at night to the gymnasium and we sneaked up the stairway and tossed firecrackers down into the gymnasium. The noise in that hollow gym sounded like mortars going off. Of course, I can't tell you all that were involved but we never got caught."

Senior Trips—Some superintendents did not like the senior trips to be called sneak or skip days. For most years, the seniors traveled by car to the Ledges, a park in Boone county. Other trips were to Arnold's Park in Dickinson County and visiting the Grotto in West Bend along the way.

Killed in Action—One hundred men from Milo and the surrounding township enlisted into the Union Army during the Civil War. There were four boys in the Spanish-American War. Eighty-four were enlisted in WWI. One hundred and fifty-five were called to duty during World War II. Frank Howe was on duty with the Seabee's in World War II and served with his three sons, Homer ('38), George ('39), and Jim ('40). Carol Barnes Kaldenberg ('56) told, "My aunt Mildred Risinger ('37) was a teacher the morning the flag outside her classroom window was dropped to half-mast. The town had just received the news that George Howe ('39) had been killed in action. She would always get teary years later remembering that she had to tell the children why the flag was at half-mast."

Servicemen killed in action from Milo and the surrounding township were:

Henry Coffman, Spanish American War
Charles Bracelin, WWI
Harvey Hall, WWI
Everett Males, WWI
Carl W. Polson ('16), WWI
Erastus B. Summy, WWI
Merrill Dean Cox, WWII
Merle Bown, WWII
Tom Ervin ('38), WWII
Richard Jacobs, WWII
George Howe ('39), WW II
Russell Thorn ('36), WWII
Floyd Wadle, WWII

Carl T. Miller Jr., WWII
William Howard Butler, WWII
Joseph Frank Wright, WWII
Donald Baughman, Korea
Art Wright, Vietnam

Drivers Education—The drivers education program was one of the first in Warren County offered as part of the school's curriculum in 1952.

Closing—Superintendent Kenneth Bryant (1949-1957) created citizen committees in southeast Warren County to inform the communities that the small schools were not financially able to conduct desirable programs. Studies, surveys, and public meetings were held. A vote in 1958 followed with 20 of the 23 contiguous school districts approving the creation of the Southeast Warren School District with the high school located at Liberty Center. The Milo High School closed following graduation in May of 1959. The Milo building was then used as an elementary and junior high site for the SE Warren district.

Superintendent Ray Elsa was responsible for helping Milo integrate into the new district. The school districts that consolidated were the high schools of Milo, Lacona, and Liberty Center. The other elemen-tary districts which consolidated were McClelland, McNeer, Locust Grove, Plainville, Motor, Belmont Center, Fairview, Pleasant View, North Central, Concord, Thorn, Round Top, Hawkeye, Burgess, Primrose, Lucas County, Whitebreast, Lawrence-burg, Mt. Moriah, and North Lincoln.

There were 867 graduates from Milo High School from 1898-1959. The largest class was 29 in 1927. The most numerous surnames of the graduates were: Van Syoc-24, Smith-18, Nutting-17, Wright-12, Clark-10, Howe-10, Graham-9, Oldaker-8, and Wells-8. The last to receive a diploma from Milo High School was Leonard Van Syoc (alphabetically).

(Author's Note: Some of the information for this story was provided by Milo 1880-1980. This book was written for the Milo Centennial. Of the many historical accounts of the towns this author has visited in Iowa, this Milo Centennial book has no equal. It was a thorough record of history.)

Milo High School
Warren County, IA

#63

Moorhead High School

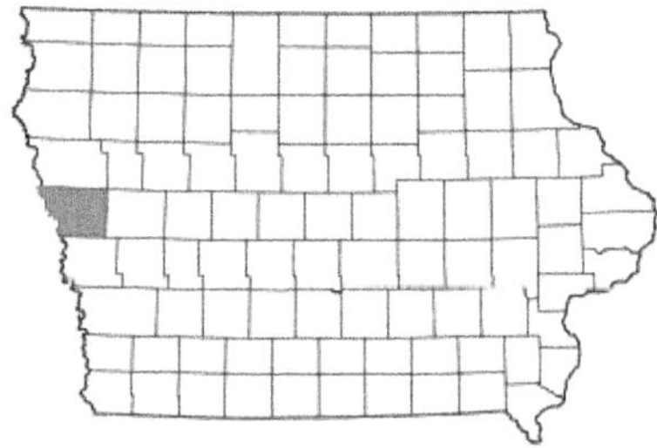

Mascot: Vikings
Colors: Black and Gold
Closed: 1962
Location: South Central Monona County

Early History—The town of Moorhead was named after John B. Moorhead. He was the son of immigrants who came to America from England. In 1861, he obtained a grant for a half section (320 acres) of land in Spring Valley Township. His first home was a log cabin near Jordan Creek.

The Mormons arrived in the area south of the town in 1847. They left Nauvoo, Illinois, and were followers of Brigham Young. They were following him to Utah until a rift occurred over polygamy in Kanesville, Iowa (present day Council Bluff). Some 60 families split off and came to an area they called Preparation (present day Preparation State Park). After their leader, Charles B. Thompson, was threatened with hanging in 1854, most of the Mormons left the area. Old log cabin foundations and a cemetery are the only remnants of their occupation.

John B. Moorhead constructed a kiln for making bricks. Out of the clay in the Loess Hills, he established a brick business. He built a remarkable "Brick House" in 1871 that stands to this day having been occupied by five generations of Moorheads. The lumber was transported by wagons from Little Sioux, Iowa. The walls were a unique characteristic of the house. They have two layers of brick on the outside, a two-inch dead-air space for insulation, another layer of brick, and then plaster, making the walls 18 inches thick. The lower floor has 10 feet high ceilings and in the center of the house is a walnut staircase. Originally, the house was heated with wood burning stoves. Through the years, the system has been modernized. The lighting was originally from oil lamps; later, carbide lights were installed, and electricity installed in the early 1900s.

Town Relocation—The *Monona County History* book of 1890 refers to Old Town Moorhead as follows:

Located on the southeast corner of Section 9 in Spring Valley Township lies the little hamlet known by the name of its founder John B. Moorhead. Although never plated as a town site, the necessities of trade have caused the springing up of one of the busiest small business centers in the county, the New Town-Moorhead.

The Chicago Northwestern Railroad came to the Soldier River Valley in 1899, so the town was moved over the hill east.

The *Moorhead Mirror* reported on Feb. 23, 1899:

The real estate is booming in this place these days. Townsite agent Torrson has sold 15 lots over at the new town during the past week and expects to dispose of many more during the next few days.

The town was incorporated in 1900 and named in honor of the original founder John B. Moorhead. Most businesses were moved within one year.

Laws Enacted—In 1907, a law was enacted that made it "unlawful" for any person under 16 to be on the streets or alleys after 8:00 pm from April-September. The rest of the year, the curfew was 7:00 pm or a $10 fine.

In 1920, a law limited motor vehicles to 15 MPH with a fine of $25 for speeding, or 5 days in jail.

A 1920 law passed prohibiting poultry from running at large. Fine was $1 to $10.

Early Schools—The first school was built in 1876 at the north end of the settlement known as Old Town. The lumber was freighted from Onawa and Dunlap. It was also used as a community center and for church services.

The township high school was organized in 1900 in New Moorhead, becoming one of the first township high schools in the state. It was a four-room brick building erected at a cost of $6,000. A 36-inch diameter school bell was provided by John B. Moorhead. The township school was changed to an independent district school. The building was located east of the present building until 1921 when it was torn down and replaced with the three-story school that stands nearly 100 years later.

Highlights of the early high school:

- Vocal music was introduced in 1924, instrumental music in 1925, and typing in 1930.
- The school first entered music contests in 1931.
- Tri Hi plays were started in 1932 with Soldier, Ute, and Moorhead participating.
- Speech and speech contests were extremely popular in school.
- FFA and FHA programs were started in the 1950s.

Notable Graduate—Ival Outhouse ('33) led the state in scoring his senior year at Moorhead. Outhouse graduated from Morningside where he starred on the basketball team. He served in the Navy during World War II before starting his teaching career. Outhouse returned to Moorhead in

1947 to coach and teach. With his great enthusiasm for the sport, he turned Moorhead basketball from just a 'fever' into a 'mania.' Ival led the 1949 boys basketball team to the sweet 16 at the state tournament by beating Charles City and McGregor in the first two rounds. In the semifinals, they bowed to Ottumwa, the eventual State Champions in 1949. Moorhead captured third place by beating Winfield. The boys repeated going to the state tournament in 1960. Outhouse's coaching career took him to Bronson, Castana, Sioux Rapids, Moorhead, Carroll, Whiting, West Harrison-Mondamn, and Alton. He coached nine different teams to sub state. His teams had 510 wind and 156 loses.

Sports—There was no football played at Moorhead. Basketball was the king of sports. The boys went to the state tournament in 1949 and 1960 when there was only one class for the whole state. They won the third-place trophy in both years.

Soldier was the greatest rival. They were the closest school on the east side of the county. And as fate happens, Soldier eventually joined Moorhead in 1962 to form East Monona High School.

Girls basketball was played for a short time in the 1920s. It was restarted again in the 1940s. Marcia Woodward ('62) was selected to the first team all-state team as a guard.

Girls track came to Moorhead when it was East Monona. Anita Kalskett Moorhead ('56) told, "Moorhead parents always supported our teams. Whether it was the 75 carloads that followed the boys to the state tournament or any other sport, the parents were always supportive and followed their children."

Cooks and Hot Lunch—Opal Hinkel or 'Grandma Opal' (as the kids affectionately called her), was the long-time head cook for the hot lunch program which started right after the war. The first meals served were soups. The townspeople donated their fruits and vegetables to the hot lunches.

Drivers Education—Nancy Ballantyne Hinkel ('62) recalled, "My Uncle had given me some lessons in driving out on the ball diamond. Our drivers ed. teacher taught us to drive a stick shift, change a tire, and where to put oil in the motor. We had to go to Onawa which is 18 miles away and try to learn how to parallel park. I hated it and still try to avoid parallel parking to this day. We had to pass out on the two-lane highway at a fast speed. The teacher had dual controls on the other side in the passenger's seat, but it still scared me."

Polio—"Connie Skow McBurney ('50) married a teacher. When they were stationed in Guam, she contracted polio which was one of the most tragic things that ever happened in Moorhead," said Nancy Ballantyne Hinkel ('62). Connie, though paralyzed, recovered and had three children.

Lottie Nielsen McGill developed polio in the early 1950s, It was thought she got it while detasseling corn. Anita Kalskett Moorhead ('56) recalled, "We all had to get the polio vaccinations, and all got stiff. School was dismissed and we all had to walk out in the main street and were told that it was to keep us limbered up."

Pranks—Two boys were credited for a chemistry experiment that affected the city water supply. Roger McCall ('63) and Charles (Chum) Kalskett ('62) used their ingenuity to collect a large quantity of red food coloring bottles. One night they climbed up the water cistern and poured all the red dye in the water tank. The next morning after the townspeople took their first drinks of water, there was quite the reaction when they started having red in their urine. Some even complained that it stained their underwear. Not being able to act innocent, the culprits were quickly identified. Winston Kalskett ('26) called the principal, Norman Miller, and said, "Throw the book at him and whatever you do to him, he's going to get double when he gets home."

Boys seem to get these ideas in pairs. Gordie Soldberg ('54) and Jerry Soldberg ('56) were credited for disassembling a manure spreader and neatly restructuring it on top of the Moorhead Bar.

John ('55) and Anita ('56) Moorhead had a farm and feedlot near town. Being a conscientious cattleman, John always tried to buy the best bargain cattle to feed out in their small feeding operation. He once bought a load of scruffy old cull Holstein cows. These cows were quite clever and could open about any gate. They escaped one morning and made their way to meander around the parking lot at the high school. They quickly drew the attention of all the students as they watched out the windows at these black and white cows lumbering around and licking and nudging the cars. The Moorhead's daughter, Ann Moorhead Forney ('84), immediately recognized the cows as her dad's and she was embarrassed and hovered down even though none of the other students knew whose cows they were. The escapees were soon apprehended by a posse, but the scars of embarrassment on the Moorhead's daughter were already organized.

Notable Teacher—Norman Miller came to Moorhead in 1952. He taught history, coached girls basketball, and became the principal for 27 years. "He ruled the roost. One time on the way to a game at Castana, while riding on the bus, we girls started singing a crazy song, 'The old gray mare went to the county fair, she sat on a Frigidaire; froze off her underwear. The old gray mare she ain't what she used to be!' We would all laugh hysterically and then sing it repeatedly," exclaimed Anita Kalskett Moorhead ('56). Anita continued, "Castana had a poor team but when we left the court at half-time, we were behind. When we got to the locker room, Coach Miller chewed us out and wondered what we were thinking about—it certainly was not about basketball—maybe the Old Gray Mare song? It scared us so much that I went out in the second half and scored 36 points. Coach Miller had so much discipline and we all dearly loved him and respected him." Gordie Soldberg ('54) remarked, "When I would see Mr. Miller over the years, I always called him Mr. Miller. He would say, 'You can just call me Norman.' I told him 'No! you will always be Mr. Miller to me.' I had such respect for him as a teacher and a person."

Closing—In the 60 years from 1903 through 1962, there were 743 graduates from Moorhead High School. The high school closed in May 1962. The largest class was 26 in 1955. The most numerous surnames of the graduates were: Johnson-35, Kalskett-14, Neal-14, Coberly-10, Mann-10, Sandvold-10, Moore-9, Moorhead-8, Ballantyne-7, LaSeur-7, and Soldberg-7. The last graduate from Moorhead High School was Marcia Woodward (alphabetically).

Moorhead High School
Monona County, IA

#64

Morning Sun High School

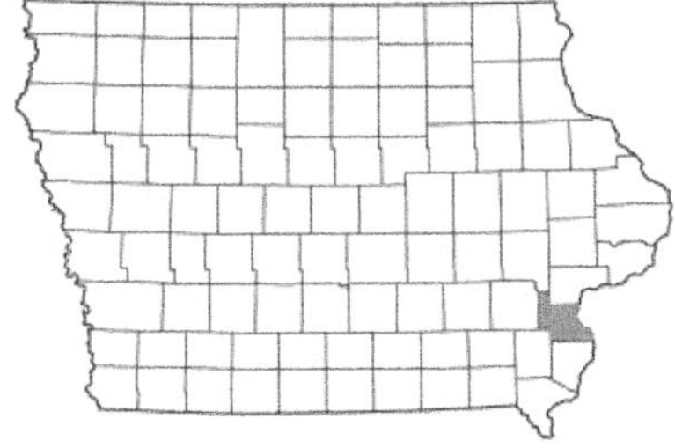

Mascot: Tigers/Tigerettes
Colors: Blue & Gold; then Green & White
Closed: 1990
Location: Extreme south Louisa County

Early History—Morning Sun is located on the southern edge of Louisa county. This county is one of the most uniquely shaped land areas in the state as it resembles a 'boot' much like the state of Louisiana.

Folklore suggested two views of how the town got its name. Early settlers from Morning Sun, Ohio, could have named it after their home. Another theory is that Cicero Hamilton had a couple of oxen that broke out one night and wandered away. He aroused his neighbors in the early dawn and instituted a search for the lost animals. When the sun peeped over the horizon, a great and glorious idea hit one of the men helping his search for the oxen, and Henry C. Blake cried, "I've got it. Let's name our town Morning Sun." The town was incorporated in 1867.

Among the early settlers were Dutch, Irish, and Scottish immigrants. The Reformed Presbyterian Church south of Morning Sun had a large Scottish congregation. The Scotch surnames of McKeever, McClure, McKee, McAfee, McKinley, McKelvey, McCune, McCarrish, McElhinney, and McDonald were among the graduates of Morning Sun school.

Two railroads met near Morning Sun. The north-south Rock Island and the east-west Minneapolis St. Louis railroads passed on the south and east edges of town.

Early Schools—Pictures of a two-story school show a wood building with several additions that were used for the first schoolhouse from 1869-1905. Graduation records started in 1876 with eight graduates.

A three-story public brick schoolhouse was built in 1905. Records indicate that there was no graduation class in 1905, suggesting that the 12th grade was added that year to the school. This building housed all the primary and secondary grades.

On May 26, 1921, the red brick three-story high school was dedicated, which stood for the next 68 years in Morning Sun.

Notable Graduates—Jack Hamilton ('56) was a high school star in all sports. He was a bruising running back and a tackling-machine linebacker. He excelled on the basketball court and became a baseball legend from Morning Sun. Hamilton played ten years in the Major Leagues possessing a bullet for a fastball. When pitching for the Phillies, he hit a grand slam home run against the Cardinals. After circling the bases and returning to the dugout, his teammates decided to give him the silent treatment. No high fives, no back slaps or congratulations, nothing! When he started back to the hill for the next inning, they made up for it with hooting and whistles. Hamilton had a no-hitter in the minors and pitched a one-hitter against the Cardinals with the only hit being a bunt single by the Card's pitcher, Ray Sadecki.

Donald Honeyman ('36), while studying at the University of Iowa for a degree in photography, entered a national competition and won the grand prize—a job with *Vogue*. This began a quarter century career in New York, London, and Paris. Following Pearl Harbor, he became a war correspondent and cameraman in the South Pacific. He was awarded a Bronze Star for bravery. His best-known front-line footage was at the liberation of Manila in February 1945. Opening his own studio in London, he is known for his most famous image of the solarized poster of Che Guevara.

Raymond Wilson ('14) received two degrees in animal husbandry from Iowa State College. He served in World War I in the Navy. He was the founder of the Quaker lobbying organization of the Friends Committee on National Legislation serving as its executive director for 30 years. He was involved with legislation affecting foreign policy, peace, world hunger, assistance to developing countries, disarmament, civil liberties, civil rights, full employment, comprehensive health insurance, and energy conservation. His papers are at Swarthmore College and a valued part of the Swarthmore College Peace Collection.

Sports—Morning Sun had football in the early years but it ended in the 1930s. Football resumed in 1953 with eight-man football. David Wilson ('55) shared, "My dad told me not to go out for football when it started my sophomore year. One month later, he found out that I was playing. I was tall and athletic, and my senior year I caught 15 touchdowns thrown by Jack Hamilton. I loved the sport and later played college football and basketball from 1955-1960 for the Colorado State University Rams."

The biggest rivals were Wapello and Winfield during the 1950s. In later years, rivals became Wapello and Mediapolis.

The girls played basketball. They made it to the state tournament in 1952, losing to Reinbeck in the first game, and in 1961, losing to Lost Nation in the first-round game. Mary Reid Zoeckler ('59) shared, "I was a forward on our team. In my senior year in 1959, we just missed going to state as we lost in the finals of the districts. I did go on to play at Monmouth College, making the transition to the five-on-five full court game. Basketball was such a great sport for girls and allowed us to compete with others and grow in our own confidence."

Boys wrestling became the leading boys sport at Morning Sun. It was the wrestling program that became well known throughout the state. Starting in 1962, the team, led by Hall of Fame Coach Bob Darrah, posted a 50 win and three loss record over the next six years. Other coaches followed with great success and Morning Sun continued to be a state powerhouse until the school closed in 1990.

Morning Sun was part of the Southeast Conference from 1925 until 1951 and rejoined again from 1961 through 1990. Other conference members were Cardinal, Central Lee, Columbus Community, Danville, Lone Tree, Louisa-Muscatine, Mediapolis, New London, Pekin, Wapello, Wayland, and Winfield.

The sports teams played in Lemosa League from 1951-1960 with conference members Danville, Denmark, Huron, Mediapolis, Oakville, Sperry, Yarmouth, and Morning Sun.

Notable Teachers—Mrs. Freda Wilson taught math and was a passionate St. Louis Cardinal fan. Mary Reid Zoeckler ('59) remembered, "I had no idea how good a teacher she was until I got to college math. I was told that I had no right to be in this class as a woman, because I was at the top of my class. With Mrs. Wilson, it had nothing to do with your ability, as she taught each student at their own level and had them all succeed." David Wilson ('55) added, "Mrs. Wilson is why I became an engineer. She was so inspiring and made math enjoyable, and easy to understand. She was one of the best teachers I had in high school."

Mrs. Donna Pittman taught literature English and directed all the school plays. Sherry Nichols Robb ('60) told, "She could give you the look and get your attention immediately." "She taught us the value of good literature and was so proper in our English and writing instruction. She is the reason that I became a writer with my lifetime career," remembered Mary Reid Zoeckler ('59). David Armstrong ('55) added, "As my junior high teacher,

I stayed after school and she drilled me on spelling words when I was in the 7th grade. I had won the Louisa County Spelling Bee and was headed for the state spelling bee in Des Moines."

John Siegel was the wrestling coach whose teams compiled a 143-17-3 record, producing 55 State meet qualifiers. This included 25 place winners, four champions, and five runners-ups at the State Wrestling Tournament. He was named Class 1A Coach of the Year in 1983 and 1989. He was inducted into the Iowa High School Athletic Association Wrestling Hall of Fame.

Bus Drivers—The senior boys at Morning Sun were some of the bus drivers. They could take the bus home at night and pick up the students on the way back to school the next morning.

Johnny Johnson ('53) was a memorable driver. "He not only taught each of his own children but everyone of his rider students to be proud of who you are and that you are from Morning Sun," told Marvin Garland ('59). Johnny Johnson became a race car driver and owner of a racetrack after graduation from high school.

Hot Lunch—Gwen Wilson Jolly ('53) remembered, "We had hot lunch when I started first grade in 1941. The mothers brought in their extra garden produce and with the government supplements the meals were always wonderful."

Killed in Action—The following men were killed in the wars:

Fred Hays, WWI
Leland Scott, WWI
Dean Bisher ('33), WWII
Joe Harris, WWII
Maurice Kerr ('39), WWII
Robert Smith, WWII
Philip Walsh ('39), WWII
Merlin McKeever, Korea
Dean Alfred Jackson ('62), Vietnam

Three Morning Sun men became prisoners of war. They were:

Richard Boyle, WWII
Howard Hobbs, WWII
Leroy Pierce, WWII

Yearbooks—The names of the yearbook varied with each senior staff choosing the names. The names included *The Tiger*, *Reflections*-1973, *Nevermore*-1974, and *Horizon*.

Senior Trips—The seniors in 1955 traveled to Chicago by bus. Three boys, David Wilson, Raymond Linder, and David Armstrong ventured off with four girls to the Cubs game at Wrigley Field. On the way back to the hotel, they walked by a burlesque show. David Armstrong ('55) chaperoned the girls back to the hotel while Raymond Linder and David Wilson let their curiosity lead them into the dark room for the show. Each claimed innocence on what the show was about, but David Wilson had an idea. Shocked by the show, they quickly left by the back door anxious to tell the others of their escapade. David Armstrong ('55) remembered, "I had met a girl from another Iowa high school who was on their senior trip also, and the two of us ventured to the top of the Conrad Hilton to have a wonderful view of the lights of Chicago."

The 1959 and 1960 seniors went to Chicago by train. They went to the Ice Capades which were showing at their Hilton Hotel.

The 1985 seniors traveled by cars to Nashville. All 21 seniors enjoyed the Grand Ole Opry and touring the museums of the city. Bill and Etta Owens were sponsors. Robin Mullen ('75) and her husband Dennis Barth ('75) were the other two chaperones, which just happened to be the sister and brother-in-law of senior Raelyn Robb Mullen ('85).

Closing—The Morning Sun High School closed in May 1990. In the 91 years from 1900-1990 there were 1,719 graduates from the high school. The largest classes had 33 in 1936 and 1965. The most numerous surnames of the graduates were Wilson-55, McElhinney-45, Kerr-30, Hamilton-24, Baird-22, Bryant-22, Allen-20, McDonald-20, Willson-16, Pogemiller-15, McClurkin-15, Brown-14, Smith-12, Hartman-10, and Thompson-10. The last to receive a diploma from Morning Sun High School was Joanna White (alphabetically). In the fall of 1990, the high school students were bused to Winfield-Mt. Union.

Morning Sun High School
Louisa County, IA

#65

New Albin High School

Mascot: Eagles
Colors: Purple and Gold
Closed: 1960
Location: Northeastern tip of Allamakee County

Early History—The northern border of Iowa is located at 43 degrees 30 minutes latitude. The determination of this border was not always this defined. The significance of the boundary was reported in the *Allamakee Journal* October 7, 1992 by Barbara Cain:

> You drive right by, and not even know that it meant anything. But there is an iron marker, found well off the beaten path in New Albin, that is on the National Register of Historic places.
>
> For many years, this obscure post stood in the Wilderness. Indians passed by it in early days; few white settlers had yet reached its territory. It is simply known as the Iron Post.
>
> The Purpose. Before statehood, Iowa and Minnesota territories disputed their land holdings. Each thought that the boundary line should be located well within each other's territories.
>
> Locals say that the Minnesotans felt the edge of the territory should be marked by the Upper Iowa River. Iowans, on the other hand, thought the Root River, much further north should be the line. The United States Congress acted and the exact location of this spot was determined by astrological observations.

Another land mark of historical interest was placed in 1849 by Captain Thomas J. Lee (brother of Robert E. Lee). He was a Topographical Engineer on the Mississippi River when he placed a cast iron obelisk, 7 feet tall and 14 inches square at the base, with the words "Iowa and Minesota Boundary, 1849 Lat 43 30'" on its sides. Minnesota is short one "n" on the marker.

The railroad came along the west side of the Mississippi in 1872. It played an important part of the settlement of New Albin. The rail was laid to State Line—a name that became the first name of the village and depot.

The name New Albin originated after a 10-year-old boy died of burns sustained while he and other boys were playing with gun powder in Dubuque. His name was Albin Rhomberg. His father was one of the organizers of the Chicago, Clinton, and Dubuque Railroad and had the town named Albin to honor his son.

When application was made to the proper government agency, it was found that other towns had similar names, so the name was changed to New Albin. To the north lay the Minnesota Bluff and to the east the Mississippi River.

•

Indians—The Indian tribes in the area were Sac, Fox, Sioux, and Winnebago. A fort was built along the Iowa River Road. At the time of the Black Hawk War, Indians lived in the Fort. Family names, such as Decorah and Thompson were taken by some of the Indians. Historical photographs of Frank Decorah and his family show him sitting with a fedora, his wife with a plaid blanket over her shoulders, a baby with a stocking hat, a son with a jacket and tam, and daughter with primped hair and earrings. Another photograph of Mrs. Johnny Thompson and her three children show the boys dressed in white jackets, a stocking hat, and a white top hat.

This region documented the Indians in the area in the local newspapers through the first 50-plus years of statehood. Some of those notes were:

1877 A "Bib Injun" dance was given by a band of Winnebago's in Robinson Hall Saturday evening.

1882 All Indians in the neighborhood have folded their tents and stolen quietly away.

1893 The Indians pulled up stakes Thursday and moved their wigwams and "dusky maidens" up just above Jefferson Drive to avoid high water.

1895 Tom Thunder and his band of Winnebago's will occupy the boards at Pohlman's Hall this Friday evening in a repertoire of songs and dances.

1899 A wandering band of Indians blew into town one day last week and had in their possession some very fine ponies.

1899 A number of Indians arrived here Friday from the north and immediately went into camps on the bottoms south of town.

1900 Died: George Waukon, at their campgrounds a few miles north of New Albin on July 8, 1900. He leaves a squaw and little papoose.

Early Schools—The first educational opportunities in the area are not well documented. Some New Albin newspaper notes report early school information:

1877 Having 500 inhabitants our school district is now entitled to six directors instead of three.

New Albin School has an enrollment of 42 students.

1880 97 students in public schools.

1891 New Albin School started Monday with Principal Miss Brady.

1901 A contract was let of new school for $1,484.

1911 New Albin schools closed for one week owing to a case of infantile paralysis.

1922 Class roll of 9 seniors graduated from New Albin High School.

Bonds were issued in the amount of $35,000 to build a new three-story red brick school in 1916. This school was built on the location of the previous school ground. The building consisted of nine rooms. The basement housed the heating unit, which was a direct and indirect system. Humidity was furnished by air blown through a curtain of water. The annual expense of fuel was $700. In the basement was a small gymnasium complete with bleachers at each end, a home economics room and a classroom. The second floor had four classrooms, and restrooms at both ends of a central hallway. The third floor had two classrooms, an auditorium with a small stage, a library, and the superintendent's office.

By 1932, the teaching staff was six women teachers and one man. The principal, Miss Veronica Cull, was the girls basketball coach, taught English, American literature, and vocational guidance.

In 1951 a new gymnasium with locker rooms and a stage was built adjoining the brick building. Several rural schools closed and those districts consolidated with New Albin—the town school

Busing—When the district was organized, it was for town children only. Families living outside of this tax base who wanted their children to go to school were charged a tuition of $6 to $8 a year. Some, living miles away, were brought to school in a horse-drawn school bus, a large wagon with benches and top and canvas side curtains to keep out the rain. This "bus" was used from 1912 until 1934. Freemont Meyer converted his farm truck into a "bus" and it was used for a few years until the district purchased a "real" school bus.

The school transported students from Minnesota. Dolores Moldenhauer Crowley ('54) lived near Reno, Minnesota, and rode the bus. Ralph Nelson ('57) lived three miles north of New Albin in Minnesota, and said, "Every day I had to walk up the hill and then down to the bus. I always tell people that I had to walk up the hill and down the hill both ways just to get to school. Even though we lived in Minnesota, our mailing address was always New Albin because that was the closest United States Post Office."

Sports—The only sports offered at New Albin High School were boys and girls basketball. A picture of the 1930 girls team shows nine girls on the team with their attractive Coach Humphrey in a two-piece suit and heels. Football was not played at New Albin High School.

The teams played in the Little Swiss Conference. Other schools in the conference were Lansing-Public, Lansing Immaculate Conception, Waukon-St. Pat's, Waterville, and Harpers Ferry

The boys basketball teams of 1954 and 1955 made it to sub-state with Mr. Dean Reed as their coach. "In 1955 we lost to a much larger Independence High School in the finals by one point. I had the onus of missing two free throws that could have changed the outcome," reflected Ray Whalen ('55), a guard on the team. In 1957 and 1958 the basketball team won the Allamakee County Tournament championship. The only other time this had been done was in 1929.

Baseball was played in the spring and fall. In 1952 and 1953, there were especially good teams. In the 1953 fall season, there were four teams in the state championship tournament. New Albin was beaten by Auburn, the eventual state champions.

Janitors—A World War I veteran who was gassed twice in France became the school janitor from 1946-1957. Leo Crowley, or "Growley" Crowley, as the kids affectionately called him, became a legend at New Albin High School. He gave nicknames to all the students. Every summer, he and his wife would strip all the floors and apply two coats of wax to the floor. He was the real disciplinarian in the school. When the students tried to slide on his beautifully waxed floor each September, his simple frown stopped them. The new gymnasium built in 1951-52 was his pride and joy. He did not allow street shoes on the floor. His son Earl Crowley ('54) told, "When I was in the 5th grade, I would help at school by standing on a stool and cleaning the black boards and erasers. I always had a job, so did not get to play sports. During high school my job was at Heiderscheit Chrysler and Plymouth." Dolores Moldenhauer Crowley ('54), who was to become Leo's daughter-in-law, said of Mr. Crowley, "We had basketball practice at 11:00 so I was always late for lunch. We ate our sack lunches on the bleachers in the gym. We would place our lunch there before basketball practice so that after taking our shower we could go straight to lunch." Mr. Crowley would clear off all the left-over lunches and waste when he would return from his exactly 30-minute lunch break that he ate at his home. Dolores continued "I had to rescue my lunch from the garbage regularly. My complaining did not help as he said it looked like it was not being eaten. I know he knew exactly what he was doing."

Harris "Shooky" Fink ('35) was the janitor following Mr. Crowley's retirement in 1957. His passion was teaching and coaching the game of baseball. He played and instructed the kids at all the recesses. His legacy was making baseball popular. Many of his New Albin Little League players played integral positions on many high school state championship teams.

Drivers Education—The drivers training program started in 1952. Jean Linzenmeyer Kurk ('55) recalled, "The cars were always provided by Heiderscheit Motors. They were manual transmission and the stick was on the column. Talk about grinding the gears when trying to downshift going up hills!" Ralph Nelson ('57) chuckled when he said. "I can still see Bernadette Mauss ('56) running over the cones in the parking lot."

Killed in Action—New Albin men lost in World War II were:

Kenneth Edmund Casey—1942 Guadacanal
awarded the purple heart

John Colsch ('35)—Killed in France, August 1944
bomber pilot

Douglas Ray Darling—Killed in Ruhr Valley,
buried in Belgium

Daniel Kelly ('36)—Killed in Holland 1944

Donald Olaf—Philippines on the
Bataan Death March, 1942

Notable Graduates—Harris "Shooky" Fink ('35) became a legend in New Albin for his love of a 'stitched horse hide' and kids for over four decades. Returning to his hometown to follow another legend as the school janitor, Shooky continued to mold the brand of baseball into generations of young boys. Playing ball and practicing nearly every day on his ballfield became the passion of every little boy who ever rode his bike to practice with the mitt hanging on the handle bars. To say that he loved baseball was only be topped by his love for boys and their development of character and confidence. Vandalism and juvenile delinquency in New Albin was never a problem as he taught respect, responsibility, and leadership to every boy who ever learned to lay down a bunt. The girls at school loved him too and the friendship pins from them in the laces of his tennis shoes were an outward sign. Heywood Hale Broun, the national sportswriter for CBS journeyed to New Albin to see this Mr. Baseball in action and for an interview for national television.

Notable Teachers—Many teachers came to New Albin for their first teaching positions. Two that made lasting impacts on the community and the students were Jim McGrew and Mike Corrigan. Jean

Linzenmeyer Kurk ('55) shared, "Mr. Corrigan was so special to all the students. He was different than other teachers. He took us on field trips in the spring and fall. Everyone who went through New Albin schools would say he was the best they ever had. He really cared about his pupils. He left to become a principal in Minnesota. Jim McGrew came my freshman year and stayed three years before going to Waverly for the rest of his career. He taught history, social studies and was the girls basketball coach. Wow, was he good looking. He became part of the community. He attended church and came to every one of our activities. He still comes back to our reunions and is much respected for all of his great teachings that he brought to NAHS."

Senior Trips—Chicago was the destination for the classes of 1954 and 1955. Harris "Shooky" Fink ('35) was working as a machinist in Chicago and came to see the class of 21 seniors while they were staying at the Conrad Hilton Hotel. "He was some 20 years older than us but loved his New Albin people. I can still see him sprawled out on our bed saying, 'I just wanted to say that I have slept at the Conrad Hilton,'" remembered Jean Linzenmeyer Kurk ('55).

Closing—The New Albin High School closed after graduation in May 1960. The closing was bitter. Students were bused to Lansing the next fall. The 1961 graduates from Lansing Kee High who were from New Albin when it closed returned to New Albin to have another graduation ceremony. They believed that they did not belong to either school.

New Albin High School
Allamakee County, IA

#66

New Hartford Consolidated High School

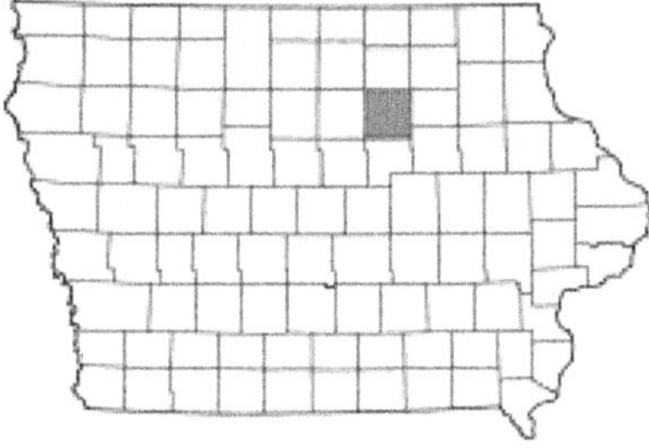

Mascot: Hawks
Colors: Blue and White
Closed: 1992
Location: Southeast Butler County

Early History—Butler County is a perfect 24 by 24 miles square. This allows for 16 townships which make up the quilt pattern of six by six miles square. Beaver Township is in the southeast corner. Titus and S.B. Ensign came in 1855 and built a mill on the banks of the Beaver Creek. A town was plated and the Ensign brothers named it after their home town New Hartford, Connecticut.

In a historical account written in 1976 for the US Centennial, Congressman Charles Grassley ('51) penned a letter to the New Hartford community on this occasion:

> . . . there's nothing more pleasant about being your congressman than coming home to New Hartford. My kids and wife feel the same way and have elected to live on our farm and go to school in New Hartford instead of moving to Washington D.C.

The railroad came to town at the end of the civil war in 1865, and a depot was built on the south side of the tracks. A sign was posted declaring Omaha-224 miles, Chicago-292 miles, and New Orleans-1,124 miles. As many as four passenger trains stopped each day. One could leave New Hartford at 1:30, travel the 18 miles to Waterloo, take care of business or shop, and return at 5:30. Tickets to Cedar Falls were 25 cents and to Waterloo were 43 cents.

Early Schools—In January 1857, Charles Ensign started the first school teaching a three-month term. County records show in October 1857, lots 3 & 4 Block 1, Roots Addition were transferred to the school. This became the site of the first school and has continued to serve as the location of the New Hartford schools since.

By 1867, the building was unsuitable both in size and accommodations. A new two-story school was built for $2,000. It was considered the most efficient in the county at that time.

The next two-story brick building was erected in 1897 at the cost of $4,000. The brick for the building was fired at a brick factory north of town. This building burned in November 1916 during a Monday noon hour. All books and equipment were destroyed. The loss was figured at $12,000 with only $4,000 insurance.

In 1901, the first graduates of the New Hartford High School were Mae Ensign and William Ressing. The school became a four-year high school in 1914. Due to the fire in 1916, there were no graduates in 1917 because the high school students relocated to Cedar Falls for the school year 1917-18.

A special dedication service was held in 1918 for the new high school with Governor W.L. Harding giving the dedicatory address. It was attended by county officials, local businessmen, and members of the board of education. The Grundy Center High School band gave a long concert from 1:00-2:30. A procession headed by the Boy Scouts carrying flags and a band marched to the city park. Dr. J.G. Evans (the town physician) introduced Governor Harding who gave a stirring patriotic address proclaiming he "thought it the duty of the state to find out the special talent of each child to help develop it, this being one so there would be no dullards." There was an open house and 1,500 people were shown through the new school.

In 1920, most of the rural schools in Beaver Township voted to close and consolidate with the town school becoming the New Hartford Consolidated School District.

New school rooms were added in 1927 and 1948.

After World War II, the army barracks in Sioux City were no longer needed. The New Hartford School District bought the barracks and sent a crew to tear them down. They were then reconstructed into a bus barn that stood where the shop was later to stand, according to New Hartford historian, Vopal Gowan Youngberg ('33).

Floods – Flooding in New Hartford seemed to come with the summer rains. The Floods of 1902 and 1947 were ones for the record books. "I remember the one in 1947 distinctly because there were drowned dead pigs streaming right down Main Street," said Kent Cuvelier ('61).

"We had been on vacation to California in July of 1947 when the flood put several inches of water in our family's hardware store. The muck it left behind was such a memory with the cleanup," remembered Lorraine Johnson Hoffman ('60). "My dad, John Johnson and my mother Grace Tencate ('26) had started the hardware store at the beginning of the Depression in 1932. They taught us to treat everyone with respect and that if we saw others being naughty, we were to walk away. This was the nature of our classmates at New Hartford."

Holger Holm ('34) enlisted in the Army at the outbreak of WW II. He was captured on Corregidor in the Philippines. He survived incredible torture and imprisonment in Japan as a prisoner of war for 3½ years. He returned to the states after the capture of the POW camp in 1945 to recover at the Clinton Iowa Veterans hospital. Back in New Hartford, he was sleeping the night of the first signs of the flood in July 1947. He is reported to have put his hand out of bed in the night to find there were several inches of water flowing through his house. The community always rallied to rebuild.

Sports—The boys basketball teams were the Butler County Champions in 1927, 1931, 1934, 1935, 1941, 1948, and 1950.

The school newspaper, *The Echo* headlines in March 1938 read:

> Greene withdraws from Tournament: Forfeits first game of Tournament to New Hartford because of some cases of scarlet fever at Greene. They have decided to forfeit their game in the first round of the county tournament which will be held at Parkersburg . . . New Hartford's first game will be with the winner of Shell Rock-Clarksville. The tournament is as follows: Parkersburg-Dumont, and Allison-Aplington.

The beautiful brick gymnasium built in 1949 was considered the biggest gym in the county and became the site of many county and sectional tournaments. Kent Cuvelier ('61) remembered, "There was no such thing as a contract for the construction and the community volunteers all had a hand in its construction. I helped my dad by handing him the bolts used in the subfloor for the basketball court." The long-awaited inaugural game came in January 1950 against Allison.

"We had a good team but playing on such a special night with a packed house it seemed we were somewhat tense and rattled. We couldn't do anything right in the first half and went to the locker room at half down by a few points. Coach Formanek chewed us out and told us we were a much better team and we came out the second half and buried Allison. It was one of those nights I vividly remember these 70 years later," reminisced Jack Hovelson ('50).

Schools in the Butler County Conference were Aplington, Parkersburg, Allison, Clarksville, Bristow, Greene, Shell Rock, and New Hartford. Parkersburg was the fiercest rival located just eight miles west on Highway 20. The boys basketball team made it to the state tournament in 1956, finishing fourth place. Not until 1991, when the boys track team won the state track meet, would a state crown come to the New Hartford Hawks.

The boys played basketball and spring and fall baseball. Football became a sport in the fall of 1959 when there were 14 boys out for 11-man football. Kent Cuvelier ('61) was on that first football team. "It was quite a learning curve, but we competed respectively. It was a coincidence that when I returned to New Hartford to teach, I coached the first girls cross country team. There was some back talk that girls should not be pushed into such strenuous sports as cross country. The controversy was shortly put to rest as the year progressed," said Cuvelier proudly.

Girls basketball became a school sport in 1954. Audrey Naber Schoeman ('56) remembered, "The first time I ever got to suit up for a game it was at Allison. The only time that I touched the ball, it went straight up in the air. I was convinced that this was not my sport."

Band and Music—The band in 1940 had 34 members. New blue and white uniforms were purchased.

Forty-five years later in 1985, the new seven-piece uniforms were worn by the high school band. A total of $14,350 was raised through selling thousands of dollar worth of pizzas, beef burgers, ice cream, and including a variety of activities from raffles to softball games. Money was also donated from school alumni, area civic groups, churches, and businesses.

The *Waterloo Courier* January 31, 1986 reported:

> The New Hartford Swing Choir is a song and-dance business . . . faded sweatpants, 16-ounce bottles of pop and music by Madonna might be on a teenagers list of favorite things. One thing is definitely not on the list is practice, for anything at 7:45 in the morning. . . " the first year I had 11 kids," recalls Nancy Allen (teacher). . . "this year we have 55 in the concert choir and 25 in the show choir (there were 110 students in the entire high school this year) . . . show choir members are also athletes, musicians, and actors."

Drivers Education—Drivers Education was started in 1953. Audrey Naber Schoeman ('56) remembered, "I got to drive for the first time. There were three boys in my driving group. We started first on the gravel road going east along the rail road track. In time, when I was good enough behind the wheel, I was allowed to drive out on the highway south of town. The boys would all duck down so that they would not be seen in the car with me, the student driver." The drivers education car was also used for transportation to away ball games. The car had a set of dual controls on the passenger side of the car. Coach Kurtt would usually drive the car out of town, but Paul Schoeman ('56), sitting on the passenger side, was notorious for accidently pushing in the dual clutch and the car motor would roar as the accelerator was floor boarded.

Killed in Action—New Hartford men killed in action were:

Leon Geyer, WWI
Ray Brickner, WWI
Leroy Bowen ('37), WWII
Ivan Case, WWII
Warren Jensen, WWII
Edwin Grotte, WWII
Charles Stickley, WWII

New Hartford men who were prisoners of war during WWII were:

Vernon Harms, Germany
Wendell Harms ('41), Germany
Holger Holm ('34), Philippines-Japan
Donald Jorgensen, Germany

Notable Teachers—A recognized teacher was Mr. Henry Eschen. However, it may not have been his excellence in the classroom that helped change one of his student's careers. "He was a great mentor to me as girls were not thought to be scientists. I had thoughts of going to medical school and Mr. Eschen was so encouraging and helped direct me to college at Wartburg. I later received my doctorate in Microbiology and taught at Iowa State. Teachers can have such an impact on student's lives," affirmed Lorraine Johnson Hoffman ('60).

A distinguished principal, Herb Hovelson, was an administrator and teacher from 1946 through 1952. Because he was a left-handed student, in his early education he had been forced to write with his right hand, which was quite common in that era. Many of his students can remember his great talent at the black board when he wrote the syllabus for the day. "He was able to start at the left side of the board writing with the left hand until he reached the center of the board. Here, he would switch hands and write the rest of the assignment with his right hand. This seemed to impress his students for years to come," recalled his son Jack Hovelson ('50).

Mrs. Roberts was the English and literature teacher in the 1950s. An extracurricular honor for the English teacher was to direct the school plays. The spring of 1960 there was to be a three-act play. "Mrs. Roberts was notorious to sit at the back of the gymnasium with the lights down and sometimes doze off while the actors were practicing. A plot was schemed. At first the girls did not want to have anything to do with the plan but finally consented to play along. When finishing the first act in practice the next night, they immediately skipped the second act and went into the third act. When Mrs. Roberts awakened, she was very complementary for the work the actors had done that night and released them early not realizing the quick rehearsal. The straight-faced seniors quickly left with theatrical composure," admitted Lorraine Johnson Hoffman ('60).

Pranks—The pranks at New Hartford High School were somewhat on the unusual and harmless nature. Gene Grassley ('59) cut down a tree at the end of the bus turn-in to the school. The downed tree prevented the buses from getting in line for picking up the students. The daughter of the town cop provided the look-out at the end of the block while the lumberjack, Gene, was doing his deed.

Several students got access to the principal's day planner. His son Jack ('50) was possibly the ringleader. They added to Mr. Hovelson's list of daily announcements for the public address. As he read the announcements, the last one by the boys added was that school will be dismissed at 1:30. It was when Gary Sells ('50) snickered that Mr. Hovelson realized the plot.

Some still-anonymous culprits dreamed up the idea to urinate in one of the school bus gas tanks. They stayed after manual arts class to relieve themselves. Of course, the next day the bus sputtered and stalled. The bus driver believed that there must be water in the gas. A bus driver started to use a siphon to suck the fuel out of the tank, the juveniles headed for the hills to forever claim their innocence.

Bus Drivers—Bus drivers were recognized in the *Hawk's Eye* on February 25, 1988 written by Michelle Fish ('89).

The School Bus Driver's Story

When you think of school you probably think of students, teachers, and homework. But there's something you forgot. How did you get to school before you started driving?

Everyday four important people get up before most of us and help make transportation available to and from school. These people are our bus drivers. Between them they have been driving our buses for a total of 74 years: Duane Wessel ('52) has driven for 38 years, Donna Payne-17 years, Fred Everts-15 years, and Carol Joblinske-14 years.

Closing—New Hartford became a bedroom city after World War II. Waterloo and Cedar Falls factory and college jobs became the primary employment for returning veterans and farm workers. The catastrophic 1980s and the agriculture crisis caused unemployment, loss of population, and decreased enrollment in the school.

The graduates from New Hartford have been successful in education at the elementary, secondary, and the university level. Contributions were made in politics, banking, industry, secretaries, farming, and journalism. The class of

1950 distinguished itself with a college biology professor, a banker, vice president of a large corporation, teachers, an entrepreneur developer, farmers, and a newspaper writer. The Class of 1961 had over half of its graduates earn college degrees.

By 1992, the vote was held to consolidate with Dike was passed. After 91 years, a total of 1,703 graduated from New Hartford Consolidated High School from 1901-1992. The largest class was 41 in 1981. The most numerous surnames of the graduates were: Johnson-29, Luck-24, Hansen-23, Chapman-20, Gersma-18, Ballhagen-14, Grandon-14, Sells-14, Ackerson-13, Bolton-13, Miller-13, Smith-13, Bergman-12, Perrin-12, Schoeman-11, Thompson-11, Bass-10, Dove-10, Grassley-10, Hersey-10, Jones-10, DeBuhr-9, DeGroote-9, Naber-9, and Schrage-9. The last to receive a diploma from New Hartford High School was Jeremy Venenga (alphabetically).

New Hartford Consolidated High School
Butler County, IA

#67

New Vienna St. Boniface High School

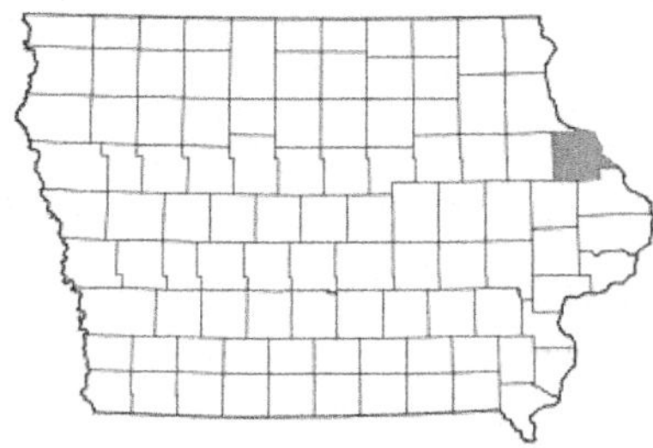

Mascot: Bonnies/later NU Hawks
Colors: Black & Gold/
later Blue and Gold (1952)
Closed: 1966
Location: Dubuque County

Early History—New Vienna is named after the Europeans' homeland city. These German immigrants came to America in 1833. They first settled near Muenster, Ohio. After ten years in Ohio the farmland became less available and five families sold their farms and headed west to Dubuque County in 1843. These German Catholics were lured for a larger settlement and government land so they could expand their farms. Under the direction of Rev. Matthias Loras, Bishop of Dubuque, they found suitable rich soil in the area to become New Vienna.

Bishop Loras, at the time, was working with Emperor Francis I of Vienna, Austria, to help relocate immigrants to America. It is because of this tie that the small settlement was named New Vienna. These settlers purchased land from the government for $1.25 an acre and built their log houses. In August 1844, four out of the five families donated ten acres to the form the village. Part of the gift was for the town and part for the parochial area.

Education for their children was very important to these German families. As the town grew to seventeen families in 1846, the St. Boniface Catholic congregation was formed. Bishop Loras celebrated the first mass in a log cabin.

First Schools—Early in 1847, John Klostermann, a well-educated farmer conducted the first school in New Vienna. School was held in a log cabin and later in a separate section of the first log church. The cabin became the parochial school and the church.

In 1870, a new school was constructed with a convent and boarding house for the students. Two years later in 1872, the Franciscan Sisters of Perpetual Adoration were asked to teach at this school and convent. With increasing enrollment, the former church building was renovated to serve as classrooms.

The long-awaited free-standing school building was built to accommodate grades one to eight on the first floor and nine to twelve on the second floor. The three-story brick school opened on September 9, 1925 with 250 students.

On May 16, 1929, St. Boniface High School received state accreditation from the Iowa Board of Secondary Schools. This accreditation allowed graduates to be admitted to the three state colleges without examination. The graduates were also recognized by all colleges in the country.

The first graduation was held in May 1929 with eleven graduates.

Religion—New Vienna families held catholic faith and education as their core values. Thirty-four men from New Vienna St. Boniface Parish entered the priesthood. Fifty-one daughters of St. Boniface became Sisters at St. Rose Convent—Lacrosse, Wisconsin, Mount St. Francis—Dubuque, Iowa, and Mt. Carmel—Dubuque, Iowa.

Mass was conducted every morning for all grade and high school students. The students were expected to be present and on time. "I had perfect attendance and was a model student," told Inez Krapfl Kluesner ('59). "Sure enough, the one time I was late was on January 22, 1955. That was the day that our family had accompanied my brother, Gene, to the train station to bid him farewell as he was going in the Army. I will always remember my mother's last words to him, 'Now watch-out for those protestants.' This excuse did not hold any water with the Sister as I tried to explain my tardiness." This incident is confirmed by Fred Westhoff ('54), who was also on that same troop train to be inducted into the Army.

From the fourth grade through high school, the schoolboys helped serve mass. Bernie Kluesner ('58) recalled, "I was a server all the way through school. We had mass server meetings and we learned how to hold our hands and to do the proper genuflect. We always looked forward to the annual Mass servers and girls chorus picnic."

The Mass server president for 1963-64 recalled a time of boyhood chicanery. "The first Friday of every month we had communion. To take communion, the students were not allowed to eat after midnight. After communion I had about ten minutes to eat my fried egg sandwich. Just to wash it down, Arnie Vaske ('64) and I would slip out to his car to spike our milk and make it a sweet tasting Irish chocolate milk. So much for being cherubs," laughed Dave Krapfl ('64).

Janitor—Andy Nefzger was a fixture at the school as the janitor and maintenance man. The church was across the street from the school. Inez Krapfl Kluesner ('59) remembered, "I can still see him hanging out that high door on the church steeple to move the hands on the clock. I thought he was always going to fall." Dave Krapfl ('64) said, "I don't think that man ever slept. The school was his palace. I remember him shoveling coal into the boiler every morning and then shoveling by hand the snow from the sidewalks at the school and church. On top of that, he had to dig all the graves for the cemetery next to the church by hand with a shovel. What a worker and example of dedication to his job, school, and church."

Sports—There was no football at the school. Baseball was played in the spring at the high school. The boys basketball team was formed in 1946.

Father Krull became the Superintendent in 1957 and was the basketball coach. However, he admitted that he knew little about the sport, so a local farmer, Kenneth Vorwald, was the actual coach. The state athletics association did not allow for non-teachers to be coaches, so Father Krull would sit on the bench next to the team and Kenneth Vorwald would be one row behind coaching.

The main school rival was Holy Cross.

They played in the Eastern Iowa Conference with the following teams: St. Mary's—Cascade, St. Martin's—Cascade, Holy Cross, Epworth, Farley, Peosta, Bankston, St. Mary's—Guttenburg, Ryan, and Worthington.

Each year, the Dubuque Catholic Diocese Tournament was held at Loras College. Bernie Kluesner ('58) recalled, "When we first stepped onto that court it was like a different world. Glass backboards, a huge shiny court, and seating that seemed like a colosseum. Winning that tournament with all of the surrounding schools involved was for bragging rights all of the next year."

The 1960 team won the great Dubuque Diocese Tournament. Henry Westhoff ('60) stated, "We had a great team. We were undefeated going into the post season tournaments. We made it to the sub-state and lost to Solon and had to settle for the consolation trophy. At those times, a team had to win 12 straight games in the tournaments to become the State Champion. We had quite a run and almost made it."

The sport for the girls was softball. They had not competed against many other schools until a call came from the Epworth superintendent who suggested that St. Boniface High School should enter the competition for the first Girls State Softball Tournament in 1956. That year, led by a great pitcher, Diane Oberbroeckling Domeyer ('58), St. Boniface High School finished fourth place in the state. Doris Krapfl Langel '(56) said, "I was the captain and played centerfield. They called me

'Homerun Doris' and I loved the sport and the competition."

In 1958, a forfeiture would occur that would be long remembered in New Vienna. "We had a great team, of course, with a great pitcher, Diane Oberbroeckling Domeyer ('58). We were to play Colesburg in the playoffs. The priest who was our coach told us that he had to stay at the church for a wedding rehearsal but that another senior boy, Tom Kramer ('59), would be our coach. Of course, we won the game handily. The problem arose when Colesburg reported us to the state for not having a teacher-coach and the game was forfeited by the state athletics association. This was a bitter pill to swallow and it was the girls that had to suffer, and our season was so prematurely over," lamented Mary Roling Sassen ('59).

Killed in Action—Six men from New Vienna were killed in World War II.

Arnold Fangmann ('37)
Donald Koth
Clarence Ries
Arnold Rahe ('35)
Clarence Schwers ('34)
Julius Schwers

Two men were held prisoners of war: Louis Heying ('36) and Julius Klostermann.

Music—Singing and music were a great love of Sister Joseph Marie. She made the choir mandatory and recruited every boy to join. Bernie Kluesner ('58) said, "When I was in the 9th grade I was told 'you boys will be in choir.' We did not resist, as she was a great teacher, and we learned to love music from Sister Joseph Marie. She also played the organ at church, so as a server I was always under her watchful eye."

Pranks—Arnie Vaske ('64) of the 'Irish Chocolate milk' fame was one for prolonging the study hall period rather that going to class. He borrowed a hair pin, wrapped it in a towel, and stuck it into the electrical outlet at the back of the classroom. The lights began to flicker and then the fuse was blown. In the ensuing time to get the lights back on, the bell would ring late and the study hall period was extended.

A typewriter with paper already in the roller was the trademark position for the Sister teaching the typing class. Occasionally, Jim 'Pluto' Conrad ('64) sabotaged the roller and placed a roll of caps neatly under the preloaded paper. The Sister diligently started to type. Each time when reaching the end of the column, she would hit the return bar. A cap exploded under the roller paper. Of course, none of the class ever looked up to catch the glare of the teacher.

Senior Trips—During the 1950s the annual bus trip took the seniors to Chicago. "We got to stay for a night or two and see the museums, Michigan Avenue stores, and take in a Cubs baseball game. My senior year we were even allowed to see a real pro team by going to see a White Sox game," chuckled Larry Westhoff ('58) (a lifelong Cardinal fan digging at the Cubs).

"Having never seen Chicago, we took the chartered bus and saw the tall skyscrapers. I was on the elevator of the new Sears Tower with Carol Pape ('59) and Agnes Reinert ('59) when suddenly it stopped. There came over the intercom a voice that said 'you boy scouts take care of those girls on there till we get the elevator started.' We sat there for about 20 minutes before it started moving again. What a welcome to the big city for a small-town farm girl," laughed Mary Roling Sassen ('59).

Drivers Education—There was no drivers education taught at St. Boniface. "Our drivers education was taught by our dads on the outfield of the baseball field," remembered Fred Westhoff ('54). Marian Klostermann ('59) added, "Since most of us were farm kids, many of us learned to drive out in the hay fields."

Snow Days—In the history of the St. Boniface school there was never a day closed because of snow. The rural students were brought to school by their parents driving a tractor pulling a wagon. "My dad took his turn in hauling us to school during the bad winter storms and heavy snows. Only he would pull us with the tractor attached to the manure spreader. I don't recall us raising much of a stink about it," laughed Dave Krapfl ('64).

Closing—St. Boniface High School closed in May 1966. The next year the students were bused to Dyersville-Beckman High School in Dyersville. There were 521 graduates from St. Boniface High School. The most numerous surnames of the graduates were: Boeckenstedt-23; Vaske-22; Lansing-15; Oberbroeckling-15; Kluesner-13; Krapfl-13; Deutmeyer-11; Heying-10; Mescher-10; Ahlers-9; Klostermann-9; and Wilgenbusch-8. The last to receive a diploma from St. Boniface was Judy Willenborg (alphabetically).

#68

Nichols High School

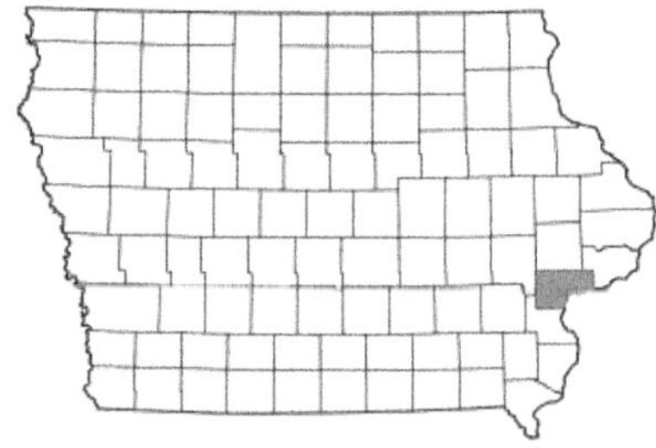

Mascot: Little Nicks
Colors: Maroon and White
Closed: 1961
Location: Muscatine County

Early History—Sam Nichols came to Pike Township from Ohio in 1838. He was a self-made man and the founder of the town of Nichols. His eldest son, B.F. Nichols, laid out the town in 1869.

The Burlington, Cedar Rapids, and Minnesota Railroad commenced construction of a north-south line through the area in 1869. In 1872, Benjamin Nichols erected the three-story brick St. Nichols Hotel. It was within sight of the railway depot.

In 1873, the east-west Muscatine Western Railway reached Nichols on its way to Montezuma which was 80 miles west of Muscatine. By 1899, both railroads were owned by the Burlington, Cedar Rapids, and Northern Railroad. In 1903 they were acquired by the Chicago, Rock Island, and Pacific Railroad.

Nichols was incorporated in 1899 and had a population of 500. The *Atlas of Muscatine County, Iowa 1899* shows a clip from the *Nichols Gazette* titled "Sketch of Nichols." Several advertisements highlight the area merchants at the time:

The Peoples Furniture Store

C.H. MILNES
Licensed embalmer and Funeral Director
West Liberty, Iowa

WR Trautman
General Repair Shop
3 mi S and 1 W of Nichols
Repairing of Ag Machinery
Promptly Attended to at all
Hours day or night

Early Schools—In 1872, a square 40′ two-story wood frame school house was erected to house a "common school" for the town. In 1883, the Nichols common school became a "graded school" with grades 1 to 8.

A three-year high school curriculum was established in September 1900. The first Principal and only teacher for Nichols High School was Thomas L. Eland. In 1903, Bessie Baker ('03), the daughter of the Nichols Savings Bank's Cashier, became the first graduate of Nichols High School. Professor Thomas L. Eland enrolled in the medical school at the State University of Iowa.

At the beginning of the school year in September 1913, the Iowa State Board of Education placed NHS on the list of accredited three-year high schools. This allowed NHS graduates to enroll in the 4th year class of any high school in the country to earn a four -year diploma. Some students took their fourth year of school at West Liberty, ten miles north of Nichols. The Nichols School Board hired another Assistant Principal thereby doubling the number of high school teachers from one to two.

On January 27, 1915, after 43 years of service, the wooden frame Nichols Public School building was destroyed by fire. Miss Mayme Foley, who taught the intermediate grades at the Nichols Public School for 48 continuous years from 1904-1952, smelled the smoke and then discovered the fire in the attic. Classes were conducted in temporary quarters in the Opera House and churches until a new building was constructed. In less than 10 months, the new Nichols Public school was constructed. It opened the Monday after Thanksgiving on November 29, 1915. The new building was located on the east side of Nichols on the north side of Ijem Avenue (later became Iowa Highway 22). On May 28, 1916, four seniors comprised the first class to graduate from the new schoolhouse. The class included Benjamin Franklin Nichols ('16), great-grandson of Samuel Nichols. Exactly 34 years later, on May 28, 1950, this Benjamin Nichols, as President of the Board of Education, presented diplomas to the six boys constituting the 1950 Class. (One member of the 1950 class, 70 years later May 28, 2020, has spent five years building the Nichols High School Digital Archives on the web site of the Musser Public Library in Muscatine.)

During the 1924-25 school year Nichols High School adopted a four-year curriculum.

Notable Graduates—Don Smith ('50) became a lawyer and practiced in Ames Iowa. His deep love for his hometown and high school made him the Nichols alumni historian and his works are preserved at the Musser Public Library in Muscatine. The Nichols High School Digital Archives at the Library is an incredible historical collection of data from the Nichols founding including the pictorial history of the community.

Alberta Metcalf Kelly ('15) became a Democratic National Committeewomen. A proud picture of her at the National Democratic Convention in Chicago shows her standing next to Mrs. Eleanor Roosevelt and Adlai Stevenson.

Killed in Action—Harry L. Ogren ('43) was killed in World War II.

Notable Teachers—Miss Mayme Foley arrived in the Town of Nichols by train from Columbus Junction to start her new employment as teacher of the intermediate grades. It happened that she would teach those intermediate grades for 48 consecutive school years, retiring in May of 1952 at age 79. Many families in the Nichols community had three generations pass through her classroom. The very first *Mirror* yearbook in 1944 was dedicated to Miss Foley. It read: Her guiding hand will be long remembered. Her advice has often been sought and often helped its seekers during her 34 years of service to the Nichols community

Notable Teacher and Graduate—Dr. Thomas Eland married his first graduate from NHS, Bessie Baker ('03), in 1907. Professor Eland was enrolled in the Medical College at the State University of Iowa where he completed a four-year program in 1907. During this same time, he maintained a social connection with his sole Nichols High School graduate. On June 11, 1907, Thomas L. Eland and Bessie M. Baker were married.

Sports—The Town of Nichols had an independent basketball team as early as 1909 which played its home games with out-of-town teams in the Nichols Opera House. In 1917, Nichols High School organized its first boys basketball team. A Nichols High School girls basketball team followed soon evidenced by a 1925 photograph.

A challenge was printed in the *Muscatine Journal* on December 6, 1917. It read:

> **Challenge Issued By the Nichols School**
>
> Nichols, Ia, Dec 6—The Nichols High School has recently organized a basketball team which is now ready to be pitted against other fires. This team has issued an open challenge to play any high school second team in this vicinity. Arrangements for games and dates can be made by letter with Robert Nolan, secretary of the team at Nichols.

In the summer of 1934, a new auditorium-gymnasium addition to the schoolhouse was constructed at a cost of approximately $12,000.

On October 2, 1934, a car carrying six members of the NHS baseball team was returning from a game in Conesville when it crashed into a vehicle parked along the side of the road. Three players died from their injuries: Virgil Poole, Clarence Carney, and Junior Nash. The other three players, Pershing Elder

('38), Lloyd Hahn ('36), and Edwin Yedlik ('35) had serious injuries but recovered. A triple funeral for the three deceased students would be the first event held in the new auditorium on October 5, 1934.

The girls basketball team won the Muscatine County Tournament three straight years from 1942-44. They were denied a fourth straight year losing by one point to Wilton in 1945.

Other teams played in 1944 were: Riverside, Wilton, Conesville, Atalissa, Springdale, Lone Tree, Carver Pump girls, Solon, and Tiffin.

No football was played at Nichols High School Spring and fall baseball was played by the boys.

Alumni Association Organized—On November 1, 1924, a meeting was held at the high school building to organize the Nichols High School Alumni Association. It was chaired by Professor Gerbrecht, the school's "Principal Teacher" for that year. The records created and maintained by the Alumni Association listing the names of graduates and their years of graduation from 1901 to 1961 proved to be the single most valuable resource for that information in building the Nichols High School Digital Archives. Willard Salemink ('51) has preserved the Alumni Association records.

Student Newspaper—The 1925 school year saw the first publications of the *Nicholite* student newspaper. The first editor of the *Nicholite* was Robert Fox. His parents were Harry and Lenore Fox and four of their five children graduated from Nichols High School: Harry Jr. ('24), Robert ('26), Lillian ('29) and Charles ('31). The father, Harry, was the station agent for the Rock Island Railroad in Nichols from 1915 to 1939. The sad part of the Fox family story is that Robert died of tuberculosis on July 5, 1936, at the Oakdale Sanitorium at Iowa City, Iowa.

Yearbook—The 1944 school year saw the publication of the first of 18 volumes (1944-1961) of the new *Mirror* yearbook. The content and the publication of the first six volumes (1944-1949) was totally the work of the student staff, including gluing black and white glossy pictures onto blank spaces left on the typed pages. The last twelve volumes were produced by a commercial publisher using content provided by the student staff that was printed on paper that was not photo quality. The irony is that the glossy prints in the six volumes totally produced by students could be scanned at a high-resolution level and added to the Nichols High School Digital Archives. They are a remarkable collection of old but high-quality pictures. That was not the case with the last twelve volumes produced by a commercial publisher using non-photo quality paper.

The 1944 *Mirror* pictured 15 seniors, and each shared their ambitions, hopes, and dreams following graduation. Their documented ambitions were: Army Air Corps pilot, Journalist, Business College, Yeoman in Navy, Officer Navy Air Corps, Business College, Nurse, Army Air Corps Bombardier, College Education, Business School, Stenographer, Officer Navy Air Corps, Designer, Flyer, Graduate from State University of Iowa, and to become Mrs. Bob Harbit.

Janitor and Cooks—Cleve Hazan started as the school janitor in 1944. He was paid $1.00 an hour. In the winter, he stayed all night in the furnace room feeding the fire to prevent the pipes from freezing. His wife, Julia brought him supper and he would save half of it for his lunch the next day. In 1946, Julia and their daughter, Loretta Hazen Hahn, became the first cooks for the hot lunch program. Cleve built the first tables and benches from scratch. The kitchen was against the wall and the 65 lunches were prepared on a two-burner gas stove. The cooks brought their own pans from home which they filled with hot water to hold the pots to keep the food warm. When the school switched from coal to natural gas, the kitchen was moved into the old coal room and this allowed for a more efficient food preparation. At the peak of serving, the lunches were prepared for over 250 students. Loretta graduated from the first class of the Iowa certifying school lunch short course. In 1976, at the annual meeting of American School Food Service Association in Honolulu, Hawaii, she was awarded a plaque for 30 years of service to the youth of America.

Closing—A notice to the Nichols Independent School Board from the Iowa Department of Public Instruction came in January 1960. Accreditation for the secondary school would be withdrawn following graduation of the 1961 class. The board was urged to engage in a voluntary reorganization by June 30, 1961.

The Nichols High School closed in May 1961 as forced by the State Board of Education. In the 59 years from 1903-1961 there were 494 graduates.* The largest class was 22 in 1961. The most numerous surnames of the graduates were Mills-16, Smith-14, Elder-12, Oostendorp-11, Kirchner-10, Schmidt-9, Kirkpatrick-8, and Pike-8. The last to receive a diploma from Nichols High School was Dennis Wieskamp (alphabetically).

*A distinguished graduate was Lloyd Mills. He received a diploma in 1923. He returned to receive a 12th grade diploma in 1926. So, for historical purposes there were 493 individuals receiving diplomas from NHS.

Nichols Public School Building, Nichols, Iowa

Nichols High School
Muscatine County, IA

#69

Nodaway High School

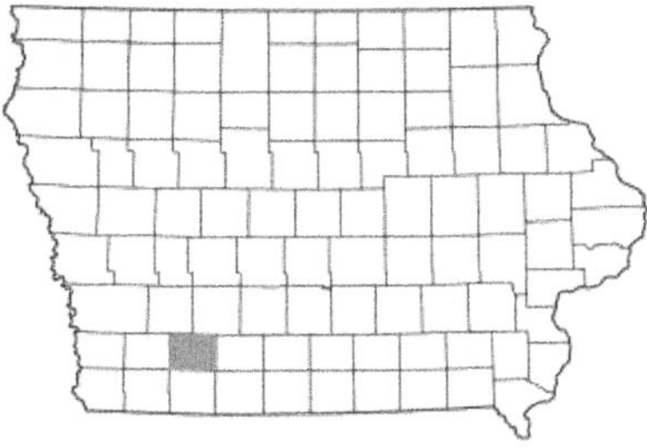

Mascot: Cardinal
Colors: Red and White
Closed: 1959
Location: Southwest Adams County

Early History—The town of Nodaway is located in Nodaway Township. It is one mile east of the East Nodaway River. A stagecoach trail, "The Blue Grass Trail," followed the East Nodaway River. The Wayside Inn was built by Noah Odell in 1856 and a small settlement established called East Nodaway. Its name was changed to Rachelle, proposed, adopted, and recorded in Washington D.C. during the 1870s. The name was not popular and changed back to Nodaway. The Chicago, Burlington, and Quincy Railroad (CB & Q) built through the town in 1869. A second track was added in 1897. Nodaway was incorporated on May 28, 1900.

The Nodaway River appears in the Lewis and Clark journals. They camped at the mouth of the river where it flows into the Missouri River on July 8, 1804. The name is an Otoe-Missouria term meaning "jump over the water." Another version of the meaning is an Indian word meaning "crossed in a canoe."

Early Schools—The first school in Nodaway opened in 1869. As settlers moved into the area and interest in scholarship increased, a new and larger schoolhouse was needed. In 1879, a two-story frame building was built on the same site as the first school. There were 65 students the first year with Professor Worley and one assistant as teachers. There were three rooms and it was considered the second-best schoolhouse in Adams County.

In 1885 with the district consisting of 13 sections, opposing factions caused the district to be divided and district size shrinking to two sections. Having lost its territory and independence, the township board was charitable and allowed Nodaway one teacher at $35 per month.

A bitter contest in 1900 resulted in the Nodaway district boundary remaining unchanged. The residents had become dissatisfied with the current two-year high school. In 1905, a four-year high school was organized. The high school department was handled by one teacher, Professor C.V. Frazier.

In 1908, a new brick building was erected at the cost of $4000. It was quite an improvement for a high school. The first class graduated in 1909 with two graduates, Bessie Norcutt and Wilbert Shipley.

By 1915, the first two extracurricular activities were added with boys basketball and declamatory. The growing interest in public speaking and debating sparked the faculty that there may be talent for orations and dramatic art for the boys and girls. A midwinter contest was planned with ten eager contestants in the race for honors. Mrs. Ida Robb of Creston was employed to train the contestants. She found several "backwoods preachers" to help. Within a week of careful training, Mrs. Robb was able to produce quality work. Harry Moore ('16) won first overall and Gwendoline Gibson ('19) was second. The first prize was a $5.00 gold piece and second was $2.50

In 1919, five rural districts (one-room schools) voted to consolidate with Nodaway school district. The enlarged district now had 24 sections and a greater wealth of students and interest in education. The school building was entirely inadequate for this increased enrollment. Vaughn's hotel building was purchased for the elementary department.

On June 14, 1921, the Nodaway Consolidated District voted $80,000 in bonds for a new school building. The new three-story brick building stood majestically on the rise to the east overlooking the town and valley. It opened in the fall of 1922.

By 1930 the enrollment had increased to the point that the eight elementary grades were very crowded. The seventh and eighth grades were moved to the third floor of the school. This was considered a 6-6 plan. It was not called a junior high school, but with this move it did create a model with the upper six grades combined for faculty and teaching.

In 1933, over 2,000 yards of dirt was moved in the south school yard. More than 80 men worked at different times with 45 horses for a complete landscaping of the grounds. Within a week, without any monetary cost, a new level playground and athletic field was finished.

Sports—There was no football or track played at Nodaway High School.

In 1916, the first girls basketball team made its performance with only one of the girls having prior experience.

The boys and girls played in the Wabanuce Conference. Other teams in the conference were Blockton, Clearfield, Conway, Gravity, Prescott, and Sharpsburg. Other towns they played against were College Springs, Coin, Braddyville, New Market, Colburn, and Wales. The biggest rival was Gravity.

Paul Barker ('57) was all-conference. He was 6' 6" and played college basketball at Northwest Missouri State. "My dad, Sylvester Barker ('29), played basketball for Nodaway in the late 1920s. He told me that when either team made a basket there was a jump ball. At my height I would have loved that game, but by the 1930s the rules had changed," said Paul Barker ('57)."

Band—The marching band performed annually at the Nodaway Corn Festival.

Gloria Ridnour Baldwin ('58) remembered, "We picked up corn that had been missed by the pickers and sold it for money to buy new band uniforms. We even got out of school to go pickup corn. It was amazing that we picked up enough corn to pay for the band uniforms."

"Harlan Kishtaugh was the band instructor and the local Methodist minister in the late 1940s. I played the e-flat Alto horn," told Emma Jeanne March Shipley ('48).

Janitor—Cloyd Shell was disabled and somewhat crippled. He lived in a house that the school district owned. Tom Shipley said, "There was not a nicer man in the world. I don't know if he wore braces, but it sure never caused any problems with his work."

Bus Drivers—Floyd Agnew was one of the first bus drivers. He drove a 1923 Model T with benches on both sides and open windows.

"Julius March was my bus driver. There was not another like him. When he looked in the mirror you knew it was time to sit down. He did not even have to say anything," reports Carolyn Walter Dixon ('58).

Yearbook—The yearbook was called the *Cardinal*. A 1957 yearbook picture showed 28 students in band.

Senior Trips—In 1948 the senior class journeyed to Des Moines. Emma Jeanne March Shipley ('48) remembered, "There were seven of us seniors. We had a grand time. Even though it was only 100 miles away, some of the class had never been to the capital city. We toured the state capitol building and other educational things. On returning to Nodaway some of us climbed the water tower and put up our class colors."

The 1954 senior class went to the Lake of the Ozarks. Chuck Bartz ('54) grinned as he told, "When we hit the Missouri border, the first thing we did was stop at a fireworks stand. They were illegal in Iowa, so we loaded up on the forbidden fruit. We were able to perfect throwing the firecrackers out the window at just the right time and having them explode under the car behind us on the highway. The Ozarks were fun with kids from other schools everywhere."

In 1957, the senior class returned to Missouri and Branson. They took two cars and drove into the night. Having stopped at fireworks stands before their arrival, they were well armed. Paul Barker ('57) at the age of 81 remembered, "Those fireworks were fun, but we were warned at midnight to stop or we would be kicked out of the motel."

In 1958, two carloads of seniors traveled on the two-lane roads to the Black Hills. They saw the Bad Lands, Mt. Rushmore, Wall Drug, and the Corn Palace along the way. One of the drivers was senior Maxine Wiley Forsythe ('58) with her mother in the front seat as a chaperone. They stayed in cabins at Keystone and spent one night on the road. Carolyn Walter Dixon ('58) exclaimed, "We had to get back for baccalaureate on Sunday night. Maxine sped all of the way home on those two-lane roads and we dubbed her 'lead foot Maxine."

Killed in Action—For such a small community, an unusually large number of boys lost their lives in World War II. Including Nodaway Township, the ten men were:

Wayne Agnew

Lester Bull
M. Lyle Conway
Fred McElroy ('32)
Wayne Lacox ('39)
Wesley Miller
Evlad Rued ('36)
Joe Strain
Josiah Thuman
Gordon Watts

Closing—With demands from the State Department of Education, Nodaway struggled to meet the curricular benchmarks. Paul Barker ('57) suggested, "The writing was on the wall. When I started as a freshman, we had 33 in my class. When we graduated three years later, we only had 15 left in my class."

In the 51 years from 1909 until 1959 there were 467 graduates from Nodaway High School. The largest class was 22 in 1942. The most numerous surnames of the graduates were Lacox-14, Northrup-13, Shipley-12, Walter-10, Kennedy-9, Agnew-8, Watts-7, Williams-7, and Windon-7. The last to receive a diploma from Nodaway High School was Thomas Watt (alphabetically).

Nodaway High School
Adams County, IA

#70

Ocheyedan High School

Mascot:	Indians, later Mounders
Colors:	Orange and Black
Closed:	1985
Location:	Northeast Osceola County

Early History—The Ocheyedan area was settled by German, English, and Dutch descendants coming from Illinois, Indiana, and eastern Iowa to claim land. Some of these settler surnames were Kout (a general merchant), Boyd (on whose land part of Ocheyedan now sets), and Meyer (blacksmith). The last local descendant of Daniel Boyd graduated from OHS in 1981, and the last local descendant of Fred Meyer graduated from OHS in 1970. Representative of Dutch surnames were Zylstra, which means eighth gate, and Jacobsma, meaning Son of Jacob.

The name Ocheyedan is an Indian name meaning "Place of Mourning." Two geographical features—the Ocheyedan Mound and the Ocheyedan River—were the landmarks as the settlers arrived. The mound is an unusual site on the rolling topography developed by the last glacial period in northern Iowa. The mound was of glacial origin, a *Kame.* During the ice age, glaciers carried sand and gravel along with larger rocks and boulders. These glaciers deposited these materials at the mouths of ice tunnels or channels. The mound arises as one of the highest points in Iowa at 1,655 feet above sea level.

In the summer of 1884, the Burlington, Cedar Rapids, and Northern Railroad crossed through the northern part of Osceola County. In the fall of 1884, building began and the prairie town of Ocheyedan was a busy place. Ocheyedan became an incorporated town in April 1891. The previous month, by a vote of 28 to 22, the residents chose to be incorporated. The public opinion and discussion was equally divided between strong and almost belligerent groups. When the vote results were in for incorporation, the conflict was over. Soon agreements for public improvements were made.

Ordinances for better government of the town and in promotion of its welfare were passed.

Early Schools—The first school was a one-room building just north of Ocheyedan. It was built before the school tax law was passed in 1872, so the students that attended paid a subscription fee. It was soon too small, and in May 1887, a vote passed to build a new two-story building. Finished in only six months, the school opened with 50 students on November 25, 1887. The only teacher had to step down because of a family illness, and E.J. Robinson became the teacher. School moved along smoothly with the advanced scholars aiding the teaching.

By 1897, enrollment had grown to 138 students with 25 in high school, 30 in grammar, 33 in intermediate, and 50 primary pupils. The high school subjects were bookkeeping, US History, general history, English literature, geometry, physics, political economy, physiology, algebra, English, and English composition. A new law went into effect which allowed school boards to buy library books.

Change came rapidly until a fire in 1902 destroyed the two-story building. The fire started in the basement coal room and in less than an hour the school burned to the ground. Reported in the *Ocheyedan Press* on January 8, 1903:

> Principal Wilson averted a stampede upstairs by taking hold of the larger pupils and jerking them into line, making them pass downstairs in order. After the upstairs had been cleared, he went through the lower rooms, filled with smoke and found two or three of the smaller children which had been so frightened that they were not able to leave. These he carried out. His presence of mind and bravery are very commendable.

Barbara Sotle Block ('50) interviewed an elderly Eleanor Meyer (daughter of the blacksmith, Fred Meyer) in 1991 for her account of the fire. She shared this with the Ocheyedan High School reunion in 2013.

> It was my first year at school and my class was writing at the blackboard, when there was a terrible noise. My teacher, Miss Smith ran to the door, opened it and thick heavy green smoke filled the room. She told us all to run outdoors, she went to the cloak room and carried all our coats outside. In one of the classrooms, two boys were acting up, the teacher went over to straighten them out, she stopped short and saw the boys sitting there fanning the smoke that was coming through the cracks. The fire had gotten such a start in this wooden building. It went up like a cracker box. Within five minutes, after all of us got out, the floor went down. It was 30 degrees below zero and the wind was blowing the kid's caps and scarves down the road. We then had classes all over town, in the church, the town hall, and even in the saloon.

I grew up with my siblings in a home not much more than a shack behind the blacksmith shop with nothing but prairie beyond. At times buffalo would come near the house.

For the rest of 1903, school was held in churches and other available buildings in town. The new high school building was erected in 1903. James Riley Wilson was the only high school teacher with three grades. A law was passed that rural school teachers must graduate from the twelfth grade and pass an examination given by the county superintendent of schools. At this time, the twelfth grade was added rather than send the students to the Sibley school to finish twelfth grade.

In 1905, the German school in Ocheyedan with 15 students was closed because the Rev. C.E. Miller became ill. The students started attending the public school.

Printed in the January 16, 1918 *Ocheyedan Press*:

> A meeting was held on Monday evening and steps were taken to make Ocheyedan High School accredited. This necessitates the engaging of another teacher and perhaps a little more equipment. If a teacher can be secured and the school is placed on the accredited list, most of the seniors who have planned to finish school elsewhere will remain and be graduated from the Ocheyedan High School.
>
> Normal school training was offered at Ocheyedan which allowed students to take the Normal classes, and then a three-month summer course which allowed the student to teach in the rural one-room schools. Ocheyedan was one of the few schools in the area to provide this training.

An election for a $12,000 bond issue was passed. An abandoned army barrack in Missouri was purchased. It was dismantled and hauled to Ocheyedan. This salvaged lumber was used to construct an annex for additional classrooms. By 1958, the post war baby boom children began moving through the schools. It was apparent that more classrooms were needed to handle the enrollment. A $175,000 bond issue passed in 1958 for the construction of a new elementary school with nine classrooms plus hot lunch facilities. With the completion of the new elementary building, more room was available in the old school for science, home economics, and music.

As the student bulge advanced to the high school, more classroom space was needed. Another bond for $100,000 was passed to build a new gymnasium. Various plans were debated including the possibility of reorganizing the entire county into a one-county district. When the attempt to reorganize failed, construction on the building was started in the spring of 1963. The old gymnasium was remodeled to provide two classrooms, a special education room and an audio-visual education room.

Notable Teachers—Betty Hembd Taylor wrote in a composition:

In the 1940s a neighbor girl, Iris Linter, brought an unusual picture to our rural school. It showed an Easter Sunrise Service on the Mound in the 1920s. Iris's mother, who was the high school music teacher at the time, was directing the choir that morning when uninvited quests appeared. Dressed in robes and hoods, members of the Ku Klux Klan approached the worshippers from two sides, then stood quietly by as they listened to the hymns. Faith Linter must have relied on the meaning of her first name as she nervously continued to direct music. When the singing ended, the robed visitors left as they had come, without a word. Iris Linter ('49) graduated from Ocheyedan and our paths crossed again when we taught together in Sutherland, Iowa.

When these country school children came to town for school, they were not considered behind academically. Betty Hembd Taylor shared, "The best teacher I ever had was Dorothy Travaille Intveld ('42). When I say that I mean 'the best' which included country school, high school and all my college years. Our school was 1 ½ miles west of town. She taught us in a manner that we all learned and helped each other learn. Since she was her own custodian, we all had jobs and enjoyed the responsibilities. Miss Travaille also taught art, PE, and music. With no electricity, audio visuals aids were manually run. We had a wind-up phonograph for music, maps, and a globe. To add interest, she provided her own flannel graph—an easel with a flannel covered board and flannel backed figures that adhered to it. With the use of the board she narrated and illustrated Bible stories. We loved it. Her education and teaching included two years of Normal Training in high school followed by summer school at Iowa State Teachers College in Cedar Falls. At age 18, she was ready to educate all grades in a one-room school and she did it well. In spite of teaching all subjects in all grades, we found time to rehearse and put on Christmas plays and make gifts for our parents." In 1948 many of the country schools were closing because of the difficulty in obtaining qualified teachers.

Buses—Bus service for pupils began in 1948 when the country schools began closing. Three buses were first used and, as enrollment increased, expanded to five buses. Elmer Schuster ran the Sinclair station in town. He started driving a bus in 1953 and for the next 24½ years proudly drove the only Ford while all the other drivers had to drive Internationals. "The kids loved him and he was a kid at heart. He could imitate people and sound just like them. He even got off the bus one day to help us girls get away from the geese that were chasing us to the bus. I was so blessed that one day after marrying I was able to call him my uncle," remembered Connie Block Schuster ('69).

Drivers Education—Drivers Education was first offered in the fall of 1950. While learning to drive with a manual transmission and the shift on the column, Shari Zylstra Jacobsma ('62) smiled and recalled, "I could change a tire but still can't parallel park." After the classwork and practice driving, the students went to the county seat Sibley to get their licenses.

Sports—Basketball was the main sport in high school. Barbara Stolte Block ('50) told her all-school reunion in 2013: "I wore the uniform that was worn by my son's teammate which happened to be the same number I wore when I played in the late 1940s. You know there seems to be a reversal in the fashion of uniforms. In my day, these little short pants were worn on the basketball floor and the baggy pants on the street. Now the baggy pants are worn on the basketball floor and the short pants on the street." Her daughter Pam Block Jacobsma ('75) bubbled as she remembered, "We were the best defensive team in the state of Iowa holding opponents to 32 points per game. I wasn't the tallest, but I was scrappy. Our scoring forward was Judy Hartwig Wolterstorff ('73) who holds the school scoring record. The other guards on that great defensive team were Jo Dreesen Bruns ('74) and Peggy Hartwig Sorensen ('74)."

Football started in 1958 after many years without the sport. The fall of 1967 was the last year for football. By 1968, there were not enough players out for football, and it was discontinued.

Band—The marching band traveled to march at Worthington Turkey days and Orange City Tulip days. Shari Zylstra Jacobsma ('62) remembered, "Those wool uniforms were so hot in the summer and so cold in the winter. I was a twirler and flag girl in junior high and played the cornet in high school band. We had one band instructor that was not our favorite. The cornet section placed their music upside down and played the notes backward."

Notable Graduate—Deanne Ostermann Schellschmidt ('60) was crowned Miss Iowa in 1962. The *Ocheyedan Press* reported:

> Deanne Ostermann was crowned Miss Iowa at the Roof Garden Ballroom in Okoboji. Miss Iowa attended the national pageant at Miami, Florida at the age of 19. The 5'7" tall girl with vital statistics of 37-25-37 lost the national title but Ocheyedan was proud of her as Miss Iowa.

Pranks—The *Ocheyedan Press* on November 7, 1963 reported:

> Halloween night the switch northwest of town carrying the feeder line in to Ocheyedan was pulled by some prankster throwing the entire town out of electricity for more than an hour.

To date the prankster remains unidentified and the crime unsolved.

Yearbooks—The first yearbooks for the high school were called the *Patriot* and later years called the *Mounders' Momentum*. The 1954 yearbook picture showed 38 in the band with 15 twirlers, and one majorette. This same yearbook pictures school groups of Future Farmers of America with 14 student members, and Future Nurses Club with three student members.

Notable Person—The student body of 1972 honored Homer Wilmarth with a commemorative plaque. He was the village disadvantaged man who was the number one fan for many and all school events. He was a devoted follower of all activities of grades, junior and senior high school. His enthusiasm, vocal support, and near perfect attendance was as important part of the school spirit.

Cook—A forever cook at Ocheyedan was Florence Jobes. "No one ever wanted to miss Thursdays because the menu was chili and cinnamon rolls. Friday was fish sticks and chocolate milk," recalled Pam Block Jacobsma ('75).

Closing—The high school closed after graduation in May 1985. The next year the students attended high school in Sibley as they did over 75 years earlier. The reorganization discussed in 1962 became a reality as the increased cost of education and the declining enrollment forced the consolidation. A total of 1,331 graduated from Ocheyedan High school in the 67 years from 1919 through 1985. The largest class was 36 in 1939. The most numerous surnames of the graduates were: Glade-45, Bremer-30, Schmidt-26, Ostermann-19, Timmons-17, Baker-15, Johnson-15, Dreesen-13, Kallsen-12, and Graves-11. The last graduate to receive a diploma from Ocheyedan High School was Glenn Zevenbergen (alphabetically).

#71

Okoboji Consolidated High School

Mascot: Orioles
Colors: Black and Orange
Closed: 1957
Location: South Central Dickinson County
4 miles west & 2 south of Milford

Early History—The school was built in 1915 in southern Okoboji Township. There was no town at this location. The district owned two homes, one for the superintendent and the other was called the teacherage, for the janitor and the single teachers at the school who had no cars. The only other structure in this rural area of the county was a gas station across from the school building. The first high school graduating class was in 1919.

The only physical remaining recognition for the location of this school is in a park called Horseshoe Bend. Two plaques have been placed there, one to honor the school and the other to honor the 1939 mighty Oriole baseball team that went all the way to the state baseball tournament in Eddyville. Orville Taylor ('42) was one of the four sophomores that made up the ten players on the team. The school only had ten uniforms for this team of four sophomores, four juniors, and two seniors. Orv's brother Glen ('42) was an outstanding pitcher on the team. He only had vision in one eye due to a BB gun accident. He could throw a blazing fastball to the tough junior catcher, Charles Gould ('42). It was Charles' son, an artist from Taos, New Mexico, who designed and placed the plaques in memory of the school and the "Okoboji Ten."

The school protest and walkout of 1939 in the rural area of Iowa was news. This story was printed in the *Hartley Sentinel* in May of 2017 written by the same Orv Taylor ('42).

> In the fall of 1938, I started high school at Okoboji Consolidated, a three-story brick school house out in

the middle of nowhere . . . located in a wooded area, six miles from Milford, Iowa, the nearest town.

The superintendent's home was on the grounds along with another building called the teacherage. The teacherage had an apartment for the custodian's family and rooms for single women on the facility.

. . . I don't recall just how many classes Superintendent Brower might have taught but from 11:00 to 11:50 each morning I was in his shop class, then called manual training. The *Des Moines Register* was delivered to school at 10:30 and Mr. Brower was the first to get his hands on it. He would show up in class with the newspaper under his arm, more interested in the reading the news than in supervising a bunch of boys.

Since we had hand tools to work with, he was quite certain we wouldn't hurt ourselves; so most of the time, he leaned back in his chair, propped his feet up on the desk, and read the morning paper. As students, we shared an unspoken agreement with him. If we didn't bother him, he wouldn't bother us.

The principal, Mr. O.R. Niffeneggar was just the opposite. He was well-educated and highly valued as our English teacher. He demanded much of his students and we respected him for it. Imagine our surprise when we learned he was not so highly regarded by some of the parents. We knew him as a happily married man, but by the time contracts came out in the spring, a whispering campaign had spread the news that he'd been divorced. A few women in the community got wind of the situation, and without checking his teaching methods, they pressured the school board to fire him.

When confronted, Mr. Niffineggar didn't deny the divorce, but was quite disappointed to think that could cost him his job. He spoke to each of his classes about the situation and told us the school board might not renew his contract the following year. He wasn't asking for help; he just wanted us to know before the news got around the community.

Hazel Thomsen ('39) was a senior and the sister of one of my classmates. She and some of the other seniors bristled at the unfairness of the situation and decided to challenge the decision. They wrote out a formal complaint in the form of a petition and organized a student walk-out. The petition stated positive regard for Mr. Niffineggar and requested that the board renew his contract for the 1939-40 school year. When the seniors approached the rest of the student body, including my freshman class we were intrigued and happy to take part. Those interested met at noon the next day and joined a march to the home of Noel Williams, the school board president. Mr. Williams had two daughters in high school, Lela ('42) was in my class, and participated in the protest. Among the two other students, her older sister Jean ('41), remained at school. Fifty-seven of us had signed the petition by the time we set out on the two-mile walk. The walk was peaceful and Mr. Williams was understanding. He offered to call a meeting for the following Friday afternoon for all interested citizens. There would be an opportunity to meet with the school board, Mr. Brower, and Mr. Niffineggar. Four sets of parents, and sixty high school students, the entire student body attended.

Mr. Williams gave everyone a chance to speak. One of the mothers gave her opinion of why a divorced man shouldn't teach school. She said it set a bad example.

Mr. Niffineggar countered her arguments and presented the petition signed by 57 students . . . Before he finished speaking, another woman interrupted him, jumped to her feet and demanded that he be fired. Unruffled, he replied, "If it hadn't been for a bunch of old hens scratching in the dirt and stirring up the school board, this wouldn't have happened."

The woman's husband retorted, "How dare you call my wife an old hen?"

Still calm, Mr. Niffinegger commented, "I didn't mention any names, but if the shoe fits, wear it."

. . . Mr. Niffineggar was rehired . . . I have never forgotten that favorite teacher, a man who could remain calm under fire. More than once I'd heard him say, "Do what needs to be done, when it needs to be done, whether you want to do it or not." It was a motto, and one I have tried to follow throughout my life.

Notable Teachers—Lois Gleason a first year teacher in Okoboji graduated from the State University of Iowa (University of Iowa) with her BS degree. Orv Taylor ('42) grinned as he shared about her influence on his life. "She was our literature teacher and loved poetry. She had very good discipline in the classroom. Duane Neuman ('42) was caught chewing gum and she firmly shouted, 'Duane Newman swallow that gum.' I still can see his throat move as he went gulp. She taught us a Scottish poem which interchanges the e'e for eye that I told her even I could write poetry if I could make up words the same way."

Then some 80 years later at age 95 (2019) Orv Taylor ('42) carefully recites from memory the Robert Burns poem:

To a Mouse

Thou saw the fields laid bare an' wast,
An' weary Winter comin fast,
An' cozie here, beneath the blast,
Thou thought to dwell,
Till crash! the cruel coulter past
Out thro' thy cell.

Still, thou art blest, compar'd wi me!
The present only toucheth thee:
But Och! I backward cast my e'e,
On prospects drear!
An' forward, tho' I cana see,
guess an' fear!

Killed in Action—When the war broke out, the class of 1942 had 12 senior boys. Four were deferred from serving because of farming, two failed their physicals, one went into the Air Force, two went into the Navy, and three into the Army. Duane Neuman ('42) was killed at the Battle of the Bulge. There were 60 students enrolled in the high school at this time.

Alumni Gatherings—The school song was:

Once again, here our school mates assemble.
We fain would lift our hearts in song to our
High School,
our dear Alma Mater.
Let gladness the moments prolong.
We are proud of our lads and our lasses
And honors won in days gone by--

So here's a cheer for our old High School;
Our dear old high school;
Our dear old High.
Here's to our classes:
Here's to the lasses; Here's to our lads and they adore;
Here's to the seniors so mighty;
Juniors so flighty, Freshies
And sophomores.
Let mirth and gladness banish all sadness
And as the days go by, you'll find us
Ready and steady, boosting for our old High.
Rah! Rah! Rah!

The words of this song resounded as the Alumni of Okoboji Consolidated High School met in the summer of 2019 at Horseshoe Bend, site of the plaques honoring the school and the 1939 baseball team. This was their final school reunion.

Yearbook—The school yearbook of 1954, called the *Oriole Tales,* was one of the better annuals of that time. This is a credit to not only the student staff but to Mrs. Wilber Sacket, the advisor for the yearbook annual editors. Some of the highlights in the 1954 *Oriole Tales* were:

- The girls basketball team is pictured with 17 members and Mrs. L.H. DeWitt-chaperone (also the music, biology, and home economics teacher). There were not many wins that year but a 70-69 overtime win over rival Everly stands out. Leading scorers that year were DeAnne Welle ('54) with 25.6 and Ruth Williams ('54) with 18.4 points a game.
- The boys basketball team had 14 players pictured with Coach-Principal Mr. John Geertsema. Their record was ten wins and nine loses. Leading scorers for Okoboji were Jerry Roskens ('54) with 20.2 and Nate Gould ('54) with 13.8 points per game. The most outstanding game and victory of the season was the 33 to 26 win over Milford. It was the first win over Milford in six years. The one heartbreaker was the 55-53 loss to Ocheyedan. "This game was in the bag for us, or so we thought at the end of the third quarter when we led 44-26. We were a bit too sure of ourselves and they caught up with us at the end of the game. They went on to win the game 55-53 in the overtime period. That taught us our lesson," reminisced a former player.
- The girls softall team is pictured with 19 team players. Mr. Geerrsman was the coach. They had a victory of 25-4 over Lake Park.

- The fall baseball team had 22 boys and is pictured with coach Mr. Geertsman. It had victories over Royal and Excelsior.

Closing—The school closed after graduation in May 1957. There were 385 graduates in the 39 years from 1919-1957. The most numerous surnames of the graduates were: Wilson-14, Meyer-11, Anderson-10, Northey-9, Johnson-10, Schmidt-7, Amundson-6 and McLaughlin-6. The last to receive a diploma from Okoboji Consolidated High School was Gary Wilson (alphabetically).

Okoboji Consolidated High School
Dickinson County, IA

#72

Olds High School

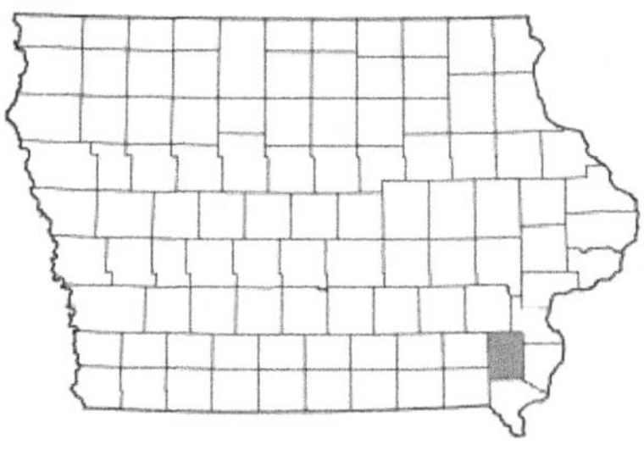

Mascot: Raiders
Colors: Black and Gold
Closed: 1962
Location: North edge of Henry County

Early History—A survey of the area in 1837 does not show any trails or habitation when Henry County was organized. John Wesley (J.W.) Olds was born in Stockbridge, Massachusetts, in 1833. His wife, Ellen, was born in 1839 in New York City. J.W. Olds gave twenty acres for the townsite and his name to the town. Olds appears in the Atlas of Henry County in 1895. Olds was incorporated in 1900. According to the census records, J.W. Olds never lived in the area as he was a farmer in Scott County, Iowa. Both J.W. and Ellen died in 1918 and were buried in the Hazelwood Cemetery in Grinnell, Iowa. *(Author's Note: While this year was during the peak of the 1918 Spanish influenza, their causes of death were not recorded).*

Early Schools—Mt. Pleasant and Henry County were once called the "Athens of Iowa," as it was also the home of Mt. Pleasant Female Seminary, Howe's Academy, Mt. Pleasant Academy, Iowa Wesleyan College, Conservatory of Music, and the German College. Other schools located in the county were Whittier Academy at New Salem, the New London Academy at New London, Institute of Science at Trenton, and the Female Academy at Swedesburg. The academy at Swedesburg was two miles south of Olds. The Academy had school from 1898-1901.

There were eight country schools in Wayne Township. Olds had a grade school but the dates are not recorded. In Henry County the consolidation movement started in Wayne Township with the formation of the Olds Consolidated School. North Wayne, Maple Grove, and Sunnyside joined Olds in 1911. The high school was built shortly after and the first graduating class from Olds Consolidated High School was in May 1914.

Notable Graduates—Virgil Peterson devoted a lifetime to exposure of organized crime. He wrote *Barbarians in Our Midst* (Little Brown 1952) which covered the Chicago Mob. The book follows his 12 years with the Federal Bureau of Investigation including his key role in the Dillinger investigation. He became the head of the Chicago Crime Commission in 1942 and became a nationally known expert on organized crime during his 27-year tenure there.

Harry F. Olson ('20) was awarded a PhD from the State University of Iowa in 1928. Both his parents were immigrants from Skane, Sweden. He became a noted acoustic expert and research engineer for RCA and held 100 patents. Olson invented the music synthesizer and acoustic electronic stethoscope.

John Harlan Lindell II, at 6′ 5″, became a major league outfielder and played in 854 games in the 1940s and 50s. He played in three World Series in 1943, 1947, and 1949. His lifetime average was .273 and World Series average was .324. He led the American League in triples and total bases 1943-44. Following a stint in the minor leagues, he reappeared with the Pittsburgh Pirates as a pitcher in 1953.

Wally Bergstrom ('34) became one of the University of Iowa's "Four Iron Men" who played for Iowa in the miracle season in 1939. With 85 out for spring ball in 1939, only 35 returned in the fall. The Hawkeyes had not won more that three games a season throughout the 1930s. The Athletic

Department was deep in debt. Yet, a new coach and Mason City native, Dr. Eddie Anderson, was hired from Holy Cross. Anderson played for Knute Rockne and was the team captain at Notre Dame. The Irish went 28-1 in his last three years. Ironically, the only loss during that three-year time was to the Iowa Hawkeyes in 1921. Anderson brought a new style offense and intense workouts to Iowa City. Led by the miracle boy and Heisman Trophy winner Nile Kinnick, the Hawkeyes only loss came at Michigan when Tom Harmon scored four touchdowns. Wally Bergstrom ('34) was a starter in the line.

Notable Teachers—Jackie Korf Hultquist ('42) was an Olds graduate. She returned after college to teach social sciences, speech, and drama at Olds High School. Jane Lindeen Wickham ('57) remembered, "She had discipline and we did not fool around in her classes. She was so knowledgeable with her subjects." Mrs. Hultquist later became a faculty member at Central Missouri State in Warrensburg, Missouri.

School Lunch—The church ladies in town provided the hot lunch one day a week to the school children in the 1940s. Malcom Alvine ('52) recalled, "In 1948, by the time I was in high school, the school lunch program was started. No more lunch buckets and it was quite a great time to have all of the lunches right there at school."

Sports—Football was played at Olds High School until the 1930s. The boys played basketball and baseball. The girls played basketball.

"Clarence Unkrich ('40) was a basketball player on the team of 1939-40 which had the distinction of being the shortest starting line up in the state of Iowa with no player being any taller than five foot six inches tall," told his wife of 54 years, Louise Tolander Unkrich('43). The starting lineup was quite different than the 1962 state tournament team which averaged at least 6′ 2″.

The 1962 state tournament was special as it was the last class to graduate from Olds High School. It was an all-senior lineup and led by Gary Anderson, Gary Olson, Dennis Anderson, Dean Eichelberger, and Mervin Roth. The coach was Don Ramig who wore his superstitious gold corduroy jacket to all the games. Olds lost to the eventual state champions, Cedar Rapids Regis, that year. Regis fouled the leading scorer, Gary Olson, repeatedly and was able to slow down the game.

The biggest sports rivals were Wayland, Yarmouth, and Winfield.

An eighth grader in 1938, Louise Tolander Unkrich ('43) started as a forward on the girls' team. At 5′ 6 1/2″ she was taller than any of the boys on their team that year. Louise recalled, "It was such a great thrill to be able to play as a forward for five years on the high school team. Our coach was the superintendent, Donald Jones. We did not make it to the state tournament, but we won many games."

Glenda Boal Alvine ('53), as a senior, won the sectionals and district advancing to the state free throw championship.

Senior Trip—Due to gas rationing, the 1943 class of 23 drove to Burlington for their senior trip. "Our sponsors were Miss Halvelson who had an unusual habit of stealing spoons and slyly putting them in the boys' pockets. We were simply happy to be able to even get out of town with the strict shortage of tires and gasoline. I remember we toured a basket factory and a biscuit bread factory," recalled Louise Tolander Unkrich ('43) at 95 years of age.

In 1952, the nine seniors with their sponsors, Glen and Caroline Brostron, boarded a train in Burlington and were off to Chicago. Malcom Alvine ('52) vividly recalled, "We saw 'Guys and Dolls' at the Shubert. We stayed at the Palmer House which was so elegant. The Science and History museum seemed huge and was educational."

The eleven seniors in the class of 1957 and their class sponsors, Superintendent Garlyn Wessell and teacher Jackie Hultquist, boarded an Ozark Airline flight from Burlington to Chicago. The class was blessed to have a large amount of cash which had accumulated from concessions at ballgames following the addition of the new gymnasium in 1955. Jane Lindeen Wickham ('57) smiled as she told, "In Chicago we did it all. We went to the Science and History Museum, shopped, and stayed at the Palmer House Hotel. The boys wanted to go to a White Sox game, but we girls went to a show. I believe we were all pleased with our choice. We all ate at the beautiful elegant Empire Room at the Palmer House. It was such a gorgeous room and we had never experienced such a dinner in our lives." The seniors returned home by passenger train to Mt. Pleasant and were greeted by their families and many students.

Yearbooks—The first yearbook in 1923 was named the *Tormentor*. The second year, in 1924, it became named the *Black and Gold*. A perspective of a few of the organizations and activities in the yearbook are shared for 2020 enjoyment:

- The Hiking Club was organized with Miss Williamson as leader, beginning of the school year, with an enrollment of about fifteen girls . . . several short hikes were taken before basketball season opened. The longest one was eight miles which was taken one evening after school . . . A number of long hikes have been planned now as soon as the roads and weather prove favorable. We hope to complete the one hundred miles so as to get a letter which will be awarded by the Letter Club . . .

- The completion of the new gymnasium marked the transition from outdoor to indoor basketball. They won games against Salem, Ainsworth, Crawfordsville, Wyman, Riverside, Mt. Union, and Morning Sun; and lost one from Morning Sun and Wayland.
- In the year 1920-21, football and track were added to athletics, and baseball was dropped.
- Home Economics Club. Early in September the ninth grade home economics girls organized a club with Esther Zingg as President and Florence Grimm as Secretary. It was the purpose of the organization to meet twice a month at the various homes. Each girl taking an interest in embroidering.
- About fifteen girls responded to the call for basketball in the fall. Superintendent Woods, our coach, worked faithfully with us, and we started the season with a brisk pace defeating Brighton, Crawfordsville, and Salem which were our first three games . . . the games at the end of the season showed a vast improvement over former exhibitions. . . Good sportsmanship was shown throughout the entire season by all the girls who came out for practice.

Killed in Action—The following from the Olds community were killed in service for their country:

Charles Boal, WWII
Chester Lundquist, WWII

Polio—Marlene Anderson ('55) contracted polio and became wheelchair bound. Jane Lindeen Wickham ('57) recalled, "The school set up a box at her home and strung a wire three-fourths of a mile to communicate and teach her at home. I remember taking Algebra with Marlene while connected by a phone line." Marlene Anderson died at the young age of thirty-two.

Janitor—Hobert Purvis was the longtime janitor at Olds High School. Jane Lindeen Wickham ('57) told, "He was such a kid at heart. We all loved him. I was in class when someone swiped one of my shoes and sent it sailing out the window. We all went to the window to see where it dropped. Who else, but the superintendent retrieved it and took it to his office? Mr. Purvis got into the superintendent's office and confiscated the shoe and he got it back to me before the end of the day. I never ratted on who did it."

Closing—After 49 years, from 1914 through 1962, the Olds High School closed following graduation in May 1962. There were 633 graduates from the school. The largest graduating classes were 23 graduates in 1932 and 1943. The most numerous surnames of the graduates were: Miller-29; Anderson-24; Peterson-22; Huston-17; Olson-16; Johnson-11; Lindeen-11; Tolander-11; Erickson-9; Abrahamson-8; and Canby-8.

In the fall of 1962, the high school students from Wayland and Crawfordsville joined the Olds students at the former Olds High School with their diplomas reading WACO (Wayland Crawfordsville Olds) High School. The new WACO High school was built in 1989 north of Olds near Wayland.

Olds High School
Henry County, IA

#73

Olin High School

Mascot: Lion
Colors: Red and Blue
Closed: 2012
Location: South Central Jones County

Early History—Olin took its name from D.A. Olin, the general superintendent of the Chicago, Milwaukee, and St. Paul Railroad. The town was incorporated in 1878. The earlier settlements in the area were named Elk Ford and Walnut Fork. The post office established in 1841 retained the name Walnut Fork. The town name was changed to Rome in 1852 as it was in section 13 of Rome Township.

(From the *History of Jones County* published in 1901). The town was incorporated in 1878 and became Olin with a population 392.

Early Schools—Early school board records were destroyed by fire. The first school in Olin was a two-story white wooden structure with a bell tower on top and was in the center of the town on a site where the post office stands today (2020).

On March 9, 1903, voters approved a bond for 5% on the assessed valuation of property for the purpose of erecting a new school building. This new school on the old site was a three-story stone building built for $9,885. It was finished in less than seven months and opened on October 1, 1903.

Only 23 years later, in 1926, another bond for $110,000 was proposed for constructing and equipping a new schoolhouse and procuring a site. In this general election 608 ballots were cast. This time the vote was much closer with 334 yes and 273 no votes. The land was purchased for $125 an acre.

The last construction project for the Olin schools was 27 years later in 1954 when the new high school was proposed with an additional six acres of land to be acquired. Each of these three bonded building projects seemed to be about a quarter of a century apart or about a generation in between. The bond for $297,000 was passed. However, it took three biddings, over a six-month period, to adjust the project and planned bids were accepted. The last cost for this acquisition was $1,000 per acre.

Sports—The football team of 1925 was exceptional. They played the much larger schools of Anamosa and Cedar Rapids. The quarterback, Dillon Story, became a star at Coe College. Football was ceased in the 1930s following a tragic death of a player. Norman Ellis was able to restart the sport in 1961 to play eight-man football.

Coach Tab Jensen led the Olin girls basketball team to five straight state tournaments from 1937-1941. Though these teams did not finish with a state championship, the 1937 team were consolation winners. Five straight appearances was a record for that time. These teams also won the Jones County Championship in those five years. Two of these players, Margaret Macomber ('40) and Helen Joura ('40), were named to the National High School Girls Hall of Fame.

The Wapsie-Eight Conference was formed in 1950 with Lowden, Stanwood, Wyoming, Oxford Junction, Mechanicsville, Lisbon, Clarence, and Olin as members. All of these towns were within a 25 mile radius of Olin.

In 1950, Howard (Tommy) Tomlinson arrived at Olin to teach business classes and coach girls basketball. Olin and Center Junction had reorganized that year and the Olin team inherited some good players from Center Junction. Olin had a great history of girls basketball, but the 1949 team had not been very successful. Great expectations were anticipated from the new coach. And he did not disappoint. The hot lunch program had just been started at Olin and the new coach was able to have the girls in the gym during the lunch hour, too. Practices featured dribbling, passing, and defense drills. The girls were not allowed to have steady boyfriends and were instructed to not go out the nights before games. Laps around the gymnasium and suspensions were handed out to violators of team rules. Three girls stepped down for one year as they did not accept the 'steady boyfriend' rule. Later, all three of them came to Coach Tommy in tears, knowing that they had not made the best choices. In just the second year at Olin, Coach Tomlinson took yet another team to the sweet 16 or the state girls basketball tournament. Two of the starters could not play because they had the mumps and flu. Others on the team were plagued with flu-like symptoms and played with fevers. Gwen Jones ('55), a cheerleader, was recruited to suit up so that Olin had ten players in uniform and as a backup in case of foul trouble. Great players on the 1952 team were: Judy Greim ('53)-forward, Janice Fairly ('52)-forward, Jean Williams ('53)-forward, Delores Andrews ('53)-guard, Greta Moreland ('54)-forward, Lela Rae Manuel ('52)-forward, La Verna Conwell ('55)-guard, and Chlona Hanken ('52)-guard.

Before the 1952 team headed to Des Moines, they stayed home one extra night to sleep in their own beds to continue to recover and gain strength. The girls were awestruck by the sight of the Drake Field House basketball court with the oval track around the outside. Some had never seen an escalator and continually rode the moving stairs at Younkers. Others were exposed to eyelash curlers for the first time. Though the team was sick and wounded, they played a close first game losing to West Liberty 36-34.

Colleen Von Behren Pope ('56) took a blow to her head in the sectionals game in 1954. She was nick-named 'Spark Plug' by Coach Tommy. Though this team did not make it to state, Colleen became the State Free Throw Champion that year. Coach Tommy told her, "I guess you had to be hit on the head to go on to make all of those underhanded shots." Her brother Gale Von Behren ('66) fondly explained, "Our dad had put up a basketball goal in our yard. Countless games and shooting were played around that old hoop. There was a mud hole at the free throw line and one under the basket to prove how much those two places had seen the action."

In the book, *Courting Girls,* Coach Tommy's account of coaching this team is eloquently recorded. He was inducted into the Iowa Coaching Hall of Fame.

A popular cheerleading yell during these years was:

Can you make it, Can you take it,
Can you Alabama shake it?
Can you move it to the left?
Can you move it to the right?
Can you Yeah team? Yeah team? Fight! Fight! Fight!

Another great girls player of that era was Lana Graf Ballou ('66). She scored 2,300 points in her high school years. She played college ball at basketball powerhouse Wayland Baptist in Longview, Texas. "My dad, Alan Graf ('34) had a business in town and when he poured the concrete for the large driveway it was marked and cut to make a perfect half-court basketball court. Hours upon hours the ball dribbled, and games were played with the lights on at nights," Lana remembered. This short little feisty *(2019 author's observation)* girl was a leader on her team for four years in high school. Her classmate and to-be husband Jim Ballou ('66) smiled as he shared, "She may have been small, but man she had a jump shot. This was from all of nights on her dad's driveway playing against the boys."

Track became a successful and popular program during the 1970s. Coach Rich Ginn groomed 19 state track qualifiers. State individual titles were won by:

1985 400 meter low hurdles, Roger Grafft—55.61
1987 800 meter run, Brian Dahloff—2:00.06
1989 Discus, Tim Johnson—157-01
2010 High Jump, Jordan Cress—6'07"
2011 High Jump, Jordan Cress—6'09"

Rich Ginn was a popular drivers education and industrial arts teacher in Olin for over 20 years.

Baseball had a great run at the state tournament in 1992. They were led by Darrin Moore ('92) with a .458 batting average and no strike outs in 96 at-bats. Matt Walshire was the ace pitcher who was 10-3 on the mound with 104 strikeouts in 83 innings. Olin High School lost in the semifinals at state to perennial powerhouse Kee High of Lansing, who had a 43-1 record for the year. Darrell Winger was the baseball coach at Olin for six years and he always credited the athletic directors Stephen Williams and Marv Ryan and the community for their support in helping make these boys winners and champions in baseball.

School Activities—The hot lunch program was started in 1951. Four families with 30 children total came to the superintendent to ask if their children could get little jobs to help defray the costs of their 25 cent meals. Prior to the hot lunch program, there had been a brown bag system for the spring and fall sessions, and a modified hot lunch program in the winter.

Drivers Education—Drivers Education started in 1956. The class was optional at the time but it was a ticket to getting a drivers license without having to take the drivers test at the county seat. Deloris Strong Wood ('56) remembered, "Judy McAtee Luckstead ('56) tapped a tree on one driving session. Of course, the story grows over the years, as it escalated from tapping the tree, to hitting the tree, to flatting the tree, to eventually totaling the car!"

Buses—Buses were used in the 1930s. Bus driver Frank Miles, who owned his bus, died in an accident while driving the bus with no students on board.

Alan Graf ('34) owned many of the other buses. A picture of the time shows seven buses lined up in his large driveway. It was this driveway where the famed basketball court existed.

Band—The band was a great program at the high school. Director Darrell Dickens was the leader and developed 19 All-Staters. Jim Ballou ('66) said "Mr. Dickens always wanted a perfect lesson. He didn't care if it took 20 minutes or an hour, he wanted it to be perfect before it ended. I played the trombone for eight years and later in bands after high school. It seemed that at least three-fourths of the school was in the band."

Making the All-State band was a significant accomplishment and honor. Two of these 19 All-State members tried out and were selected for the All-American Band. They were Mary Zimmerman Weaverling ('65) and Judy Strong Tsui ('66). This feat from a little town of 700 population was unheard of anywhere. Practice does make perfect lessons and with the 25 cent coupons for the summer playing may have returned special dividends.

Lana Ballou Graf ('66) shared, "On Wednesday nights in the summer the band played downtown. I played the trombone (interesting note that two trombone players graduating in the same year, married, and celebrated over 50 years of marriage together). We were given 25 cent coupons that we could save up and get pop and hamburgers at the local cafes. We played everything from John Philip Sousa to Beethoven. What a lifelong thrill to be part of that program."

Notable Graduates—Carol Coleman Zigler ('54) became the first woman high school referee in Iowa. She also played college basketball.

Two boys were selected for the All-American Band. Lynn Postel ('63) played the tuba in the Navy Band. David Lasack ('66) made the Air Force a career and played in the Air Force band.

The Olin High School Alumni Association held its 130th annual banquet in 2019.

Pranks—There were the usual Halloween pranks played in Olin. The crime of placing of a skunk in a teacher's car and a snake in the music teachers desk drawer have not been solved to this day (2019).

Closing—The high school closed following graduation in May 2012. The students were bused the next fall to attend high school at Anamosa. In the 125 years from 1888 until 2012, there were 2,498 graduates from Olin High School. The largest classes were 39 in of 1966, 1969, and 1970. The most numerous surnames of the graduates were Ahrendsen-34, Hansen-27, Rohwedder-27, Levsen-26, Taylor-25, McCormick-23, Smith-19, Ballou-17, Miller-17, Wood-17, Starry-15, Fall-14, Freeman-14, McAtee-14, Moore-13, Hartwig-12, and Moreland-10. The last to receive a diploma from Olin High School was Tommy Townsend (alphabetically).

Olin High School
Jones County, IA

#74

Orange Township Consolidated High School

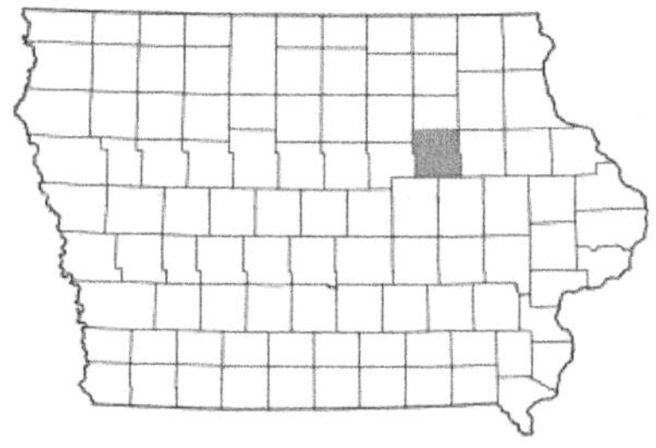

Mascot: Tigers
Colors: Black and Orange
Closed: 1964
Location: South Central Black Hawk Co.

Early History—Few townships in Iowa have a written history as complete as Orange Township in Black Hawk County. This rich farmland was first settled in 1856 by families from the Somerset County, Pennsylvania. The Pennsylvania Dutch were a religious group. Many of them belonged to the German Baptist Brethren Church founded by Alexander Mack in Germany in 1708. Nearly the entire membership migrated to Pennsylvania and neighboring seaboard states between 1719 and 1730. They brought to Iowa not only their farming abilities but also language and religion. The German Baptist Church in Orange was built in 1868. There were at least 30 Brethren families in the township. The church became the South Waterloo Church of the Brethren.

Orange Township Lore, written by Ida B. Snavely in 1966, pieced into a patchwork the history of this perfect 6 x 6 square-mile township. Some of the following is a chronicle summary of the beginnings of Orange High School.

After the final section of the railroad was completed between Dubuque and Waterloo in March 1861, the stream of emigration from Pennsylvania picked up speed. The earliest settlers were four Miller brothers, plus others with the surnames of Lichty, Klingaman, Shaulis, Fike, Bueghley, Hoff, and Berkley. These last names appear among the high school graduates a century later.

Early Schools—After building their homes, the early settlers provided a school for their children. The first school buildings emerged according to convenience rather than a plan. By 1875, there were thirteen schools in the township. The next year they were consolidated into nine "little red schoolhouses." Initially, they were on skids, so they could be moved easily. They were replaced by permanent brick buildings.

The number of pupils varied from two to over forty. Pupils ranged from four years of age up to twenty. The older ones were the grown-up girls and boys who lacked a chance to go to high school.

The teachers of these first schools in Orange Township had a language problem. Many children came from homes where only Pennsylvania Dutch was spoken. The teachers insisted that all must learn English.

Planning was needed to change the pastures and cornfields into the eventual well-kept grounds of the Orange Consolidated School and athletic field. There was the question of what to do with the ever-increasing number of eighth grade graduates. Some were driven by horse and buggy to West Waterloo High School. An academy of the Brethren faith at Mt. Morris, Illinois, was another option for secondary education.

O. Stuart Hamer, a graduate of Mt. Morris college, was active in helping find a solution. He knew of a school consolidation plan in Indiana. This information was presented to the public at some of the local literary society meetings. Township citizens did not know what to think of the idea of building one large central school to replace all the little school districts. There was also the suggestion that a high school might be included in such a movement. The skeptics countered, "It might work in Indiana, but not here in Orange Township with our mud roads." Another opinion was, "We have our good schools; they are paid for and we are making improvements every year. Why not leave good enough alone?" Or, "If we build such an expensive school it would saddle a debt upon our children that could never be paid off." Those in favor argued, "But what are we going to do with our young people? It is our responsibility to give them a chance. We should build both a consolidated school and a high school. They need both."

The public was given a chance to choose at the ballot box. The first petition was voted down three to one. A second vote held a year later passed by the same margin.

A bond of $55,000 was approved and a five acre tract at the center of the township was purchased at a price of $500 per acre. The school was ready by September 1916. The first day of school, a line of horse-drawn hacks moved slowly up the muddy road and brought more than two hundred children into one school system for the first time.

Three years of high school subjects were offered the first year. The following year a full four-year course was provided. Sixty high school students were enrolled the first year. In the spring of 1918, there were nine seniors in the first graduating class from Orange High School.

In 1936, the final payment on the bonds was made twenty-one years after they had been issued. A ceremony of the burning of the bonds was held in the high school assembly room.

Sports—The first girls basketball team was formed in 1917. The Orange Literary Society and a Soils Club were formed this first year of the high school.

Boys sports were basketball and fall and spring baseball. Track was added in 1961. The first football game was played in 1962.

Yearbooks—The first year book was published in 1917 and titled the *Orange Reflector*. Later yearbooks were called *The Tiger*.

The 1958 yearbook lists a Drama Club with 17 members. The band that year had 58 members, including the majorettes.

The 1959 yearbook pictures the boys basketball team with a record of 15-5. The Future Teachers Club had ten members, Science Club had 23 members, and Speech Club had 16.

The school newspaper was called *Orange Peelings*.

Closing—The school closed after graduation in May 1964. The district was absorbed into the Waterloo

Public School system that fall. The Orange High School building remained open until 1972, but the name of Orange Consolidated School was dropped and no class composite pictures were allowed. It was then part of the Waterloo District though the name continued as Orange High School until it closed for good in 1972 when Waterloo built the Central High School seven miles away. A total of 957 students graduated from Orange Consolidated High School from 1917-1964. The most numerous surnames of the graduates were: Miller-35, Lichty-21, Saylor-17, Pullin-15, Klingaman-12, Trent-11, Blough-7, and Fike-7.

The three-story building continued to be used for the elementary grades until 1973 when it was torn down and the students attended the new Orange Elementary School.

Orange Consolidated High School
Black Hawk County, IA

#75

Palo High School

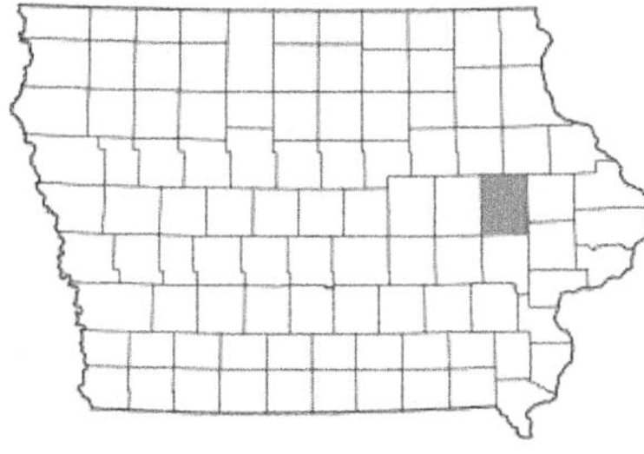

Mascot: None
Colors: Orange and Black
Closed: 1961
Location: Extr. West Central Linn County

Early History—Palo was named by Dr. Thomas Bardwell from Marion Iowa. He named the post office in the area Palo in 1849 after the battle of Palo Alto in the Mexican-American war. The town adopted this name.

The earliest white man to come to Fayette Township was Joseph Strawn in March 1839. Strawn settled three and one-half miles north of the later site of Palo. John and Thomas Lewis arrived on

March 28, 1839 in Fayette Township. They paid $1.25 an acre for three sections of government land. Much of the work clearing the land was done with oxen. They built a log cabin to bring all the family. There were around twenty members (three generations) including their parents, Levi and Sarah Lewis, two brothers, and four sisters who joined them. The youngest married Joe Strawn in 1845. They had nine children. The region and cemetery were called Lewis Bottoms. John's daughter, Melissa Tabitha Lewis, wrote in her diary of coming to Iowa:

> *Father and Uncle Tommy came in the spring and broke up the prairie and planted corn and grains. Father returned (to Ohio) for us. When we moved to Iowa, we came in covered wagons drawn by horses and oxen . . . When we came to the Mississippi River, we had to cross it by ferry. The boat was on the west side of the river, and we called it by blowing on a conch shell that hung on a tree for that purpose . . . Father was a blacksmith. He built the first grist mill, and the burrs himself. The first post office was at Marion (14 miles east) and it cost 10 cents for letter postage . . . We held the first church in our cabin. It took four weeks for a Methodist minister to make the circuit and arrive at our home. At one of the meetings some of the boys put red peppers in a kettle and everyone began to cough . . . I was 8 years old before I went to school. My mother, Martha, taught the first school in our cabin (circa 1845).*

Palo is unique as a center for many sources of energy. Water power, steam, railroads (steam and diesel), and nuclear. These events happened in a little over 100 years.

- John Lewis grist mill—water powered.
- Steamboat—powered by steam on the Cedar River northward past Palo's Main Street to Waterloo in 1858-61. The government bought the steamboat "Blackhawk" and took it south for use as a supply ship on the Tennessee and Cumberland Rivers during the Civil War.
- Railroads bypassed the village by a mile and a half to the west in 1870. Palo was one town that did not pick up and move to the railroad. This may have helped prevent fires as the embers from the train boilers often caused fires that burned many town main streets.
- In 1964, the construction of the Duane Arnold Nuclear Plant started. It took nearly ten years to complete.

Railroads—In 1861, community leaders joined forces with other towns in the area to form the Cedar Valley Railroad Company. The purpose was to attract a railroad line through the area. From the *Cedar Valley Times* on February 21, 1861:

> While railroad men abroad are debating and settling down on their schemes, the Cedar Valley Railroad Company will push forward the portion between Vinton and Palo and get it in readiness for the track at as early a day as possible. This will not only render it certain that the North end of Benton County will ultimately possess a railroad but insure its completion before the lapse of many years.

That lapse of years did occur as the Civil War stopped any railroad construction for four years. It was not until December 22, 1869, that the first wood-burning engine and passenger cars of the Burlington, Cedar Rapids, and Minnesota Railroad (BCR&M) made its inaugural journey from Cedar Rapids through Palo and Shellsburg to Vinton. At each stop, the train picked up people who had subscribed toward the railroad building fund. At Palo, the BCR&M Railroad built its tracks and depot about one-half mile west-southwest of the village.

Early Schools—The first town school in Palo in 1858 was called No. 5 Palo Independent School. It was a red brick, one story, 28′ x 30′ building. It was replaced in 1871 by a two-room wooden frame building.

Consolidation of the rural country school districts into Palo was put to a vote in 1917. Due to an illegal ballot being cast, the election was annulled. At another election in 1920, the consolidation vote carried. By this time there were 179 students in the present building. Palo Consolidated School District was formed by merging some Linn County schools and those located in southern Fayette and northern Clinton Townships. Debate lingered about where to build the new consolidated school building. One choice was in the town of Palo. The other choice was a location in the northwest corner of Clinton Township along the border between the two townships. The first class to graduate from the Palo Consolidated High School had seven graduates in 1922.

A bond election on March 15, 1922, for $75,000 was passed for a new three-story brick building. The new school was built in 1922 in the northeast corner of Palo. During the time of its construction, students were attending school in the old wooden schoolhouse, Woodman Hall, and a temporary building known to the students as the "Sheep Shed."

In 1956, due to increased enrollment in the grade school, a new addition was added to the north. This addition included two restrooms, four classrooms, and a gymnasium with an elevated stage.

Notable Graduate—Sylvia Mobray ('29) learned to speak words which she never heard. She was deaf and mute from birth. She started her education in 1917 at Palo and graduated in 1929. In a *Cedar Rapids Gazette* article in May 1929:

> She listens with eyes instead of ears, reading people's lips as they carry on a conversation. And to learn to talk herself, she had to use her fingers, placing them on the face and throat muscles of her teachers at the Iowa State School for the Deaf at Council Bluffs so that she could make her own voice imitate the sounds which she has never heard . . . Her fingers are especially talented. She has trained then to be particularly adept at drawing, writing, printing, sewing, cooking, and music . . . although she does not have a piano at home she learned and liked to play the instrument at the Council Bluffs school. Nor has her handicap kept her from taking part in extra-curricular activities at school. She was the treasurer of her class this year and took an active part in athletics.

Sports—Football was not played at Palo High School. The 1931 Boys basketball team won the Linn County Tournament and the sectional to make it to the districts. They lost to Elma by one point. They were coached by Superintendent W.P. Glasgow.

The girls basketball teams of 1939, 1940, and 1953 won the Linn County Tournament. In 1939 they played in the sectional's tournament at Newhall. The 1940 team progressed to the sectionals and played three games in one day. They were defeated by Center Point 20-19 in the sectional consolation game. They were coached by Superintendent Walter Wagner.

Music—William Julius, the music instructor in 1934, organized the first high school band.

The Palo Band Association was organized by the parents in 1937. They were led by their president, Loyal Melton, the same boy who drove a horse-drawn bus in 1918. Howard Ellson of Coe College was hired as the band instructor. Band members from the third grade to the twelth grade performed with the Palo band at the Chicago Music Festival held at Soldiers Field.

Memorable Teachers—Superintendent Carl McCauley and his wife, Vivian McCauley, taught in Palo from 1947-1958. Eloise Beatty Dennis ('52) recalled, "They were so kind and took me to Cedar Falls to the Iowa State Teachers College to get me a grant and scholarship. It was such a great start for me as I got my two-year degree and later finished a baccalaureate degree in California.

Community Trivia—

- Chief Kennesaw of the Mesquakie tribe wanted to stay in the Palo area and be buried near his forefathers. He went to seek advice from his Palo friend, John Mills. The Chief handed over his own gun to John Mills and said, "Kennesaw not go—you shoot." He stood facing John, waiting for him to shoot. John paused, then raised the gun. Kennesaw looked him straight in the eye—not a muscle moved. Then John lowered the gun and asked him to go with the tribe, that he could come to visit here. Later, Kennesaw did return and groups of Indians from Tama pitched their tents and camped in the timberland for weeks or months at a time. When Chief Kennesaw died here, he was buried in a wooden coffin. His white friends attended and helped with his burial in the cemetery (by Georgia Mills, author, teacher, and granddaughter of John Mills).

- August 28, 1917, school was postponed for two weeks due to diphtheria.
- September 1920, 170 students enrolled at Palo schools.
- June 8, 1921, Palo paid Shellsburg $880 for tuition.
- Bus Drivers—In 1918, a student at Palo Consolidated School, Loyal Melton, was a driver of the first horse-drawn bus that delivered students from the Round Prairie District to Palo. Fred Ashlock and Bill Kueger were hired in 1922 for $125 a month to drive the first motorized buses.
- 1936—A big blizzard closed the schools for six weeks.
- Fourth grade students made a map out of wood. Each state was made with wood native to the state, which was obtained by writing to lumber yards in each state.

Closing—In 1961, the Department of Education determined that Palo High School no longer met the minimum standards set by the state of Iowa.

The Palo High School closed in May 1961, following graduation. The largest class was 17 in 1931. The last class in 1961 had 11 graduates. There were 406 graduates in the 41 years from 1921-1961 from Palo High School (the numbers from 1921 through 1925 are missing). Dick Minor ('61) was the last to receive a diploma from Palo High School (alphabetically).

Palo and Shellsburg started whole grade sharing. The high school students attended school in Shellsburg, and the seventh and eighth grades attended in Palo. The buses met at the halfway point and the bus drivers switched buses and continued to the respected school.

Negotiations to consolidate with Shellsburg broke down in 1966. The Palo Consolidated School became part of the Cedar Rapids Community School District. This was a bittersweet relationship. The promised continuation of the grade school in Palo ended in 1972. To make matters worse, the most shocking news in the Spring of 1973 came when the four remaining grades were sent to Jackson Elementary School in Cedar Rapids. The doors to the Palo school were closed. The heart of the community came to an end and with it an end to an era. The beautiful red brick school building was razed by the Cedar Rapids School Board. Even though the community of Palo had built the building, they had no say in its demolition. The 1956 addition on the north remained until the entire community was devastated by the 2018 flood and the building also was razed.

Palo High School
Linn County, IA

#76

Paton High School

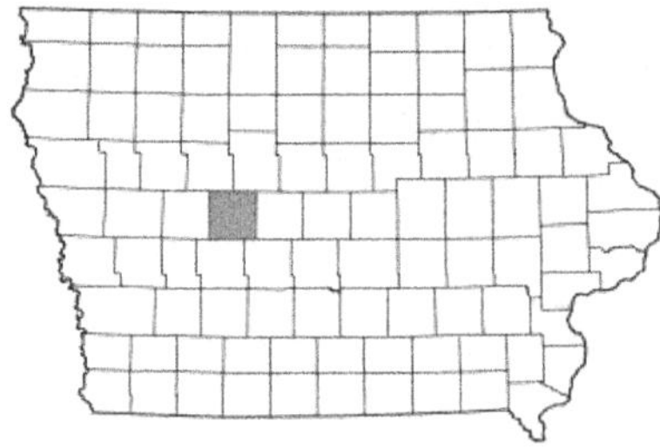

Mascot: Black Panthers/Pantherettes
Colors: Scarlet and Black
Closed: 1962
Location: Northeast Greene County

Early History—No other town in the world has the name Paton. Paton owes its unique name to William Paton, a Scottish born Presbyterian who came to New York City at the age of 14 in 1832. He established himself in a business known as Paton & Company. He traveled by rail to Iowa in the 1870s during the years of the ubiquitous railroad building expansion. Whether he had a direct monetary stake in the Keokuk, Des Moines, and Ft. Dodge Railroad (KDM&FD) is not clear. After traveling by rail to Grand Junction (ten miles south of Paton), he took a side trip to the eventual Paton area on the KDM&FD track. The vastness of the prairies and the newly broken land may have inspired him to contribute to the culture of the area. He was very interested in writing and books. He challenged the people in the area, if they would move the location of the present village (unnamed at the time) further north (two miles) to higher land, he would start a library for the town. The new town was named Paton in his honor.

Platting started in the new town in 1874. The sod was broken in this part of Greene county and sloughs were drained by teams of men laying tile to aid in the drainage of the land.

William Paton's travel and subsequent request was commissioned on his son, David Paton. David had just graduated from Princeton University in 1874 and became a scholar, world traveler, and historian. At his father's request, he sent 1,500 books from William Paton's library to start a library in the little village of Paton.

The townships of Thompson and Dawson were settled by German, Irish, and Swedish immigrants. The first child born in Paton Township was Margaret Conroy in 1875. She became a teacher at the age of 14 and taught in the rural Greene County schools.

A perspective of the diverse backgrounds of the settlers is found in the *Paton Centennial* book. A few highlights of the beginnings of these settlers:

- born in Madison, Wisconsin, came to Paton at one year old.
- native of West Virginia, moved to Pennsylvania, dreamed of a steamboat on the Des Moines River. Tried to start one, lost $4,000, started over farming.
- born at Canal Winchester, Ohio, Civil War, attended school at Mt. Vernon . . . taught three years . . . farmed.
- from Richmond, Indiana.
- born County Galway, Ireland.
- Vermont reared, farmer, educated in subscription school in Vermont.
- from Cornwall, Canada.
- from Dundee, Scotland.
- born in Niedermollrich Kirhessen, Germany . . . to US at age 31 . . . shoe repair doctor.
- born in Switzerland County, Indiana.
- others from: Boston; Mecklenberg, Germany; Pennsylvania; New Hampshire; Genesee County, New York; Bern, Germany; Toronto; and Ihringshausen, Germany.
- The northeast quarter of Paton Township was almost entirely Swedish.

Early Schools—The first school in Paton was held in a box car until winter arrived and then it was moved to a millinery shop on Main Street.

A two-room school was built in 1877. The teacher turnover was high. The pay range was from $30 to $90 a month for the superintendent. The bell from this first school was still in place and used 100 years later (2020).

The Paton Consolidated School District was formed in 1920. The new high school was built in 1922. The Dawson Township schools became consolidated into Paton in 1943. A bond vote in 1954 passed to join the two groups.

Music and Band—The school orchestra under the direction of John Miller went to the state contest in 1930 in Iowa City. Miller was also the band instructor and guided the band to Madison, Wisconsin in 1935 to participate in the National Music Contests.

Twenty years later, Carl Whitson directed the band to march at Iowa State Band Days, and the Jefferson Parade. Judy Darling Wilson ('62) remembered fondly, "I was an oboe player, but I was needed as the majorette for the band to lead them. Our mothers made the majorette and twirler hats worn by Barbara Wilbur Hansen ('47), Jean Anthony Fox ('46), Zeta Ladd, and Lois Darling. That majorette uniform was beautiful, and man were they hot! So much for being able to count and the oboe would have been much less taxing. Mr. Whitson was a great teacher and motivator."

Notable Teachers—Robert H. Meyer taught office practice or bookkeeping. He was precise and expected perfection of every student. Judy Darling Wilson ('62) recalled, "Every Sunday night, five boys would come to my house and copy my bookkeeping. They spent the rest of the night talking to my dad about World War II. One Monday morning, Mr. Meyer looked up over his glasses and said 'there's something rotten in Denmark! This work does not match the answer.' Jerry Erickson ('62) was busted. Seems he couldn't even copy my perfect work and had gotten one line off and his answers were all wrong."

Mrs. Donna Blair was an elementary teacher who would stand over the students and demand that they learn their math. She did have a paddle and was known to use it on Bill Bertelli ('62).

Polio—Carl Mackey ('56) contracted the dreaded polio virus. He became the parts manager in his dad's Allis Chalmers business. Using Mr. Meyer's learned bookkeeping skills, he became a legend in the parts department. Dave Cunningham recalled, "He was such a smart man. Even though it was a time before so many thousands of parts, Carl knew the exact shelf, the parts numbers, and the inventory in his head."

Jon Ryberg ('31), his brother Jimmy Ryberg ('34), and Duane Shriver ('55) contracted polio and recovered.

Notable Graduates—Loren Shriver ('62) was a graduate of the Air Force Academy. He became an astronaut and commanded three space mission. His last mission was to put the Hubble space telescope into orbit. Shriver retired from the Air Force as a colonel.

Three brothers—Leonard ('28), Harold, and Ted Lindgren ('27)—and Howard Judd won team honors at the National Livestock Judging contest in Kansas City in 1925. They represented Paton, Greene County, and then the state at the national competition. To get to Nationals they had to win the Iowa State District against 45 teams in Ames. At Nationals, Harold was first overall out of 108 boys, and Ted finished second.

There were three Walker sisters in the graduating class of 1923: Blanche, Evelyn, and Bernice. Two more sisters, Iola ('25) and Alberta ('26), were in high school to make five Walker sisters in high school at the same time.

Alumni Reunions—The first Paton alumni organization started in 1924. The annual event started with a potluck. The minutes for five years during the 1930s show the meal cost 35 cents. During the next four years, the cost rose to 40 cents for the meal. By 1975, the meal was $3.00.

Sports—Football was not played at Paton. The 1930 boys basketball team went to the state tournament. Three players from that team were named to the All State teams. They were Walter Pack ('30), Vernon Grant ('31), and Harold Magner ('31).

The boys and girls played basketball in the Little Central Conference with Churdan, Rippy, Grand Junction, Callender, and Boxholm.

Cooks—Ethel Grimes was a single lady and an institution for the Paton hot lunch program. She also ran a boarding house for teachers. Dave Cunningham shared, "Miss Grimes always wore a dress with a white apron. One of the things we will always remember are the lettuce and mayonnaise sandwiches. She stacked them up and had to limit them to three for each student until everyone was served because some boys were taking six at a time. Another specialty was the peanut butter and dill pickle sandwiches. Creamed eggs on toast was loved by all of us. We also had a meat that the boys called horse meat!"

Yearbook—The first yearbooks were called *Scarlet and Black*. The last yearbook in 1962 was the *Panther*.

Closing—The Paton High School closed following graduation in May 1962. In the 43 years from 1920-1962 there were 692 graduates from Paton High school. The largest class was 32 in 1936. The most numerous surnames of the graduates were Wilson-15, Smith-14, Premble-13, Anderson-11, Fields-10, Walker-10, Carlson-7, Hanson-6, and Taylor-6. The last to receive a diploma from Paton High School was Ardith Wolf (alphabetically). In the fall of 1962, the high school students were bused to the new Paton Churdan High School in Churdan.

Paton High School
Greene County, IA

#77

Pisgah High School

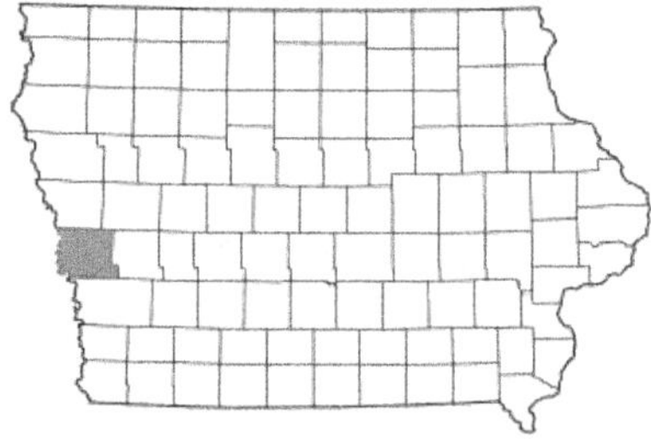

Mascot: Pirates
Colors: Purple and Gold
Closed: 1961
Location: Northwest Harrison County

Early History—Though miles from the Holy Land, the town of Pisgah derives its name from the Bible, Deuteronomy 3:27: "Get thee up into the top of Pisgah, and lift up thine eyes westward, and northward, and southward, and eastward, and behold it with thine eyes: for thou shall not go over this Jordan." After some 10,000 years, a splinter group of Mormons under the leadership of Charles B. Thompson, came to this beautiful valley along the Soldier River in far Western Iowa. These 60 families of Mormons settled in the area in 1853 for a few years. The first village just north of Pisgah was called Preparation. Thompson's community of 150 men, women, and children grew until serious problems with his leadership developed. Thompson and his family left in 1858. The only remnants of this Mormon village is Preparation Cemetery near the location of the Preparation Village and a 327 acre Preparation State Park along Soldier River.

Pisgah is in the heart of the Loess Hills, a unique landform up to 15 miles wide and 220 miles long. It was formed by wind blowing soil from the Missouri River flood plain to form steep hills.

The Chicago Northwestern Railroad came through Jackson Township in 1899. The town of Mt. Pisgah was platted by the railroad. The train was called the Punkin Vine and operated from 1899 until 1951. One resident in the town's centennial book noted that the high school girls of the 1920s used to trek to the depot after school. They wanted to see if any good-looking young salesmen got off in town to spend the night at the local hotel.

The first general store was opened by Ezra Miller in 1899 and was operated by his son and then grandson until 1988.

Early Schools – The first school was built in 1904. It was a two-story white clapboard building. A dark brick three-story building was built across the street from the playground in 1915 and became the high school.

An addition to the school was made in 1951 for the grade school and a new gymnasium. This gymnasium was built over the top of the elementary classrooms, home economics room, and the lunchroom. Joyce Hall remembered some 65 years later (2020), "The gymnasium was the most beautiful in the area with a rounded dome ceiling that had exposed knotty pine wood, graceful arched beams, and a beautiful hardwood floor. The architects assured the school board and superintendent, though the gym was above the classrooms, it would be soundproof to the classrooms below. This assurance was incorrect as the noise below from the pounding of thundering feet of 25 students running and bouncing balls in the physical education classes reverberated from overhead."

Killed in Action – The following from Pisgah were killed in service to their country:

Niles Raymond, WWI
Elmer Weber, WWI
George Nuzum, WWI
Harvey Pierce, WWI
Bernard Rogers, WWII
Roy Nuzum, WWII
Fred Wood, WWII

Vernon Carson, Korea

Sports—Pisgah was a baseball town. The barber in town was Orson Babe. After moving to town at the age of 14, he started playing outfield for the Pisgah town team. He became infatuated with the game of baseball. Quoted in the *Omaha Journal*, "I don't know why I got so crazy about baseball . . . I had to throw the ball on top of our house, then catch it coming off. But I used to eat, sleep, and talk the game. Later, I said if I ever had a boy, I was going to make a major-leaguer out of him." His son, Loren, was born in 1928. He did indeed make it to the major leagues and played in the 1952 World Series for the Yankees. Babe instilled into the boys of Pisgah a love for the game. Few towns in Iowa would ever send one, much less two of its boys to the major leagues. Bob Wiltsie ('47) from Pisgah also became a pitcher for the Yankees.

Loren Babe did not make it to the Hall of Fame at Cooperstown, but his bat did. He hit his only two major league home runs with the bat in the spring of 1952. Late in the season, Mickey Mantle asked to use the bat and he let him use it once. With one swing, Mantle hit one of the longest home run balls in history out of Griffith Stadium in Washington DC. The Hall of Fame picked up the bat and placed it in Cooperstown with Loren Babe's signature on it.

The boys baseball team went to three straight state tournaments in 1940, 1941, and 1942. The 1942 spring baseball team was led by three pitchers who each played in the outfield when not pitching. They were Howard Harmon ('42), Rex Hester ('42), and Delbert Nuzum ('42). The freshman, Loren Babe, held down the hot corner at third base. He was already being scouted by the St. Louis Cardinals at the age of 14. Howard Harmon ('42) was All Southwest Iowa in basketball in 1942. In the spring 1942 state baseball tournament, Pisgah lost in the finals to Martindale, 4-3.

Pisgah played in the Soldier Valley League with Mondamin, Modale, Magnolia, and Little Sioux. Castana and Blencoe were added in the spring round robin schedule.

Football was not played at Pisgah High School.

The girls played six-on-six basketball. The 1959 team went to the state tournament behind their high school All-American, Philis Bothwell Blazek ('60). Pisgah played Bondurant-Farrar in the opening round and lost. Philis was named the 'Blonde Bomber' by the newspaper for her great shooting and later played for Commercial Extension in Omaha. She was inducted in the Iowa Girls High School Hall of Fame.

Yearbook The yearbook was named the *Estudiante* which is Spanish for 'student.'

The 1957 yearbook staff believed that the company which published the 1956 annual had done a poor job of printing. The yearbook staff asked to have a different company print theirs. Superintendent Ruetter and class sponsor, Mr. Rickman, told the staff that the contract with the 1956 company had already been signed. Mr. Ruetter sent all the copy, pictures, and advertisements to the publishing company. "In the spring when the yearbooks arrived, the books were refused by Mr. Ruetter and Mr. Rickman, and the school returned the books without payment to the printing company because they were so poorly printed. We did not even get to see them. The company refused to send back our materials without payment. We had designed a wonderful yearbook and sold the ads to all the area merchants. We wanted to return the money to the merchants, but we were told the money would be kept and the next class could use it. We got blindsided. I am still angry at the superintendent these 63 years later," were the words from Linda Seabury Herman ('57).

Band—The town festival celebration called 'Play Days' started in the 1940s and continues to this day (2020). The marching band was the centerpiece for this celebration. Larry Green ('58) told, "I was the biggest and strongest, so I got to play the bass drums." Robert Hall smiled as he remembered, "I played the tuba and since it was so big, I didn't have to take it home to practice."

Senior Trips—"The seniors for 1957 took four cars to Colorado on their five-day senior trip. There were two girls' cars and two boys' cars. My parents, Ed and Pauline Seabury, drove our family car. Other drivers were the parents of Nancy Cross, Mr. Rickman, and a new teacher-coach, Mr. Seward. We toured the Denver Natural History Museum, Thompson Canyon, had Easter Sunrise at Red Rock, and went to the Garden of the Gods. The most afraid I have ever been is when our cars stopped half-way across the Royal Gorge Bridge," shared Linda Seabury Herman ('57). Larry Ramsey ('56) said, "We started the Colorado trips. We sure worked at about every concession stand and car wash in the community to raise the money to go."

By the next year in 1958, the seniors were limited to a three-day trip to the Lake of the Ozarks. "And, two of those days were spent driving. Guess the beer incident from the year before may have caused our abbreviated trip," remembered Larry Green ('58).

Teachers—Maurice (Mo) Jungck was an English teacher. Jean Jungck (his wife) reflected (in 2019), "We came from far Western Nebraska to interview for the job. Mo had forgotten his tie and we stopped in Blencoe to buy one. We stayed with the superintendent who lived in the house the school district owned next the school. Mo later became the elementary principal and taught in the district for 40 years."

Joyce Hall said of Mr. Jungck, "He was one of the best teachers I ever had. I knew he was good, but when I had to finish my last two years at West Harrison, it became evident. Those kids had not been taught a noun from a verb, much less the parts of a sentence." Robert Hall said, "His favorite saying was 'Oh kids, quit the mickey mouse stuff.' Another one was, 'Ya, I'd hope to kiss a duck.'"

Irma Woodward Pape ('29) returned after college to teach first and second grade for over 40 years at Pisgah. "She was so kind and dedicated. She was always concerned about every student. She came to all our graduations and plays," remembered Linda Seabury Herman ('57).

Pranks—Numerous Halloween's were so mischievous in Pisgah that several of the town fathers hired two out-of-town men to try to police the actions in town. One of the men was reported to have been a 'chicken thief' and only seemed to instigate more shenanigans for the night. Complete John Deere implements were dragged into the streets, a new single teacher's car showed up on the front steps of the school, and cherry bombs were launched from the top of the water tower by sling shots. Larry Green ('58) remembered, "Those two guys were the laughingstock with all of us kids. They were like 'Barney Fifes' and would fall for any act we pulled off on those nights."

Community Attractions—The Metz Baking Company from Sioux City made Old Home Bread and brought a legend to Pisgah, with the commercials for the Old Home bread featuring C.W. McCall, Mavis, and the dog named Sloan. The café in town, featured in the commercials, became an immediate regional attraction and was named the *Old Home Town filler up and keep on trucking Café.* It still serves food today (2020) and the country song is still a YouTube hit. Old Home Bread advertising continues to be current over 50 years after the first song was released.

A community icon was restored in 2017. The former ballfield that had seen so many years of town team, Pisgah High School, and West Harrison High School baseball, fell into disarray and became overgrown with weeds. A social media appeal was answered with $90,000 to restore the ballfield, bleachers, and dugouts. The Harvey Stueve-Orson Babe ballfield was restored to its glory and stands again (2020) for Pisgah's great baseball tradition.

Closing—The high school closed in May 1961. The district unified with three other districts: Little Sioux, Modale, and Mondamin to form West Harrison High School in Mondamin. Since the building was really not finished until the next year, the 1962 Pisgah class attended school and graduated from the Pisgah High School building. In the 49 years from 1913-1962, there were 684 graduates from Pisgah High School. The largest class was 24 in 1954. The most numerous surnames of the graduates were: Hinkel-26, Nuzum-12, Shepard-12, McWilliams-11, Johnson-10, Smith-9, Babe-8, Clark-8, Hildreth-7, and Harmon-7. The last to receive a diploma from Pisgah High School was Sharon Wakehouse (alphabetically).

Pisgah High School
Harrison County, IA

#78

Prescott High School

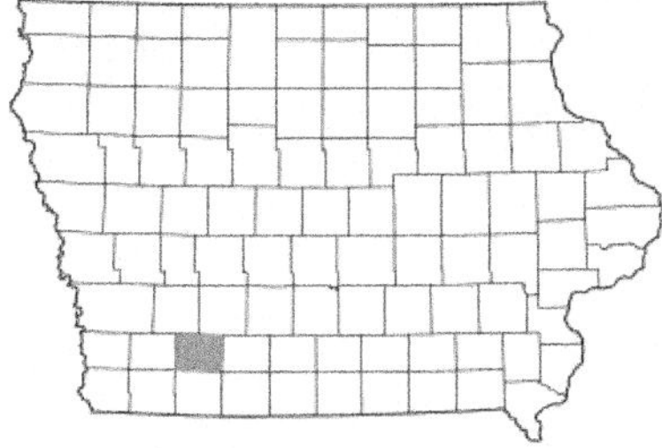

Mascot: Eagles/Eaglettes
Colors: Black and Gold
(originally Purple and White)
Closed: 1991
Location: East Central Adams County

Early History—Located on the banks of the East Nodaway River in northern Adams County, the town of Prescott originated with the coming of the Burlington Railroad in 1868. The site of the town had been called Matleu and Glendale, but in 1869 its name was changed to Prescott in honor of one of the men instrumental in building the railroad. Prescott

Township was called Queen City Township in December 1857. The township name was changed to Prescott in September 1868. The original plat of Prescott was recorded on June 6, 1870.

With the building of the railroad, the first terminal point in 1868 was Afton. As the track was laid west, the next terminal point was Cromwell (Creston was not there at the time). The railroad considered building a roundhouse at Prescott because of the water supply. The company intended to locate the roundhouse on the bottom by the river. When they found that flooding was frequent, the idea was abandoned. Afton and Cromwell became rivals for the roundhouse. The railroad company compromised and built it on the highest point between them and called it Creston.

In 1870, there were 82 votes (male) in Prescott Township. Every year one of the pressing issues regarded allowing cattle to run at large.

Early Schools—The first schoolhouse in Prescott was built in 1870. A few years later, a two-room school building was built. In 1890, a new principal, A.C. Peckham, reorganized the curricula to form a ten-year school.

The first tenth-grade graduation was held in June 1891. In 1894, a new brick veneer building was erected. This building was razed and on this site a new $16,000 brick building was constructed. A twelfth-grade curriculum was organized in 1915. In 1918, the district was consolidated and named Prescott Consolidated School which included the former Prescott Independent District and twenty rural sections. At this time Prescott #1, #2, and #3—rural one-room schools—came to Prescott to attend high school. In 1925, the high school enrollment was 46; by 1940 it increased to 90.

In 1925, an addition of six rooms and a gymnasium were built at a cost of $3,000. A larger gymnasium was built in 1952 for $60,000. It had a seating capacity of 800 and had a gray concrete floor.

In 1961, students moved into a new brick building which was constructed west of the original school. It housed the shop classes, kindergarten, first and second grades, and the superintendent's office.

Sports—Prescott High School had the distinction of being the first school in Iowa to play six-man football. It was discontinued by the 1950s.

Spring and fall baseball were played by the boys. In 1979, coach Ron McNeill led the team to the state tournament, but they lost to the perennial champions, Norway.

The girls played basketball and softball. Volleyball was added as a girls sport in 1979. With a renovation of the gymnasium in the 1980s, a new wooden gymnasium floor was added. The old gray concrete basketball court was the bane of many visiting teams.

Blake Cooper ('57) laughed as he remembered, "In 1952-53, when the new gymnasium was being built, we had to play all our games in Corning. There was no such thing for a home court advantage."

The teams played in the South Central 8 Conference which formed in 1967. The original members of the conference were Clearfield, Diagonal, Grand Valley, Lineville-Clio, Martinsdale-St. Marys, Murray, Russell, Van Meter, and Prescott.

Notable Graduates—Bradford I. Daggett ('54) received the Who's Who Among Students in Universities and Colleges Award. He is also listed in the Who's Who in American Colleges and University Administration. He held certificates in a variety of technical specialties from 27 technical institutes.

The Ryan sisters, Betty ('52), Joye ('54), and Patricia ('56) became well known as the "Ryan Sisters Trio." Their singing career began when they were quite young. They were invited to be on the radio with the Everly family (Everly Brothers) broadcasting over KFNF in Shenandoah, Iowa. When President Truman and his daughter Margaret were in Shenandoah, they were invited to sing with the Everlys. The Ryan girls had a half-hour weekly radio show on KSID in Creston, Iowa. Mr. Eugene Bundy, the school music instructor accompanied them for a while, until the oldest sister Betty took over. Betty was married while they were on the radio program. The staff at KSID insisted the wedding should be in the studio and part of the broadcast.

Carol Ann Campbell ('61) scored 59 points in a single basketball game in 1961. She averaged 45 points a game that year which ranked third in the state. She attended Commercia Extension in Omaha after graduation and played for three years. She was named to the Midwest AAU All-Star team.

Thurman Chapman ('00) became a student at Drake University in Des Moines. On April 25, 1903 he cleared the bar at 12 feet to set a new world record in the pole vault. This surpassed the old record by Capp from Yale by one and a half inches. His poles are placed in the "D" Club trophy room in the Knapp Field house at Drake.

James Briles ('44) was a US Army combat infantryman in the Asia-Pacific theater for two years. He won four Bronze Stars and the Meritorious Service Medal. He was an auctioneer. He became a state representative and state senator in Iowa from 1956-1984. He was well known in southwest Iowa and significantly helped the area in the legislature.

Horace Daggett ('48) served thirty-one years in the National Guard, attaining the rank of Sergeant Major. He was a lifelong farmer and served in the state legislature for 24 years as the Republican representative. He served with the longest continuous record as a member of the Iowa House of Representatives. His most noted piece of legislation was a bill which passed in 1980 which forbids foreign ownership of Iowa farmland. This same legislation later passed in 27 other states.

Community Events—"Prescott Welcomes the World" as 350 inhabitants prepared to welcome the 32nd Annual Pipe Smokers convention of the International Association of Pipe Smoking Club and the World Pipe Smoking Contest in 1980. The Prescott Pipe Puffers Club hosted the event. Contestants heard the words "Smokers Load your Pipes" at 2:30 PM. Each contestant was given 3.3 grams of prepacked tobacco and two matches. After 32 minutes and 34 seconds a new world champion, Bob Richer Jr, age 25, from Clinton, Iowa, was crowned. Three Prescott men finished in the top 11. They were Richard Luther, 5th; Donald Shires, 7th; and Edward Blazek, 11th.

In 1987, "Kline's Sale of Sales" was held to auction off the collectibles of Clarence Kline. The event took three days into the twilight each evening to sell 3,000 unbelievable collectibles. A crowd of 2,500 people attended. Part of the collection went to establish the Kline Museum in Prescott. The city selected some of the items prior to the sale.

Bus Drivers—Don Daggett drove a bus for the school many years. He was a farmer and is shown in a 1924 picture driving the bus through flood waters that stretched nearly a half mile.

A bus wreck on the first day of school in 1953 occurred when a tie rod broke and the bus careened into the ditch. It did not roll over as it came to rest against a row of trees on the upside of the ditch. All the students on board were thrown forward. Rosalie McMorran Phillip ('59) said, "My sister Pam and I were taken home in a car and our parents met us at the end of the driveway. Dr. Brunk came to our house and sewed up my head and examined Pam. She was pale and scared. The next day she was taken to the hospital. She recovered following a miraculous surgery which repaired her torn intestines.

Senior Trips—In 1957, the seniors went to Kansas City by bus. A highlight of the trip for Blake Cooper ('57) was going to a Kansas City Athletics baseball game.

Rosalie McMorran Phillips ('59) recalled, "My senior class went to Kansas City. We toured the massive Chevrolet car manufacturing plant. I had heard of assembly lines but this continual movement of the cars being built down a conveyor line was fascinating."

Bill Birt ('71) said with a wink, "My year the seniors all went to the Lake of the Ozarks. We must have been angels because no misconduct is remembered. We did go-carting and all were given a neat helicopter ride over the lake area."

Every year groups of students went to Des Moines and toured the state capital as hometown Representatives Daggett and Briles from Prescott met the Prescott students and gave them a personalized tour.

Pranks—An innocent goat somehow appeared on top of the roof of the high school. It had been coaxed up the fire-escape by still unidentified pranksters. This seemingly harmless act was punctuated by the sharp hooves of the goat penetrating the tar roof of high school.

Drivers Education—Blake Cooper ('57) took drivers training in 1954 and recalled, "The thing that I remember is the blue 1953 Ford with a stick shift." Rosalie McMorran Phillips ('59) told, "Our instruct-tor was David Miller who was also the history teacher. He had a little box that he put on the dashboard that we all called 'Casper' (the friendly ghost). We had to start the car from the bottom of a hill. If the chain inside the box made noise when we started and shifted, our grade would reflect it."

Notable Teachers—Robert Kiser was the superintendent and taught Typing I and II. Rosalie McMorran Phillips ('59) related, "He was outstanding and ran a strong ship."

Bob Hinrich was the principal who taught German and directed the band. He came to Prescott in 1965. "I played the baritone sax and the electric bass. We had over 50 in the band which was over half of the student body. Mr. Hinrich really was a great leader and inspired so many of us," remembered Randy Cooper ('79).

Closing—Randy Cooper ('79) served on the school board in 1990 when the decision to close the high school came before the board. He told, "The state did not want schools with less that 1,300 students to exist. They wanted the schools to all be on one level and at least two or three people handling the money. We were sharing sports with Corning and they wanted to stop the busing expense. We had been sharing a superintendent with Orient, but we could not afford the expense of one on our own. When we were forced to close, we still had money, but were not able to hire enough qualified teachers to keep the school going."

By a vote of 3-2, the Board of Education dissolved the district. Students in grades 7-12 were given the choice of going to five different schools: Lenox, Bridgewater-Fontanelle, Creston, Orient, or Corning. The grade school was consolidated into the Creston School District. Creston left the town with the option of buying the school. Due to asbestos in the schoolhouse and an estimated cost of $200,000 to tear down the structure, five individuals from Prescott paid $50,000 to purchase the school. It is still (2020) being used as a community center and large meetings and dinners are held at the school for reunions, Thanksgiving, and Christmas gatherings.

The high school closed in May 1990. A total of 1,247 graduated from Prescott High School in the 100 years from 1891-1990. The most numerous surnames of the graduates were: Brown-28, Blazek-27, Walter-21, Miller-17, Campbell-14, Brandt-13, Green-13, Peterson-13, Young-13, Lane-12, and Wood-10. The largest graduating class was 28 in 1979. The last to receive a diploma from Prescott High school was Daniel Wood (alphabetically).

#79

Quasqueton High School

Mascot: Indians
Colors: Black and Red
Closed: 1960
Location: Southeast Buchanan County

Early History—Quasqueton; quaQUEton; QUA-quaton: The correct pronunciation, even among the residents of the town, can spring a debate. They find it much easier to just say Quasky. It was named after Quasatuk, a chief of the Mesquakie Indians who were inhabitants of the Wapsipinicon River area when the 'white' man settled into this area in the 1840s. It is the oldest town in Buchanan County.

The Chicago, Anamosa, and Northern Railroad (CA&N) laid tracks through the town. It was short-lived, running from 1913 to 1916. When it went bankrupt, the iron rails were torn out and shipped to France for the war effort.

Floods on the Wapsipinicon, or Wapsie, were mostly in the lowlands west of downtown Quasky. Main Street was flooded by the memorable 1947 flood. However, the 1999 flood became the record.

Early Schools—Education has been documented with the first school taught in the county at Quasqueton area in 1844 by Alvira Hadden. This was two years before statehood in 1846. Few books and resources were available. Printed in the *History of Buchanan County*:

> The Bible was largely used for a text for spelling and reading lessons. Sometimes a dictionary was added to the equipment, and always either the birch, the hickory, or the strap or the cat-o'-nines-tails was a necessary and essential adjunct.

Many of the immigrants hailed from old rock-ribbed New England. They left behind their schools and churches, which were marks of advanced civilization. By 1858, the county superintendent (salary $500) record showed a total number of school age children in the county at 2,445, the total number of those attending 29 schools, and 27 schoolhouses was 1,015. By 1864 (last full year of the civil war) those numbers rose to 3,435 students, 120 schools, and 59 school buildings. By 1880, these numbers more than doubled again.

In 1870, debate in the county to establish a county high school was proposed by the Buchanan County Teachers Institute. A vote in 1873 found overwhelming opposition with 256 in favor and 1,954 against taxing to establish a county high school. (*Author's Note: these were probably all men voting.*)

A two-year high school was started in the two-story public school in 1891. The first graduation class from this school had two graduates in the spring of 1893. The school was expanded to three years in 1909.

In 1915, a bond was issued for construction of a new school to add the fourth year for high school. This school was finished in time for school in the fall of 1915. A graduation class of eight received their diplomas from the newly accredited Quasqueton High School in 1917.

Sports—Basketball and softball became the girls sports, while basketball, and spring and fall baseball was played by the boys. The sports teams played in the Buchanan County League against Winthrop, Hazelton, Fairbank, Rowley, Jesup, Aurora, Lamont, Brandon, and St. John's of Independence.

The 1936 boys team made it to the state basketball tournament (only one class division for the whole state). Roy Love ('36) was a player on this team. His son Orlan said, "Quasky never had a very tall team. After every made basket, the ball was taken to center court for a jump ball. At state we came up against a taller team in Mason City. Not only was the school much larger enrollment, but they seemed like giants. Their center was 6'3" and later played at UCLA and seemed like an All-American. We were drubbed 40-7. That ineptitude still gives us some notoriety as having scored the least points ever at the state tournament."

The year was 1933. In depth of the depression, a small pasture outside of town was the gathering place for the creation of a small town legend. A bat and a leather, raised-seamed ball, called a 'kitten-ball', was the beginning for a group of girls and their famous Quasqueton Kittenball team. The mayor and the coach, Carl Walter, organized this ball team to "take on all comers" for the next two summers. They played in Prairie du Chien, Wisconsin, and all-over rural Iowa and at home. The team was undefeated in 1934, and in 1935 only lost one game to a team in Des Moines.

The following is an excerpt from a *Cedar Rapids Gazette* article dated September 16, 1934.

Quasqueton Girls Unbeaten at Kittenball:
Played before crowds of 1,600 in Little Town of 360.

A kittenball game and a girls' mix of high school girls, farm girls, married girls, and college girls ranging in age 14 to 21 years old. All enjoyed letting off steam and participating in "America's Favorite Pastime" whenever time allowed.

Also incredibile about this legacy during this era is the high graduation rate among these girls. The following is a list of the team and their graduation years from Quasqueton High school:

Luella (Sal) Sherrets Buck ('29)
Irene Sherrets Vig ('35)
Gladys Turner Walton ('29)
Donna Hekel Buchanan ('36)
Edna Walter Van Etten ('30)
Josephine Turner Mahnke ('36)
Dorothy Wade Clark ('31)
Saloma Sauer Schantz ('36)
Marian Sherrets Scott ('33)
Della Matteson Fairchild ('37)
Bernadine Hekel Willert('33)
Alma Sherrets Kimmerle ('37)
Ona Bender Kress ('34)
Thelma Pilcher Ross ('37)
Geneva Clark Newkirk ('35)
Veta Butterfield Ferreter ('38)
Francis Foster Towlerton ('35)

One of the three Sherrets sisters on the team and third baseman, Irene was the last surviving member of the team when she gave an interview at the age of 95 about the Kittenball team. Irene remembered,

"We all got along so well. We won a lot of games, and it didn't hurt that we had the great pitcher with Geneva Clark. I was often remembered on an occasion when I hit a homerun. Upon rounding third I just excitedly, unrehearsed turned a cartwheel on my way home." Irene passed away the following year in 2014.

Drivers Education—Quasquetion High School did not offer drivers education. Jack Stanford's ('50) eyes twinkle as he quipped, "The first time I had ever driven a car was for my driving test to get a license. I sure had logged a lot of hours behind the wheel of a tractor, though."

Notable Graduates and Teachers—The Manson family (Nedra Manson Chesmore ('58) and parents) gave many years to the Quasqueton schools and community. Edwin Manson ('34) provided all of the buses for the district. He also drove one of the bus routes, along with running his service station and the farm service oil truck. Velma Manson was a favorite teacher, instructing all the commerce and typing classes as well as directing the band. The 1958 yearbook, named *The Quasquetuk,* was dedicated to her. It read: "Having taught us here for 20 years, your willingness to help all of us in our everyday problems and unlimited guidance which you have given us so that we could obtain an education. We extend our gratitude and wishes for every best in life and to you we give our great appreciation." Mrs. Manson's band marched at numerous parades such as the National Cattle Congress, Mason City, and Memorial parades. The Manson's daughter, Nedra ('58), was chosen for the All-State Band playing the saxophone. Donita Kress Scott ('57) added, "I played the drums and clarinet. We had 32 in band when there were only 50 to 60 in high school. Mrs. Manson even taught baton. She made it such a great learning time together and helped us have an appreciation for music."

R.L. Helt was the superintendent for 14 years, from the end of WW II until the school closed in 1960. At an all school alumni reunion he commented, "I know you all used to hate me." A quick tongue in cheek response was heard, "No we only hated you because you got us in to Winthrop (consolidation)."

The class of 1958 spawned one lifelong romance. Harvey Chesmore ('58) and Nedra Manson ('58) were married after school. They were blessed with two children and then triplets. All the children were provided with a college education even with four children in college at the same time.

Pranks—In Quasky, the usual Halloween pranks ranged from the cow in school and a merry-go-round on top of the high school. Just as much fun occurred when cleaning up the devious acts the next day by the students. One prank with an unusual ending was told by Jack Sanford ('50). With a twinkle in his eye he remembered, "There had been a beer can down at Reece's place for weeks just sitting on the table. We took it to school and put it on a teacher's desk. Somehow the poor old janitor got blamed and he got fired."

School Closing—The high school closed after graduation 1960. The remaining students were transported in the fall north to a renamed East Buchanan High School in Winthrop. There had been 497 graduates from Quasqueton High School from 1893-1960. The largest class was 21 in 1935. The most numerous surnames of the graduates were: Franck-19, Manson-12, Chesmore-10, Sherrets-10, Crawford-9, Melick-9, Clark-8, Gemmell-9, Polk-8, Smith-7 and Turner-7. The last to receive a diploma from Quasqueton High School was Helen Sucher (alphabetically).

Quasqueton High School
Buchanan County, IA

#80

Ridgeway High School

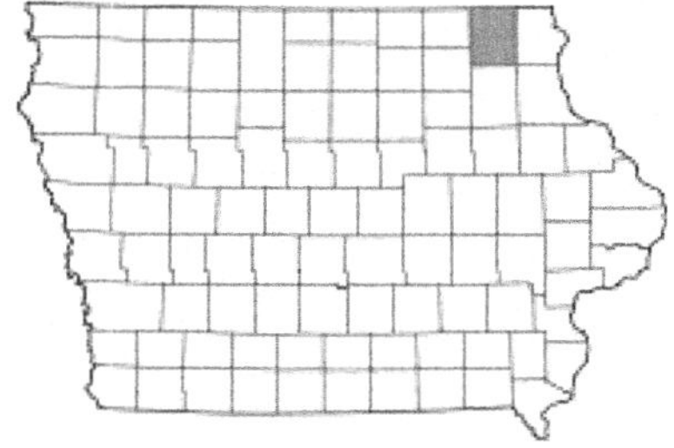

Mascot: Mustangs
Colors: Black and White
Closed: 1959
Location: West Central Winneshiek County

Early History—Ridgeway is located on a ridge in a driftless area that was not glaciated. Half of the townsite is drained north to the Upper Iowa River and the half south to the Turkey River.

English and Norwegians settled in this area of the county. There were Irish settlers north of town and Czechs to the south. An unsubstantiated story is that there were 13 saloons in Ridgeway in 1880.

Dramatic decline in the farming community after World War II was reflected in the Ridgeway population. Rosemary Hovden Vopava ('48) recalled, "My freshman year in 1944 there were 24 freshman and only 17 graduated in 1948. Maynard Hovden ('52) remembered, "When I was a freshman in 1948, we had 27 in our class. By graduation four years later we had five graduates."

Early Schools—The Independent School District of Ridgeway was organized in 1875. In the early 1880s, it consisted of a one-room school in town. A second room and second teacher were soon added with the increase in enrollment.

A long-time story is retold of Rollin Baker serving as the school janitor when he was a boy. He swept both rooms each day and built fires in the box stove. His salary was $2 each month. This two-room school burned in 1898. The district voted $5,000 in school bonds to construct a two-story brick schoolhouse. In 1936, a gymnasium was added to the structure.

Electricity was added to the school and town in 1914. City water was pumped in 1930 to replace the well water at the school.

The school became a four-year high school in 1932 after passing requirements for accreditation by the State Board of Education.

Sports—Six-man football was played 1940. Due to lack of boys out for football, the sport was dropped by 1943. The boys played baseball in the spring and fall and basketball in the winter.

The girls played basketball and kittenball. In the early 1940s, the girls rode in the back of a truck to out-of-town games. The 1948 annual shows 24 girls out for basketball.

Band—Band members wore black and white uniforms. There were 21 in band in 1948, 28 in 1952, and 30 in 1959. Maynard Hovden ('52) smiled as he said, "I played the clarinet. We were not much into marching but played at the Ridgeway Celebration. We did not take the band out of town."

In the last year of the high school, Kenneth Nesvick and Donna Anderson took part in the Dorian Festival at Luther College.

A special concert was held in March of 1959 with the combined band from Elmo in the school gymnasium.

Several students (Roger Bergan and Kenneth Nesvick) kept band uniforms the last year of the school. They knew the uniforms would be thrown away by the new Howard Winn District.

Notable Teachers—Ed Shileny was a beloved and special teacher at Ridgeway High School. He was proud of his Czech heritage and his love of music was shared with the students. He was the band director and taught history. Maynard Hovden ('52) recalled, "He was very dedicated and brought his enthusiasm to the classroom. He brought history into the classroom. I was in the Army in 1954 in France and when our unit bivouacked on the Normandy beach ten years after D-Day, I could not help but think of Mr. Shileny. There were still helmets on the beach and the destroyed hulls of the ships were all along the beach." Mr. Shileny later became the principal and taught French, social studies, and vocal music

Miss Cray taught in Ridgeway in the 1940s and 1950s. She stayed in town during the week but returned to Lime Springs on weekends. She caught a ride with Lars Rue who drove a truck to Austin, Minnesota delivering hogs to the slaughter plant.

Busing—The first buses for the district were purchased in 1946. Tony Snyder took the train to Ft. Wayne, Indiana, to pick up a new bus. He drove by himself all the way home. When he arrived home after all those hours 'his eyes were as red as cherries.' He was so proud that he could drive the kids to Ridgeway to get their education. Clifford Bakken drove another 36-passenger bus purchased from Camp Dodge which had been used to shuttle soldiers. Clifford remembered, "The first year that bus had 11 flat tires on our gravel roads." The route was 35 miles twice daily. He was paid $50 a month.

Closing—The Ridgway School District was limited in size. The Calmar District came within one mile of the south edge of Ridgeway and the Decorah District came within a mile and a half from the eastern edge of Ridgeway. The Ridgeway High School closed after graduation in 1959. It became part of the Howard Winneshiek District with the high school students bused to Cresco.

Ridgeway High School
Winneshiek County, IA

#81

Ringsted High School

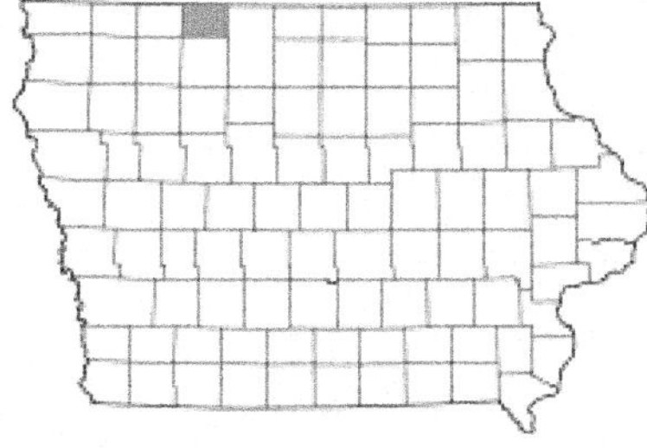

Mascot: Great Dane
Colors: Purple and White
Closed: 1979
Location: Emmet County

Early History—Ringsted is a unique name for an American town and shares the name with Ringsted, Denmark. It is the story of the American dream, when Danish immigrants brought their Danish heritage to a small town in Iowa. Ringsted is in the center of Denmark Township in the southeast corner of Emmet County. A few months before the organization of the township in 1883, several Danish families came and settled in the area. The first settlement was in an area called Angola. Most of the Danes came from Clinton County, Iowa, and purchased land from the Chicago and Milwaukee Railway.

Ringsted was incorporated in 1899 and the first post office was in the home of John Larsen. He named the town after his wife's hometown in Denmark. When the Chicago and North Western Railroad came through the area, the post office was moved to the station location.

Early Schools—The first schooling was in the upstairs rooms of the home of Peter Schulz. The ceiling was so low that there was only one place to stand upright in the middle of the room. The families were satisfied to have a chance to learn the American language.

The first teacher in Denmark Township was Brad Jenkins from the Swan Lake area. He walked to and from the area, staying a week at a time. The first school in the township was started in 1884. By 1915, there were seven school buildings in the township.

The first Ringsted school building had an interesting history. Since the center of the community was located around Black Cat Creek, where the St. John's Lutheran Church later stood, it was believed the town would be built in this area. In 1886, in order to have one-room schools in the township two miles apart, this first school was relocated to the west. Then a second relocation occurred in 1910, so the school then was within the original plat of the town of Ringsted. The school had eight rooms. High school was not considered important as most of the children returned to farming after the eighth grade.

In 1908, another wing was added to the west side of the building. The extra room allowed for the inclusion of grades nine and ten. After finishing the tenth grade in Ringsted, those students seeking the full four years of high school enrolled at Halfa or Armstrong.

Bathroom facilities were still out of doors with one outhouse for each gender. The school had no running water and the well was in front of the school. Each room had a drinking bucket and dipper. Every child was to have their own drinking cup.

By 1919, this wooden school building needed repair. Discussion ensued that it was time Ringsted have its own four-year high school. It was not a unanimous decision. Since it was right after World War I, there was pessimism about the future. Some citizens believed that a new, larger school could not be filled. The vote for a new school passed by a very narrow margin.

The cornerstone was laid in 1922. The Ringsted Independent School District at last had its high school. Within two years, the new school was overcrowded with students.

Notable Teachers—Students remember their outstanding teachers, administrators, and coaches. Several of these great teachers blessed the hearts and minds of Ringsted and are remembered fondly.

Alice Ulrich Sorensen taught three generations of students in Ringsted. Del Matheson ('58) wrote, at the time of his fifty-fifth-class reunion:

> Mrs. Sorensen started teaching at Sunnyside School, a rather outstanding country school two miles east of town. It was here that she taught the Sorensen, Henricksen, and Heerdt children. That school was unusual because it was large and had a full basement, running water, and two restrooms. Most country schools had one room and a path. She moved onto another teaching challenge in western Minnesota. And returned to Ringsted in 1950 and married James Sorensen ('40), a Sunnyside kid, who had grown up in the meantime. Ironically, I knew one of her Minnesota students at MSC (Minnesota State College). Later in life, as a pilot, he'd often land in Fairmont, rent a car and bring Mrs. Sorensen lavish bouquets of flowers—like one hundred long-stemmed red roses. Or he might call her in the morning and invite her to lunch in Fairmont at a given hour. Alice's life was steeped in drama. She was indeed Ringsted's Grande dame.

This same class of 1958, sixty years after leaving Ringsted wrote back about Mrs. Sorensen:

- She liked to drive big cars ***fast.*** The county sheriff stopped her more than once . . . oh, yes, she laughed.
- She had a wardrobe that made eyes follow her.
- She had a ready answer to almost any comment.
- Let's say she liked showy shoes.
- She was a hard worker—even diligent.
- She helped lots of students who needed an extra jump-start.
- Her sense of humor was outstanding.
- She had a very distinctive laugh.
- The timbre of her voice was "Hollywood." She loved to dance.
- Her handwriting was "classic."
- She was a spellbinding storyteller.
- People usually felt better about themselves after visiting with her.
- She often said, "I've had a wonderful life," and she meant it.
- She did lots of things behind the scenes that benefited students.
- She would hire kids to help with projects to boost their morale and to provide them with some spending money.
- She was reasonable in her expectations of students.

- She challenged students to think outside the box and to go the extra mile.
- Her art projects for students were often keepers.
- The school budget did not include her plaster items which we painted. That was out of pocket.

Julie Johnson Laidig ('73) remembered, "I was in FTA (Future Teachers Association) which Mrs. Sorensen was the sponsor. I was elected president at a meeting and I wasn't even there. Mrs. Sorensen was so patient and helped me learn to run a meeting and gave me leadership."

John Manson came to Ringsted in 1951. He was a World War II veteran and taught math and coached both boys and girls basketball. He was well liked and had a professional air about him. Del Matheson ('58) wrote:

> He would stride into the classroom with the lanky grace that was his alone and take charge. He was endlessly tall, maybe 6'7". I had him for eighth grade math and luckily skipped algebra my first two years in high school. I can still remember his quote, 'If you know the formula, you can build an atom bomb.' I always called him Mr. Manson when most kids just yelled, 'Hey, Manson." He did condone that, but I often wondered if he even noticed the little edge of respect that I felt was important. All of my teachers got that from me. My mom would have beaten the hell out of me with her fists if she thought I had called a teacher by his or her last name only.

The basketball teams under Mr. Manson always seemed to have their chief rival, Armstrong's number. Lowell Christensen ('55) told, "Mr. Manson would always tell us that it was because he always played our best players, but Armstrong had to play the school boards' sons. And then he would laugh." Lowell continued, "when he came to town in the fall of 1951, he drove a beautiful new green two-door Ford. All of the boys were instantly impressed with him."

Connie McKay Wilson ('68) laughed when she told, "After basketball practice we were required to take showers. We hated that, but Mr. Manson would yell, 'girls, if I don't hear that water running, I'm coming in there to turn it on myself.' We would have to walk through some solution to prevent athlete's foot. How Mr. Manson would have yelled if he would have known that some of us tried to make it through the whole semester without washing our gym clothes."

Mr. Phil Lachelt taught government and directed the band. Julie Johnson Laidig ('73) recalled, "He was good. Everyone wanted to be in his band and choirs. We marched every Fourth of July at the Wallingford Parade. How hot could it be in those wool band uniforms?" Irma Justice Ostergaard ('55) said, "I played the bass drums and cymbals and Norm Rasmussen ('57) played the snares. We felt that with us in the rhythm backup, that the marching band was always in step." Connie McKay Wilson ('68) remarked, "Every Wednesday night in the summer we played downtown on a trailer bed for the whole community. Afterwards we were treated to ice cream." Nearly half of the student body was involved in music or band. The 1954 annual included a picture of the band with 44 members, 34 girls in glee club, boys chorus with 19 members, and the mixed choir with 47 members.

Dorothy Underwood was a beloved principal and English teacher. Her husband had left her with five boys to raise on her own during the depression. All the boys graduated and went into the service. They were William Underwood ('39), Howard Underwood ('41), Max Gordon Underwood ('43), Herbert Underwood ('45), and Raymond Underwood ('47). "She was a great English teacher," remembered Irma Justice Ostedgaard ('55). "We were required to give speeches in class on any subject of our choice. Some us took this quite seriously and gave our best efforts. The superintendent's son, Chuck Bredeson ('55), was always a cut-up and one day in 1953 he stood up for his speech and said, 'The King is dead-long live the Queen!' and sat down. Who would have thought that Queen Elizabeth would still be reigning over 66 years later?"

Drivers Education—Bob Scott was the first drivers education teacher in the fall of 1954. He also taught industrial arts. Irma Justice Ostedgaard ('55) smiled as she told, "Even though Dorothy Petersen Anderson ('55) and Jackie Christian Chambers ('55) already had their drivers license and did not have to take drivers ed, they took it anyway. They said it was because Mr. Scott 'was hot.'" Norm Rasmussen ('57) winked as he told, "In shop we had just finished overhauling Dick Smith's ('57) big old 'Olds when the bell rang. Mr. Scott says, 'Okay boys, you can break out the smokes because school is officially out for the week!'"

Sports—Basketball and baseball were the sports for boys. Basketball was the girls sport. Neither football nor wrestling were played at Ringsted.

The 1976 boys basketball team lost to Graettinger in the finals of the boys sub-state, thus denying a state tournament appearance. "It broke our hearts," remembered Lowell Christensen ('55). "My son, Terry Christensen ('76) was on that team. We can replay that game to this day in our minds."

Bus Driver—Harold Kramer drove the school bus for many years. He also had other businesses in town including a feed business and a restaurant. A teacher, Sylvia Hansen remembered, "I loved him on field trips, because he would take all of the boys to the restroom while I would lead the girls toward their direction."

Senior Trips—David Solberg ('79) was in the last graduating class and told, "We chartered a bus and were chaperoned by Gordy Howe and his wife, and Mr. Richard Newkirk and his wife. The senior boys had been called on the carpet and warned not to even think of any beer. So it was quite to our surprise, as it was the girls in the class that brought the beer. The boys thought of themselves as angels." David continued, "I vividly remember working as a class at the Stokley's canning plant in Fairmont, Minnesota, to raise money for our senior trip. I was to pick off the bad ears of corn as they came along on the conveyor belt. In no time at all we started getting dizzy with the continuous motion. So much for my assembly-line days."

"My class picked up rocks in the glaciated fields in the spring to make money for our prom," recalled Connie McKay Wilson ('68).

Notable Graduates—The class of 1958 demonstrated dedication and longevity. All 14 graduates came back for their 60th class reunion alive and well. An actuarial mathematician friend of Del Matheson ('58) did the calculations of the chances of this happening. He reported back to Del on the phone, "You won't believe this. Your class is like a lottery winner. You have 5.6 chances out of one billion to hit this jackpot . . . and you did it."

Closing—The high school closed following graduation in May 1979. High school students the following year were bused to Armstrong. A total of 1,285 graduated from Ringsted High School in the 58 years from 1922-1979. The largest class was 41 in 1965. The most common surnames of the graduates were: Jensen-84, Petersen-46, Hansen-32, Christensen-26, Anderson-25, Johnson-24, Christiansen-23, Madsen-23, Nielsen-21, Nelson-21, Sorensen-20, Larsen-18, Henricksen-17, Nelsen-17, Jorgensen-16, Pedersen-14, and Bonnicksen-13. The last to receive a diploma from Ringsted High School was Dale Ziemer (alphabetically).

Ringsted High School
Emmet County, IA

#82

Roland High School

Mascot: Rockets
Colors: Red and Black
Closed: 1969
Location: North Central Story County

Early History—The concentration of Norwegian heritage is deep-rooted and strong in Roland. In 1846, (the same year Iowa was admitted to the Union) Torkel Henryson, a young schoolteacher in Bergan, Norway, gathered 165 passengers from 29 families and 16 single men to come to America. They chartered a boat and sailed across the Atlantic Ocean in six weeks. Landing in New York, they took another boat trip to Chicago where they were outfitted with ox-drawn covered wagons to Lisbon in Kendall County, Illinois. Disappointed that all the government land in that area had been claimed, they listened to rumors that good land could be bought from the government west of the Mississippi River.

Early in the spring of 1855, six Norwegian men traveled overland in two horse-drawn covered wagons. They forded the high springtime Mississippi River and traveled overland to the northern part of Story County, Iowa. These men stopped at a place along Long Dick Creek and made their headquarters at the home of James Smith. This was one mile east and one mile south of present-day Story City.

The men traveled back to Lisbon, Illinois, and returned the next year with twelve Norwegian families. Many more Norwegian immigrants followed in the ensuing years from Wisconsin, Illinois, and Norway into Palatine and Howard townships in Story County.

John Evenson, the postmaster, bestowed Roland with its name, because it was easy to pronounce in both English and Norwegian and easy to spell. Folklore credits the Roland name to Evenson from an epic character in Charlemagne's day who was a Frenchman and not Norwegian.

Early Schools—In 1862, a school district was organized in the community. A building was erected on Main Street. In 1871, when the school districts of the townships were arranged, this school was moved one mile east of town. Another school was built one mile west of town (complying to a school every two miles).

By 1885, Roland had become quite a village and the school building did not accommodate all the pupils. An independent school district was organized and, during the summer, a second school was erected at the Main Street site of the original schoolhouse. This school was graded and soon outgrew its quarters. The school which had been west of town was moved back into town to be used for intermediate grades. In 1891, the school had reached the standard for organizing a high school. A three-year course was added, and the first graduating class was in 1891.

An election was held in 1915 to consolidate four rural school districts with the Roland Independent School. At a construction cost of $52,000, a two-story, red brick rectangular building was dedicated on September 29, 1916. The first floor had a great hall with large windowed rooms and a teachers' lounge. The second floor was a central assembly area where every student had a desk. Elementary teachers received $50 per month, the superintendent received $108 per month, and the six bus drivers were hired at $45 to $60 a month. The school furnished wagons with a capacity of 20-24 students. The drivers had to furnish the horses.

The class of 1917 was the first to graduate from the new school. Curriculum consisted of having completed four courses each year for four years. The courses offered were English, German, Norse, algebra, geometry, physics, agriculture, manual training, domestic science, history, civics, and bookkeeping.

Improvements to the school over the years:

1940 Six lots were purchased for additional playgrounds.

1941 A new gymnasium/auditorium was built with $20,000 in school funds and $28,000 in federal works funds.

1950 A school dwelling was purchased at a cost of $9,000.

1953 A six-stall bus garage was constructed for $15,000.

1956 Roland Consolidated School became a community school district with the annexation of land in Hamilton and Hardin Counties.

1963 A new addition and remodeling to the school was made for $150,000.

Sports—The girls basketball team was called the Rockettes. They played on an outside dirt court until the new school was built in 1917. These early basketball teams were called "The Invincibles." Girls basketball was discontinued at Roland in 1925. It restarted playing interscholastic again in 1942 until the school closed. In the next 28 seasons, the girls compiled a most impressive record with 414 wins and 177 loses for a 69.8 winning percentage. They competed in the state six-on-six tournament in 1960, 1962, and 1963. Carol Holland ('58) led the Rockettes in the state free throw championship in 1958 making 24 of 25 attempts which tied the record at that time.

The 1951 boys basketball team entered the sweet sixteen state tournament in Iowa City as a little heralded small school. (There was only one class and all teams across Iowa played in the state tournament regardless of the school enrollment.) They were a team which averaged 5′ 10 ½″ and played against a very tall Hull team in the opening round of the tournament. Their fast break, full court press proved too much for the team from northwest Lyon County. The next game was against heavily favored and top ranked Waterloo West with a 6′7″ center. Roland upset the Wahawks 43-40. The next giant to fall was Des Moines East in the semi-finals. In the championship finals, the Rockets were defeated by the top team in the state, Davenport Central Blue Devils, before a packed fieldhouse crowd of 15,000. Most of them were cheering wildly for the Roland Rockets. Little 5′ 6″ sophomore, Gary Thompson, with his crewcut and floppy socks hanging over his converse all-stars, had become the darling of Iowa high school basketball. This start and his renown continued through two more state championship tournament runs in 1952 and 1953. His legacy as the "Roland Rocket" continued, and Gary Thompson ('53) became a three-time basketball first team All-Big 8 and all-American in baseball at Iowa State University in 1957.

The boys played in a total of six state tournaments in 1951, 1952, 1953, 1957, 1958, and 1959. They finished second in the Cinderella year in 1951 and won the tournament in 1958 with the Class B title.

The boys baseball teams went to state in the spring seasons of 1936, 1944, 1951, 1952, 1953, and in the fall of 1952. The Rockettes softball teams went to state in the summer seasons of 1959, 1960, 1969, and in the fall seasons of 1959, 1960, and 1968. The Rockettes won the state championship in the summer of 1959, the fall of 1959, the fall of 1960, and finished second in the summer of 1960. The athletes and the community enjoyed the teams' successes.

An article in the *Fort Dodge Messenger* by sports Editor Bob Brown epitomized the Roland Rockets basketball teams:

> Before closing its doors, Roland left a record of success that perhaps will never be matched or even approached by any school. Roland is now consolidated

with neighboring Story City so the Rockets as we knew them in the 1950s are no more.

During the glory years, a 10-year period starting with the 1948-49 season to and including the 1957-58 season, Roland won a fantastic 297 games and lost just 25. That's a winning percentage of .922 and an average of 29.7 victories and 2.5 loses a year.

The records for the 10 seasons went this way: 1949 (29-2); 1950 (29-2); 1951 (35-1); 1952 (31-3); 1953 (32-2); 1954 (28-3); 1955 (30-2); 1956 (22-5); 1957 (27-4); and 1958 (34-1).

Seventeen Roland athletes were selected to the first team All-State during those years. They were: Shirley Auld ('66), Marcia Bakke ('63), Norma Christian ('64), Allen Erickson ('55), Susan Erickson ('64), Donna Hagen ('53), Charlene Hall ('60), Janet Hansen ('60), Janet Hanson ('58), Patty Morgan ('60), Deanne Hill ('63), Debbie Holen ('69), Duane Hovick ('59), Rod Larson ('66), Ralph Johnson ('51), Gary Thompson ('53), and Paul Twedt ('58).

Football was not played at Roland.

McCallsburg was always the biggest rival. In the 1960s, South Hamilton and Nesco became big rivals. Gary Thompson ('53) stated, "We didn't have many friends from other towns because we always beat them in basketball."

Notable Teachers—Coach Buck Cheadle came from Oklahoma and was part Cherokee with high cheek bones. He demanded dedication and no smoking, drinking, or candy bars. Duane Weltha ('52) wrote, "His players played together and were much better than they thought they were. They were steady and never had a bad game." Jerry Twedt ('53) said, "Had he put on eagle feathers and called us to do battle we would have followed. He believed that we were not a champion without a superior defense."

C.P. Thompson was the superintendent from 1944-1956 and taught typing and instructed the bands. Ralph Johnson ('51) shared, "He ran the show. He took the band to the state fair. Three of us who were not in band conjured up a plan to take in permission slips to get out of school for the day, while they were away. We took in the slips and presented them to the secretary, and we headed off to Des Moines and the state fair, too. The next day I got to see Mr. Thompson's bad side. He was tough, though he always wept at all graduations. He was so patient with such self-control."

Rosemary Hennessy told the story that Linda Braathun Donahue ('65) remarked of the rule that "no slacks were to be warn in school." Paula Chrisitian Sampson ('71 from Roland-Story) recalled, "so, we would roll up our slacks under our skirts and wear them anyway."

Mrs. Johanna Finch was the principal and taught math and vocal music 1-12. "We were just as good at music as we were in sports. Mrs. Finch had us ready for contest and at least 75% of her Roland music contest entries scored a top-rated first," wrote

Duane Weltha ('52). Pete Twedt ('48) remembered, "She had wit and charm. We all loved her. I gained a great deal of affection for her. She took us to Grinnell for a music contest. It must have been a big event because after the contest there was a dance. Arlene Erickson Sampson ('46) asked me to dance with her. Since we had not been allowed to dance at home, it was not the smoothest, but it sure was a music lesson for me."

Bill Hennessy taught government, civics, Iowa and US history. He coached the girls softball and basketball teams. He wrote the *Iowa Softball Rule Book*. He became the first coach in the Iowa Athletic Union Hall of Fame and was named the National coach of the year in softball. "One of our class requirements for class was naming the countries in the world. I had nightmares about naming the counties and county seats of Iowa. But did we ever learn our history. He was such a thorough and great teacher," recalled Martha Bakke ('66).

Notable Graduates—DeLon Thompson ('60) pitched in the Minnesota Twins organization. Gary Thompson ('53) stated, "My brother was a great ball player at Iowa State. He pitched in both ends of a doubleheader against Oklahoma and won both games. At Roland, he once struck out 23 batters in a seven-inning game. That's right, there were two third-strike pitches that got away from the catcher and the runner ended up on first base." DeLon makes his living as a musician playing the piano and sings professionally. He had the number one hit on Eucap music.

Killed in Action—Many from the Roland area lost their lives in service for their country.

Donald Alvestad, WWII
Dean Bakka, WWII
Boyd Christian, WWII
Sterling Seymour, WWII
Carrroll Gjerda ('35), WWII
Robert Larson ('40), WWII
Virgil Twedt ('38), WWII
James Twedt ('43), WWII
William Quam ('43), WWII
David Quam, WWII
Wayne Holland, Korea

Buses—Harry Amenson started school in 1931 and reported of that year, "The school hired senior boys to pick up kids in their family cars. The school purchased two buses that came in kits. John Thorsness in Story City assembled the kits onto the chassis. One was a 1932 B Ford four-cylinder and the other was a 1935 International. There were two rows of seats on the sides and a very poor heater in the middle. Each bus was able to carry about 20 students."

Community Stories—With World War II taking many men and workers away from the country, the Marshalltown Canning Company in Roland employed high school boys for the summer and weekends. Gary Thompson ('53) remembered, "At the canning company they had German POW's who helped in the plant. There were also many Jamaican workers that came to town to work in the plant as well. I loved working with the Jamaicans, because we played catch and ball with them. They were great ball players because they had played cricket back home in Jamaica. The POW's would help on the farms in the area and never even had a guard looking over them. They were great people."

Television came to most of the homes by the mid-1950s. With the televisions came commercials. A good churchman, Harris Twedt Sr., became part of one such commercial which repeated over and over on TV for some time. Harris had been caught on camera at the Nevada Liquor Store which used this footage in their TV commercial. Back home in Roland, he became the tongue-in-cheek legend, "There is good 'ole Harris buying communion wine for church!"

Religion—With two deeply committed Norwegian Lutheran churches in town, religion classes were taught in the school. Dancing was not permitted. On a visit by the State Board of Education, they questioned what was held in that classroom. The superintendent said, "Oh that is just the religion class." With separation of church and state, the religion class was then moved out of the school and into one of the Lutheran churches. The junior-senior banquet was a dinner provided by the junior class mothers. Pete Twedt ('48) recalled, "We all brought pennies to school for missions. During my years we were brave enough to lobby the preachers if we could have a dance at school. We were turned down and permission was denied. By the 1950s, this strict rule was loosened and there was a Prom dance after the junior senior banquets."

Yearbook—The yearbook was named *The Rocket.* The first yearbook was printed in 1920. It was dedicated to Superintendent Karl Hanson who had been at Roland for eight years overseeing the building of the new school. The dedication read:

Whom we love as a friend, respect as a
teacher, admire as a leader, and
honor as a faithful promoter of
the welfare at Roland High
School for eight successive years,
we affectionately dedicate
this, our first
Annual

Organizations in the 1920 yearbook included; two literary societies, Declamatory, Debate, Glee

Club, Parent-Teacher Association, Girls Basketball (wins over Radcliffe, Hubbard twice, and splitting with Nevada); Industrial Department with Agriculture; Shop Work; Judging team; Corn judging; Domestic Science; and Domestic Art. The boys basketball team played Story City, Gilbert, Fernald, Hubbard, Radcliffe, Nevada, Ellsworth, Zearing, and Colo.

The final yearbook in 1969 lists all the extracurricular activities in the school. They were band, music, class plays, homecoming (decorating the store windows), snake dances, pep assembly, school musical—"Oklahoma," junior class play, awards day, annual staff, newspaper staff, Honor Tea, Boys Glee, Girls Glee, trios, sextets, octets, and quartets.

The sports teams played the following towns in 1968-69: Radcliffe, Story City, Urbandale, Nevada, Steamboat Rock, Stratford, Nesco, Guthrie Center, Grand Community, West Marshall, North Polk, Eldora, West Des Moines, Bondurant, Ballard, Hampton, South Hamilton, Hubbard, and Gowrie.

Closing—Roland and Story City voters passed a proposition to become the Roland-Story Community School District effective in July 1969. (the Roland Girls softball team was still playing in the state tournament after that date). In the 77 years of the Roland High School from 1893-1969, a total of 1,309 graduated. The largest class was 35 in 1941. The most numerous surnames of the graduates were: Anderson-43, Thompson-40, Johnson-37, Olson-36, Twedt-33, Larson-31, Hanson-29, Eggland-29, Jacobson-25, Nelson-21, Rod-21, Hill-16, Erickson-15, Michaelson-14, Teig-14, Hegland-13, and Duea-10. The last to receive a diploma from Roland High School was Steve Wierson (alphabetically).

A poem written by Pete Twedt ('48) gave a parting to the Roland High School. Jerry Twedt ('53), Pete's brother, called this "not bad for an Iowa hog farmer.

End of an Era

I saw an era end this night,
A night I knew must come,
But the heart is a bit more stubborn
To accept progress's total sum.
I watched the colors black and red
Leave the court, their final bye;
My heart bled just a mite,
'Twas the end of Roland High.
My thoughts flew back to many years
Before I wore the colors,
To the early "stars" of Roland High,
The bloomer gals and their big, strong fellers.
Then came the '40s and the '50s,
A dynasty emerged.
A name to be feared by other towns,
A greater spirit surged.

"Super Stars" wore the black and red,
Put Roland on the map;
The crowds were big, the fans fantastic
For every gap on tap.
Still the colors go on to further glory,
For time cannot stand still;
Reorganize is the cry-the thing to do-
To ease the till.
That fateful day has now arrived,
For Roland High to cease;
The conflict has ended, the race been run.
Black and Red may rest in peace.
Back to reality my thoughts were jarred.
The bleachers nearly bared.
With "Roland High" ringing in my ears
Had others my thoughts shared?
Yes, Roland High, we'll sing to you
Of great times old and new
For the honor was mine to walk your halls
My heart will be with you.

#83

Rudolphinum High School

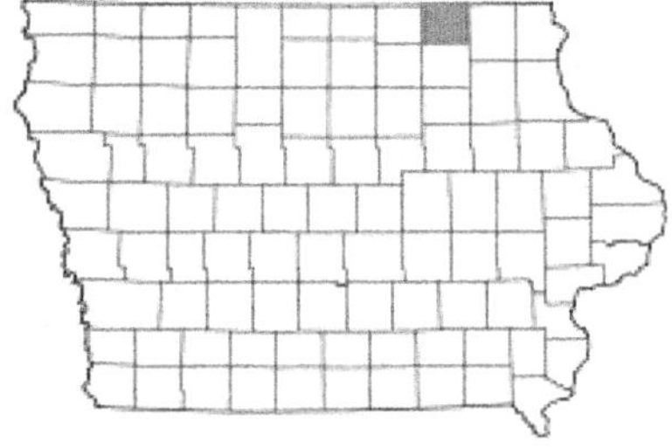

Mascot: Rudohawks/Rudogirls
Colors: Purple and Gold
Closed: 1968
Location: Southeast Howard County

Early History—The name Rudolphinum is unique and primarily known in the Northeast quadrant of the state. In the town of Protivin, Rudolphinum High School was part of a beautiful Czech community that celebrates its heritage. The first Czechs came to Iowa in the 1850s. From 1860-1862, the state of Iowa had a Commissioner of Immigration living in New York to persuade foreigners to locate in Iowa. Pamphlets were published in foreign languages describing Iowa as ideal for settlement. By 1880, over ten thousand Czechs had settled throughout Iowa when railroads made travel more convenient.

In 1872, Frank Chyle Jr. married Mary Jira and they purchased a farm in southeast Howard County. Mary Jira was born in Protivin, Bohemia, and it was in her honor that the new town was named. While common among other nationalities to name settlements in the United States after their homelands, the Czech immigrants named very few settlements. Chyle was urged to name the new settlement Pisek, another town in Bohemia. However, he continued with his plan to name Protivin in his wife's honor. They donated land so that a Catholic Church could be built. In June 1878, Frank Chyle Jr. filed a plat of the town and became the town's first postmaster.

Spillville, eight miles to the east, was a center for Czech families, and the St. Wenceslas Church majestically stands on a hill overlooking the community. The early Czech-Catholic families around Protivin attended church services at St. Wenceslas. Spillville families offered help to Protivin Czechs to build their own church.

The Protivin Parish was named Holy Trinity Parish on May 29, 1878. The cornerstone of the new church was blessed, and Holy Trinity Church was dedicated four months later.

Early Schools—In 1895, Reverend John Broz was appointed to the Parish. He immediately began work on building a Catholic school. The people responded. In 1896 the first parochial school, Holy Trinity Grade School, was built.

Reverend Rudolph Lakomy came to the Parish in 1906. He was also an architect by profession and drew plans and supervised the construction of the new church. This church still serves the Holy Trinity Parish today (2020). At the time of his death in 1925, the parish numbered 280 families. A meeting was held on January 16, 1927 to determine if the parish should proceed with construction of the school. By a vote of 83 for and nine against, the new school was approved. Contracts were awarded to W.L. Yokum Company of Dubuque, general contractor for $35,500; Charles Mallat Company, Decorah, heating and plumbing contractor for $5,458; and United Electric of Dubuque, electrical contractor for $1,045. The new grade and high schools were called "Rudolphinum" in honor of Reverend Rudolph.

At the time of its construction, Rudolphinum school was described as a massive brick structure standing as defiance to storm and fire, dressed in Bedford rock at the main and side entrances. On April 25, 1928, a flag pole was dedicated by raising the American flag and playing the "Star Spangled Banner," thereby making the school complete. Rudolphinum was dedicated on May 5, 1928.

High School Days—The first attempt at journalism was called the *Rudograph* or the school newspaper. It was published monthly. The first yearbook was published in 1928 and called the *Oh-Kay*.

The first graduating class of two students was in 1928. By the next year, 40 students were enrolled.

In 1936, the United States War Department gave the Protivin community a cannon in memory of one Civil War veteran and four WW I veterans buried in Holy Trinity Cemetery. In the early 1940s, this monument, located on the school grounds, went off to WW II. The old war relic was sold for scrap and, like other scrap metal gathered by patriotic citizens, it was recycled into war materials and never returned.

Sports—Boys and girls basketball were the only sports offered at Rudolphinum. There was no football or baseball in the school curriculum. In the first years, they played Assumption, Cresco, North Worthington, Lawler, Chester, Ft. Atkinson, Elkader, Elma, Ridgeway, and St. Joseph's of Elkader.

From the 1929 *Rudograph,* the importance of girls basketball was highlighted:

> The physical as well as the mental powers of young women must be strengthened and cared for. In order to do this, athletics have been introduced into our high school. It is the foremost sport in our state, and particular of our town. Every muscle is thrown into play in the game and from the standpoint of exercise it is one of the most excellent for the purpose of developing strength, grace, precision, skill, and alertness . . .

From the 1934 *Rudograph*:

> . . . Like in Southern California there is annually a great game at Rose Bowl. Protivin also boosts of this kind of a game in the Protivin Soup Bowl every New Year's Day when the Rudohawks and Rudogirls play the Alumni and Alumnae. The Rudogirls defeated the Alumnae 23-20 in an exciting game.
>
> The Rudohawks fell under the heavy artillery of the Alumni. The Alumni with four captains and the cream of the crops of all RHS basketball teamed to defeat the Rudohawks . . .

The teams played in the How-Win Conference tournaments in the 1950s. There were four schools from Howard County: Rudolphinum, Crestwood, Lime Springs, Chester, and four schools from Winneshiek County: Ridgeway, Ossian Public, Desales, and Ft. Atkinson.

In the 1960s, the new North Iowa Catholic Conference was organized. Other conference members were Desales (Ossian), Immaculate Conception (Charles City), Notre Dame (Cresco), St. George (Lansing), St. Lukes (St. Lucas), St. Patrick's, (Waukon), and Visitation (later Marion-Staceyville). This concentration of Catholic schools was unique. The opportunity for a sports conference of like-sized student enrollment captivated and energized the area.

In 1965, Art Sweska scored 64 points in a game against St. Mary's of New Haven. This scoring record remains the seventh highest scored by an Iowa prep in a single game.

The Rudophium gymnasium was built in 1928 and was a small court with a row of benches on both sides. The stage was on the east end and a balcony on the west end. This balcony also was the changing room for the teams getting ready for the basketball games.

Service to the Country—Five from Protivin died during World War II. Lest they be forgotten.

Lester Schmidt ('42), 1944, by a Japanese sniper on Saipan Island
Quentin Wagner ('38), bomber pilot—Guadalcanal
Arthur Tuchek Hanchow, China
Richard Pecinovsky, pneumonia 1945
Joseph Houdek, Leyte Gulf, Philippines

Busing—The school did not have buses for transporting students. Spillville, which had no high school, paid tuition to send their students to Rudophium. The Parish purchased a small bus which held six students on each side. It met each morning at the Spillville Ford garage, and the parents transported their children to that location to catch the bus. Joe Spalla ('63) was one of the student drivers. He was driving the bus before he was 16 years old. After school, he was instructed to leave immediately to get the students back to Spillville to meet their rides home. This proved very handy. Detention after school for any disciplinary actions could not be served by bus students. Spillville kids would rush to their bus much to the frustration of the priest giving them chase.

Notable Graduates—Bill Prochaska ('55) was elected to the Iowa High School Hall of Fame for his four-year scoring record of 2,124 points. This state record stood for nine years. Bill's record still stood as the eighteenth best of all time as of 2004. He became a professor at Upper Iowa University, athletic director, coached the Upper Iowa basketball team for 21 years, and the Upper Iowa baseball team for 16 years. In a 2019 interview, he credited his school coach, Fr. Jerome Trizil, who also taught religion at Rudophium, and Sister Vitaor, the principal, for encouraging him to become a teacher. Bill said, "My father, Joseph ('35) and mother Wilma Kalishek ('36) Prochaska wanted all of us kids to continue our education and contribute to society. Something must have stuck as all four of us; Jane, Jim, Mary, and myself, graduated from Rudolphinum and became teachers.

Polio—Gerald "Jerry" Pecinovsky ('62) had polio when he was ten years old. He missed a month of school and when he returned to school no one wanted to be his friend. The students had been warned by their families to not get too close to someone who may have polio. There was no vaccine at the time. This stigma passed and Jerry made a full recovery, except for one shoulder being slightly lower than the other. He graduated from Loras College and later obtained a master's degree and worked in market research. He distinguished himself with career as a specialist in local and city governments in Oregon, Minnesota, and Iowa. He wrote and accumulated some of the history of Protivin used in this story.

Pranks—Father Jarislaus Skluzacek held mass for all the students each morning at 11:30, just before lunch. He was quite elderly and sang the 'Gloria' at mass and his voice vibrated with a rumbling cadence. Gerry Lentz ('63) recalled, "Sister Herman Joseph was our accompanist for our boys' quartet. There was one of the cables on the organ pipe that was stuck or was broken. So, when she accompanied us, we had been instructed to pull on that cable when she gave us the nod. One morning at mass when Father Skluzacek was in his warbling rendition of the 'Gloria', all four of the angelic quartet of senior boys, Jerry Wagner ('63), Jim Prochaska ('63), Edmond Samec ('63), and myself had stationed ourselves behind the wall of the organ ready for action. Not only did we pull on the stuck cable, we gave every one of them a yank. Since Sister Herman Joseph could not see us, she was not able to give us the eye. The laughter throughout the church surely still echoes to this day, as a perplexed Father did not quite see the humor in our mischievousness."

The class of 1963 had some less than serious students. Gerry Lentz ('63) admitted there was another stunt that drew the ire of the nuns, "Every year the sisters would sell candy. It seems that on the lower level where the building was half below ground and half above with the window on the side, the tile floor slightly angled to the front of the room. This made a perfect ramp for the round candy starting at the back of the room to roll slowly down the tile flooring. It gained momentum to hit the front wall with a resonating ping. When Sister Mathias would jump at the noise, every one of the pupils would be diligently studying with our heads in a book or working. It was such an honor system that no one ever ratted on the back row boys."

The pranks were all harmless and yet rather symbolic of the times. Aging Father Skluzacek also taught the religion class. Jerry Pecinovsky ('62) remembered, "Religion class was such a dull and boring class and Father was not too with it about the new things of our time. The transistor radio had just come into use, and we would often bring one to class and set it on the radiator playing music. It would seem to amplify the music through the pipes and Father would ask where is that music coming from. Innocently, we would say it must be coming from a car out on the street. He never did catch on. Neither did he catch on when we would cut up rubber bands in small pieces and mix it in with his pipe tobacco. Talk about a putrid smell, and it surely must have tasted just as rotten but he never seemed to notice."

Closing—The high school closed following graduation in 1968. The next fall the students were bused to Cresco, New Hampton, and Turkey Valley depending on their location in the district. In the 41 years from 1928-1968 there were 476 graduates of Rudolphinum High School. The largest class was 25 in 1965. The most numerous surnames of the graduates were: Pecinovsky-28, Bouska-22, Lukes-15, Kalishek-14, Fencel-12, Zahasky-12, Svoboda-10, Prochaska-8, Hubka-7, Novak-7, and Klimesh-6.

Rudolphinum High School
Howard County, IA

#84

Sabula High School

Mascot: Panthers (black)
Colors: Orange and Black
Closed: 1972
Location: Jackson County

Early History—Sabula is an 'island city' at the extreme tip of eastern Iowa where it touches the Mississippi River. This land was part of the Wisconsin Territory before the area was conveyed in a treaty with the Sac and Fox tribes in September 1832. This treaty was known as the Black Hawk Purchase which opened the first land in Iowa for settlement. The Dubuque and Maquoketa countryside was home to the Fox Indians. Except for Winnebago Indians, there were few Indians seen in Jackson County after the immigration of the white people.

The land Sabula now stands on was an Indian village. There were several families of Indians living here at the time the settlers came. The spot was known to the French as 'Prairie La Pierre.' This was the only point on the west bank of the Mississippi River between Bellevue and Lyons which afforded a good site for a town. The site is situated only a few feet above the high-water mark and yet it is perfectly safe from overflow due to this location.

At first the town was called Carrolltown. When a shipment of goods from St. Louis was delivered by mistake to "Carrion Point," the name was changed to Charlestown. This seemed quite appropriate because there was a Savannah (Illinois) directly across the river to the east. But new troubles were ahead as a town in Lee County, Iowa, bore the name Charleston and annoyance resulted once more from misdirected letters, freight, and packages.

In 1846, the year that Iowa became a state, William Hubbel thought the name should be changed to reflect the quality of the ground's surface deposit. He examined his dictionary for the word 'sand' and found the Latin word for sand was 'sabulum.' It was decided to change the name Charleston to Sabulum. However, a lady at a tea party proposed the name Sabula which was elegant and more easily pronounced. Her suggestion was adopted. Thus, the legend of Sabula was determined.

River traffic and ferries were significant for this small town. The first ferry across the Mississippi was a scow ferry running as early as 1837. A horse ferry was established in 1850. By 1860, a steam ferry across the river was the best mode of transportation.

There were struggles to attract railroads to the river towns. As the towns grew, they groaned, bargained, and held elections to persuade different railroads to locate through their towns. The Sabula, Ackley, and Dakota Railroad began in 1870. Only eleven and a half miles of this railroad was in Jackson County. Rail cars were transferred across the Mississippi by ferry boat. Another railroad ran north-south along the bluff west of town, but bypassed Sabula.

Newspapers—The first newspaper was founded in 1856 and called the *Sabula Tribune*. In 1862, the *Gazette Company* formed, and the name was changed to *Eastern Iowan*, then *Sabula Union*, and finally to the *Sabula Gazette*.

Industries—The Iowa Packing Company was operating in Sabula by 1860. It was a pork plant which occupied up to two acres and employed 200 men. It was the fourth largest packing house in Iowa after Dubuque, Des Moines, and Cedar Rapids.

First Schools—The first schools were in private homes as early as 1838. In 1844, the Methodists were having financial problems in completing their church. The church joined with the citizens to let the building be used as a school during the week and as church on the weekends. This arrangement proved very satisfactory for both parties. The town contributed to the cost of furnishing the building.

The first stone school was erected in 1856. There were 57 male students and 93 female students enrolled the first year in this building. Summer tuition was 78 cents and winter tuition $1.18. The school consisted of 60 days in the summer, and 60 days during the winter months. The first year a total of $165 was spent on teacher salaries.

In 1860, an independent school district was formed. By 1869, a tuition free public school was supported by the taxpayers. A contract was awarded for the construction of two frame buildings, one at the north end of town and the other at the south end. Repair of the stone building was $2,953. There were two wards created, a north ward and a south ward. The two schools taught grades one through eight and the stone school had grades nine, ten, and eleven.

There were demands for a new high school. An election on August 12, 1879 to approve bonds for such a building was defeated 94 to 40. Three years later, on March 15, 1882, an election was held on bonding the town in the sum of $10,000 for building purposes. The new high school opened with regular sessions in January of 1883. The first graduation was held in June 1888. The high school became a 12-year high school in 1907.

During World War I, with patriotism running high, the study of the German language was discontinued and a huge bonfire destroyed the German textbooks. Domestic science was added to the curriculum with sewing and cooking for the girls. A room in the basement was designed for manual training for both boys and girls.

By 1920, the school was becoming overcrowded, but an election for an addition was defeated. The old stone building was once again used. On July 25, 1925, a bond election for $30,000 was approved and the building was completed in January of 1927. This addition was for a new gymnasium and four classrooms.

Sports—Football was not played, but boys and girls basketball was organized with the first team years not recorded. Practice was held outdoors on the school grounds. When it was too cold, games were played at the Sabula Opera House.

When the new gymnasium was completed in 1927, it was one of the nicest gyms in the area. The biggest rivals were Miles, Preston, and Bellevue.

The Preston team expressed their frustration after a loss at Sabula by dropping cherry bombs into the toilets in the locker room and blowing the porcelain toilets apart.

In 1963, the girls basketball team had a challenging season. They had not won a game all year. This was during the Kennedy administrations initiative for more physical education and exercise for all school age children. The boys high school team challenged the girls. If the girls won a game, the boys would do a 50-mile walk in the dead of the winter. Sure enough, in the Jackson County Tournament in February, the girls got an upset win over Ellwod. Denny Hoyer ('65), Dick Haynes ('63), Gary Marburger ('67), Dave Behan ('66), and Bob Gillespie ('65) walked the 50 miles to Maquoketa and back to Miles on February 12, 1963. The following night the boys had a basketball game and Denny Hoyer ('65) was still limping from the hike the day before.

Notable Teachers—Miss Anna Busch ('07) taught at the elementary level for nearly 70 years. She had been a graduate from Sabula in the first 12-year high school class of 1907. Every student at Sabula had Miss Busch for a teacher. Carl Haynes ('53) wrote, "One event I remember well was during the summer of 1944. Jimmy Schroeder's mother had died of cancer. We all felt bad, with Jimmy's dad, Eddie being in the Army and overseas. Jimmy was sent to live with his grandparents Earl and Rose Rogers. Then that same year in December of 1944, when I was in the fourth grade, the principal came to our room calling Miss Busch out into the hall and giving her the news that Eddie Schroeder had been killed in the Battle of the Bulge in the Ardennes forest in Belgium. Her job was to tell Jimmy. I don't know how she did it, because she never told, nor did he. I just remember her telling the rest of the class and what a sobering effect it had on all of us."

Superintendent Neil Mansfield came to Sabula in the fall of 1961. Dan Miller ('64) stated, "He was a free spirit and very kid friendly. He was a promoter. He bought us a trampoline and wrestling mats for the school. He encouraged community events for the promotion of the high school. He brought 'donkey basketball' to the school gymnasium. He put on a dress and was competing in the game when he fell off the donkey and was knocked out. For Bingo nights, he traveled to nearby Clinton, driving his Chrysler Imperial with the push button drive, to help us get prizes. When we went into the businesses to ask for prizes and were turned down, he would go right back in the same store and come out with a free prize for the Bingo night. We had a school walkout and marched to the City Hall because there was a rumor that he was going to be fired. It never happened and Mr. Mansfield stayed as our Superintendent until the late '60s."

Notable Graduates—Herman Schepler ('31) became a professor at the University of Dubuque teaching physics and optics. He invented the rear-view mirror with the dim-bright flip mode.

Joe Taplin ('64) served in the army in Vietnam. He was later employed by the Central Intelligence Agency.

Roger Knapp ('64) was a star baseball pitcher for the Sabula High School team. After serving in Vietnam, he married a Thai native and taught school in Thailand.

Killed in Action—The following lost their lives in service to our country:

Joe Dion, WWI
Alfred Clark, WWII
Robert Clark, WWII
Floyd Guyer, WWII
Clifford Robinson, WWII
Edward Schroeder, WWII
Henry Schroeder, WWII

Pranks—Halloween and turning over outhouses was a universal act in about every town. The perpetrator was seldom identified or caught in the act. One unfortunate incident occurred that chilly October evening, was related by Dick Haynes ('63). "We were out prowling in the alleys and playing around the park. An outhouse became our target. Only this time the joke was on us. Ben Highstrom ('61) was helping turn over an outhouse and his shirt got caught on a nail and he was pulled into the stinky pit."

Though not necessarily a prank, but a memorable science project, was shared by Carl F. Haynes ('53). "One night at the annual school carnival, Dick Lewis ('54) claimed that farts burned blue. We disagreed with him, so he offered to prove it. A group of us snuck upstairs to the darkened science room. Dick laid on his back on the teacher's desk, pulled his legs up to his chest, held a lighter to his butt, farted, and proved he was right. Others attempted that night to out-do him, but he apparently had been practicing and so we were no match for him. The flame was truly blue. Every time I see the Gas Industry advertise the Blue Flame Kitchen, I think of Dick Lewis, the champion."

Closing—Miles and Sabula entered into a reciprocal agreement with the schools exchanging classes. Students were bused either to Miles or Sabula wherever classes were held. James House, the superintendent at Miles, also became the superintendent at Sabula. The Sabula High School closed after graduation in May 1974. In the fall of 1974, the students were bused to Miles to form a new school named East Central High School. In the 87 years of Sabula High School there were 1,009 graduates. The largest class was 29 in 1972. The most numerous surnames of the graduates were: Petersen-22, Johnson-16, Thompson-15, Smith-9, Stoddard-9, Wall-9, and Gage-8. The last to receive a diploma from Sabula High School was Susan Weber (alphabetically).

#85

Sac City High School

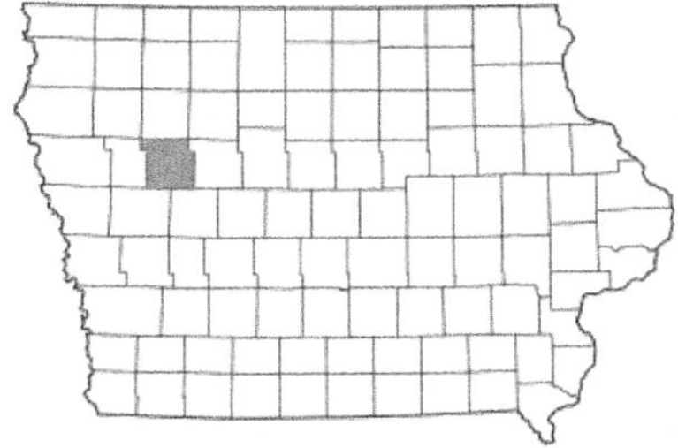

Mascot: Indians
Colors: Red and White
Closed: 2007
Location: Northeast Sac County

Early History—Lands that the Sac and Fox Indians ceded to the United States Government in 1842 encompassed the eastern part of Sac County. Under the terms of this treaty, signed at the Sac and Fox Agency, the Indians living west of a line that ran roughly from present day Ackley (Hardin County) through Seymour (Wayne County) retained the right of occupancy for three years. Also, under the treaty, the Sac and Fox Indians living in the eastern part of Sac County were not legally bound to leave their land until 1845.

Before 1856, Sac was attached to Greene County to the south for political and judicial purposes. The first election for county organization was held on April 27, 1856, when 37 votes were cast for the entire county.

The town of Sac City was platted in 1855 by John F. Duncombe of Fort Dodge, Iowa. The town was named because the Sac and Fox Indians were in possession of the land at the time of the Louisiana Purchase. The names "Sauk and Sac" were interchangeable and derived from the Indian word "Osakwugi" meaning "People of the Yellow Earth."

Railroads—Unlike many towns and cities in northwest Iowa, Sac City's progress was not synonymous with the coming of the railroad. The voters unanimously rejected a bid to subsidize local railroad construction in 1859. Sac City remained unconnected to rail service for 20 years. Numerous rail companies bypassed the county seat. In 1879, the Chicago and North Western (C&NW) constructed the Maple River branch line from Carroll to Wall Lake and extended it north to Sac City. After the C&NW came to town, the population doubled in five years from 595 to 1,200.

County Seat—The first Sac City courthouse was built in 1860. In 1873, the county was obliged to lease rooms to private individuals for accommodation for the County Clerk and Recorder. The bids for the erection of the second courthouse were let on March 13, 1873. A new courthouse was built for $30,000 with a limestone foundation and was considered one of the best buildings in Northwest Iowa. Sadly, the headline in the *Sac Sun* on October 3, 1888 read:

**Sac County Courthouse burned in an hour—
only the bare walls were left.**

While the county was without a courthouse, the citizens of the southern part of Sac County sought to move the county seat and erect a new courthouse in Wall Lake.

Using the $15,000 insurance money and another $15,000 pledged by eight men from Sac City, a third courthouse was constructed on a new foundation. The building was a duplicate of the recently erected Buena Vista County courthouse in Storm Lake. It still was in use 140 years later (2020).

Grand Army of the Republic (GAR)—Sac City organized a Grand Army of the Republic Post in 1884. They erected a substantial brick building named General Sherman Hall. It is the only building in Iowa that stands today as a Memorial in memory of the GAR. A picture taken 19 years after the end of the Civil War shows 64 veterans dressed in their black and blue uniforms in front of the courthouse.

Sac City Institute—In 1892, the Oak Park Normal College was established through the "cooperation of the progressive element" of Sac City. The Baptist denomination accepted the offer of the stockholders to turn the institution over to them and renamed it the Sac City Institute. The doors closed in 1912.

Chautauqua—The white octagonal landmark standing majestically at the entrance to the Sac City fairgrounds is the only complete Chautauqua Building in the state of Iowa. This grand assembly graces the banks along the Raccoon River. Programs, speakers, singers, and men and women of renown entertained there. It was a center for the performing arts and a resource for the discussion of the important issues of the time. A few highlights from the Chautauqua:

- Chautauqua began in 1884 in Chautauqua, New York, as the Chautauqua Lake Sunday School Assembly . . . an educational experiment in the out of school vacation learning.
- Sac City Chautauqua was founded in 1904 with 120 members . . . The first was to secure high-

class entertainment for the area . . . 7-10 days summer shows.

- The octagonal building was built in 1908 on the site of the original tent.
- Best talent in America came to Sac City including; John Philip Sousa, Robert LaFollette, Sweet Shows, Madame Schumann-Heink, William Jennings Bryan, top notch lecturers, comedians, and instrumental solos.
- 80,000 feet of lumber, 120 squares of roof materials, one ton of nails were used in construction of the building. Seating was for 3,000.
- Funds were raised by selling $10 certificates which guaranteed a season ticket for five years.
- Bus tours hosted each year . . . visitors on bus tours declared this structure, "one of Iowa's hidden treasurers."

Early Schools – A two-story frame schoolhouse was built in 1865. This was one of the earliest two-story schools in this part of Iowa. In 1871, a two-story brick schoolhouse was built with the top floor used for a high school. The first commencement was held in 1886 at the Presbyterian Church. Commencements were later held at the Opera House. Every graduate participated in the program with musical or oratorical presentations.

In 1903, a brick high school was constructed. When the doors of the Sac City Institute were closed, a portion of that building and property was sold to the Sac City School District and used for high school purposes until 1936.

The first bond issue to construct a gymnasium failed in 1915. A popular saying in the community was, "Boys do not need a gym to exercise in. They can get plenty of exercise cutting wood." The next time the bond was presented to the community, it passed and a new gymnasium was built in 1921. (This building has stood the test of time and was still being used by the community 100 years later in 2020.) In 1924, a swimming pool was built for $3,818 by excavating under the gymnasium. It is still being used today (2020) with the original tile and pool integrity good after generations in the community.

In 1935, a $50,000 bond issue passed for the construction of a new high school. With the cooperation of the WPA (Works Progress Administration) and the government's $45,000 grant, the new school was built and dedicated in 1937. In 1938, a highlight for the high school boys basketball team was beating the state champion Davenport team in a post-season game in the home gymnasium.

In the twenty years from 1938 to 1958, the enrollment in Sac City Schools had increased from 858 to 1,225 students. That year, two kindergarten classes were held in the bus barn, two classes in the city library, one in the hallway, and others in the gymnasium. In 1960, a bond for $379,000 passed for the additions to the junior high and senior high building to make room for the increased enrollment.

A vote to consolidate the country school districts passed in 1957. With this consolidation, the country schools were closed. One holdout for one more year was Jackson #2. "Jackson #2 was my school, so I was able to finish the eighth grade that last year and the school closed the next year. Every year the eighth grade graduates from the country schools had to take an examination to be allowed to attend high school. I can not remember anyone ever failing the test, though everyone was very apprehensive about having to pass the test. As much as we were quizzed that whole year before, we were very well prepared for any test," remembered Russ Hass ('62).

Sac City Realty, Inc.—In 1968, an 80-acre tract of land which the FFA had been farming, located just south of the school, became available for sale. This site had been designated on different occasions by study groups as a site most logical for future expansion of the Sac Community School building facility. After considerable discussion, it was determined there was no way the Board of Education and superintendent could enter an installment contract which the owners of the property requested. Eight Sac City men organized the Sac Reality, Inc. and acquired the property under contract and then sold it to the school district. The school was able to acquire the funds through the ten mill levy which was voted on and passed by the community to acquire the land.

1970s Bond Failures—Five different proposals were presented to the community in the 1970s. Each time they passed by over 50%, but Iowa law required a 60% supermajority for a school bond to pass. With each subsequent proposal, the project request was changed, but it led to failed votes. Finally, in 1982, the bond passed, and a new elementary building was opened in the fall of 1984.

Yearbook—The school yearbook was called the *Chieftain*. Like most school yearbooks, the students sold ads which helped pay for the publication. The 1917 yearbook had advertisements for Cornell College (Mt. Vernon), and Leander Clark College in Toledo.

The *Chieftain* fifty years later was quite different than the first one in 1917. The following groups and activities were represented in the 1967 yearbook:

- Band with 75 instrumentalists
- AFS Club (American Foreign Study)—24 members with goals of sponsoring a Sac City student abroad, to inspire responsibility to our

foreign student staying here and to instigate interest in AFS

- National Honor Society—14 members
- Thespian and Debate Club—7 members
- Sentinel School paper staff—20 members
- FFA (Future Farmers of America)—46 members
- FBLA (Future Business Leaders of America)—45 members
- FHA (Future Homemakers of America)—42 members
- FTA (Future Teachers of America)—37 members
- Careers in White (Medical-Nursing) Club—29 members
- Dolphin Club—16 members (Swimming Club)
- The football team was winless scoring 6 touchdowns for the season
- Golf—17 boys participated
- Track—27 boys participated
- There were no girls sports

Music—Dean Marshall played professionally with the John Philip Sousa band. He was the band director from 1957-1984. His bands were renowned, and his leadership was directed to each member of his concert and marching bands. Every four years the marching band traveled to Washington, D.C. to participate in the Cherry Blossom Festival and parade. In later years, the marching band traveled to Disney World to perform in early June. The black wool band uniforms were certainly not adapted to the hot Florida sun.

George Glass ('53) told, "We all wanted to be in the band. I can still remember the '1812 Overture.' We practiced it the whole year just for contest. The practice paid off as we got a first at contest. I can still hear that French horn part. We marched and played at VEISHA in Ames that spring, as well."

Sports—The first sports conference was named Coon Valley in the 1920s. After it was dissolved, Sac City joined the Tri-Valley Conference with the five other county seat towns of Carroll, Ida Grove, Denison, Jefferson, Storm Lake, and Sac City.

The next conference affiliation was the Mid-western Conference which was mostly the larger schools of Harlan, Audubon, Denison, Lake City, Carroll, Ida Grove, Jefferson, and Sac City.

Girls basketball was played in the 1920s but was dropped in the 1930s. It was restarted in the 1970s. The 1923 team went to the state tournament but lost in the second round to Cresco 15-13. Audubon became the state champions that year, defeating Mallard 15-11. The 1998 and 1999 girls teams advanced to the state tournament, each time losing in the first round.

Jean Lang ('38) played basketball at Iowa State until called to the service in World War II. After the war, he returned to Iowa State and played football.

The biggest sports rivals were Harlan and Denison in the 1940s. In later years, Ida Grove and Carroll became the big rivals.

Duane Fort ('47) at the age of 90 smiled and said, "My senior year in football we had a perfect record- no wins." The 1959 through 1961 brought another long drought of 25 straight losses.

Bus Drivers—"Sit down, Shut up, and get your feet out of the aisles," was the barking welcome from bus driver Jack Stone. This was the recollection of one his former student riders. Though this may sound rather militaristic, it was the discipline requested on his bus.

Kenny Rahn was also very strict. Frank Richardson ('73) recalled, "One morning we all zipped our coats up over our heads so that he could not see us underneath the coats, and he went ballistic. He made it a big deal. However, when Byron Stone opened the emergency door in the back and hung out, it did not seem to phase him. Dealing with a bus load of noisy children and trying to drive safely would not be everyone's cup of tea."

Teachers—Merwin Rummels was an English teacher in the 1940s and '50s. Duane Fort ('47) recalled, "He had a wonderful demeanor, but he could get your attention." George Glass ('53) commented, "He taught us literature that I still enjoy to this day and how to interpret prose."

Mary Farmer was an English teacher from the 1950s into the 1970s. "She was also the librarian during my years from 1959-62. Her guidance on reading was significant for every student," told Russ Hass ('62). "Mrs. Farmer was the most influential teacher I ever had. She taught Advanced English as well as the general English classes. She was very thoughtful in everything she said, and everything she said was thought provoking," said Mary Richardson Lyman ('67). Mary Richardson Lyman ('67) also became an English teacher and taught over 35 years. *(Author's Note: She had the same wonderful influence on her students.)*

Marian Erhart was the math teacher in the 1950s and 1960s. Her husband, Fred Erhart, was the principal. Russ Hass ('62) recalled, "She made math so interesting. She was really strict, too. It was because of her that I became a math teacher for ten years before coming back to Sac City to farm."

"She was the kindest and most patient person I ever met," shared Mary Richardson Lyman ('67).

Notable Graduates—Wrestling was a sport in the 1920s. Maynard "Spade" Harman ('29) was on the 1932 Olympic wrestling team. He was one of the five original inductees into the Iowa Wrestling Hall of Fame. He was inducted into the National Coaches and Officials Hall of Fame.

John Criss ('45) owned the clothing store in Sac City. He gifted $6 million dollars to the city. Each year his foundation funds projects for the betterment of the community.

Claire Jennett ('46) set a pole vault record (for the time) at the state track meet his senior year in 1946. With his upper body strength, he became a member of the University of Iowa gymnastics team though he never had any training in high school.

Jack Simpson ('44) set a national record in the 100-yard dash at the Compton (California) Relays. His speed was so famous that he was challenged to a race against a horse the following summer at the Sac City fairgrounds. The results were never recorded, so the legend that he raced a horse will just have to stand on its own merit.

Another dash man some three decades later was Frank Richardson ('73). Frank set the class state record and third all-time best record (at the time) in the two-mile run. Following a serious accident, he went to MIT where he won the Division III 10,000-meter championship. He later won the Chicago Marathon and finished 9th at the 1980 US Olympic Marathon Trials. After earning his degree from MIT, he graduated from Iowa State College of Veterinary Medicine with a D.V.M. and received a PhD from Duke in Biotechnology. He was a scientist in Pharmacology, Carcinogenicity and Safety Industry for 30 years.

Killed in Action—Lest we forget, the following Sac City men were killed in action in service to our country:

Harold Brownell ('18), WWI
Glenn Criss ('16), WWI
Bayard Fuller, WWI
Charles Rowe ('06), WWI
Russell Williams ('17), WWI
Norman Bruning, WWII
Guy Conger, WWII
John Currie, WWII
Burton Englis, WWII
George Hansen ('43), WWII
Robert Hink, WWII
Bruce Irwin, WWII
Wilbert Jackson, WWII
Lavern Krenzien, WWII
Donald Lake ('41), WWII
Eugene Lennon, WWII
Vernon Perry, WWII
Richard Skarin, WWII
Jerry White, WWII
Orville Wirtjes, WWII
Russell Wright, WWII
Gerald McKeen ('62), Vietnam
Jimmy Buckley, Vietnam
Randall Freeman, Vietnam
Adrian Hike ('00), Afghanistan

Pranks—Halloween mischievousness in Sac City was not a significant problem. Each Halloween, work on set-up and participation by both the students and parents for the school carnival brought all the students to the gymnasium for the night. The parents helped with the carnival booths. Synchronized swimmers in the school pool would put tokens on the hooks of the children who would redeem them for prizes. Frank Richardson ('73) remembered, "As a kid it was a really big deal to drop the fishing pole line in the water and get a token on the hook from a big high school girl."

Closing—The high school closed following graduation in May 2007. A total of 5,324 graduated from Sac City High School in the 122 years from 1886-2007. The largest class was 98 in 1967. The most numerous surnames of the graduates were: Johnson-51, Irwin-45, Zimmerman-31, Meyers-28, Anderson-25, Smith-25, Glass-24, Lange-24, Hansen-23, Olson-23, Shull-20, Simpson-20 Crabb-19, Larson-19, Miller-18, Russell-18, Baker-17, Lewis-15, and Roose-15. The last to receive a diploma from the Sac City High School was Dawnielle Wallace (alphabetically).

In the fall of 2007, Sac City consolidated with Lake View, Auburn, and Wall Lake to form the East Sac High School at Lake View.

Sac City High School
Sac County, IA

#86

Sacred Heart High School (Templeton)

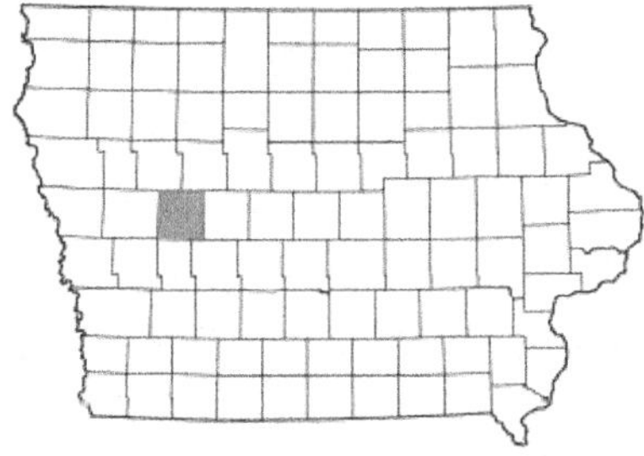

Mascot: Aces
Colors: Red and White
Closed: 1959
Location: Southwest Carroll County

Early History—German settlers came to the Carroll County prairies in the 1870s and '80s. They arrived with their families, culture, and predominantly Catholic faith. Large beautiful Catholic churches were built in the rural towns throughout the county.

Templeton came into existence when the Chicago, Milwaukee, and St. Paul Railroad laid out land for town lots in 1882. It was named after a brakeman and conductor for the railroad. Templeton is in Eden Township and was incorporated in 1883.

In July 1882, prohibition came early to Iowa. Carroll County voted it down by a large majority. This started decades of means and ways to sidestep the law. Injunctions were issued against saloons and wholesale house permits revoked. County revenues to the treasury dropped, as the liquor sales continued to grow. Templeton had four saloons by 1883.

The German farmers of Eden Township were known for distilling alcohol for their own use. The name "Templeton Rye" conjures many images of the special recipe. David Kerkhoff ('56) said, "My father, Alphons Kerkhoff, had the original recipe for what is called Templeton Rye. The distilling of spirits in the countryside allowed struggling farmers to feed their large families during the depression years."

Monsignor Fredrick H. Huesmann was as popular as the distilled "Good Stuff." He was not a fan of prohibition so he lent a hand to the locals when he could. He looked the other way when it came to the still in the basement of the church. He was even known to give a taste to people passing through town. His support was important to his flock and the rest of Templeton.

The years of prohibition enactment were as follows:

1882 The state voted to ban saloons and the sale of alcohol.

1919 Prohibition, the 18th amendment to the constitution, became law.

1932 President Hoover stated Prohibition should be over.

1933 21st amendment, lifting prohibition, passed.

Interesting items from the *Templeton News* and published in the book *Century of Memories 1892-1982*:

1909 Mr. A.W. Stotts reported Templeton was the only lively town along the Milwaukee railroad between here and Council Bluffs.

1920 Smallpox invaded Templeton.

1932 "Little Brown Jug" caused excitement throughout the state, but "now that season is over and all is back to the other 364 days until we celebrate again. Hanging the replica of the 'LBJ' with our Christmas decorations aroused the feeling we are not a law-abiding town. We are proud of our town. We get blamed for every bootlegger in Western Iowa that is arrested, even if he had "Rhubarb Hooch" or the real Templeton Rye."

1932 Preparations were being made for 3.2 beer in advance. Alcohol played a part in the area.

1933 In October, Sacred Heart Church celebrated its 50th Anniversary. Two thousand people attended.

1933 November—Dust storms sweep the area. Was dark at 3:00pm—chickens went to roost.

1935 Carol Heitman, senior at Sacred Heart, had an outstanding record of never missing a day of school and for ten years not missing Mass.

1941 September—Local fans attended a baseball game at Storm Lake. Dizzy Dean pitched. Some were lucky to get his autograph.

Early Schools—In 1883, the first Catholic church was established in Templeton (from the country church which was dismantled and moved). Catholic education began three years after the town was settled. Rev. B.A. Schulte, Mr. Joseph Hunkler, and another lay teacher taught school in the church.

In 1889, a brick structure was built providing adequate classroom and living quarters for the Sisters of Perpetual Adoration from LaCrosse, Wisconsin. Other orders that served the church and school were Sisters of Precious Blood and the Sisters of St. Francis of the Holy Family from Dubuque.

In 1916, an addition to the school was led by Father Erdman that more than doubled the size of the school.

In 1917, Rev. F.H. Huesmann became the pastor. Ninth grade courses were begun under his leadership. The school became accredited in 1924 as a four-year high school.

Music—From the 1934-35 school newspaper, *The Wheel:*

> New members of the Sacred Heart High School Orchestra were James Gerken—trumpet, Raymond Thielke and Gerald Storrs—drums, and Ruth Lechtenberg—piano.

The Wheel was discontinued for the next ten years so activities of the school are not well preserved.

Notable Graduates—Irene O. Galloway attended Sacred Heart High School for two years. She graduated from St. Joseph's Academy High School in Des Moines and was the first girl from Carroll County to be accepted into the Women's Army Auxiliary Corps (WAAC later the WAC) in 1942. Upon enlisting she was asked why, and she simply responded, "because my brother is serving in the Pacific and I saw an article in the *New York Times* regarding opportunities for women." She became a special Assistant to the Secretary of Defense and Director of the WACs. She served in Europe as an advisor for the US Army in Europe. She was awarded many commendations. She played an instrumental role in increasing military pay and re-enlistment bonuses. Colonel Galloway oversaw the establishment of the WAC training facility at Ft. McClellan, Alabama. The north gate entrance to Ft. McClellan is named Galloway Gate, and the road leading to it is named Galloway Gate Road.

Gerald Schreck ('49) served in the Air Force for five years during the Korean conflict. He returned to Creighton University to graduate from the School of Dentistry. He joined the Army Dental Corps during the Vietnam war and retired with the rank of Colonel. His specialty was orthodontics.

Notable Teachers—Sister Margretta was young and tall when she came in the 1950s. Karen Irlbeck Blaha ('59) said, "Girls were not supposed to talk to the boys as they sat in their cars over the noon hour. When the bell rang, I was on my way up the sidewalk and Larry Hicks yelled at me. Of course, I yelled back. Eagle-eyed Sister Margretta was on patrol and I was busted. She made me write 1,000 times the sentence, 'We must abide by all school regulations.'"

In 1950, the first and only lay teacher joined the teaching staff. Mr. Willis Jensen taught social studies, history and coached both basketball teams. He was originally from Audubon and led the red and white Aces to many wins. "We were very fortunate to have had him serving us. He was a very pleasant and talented teacher," remembered Judy Schaeuble Balk ('56).

Killed in Action—Templeton lost six boys in World War II. Of the over six thousand that died on D-Day, there were two from Templeton. They are listed below including where they lost their lives:

Vernon L. Bock, WWII Aleutian Islands
Donald L. Bock, WWII Romania
William Bellinghausen, WWII D-Day France
Robert Bonnesen, WWII D-Day France
Thomas Fox, WWII Battle of the Bulge
Benjamin Wagner, WWII South Pacific

Latin Class—Latin was taught for two years to the freshmen and sophomores. Those not proficient after the first year were required to take a general business course the second year.

Pranks—Just because one graduates from high school does not mean they have the best judgement. The infamous boys of the 1957 graduating class joined the National Guard in Audubon. One night after Guard drill, they dognapped a pooch and brought it back to Templeton. As Rose Mary Greteman Frahm ('59) remembered, "When I came into the school the next morning, Father Buchholz was rushing down the stairs and mumbling, 'Those God damned thieves!' I next met Sister Ermelinde and said, 'Father must be having a bad day.' She said, 'Well you might say that because the County Sheriff is sitting in his office!'" Across town innocent Gene Rupiper was found feeding a hungry dog at his feed store.

Wayne Reiman ('57) admitted, "Though maybe not a prank, I was covered by my mother. I was driving my grandfather's 1937 blue Desoto and had been asked by Leo Schoeppner if I could get out of school to drive a tractor for him. At $1 an hour, it seemed like a deal. So, at noon I jumped into the Desoto and crept around the back side of the church and headed for the country. That night, when I walked into the house, I was met by my mother who said Father Buchholz called this afternoon. I covered for you-but try that stunt again and you will swing for it."

Sports—Football was not played at Sacred Heart. The boys played basketball and spring and fall baseball.

The girls played basketball. The biggest rival was Breda. Other schools played were Arcadia, Viola Township, Bayard, Westphalia, and Panora. A Catholic Youth Organization Tournament was played annually at Ft. Dodge.

The gymnasium was located on the third floor above the grade school. Wayne Reiman ('57) smiled as he recalled, "Every school hated our gym because there was a center beam across the court. You had to shoot from the corners to clear the beam. Of course, we practiced from there a lot, so you might say we had a home court advantage."

Karen Irlbeck Blaha ('59) shared, "I remember as a freshman we had new red and white satin uniforms in 1956. It seemed that the nuns overruled the coach and said that basketball was bad on girls, so we stopped playing basketball at Sacred Heart after that year."

Scrub Day—Every spring, a general all school cleaning day was traditional. David Kerkhoff ('56) told, "We had to carry water across from the church to the school in buckets. We also had to furnish our own buckets and soap. Much of the soap at that time was handmade. Since it was done every May, it didn't seem too much of a chore. As we always looked at it, we got out of class to do Scrub Day."

Polio—One of the six in the all-girl class of 1954 came down with polio. Carol Zubrod Rupiper ('54) was the only one from Templeton to contract the disease. She recovered from the paralysis.

Janitor—A long time and beloved janitor was Matt Daeges. He lived in the house owned by the church. Templeton had one stop sign and it controlled the intersection quite well. Mr. Daeges met another car sideways in the intersection. He is reported to say to the state patrolman in his defense after the accident, "He should have known I never stop at that stop sign!"

Closing—Sacred Heart High School closed after graduation in May 1959. In the 36 years from 1924-1959 there were 301 graduates. The largest class was 20 in 1956. The most numerous surnames of the graduates were: Schoeppner-16, Greteman-8, Trecker-8, Domayer-7, Gerken-7, Schwaller-6, Horbach-6, and Schreck-6. The last to receive a diploma from Sacred Heart High School was LeAnn Wiskus Wessling (alphabetically). In the fall of 1959, the students were bused to Carroll Kuemper High School.

Sacred Heart High School
Carroll County, IA

#87

Sanborn High School

Mascot: Bulldogs
Colors: Maroon and Gray
Closed: 1988
Location: North Central O'Brien County

Early History—Sanborn owes its existence to the western railroad expansion in the 1870s and 1880s. A town site was surveyed in November 1878 when the Chicago, Milwaukee, St. Paul, and Pacific Railroad came through the county. The new station was named Sanborn in honor of George Sanborn, the industrious and energetic superintendent of the Milwaukee Road. There was an 18-stall round house with machine shops, icehouse, and mammoth stockyards built providing many jobs. At one time, there were 21 freighters and four passenger trains that chugged their way into Sanborn every day.

Ray Huibregtse ('54) said, "This community is on the eastern edge of the large populations of Dutch that settled in Northwestern Iowa farming counties." Many Dutch graduated from Sanborn High School. Some of surnames were Van Engen, Vander Vliet, Vandeberg, VanZanbergen, Van't Hof, Van Syll, Vander Heiden, Van Kley, Vander Schaaf, Vander Naald, Vander Woude, Van Wyke, Bruxvoort, Van Roekel, DeJoung, De Berg, Vander Griend, Van Wyk, Van Veldhuisen Van Rees, Verhoef, Vander Haag, DeGrooyer, Van Slot, VanZyl, VanSlot, DeVries, DeVoll, Uitternbogaard, and Huibregtse. (Centennial books written for many communities are an excellent source for history of Iowa towns).

Early Schools—From the *Sanborn Centennial* collection:

> On November 10, 1879 classes began in a school in Franklin Township just outside of town with 21 students. Mr. D. Algyer was 'chosen to learn young ideas how to shoot.' By the next year there were 50 students. By the spring of 1881 there were 95 students attending. . .
>
> C.E. Foote began teaching in Sanborn at this time. The school year was divided into two sessions of four months each, known as the summer session

and winter session. Pupils who wished to study Latin and foreign languages were heard outside of school since the teacher was not permitted to hear them during the school hours.

In July 1881, a contract was issued to erect the first schoolhouse in the new Independent Sanborn District for $4,000-5,000 including furnishings. Controversy over location caused a delay in the construction as some thought the eventual site was too far out of town. The school was completed in January 1882 with only the grammar grades. By 1887, enrollment jumped to 285 students.

In October 1896, the school year started in a new block school which was built for $13,900. It was constructed of Mankato stone, Sioux City brick, and stucco. There was a bell tower. This new building had a large basement for a playroom, fuel (coal) room, and a heating plant. Steam radiators heated halls and rooms.

The first graduating class from the two-year high school was in 1888 with four graduates. The next year there were 15 graduates. In 1888, Superintendent W.I. Simpson started the four-year high school to meet the new accreditation system in the state so there were no graduates that year. The students from the '88 and '89 two-year schools were asked to come back to fulfill the four-year diploma. Some did return. The graduation ceremony was held in the Presbyterian Church.

A model hammer was established in 1912 with ribbons of the 1912 class on it. The hammer was then handed down to the junior class at the Junior-Senior banquet. It symbolized the passing of the senior power to the junior class for the next year. The 1913 class continued the tradition. In 1914, a larger gavel in the form of a croquet mallet was obtained and handed down through the years into the 1970s.

In 1914, an addition to the building with matching block and stucco was completed. The basement was converted into a gymnasium and a floor was laid by the manual training boys for basketball and other athletic events.

Forty-three years after it was built, the school building was condemned, much to the distress and dissention of many community members. In September 1938, a proposal to build a new building in the same block was presented to the community. A bond for $55,000 and a WPA grant for $45,000 to furnish a new building was passed by the voters. One year later, November 10, 1939, the dedication ceremony was held.

Band and Music—An orchestra was organized in 1915. The first *Silver and Maroon* yearbook was first published in 1920. It has an early picture of the school band. Superintendent Edna Putman was the drive behind the band. It played concerts at the park on Saturday evenings at 7 o'clock. Horns honked from the cars around the park and people clapped after each musical selection.

The Sanborn band had many participating students. Mr. Bill Redman was the teacher and he had a dance band. He came in 1956 and was said to be the best thing that ever happened to Sanborn. In 1960, a swing band was started. By 1964, there were 57 in the marching band. The band marched every summer at the Miss Iowa Beauty Pageant in Okoboji. The students secured tickets for the Roof Garden. The band also marched at the Orange City Tulip Festival and the Turkey Days parade in Worthington, Minnesota.

Busing—By the late 1930s, Bob Rozenboom's family lived on the very edge of the Sanborn district. It made for a very long walk to school each day for Galen and "Cork" Rozenboom. Bob planned for a bus transporting the neighborhood children and presented it to the Sanborn School Board. It was approved. He remodeled a Model A Ford car and converted it into a bus large enough to hold seven children. The oldest child would sit in the bucket seat beside the driver and the other children climbed into make-shift seats in the back. According to Galen, each child had a special place to sit. Regulations required that a "school bus" sign be posted on the vehicle while transporting the children. Leola Rozenboom became the bus driver.

Galen remembered walking due to poor visibility and trudging through the blowing snow to the Maranell farm and staying there several days until the fury of the storm was spent. The bus route was discontinued after WW II when the district obtained a manufactured bus which picked up all students. Leola "retired" and never got behind the wheel of a bus again.

Yearbook—The first yearbooks were called the *Dogmatizer*. In 1941, a letterman club—the "S" Club—was organized with maroon and gray for the school colors. By 1949, the yearbook was called the *Bulldog in Review* and in 1953 it became the *Bulldog*.

Notable Teachers—A group of teachers came together to Sanborn in 1953. They each had South Dakota roots and education and taught for many years. It was said at one time that Sanborn teachers had the greatest longevity of teaching in one school in the state of Iowa. That year Harry Elletts, the principal and Henry Glover, Don Noll, and Leonard Anderson joined the faculty.

Mr. Don Noll was a former Marine. He graduated from Drake and coached most sports during the school year and the summer programs. The girls reported that he did not like girls, though he did have some very successful teams. Merne Haack ('61) recalled, "If you were a kid in Sanborn, somewhere along the line you had Mr. Noll for your coach. He was raised in Wisconsin and graduated from York, Nebraska and Drake. He was a great teacher and was such a role model."

One of the South Dakota teachers was Mr. Henry Glover. He took the boys every summer to either Canada or later to Pierre, South Dakota fishing. He had a glass eye. He taught manual arts starting the students in seventh grade with making bread boards. "I still have that bread board," remembered Chuck Comstock ('63). "One day in shop we noticed that Mr. Glover had his glass eye in crooked. The more he would move around the classroom and gesture the more snickering we did. Whispering started as to who was going to tell him that the eye was a kilter. I think we all chickened out, and poor Mr. Glover had to discover it on his own."

Drivers Education—Drivers education was started in 1953. The new first year teacher, Mr. Elletts had the honor of being the first teacher for the program. Glena Oosteenburg VerBrugge ('63) was a student in the car stopped at the only blinking red light in town. After some time being stopped, Mr. Elletts asked politely, "Are you going to go soon?" To which Glena confidently replied, "I'm waiting for it to turn green."

Hot Lunch—Hot lunches were first served in 1946 to students that lived more than a mile from school. The kitchen was located under the stage. The school lunches were served in the basement of the Presbyterian Church. In 1957, with the new addition to the school, lunches became available to all students in a new kitchen and lunchroom. In 1958, in order to educate the large number of 'baby boomer' children, a new elementary building was built. The high school classes were on the top floor of the school building. Music and the lunch room were on the first floor.

Janitor—A legendary janitor was Oscar Gacke. Merne Haack ('61) remembered, "At 6' 5" he ran the show. He was a disciplinarian. He always dressed in blue overalls. He was like a counselor to all of us and had our respect. His daughter Thelma (Babe) Gacke Bagley ('56) was also tall and was a great basketball player for Sanborn. Oscar had three other children who graduated from Sanborn: Grace Gacke Dully ('48), Howard Gacke ('54), and Loren Gacke ('58). Loren was an outstanding athlete.

Sports—Track was started as a sport for the boys in 1913. Girls basketball was started in 1914. Other sports played by the boys were basketball in 1916, football in 1918, and baseball in 1920.

The football program was dropped for one year in the 1970s because of lack of players out for football. Recovery was soon in place and the 1985 football team took second place in the state of Iowa.

The teams played in the Sioux Valley Conference. Other teams in the conference were Aurelia, Alta, Milford, Sutherland, Primghar, Hartley, and Paulina. "It was a tough conference, but it was fun," recalled Mary Loafman Japenga ('65).

The 1970 girls basketball team made it to the state tournament but lost the first game to Farragut. The coach was Don Davis. Alvina Potsma Reitsma ('71) said, "I was really tall as a freshman and played a lot. The education came that year when I got to guard the Everly star, Jeanette Olson. It was no contest for this green freshman."

The boys track team was quite competitive even though Sanborn did not have a running track until the 1970s. Chuck Comstock ('63), nick-named 'Charlie Horse,' was a four-time state indoor runner in the mile and a two time outdoor participant. He told, "Since we had no track, all of our running was done on gravel roads and the railroad right of way. One practice Coach Noll told us to warm up by running the four miles around the section. At another practice, the senior co-captains, Comstock ('63) and Roger VanVeldhuizen ('63), decided to cut it in half by running back along the railroad. The straggling freshmen followed. Waiting at the edge of town was Coach Noll. He grabbed the freshman and told them to rerun the section again but this time do not take the shortcut. When they protested that the seniors did not have to do it, he told them 'when you can run as fast as Comstock you won't have to rerun the section." Chuck continued, "Coach Noll often drove the bus to out of town games and sporting events. He was notorious for claiming he knew of a short cut, which would often get us lost and take much longer to get home. At one such event at the state indoor meet in Iowa City, we stopped to eat at the Amana Colonies at the Old Yoke Inn. One of our players stuck a dinner knife in his pocket when we left the table. One week later, a bill arrived at the high school for the cost of the knife. Merle Vander Woude ('62) fessed up and paid the bill."

Killed in Action—Michael Schultz '64 was killed in Vietnam and is buried at the Sanborn cemetery.

School Closing—The Sanborn High School was closed in May 1968. The most numerous surnames of the graduates were: VanVeldhuizen-19, Raymond-16, Hakeman-15, Potsma-15, Kroese-14, Wright-13, Peterson-11, Smith-10, Reitsma-9, and VanderVelde-7. The largest graduating class was in 1966 with 39 graduates. The last to receive a diploma from Sanborn High School was Diane VanVelduizen (alphabetically). In the fall of 1968, the high school students were bused to their new high school in Hartley called HMS or Hartley-Melvin-Sanborn.

Sanborn High School
O'Brien County, IA

#88

Shelby High School (Shelby Tennant)

Mascot: Cardinals
Colors: Red and Black
Closed: 1991 for Shelby-Tennant
Location: Southwest corner Shelby County

Early History – The town of Shelby dates its origin to the organization and naming of the county by the Iowa legislature in 1851. The county and later the town were named after Isaac Shelby, the Revolutionary War hero, and first and fifth Governor of Kentucky.

The Chicago, Rock Island, and Pacific Railroad laid track through the area in 1868. This connected eastern Iowa from Davenport to Council Bluffs the next year in 1869. The Old Stone Arch railroad bridge east of town over the Little Silver Creek is on the National Historic Registry. This railroad was one of the four that were awarded grants of land to construct their tracks across Iowa east to west. These land grants or right-of-way were in alternating sections on six miles on either side of their tracks. They could be sold to raise monies for the construction of the railroads. At one time this included 4,069,942 acres or 1/9 of all the land in Iowa. In exchange for this land grant, the railroads were to haul government materials and personnel at half price. This agreement continued from 1856 until 1952 when it was canceled. A railroad magazine stated the reduced rates that the government benefited from amounted to one and a half times the price of the land even at the 1990s prices for the land.

In 1866, the first settler in Shelby Township was an Englishman, James Hawkins. He obtained the land on which the town of Shelby now stands from the government for services rendered in the Mexican and Civil Wars.

Shelby townsite was platted in 1870 by Benjamin F. Allen and Thusie Allen on land purchased from James Hawkins. The town was incorporated in 1877.

The railroad's significance to the town and agriculture development are illustrated in the freight transported from Shelby. During the month of September 1880, the company received $15,780 on freight and express charges. A January 1881 news item stated that 14 carloads of livestock were shipped from the Shelby station one morning. In 1882, three hundred eight-five cars of grain were shipped during September, October, and November.

Much of the land not owned by the railroad was an outright gift to soldiers who had rendered distinguished service to their country in the Mexican and Civil Wars. Records from 1881 show that the land was selling from $7 to $12 an acre. The breaking of the prairie was sometimes done by professional prairie breakers at $3 to $4 per acre, but usually each settler had a team and broke his own land.

Early Schools—On February 3, 1870, Shelby Township was divided into two public school districts, North and South. Two years later a portion of Pleasant Township in Pottawattamie County was annexed to the South Shelby District. In the fall of 1870, the first organized public school met with 17 children in a building which was used as a store and hotel. Lizzie Wright from Avoca was the teacher. The next year the school was held in another store that is today (2020) the Farmers

Savings Bank. Twenty-one students were enrolled the second year.

As enrollment increased, it became necessary to build and construct a schoolhouse. Groundbreaking and construction of the first schoolhouse was in 1872.

With continued enrollment increases, a bond for $3,000 was issued for the construction of a two-story square building with a bell tower on the west side of town. (This building was located on the playground just east of the present-day building-2020). The school consisted of primary and intermediate grades. By 1882 an elegant four-room school was occupied

The *Shelby Times* reported on December 20, 1881:

> A brass band added much to the success of school programs . . . This closes a very successful term in our city schools which at present retain their high degree of excellency and rank among the best in western Iowa. Shelby may be justly proud of her public school and the edifice which stands as a monument to the enterprise and literary refinement of its public-spirited citizens.

Graduation exercises were held for the first class of six in 1885. By 1891, another year was added to the high school course.

Two women were elected to the school board in 1887, Agnes Gochenour and Katherine McGwen. Their interest in the educational needs of the youth in the community qualified them to serve well as members of the Board.

It became apparent by 1895 that a separate four-year high school was needed. The enrollment had reached 267 of which 84 were in high school. Bonds were voted and a wooden two-story structure was built for $6,148 and occupied on the first week of October 1899.

Several highlights of this high school building and the times were:

- Literary societies under the names 'Whittier and Lowell' presented many programs to the public on Friday afternoons . . . declamatory contests of orations and recitations were held as early as 1882 . . . entertainment to large audiences were held at the Opera House.
- Latin was studied by many of the high school students . . . school notes of October 5, 1900 state: "We have a Caesar Class of seven students . . . with a beginning class of 19 students, making a total of thirty-eight out of the seventy-seven high school students taking Latin.
- Football in the fall and baseball in the spring were the boys sports.
- A girls basketball team was organized in 1913. Their games were played on an outdoor court until the old Opera House was fitted with equipment for use as an auditorium and gymnasium in 1920.

By 1919, the school buildings were rated inadequate by the state inspectors. By a new law, Iowa school districts could consolidate. The Board of Education proposed consolidation to better serve rural families. On July 28, 1919, after many meetings and discussions, the Consolidated Independent School District of Shelby was formed. It was comprised of eight school districts in Shelby, Harrison, and Pottawattamie counties. The total area was 26,270 acres with an assessed valuation of $3,182,824. That December bonds were voted for a new schoolhouse and site for $175,000. The architect for the building was the famed John Latenser and Sons of Omaha. It was 192 feet long and 122 feet wide and three stories high. This U-shaped neoclassical building was typical of many school buildings that Latenser designed. It is the only known extant building by the firm in Western Iowa. The new building was completed in the fall of 1922.

The school year of 1920-21 opened with 328 children, 205 came from the country and 123 lived in town. The faculty had fifteen teachers and Miss Alice Frum ('03) was the superintendent.

School Lunches—Most schools did not have a school lunch program until after World War II. In the 1920s, the Home Economics class supplemented the lunches brought from home with one five-cent hot dish daily. In 1945, Shelby took advantage of the supplemental help from the government and started serving school hot lunches for all students.

From the *Shelby News* of January 16, 1948:

> Now in its third year, Shelby's hot lunch program has developed into one of the finest in the state and is the largest of any Consolidated school in Iowa. Last year (for the nine-month school period) 41,000 meals were served and $10,010 collected. The grocery bills were $5,447, labor costs $2,313 and new equipment including a refrigerator, roaster, electric mixer and automatic dishwasher cost $1,429. Government support totaled $3,453 . . . Shelby still served its students for 17 cents per meal.

Notable Graduates—Clyde Williams ('97) was an outstanding high school athlete in baseball and football. As the quarterback and Ray Morton ('98) as the halfback, they continued playing at the University of Iowa. While at Iowa, Williams, at five feet 10 inches and 175 pounds, quarterbacked two undefeated teams against the dreaded powerhouses of the time, Michigan and Chicago University (coached by the great Amos Alonzo Stagg). Williams earned ten varsity letters at Iowa: four each in football and baseball, and two in track. He would have owned three more had they awarded the monograms in basketball at the time when he played. In track, he broad jumped over 21 feet when the National AAU record was 23 feet. At the close of his career at Iowa, he was awarded the Max Mayer Prize for excellence in scholarship and athletics.

Clyde finished at Iowa with a Bachelor of Science degree and a degree in Dentistry. He practiced dentistry in Knoxville, Iowa, for two years. He passed up a major league baseball contract and turned to coaching. He was the head coach at Cornell College in Mt. Vernon. In 1906, he went to Iowa State as the assistant football and basketball coach. The next year he became the head football coach and athletic director. The football field at Iowa State University was named Clyde Williams Field until it was demolished in 1975.

Mary Alice Frum ('03) graduated in 1903 at the age of 16. She taught country school for one year before attending Iowa University for two years. She transferred to the University of Nebraska where she received her degree with honors and was an honored member of Phi Beta Kappa. She taught at Lincoln High School and became the superintendent at Carson for five years. Frum returned to her hometown of Shelby where she taught and was the principal for twenty years. She was the named the superintendent in 1920, the year the new three-story high school was built. While walking, she was hit by a car in Omaha and killed. Until the day she died, Alice was a leader in the DAR, Phi Beta Kappa organization in Omaha, and the Eastern Star. At time of her death in 1963 at the age of 77, over $10,000 in memorials were raised by her former students for an annual scholarship.

Janitor—Harold Norman was the janitor for the school for over thirty years. Much of the credit for the excellent condition and general appearance of the school building, the athletic field, and playgrounds was due to his care. Nancy Evans Collins ('68) said, "Harold's love for the school could only be paralleled by his love for all the students. He was respected as much as the superintendent. There wasn't a thing he couldn't fix. He cared for the huge building all by himself. Every morning he stood under the clock and told every student 'good morning!' He walked home for lunch every noon."

Sports—Football was the first sport offered at the school in the 1890s. Enthusiasm for the sport was so popular because of the early great teams and stars Clyde Williams and Ray "Buck" Norman.

The 1947 football team led by their star halfback Dick Norman ('48) was undefeated. In 1948, the Shelby six-man team went to Prairie City for a game which was billed by the *Des Moines Register* as the one to determine the state champion. Shelby lost the game. Shelby had an earlier loss that year to the Nebraska State Champions, Nebraska Deaf 34-33.

A transition from six-man to eight-man to eleven-man occurred upon joining forces with Tennant in 1959. Two outstanding players in the early 60s were Dave Robinson ('63) and Dan Messerschmidt ('63). Messerschmidt once made 50 tackles in a single game. They both had many school records in track and field.

Boys basketball began in Shelby in 1914. They first played outdoors on a hard-packed dirt court. The next year, 1915, they were invited to an invitational tournament at Simpson College in Indianola to include the fastest sixteen teams in the state of Iowa. The first game was won by Shelby before bowing to Garden Grove in the quarter-finals. They were invited back in 1925. This time they took second place. In 1941 the Shelby boys reached sub-state in Des Moines. Sub-state consisted of 16 teams—eight "A" and eight "B" with two of each advancing to state. Shelby and Wiota were in the "B" division, and Wiota won the game on a shot at the buzzer.

The 1950 boys basketball team, under first-year head coach, Charles Hess, found their way to the state tournament in Iowa City. After winning their way in the class "B" competition, they drew "AA" Keokuk for the first round. Shelby shocked the state by defeating the giants from that city. The Keokuk team included Bill Logan, who later became the all-time scoring leader at the University of Iowa.

In 1956, under the direction of the new head coach, Dallas McLaughlin, the Cardinals made it back to the state tournament. The squad did not have any seniors. In 1957, the boys went undefeated and again made it back to state. They were eliminated in the first round by St. Marys by one point.

The girls basketball was organized in 1913 and won many county, conference, and sectional competitions. They were just one game away from state in 1938, when they lost in the district finals to Coon Rapids. Pat Messerschmidt ('70) held the one-game scoring record for the school of 67 points.

Killed in Action—Shelby men killed in action were:

Rose Buman, WWI influenza
Willis Coker, WWI influenza
Clyde Howard, WWI influenza
Harry Johnson, WWI influenza
Howard Movery, WWI
Wilson Arnold Morris, WWI
Daniel Branstiter, WWII
James Dea, WWII
Everette Delph, WWII
Miles Miller, WWII
John Rihner, WWII
Russell Starner, WWII
Donald D. Noehren, Korea
Allan Pittman, Vietnam

Notable Teachers—Lynn McBride taught English, Speech, and Drivers Education. Pat Dea Honeywell ('70) rememberd, "He was a wonderful teacher. He prepared us so well for college that his students often did not have to take English in college."

Ernst Fuhs was the principal and coach in the 1960s and 1970s. There were no counselors at the school and Mr. Fuhs guided the students in their future career aspirations. Pat Dea Honeywell ('70) fondly recalled, "Mr. Fuhs called me in to his office because I had not signed up to take the ACT test. I told him, 'I can't afford to go to college so why would I pay money to take the test if I wasn't going to use it?' He encouraged me to take the test anyway and I did very well on the test. Twenty-five years later I was able to use those test scores when I went back to college at Iowa Western and got my degree."

Pranks—An incident was avidly watched from the windows of the high school in the spring of 1969. A possum somehow had been hoisted to the top of the flagpole and the cords were cut at the bottom. The culprits were never apprehended but the entire school watched in amusement as the janitor, Harold Norman, tried to get the possum down. The flagpole fell over after his long attempts standing on a ladder had failed. Class of 1969 was suspected to be involved because they collected funds to construct a new flagpole for the school.

Senior Trips—The senior classes of 1962, 1963, and 1964 went to Chicago by train. The 1965 class journeyed to Okoboji and all returned sunbaked.

The 1968 seniors chartered a bus to Colorado. They worked hard at magazine sales and concessions to help pay for the trip. Edna Pike was the English teacher and the class sponsor and chaperone for the trip. One activity she scheduled for the tour was a visit to the Open Door Mission revival meeting. Nancy Evans Collins ('68) vividly recalled the event, "We all sat down with these individuals. It was something that none of us had ever imagined. They reeked with body odor and the speakers were so passionate. It was a wonderful education for me that I will always remember. Mrs. Pike was quite clever as she would hear the doors of our motel room creak open at 2:00 am and she too would poke her head out of her door and wave to us to not try it."

The class of 1970, with 36 seniors, also went to Colorado by bus. The highlight was a trip to a dude ranch. Not that girls always get credit for their hijinks, but as Pat Dea Honeywell ('70) remembered, "Somehow all of the boys 'flies' on their underwear got sewed shut. It was really the start of the 'hippy' thing. We did not do any great educational things as I recall but that dude ranch was a spectacular setting and the mountains were incredible."

Closing—In 1959, negotiations with the school boards from Tennant, Minden, and Shelby were held to consider reorganization. The Shelby and Tennant districts agreed on reorganization. By a vote of 384 to 12 on May 29, 1959, approval was given by the citizens of the two districts to join. The high school continued in the fall of 1959 at the Shelby location and was called the Shelby Tennant High School. After graduation in 1991, the high school students started whole grade sharing with the neighboring school in Avoca. This sharing continued for five years until July 1, 1996, when the Shelby-Tenant and Hancock-Avoca Community School District consolidated to become AHST High School in Avoca.

In the 107 years from 1885-1991, there were 1,895 graduates from Shelby and Shelby-Tenant High School (which included 830 after the school combined with Tennant in 1959). The largest class was 39 in 1977. The most numerous surnames of the graduates were: Dea-28, Peterson-28, Jensen-23, Messerschmidt-22, Robinson-22, Evans-21, Kern-20, Anderson-18, Linn-18, Thies-17, Miller-15, Petersen-13, Von Eschen-13, Davis-12, Johnson-12, Brown-10, Hansen-10, and Young-10.

The last to receive a diploma from Shelby Tenant High School was Carrie Coleen Wahling.

Shelby High School
Shelby County, IA

#89

Shueyville High School

Mascot: None
Colors: Maroon and Gold
Closed: 1955
Location: North Central Johnson County

Early History – The town of Shueyville was named after Jacob Shuey who, with his family, donated the land for the town site in Jefferson Township. He also donated the land for Western College in southern Linn County. Western College was affiliated with the United Brethren Church. It became the Leander Clark College in 1867. Leander Clark College was moved to Toledo, Iowa, and went bankrupt in 1919. The College was absorbed into Coe College and came back to Linn County in Cedar Rapids.

The railroad bypassed Shueyville when it was laid one mile north of town and on west through the town of Swisher.

The town had a population of 108 in 1880. In the 1880s, immigrants from Czechoslovakia settled in Linn County and the Shueyville area to farm the rolling prairie lands. "When I was in the first grade in 1943, every one of my classmates had a Czech last name," remembered Marvin Prachar ('54). He told, "It was said that my ancestors came to the Shueyville area when it had a population of 28 people living in the town. With all of the Czech's in the area it is believed that others did not feel comfortable moving into the town."

Early Schools – At a teacher meeting in the summer of 1888, a paper written by Frank Sulek, Sr. addressed his ideas about education. Public sentiment became so strong that the Jefferson Township established a high school located in District #2. They procured a teacher and provided a course of study for a high school.

After a five-month trial, the electors decided to add three more months. It was voted to continue the high school under the community management for a period of five years.

In June 1927, the board approved plans for the Jefferson Township High School. Approximately $1,200 of donated work and money was raised to relieve some of the burden to the taxpayers. This made the total cost to the taxpayers $2,000 for the new four-room building. This building still stands (2020) and is on the National Historical Register. It is used for a community building and city hall.

In 1936, a room in the basement was added for $3,000 with running water and indoor sanitary toilets. The outside toilets were moved inside using big metal containers. Water flush toilets were installed in 1949.

Sports—Football was not played at Shueyville. Boys and girls basketball was played at Western College against rivals Ely, Walford, and Solon. Later games and practices were played at the CSPS (Czech) Hall in Swisher. Kathryn Poula Birky ('54) recalled, "We had to drive cars over to Swisher for basketball practice at the CSPS Hall. It was small but fun to play six-on-six on that court. We were creative in some of our fun. On the way back to school we would stop our cars and pickup the orange and black caterpillars crossing the road. Back at school, we would quietly release them, and they would be all over the rooms. Superintendent Earl Silka became perplexed and furious by this invasion of the cute little caterpillars."

Band—A Shueyville school band played in the summer at Riverside, Washington, North Liberty, and Lone Tree communities.

School Activities—Oratorical contests, class plays, and band concerts were all offered at the high school. Skip days by the seniors were occasions when they headed to Wisconsin, Minnesota, and various places in Iowa.

An article in the *Cedar Rapids Gazette*, December 1, 1942, told the story of the early war years and how it affected all Americans:

Zalesky, Supt. Sedlak Leave for New Orleans on their Victory Trip

The "Victory vacation" started this morning when Superintendent William Sedlak from Shueyville high school and senior Joseph Zalesky left for New Orleans to assist in the christening of a Liberty ship there on Thursday December 3.

They will represent the 28 students from Shueyville high school who gathered a total of 135,927 pounds (68 Tons) of scrap metal or 4854.5 pounds per students to the recent October scrap drive. The Shueyville students topped all Iowa schools in last falls scrap drive on a per capita basis. As a result, they sent a representative to New Orleans to attend the christening of the victory ship Samuel Kirkwood, named after Iowa's Civil war Governor. The first basketball game of the season between Shueyville and Tiffin has been canceled because of the trip. Sedlak is the coach of the team and Joe as the center and there are only 9 boys out for the squad.

A total of 3,200 Tons of scrap from Johnson County was collected.

To make the scrap collection possible, farmers dragged their scrap iron to the ditches to augment the effort of the school students.

Yearbooks—A copy of the 1913 yearbook for Jefferson Township High School showed graduation at the Shueyville United Brethren Church directly across the road. There was a special relationship between the church (later to become the Methodist Church) and the school. The church was the site of baccalaureate and graduation ceremonies.

Alumni Banquet—Each May, starting in 1895, the Alumni of Shueyville met for their annual reunion. The following song is sung at the closing of the alumni banquet:

Shueyville Will Shine
Shueyville will shine tonight
Shueyville will shine tonignt.
She'll shine with beauty bright
All down the line.
Won't she look neat tonight
Dressed up so fine?
When the sun goes down
And the moon goes up
Shueyville will shine!

Notable Teachers—Cleo Engrave taught English from the 1940s until the school closed in 1955. She directed the school plays and was an uncertified school counselor helping students with their choices for careers after high school. Kathryn Poula Birky ('54) said, "When we were practicing for the school plays at night, Mrs. Engrave would come to our house so she wouldn't have to drive home and back to school for practice at night. She had much in common with my mother, as they were both teachers."

Notable Graduates—Marvin Sedlacek ('48) was called to the office of Mrs. Engrave a few weeks before graduation. She asked "What career do you plan to pursue? Do you want to be a farmer? 'NO', he replied. Do you want to be a factory worker? 'Again, the answer was 'NO!' Then you better consider going to college," she suggested. "I believe you should pursue mechanical engineering as a field of study." Marvin followed her advice and receive his BSME from the University of Iowa. One week after receiving his MSME, he reported to Ft. Riley, Kansas, and was assigned to the Corps of Engineers unit. Overseas assignments were in France and Germany where he helped plan and build runways. After discharge from the Army, he spent a career in the Space Division of General Electric as a propulsion engineer on the Nimbus

Weather Spacecraft, the Defense Systems Communication Spacecraft, and Upper Atmosphere Research Space Craft. Certainly not quite like a farmer or a factory worker, thanks to Mrs. Engrave, his contributions to our county may have been much different.

Edna Bowersox ('25) received her PhD and taught in college in Michigan and the University of Iowa. She was also a missionary abroad with the Methodist Church.

Arlene Reyman Boddicker ('46) was noted at the Accordion School of Music in Cedar Rapids. She took students all over the Midwest to perform.

Leonard Reyman ('43) had his own big band and played pop and big band sounds throughout the Midwest. He became a large and successful farmer in the area.

Kathryn Poula Birky ('54) graduated from Coe College School of Music. She taught piano and organ to students for 60 years and continues to this time (2020) at the age of 83.

Pranks—Marvin Pospisil ('53) is remembered for picking up a dead skunk when returning from basketball practice in Swisher. He placed it, with the encouragement of fellow pranksters, between the radiator and engine of Superintendent Earl Silka's car.

Closing—The Shueyville High School (Jefferson Township High School) closed following graduation in 1955. The students were bused the next year to the newly opened Prairie High School. There were 386 graduates in the 61 years from 1895-1955. The largest classes were 14 graduates in 1939, 1943, and 1945. The last class in 1955 had four graduates, all with Czech last names—Hadacek, Prachar, Serbausek, and Teslik. The most common surnames of the graduates were: Bowersox-35; Novotny-15; Netolicky-12; Jansa-8; Louvar-8; Yessler-7; Smahel-6; Vavricek-6; Tureck-5; Ziskovsky-5; Kephart-4; Volesky-4; and Zalesky-4. Edward Teslick was the last to receive a diploma from Shueyville High School (alphabetically).

Of the graduates there became 50 farmers, 46 teachers (including professors), 45 business executives and salesmen, 20 skilled workers, 15 secretaries, 7 doctors, 5 public officials, 7 builders, 3 engineers, 3 full-time religious workers, 2 career Army, 1 lawyer, and 1 funeral director. *(Author's Observation: there are no homemakers counted in this listing.)*

Shueyville High School
Johnson County, IA

#90

St. Charles High School

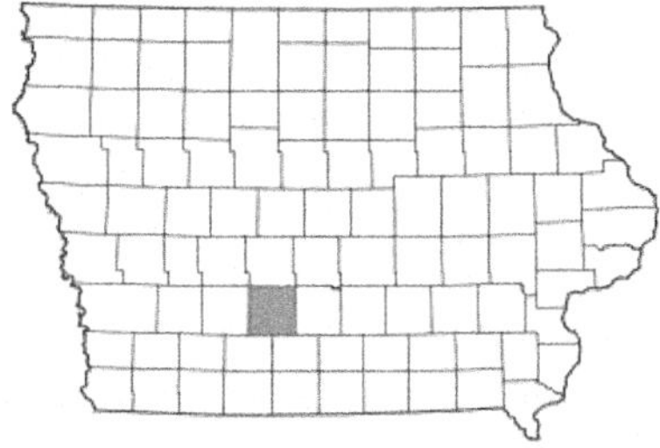

Mascot: Travelers/Travelerettes
Colors: Blue and Gold
Closed: 1958
Location: East Central Madison County

Early History—St. Charles is in South Township and named after St. Charles, Missouri. In 1846, the large Clanton family, including Joel M., Isaac, and Charles, and Caleb Clark along with their wives made claim and built homes near the present-day St. Charles location. This was the same year the Mormons headed west across southern Iowa, as well as the year the state was admitted to the Union as the 29th state on December 28, 1846 in a bill signed by President James K. Polk. St. Charles was laid out in 1851 by George Hartman and Jesse C. Young. It was platted in 1852 and incorporated in 1876.

Early Schools—St. Charles was a subdistrict of South Township school district. The first structure was a one-room building erected in 1858. It was replaced in 1877 by a two-room building. In 1888 another two-room structure was added, and a three-year high school was organized. In 1889, St. Charles became an independent district. The school became a four-year high school in 1908.

A beautiful two-story brick structure consisting of eight rooms and a basement was erected in 1911-1912 for $15,000. At this time St. Charles boasted of a school as good as any town of its size in the state of Iowa.

School Board Minutes—Exceptional school board minutes beginning in 1917 are preserved and the following represent a few of the items brought to the board over 40 years:

December 17, 1917—The matter of grades talked over . . . Mueller moved that an average of 80% with none below 65% be recognized. Motion carried . . . teachers wish to know whether they will be paid for the time school was closed for repairs of the boiler and furnace. The school board said no, but the teachers are to teach the full time and be paid full time. The school board decided no school Monday and Tuesday December 24 and 25, and then have school the rest of the time.

President Brooks stated that there was a petition to discontinue the teaching of German and removal of all German books at once. The above is copied by the Secretary after its receipt December 18, 1917. The school board said they could not act on a petition of that kind without consulting the State Superintendent even if they have the petition present.

July 5, 1918—German books in hands of F.B. Graves and any at the schoolhouse belonging to the school are to be burned Saturday evening in Street by members of School Board. On account of rain and bad weather the German books were not burned Saturday evening but were burned Monday evening as directed above.

July 24, 1918—The securing of teachers was discussed, and collection of Jackson Township tuition was discussed. It was decided that all or as many of the School Board as can go shall go in a few days to Indianola (Simpson College) to source teachers and see about tuition (finding qualified teachers was difficult at this time).

October 4, 1918—Paul Lindsley ('19), Bennie Como, and Paul Anderson ('20) came in to ask the School Board to help them or source a place to play basketball.

August 22, 1931—motion to buy 24 seats, 6 chairs and a toilet for $21.00.

April 9, 1934—motion that hauling water from school well be stopped and that pump shall be pad locked at night, and that notice be published in *St. Charles News*.

July 1, 1936—motion to hire Willard Collins and Nick Dorrell at 35 cents per hour to paint the building.

September 20, 1936—motion to trade typewriters if get $35 trade in value . . . new typewriters to be four noiseless and one standard.

October 27, 1938—motion to install two urinals in boys' toilet at $165.

April 21, 1939—motion to buy six ball bats & 100 folding auditorium chairs.

October 30, 1939—motion to dig and well, 6 feet in diameter at $3.50/ft to sand and $8/ft. thru sand.

March 18, 1940—motion to pay Dr. Sayre bill for vaccinations—$63.00.

November 4, 1940—Board decided to discontinue Normal Training as not a sufficient number of students wanted it.

March 19, 1945—motion to buy a power lawnmower . . . motion that Eleanor Parker be permanently dismissed from school on account of her physical condition.

July 1, 1947—resolved that the school district cooperate with the Burch-Osceola Railroad committee in opposing the abandonment of the Burch-Osceola branch of the Burlington Railroad.

July 26, 1948—petition to vote bonds for $10,000 for purpose of building or buying a dwelling for residency of School Superintendent or teachers presented.

April 27, 1950—payment for new dwelling for superintendent $5,000.

March 30, 1953—motion to pay $35 for T.V. aerial for Superintendent's house.

April 4, 1955—motion to bus students to Winterset for polio vaccinations.

January 9, 1956—motion that school owned instruments rental fee (band) for $1.50 per month.

November 18, 1959—letter from the State Board of Education demanding consolidation, signed by State Superintendent J.C. Wright and assistant State Superintendent Paul Johnson.

August 29, 1960—a follow up, curtly written letter to the School Board demanding closure of the high school and again signed by the State Superintendent of School J.C. Wright.

Bus Driver—Charlie Clark was driving a 1937 4-Cylinder Chassis school bus on February 10, 1943. He was paid $80 per month for driving the bus. The bridge on the north side of Hanley over the Clanton Creek had been constructed in 1885 and last repaired in 1911. Charlie was in low gear as he approached the bridge when a cracking, splitting noise told him the bridge was going down and in a split second he pressed on the gas and shot the bus across. The boards under the rear wheels went down. The increased speed carried the bus out of danger. Added to the crashing of the breaking timbers were the screams of terrified children riding the bus. Charlie later admitted it was a nerve-racking experience, and one he did not care to repeat. The bridge was finally closed by the Board of Supervisors seven months later in September 1943.

There were seven bus routes in 1921 with driver wages ranging from $65-$105 a month. By 1929, there were eight routes with the wages ranging from $75-$100 a month. During the Depression years there were eight routes, but the wages had dropped to $50-70 per month.

Notable Graduates—Van Melvin Davis ('61) was a Rhodes Scholar graduating from Simpson College 1965. He received his BA and MA from Oxford University in London and a PhD from the University of Virginia in 1972. He became a professor in history and political science at National Park Community College in Hot Springs, Arkansas for 38 years. A well-published writer of Civil War history and the Presidents Washington, Jefferson, and Lincoln, his works are at 14 prominent universities from Harvard to around the country. He was a lover of animals and ran in 60 marathons. He finished the Boston marathon five times and the Pikes Peak Marathon eight times.

Following graduation Theodore McClure ('54) enlisted in the United States Army. He graduated from Simpson College Summa Cum Laude in Biology and then attended the University of Oklahoma College of Medicine and received a PhD in neuroanatomy. He became a professor at the University of Oklahoma and University of Missouri College of Medicine and continued research in neurological diseases.

Killed in Action—These Charles City men lost their lives in war. Lest we forget:

Ralph Glen Eppard, WWI Influenza in training in Arkansas
Alva C. Gripp, WWI France
Plennie H. Williamson, WWI Influenza at sea to France
Earl Smith, WWII
Gerald Stump, WWII France

Notable Teachers—Orma Howard was a legend at St. Charles who taught at the elementary level for many years. Doris Lathrum Downs ('57) recalled, "She had never married, and we all loved her. She was one that we all could hug, and we carried such respect for her all the way through our school years."

Lyla Woolery Lynch was another elementary teacher. Ed Downs remembered, "She told me at the beginning of the second grade that if I ever did anything wrong that she would tell my parents. And she did." She later became a principal in the Des Moines schools.

Sports—Football was not played at St. Charles. The girls basketball team surprised Kathy Seibert Beaman's ('59) mother. She challenged them if they would beat St. Marys she would serve the whole team a chicken dinner. They faced the challenge and Mrs. Seibert had a delightful chicken dinner at her home for the team and Coach John Warren.

Pranks—In the middle of the night an innocent little goat was tied to the school bell at 1:00 AM and the bell could be heard ringing throughout the town. The goat's owner was Dale Beaman ('50), however, he was never implicated in the deed. Art Faust, the janitor, was summoned to remove the bleating caprine. When Mr. Faust dragged the goat, it planted its feet and damaged the gymnasium floor. Dale may have been innocent to the event, but his father had to pay for the damage to the floor since the goat came from the Beaman's place.

A flock of chickens made their way up the fire escape and were fluttering around the books in the study hall. Ed Downs, Fred Smith, and Wally Seibert had crawled up the fire escape with the hens and were to hand them off to two guys inside the unlocked door into the study hall. In trying to hand off the frightened birds, they escaped. The chickens' overnight in the study hall did not do a large amount of damage as they just roosted the night away. Interrogations the next morning found Harold Davis grinning and the chicken caper was busted. These boys did not graduate from St. Charles, not because of their chicanery but because the high school was closed after their junior year.

Dale Beaman ('50) had found a warm place to hide out along the heating ducts above the home economics room. As he slept above the classroom with his comrades John Ayers ('50) and Donal Bryant ('50), the ceiling gave way and they came crashing into the home economics room. With girls screaming and the dust flying, the boys were identified as they ran from the room. "Following a half hour dressing down by the superintendent, it wasn't anything like the hour-long lecture that I received when I got home," remembered Dale Beaman ('50).

Senior Trips—The annual school trip or skip day was a time honored event. The class of 1950 made it a day to the Ledges in Boone County. The 1957 class took a school bus to the Ozarks. The 1959 class headed to Chicago by bus. Either by being in the good graces of the chaperones or they were angelic seniors, no significant stories could be remembered by three class members on these senior trips.

Yearbook—The first school yearbook was published in 1947 titled the *Atomic Bomb*. It is not known the significance of the title (18 months after the Japan bombings). The names of the yearbooks were in the hands of the yearbook staff as the names changed to be called the *Blue and Gold*—1955, *The Echo*—1959, and the *Charger*—1960.

School Plays—In many schools the English department teacher directed the junior and senior plays. The senior class play of 1959 was *The Case of the Missing Heirs*. The main character was a Mrs. Allerdyce Beaman played by Kathy Seibert ('59). The irony in acting as Mrs. Beaman in the play is that Kathy married a Beaman—Dale Beaman ('50)—four years later.

Polio—Jack Roland Daniels ('56) and Dave Young ('56) contracted polio in 1953 and 1954. Both recovered from the disease with only slight issues.

Closing—St. Charles High School closed in May 1961. In the 69 years from 1893 through 1961 a total of 741 graduated from St. Charles High School. The most numerous surnames of the graduates were: Pickin-20, Downs-17, Johnson-15, Lathrum-15, Anderson-13, Armstrong-13, Strable-11, Gamble-10, and Young-9. The largest classes were 20 graduates in 1939, 1956, and 1960. The last to receive a diploma from St. Charles High School was Don Smith (alphabetically). In the fall of 1961, high school students were bused to the new Interstate 35 High School at Truro.

St. Charles High School
Madison County, IA

#91

Thompson High School

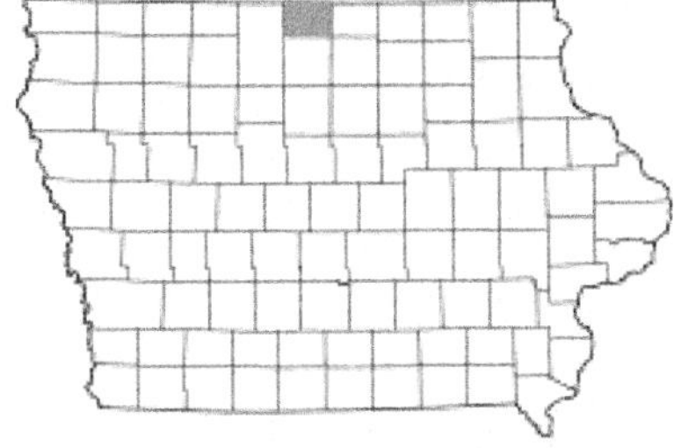

Mascot: Cubs
Colors: Green and White
Closed: 1989
Location: Winnebago County

Early History—The town of Thompson started in 1892. A pair of brothers who were land owners and connected with the new railroad coming through northern Iowa arranged for a new town. It was to be named after Jasper Thompson. Mr. Thompson's initial presentations on the new town were published in the *Winnebago-Hancock Summit* (Forest City) in late February or early March 1892.

> The Chicago and Iowa Western Land and Town Lot Company owns 4000 acres in the geographical center of Winnebago County. Upon this large body of land they have located the town of Thompson. This company has secured the publication of a newspaper, the "Thompson Herald". . . has organized the Bank of Thompson . . . contemplated the building of a system of water works... Don't dream for a moment that we will creep along for two or three years to have a town of 1000 people—we expect to reach that in a year . . . to push the town of Thompson and spare no expense in doing so . . . surrounded by a vast stretch of beautiful rolling prairie and native timber . . . town at this date has but one hotel, one store, Post Office, Bank, and printing office... It is so far without a railroad . . . now one being constructed that will be running through Thompson by June 1, 1892. The natural situation of this new "Los Angeles" . . . rivaling the booming towns of California in her balmy days . . .

Many Norwegian immigrants were attracted to this area. One was the druggist, C.T. Fletcher, who wrote this version of first setting his sight on Thompson:

> The town of Thompson first showed its life in the spring of 1892. From the top of a freight caboose, as we pulled over the hill east of town, I first beheld its budding life. This was the last days of October 1892. By my side was my beloved and life-long friend, the late F.W. Thompson, who was active in the early years of the town . . . buildings of the town mirage to view . . . one of them showed large and brick red . . . later in the day I learned that this was the hotel, and I also discovered the deception of Mr. Thompson, as the building was not

brick, but a framed covered with sheet iron and painted in imitation of brick . . .

Early Schools—The Independent School District of Thompson was formed in 1894. School was held prior to this in two locations. The first school met in a room over a store. Later, a temporary place was provided with three lots south of the first school. This building was erected by the parents with school age children and had one room with one teacher.

With the formation of the independent district, plans were made for the construction of a new building. In May 1894, work began on a new two-story, four-room school. Only the first floor was used until 1897 when a ninth grade was added to the school. Within two years, a tenth and eleventh grade were added.

The textbooks used were *Harper's Reader* and *Baldwin's Reader, Maxwell's School Gram-mar,* Arithmetic by Milne, *Harper's Natural Advanced Geography;* History: Montgomery and Barnes Advanced, *Steele's Science: Hygienic Physiology and Pathfinder Physiology;* Music: oral and written.

In July of 1902, a special Norwegian school opened in the Thompson Public School. Children became acquainted with knowledge of their native country by attending this four-week session. There is no account if this was for one summer session or continued in later years.

The first graduating class of the three-year high school was in 1900. The commencement in the spring of 1905 had two graduates in the class.

Another early graduation announcement presented four female graduates. It listed their graduation theses which was part of the ceremony. The theses were memorized and 30 minutes in length.

Ora Hamlin—"Why women Should be Educated"
Stella Severs—"Influence"
Ida Peterson—"Luck and Puck"
Emma Hanson—"Women in History"

By 1915, the school building needed an update. An election was held in February of that year for the purpose of issuing $30,000 in bonds for the construction. Construction began three months later, and the old building was sold and moved. Since the new building was not completed over the summer, classes were held in various places throughout town. In the fall of 1915, the school became a four-year high school. The new building was completed by December 20, 1915. It consisted of 23 rooms in a four-story building: a 30′ x 50′ gymnasium and a 50′ x 70′ assembly with a 12′ x 30′ stage. In 1924, enrollment had increased so much that another two-story building was erected across the street north of the high school.

When the four-year course of study was introduced in the fall of 1915, both Norwegian and Latin were included in the required curriculum for all juniors and seniors.

The mortgage for this new brick school built in 1915 was burned in November 1934 during a jubilee banquet held at the school. A photo of this mortgage burning banquet shows 131 attending with the men in their coats and ties and the women in their dresses and hats for a sit-down dinner. They were served by 20 cooks and waitresses dressed in white.

These schools adequately served the school system for another ten years when a $6,000 addition was constructed and connected to the south side of the street. A grant from the WPA was received to help pay for the construction. The gymnasium was the largest in the county. Two more additions were completed in 1952 and 1953. Enrollment peaked in the 1950s. In 1955, Thompson had an enrollment of 444 students and employed 30 teachers.

Construction of an industrial arts and a vocational agriculture classroom and additional general classrooms were completed in 1967.

Band—The band was pictured in a 1935 photo with 35 members. The drum major wore a tall white hat and director Leonard Miller wore a white uniform and band hat.

A Drum and Bugle Corps was formed in the 1950s. Following an appearance at Fort Dodge, the group received a congratulatory letter from Vice President Richard Nixon. A proud photo of the Corps showed seven twirlers, a majorette, six drummers, and eight buglers.

Yearbook—The first yearbook, *The Cub*, was in 1933. Features in the yearbook were:

- Dramatics Club with so many members (29) that the group had to be divided in half with each meeting on alternating Wednesdays.
- A glee club with 57 members with the boys all dressed in coats and ties and the girls in their pretty dresses.
- Orchestra had 29 members and there were nine boy violinists and six girl violinists.
- The girls basketball team had to take an oath before the season stating: "These girls 'solemnly swear' to keep all basketball rules and keep them with a good attitude."

Janitors—A father and son were dedicated custodians at the Thompson community school for over 70 years. When Walt Pierce retired after thirty years in 1969, his son Brice Pierce ('51), who had already been working at the school as a custodian for 17 years, continued in his footsteps. Brice continued in service to the buildings and property of Thompson schools for a total of 40 years. Brice took his son, Gary Pierce ('71) with him each morning at 5:00 AM to peel potatoes in the boiler room for the hot lunch program for that day. Besides his custodian duties, Brice drove the school bus for nearly ten years. He had morning and afternoon routes plus the kindergarten route at noon. He rushed to get his cleaning done to drive the night activities bus for out of town ballgames.

Killed in Action—The Thompson community had a large number of servicemen lose their lives in the wars of the 20th century. Lest we forget:

Albert Christopherson, WWI
James Dray, WWI
Donald E. Brown, WWII
Kermit Dahlen, WWII
Carroll Fisher, WWII
Arthur Johnson, WWII
Joseph Klei, WWII
Robert Larson ('44), WWII
John Chester Myre ('35), WWII
Irwin H. Penning ('35), WWII
Claire Tapager, WWII
Bevis A Underbrakke, WWII
Arlyn Burke, Korea
Dean Holland ('50), Korea
Daryl Dean Green ('61), Vietnam
Keith F. Smith ('53), Vietnam

Sports—Thompson played in the State Line Conference with Ledyard, Rake, Ringsted, Wooden-Crystal Lake, Lincoln Central, Sentral (Fenton), Burt, Armstrong, and Swea City. The greatest rivals were Lakota, Burt, Crystal Lake, and Titonka.

The boys basketball team of 1967-68 was an exceptional team led by junior John Harlson ('69). They defeated Buffalo Center, a team Thompson had lost to twice during the regular season. A score of 76-72 allowed the team to reach the sectional tournament. In the first two rounds, Thompson defeated Garner and Emmetsburg, setting up a substate tilt with Dumont who was undefeated at the time. Coming from behind, led by Harlson's 43 points, the final score was 80-71, and the Cubs were off to their first and only state tournament. Harlson entered the tournament as the state's leading scorer. The 6′ 2″, 220 pound Harlson averaged better than 35 points per game during the season. Wapsie Valley had a 6′ 2″ center and a 6′ 1″ forward. The game went into three overtimes with Thompson behind Harlson's 35 points, outlasting Wapsie 85-76. The following night, Thompson fell to powerhouse Paulina and then lost to Blairsburg 74-72 in the consolation game. The fourth place trophy for the 1968 Boys State Basketball Tournament would come home to Thompson. Over 800 fans packed the school gym in Thompson to welcome home their basketball heroes. A caravan of 100-plus cars lined up at the junction of Highway 69 and 9 to parade the boys into Thompson. At that time John Harlson entered five new records into state tournament records. His records of 46 points against Blairsburg and total of 106 points (three games) in the tournament remained records for years.

Also in 1968, Marcia Engebretson ('69) went to the state free throw contest and placed second. She won the sectional free throw contest with 24 out of 25, the district with 22 out of 25, and was the runner up at the state with 24 for 25, and 12 for 20.

Thompson made it to the sub-state football play-offs in both 1968 and 1969. The coach was Jerry Jenkins and the star player was Doug Peterson ('69).

The girls basketball team, the Cubettes, went to the state tournament in 1979.

Notable Graduates—A letter sweater of Judy Endreland Nygard ('67) is on display at the historical museum in Thompson. It is representative of the time. This pretty, white sweater with the school pin and the graduation year embossed in the crest, a band shield, cheerleader shield, and an FFA sweetheart shield.

Fairy Ann Florence ('70) was the band president and queen in 1970 when the band competed at the Mason City Band Festival. She played the French horn in the large Thompson high school band. Several years later, she gave up her career and returned to Thompson to care for her elderly parents, Marshall (Bud) Florence ('32) and Ruby Van Dusen Florence. Her father Marshall returned to Thompson after working as a dragline operator for the government building the Alaskan Highway during World War II. Marshall and his brother Oral were very successful businessmen in Thompson with a drainage business and later Thompson Ready Mix.

Forest and Emma Fisher had eleven children attend school in Thompson. Many graduated from Thompson: Maurice ('31), Carroll, Marlin ('32), Doris ('34), Ruth, Faye (37), Robert ('39), Geraldine ('41), Dorothy, Richard, and Ramon. They had 42 grandchildren and many of them also graduated from Thompson. For 64 consecutive years there was a Fisher in the Thompson school system. The last to graduate was Kathy Fisher ('83) (Marlon's daughter).

Notable Teacher—Miss Charlotte Stengerd was a long-time home economics teacher and later the guidance counselor. "She taught us to sew, cook, be a lady, all things proper, how to sit down, talk proper, and how to be nice and not say things off cue," remembered Mary Kurll Green ('67).

Closing—By the 1980s enrollment was declining. One of the six-room elementary buildings was abandoned and sold to be remodeled into apartments.

The high school closed after graduation in May 1989. That fall the students joined Buffalo Center-Rake High School which was then renamed North Iowa High School in Buffalo Center. In the 90 years from 1900-1989 there were 1,799 graduates from Thompson High School. The most numerous surnames were: Johnson-57, Anderson-43, Larson-43, Olson-23, Halverson-18, Erickson-17, Smith-16, Branstad-14, Peterson-14, Swenson-14, Robinson-13, Hagenson-12, Ulsted-12, Nelson-11, Bell-11, and Jacobson-11. The largest graduating class was 41 in 1969. The last to receive a diploma from Thompson High School was Carol Weaver (alphabetically).

Thompson High School
Winnebago County, IA

#92

Troy High School

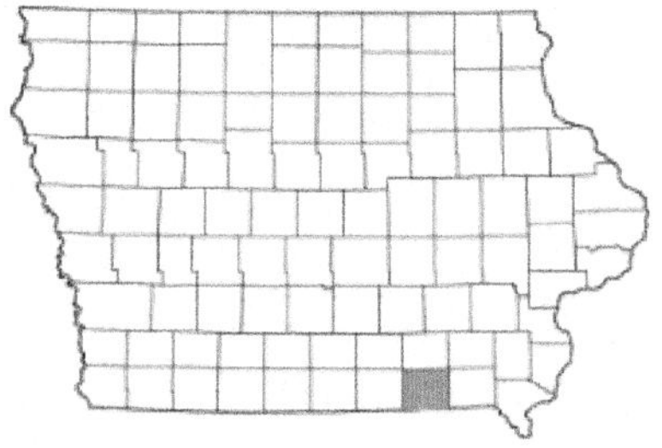

Mascot: Trojans
Colors: Purple and Gold
Closed: 1960
Location: East Central Davis County

Early History—The Treaty in 1842 with the Sac and Fox Indians established for settlement a fifty-mile strip of land running west from the Mississippi River along the border with Missouri. The white man purchased land from the government for $1.25 an acre. Much of this land was purchased with land warrants issued by the government and given to military veterans from the War of 1812, the Mexican-

American War, and the American Indian Wars. These warrants were often sold to speculators who then resold them to settlers who desired to have land in Iowa. The fifty-mile strip of land ended just west of Troy.

Troy was surveyed and platted by John W. Ellis, the county surveyor, on February 15, 1848. This land was owned by four men, one being J.I. Earhart who named the town Troy after his former home in Troy, Ohio. By 1851, the population was 101. During the next few years, a dream of these early citizens was to establish a school for higher education for teachers. The Troy Academy was opened in 1853 with the first two-story school building constructed in a Greek revival style. The term was 11 weeks. Students came to Troy to attend the Academy from every surrounding county and from Missouri. Initially, it was governed by the Des Moines Presbytery and then became independent. Two-year and four-year degrees were awarded for the next 35 years.

A bill was introduced in the Iowa Legislature to locate the Iowa Normal school at Troy. This measure called for the establishment of a teachers' college, replacing the Troy Academy. The bill was defeated by one vote. The Normal School was established in northern Iowa at Cedar Falls in 1876 at the former Iowa Orphans Home and became the Iowa teacher education school.

The Troy Academy was closed in 1888. In 1904, the buildings became the property of the Troy Independent School District and were remodeled for public use.

Early Schools—Union Township had nine independent school districts including the town school at Troy. In the early 1900s efforts were made to merge these country schools with Troy into a consolidated school district.

In beautiful cursive handwriting using a fountain pen, an account of the consolidation of the Troy school is described. It is written on the letterhead of Garrett Stock Farm, owners E.E. and C. E. Garrett, on October 9, 1916, likely by Mrs. Garrett:

> *Mr. I. C. Evans was the original advocate. He asked Dr. E.E. Garrett to act as Chairman of the 1st Consolidated meeting called for Nov. 14, 1913. A bond election was held on March 28, 1914 and bonds to the amt. of $1700.00 to build a schoolhouse were voted by a majority of 90 . . . legal action began . . . if possible, to dissolve the district. The plaintiffs were men from Walnut, Spring Grove, Antioch, Miles Oak, and Spring Grove country districts . . . district court . . . to Iowa supreme court. Ruled in favor of the district.*
>
> *After this 18-month delay from the legal case failed, a second election was needed because the school board found the $17,000 was short by $500.*

So, another election for $17,500 carried by 51 votes. Another suit was filed against the district, but it was thrown out by Judge Cornell as having no merit.

The new two-story brick high school (plus basement) was dedicated in June 1916. The building was designed by James Craddock from Omaha and completed and furnished for $18,000. Located adjacent to the old academy, the new school had six classrooms, a library, and a combination gymnasium and auditorium. The Troy Consolidated School District, in addition to Troy, included the rural country school districts of Brush, Star, Whippoorwill, Antioch, Springtown, and Walnut Grove.

The dedication was held in conjunction with the reunion of the Troy Academy alumni. An estimated 1,000 attended the two-day event.

In the late 1940s, the home economics and manual training building was acquired from Jefferson Barracks military post in St Louis. It was taken down in sections and transported back to Troy, where it was reassembled, mostly by volunteer help. The old Academy was moved to the east and south about this time.

In 1952, a Quonset gymnasium was constructed.

Buses—Six wagons were purchased in 1916 from the Studebaker Company in Des Moines at a price of $172.50 each. The horse-drawn wagons were used until 1940. They were replaced by the first motorized bus for the Troy district in 1940.

Shirley Kay Bollman Porter ('58) remembered, "My first bus driver was Pete Brooks. We lived in the country and had a long lane to our house. When I started school, the bus had two benches on the side. I had to walk to the corner about a third of a mile to get to the bus. When my brother Larry Bollman ('59) came along the next year, Pete came all the way down the lane to our house to pick us up. I didn't think that was fair."

Sports—Girls and boys basketball was played in the new high school in 1916. Football was added in 1919. It was discontinued in an undetermined year.

The 1952 girls basketball team had a great year. They lost to Seymour in the final of the sectionals. Seymour, who had a 6' 7" forward, went to the state tournament following the win over Troy.

Both baseball and basketball were popular in Troy. The earliest newspaper sport article found was written in 1873. It noted "a baseball game between the Trojans of Troy and the Stars of this place [Bloomfield] resulted in a victory for the latter by a score of 44 to 45." *(Author's Note: Troy, at the time, was less than a four-year high school.)* In 1894 "our boys looked well in their new suits of blue" and by at least the 1920s, the Troy Independents were playing Missouri teams and other neighboring towns. The 1928 boys team made it to the sectional tournament before being defeated.

The boys 1950-51 basketball team had a good year. They played Selma, Agency, Pulaski, Douds, Eldon, Moulton, Blakesburg, Bloomfield, Cantril, and Milton. They were led by seniors Robert Vanderlinden ('51), Don Williams ('51), and James Ensminger ('51). The coach was C. W. Augsburger. There were only six girls out for basketball that year.

War Stamp Club—The Troy Consolidated School organized a War Stamp Club in 1945. The officers chosen were President Robert Shobe ('45), Vice President Helen Farres ('45), and Secretary-Treasurer Dorothy Fickel ('45). Each Friday was a designated stamp buying day. During the year, $750 worth of bonds and stamps were purchased.

Notable Graduate—Joan Rector Hutchings ('51) worked for the *Bloomfield Democrat* for seven years. She took time off to have a family and returned to work at the newspaper as the writer of the society column for another 30 years, retiring in 1999. A Troy native and historian, Felicia Campbell, remarked about Joan Hutchings ('51). "She is 85 years old and has 95 percent recall of history and is very delightfully proud of her Troy education and heritage."

Senior Trips—Seniors in 1951 went to St. Louis for a day trip by cars. Their day was spent at the Lafayette heritage area and the zoo. They had a Junior and Senior banquet at a restaurant in Ottumwa. The girls dressed in formals and the boys in coats and ties. There was no prom, but this banquet was a special occasion for the seniors.

The 1958 and 1959 classes went to Ottumwa to eat out for their senior trips.

Though not exactly a senior trip, the boys did travel to the NCAA basketball tournament in Kansas City. Larry Bollman ('59) remembered, "Our coach, Jim Premer, was from Cameron, Missouri, and was quite a basketball enthusiast and knew Kansas City well. We got to stay in hotels and considered it a reward for going out for basketball. That old Municipal Auditorium was a wonderful place to see games for three or four days."

Notable Teachers—Irolene Roberts taught English at Troy. Her husband, Walter Roberts, was the superintendent, taught typing, and was the janitor. Joan Rector Hutchings ('51) told, "Mrs. Roberts was special and helped me with my endeavors as a newspaper writer. She was such an excellent teacher. I loved to read and write. She identified with my interests. She directed me to good literature and was so precise with our grammar and sentence structure."

Helen Brown started teaching history at Troy High School in 1943. Two of her pupils were sisters, Betty Fickel Spilman ('44) and Dorothy Fickel Fleming ('45). Mrs. Brown had stopped teaching for a few years but was drawn back into teaching because of World War II and the teacher shortage.

Sue Spilman (DCCHS '68) said, "Mrs. Brown was in charge of her classroom—no talking when she was talking, no passing notes, and *no* you did not need to leave the classroom. Students were seated in alphabetic order and were expected in their seats when the bell rang. They were to have a pencil, paper, English book, and homework ready to turn in. Mrs. Brown was strict but not without some fun and laughter. My mother, Betty Fickel Spilman ('45), became a teacher right out of high school with an 8-week training course from a nearby college and several years later worked for the Davis County Community School system. She became a colleague of Mrs. Brown. I returned to teach with Mrs. Brown, and my mother. We all three taught at the same time at Davis County High School. The circle of education continued."

Yearbooks—The 1943 yearbook was titled *Trojan Memo.* The yearbooks from 1951 through 1960 were called *Trojan Echoes.*

Janitor—Harold Schlotter ('43) started after high school as the janitor and stayed until the grade school closed in 1976. Dorothy Gardner (DCCHS '71) attended grade school at Troy and went on to Davis County Community High School in Bloomfield. She remembered, "Harold was ornery as all get out. Mrs. Miller was our teacher in elementary school and always dressed to the nines. On one occasion, she stepped on the floor grate over the furnace outlet and caught her high heel. She struggled to get her foot out and was so emphatic about not wanting to break the heel. Harold, the janitor was called, and it seemed like an hour while he worked carefully trying to dislodge the long-spiked heel. We kids all thought it was funny seeing Mrs. Miller hobble around with one shoe off and one shoe on."

Killed in Action—Many Troy area men were killed in service to the country. Lest we forget:

Marshall Sapp, WWI
Clyde Comer, WWI
John Russell, WWI
Clyde Moughler, WWI
Walter E. Reed, WWI
Erbert Sommer, WWI
Jr. Leonard Camp, WWII
Robert W. Gardner, WWII
Neil R. Harmon, WWII

Robert McMickle, WWII
William Yoder, WWII
Ralph Robert Baker, WWII
Dickie Obern Bish, WWII
Robert L. Birchmier, WWII
Harold E. Christy, Jr., WWII
Harold Casset, WWII
Joseph D. Elesnsohn, WWII
Neil R. Haney, WWII
Ira Laverne Ritz, WWII
Gerald G. Heither, Korea
Richard Clendenen, Vietnam

Closing—The Troy Consolidated High School closed following graduation in May 1960. In the fall of 1960, the high school students were bused to the newly formed Davis County Community High School in Bloomfield. This became the first county-wide consolidated school district in the state of Iowa (62 school districts consolidated into one). In the 43 years from 1918-1960 there were 396 graduates from Troy Consolidated High School. The largest class was 17 seniors in 1942. The most numerous surnames of the graduates were: Barker-12, Hendricks-9, Roberts-9, White-9, Richardson-8, Ensminger-7, Erhart-7, and Jones-7. The last to receive a diploma from Troy High School was Carol Stone (alphabetically).

Troy High School
Davis County, IA

#93

Udell High School

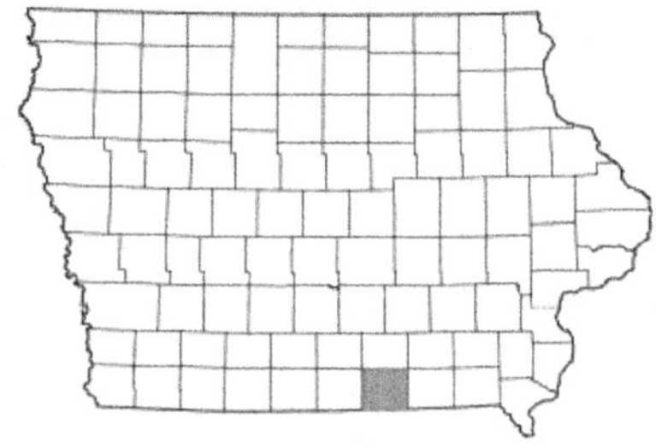

Mascot: Wildcats
Colors: Purple and Gold
Closed: 1959
Location: Northeast Appanoose County

Early History—The first white family to live in Appanoose County was the Clancy family from Scotland. Their descendants were still living in the Udell area in 2020.

When railroad construction crossed Iowa in the 1870s, Udell was a center for the intersection of two railroads. The line on the north edge of town was the Wabash, which ran from St. Louis to Des Moines. The track on the south edge of town was the Chicago Burlington Rock Island. Each had a depot and switch operators. There were several section crews that worked out of Udell and all brought their business and added to the working population of Udell. Grain and livestock were shipped to the Kansas City, St. Louis, and Chicago markets.

Early Schools—There were numerous country schools in Udell Township before there was one established in Udell. Some of those country schools were named Centennial, Streepy, Taylor, Salem, and Ulrick.

In 1907, a two-room, two-story school was opened in Udell. The lower grades were taught by Stella Chambers Cridlebaugh on the main floor and the upper grades on the second level by Jay Leonard.

A Udell native, Frank Clark, came home to visit from northern Iowa where he had been teaching. He suggested building a consolidated school building with the organization of the district. The suggestion was accepted and the districts were consolidated with a levy of 29 mills. The site was chosen, and a new three-story building was built in 1914 for $11,760. The building was finished with Kellastone stucco which was the first in Iowa. The first day of classes in the new school was December 26, 1914.

(Author's Note: no such thing as a Christmas break.) The same Frank Clark was the Super-intendent for the next three years.

Eight school routes were established and horse-drawn buses were purchased from the Marshalltown Buggy Company for $180 each. Each bus could transport 20 children. During the first year, a total of $699.40 was spent each month for the bus drivers and teachers. These horse buses were used until the late thirties when modern motorized buses were purchased by the Udell School District.

In 1951, the district voted to build a gymnasium. It was completed in 1952 for $50,000. The gymnasium was connected to the school by "the tunnel" as labeled by the students.

(Author's Note: A paper written by Marie Spurgeon Weber, "History of Udell Schools," was the source of some of this early school information.)

Sports—No football was played at Udell High School. The boys played basketball and baseball. The girls played basketball.

The 1927 boys basketball team won the Appanoose County Tournament. Their home games were all played on the dirt court at Udell. Starters on this outstanding, memorable team were brothers George and Woodrow Duty, Thayne Bryant ('27), Earl Hedgecock ('27), and Dwight Odgen ('29).

Kathryn Clancy Carr Batterson ('55) recalled, "My freshman year we had a new coach, Max Buzzard. Was he ever good looking. He also taught Industrial Arts. He had been a minor league baseball player and only stayed a few years. He may have been the reason I stayed out for basketball. By the time I was a senior, I was a forward on the basketball team. One game, coach Fay Dorsey put me in as a forward and I scored 15 points. The next game, he put me in the starting lineup. Reality was revealed and that was the last game I ever started."

Udell High School joined the Appanoose County Athletic Conference in 1940. The ten original members were: Moravia, Unionville, Exline, Jerome, Moulton, Mystic, Numa, Rathbun, Cincinnati, and Udell. The Conference was renamed Appanoose-Davis Athletic Conference in 1953, when Pulaski and Troy were added, and Unionville, Exline, Jerome, and Rathbun dropped out.

Bus Drivers—Howard Burkland was a bus driver in the 1950s. He was also the Mayor of Udell and owned a building which had a big handmade sign leaning on the side of the building with the word BANK. When Burkland introduced himself he often said he was 'the Mayor and the owner of the Bank.'

Max Batterson ('54) related "When I came over from Unionville in 1952, after that high school closed, I rode on the school bus. One night after ball practice on our way home, the bus took a sharp right and crashed. It landed on its side and we were all transported to the hospital. We were all released and not in serious conditions. As I remember it, the driver may have had a health condition and never drove the bus again."

Killed in Action—Barrack Cridlebaugh from Udell was killed in the Civil War.

Pranks—Call it a 'snipe hunt' gone bad with a happy ending. An unusual prank in 1953 led to a marriage 48 years later. Max Batterson ('54) shared the story. A friend, Joyce Watts, wanted a date with Max's friend. Joyce's mother said the only way this could happen was if there was a double date. To make this double date work out, Joyce invited Kathryn Clancy ('55) along to be Max's date. The rendezvous was all set and the boys drove the innocent girls out into the country to go 'snipe hunting.' They dropped them off and about a half hour later they returned to rescue their sweet girls. They were surprised at the girls' fury. Kathryn Clancy ('55), with fire still coming from her face, told in 2020, "We were madder than wet hens!"

Now for the happy ending. Max Batterson ('54) graduated from Udell and later retired from a military career. He had lost his wife and Kathryn had lost her husband. Out of the blue, he called the Kathryn Clancy Carr phone number in the phone book and reached her 15-year-old grandson, Brad, who was living with her at the time. He carefully explained who he was and left a message with him for his grandmother to call him. Upon returning home, Kathryn asked if anyone had called and Brad gave her the message. His words to her were, "Grandma, you don't need another man in your life, I will take care of you." Several months later, Max, the wise gentleman, took Brad aside and told him, Brad, I can't replace your grandpa, but I sure would love to share my life with your grandma." Max Batterson ('54) and Kathryn Clancy Carr Batterson ('55) have now been happily married for nearly 20 years (2020).

Yearbooks—The 1948 and 1949 yearbooks were named *Memories*. The 1951 yearbook was the *Mirror*. In 1953, it was the *Rambler*.

The 1958 Udell *Rambler* yearbook was dedicated to Anna Mae Burger:

> We, the seniors of 1958, are happy to dedicate our annual to Mrs. Burger who has been our music and modern problems teacher during our senior year. She has been the driving and inspiring power which led our music groups to a successful year in both community and the State music contests. Her teaching ability is surpassed by few in Udell High School and will count it a great loss when she leaves the Udell teaching staff.

The last yearbook in 1959 shows a band with eight members. The enrollment that year was 34 students. The glee club had 14 members.

Music—A boys quartet at Udell High School was remembered for years. Larry Hedgecock, Ronald Silliman, Roger Labertew, and Lanny Daggett from the class of 1958 were the school's entertainment. As juniors, they were under the direction of Miss Correll as they entered the Bill Riley teen-talent contest in Des Moines. They appeared on KTVO, an audition show, and performed for the PTA, church services, and school functions. Their senior year under the direction of Mrs. Burger, they earned a #1 division rating at the state music festival.

Senior Trips—The seniors from 1954 through 1957 went to the Lake of the Ozarks for three-day trips after graduation. Loren 'Larry' Walker ('56) shared, "We all took our parents' cars. It was fun in the sun with other schools' kids everywhere. Roger Silliman ('56) and I innocently found a dead snake and thought it needed to be placed in one of the other guy's beds. After a day of swimming, we were all back in our room cleaning up when there was a knock at the door. Rose Clancy ('56) asked to come in and we said 'of course.' At that very moment, Larry Whisler ('56) was just stepping out of the shower with a towel somewhat wrapped around him. He panicked and jumped into a bed and pulled up the covers only to be surprised by that dead snake. Did he ever come flying out of that bed! I really can't remember if he still had a towel around him or not, but he was a flash."

Notable Graduates—Udell had many alumni who were in the armed forces, were engineers, teachers, business men and women, doctors, nurses, farmers, ministers, missionaries and, perhaps the most important of all, became parents and housewives. All of these people were solid citizens in the community striving for a better school for their children. Muriel Arbuckle Spurgeon ('27) became the historian and leader in forming and maintaining the Udell High School Alumni Association. Her efforts to organize and communicate with hundreds from all over the country made the annual reunion possible. This is why to this day, 61 years after the closing of the high school, a group of faithful loving Udell grads meet each year the Saturday of Father's Day weekend to once again welcome friends and share their loving memories of Udell High School

Richard Burger ('38) graduated from McPherson College, a church of the Brethren school in Kansas. He went to Bethany Seminary and became an ordained minister and missionary. After 12 years as a missionary in Nigeria, he and his family returned to Udell where he farmed. His no-till and conservation practices were new to agriculture in the area. In college, he won the KCAC Conference two-mile title. At 100 years of age in a 2020 interview, he said, "I married a beautiful Missouri girl who was such a part of our missionary group in Africa. We had always been very frugal, and I learned to farm under different climates."

Carl Benz ('28) became a lead scientist working on the Manhattan project which developed the nuclear bomb used in Japan in 1945.

Closing—Beginning in 1957, legislation was passed which forced schools to become consolidated by 1962. Under the leadership of a committee chaired by Richard Burger and Superintendent Raymond Byers, a plan was formed to consolidate with Moulton to become the Moulton-Udell School District. The high school closed after graduation in May 1959. In the 44 years from 1916-1959, there were 377 graduates from Udell High School. The largest classes were 16 seniors in 1952 and 1956. The most numerous surnames of the graduates were: Whisler-21, Price-10, Gorden-7, Cridlebaugh-6, Hornaday-6, and Spurgeon-6. The last to receive a diploma from Udell High school was Lowell Scott (alphabetically).

Udell High School
Appanoose County, IA

#94

Union High School

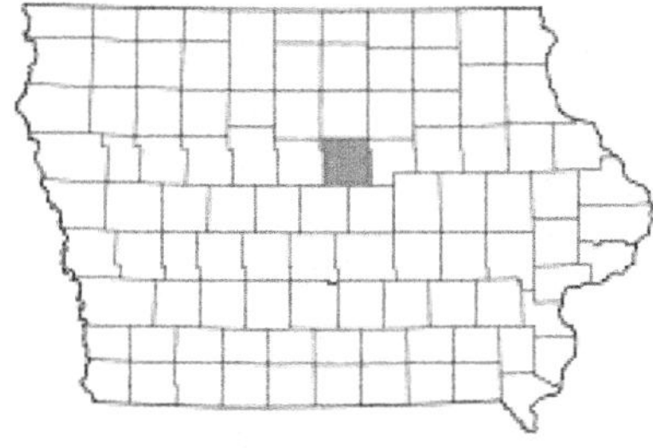

Mascot: Cobras
Colors: Green and White
Closed: 1971
Location: Hardin County

Early History—The village of Union is nestled along the Iowa River and the rolling hills of rich farmland in extreme south central Hardin County. The annual Tar Heel festival held each July is representative of the founding of the town. Among the first settlers in the area were people from North Carolina after the end of the American Civil War in 1865. These people brought their southern heritage and the nick-name of their former state as it was called due to the world's leading producer of tar (turpentine, pitch, and tar) for the navy stores. The names of these farmers are not well documented.

The first post office in Union Township was established in 1855 with Postmaster Thomas N. Hauser. This name Hauser remained significant for the next 175 years in this region. The post office was at Thomas Hauser's home south of the Hauser cemetery. Everyone in Union Township went there for their mail. His eldest daughter, Jennie, helped put letters and papers in the boxes for the settlers. She was helping one evening and pulled out a paper with black headlines reporting of the death of President Lincoln, April 14, 1865. In telling this later she said, "We all felt we had lost a good friend." The post office was moved to the village of Union in 1869.

Early Schools—The first school and library was in the home of James Dawdy in 1853-54 and was taught by Mr. Whitehead. In 1854, a log house was erected on Section 14 for a school. This was located just west of the Hauser Cemetery.

In 1868, according to the County Superintendent's records, there were 2,166 boys and 2,054 girls in Hardin County schools. Union Township had 214 girls and 200 boys. School money raised for each child was $1.82. The apportionment to Union was $768.62 for the teachers fund and $1,212.40 for the schoolhouse fund.

In 1871, Union voted to have an independent school district. The legislature legalized the issuance of bonds for the district. The school was a 30′ x 50′ frame two-story. It cost $2,350 and was completed in 1875. This school had three rooms, with two down and one up, and was located on the site of the present building (2020). Primary grades were to the south and grammar grades to the north of the hallway. The room above was called "upstairs." There was no high school. By 1877, there were 144 boys and 161 girls in school. There were ten schools in Union Township at this time. Nearby Whitten (two miles east across the Iowa River) formed an independent school district in 1881.

A long coal house stood north of the school building and on the west end was a smaller building with two doors. There was a sign nearby which read, "Boys north Girls south." The school building was heated with large stoves in cold weather. The janitor was busy carrying in coal and carrying out ashes. In 1899, it was heated by steam.

Modern conveniences were brought into the Union building in 1908 when Professor Tisdale and his physics class students installed an electric fire alarm in the school building with "push buttons" conveniently located in every room. Fires in the wooden school structures were prevalent in the early 1900s. Many schools were burned to the ground as the fire prevention and fighting was limited to the volunteer fire departments in most towns. This concern was significant. In February 1910, the school building was destroyed by fire. Classes were then held in various places in town. High school was held in the Odd Fellows Hall and part of the grade school in Town Hall and some in the Methodist and Congregational Church basements while a new building was being constructed.

O.B. Chapin gave $5,000 to the school. $4,000 was to be used for the building and $1,000 to be used for Chapin School and Circulating Library for an addition of a half-block of land south of the school. The new school building was built and ready for school in the spring of 1911. Consolidation of the country schools was completed in 1917.

In 1935, a gymnasium was added onto the building which would double as a Community Hall.

In 1955, to meet state department requirements, the Whitten High School merged with Union to become the Union Whitten High School.

Buses—The first school bus was purchased in August 1900. It was noted that A.L. Wood was fitting a bus for the school district to transport pupils in the south ward to the Union school building. Enrollment at that time was 22 in high school, 43 in grammar school, 41 intermediate students, 3 in second primary, and 40 in first primary for a total of 149 students.

Motor busses were being used in the early 1920s.

Sports—The boys played football in 1905. Union played against a team from Eldora. An amphitheater east of town was unique for the players and spectators because most places they played in had no seats.

Henry Hanson ('08) made a national reputation as a football player, but he did not play the game until he went to the State University of Iowa in 1910. As told by John Hanson ('11), "Henry was thought to be too light-weight to play football when he attended Iowa City."

The 1910 boys basketball team was the first to organize at Union. In 1921, there were winning records for both boys and girls teams. In March 1923, the boys basketball team with Harold Hauser ('10) as the coach, traveled to Manhattan, Kansas, to play for honors in the Missouri Valley. The tournament was between teams from Kansas, Missouri, Nebraska, and Iowa. These states had been invited to send their best teams. Businessmen filled the purse to help pay expenses. Vaugh Reece ('23), Myron Lepley ('23), Paul Dillon ('23), Paul Hauser ('23), Heath Hauser ('23), Ted Brown ('23), and William Cobb ('24) were the team members.

The 1968 season brought the Girls Basketball State Championship trophy to Union Whitten. The coach was Paul Eckerman and the team was composed of Mary Hammill ('68), Carol Haunusch ('68), Pam Paglia ('69), Denise Long ('69), Cyndy Long ('70), Debbie Callaway ('69), Diane Sparks ('69), Diane Maronn ('71), Elaine Hauser ('69), Marla Drury ('71), Debbie Maas ('70), Ann Eggleston ('68), Mary Hellmich, Dawn Lewis ('70), Carolyn Freed ('68), and managers Carol Haywood ('69), and Candy Clemens ('68). Though the names of the players changed some, the 1969 team placed fourth in the state tournament.

The full-page article of the February 11, 1969 *Sports Illustrated* read:

Les Girls in Des Moines

Come March and most of Iowa is in a frenzy over the State High School Basketball finals—for girls. The young women pack the house in the capitol city with their furious play, then depart as the boys take over-before fewer fans.

Phenomenal scorer, Denise Long—who as a junior scorer got 93 points in her opening game of the '68 tournament, was devastating against Pocahontas and Everly in the finals.

The fiercest rival in all sports was New Providence, a school just ten miles to the northwest.

Graduate Stories—Mary Hager Rogers ('52) told of Initiation Day 1948, "The girls all had to dress in boys clothes and the boys in girls clothes including dresses. To make matters worse we had to wear these clothes backwards. The boys then had to go through a belt line with the senior boys. This belt line was later discontinued when the buckles got much bigger."

Lyle Spurlin ('47) made quite an impression on the girls. Mary Hager Rogers ('52) eyes danced as she remembered, "There was a tree just out of the high school that reached up to the top floor. There were no screens on the windows of the classrooms. Lyle reached out the window and grabbed a branch and shimmied down when the teacher was out of the room. The first time he did it, I screamed as I thought he was going to kill himself."

"On Sunday morning December 7, 1941, my dad was listening to the radio and told us kids to hush up as he was trying to listen to the announcement about the bombing of Pearl Harbor. For days afterward I was afraid to go down to the hog house lest the Jap's would bomb us too. Every time a plane flew over, we all worried that we were being attacked," reminisced Mary Hager Rogers ('52).

There was a POW camp just north up the river at Eldora. In the fall the Germans were released to help farmers do field work. The POW's were welcomed to the farms in the Wellsburg area (20 miles northeast of Union) because this was a predominantly German ethnic area. They were allowed to speak German with the farmers. Years later after the war, these former prisoners came back for reunions with their American farmer friends.

Driver Education—Paul Eckerman was the first drivers education teacher. He also taught science and was the coach that took the girls to state in basketball. Mary Hager Rogers ('52) beamed as she recalled, "I had driven a tractor, so the car was no problem. We had to learn how to change a tire. My first try was bad as someone had put on the lug nuts too tight. I once screamed in fright as Barbara Rash nearly drove into the filling station."

Closing—Union-Whitten High School closed after graduation in May 1971. In the 85 years, from 1887-1971, there were 1,167 graduates which includes the 391 graduates after Whitten joined in 1956. The largest classes were 36 in 1968 and 1969. The most numerous surnames of the graduates were: Hauser-28, Reece-18, Norman-17, Rash-14, Rogers-13, Johnson-10, Smith-10, Miller-9, Barnes-8, and Schwarck-8. The last to receive a diploma from Union-Whitten High School was Dan Yordy (alphabetically).

#95

Ventura High School

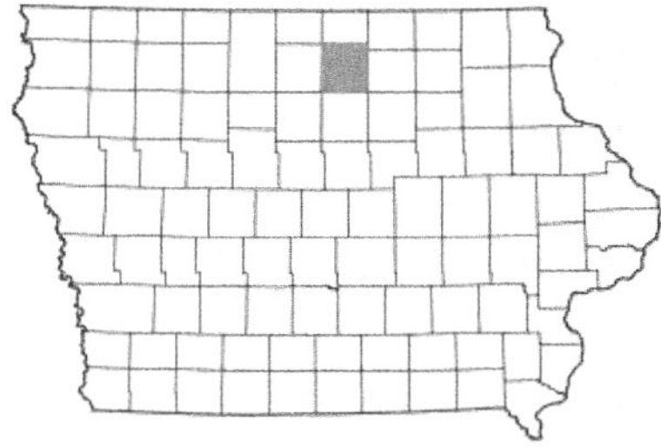

Mascot: Vikings
Colors: Blue and Gold
Closed: 2012
Location: West Cerro Gordo County

Early History—The original name for the town and area was Thayer's Siding. Mr. Thayer cut wild hay from the marsh area and baled the grass along the railroad siding. It was shipped east for its great quality for horse hays. When the railroads came through, they passed through land obtained by land grants. The Skene brothers said this area was quite a "venture." To identify freight landing for the railroad, the town name needed to be included. In the process, "Venture" was changed to "Ventura" and the name stuck.

Early Schools—A little red schoolhouse was located one mile north of town in 1870. It was later moved to Ventura by teams of oxen. A two-room brick school located in the northeast part of town was constructed in 1916.

The 1918 building was constructed on a five-acre hill overlooking beautiful Clear Lake at a cost of $62,500. This building still stands and remains in use (2019). The District consisted of 32 sections in Cerro Gordo and Hancock counties. There were 200 students and nine teachers in the first year of the new building. The first graduate from the new high school was in 1919.

A new gymnasium was built in 1940 with the help of 52 WPA workers. There was a requirement that 95% of the workers had to be from Cerro Gordo County.

Buses—In 1918, a horse barn was converted into a bus barn. It was first used for hacks, or farm wagons covered by canvas. In 1927, the first two motorized school buses were purchased. By 1969, there were nine buses in the fleet, and a total of 493 students in the schools.

Maurice Buckley was a longtime bus driver and head mechanic for the buses. He drove buses to the away games for years. During the run of the great girls basketball teams of the 1980s, with only three games lost in four years, Maurice was quoted as saying that he was the "All-State Bus Driver." When he died during the school year, a special busload of students went to his funeral in Mason City.

Sports—There was no football played at Ventura until 1946. They played eleven-man until 2008 when declining enrollment led to an eight-man team.

Basketball was the game of choice for both the boys and girls teams. "Championship fever was in the air in the school and community in 1945-46," wrote Lois Dorow Druhan ('46). The coach was the superintendent, Leo J. Esbeck. The boys team made it to sub-state but both teams were denied the trip to the state tournament. Willard Gisel ('46) was named to the All-State First Team.

The main rivals were Dows in the 1950s, Boone Valley, and Sheffield in the 1960s, and Meservey-Thornton in the 1970s. "It just seemed the biggest rival were those schools that had the best teams," quipped Danny Miller ('78).

The quest for the girls state tournament was met in 1961, 1984, 1985, 1987, and 1989. The first-place trophy was brought home in 1987 and fourth place in 1989. Though six-on-six basketball featured several players, it was team basketball. They were coached by Chuck Bredlow, who was also the football coach.

Lynda Larson ('86) was recognized by the National Girls Basketball Association for a record of 857 assists from 1983-86.

Lynne Lorenzen ('87) became the national all-time scoring leader in 1987. This national record stands today (2020) and will likely stand forever as the six-on-six game often featured a scoring forward in the game, and that game is not played today.

Band and Music—A Drum and Bugle Corps was started in the 1930s. John Kopecky from Clear Lake, a well-respected band leader, was hired on a part-time basis to lead the band. With his enthusiasm, he taught music—playing instruments and marching. The Band Mothers Organization was formed to raise money through community and school functions for uniforms for the musical groups. They also designated their funds to the more expensive instruments, the bass horn, baritone, and drums for the students to rent. The Band Mothers group was later renamed the Boosters Club and raised money and support for athletic and drama departments.

Jim Reynolds was an outstanding band instructor. He led the marching band. "We were amazing and won everything at contests. We took a trip to Winnipeg, Canada, to march in a festival. What a fantastic experience. And of course, the North Iowa Band Festival at Mason City was the major competition every year," remembered Becky Boehnke Ziesmer ('75).

Milan Brouzek became the new band instructor in 1974. Coming in after the legendary Mr. Reynolds, he attempted to control the students in the band. Snickering at funny statements from the trombone section drew his attention. David Ziesmer ('76) said, "I was always one to get caught at the wrong time having a good time. One practice session the instructor yelled, 'Ziesmer, you laugh one more time and you are out of here.' At the next rest in my music, sure enough, Charlie Roenfanz ('74), a senior in our section, mumbles under his breath a comment, and I laughed. I was instructed to leave band practice. I was just a sophomore and I hid out on the stage trying to figure out how to get myself out this pickle. Of course, my dad was the president of the school board. My band days were over for good."

Band queens were elected each year. They represented the band at the North Iowa Band Festival where an overall band queen was chosen. Gwen Johnson Boeke ('52) was named the 1952 North Iowa Band and Festival Queen. In 1990, Jody Schichtl Jones ('90) was the North Iowa Band and Festival Queen.

Pranks—Each month a teacher was selected to receive the "teacher of the month" award. Larry Costello was the school board president and served on the board for nearly forty years. He came each month to award this honor to the teacher selected in class in front of the students. One month, the band instructor, Milan Brouzek, was honored. The students caught wind of the timing and schemed up a plan. The award was to be given by Mr. Costello on the stage with the curtains pulled and the band students in place for the award and picture. When the announcement was made with the teacher and Mr. Costello standing on the stage, the curtains were pulled. And sure enough, there was no band there and the chairs were all empty and the students were hiding.

Drivers Education—The first drivers education instructor in the 1950s was Bob Jackson. Each session included three students who practiced driving for about 15 minutes each class period. Kenny Coe ('62) told, "I was in a group with Norma Graham Kenworthy ('62) and Gayle Westcott Stokes ('62). When it became my turn to drive, Mr. Jackson mumbled to me 'I am so happy you are behind the wheel.'"

The instructor in the 1970s was Mike Kavars. "He was known for making us go out on Highway 18 and going 75 miles per hour because that was the speed limit at the time. It scared me to death as a 15-year-old freshman. It may have been a good teaching method, but looking back I wonder if it was very safe," remembered Becky Boehnke Ziesmer ('75).

Notable Graduates—Kim Krause Haddow ('73) was named the NCAA Women's Golf Coach of the year in 1992.

In 1987, Robin Wolfgram ('81) was crowned Miss Iowa and competed in the Miss America contest.

Mr. and Mrs. W.F. Dorow had seven children that were all named Ventura Valedictorians for their classes. They were Edgar ('38), Norbert ('39), Hilda ('40), Edna ('41), Lois ('46), Maynard ('47), and Winton ('51).

Killed in Action—The Ventura community lost seven men in the service to our country. They were:

Joseph Blanchet, WWII
Arnold L.Cooley ('36), WWII
Orval Grell, WWII
Thelen Osnes, WWII
Swen Oswald, WWII
Eldon K. Steuerwald, WWII
Joseph Zeiger, WWII

School Activities—The Junior-Senior Banquet began in the 1940s. For several years, it was limited to just a banquet and no prom or dance due to St. John's Lutheran Church's frowning on dancing.

An experiment was started with Clear Lake in 1963. The two districts shared classes in physics, art, industrial arts, shorthand, auto mechanics, and vocational agriculture. This was the first case of sharing classes in the state of Iowa.

In 1992, Japanese I was taught by Sarah Schaefer to ten students in the fall. Japanese II was taught in the spring semester to two students.

Closing—The last graduating class from Ventura High School was in 2012. The students were bused to Garner seven miles to the west in the fall of 2012.

Ventura High School
Cerro Gordo County, IA

#96

Villisca High School

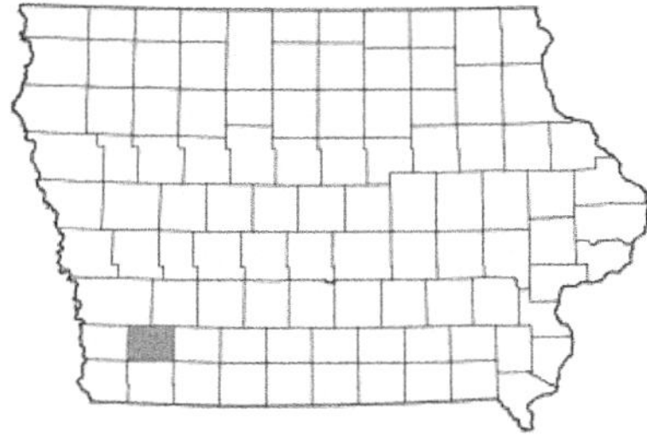

Mascot: Bluejays/Jayettes
Colors: Blue and White
Closed: 2013
Location: Montgomery County

Early History—Villisca is an Indian word meaning beautiful or pleasant place. Villisca truly is in a beautiful place located in East Township, the most southeast township in Montgomery County. It is on the northeastern rise overlooking the confluence of the Middle Nodaway and West Nodaway Rivers, and was relocated from the forks of the rivers after the town was platted. The Chicago, Burlington, and Quincy Railroad came through the area in 1869.

Early Schools—The first public school in Villisca was built in 1866. It was a one-room frame building. The next school was a three-story brick building constructed in 1872 with the primary grades on the lower floor and the upper grades on the upper floors.

In 1882, a bond was passed to add four rooms to the 1872 building. Professor A.E. Hughes was the founder of the Villisca High School (also called the East Side School). An account in the *Villisca Review* on November 23, 1882:

> The course of study recently accepted by the School Board, as recommended by Prof. Hughes, is made up of twelve grades, that is, twelve years to complete the course. When a pupil has finished it, they are prepared to enter the State University as a full-fledged freshman. The eight rooms of the school are not "Departments" as formerly known, but are known simply by the grades.

The first graduation was in 1884 with four graduates. Each student was required to give a 25-minute oration at the ceremony before they received their diploma. Nearly fifty years later May 19, 1933 an article in the *Villisca Review* recalled the event:

> . . . The first graduating class, composed of four members, received its diplomas just 49 years ago this spring after a spirited commencement program in the town hall which drew scores of townspeople to view the first finished products from their young public school system . . . in recalling the events of the first commencement here, (the current state clerk) at the

> age of 69, Edwin Jenkins ('84) said that the class presented a play which was well received, although it could not be described as a polished production . . . Professor A.H. Hughes launched the school with a staff of two teachers and offered diversified courses in physics, chemistry, geology, composition rhetoric, zoology, botany, geography, history, and geometry . . . By a vote of the student body, Latin was abandoned for trigonometry . . .

Linda Artlip Weinstein ('66) wrote: "The first real dedicated high school was built in 1888 . . . All of the classrooms were hexagonal in shape. Although it was supposed to be dedicated to high school scholars, the overall school population was so large, that the junior high students were assigned to rooms at the Eastside School."

Yearbook—The first senior yearbook was published in 1896. It was called the *Senior Annual*. Other names over the years were the *VI-HI SCA*, *Cycle I* and *II*, and lastly, *The Bluejay*, from 1948 until the school closed in 2013.

Women's Events—Villisca women were instrumental in the school and community.

- The first woman, Miss Emma Alger, was appointed temporary principal in 1875. The first woman elected principal in 1888 was Miss Kellogg.
- By 1894, Iowa women were allowed to vote on issues in which there were no candidates involved such as school bond issues; their ballots were counted separately.
- From the *Vilisca Review* March 27, 1913: The Women Saved the Day. A majority of men voted against the high school. At the bond election held Tuesday afternoon, a majority of 41 favored the issuance of $45,000 in bonds, but the women saved the day. There were 112 men who voted for the bond issue, and 133 against it. Of the women, 84 favored the bond issue and 22 were opposed. The total vote was 351, of which 245 were men and 106 women. The final vote 196 for, and 155 against. The women carried the day.
- At the dedication in 1914, the school building was dedicated to the women of Villisca. Having been given the right to vote by the Woman's Suffrage 19th amendment in 1920, the first two women were elected to the Villisca School Board in 1921. They were Miss Clara Cowgill ('96) and Mrs. S.C. Boise.

Superintendent Anderson—In a letter from former Superintendent, Bill Anderson, is a post-war account of the Villisca schools:

> *My first teaching was directly after being decommissioned in 1943 and my wife, a vocal music teacher, and I applied at Villisca. Since their*

science and math secondary teacher had had a nervous breakdown in the previous March, the school had decided to let the Seniors of that year receive credit in those courses while the Juniors were required to retake the course the following year . . . the science lecture room was overcrowded and chairs in that elevated area were added. My teaching assignment was Chemistry, Physics, Advanced Algebra, Trigonometry, and Advance Biology. At that time, I had no idea what a normal teaching load was as I was just off training 250 soldiers at a time. I think they (School Board) felt it was perfect for them and we were signed on the spot for $2,000 each for the year. After teaching two years and getting a principal's certificate (only required 2 courses in Iowa at that time) I was made superintendent and served in that capacity for six years . . . My thesis upon graduating from Iowa State in 1951 was, "A Proposed Community School for Villisca, Iowa" and we were one of the very-very first districts in Iowa to do so. As a result of my inexperience at that time, I did not realize that I needed an attorney or had any model to follow in my first year as superintendent. I worked on implementing the play and it passed the next year.

Sports — Boys began playing interscholastic football in 1894 and were called the Villisca High School Eleven. In 1899, the sport was disbanded for one year due to "rowdyism." In 1906, Villisca High played Corning under new rules that "tamed" football brutality. Football was again canceled in 1914 because a majority of the team was ineligible because of poor grades.

Villisca played sports in five different athletic conferences. It usually was one of the only schools that was not a county seat town. In 1926, Villisca joined the Southwest Iowa Conference: Clarinda, Corning, Red Oak, Shenandoah, Stanton, and Villisca. The next year in 1927, Villisca changed conferences and became a charter member of the Little Ten Conference: Atlantic, Bedford, Clarinda, Corning, Glenwood, Red Oak, Shenandoah, Sidney, and Villisca.

By 1930, another conference realignment formed the Hawkeye Six Conference which would last for nearly 70 years. An expansion was to add schools to become the Hawkeye Ten. The original schools in 1930 were: Atlantic, Clarinda, Creston, Red Oak, Shenandoah, and Villisca. Corning was added in 1946 to become the Hawkeye Seven. Glenwood was added in 1951 to become the Hawkeye Eight.

Villisca became a charter member of the Tall Corn Conference in 1962.

By 1988, the Corner Conference was formed with eight original schools: Bedford, Carson-Macedonia, Farragut, Hamburg, Malvern, Nishna Valley, South Page, and Villisca.

Some firsts and highlights at Villisca include:

1915 Girls Basketball begins playing against other teams.

1921 Floyd Watt Jr. dies from injury in football game with Clarinda.
1925 Girls basketball begins again (lasting for two years).
1930 First night football game played at Sidney with Villisca winning 18-0.
1933 Lights added at the Villisca football field.
1938 First track meet at Villisca in 30 years.
1947 Girls basketball starts again.
1954 Girls volleyball starts. It was started again in 1988.
1958 Girls golf added.
1975 Boys wrestling added.
2000 Changed to eight-man football.

The girls basketball team in 1968 went to the state tournament, losing in the first round to Paton-Churdan 62-61. This tournament was for all schools of all sizes. The girls team went to the state tournament again in 2013. They lost in the first round. This was the last year of the high school as it closed two months later.

Notable Teachers—Bill Anderson was a teacher, principal, and superintendent from 1943-1957. John Focht (49) told, "Mr. Anderson was the most intelligent and prepared teacher that I ever had through high school and college. I had physics, chemistry, biology, and psychology from him. He was able to bring me through those courses even though I was a severely 'challenged' kid. After teaching for eight years, I became an elementary principal. I feel that I owe a lot of my drive to be a principal to him. He was an exemplary role model. His concern and care for each and every student and staff member was something that I tried to emulate as a teacher and administrator. He had such command of the classroom and the students had high regard for him."

Teresa Nook was an English teacher and the first female superintendent at Villisca. Carol Patterson Greenfield ('55) remembered, "Kids back from college always stopped in to see Ms. Nook and thank her for her giving them the foundation in English and composition."

Marjorie Stillians ('18) was an English teacher and taught for 44 years from the 1920s into the 1960s. Marie Stephens Weddle ('68) recalled, "She was strict in all her presentations and in the classroom. She moved to Clarinda to teach at the Junior College before returning to Villisca for many years." Mary Moore Lissandrello ('43) wrote, "It was an unwritten law that a female teacher in my days had to be a Miss. Very rarely one of these maiden teachers would marry. Some refused to give up their title of Miss. Miss Stillians was one of them. Her nieces found it hard to call her Miss. So she became Aunt Marj to everyone, although in the classroom she was Miss Stillians."

Duane Johnson and Gaylin Sudik were directors of band and music from the 1950s into the 1970s. Band practice started at 6:30 AM for the marching band. Marie Stephens Weddle ('68) said, "Mr. Sudik led us at the Clarinda Band Days. I played the flute. He was so proud and motivated us all to perfection. We won the Clarinda Band Days top band several times. It was so difficult to have to decide between band and music class."

Jacob Grasmick taught history and coached football in the 1960s. Delbert Schroeder ('52) told about the students at that time, "Mr. Grasmich was very firm but his students could always get him off subject by asking about football games and players. Of course, he would surprise them by testing them over the parts of the lecture he was not able to cover while we had interrupted his class about our football conversations. He once told a mother in the stands at a game, 'be quiet or I'm going to suspend this game.'"

Reno Smith was the FFA instructor and taught agriculture. He sponsored many groups to the annual FFA convention at the Kansas City American Royal. In 1956, the school changed the name of the FFA Chapter to Reno Smith FFA.

Notable Graduates—Walter Kennedy ('90) brought football to VHS as both a student and the first coach. He played collegiately for Amos Alonzo Stagg at the University of Chicago. He was named by the Chicago Herald in 1915 as the greatest football player that ever wore a Chicago University football suit. He was also named the greatest Iowa Football player by the Des Moines Register & Leader in 1915.

Margaret Williams Posten ('31), taught in Villisca as a teacher for many years. She was a huge influence not only on the students in her classroom, but on students throughout Iowa who learned about Iowa's history through Mrs. Posten's textbook for fifth graders,"*This is the Place: Iowa.*"

Paula Means Lund, after an outstanding high school athletic career, played professional basketball for *Look Magazine* in Des Moines in the AAU League from 1968 to 1969.

Phil Wertman ('67) was one of the best high school athletes to come out of southwest Iowa, setting state records that held for years. He was conference pole vault champion in 1971, setting a University of Iowa pole vault record as well as a Big Ten record. He continued setting records as a coach in Colorado, coaching individuals and teams to numerous championships.

Patricia Knoke Shipley ('71) served as Iowa State P.E.O. president from 2017-2018. She represented

Iowa on the National Education Association Board of Directors in 1987-91, one of the first two women to serve in that capacity. She currently is the State Clerk of her Presbytery, the first woman ever in that position. She is presently the mayor of Nodaway, Iowa.

Robert R. Moore Sr. ('23) was a hero of WWII. After being wounded, he returned to the states and joined an elite group of military leaders who developed a course in instructing other officers in small unit tactics. Those operational procedures are the foundation of small unit tactics in today's US Army. He returned to Villisca and retired in 1962 as a Brigadier General of the Iowa National Guard.

Colleen Means Dempsey ('69) was an outstanding high school athlete who continued her sports career in college at Northwest Missouri State University. She was instrumental in organizing the Women's sports programs at NWMU in those pre-Title IX years.

Richard Hart ('50) was for 39 years, an agronomist and rangeland ecologist with the US Department of Agriculture in Wyoming, and was recognized as a world-renowned forage and range management scientist. He is a poet, author, and performer, and was named the Cheyenne, Wyoming Poet Laureate in 2001.

Lynn King ('26) was an All-State high school track star and Villisca quarterback, superstar at Drake University, professional baseball player with the St. Louis Cardinals for three years, and was in the first class of athletes named to the Iowa Sports Hall of Fame.

Teachers Handbook—With the consolidation in 1959 with Nodaway, the Villisca Community School District No. 2 printed its first Teachers Handbook. That year there were 17 high school teachers and 17 bus drivers. Aron Laipple was the Superintendent and the high school principal was Louis Sullivan. Here are several interesting highlights of the handbook:

> Every teacher should have membership in the local, state, and national professional associations participating actively and unselfishly.
>
> **What is expected of a teacher in Villisca Schools?**
>
> Every teacher puts his heart into his work and does his best.
>
> A high standard of professional ethics is maintained by every member of the faculty.
>
> Our keyword is friendly cooperation and we will work together.
>
> We present to the community a high standard of conduct.
>
> High school substitutes will be paid $14 per day. Elementary teachers $12 a day.
>
> All teachers should take an active interest in community organizations. This is your home and gives you the chance to work and earn your livelihood; we have a

responsibility to the community as great as any other citizen.

Suggestions for better Discipline

1. Avoid making rules as much as possible
2. Never threaten students
3. Friendly discipline is usually the best
4. Use common sense
5. Never plead with students and, above all, don't resort to tears.

Wednesday night of each week is reserved for church activities. No school activities are to be scheduled for that evening or on Sunday. The school building will be closed on Sunday also and no students are to be admitted then.

Villisca Volcano—The school newspaper was first printed in 1931. Its motto was "Always erupting, never corrupting." The class of 1932 believed that there was little opportunity for high schoolers to corrupt anything, so they changed the motto to "Always Active."

Bus Driver—Lois Frazee drove the rural routes with a stick-shift. Martha Stephens ('81) told, "I learned to drive a stick just by watching her. I sat up front because I got car sick. We lived on a muddy country road. Lois often got stuck and had to come to our house to have someone pull the bus out of the ditch."

Lester Focht drove for Villisca for many years. He drove the south route and the kids loved him. He once went down an embankment with a bus load of students, but no one was injured.

Polio—Jeanne Palmquist Artlip Schenk ('60) had to be in an iron lung during the polio epidemic in the 1950s. She recovered but had to wear a leg brace.

Bill Anderson ('53) was stricken with polio. He recovered but later in life had health problems due to the disease.

Killed in Action—The following from Villisca and Scott Township area were killed in action in four 20th century wars:

WWI

Marion Campbell
Lawrence Gridley
Glenn Kendrick
Orville Winter ('13)
Victor Frist
Rennie Henry ('16)
Joe Thuman

WWII

John Baker ('41)
Clyde Braden
William Braden
Lester Bull ('39)
Manford Cooney
George Comley
Harlan Delaney
Stanley D. Focht ('41)
Donald Hale ('38)
Byron Jackson
Wesley Miller
Harlan Peterson
Albert Ryder
Roy Shield
Wayne Shrimpton
Clarence Storm
Loren Taylor
Roy Wright

Korea

Clark Schaffer
Ivan Winter

Vietnam

Lee Gourley ('62)
Jerry Ziehe ('50)

Pranks—Jerry Greenfield ('50) had a less than stellar career in typing. When the fire alarm sounded during a drill, he threw his typewriter out the third-floor window. He innocently claimed that if the school burned down, he at least wanted to save the typewriter.

Amy Lemkuhl's ('81) light yellow VW occasionally found its way mysteriously into the hallway of the school. There were at least ten steps up to the school doors. By removing the center post of the double doors, the little car could be carried up the steps and pushed into the building. To date, the culprits have not been identified.

Villisca High School
Montgomery County, IA

Closing—Villisca High School closed after graduation in May 2013. In the 130 years from 1884 through 2013, there were 5,131 graduates from the school. The largest class was 72 graduates in 1970. The most numerous surnames of the graduates were: Johnson-58, Smith-58, Peterson-53, Means-47, Taylor-47, Anderson-45, Gourley-45, Williams-43, Brown-34, Focht-34, Gray-33, King-33, Scott-33, Sunderman-30, Marsh-27, Fast-26, Carlson-25, Enarson-25, Greenley-25, and Shipley-24. The last to receive a diploma from Villisca High School was Jeffery Stephen Whitt ('13) (alphabetically). Jeffery Whitt was not only the last graduate, he was the only Whitt to ever graduate from Villisca.

"New" High School 2000-2013

#97

Visitation High School

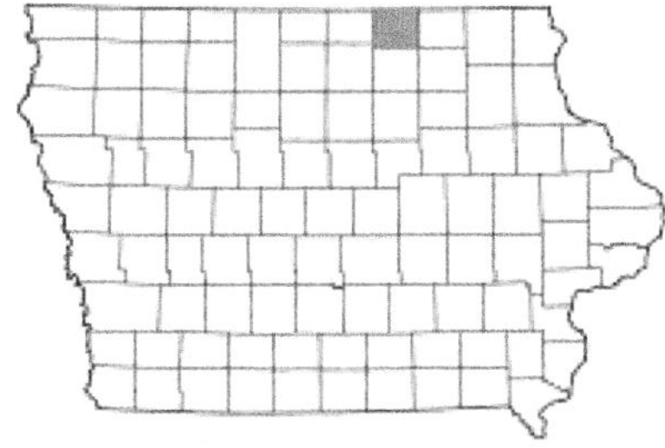

Mascot: V-Hawks/Mustangs
Colors: Blue and Gold
Closed: 1968
Location: North Central Mitchell County

Early History—Stacyville is located along the banks of the Little Cedar that flows from Mower County, southwest of Elkton, Minnesota, and drains into the Cedar River just south of Nashua in Chickasaw County. It is named after Homer Stacy who, with his brother, came to the area in 1855. The *History of Mitchell County Iowa* provides:

> Homer came to Iowa on a "prospecting tour," and after a careful examination of the claims in different portions of the state, he bought 600 acres on the Little Cedar from a man named John McIntire. Homer bought the land tract for $3,000. Mr. McIntire had purchased the land only a short time prior from the government for $1.25 per acre. (Nice profit for a short holding.) Homer then selected and located for himself and his brother 1,500 additional acres including the present site of Stacyville. By 1857 "seventy or eighty" families settled along the banks of the river in and near Stacyville.

By the fall of 1857, Homer Stacy recounted in a document found among his papers that there were over 20 frame buildings in the village.

Newspapers—The *Stacyville Sentinel* published its first issue of a weekly paper on November 18, 1897.

Another paper, *The Herald*, showed a subscription rate of $1.00 per year to be paid in advance. Obituaries were published free for the first 30 lines and then five cents for each line after that. Although *The Herald* publisher promised not to discuss religion in the newspaper, he could not resist commenting in an editorial on May 12, 1910, "As a tribute to the teaching of the Catholic Church, there was not a divorced person in Stacyville or Stacyville Township."

Yet another paper, *The Monitor*, was published in 1910 and continues as a community paper to this day (2020).

World War I with Germany—When the United States entered WWI, Stacyville residents lived in a somewhat isolated world. In May 1917, *The Monitor* reported that men between the ages of 21-30 must register with the US government for military service. Ninety-six Stacyville men complied. By August 1917, twenty Stacyville men were called up for service. Four more left for training at Camp Dodge in 1918. After May of 1918, farmers lost their deferment and 25 more were called up.

Soon the first casualties for Stacyville men came with the reports back from France. Peter Gartner was killed in action and Hal Fuller died in a hospital with the deadly Spanish influenza. Both of their remains were returned in 1921 to be buried in the St. Mary's cemetery. Peter was buried next to his brother, Frank Gartner, who was also killed in action.

By the summer of 1918, The German Savings Bank changed its name to the American Savings Bank. Traditionally, the people living on the west side of town spoke English or Irish. On the east side of Main Street there were more German speakers and many stopped speaking German in public at that time.

Chautauquas, community bands, revivals, baseball, the first woman dentist, Dr. Esther Brown in 1916, and a new butter-maker in town from Luxemburg, were the Stacyville scenes in the second decade of the century.

Stacyville Election Results—The national election for the president had some interesting results in Stacyville. Voters did not always vote for the winner as the election results were reported in *The Monitor:*

Year	Candidate	Votes
1912	Wilson	157
	Roosevelt	34
	Taft	17
	Claflin	4 (prohibition candidate)
1916	Hughes	113
	Wilson	97
1924	LaFollette	380 (Progressive)
	Coolidge	76
1928	Hoover	21
	Smith	459 (1st Catholic candidate)
1936	Roosevelt	466
	Landon	55
1944	Dewey	249
	Roosevelt	234
1948	Truman	371
	Dewey	130
1952	Eisenhower	315
	Stevenson	222
1956	Eisenhower	270
	Stevenson	259

Early Schools—A school district was organized in 1856. The new log schoolhouse was dedicated "to education and religion" in January 1857. The Stacy brothers donated 25 acres of land adjoining the village for an academy. The academy was never built on the tract and the land reverted to the Stacys. It was donated to the Stacyville Independent School District. A public high school was built on the tract in 1869 (either a 9th or 10th grade school) at the cost of $4,000.

The Stacyville schoolhouse was typical of other schools of that time. There were two outhouses on the grounds and an outside pump providing water.

Early Catholic settlers worshiped in the public schoolhouse located 2 ½ miles north of Stacyville. By 1873, there were 27 Catholic families in and around Stacyville. They made plans to build a church. Work began on a 30′ x 46′, two-story frame structure in 1874. Every church member helped by hauling materials to the site; some donated money. The total cost to build the church was $2,000. A German speaking priest from North Worthington served the church from 1875-76. The next priest lived in the second story of the parochial school building. Ten years later in 1883, the Catholic parish comprised of 100 families.

At the cost of $32,000 a new brick church was built in 1905. It was a Gothic style and measured 62′ x 118′. The tower had a base of 18′ square and rose to a height of 140′.

The St. Mary's school was located in two wings on either side for the church. This school was called Visitation after the Visitation Parish. Some students entering first grade faced a big adjustment at the Visitation school. In these early years of the decade of the 1900s, English only was spoken at the school. For those students that only heard German at home, school was challenging. Older students at Visitation usually completed eight grades and then took an examination at the public school. If they passed, they were given a diploma at the fairgrounds in Osage.

The public school and the Catholic school were central to the lives of the residents through the early decades of the 20th century. In 1913, the Stacyville Independent School District voted to reestablish the two high school grades that had been dropped the previous year and added a 12th grade to the school.

The Opera House was packed for the first Visitation High School graduation in 1916 with five graduates: Albert Wolf, Benedict Faas, Anton Bawek, Anna Mayer, and Irmina Halbach. (Note the German surnames.) Albert Wolf ('16) had a job waiting for him and became the new assistant cashier at the German Savings Bank. The graduating class of 1917 had three graduates: Arthur Halbach, Robert Adams, and Rose Frein.

From *The Monitor* November 23, 1923:

> The dedication of the new parochial school for Visitation was held. The new 2 story building with "six light and airy" rooms on each floor was built at a cost of $45,000.

The first graduation for the new Visitation High School was in 1925.

That same year in 1925, the last Civil War veteran, Baltes Schaffer, was laid to rest in St. Mary's cemetery. He was born in Germany and came to America when he was seven years old.

Some highlights of the Visitation High School years:

1930 The Visitation football team played a game against Adams.

1932 Visitation girls had new school uniforms. They were "bright blue Indian heads with tan collars, cuffs, belts, and ties." It was reported that 24 girls in the uniforms were a "pretty sight."

1933 Five grads in the public high school—only two teachers.

1935 14 grads at Visitation High School.

1938 160 vaccinated for smallpox at Visitation. 17 graduates.

1940 Selective Service reinstated for men 21-35. 109 registered in Stacyville.

1941 Visitation 15 graduates.

1942 Visitation 12 graduates.

1943 Mr. and Mrs. Ray Giles with 5 sons and 2 daughters in "war services".

1945 Visitation enroll. 300, Public school 11 students, Methodist church sells.

1950 Public school closes.

1950 New Gymnasium at Visitation. 500 parishioners attend dedication.

1955 15 graduates.

1957 16 graduates.

1958 17 graduates.

1959 BB team lost to New Albin 60-59 semifinals of the District Tournament.

1960 Enrollment at high school-130 students.

1964 29 graduates.

1965 Became Marian High School the next year which became a central Catholic high school for parishes St. Peter's at New Haven, St Mels at McIntire, Sacred Heart at Meyer, St. Ansgar at St. Ansgar, and Visitation.

1966 39 graduates from New Marian High School.

1967 Fall—2nd place in the state in baseball tournament.

1968 26 graduates at Marian High School.

Closing—In March 1968, an announcement came from the Dubuque Diocese that the school would be closing after graduation in May. This came as a shock to the community. Protests by the students and parades to encourage support had no effect. There were 741 graduates from 1925-1968 from the Visitation-Marian High. The largest class was 36 in 1966 and 1968. The most numerous surnames of the graduates were: Pitzen-35, Adams-29, Blake-25, Brown-22, Koenings-20, Hemann-18, Halbach-16,

Weber-16, Mayer-15, Falk-12, Durban-11, Throhold-11, Wolf-11, and Hackenmiller-10. The last to receive a diploma from the Visitation-Marian High School was William Wold (alphabetically). In the fall of 1968, the remaining high school students were bused 12 miles west to St. Ansgar.

Visitation-Marian High School
Mitchell County, IA

#98

Weldon High School

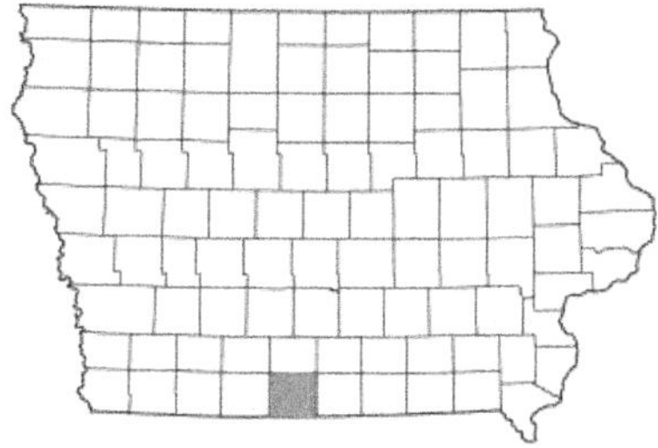

Mascot: Wildcats
Colors: Black and Orange
Closed: 1958
Location: North Decatur County

Early History—The founding of Weldon and the early settling of the area is not well documented. Weldon is located on the south edge of the Decatur-Clarke County line. Mormons traveled west from Nauvoo, Illinois, in 1846 and established an encampment at nearby Garden Grove (12 miles southeast of Weldon). There are still foundation remnants from those families who stayed at the Garden Grove area for at least a year before going west to join Brigham Young in Utah. There is no history that indicates the Mormons were in the Weldon part of Decatur County.

In the spring of 1880, the M.J. and N. Railroad was built through northern Decatur County. The rail-road built a station on 70 acres of land and platted the town of Weldon.

Weldon was known for its newspapers and lodges. The first newspaper, the *Weldon Witness* was issued on May 26, 1881. It was a weekly and published by Ed Burleigh for $1.00 per year. The paper byline was "Independent in all things. Neutral in Nothing. Devoted to the Interest of Weldon, Decatur and Clarke Counties." But this paper was short lived and was bought out by a man from Humeston in March 1883.

The next paper was the *Weldon Hornet*. It was first published by J.R. Critchfield on June 10, 1885. This was a five-column independent in politics and published weekly on Wednesdays for $1.50 per year.

Over the next 30 years there were a succession of newspapers—*The Hornet, The Expositor, The Weldon News, Weldon Bulletin*, and *The Weldon American.*

For a small town, Weldon had a preponderance of lodges: Grand Army of the Republic organized in 1883, Knights of Pythias, Good Templers, Woman's Christian Temperance Union, Royal Neighbors, and Order of the Eastern Star.

Early Schools—In the fall of 1881, Emma DeSelm taught a subscription school in the I.O.O.F. Hall. The next spring the children were sent to a country school located one mile south of town. The following spring, William Morrow was hired to teach in town. The expense of this school was aided by the township school funds. October 1, 1882, the town became an independent School District. Classes were held on the second floor of a business before a permanent school was built.

Notable Teachers—Superintendent Wayne Exley had a huge paddle with holes in it hanging on his office wall. It was occasionally used. Larry Siefkas ('58) shared, "No one gave him any lip. I never experienced the 'paddle' though I am sure I deserved it a time or two. He had a way of disciplining a student and a few minutes later you were his friend. He also was the girls basketball coach and history teacher. I didn't learn anything in history till I got to his class. He just had a way."

Pranks—It was midnight when the bombs were bursting in air. These were aerial bombs, or the kind of fireworks that explode high in the air without leaving any light. Larry Siefkas ('58) reminisced, "There were four of us who hung together, Elmer McCann, Don Hoffman, Jim Ellis, and me who would pool our money and go down to Missouri and buy Arie Bombs. They were pricey, maybe $4 or $5 each at that time. They came in a tube with nine loads in each one and shot off like a Roman candle. Each of us would go to the four corners of town about midnight and place the artillery. Using a cigarette for a slow fuse, we would rocket the town. We never got caught, but I think many people may have suspected who the culprits were." Larry continued, "One of those nights after getting our thrill, I headed home which was about five miles away on a country road. Suddenly, there were headlights following me. They got closer as I sped down the dusty road looking into the rearview mirror. As I pulled into our farm driveway, these headlights slowed down too, but they pulled into my uncle's drive across the road. It was my Uncle coming home from one of his stag poker parties. My heart was beating pretty fast, because I just knew it was the County Sheriff. I don't think we ever tried to bomb Weldon after that."

Sports—Football was not played at Weldon High School. The boys and girls each played basketball. The biggest rivals were Van Wert, Leroy, and Garden Grove. The Van Wert rivalry was so heated that a fight broke out on the basketball court that left future businessman and pharmacist, Elmer McCann with a shiner. The 1951 boys team had a perfect record. They won no games that year. Boys also played spring and fall baseball.

Yearbook—The yearbook was called *The Spotlight.*

Senior Trip—The seniors from the class of 1958 went to Rockaway Beach, Missouri. Table Rock Lake was being built and the spillway dam floodgates had not been closed yet, so there was no water backed up until later that year. Larry Siefkas ('58) recalled, "Mr. Exley and his wife Marie drove the station wagon that we rented and all five of our class headed for Missouri. That town of Rockaway Beach was hopping with kids from a five-state area acting like spring break at Ft. Lauderdale. Rockaway Beach was just a small little town there on Lake Taneycomo. There were dances and chasing girls was a big thing. We went to Marvel Cave which was the only thing there at which was soon to become Silver Dollar City. When Branson became a boom tourist town, Rockaway Beach started to dwindle in its popularity for senior trips."

Closing—As students started transferring to Leon and Osceola so they could take chemistry and science classes, the enrollment at Weldon declined. Weldon High School closed in May 1958. There were 422 graduates in the 66 years from 1893-1958. The largest class was 18 in 1910. The most numerous surnames of the graduates were: Smith-13, Mitchell-9, Kline-8, Wallace-8, Evan-7, Snider-7, Westfall-7, Coffey-6, and Marshall-6. The last graduate from Weldon High School was Larry Siefkas (alphabetically).

Weldon High School
Decatur County, IA

#99

Williams High School

Mascot: Tanager
Colors: Scarlet and Black
Closed: 1962
Location: Northeast Hamilton County

Early History—Western settlement into central Iowa expanded after the Civil War. The Homestead Act of 1862 encouraged settlers to come to the Midwest to buy land. In 1867, the Illinois Central Railway Company leased its right of way to the Dubuque and Sioux City Railroad, which was the name used in its early history. By 1868, the railroad was built through the present site of Williams. The next year it was completed as far west as Ft. Dodge. Eleven families came to the area that first year.

The promise of a railroad encouraged settlement. The Illinois Central Railroad came through this area as well in 1868. The town of Williams was laid out in the winter of 1868-69. It was named in honor of Major William Williams, who came from Pennsylvania to Iowa in 1850 with a party of immigrants. His group arrived with three companies of soldiers to establish a fort on the banks of the Des Moines River. Major Williams became the founder of the city of Ft. Dodge. John Blair, an official of the Illinois Central Railway, platted the town. An election was held to incorporate the town of Williams.

Disasters and Events—Fires were a regular occurrence in Williams which dramatically affected its growth and prosperity. The following are a few of those devastating fires and events in the town:

- February 1882—A fire starting in Pat Malloy's saloon ripped through town. In less than an hour, the entire west side of Main Street was in rubble. Only two buildings were saved.
- 1895—St. Mary's Catholic Church was destroyed by a violent windstorm.
- November 8, 1899—Fire stuck again. Starting in the post office, it was fanned by a strong northwest wind and temperatures of -36 degrees. The whole west block of Main Street was flattened.
- 1909 and 1910—There were fires in other buildings with a café and restaurant destroyed.
- 1915—William Jennings Bryan spoke to a crowd of 10,000 at a Chautauqua in Williams.
- 1916—William Jennings Bryan came to town again. This time he spoke to 500 at the Methodist Church.
- 1919—The Davis-Hughes Café and Hotel was engulfed by fire.
- 1924—The second Methodist Church, of brick construction and less than 20 years old, was destroyed by fire.

Early Schools—A country school was built in 1870 near Williams. By 1875, a one-room frame school was built. The first teacher was Mr. J.M. Blake who later became the county attorney. A two-story structure was built in 1881.

In 1891, the school board voted to establish a grade school and added an intermediate department in one of the rooms.

In 1893, the school board asked the question, "Shall we bond the district for money to build a new school?" At the election there were 68 votes cast in favor, and no dissenting votes. This new building was completed the next year at a cost of $7,500 of which $5,000 had been raised by the bond.

In this new building another department was added, a grammar department. A department in the school was added in 1902 when the assembly hall on the upper floor was partitioned, and a recitation room formed for the accommodation of the high school department. More teachers were added and the curriculum was expanded, including Latin.

The last part of the school building was added to the south in 1918. A progressive schoolboard interested in education is credited for the completion of the high school.

In the depths of the Great Depression with growing numbers of pupils and a demand for more room, a bond proposal for building a new auditorium and gymnasium was defeated. It was 18 years, until 1957, before a new gymnasium and auditorium was built. The first game was played in the gym in 1958 to a capacity crowd.

Yearbook—The yearbook was called *The Tanager*. The final yearbook in 1962 gave a pictorial history of the events of the country and world at the time. Some of those photos showed:

- Roger Maris (who had hit 61 home runs that October).
- the John F. Kennedy cabinet.
- the Redstone Rocket with Virgil Grissom in front.
- the Bel Air Section fire in Los Angeles.
- Mercury Capsule with John Glenn and Carpenter.
- the Twist.
- Alan Shepard dangling from his harness.
- the devastation from Hurricane Carla.

Sports—Williams did not have a football team. Boys and girls played basketball. Boys played baseball. The girls made it to the 1954 state tournament, losing in the first round to Tingley 54-52.

Don Williams ('53) shared, "I thought I was a fairly good player until I had to guard the legendary Gary Thompson from Roland. It was no contest, but what an experience and privilege to even be on the court with him."

The biggest rivals were Kamrar and Blairsburg. It was fate because of proximity, these three schools consolidated in 1962 to form the Northeast Hamilton School located in Blairsburg. The last *Tanager* yearbook for 1962 showed the boys with a basketball record of 6-13 and the girls with a record of 1-18. They played the following towns that year: Stratford, Alexander, Blairsburg, Randall, Jewell, Dows, Ellsworth, Stanhope, Alden, Franklin, and Goldfield.

Senior Trips—The 1953 seniors traveled to Des Moines for the day. The 1958 class went to Chicago by train leaving from Iowa Falls. They slept on the train going, spent the day sightseeing in Chicago, and boarded a late train home, all in the same day.

Teachers and Superintendent—Lyle Shelton was the superintendent from the early 1950s until the high school closed in 1962. Don Williams ('53) was elected to the school board in 1960 and remembered his first school board meeting, "We met in the home economics room that September evening. Mr. Shelton took one look at me and started laughing uncontrollably. He finally spoke and said, 'Williams, you are the last person I wanted to see again in this school after all the times you sat in my office as a student. And now you are my boss.'" Harmony was activated and Don Williams ('53) was on the school board when the high school closed in 1962.

Notable Graduate—Alan McCoy ('51) was a radio announcer for the Phoenix Suns and became known as the "Voice of the Phoenix Suns." For 47 years (through 2020) his patented "Shazam! Oh Brother! Wham Bam Slam, Wham O! Sing Go the Stings, Swish-o-roo-for-two!" has been enjoyed on the radio by millions of Phoenix Sun fans. He is a member of the Broadcasters Hall of Fame. He was inducted as the 15th member of the Phoenix Suns Ring of Honor and honored with the inclusion in Iowa Hall of Pride.

Killed in Action—Ten service men from Williams lost their lives in war. They were:

Edward J. Franklin, WWII
Wilbur C. Vey, WWII
Keith Ose, WWII
Joe L. Cady, Jr., WWII
Donald E. William, WWII
James I. Watt, WWII
Milo K. Shaner, WWII
Willard C. Akers, WWII
Paul Jacobson, WWII
Clair V. Keane, WWII
Donald Buntenbach, Korea

Closing—Several town votes were needed to close the high school. The arrangement was to form a new district called Northeast Hamilton with the high school located at Blairsburg. There were three bitter rivals; Kamrar, Williams, and Blairsburg united. The Williams community was quite upset at losing the high school but was assured that the junior high school would be in Williams. This continued until 1968 when the junior high was also moved to Blairsburg. Williams was the larger town and had a thriving business district. Williams had the newest gymnasium and facility, but the votes were determined based on the three uniting schools and Blairsburg was more centrally located of the three towns. In the first year of Northeast Hamilton district, there were over 700 students. For the next 53 years until 2015, the Northeast Hamilton district thrived. By this time, the enrollment had dropped below 200 for the K-12 school and it also closed to merge west with Webster City.

Williams High School
Hamilton County, IA

#100

Woodburn High School

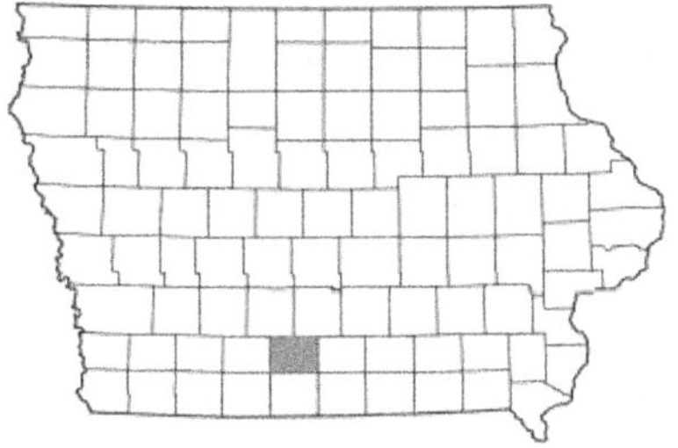

Mascot: Wolves/Wolverines
Colors: Red and White
Closed: 1958
Location: Clarke County

Early History—Clarke County was formed in January 1846. It was one of 12 counties established by legislative action in a comprehensive act by the territorial legislature. This was 11 months before Iowa became the 29th state admitted to the Union.

John Lewis, his wife, and their three children, were the first settlers in Jackson Township in 1850. They later had a total of ten children. The Lewis cemetery and Lewis school were the first in the township.

The 1856 census recorded a population of 232, 122 men and 110 women. They came from Indiana-72, Pennsylvania-28, Ohio-28, Iowa-42, Virginia-17, Illinois-14, Ireland-2, England-1, and Canada-1.

Travel to the area was by stagecoach for the first 20 years after the establishment of the county. At first, the stagecoach came three times a week. Eventually, daily stages from the east and west became regular. The stagecoach was replaced in 1867 when the Chicago, Burlington, and Quincy Railroad was built through Clarke County. The railroad followed the natural valley south of the village of Ottawa. At the fork of the Brush and Gooseberry Creeks, a depot was built. To feed the engines there were great piles of wood along the tracks which led to the naming of Woodburn. Grace Marquis penned another story for the name. There was a railroad shack alongside the track that was being built. A wood pile next to the building caught fire and the workers retreated saying, "Look at that wood burn." This was the only station in Jackson Township. The town was officially created when 22 lots were platted; the town of Woodburn was born.

The coal fields and mining in Lucas county, the adjacent county to the east, created speculation in 1876. A 4′ x 6′ shaft was dug within the city limits of Woodburn. When it reached the depth of 220 feet, water was hit and filled the shaft up to within 50′ of the top, and the hole was abandoned. This was considered a dry hole, and there was never any coal found in Jackson township.

Early Schools – The Woodburn Independent School began in two houses: one house for the older pupils and one house for the younger children. In 1879, the lower school was moved to Dr. Martin's house. In 1880, the west section of the schoolhouse was built for $3,000. There were two rooms, one up and one down. There were 70 students and one teacher in each room. Two additional rooms were added in 1897. This formed the middle school. In 1922, another room over the top of the primary room was added for the school to become a 12-year school.

The first graduation was held in 1901 with four graduates. The Osceola Orchestra played six numbers. Their selections were enjoyed, and the audience manifested their appreciation with liberal applause. Each student gave a 25-minute oration speech. Their titles were, "Washington Irving," "Modern Inventions," "Old stories Grandma Told," and "Three Immortals (Washington, Lincoln, and U.S. Grant)." The President of the school board, W.H. Duke, presented the first diploma from the school to the valedictorian, his son, Lloyd Duke.

Notable Teachers—John Agans was the superintendent from 1948-1952. His education was from Afton College, Highland Park College, and Parsons College. He taught math, science, and coached the girls basketball team. "Mr. Agans taught me in engineering. He was focused and determined to do the right thing," remembered Clare Keeney ('50). Gloria Marquis Steele ('50) added, "Mr. Agans was strict. He worked extra with the boys who needed it in math so they could graduate. At the time I was praised by him for helping the boys. He was the best teacher I ever had."

Horace Oliver ('24) started teaching at Woodburn in 1925. He became the principal from 1930-1936 and the superintendent for the next two years.

A tribute to Horace Oliver was written by Lynnette Davis for the community of Woodburn web page.

Who we consider to be the first chronicler of Woodburn history.

Horace never forgot his roots and regardless of where he lived, he came back to Woodburn often to visit family and to participate in the Woodburn High School Alumni banquets, and Woodburn Homecoming events, etc. It was his love for his hometown of Woodburn that prompted him to write two books, *Boy Life Along the Burlington*, and *Spring in Autumn, or the Hills of Home*, which were published in 1969 and 1972. Horace taught at a small rural school near Woodburn for one year, 1925-1926. He taught 7th and 8th grade in Woodburn from 1927-1929. He stopped teaching for two years and was hired as Woodburn's HS Principal for six years, 1930-1936. He was also superintendent at Shannon City, Runnells, and Saydel, also Assistant Polk County Superintendent of Schools for seven years . . . His former students were always special to him and he always looked forward to the opportunity to meet and visit with them. He will always be remembered as a strong supporter of Woodburn.

Great teachers can influence their students long after their years in the classroom. "Wilma Mackey was my great teacher when I was 12 years old. She assigned reading for us, including some of the great classics like *Invictus* and *Crossing the Bar*. I felt that if those guys could write like that, I would try writing something. Woodburn was my life at that point, and I was proud of the town, so I wrote about it," shared Clare Keeney ('50) 75 years later. This is his poem written at the age of 12.

WOODBURN, by Clare Keeney (1944)

Deep in the heart of the U. S. A.,
Far from the ocean wide,
In the fertile land of Iowa,
With hills on every side.
In that valley lies a town.
A town small and serene,
Its hills so gently sloping down,
Its creeks so clear and clean.
Its life so quiet yet full of fun,
Its citizens satisfied,

With room to think and climb and run,
Where the birds and beetles fly.
No other town would satisfy,
Nearly as well as ours.
No other town would catch our eye
As Woodburn and its flowers.
With the schoolhouse on the hill,
The wide green landscape looking on.
Flowers on the window sill,
All in our one little town.
Off we wander through the hills
Of Woodburn with its many scenes.
Through the many rocks and rills
And trees and grass and golden greens.
Many towns may win your heart,
Many towns may look so good,
But never one would ever start
To pass by Woodburn, It never could!
Let us live our life right here,
Never leave our little town.
No other town could ever be so dear
As Woodburn.

Sports—The county seat town, Osceola, was always the biggest rival, though they were not in Woodburn's conference for basketball. "I was a starter forward all four years in high school," said Gloria Marquis Steele ('50). "Coach Agans was a wonderful girls coach. We did not make it to the state tournament, but we were competitive. We played Lucas, Weldon, LeRoy, Garden Grove, Millerton, Van Wert, and Russell."

Glenn Mason ('39) wrote as a contribution for the *Woodburn, Iowa: Life in a Railroad Town* (1968), "Until my senior year ('38-'39), we played our home basketball games on a sand court on the south side of the school building. For out of town games, we rode in the trunk of Mr. Oliver's Chevrolet coupe in rain, snow, or whatever winter weather had to offer. That year we initiated our new gymnasium. To us it was like Veteran's Auditorium. It was made possible by a coordinated community effort led by Superintendent C.E. Nichols with all volunteer help."

A girls basketball uniform is remembered by Grace Boyles Peterson ('58), "In about 1949 or 1950 the old school color red and white girls basketball uniforms were looking rather old. Another school had ordered some green and white satin uniforms and didn't take them. So, Woodburn bought them. They were quite daring and had short skirts with shorts attached. The tops were bare midriff with round necklines, short sleeves, and button fronts. Everyone sewed the cut-outs in the shorts shut, because if you jumped, the pleated skirt sometimes flew up. When it was our chance to wear them, I was #32."

Woodburn Cheers—The basketball teams were encouraged by the cheerleaders and pep club. Some of the more interesting cheers were:

How do you like your beefsteak? Raw, Raw, Raw
How do you like your cabbage? Slaw, Slaw, Slaw
How do you like your sugar? Sweet, Sweet, Sweet
How do you like your opponent? Beat, Beat, Beat

Step on the starter, Push on the gas,
Here comes Woodburn,
Let them pass.

Strawberry shortcake, Raspberry pie,
V - I - C - T - O - R - Y
Are we in it? Well, I guess,
Woodburn High School, Yes! Yes! Yes!

Go back, go back, go back to the woods,
You haven't, you haven't, you haven't got the goods,
You haven't got the pep and you haven't got the jazz,
You haven't got the team that Woodburn has.

Rah Rah Hoop a Tater
Half past alligator
Ram Sham Monkey Sham
Chick a lick a dah
Woodburn High School, Rah Rah Rah!

Yearbooks—The first yearbook published was post war in 1948 titled, *Archer.* It was followed in 1950 and 1951 by *Archer II* and *Archer III.* In 1954 it became the *Echo,* 1955 *Archer,* 1957 *Memories,* and 1958 *Resume.*

Notable Graduates—Glenn Mason ('39) served four years in the Marines during World War II. He earned a B.A. from Simpson College and M.A. from Drake. Glenn taught school and was a school superintendent at Murray, Tabor, Fremont-Mills, Lowden, and Villisca. He coached the Lowden girls to the state tournament in golf in 1971. Following his retirement, he served for six years on the Chariton school board with three of them as the President. Glenn received the Double S Award from Simpson College for a sports scholarship and service to communities while he was at Simpson and through his years in education.

After graduating from Iowa State University with a degree in Electrical Engineering, Clare Keeney ('50) worked for Sylvania in Pennsylvania and California. He spent four years in the Navy on a destroyer in the Mediterranean and Caribbean in submarine patrol. Following the death of his mother when Clare was three, he was raised in Woodburn by his grandmother, Maude Davis, who started him in piano lessons. His father, Morris Keeney, had a master's from Drake in music but was unable to find a music job during the Depression. He sent Clare on Saturdays for piano lessons in the precollege student on-campus program at Drake University. Clare won the youth division piano contest in Des Moines Cavalcade of Music in 1951. He was considered a concert-level classical pianist. This ability made Clare the accompanist for music classes, ensembles, and he played popular songs for groups singing around the piano. He was a fourth generation from Clarke County and Woodburn on both sides of his family, Davis and Keeney.

Hot Lunch—The first hot lunch at the Woodburn schools was November 22, 1954. The first cook was Fern Boyles. Mary Lou Mason joined her in 1957. The first meals were 25 cents and the students had to bring their own table service. Lynnette Davis remembered, "School lunches were like home cooking. These cooks were loved by all of the students."

Bus Drivers—Don Wright ('49) started driving an old school bus when he was 17 years old. Clare Keeney ('50) laughed as he told, "Being a city kid (Woodburn), I often rode along with Don on the bus route because I wanted to see what the country was like." Gloria Marquis Steele ('50) commented, "Don Wright drove that old bus to away ballgames. Before that bus, we had to go in our parent's cars. When he graduated, the district got a new school bus in 1951."

Orville Gardner and his wife, Vera, and family moved from Van Wert to the Woodburn area in 1933. In 1935, he and his father opened Gardner and Son Grocery in Woodburn. They had a big egg and cream route to the neighboring farms and delivered groceries. Orville was a school bus driver until 1955. He was on the Woodburn school board and served as the board president.

Senior Trip—Fourteen seniors traveled to Kansas City for a one-day trip in 1950. "We toured the Ford assembly plant, Swope Park Zoo, and Kansas City Municipal Airport. We also drove through Mission Hills where all the rich people lived. On the way home, we stopped in Cameron, Missouri to roller skate. Getting home after midnight made for one jam packed, educational, fun, and memorable venture," Gloria Marquis Steele ('50) laughed. "A big deal was going to the drive-up Dairy Queen. Mr. Agans drove one of the cars. His niece, driving the other car, got sideswiped by a hit-and run driver in downtown Kansas City."

Killed in Action—The following Woodburn men were killed in action in service to the country. Lest they be forgotten:

Isaac Davis, WWI-France
Earnest Herndon, WWI-France
Herschel Allen Oehlert, WWII-Pacific

Fargust Earl Lamb, WWII-Philippines
Art Echund Jr., WWII-Belgium
Stanley Paul Carson, WWII-Germany
Jack Cooklin, WWII-Aircraft training

Pranks—An incident in 1942 left an indelible mark on a young grade school girl. "I was in the fifth-grade when one morning as we were walking into school, some senior boys led by Bob Oehlert ('43), were out on the sidewalk, cracking eggs, and swallowing them raw. I thought those boys were crazy!" recalled Gloria Marquis Steele ('50). The boys were never reprimanded and the mystery of which came first, the chicken, or the egg remains unsolved. But, for these boys it surely was the last raw eggs they would ever suck.

Closing—Woodburn High School closed in May 1958. There were 408 graduates in the 59 years from 1901-1958. The largest class was 15 in 1941. The most numerous surnames of the graduates were: Mason-19, Ewoldsen-10, Carson-8, Davenport-7, Heston-7, Johnson-7, Lowe-7, Marquis-7, and Wright-7. The last to receive a diploma from Woodburn High School was Lois Showers Keller (alphabetically).

In the fall of 1958, the high school students were bused to Osceola to attend the Clarke Community School.

Woodburn High School
Clarke County, IA

#101

Woolstock High School

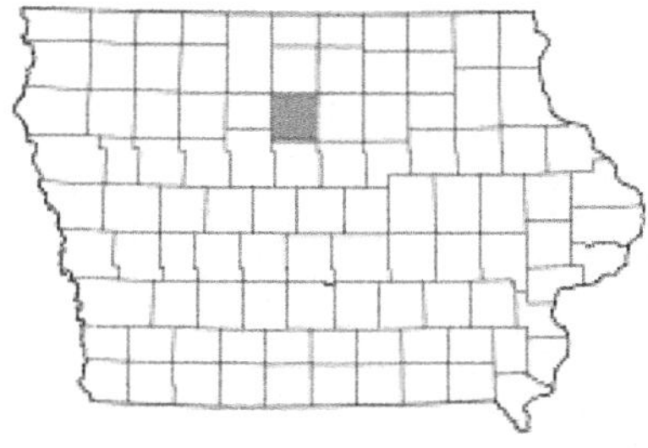

Mascot: Wolverines
Colors: Green and Gold
Closed: 1954
Location: Wright County

Early History—The first settlers near Woolstock located themselves on tracts of land along the river and streams in Troy Township in 1854. These settlers attempted to raise sheep. They traveled to the southwestern part of Woolstock Township near the old hamlet of "Wool Stock" on White Fox Creek. They met with traders who selected from the wool they brought with them to sell. Unfortunately, the wool trade was a failure due to the harsh winters and lack of prepared shelter for the herds. Many sheep died or were killed by wolves. The name Woolstock came from these early settlers and their sheep. Woolstock Township was settled by families with surnames of Perry, Boring, Brewer, McDaniels, Metz, Allen, Watterman, and a Frenchman, Louis Bernard. Sheep auctions were held in Woolstock.

More French immigrants arrived from the Alsace Lorraine area of France following the defeat of Napoleon III by the Germans in 1871. Because these provinces went back and forth between France and Germany, many settlers had both French and German sounding names such as: Becker, Bernard, Caquelin, Claude, Hanus, Hilpipre, Hisler, Krieger, Loux, Malaisie, Marchal, Schmidt, and Wolfe. They brought with them their language, traditional dress, and their Lutheran religion. In 1896, they built their own church in rural Woolstock. More families arrived from Alsace Lorraine following the two world wars. French speaking community members could be heard on the main streets into the 1920s.

Early Schools—Woolstock was platted in 1880 and incorporated in 1895. The first schoolhouse was located one-half mile north and one-half mile east of Woolstock. The school was under the jurisdiction of the township and known as Woolstock No. 9.

From the *Woolstock Freeman* on March 29, 1895, the following news item was printed:

> Necessary steps to incorporate the town of Woolstock are being taken. We will find it an advantage to improve our school as no doubt we can have an independent school and get what belongs to us to use in our own district.

In the early 1900s, the two frame buildings were replaced by a two-story brick building. It was known as the Woolstock Independent School. This schoolhouse had two large rooms on each floor.

Another school of significance was the rural school located on the Claude farm east of Woolstock and west of the French Church. O.H. Benson arrived in Rural Woolsock in 1898 and taught for three years. He then became the county superintendent of schools. He founded the 4-H organization in 1907. This little school was purchased by the Woolstock boys and girls 4-H clubs as their clubhouse. This was the first club in the state.

From the *Eagle Grove Eagle* on March 10, 1921:

> Woolstock School House Destroyed. Fire destroyed the Woolstock School building Wednesday morning. The blaze was difficult to locate and it was also found that the pump was frozen . . . All the children got out . . .

Following a successful bond vote in December 1921, a new school was built, and the first classes were held there in early 1923. By 1926, the school had a fully accredited four-year high school and a graduating class of seven students.

Sports—In 1926, the first year of the four-year high school, the boys had a good basketball team. After winning the sectional tournament, this team went onto the district tournament in Ida Grove. There were four teams in the tournament, and they played a round robin tournament and Woolstock lost. This was a new experience for the team. Some of the Woolstock girls traveled to Ida Grove on the train and others went with their parents in cars to cheer on the team.

The girls team of 1924 had three Grady sisters, Daisy ('26), Pansy ('27), and Rose. Daisy was in the first graduating class of 1926.

The Woolstock cheerleading calls were very interesting.

Rip, saw, rip saw!
Thunder, thunder, thunderation
Rip saw, bang!
We're the high school congregation
We belong to the Woolstock gang.
We create much consternation
Are we in it?
Woolstock high school is our station.
Well, I guess
Woolstock High School
Yes! Yes! Yes!

Activities—One year the Junior-Senior Banquet had a special French theme for the decorations, menu, and program. The menu included *Hors d'oeuvres, Fraises au sucre poudre', Pommes de terre a la francais, Chou froid, Pommes d'amour, Boeuf à la seusse, Pain a la francais, Salade de fruits, Glace au chocolat, avec petits-gâteaux*, and *Bonbons Moisette.*

The Talkateer society was organized in 1937 to aid students in public speaking and help obtain a band of unity between students and teachers.

The sophomores took their turns in initiating the freshman. The girls were requested to dress as tramps and the boys as sophisticated ladies. A crowd enjoyed the parade downtown, and the freshmen were treated with all-day suckers by Caquelin's Café.

Hot Lunch—Beginning in January of 1941, hot lunches were served at the school at a cost of four cents a day or 20 cents a week.

School Plays—The Senior class of 1928 presented the three-act play, "*Aaron Boggs, Freshman.*" The play was under the direction of Superintendent O.G. Thompson.

The Senior play in 1938, "*Look Me in the Eye*", was presented at the IOOF Hall. Admission was 30 cents for adults and 15 cents for students. The 1953 Senior class play was "Take your Medicine."

Enrollment—The school enrollment never reached large numbers. In 1941, there were 37 high school students. In 1952, there were 25, with twelve girls and thirteen boys enrolled.

Yearbook—Highlights of the yearbooks through the years showed:

- An orchestra picture in 1939-40 with 11 members under the direction of L.G. Sweitzer from Webster City.
- The Girls Glee Club in 1937-38 had 21 members.
- The Band in 1941-42 had 21 members.

The 1949-50 yearbook showed the basketball teams playing: Duncombe, Lehigh, Dows, Stanhope, Rowan, Williams, Popejoy, Alden, Stratford, and Blairsburg. The boys also played the Eldora Training School and won 55-54. The boys defeated Bradgate in the first game of the sectionals but lost to Des Moines Township in the second round of the sectionals.

Opponents during the last year of the school in 1954 were against Pilot Mound, Otho, Goodell, Sacred Heart, and Kamrar.

Student Recollections—Jenny Soop Letts told, "My mother, Doris Anita Doughten Soop ('26), was a graduate in the first class from Woolstock in 1926. She died when I was four years old on December 2, 1941, just five days before Pearl Harbor. I was raised by my grandmother who was the postmaster and had been appointed by President Wilson two months after he took office in 1913. She was always a Republican. I married Kenneth Letts ('54) who was in the last graduating class. I guess I spanned the entire years of the Woolstock High School years. I was a junior when the school closed so I finished at Eagle Grove."

Jenny Letts, continued, "Kenneth Letts ('54) drove the school bus his senior year because he was 18-years-old. He even drove it to away ball games. When I was in school, we had no band and no drivers education, but could we play girls basketball. We were not very tall, because with all of the French influence in Woolstock, we were called 'the little Frenchies'."

A notable early child in Woolstock was George Reeves. He was the child of Don and Helen Brewer. Don was a pharmacist with Reed and Brewer Drug Store. Helen had come from Galesburg, Illinois and met Don while in Pharmacy school. She was a child from a wealthy and prominent Galesburg family. She moved to Woolstock after her marriage to Don Brewer in August 1913, and after she became pregnant with George. She disliked Woolstock because of its small-town setting and her desire for more attention and fancy flare. After their divorce, Helen moved with young George to Pasadena, California. She never identified her son's true father or his whereabouts. George grew up to become the television Superman and played in movies such as *Gone With The Wind*.

Alumni Reunions—On August 2,1969, fifteen years after the closing of the high school, 225 graduates and guests were present for the Woolstock High School reunion honoring all the classes from 1926 through 1954. The reunion was held at the Community Hall. In addition to Iowa, guests came from Massachusetts, Florida, Washington D.C., Minnesota, Colorado, California, Montana, Nebraska, Illinois, and Missouri.

The next all-school reunion of the Woolstock High School alumni from the classes of 1926-1964 was held on August 3, 1974 at the Woolstock Community Hall. A total of 205 alumni and guests attended from Iowa, Minnesota, Illinois, Indiana, Missouri, Kansas, Virginia, and California. Special recognition was given to Bernadine Jones Knuckling ('26), the captain of the first class and the only class having all members making banquet reservations.

School Closing—The high school closed following graduation in May 1954. From 1926 through 1954 there were 250 graduates from Woolstock High School. The most numerous surnames of the graduates were: Claude-27, Schutt-11, and Parrish-10. The largest graduating classes were in 1933,

1934, 1939, 1945, and 1949 with 12 graduates in each of those years. The last to receive a diploma from Woolstock High School was Joan Williams (alphabetically).

Woolstock High School
Wright County, IA

#102

Yarmouth High School

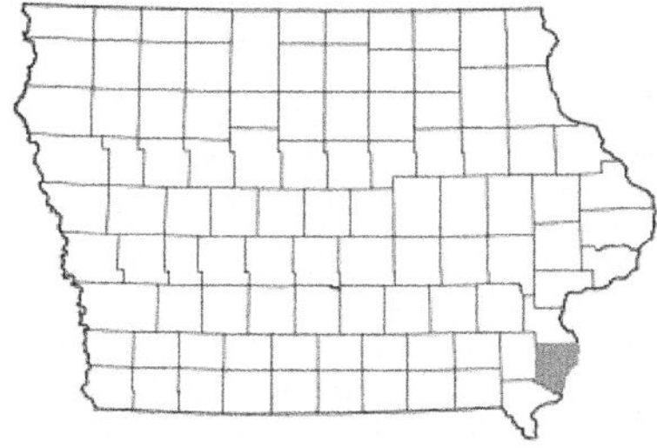

Mascot: Tigers
Colors: Purple and Gold
Closed: 1961
Location: Northwest Des Moines County

Early History—Washington Township is in the northwest corner of Des Moines County. It was settled last in the county which was farthest from the river town of Burlington. It had very few trees and no water. It was once part of Pleasant Grove Township when it was formed in 1841. With a petition from area settlers, a county judge established Washington Township in 1852. This township was the last to be settled in the county.

Some dates and events that were significant in the settlement of the area were:

- With the signing of the Black Hawk Treaty on June 1, 1833, people could move into six million acres in Iowa.
- Thirteen families ignored the law. Troops led by Jefferson Davis removed them and burned their cabins.
- Burlington was surveyed and platted in November 1833.
- Thomas Hedges was one of 46 men who acted swiftly and decisively to get a railroad land grant for Burlington. Land grants were passed to the states, then turned over to the railroads as each 20 miles of track were completed.
- In April 1870, the Burlington and Missouri River Railroad made a concerted effort to sell 300,000 acres and establish a population along the line for their proposed railroad, with track from Burlington west to Mt. Pleasant. Prominent ads read, "English, German, and Scandinavian Emigrants!" Average price of land was $2 an acre.
- Yarmouth was formed as one of the train stops at mile number 24.
- Thomas Hedges was an eastern railroad official who helped in naming the stops along the way. He had been raised in Yarmouth, Massachusetts. This may have been the reason for the name of Yarmouth. Another possible reason was because of his ancestry in England at Yarmouth on the Yare River.

A post office at the small village of La Vega (meaning flat land) was the first to establish in the township one mile east of Yarmouth. It was moved to Yarmouth on November 18, 1881.

Early Schools—The La Vega country school was one mile east of Yarmouth. The first classes in the one-room school were held in 1865. La Vega was one of nine country schools in Washington Township. The principal was Gerald Dillavou, and the primary teacher was Nellie Carlson. His school was called La Vega. It grew to include a few years of high school instruction. To receive a four-year high school diploma, students had to travel by train east to Burlington or west to Mt. Union.

In 1920, all the country schools were closed, and a large consolidated school was built in Yarmouth. This required hiring eight teachers and a superintendent. The La Vega school was moved to Yarmouth and remodeled as a house for the new superintendent. He was also asked to house as many of the single teachers as possible. The teachers boarded at restaurants or at homes for meal service.

When no deed was found for the new building, five directors bought the school from the landowner. These directors were Ray Redfern, Claude Oberman, Joe Tonkinson, Charley Brown, and Pearl Gabeline. They bought six lots in Yarmouth for the new school building. The new school was completed in 1922 with the first graduating class from Yarmouth High School in 1923.

In 1953, a $100,000 addition was completed for a new auditorium, gymnasium, expanded lunchroom, and locker rooms.

Activities and Events—The Yarmouth Café remained a fixture in town for over 77 years. It was opened in 1938 by Grace Coppes in the old bank building where her young son was able to sleep in the bank vault during business hours. In 1945, Grace moved the Café across the street to a building which had previously been a dance hall (pool hall) and then a tractor shop. Grace Anna Marie Kolbman was born in 1896 and died a few months before her 100th birthday. She married Forrest Coppes and they had five children that graduated from Yarmouth High School: Earl ('36), Laurel ('36), Milo ('39), Cecil ('42), and Leota ('48). Grace retired at the age of 80 in 1978. She was still putting in 12-hour days from 8:00 AM to 8:00 PM until she retired.

Christmas time in Yarmouth was clogged with traffic for miles. Tour buses idled in lines up to a half mile trying to get into town to view the extravaganza of Christmas lights. Once started as a friendly competition between two neighbors, the Christmas light display expanded from their front yards to line the whole town with the ingenious light show. Paul and Pauline Tonkinson and Don ('41) and Evelan ('41) Jarvis gave the town and Yarmouth a tourist attraction which lasted nearly 30 years until 1986. An unincorporated village with no stop lights, and only three stop signs leading onto the blacktop, was host to well over an estimated 100,000 out-of-town visitors who came to ogle at the Christmas light display. "We lived in town and often had out-of-town people knock at our door asking to use the bathroom. One time a carload of five knocked to see if we would drive them to Muscatine as their car had broken down. Being good town hosts, we drove these people, who we had never met, to their home," told Jane Irwin Crough ('57).

"I was teaching school in Mediapolis and trying to get home after work. From December 1 until the first of January it was like a traffic jam in Chicago. The Yarmouth locals had to take the round-about ways through the countryside to get home without having to be stalled in the lines of cars coming to see the lights." Jean Coppes laughed.

Notable Graduates—Darrell Kolkman ('57) became a career teacher but also had a hobby that brought international fame in the horse world. His specialty was hackney ponies. He raised, bred, and trained ponies and competed throughout the United States. People came from around the world to buy horses. Many came to train and observe Darrell's stable operations near New London, Iowa.

Major Watkins ('34) became the 'unofficial mayor' of the unincorporated village of Yarmouth. He married Hazel Wasson ('35). Together, they contributed to the enjoyment of parades in Illinois, Missouri, and throughout Iowa with their antique vehicles: two Model T's, a Model A, and a delivery truck. Major was another resident who lived to be a centurion. He died in the spring of 2020.

Yearbooks—The 1959 yearbook was called *Tiger Tales*. A picture shows 22 musicians in the band that year.

The final yearbook from Yarmouth High school in 1961 and was titled, *Echos in Time*. The yearbook was dedicated to the memory of Georgia May Tonkinson who would have been in the senior class that year. She had tragically been electrocuted on May 28, 1958. Her twin brother, Joe Paul Tonkinson ('61), was also a senior in the class of 1961.

Sports—There was a football team for a few years at the new high school. However, when Fred Brown ('26) broke his leg during a game, the sport was discontinued at Yarmouth High School.

The boys played basketball and baseball.

The most successful sport was girls basketball. The Yarmouth six-on-six teams made it to the state tournaments in 1946 and 1954. The '46 team lost in the second round to the eventual state champion, Coon Rapids, by 48-44. The '54 team lost in the first round to Farnhamville. The girls' teams often had boy cheerleaders. Some of the more renowned boy talents as cheerleaders were Jerry Talbott ('60), Fred Vantiger ('60), Larry Flarr ('60), and Don Fischer ('60).

The biggest sports rival was Sperry. The teams played in the Lemosa League (short for Lee, Des Moines, and Louisa Counties) against the Bears, Demons, Chieftains, Bulldogs/Bulletes, Tigers, Wildcats, and Bombardiers. Those mascots were for Danville, Denmark, Huron, Mediapolis, Morning Sun, Oakville, and Sperry, respectively.

The gymnasium was also used for a few years as the home court for the New London High School (10 miles southwest of Yarmouth) for their boys and girls basketball games.

The girls basketball team in 1958-59 had another great season. They won the Des Moines County Tournament by defeating Mediapolis, Mt. Union,

Denmark, and New London on their way to a 17-4 won-loss record for the year. The neighboring Danville High School team knocked them out of the sectional tournament. Other schools they played that year included Argyle, Morning Sun, Huron, Olds, Oakville, and Sperry.

Pranks—Play practice at nights at the high school provided not only time for the actors to work on their scripts, but also for a time of mischief. Richard Robb ('57) and Marvin Robertson ('57) thought it would be exciting to set off fireworks in the school during the Senior class play practice. "I was just a freshman but had a part in the play. During a time of quiet rehearsal came an explosion from the hallways. A lighted cherry bomb had been thrown into a boys' bathroom toilet. We were all shocked and when the two seniors came running out of the bathroom when the mystery of the explosion was exposed. The cherry bomb had blown the toilet apart at the floor level and water was flooding under the door and down the hall. These two seniors may have been older than me, but they were certainly not wiser!" extolled Anita Wilkerson Vantiger ('60).

Another incident involving a goat was remembered. This bleating caprine somehow made it to the rooftop of the high school. After some 65 years, there were various recollections of how it got there and, more importantly, how it got down. The most dramatic versions are that it jumped the three stories to the ground, while a less dangerous script is the goat jumping through a skylight to safety. No human help was identified.

Senior Trips—Going to New Orleans and Biloxi, Mississippi, by train were enjoyed by the seniors of 1958 and 1960. "We boarded the train in Burlington, and along the way through Illinois another senior class joined our train. In New Orleans we ate at the Court of Two Sisters. Some of us were shocked to see people sleeping in the doorways in the French Quarter. Of course, the boys' eyes were more drawn to the open doors of the businesses along Bourbon Street," recalled Anita Wilkerson Vantiger ('60).

The 1959 senior trip was to Washington D.C. and New York City by train. Arnold Crouch (59) keenly remembered, "We rode the elevator to the top of the Washington monument. Then we all took the steps down. In New York, the girls all bought makeup and some fancy clothing which was all-new to all of us back in Iowa."

Anita Wilkerson Vantiger ('60) shared, "On our trip to New Orleans and Biloxi, Mississippi, we were accompanied by the Superintendent Kenneth Grinstead and his wife. There were 18 in our class and most of us went on the trip. I remember some of the boys disappearing at night and heading back down to the French Quarter. They were so young and did not get into any trouble. We all had our eyes open while our tour bus drove us up the streets seeing the 'girlie shows' going on inside through the door openings and the windows. It was then onto Biloxi and the beaches and the motel shamrock shaped swimming pool. What a great educational time and memories with our classmates!"

Closing—The Yarmouth High School closed after graduation in 1961. In the 38 years from 1923-1961, there were 442 graduates from the school. The largest class was 19 seniors in 1933. The most numerous surnames of the graduates were: Brown-13, Oberman-13, Hollingsworth-13, Coppes-11, Gabeline-10, Redfern-9, Funk-8, and Wasson-7. The last to receive a diploma from Yarmouth High School was Karen Wallman (alphabetically).

In the fall of 1961, the students were bused to Mediapolis High School.

Yarmouth High School
Des Moines County, IA

Acknowledgments

Albion-Marshall Co.—Dorothy Thomas Keeler, Janell Walker, Merle Mann

Alleman-Polk Co.—Bonita Barr, Bill Haglund, Judy Bortz, Willard Lehman

Allerton-Wayne Co.—Lorena Blount, Richard Henderson, Clell Bryan

Alta Vista-Chickasaw Co.—Kristie Roether

Anthon-Woodbury Co.—Joanne Reimert

Arnolds Park-Dickinson—Verne Eckman, LaVonne Siemers, Allen Smith, Don Gregerson, Patricia Schumeman, Sharon Kay Wilson

Aurelia-Cherokee Co.—Sue Fett Johnson, Duane Kent, Sharon Stevenson, Bonnie Lewis, Lee Langlitz, Rod Hasenwinkel, Lynn Evans

Batavia-Jefferson Co.—Judy Major Dovico, Randy Major, Mary Dunne Campbell

Beaman-Grundy Co.—Pat Rueter, Sharon Ziesman, Richard Stewart, Barb Ream, Ann Miller, Leon Webb,

Beaver-Boone Co.—Larry Adams, Kim Paulsen Downs, Bob Powers, Harold McCombs, Don Paulsen

Benton-Ringgold Co.—Shirley Graham Klejch, Louise Groves Frost, Mary Gepner

Bonaparte-Van Buren—Roberta Genterman

Bussey-Marion Co.—Susan Bacon, Carolyn Decora, Orville Dunkin, Teddy Sprau, Sherill Peters Sprau

Casey-Guthrie Co.—Jeff Smith, Tom Cline, Collen Stolk, Kenneth Schmeling, Earl Joint, Judy Wedemeyer, Verdell Nelson, Joan Acker

Clearfield-Taylor Co.—Marketta Baker, Dick Stephens, Leann Baker, Carroll Baker, Jack Baker, Marvin Baker, Darrel Stephens, Doug Boyer

Clutier-Tama Co.—Dorothy Hayek, Delbert Caloud, Richard Wiebbeke, Dennis Hosek, George Hayek, Carol Vokoun, Jim Kupka, Marcia Kupka

College Springs-Page Co.—Gene Ripley, Elaine Christensen, John Christensen

Dayton-Webster Co.—Diane Epperson, Joe LeValley, John Skoglund, John Hambleton, Gordon Lundberg, Phyllis Kinsey, Lynn Schlief

DeSoto-Dallas Co.—James Riley, Betty Gustafson

Donnellson-Lee Co.—Roberta Krehbiel, Daryl Smith, Bob Leisy, Lillian Schweer, Donald Scheeer, Diane Kruse, Marge Wilhelm, Marty Miller,

Doon-Lyon Co.—Darrell VandeVegte, Carine Schroeder, Angie Keizer, Louie Kopsas

Dow City-Crawford Co.—Nancy Rosberg, Andi Sharp, Jeri Vogt, Linda McCutcheon

Earlville-Delaware Co.—Jim Clifton, Connie Clifton, Lucille Holtz, Eldon Sassen, Laurie Boies

Eldon-Wapello Co.—Bill Campbell

Emerson-Mills Co.—Kirk Hascall, Bud Ekins, Vivian Fleming, Mary Bolton

Everly-Clay Co.—Marilyn Meyer, Chela Rafdul, VerDon Schmidt, Nancy Patrick, Amy Byro

Farragut-Fremont Co.—Jeff McQueen, Penny Budenstein, Roger McQueen, Jan Wilson, Harold Dinsmore

Fertile-Worth Co.—Joyce Russell, Gwen Scott, Betty

Waddington, Viola Roberts, Harriet Winder

Floyd-Floyd Co.—Larry Stewart, Eleanor Mills Waid, Chuck Thorson, Judy Thorson

Fontanelle-Adair Co.—Deb Miller Gevock, Melissa Menefee

Fremont-Mahaska Co.—Jackie Perkins, Greg Perkins, Bill Ward

Frederika-Bremer Co.—LaDonna Bergmann, Helen Schumacher, Darlene Andrews, Mary Rewoldt

Galva-Ida Co.—Gary Wanberg, France Wanberg, Virdene Otto, Kathy Breyfogle, Randy Hustedt

Garnavillo-Clayton Co.—Jane Thein, Carolyn Koopman, Carol DeSotel, Marjorie Jensen, Sharon Stade

Garrison-Benton Co.—Dorothy Readnour, Steve Young, Dick Grimm, Elsie Grimm, Bruce Gardner, Zelda Sacket

Hansell-Franklin Co.—Ken Armstrong, Delores Benning, Ron Schult, Joann Young

Hawkeye-Fayette Co.—Shirley Gibbs, Dorothy McIntyre, Evelyn Schultz

Hedrick-Keokuk Co.—Harlan Millikin, Joyce Millikin, Mary Spears

Kalona-Washington Co.—Gary Kallous, Louise Kallous, Angela Hofer, Tom Hofer, Steve Reif, Larry Kern

Kimballton-Audobon Co.—Annette Anderson

Klemme-Hancock Co.—John Schwichtenberg, Kathy Olthoff, Luverne Schmidt, LaVern Velau, Rick Hartzell

Ladora-Iowa Co.—Ardillo Fay, Bernna Deane Hawkins, Lois Kovar, Vera York

Lakota-Kossuth Co.—Gwen Bierstedt Good, Sharon Price, Linda Nydegger, Bruce Meurer, Joyce Paulsen, Royce Janssen

Laurens-Pocahontas Co.—Connie Dallenbach, Leslie Stewart, Jerlynn Sruba, Kelly Tate, Mary Wright.

LeClaire-Scott Co.—Dick Wales, Marie Brand Spinsby, Ellen Miller

Lewis-Cass Co.—Roy Marshall, Robert Jobe, Lila Mudorf, Emily Jobe, Randall Breckenbaumer

Livermore-Humbolt Co.—Doris Gillespie, Nancy Kellner, Katie McKibban, Byron How, Paul McKibban, Ted Beach, Kenneth Underberg, Shirley Fox

Lohrville-Calhoun Co.—Jon Johnson, Ronald Brown, John Anderson, Tim Blair, Lois Irwin, Gene Kinney, Linda Gentry

Lorimar-Union Co.—Lee Decku, Wayne Tucker

Lost Nation-Clinton Co.—Pamela Crawford, Ron Semran, Enos Ihns, Nancy Dake, Jean Scott, Phyllis Carraher, Gary Mohl, Janet Burke, Nancy Hertner

Lovilia-Monroe Co.—Fred Kraber, Goldie Walter Kraber, Bill Barnes

Lucas-Lucas Co.— Becky Allen, Dan Allen, Roger Allen, Mike Gober, Janice Heston

Lynnville-Jasper Co.— Garnet Gertsma, David Gertsma, Ila Mae Sprouse, Wilbur Terpstra, Joan Eysink, Wanda Terpstra, Barbara Hoovegren

Macedonia-Pottowattamie—Kandis Cole, Donna Cole, Earnest Carley, Ruby Zey, Joan Scott, Melinda McCready, Bonnie Pilling, James Pope

Malcom-Poweshiek Co.—Denise Baustian, Rick Puls, Arlene Reimers, Lucy Lu Axmear, Jane Sherwood, Dick Puls, Norman Schroeder, Jane Schroeder, Nedra Goeke

Mallard-Palo Alto Co.— John Hartman, Jane Hartman, Peggy Kenyon, Judy Miller, Kenneth Lyon, Bev Goodchild,

Dorothy Lyon

Marathon-Buena Vista Co.—Darel Burns, Carol Schulz, Shirley Smith

Maurice-Sioux Co.—Don VanHorsier, Eilieen Wickers, Evelyn DeVries, Betty VanDerWiede

Mechanicsville-Cedar Co.— David Ferguson, Betty Emrich, Dorothy Hering, Janet Mahe, Meredith Dehmer

Melvin-Osceloa Co.—Fay Schmidt Schall, Phyllis Benz, Robert Benz, Julia Michelson

Merrill-Plymouth Co.— Margaret Marienau, Glenda Vanderloo, Laura Jane Hauff, Al Fagan, Maurice Blum, George Kale, Janice Bolte

Milo-Warren Co.—Carolyn Fellows, Ardel Keeney, Sharon Young, Henry Nutting, Frank Nutting, Carolyn Lundberg, Gene Lowe, Joe Kuhn, Carol Kaldenberg, Robert Lyle Davey, Betty Coffman

Moorhead-Monona Co.—Anita Moorhead, Nancy Hinkel

Morning Sun-Louisa Co.—David Wilson, Kathy Vance, Gerri Wole, Marvin Garland, Mary Zoeckler, Shirley Robb, Merry Robb, Beth Shenpolk

New Albin-Allamakee Co.— Ray Whalen, Jean Kurk, Delores Crowley , Earl Crowley, Ralph Nelson

New Hartford-Butler Co.— Jack Hovelson, John Brokay, Clyde Luck, Larry Bass, Lavern Holm, Kent Cuvelier, Audrey Schuman, Lorraine Hoffman

New Vienna-Dubuque Co.— Marian Klostermann, Henry Westhoff, Dave Krapfl, Larry Westhoff, Fred Westhoff, Kay Klostermann, Doris Langel, Inez Kluesner, Bernie Kluesner

Nichols-Muscatine—Don Smith, Ellen Oosendorp

Nodaway-Adams Co.— Pat Shipley, Maxine Forsythe, Chuck Bartz, Shirley Bartz, Christine Dunn, Paul Barker, Gloria Baldwin, Carolyn Dixon, Emma Jeanne Shipley

Ocheyedan-Osceola Co.—Barbara Solte Block, Connie Schuster, Shari Jacobsma, Pam Jacobsma, Betty Hembt Taylor, Margaret Dau

Okoboji-Dickinson Co.— Orv Taylor, Betty Taylor

Olin-Jones Co.—Richard McAtee, Deloris Wood, Gene McAtee, Gale VonBehren, Jim Ballou, Lana Ballou, Mike Hansen

Olds-Henry Co.— Louise Unkrich, Pat Woepking, Glenda Boal Alvine, Malcom Alvine, John Wickham, Jane Lindeen Wickham

Orange-Black Hawk Co.—Merlyn Harbaugh, Soo Grieman

Palo-Linn Co.— Eloise Beatty Dennis, Bill Zeller

Paton-Greene Co.— Judy Wilson, Dave Cunningham, Kyle Niles, Becki Drayer

Pisgah-Harrison Co.—Joyce Hall, Larry Green, Wes Hall, Bob Hall, Linda Herman, Larry Ramsey

Prescott-Adams Co.— Blake Cooper, Randy Cooper, Bill Birt, Roaslie Phillips

Quasqueton-Buchannan Co.—Jack Sanford, Connie Love, Harv Chesmore, Nedra Manson Chesmore, Richard Scott, Donita Kress Scott

Ridgeway-Winneshiek Co.—Roger Bergan, Rosemary Vapava, Maynard Hovden

Ringsted-Emmet Co.— Robin Hansen, Mark Larsen, Norman Rasmussen, David Solberg, Irma Ostedgaard, Sylvia Hansen, Jane Christensen , Lowell Christensen, Julia Laidig, Connie Wilson

Roland-Story Co.— Bob Higgins, Paul Twedt, Harry Amenson,

Paula Sampson, Ralph Johnson, Harris Twedt, Martha Bakke, Rosemary Hennissy, Gary Thompson

Rudolphinum-Howard Co.—Eileen Tlusty, Steve Klimesh

Templeton-Carroll Co.— Rhonda Schwaller, Elaine Schwaller, Rose Mary Greteman, Judy Balk, Karen Blaha, David Kerkhoff, Duane Bueltel, Carrol Schoeppner, Wayne Reiman, David Friedman

Sabula-Jackson Co.—Dan Miller, Dick Haynes, Judith Bowling, Wayne Johnson, Bill Johnson

Sac City-Sac Co.— Lance Wilhelm, Frank Richardson, Russ Hass, Marvin Janssen, Duane Fort, George Glass, Shirley Kilsmiller, Mary Lyman

Sandhorn-O'Brien Co.— Chuck Comstock, Tammy Ginger, John Haack, Merne Haack, Ray Hubegtse, Alvina Reitsma, Harriet VanVeldhuizer, Evelyn Kroese, John VanderHaag, Mary Loafman

Shelby-Shelby Co.—Pat Honeywell, Nancy Collins

Shueyville-Johnson Co.—Katherine Birky, Marvin Prachar, Margaret Probasco

St. Charles-Madison Co.—Dale Beaman, Kathy Beaman, Kim Downs, Ed Downs, Doris Downs, Jan Downs, Larry Downs, Steve Downs, Karen Winkelmann

Thompson-Winnebago Co.—Fairy Ann Florence, Mary Kuril Green

Troy-Davis Co.— Pat Howk, Felicia Campbell, Shirley Porter, Larry Bollman, Sue Spilman, TerriJo Weideman

Udell-Appanose Co.— Barbara Bare, Kathy Cridlebaugh, Kathryn Batterson, Loren Walker

Union-Hardin Co.—Toni Kinney, Candy Wait, Mary Rogers

Ventura-Cerro Gordo Co.—Becky Ziesmer, David Ziesmer, Danny Miller, Larry Costello, Arnold Pueggel, Nancy Watson, Kathy Pueggel

Villisca-Montgomery Co.—Carol Greenfield, Delbert Schroeder, Marie Weddle, Linda Weinstein, Martha Herzberg

Visitation-Mitchell Co.—Mary Hanke, Mary Blake

Weldon-Decatur Co.— Mary Jane Lillibridge, Bob Bixby, Larry Siefkas

Williams-Hamilton Co.—Don Williams, Joan Williams, Charlotte Brim, Viora Welch, Jeanette Ratzke, Wayne Tapper

Woodburn-Clarke Co.—Grace Peterson, Bonnie Mason, Gloria Steele, Lynette Davis

Woolstock-Wright Co.—Ginevra Soop Letts, Veronica Guyader

Yarmouth-Des Moines Co.—Jane Couch, Mike Miltenberger, Ronald Fortune, Anita Vantiger, Jean Coppes

About the Author

James Kenyon was born and raised on a third generation family grain and livestock farm. He grew up caring for cattle, pigs, chickens, and horses near the small town of Bogue, Kansas, population 300. His roots make him a natural candidate for recording the histories of small-town schools and stories from the past decades of these communities. From his grandfather, John Gibbins, who was the superintendent of four high schools in Kansas and a college professor, to his three aunts and two sisters who were teachers, James was raised in a community that valued education. His mother, Anita Kenyon, was a school nurse for twenty years. James grew up in an era when the whole town was involved in raising a child. He was taught by aunts and neighbors throughout his school years. There were six students in his high school graduating class. He was taught trigonometry by Mrs. Fischel during her planning period and study hall, as she knew that he would need it for college.

James was a veterinarian for thirty-five years in a mixed animal practice in a beautiful Iowa college town. Through his mentoring, eighteen student workers went on to become veterinarians. He is a seven-time veterinarian for the Alaska Iditarod Dog Sled Race, was named Iowa Veterinarian of the Year, and was the state president of the Iowa Veterinary Medical Association, as well as the chairman of the Iowa Veterinary Medical Examining Board.

Today, James continues the family tradition of community involvement with twenty-four years of service on his local school board. This made him the fourth generation (spanning three different centuries) of his family to serve as a school board member. He credits the importance of team work and leadership learned in school as having guided him through his adult years.

His wife, an education doctorate, is a retired secondary level and college teacher. His oldest daughter is an elementary school counselor; her husband a judge. His second daughter is a veterinarian; her husband an architect and commercial real estate broker. His son and daughter-in-law are graphic designers.

James has six grandchildren.

www.jamesrkenyon.com

hi@jamesrkenyon.com

Index

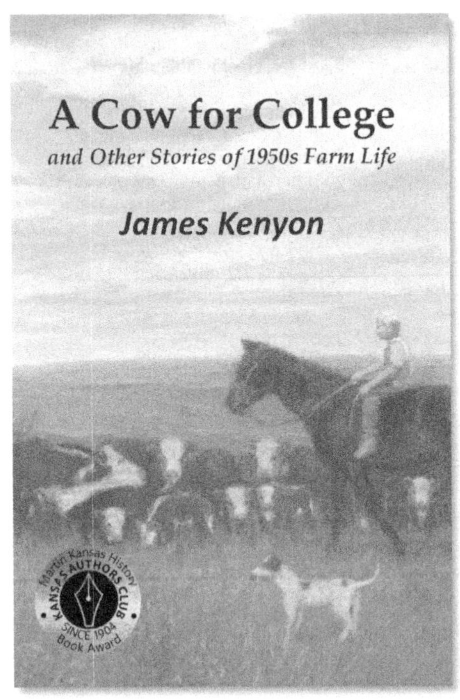

Winner of the 2018 Martin History Book Award

A Cow for College, and Other Stories of 1950s Farm Life

By James Kenyon

- **Paperback:** 166 pages
- **Publisher:** Meadowlark (September 2017)
- **Language:** English
- **ISBN-13:** 978-0996680141

James Kenyon, a born storyteller, writes an account of growing up in 1950s rural America that will make a reader laugh, smile, and occasionally shed a tear. As a young farm boy raised on the high plans of western Kansas, James shares memories of learning to care for cattle, ride (and fall from) the family horse, nurse a piglet back to health, and drive a tractor. Whether selling eggs from the back of his red wagon to the women in the nearest town of Bogue (population approximately 300) or saving the family cow from death by bloat, readers will enjoy these glimpses of a farm boy's life, a look back on simpler a time in America, post-depression, post-war.

"James Kenyon's vivid description of 1950s farm life is the perfect tonic for those craving a connection to old-time rural culture. Farm chores are told in such detail that the reader will feel like they are working alongside young Jimmy as he milks the cows by hand, cleans the chicken house, or weeds the garden with his puppy by his side. We're invited to experience the death of a favorite horse as well as the excitement of this author's first kiss. Reality will bring laughs and tender moments as you work your way through this portrayal of a life well lived."

Marci Penner, Executive Director, Kansas Sampler Foundation, and author of the *Kansas Guidebook for Explorers* and *8 Wonders of Kansas Guidebook*

Copies of this book may be ordered from the Meadowlark Bookstore online:

https://meadowlark-books.square.site/ ***or***

Mail this form with check to:

Meadowlark Press, LLC Phone: 620-794-9320

P.O. Box 333 Email: info@meadowlark-books.com

Emporia, KS 66801 **Please contact us for bulk orders or discount pricing for resale.*

Please send me _____ copies of *Echoes in the Hallways* @ $25.00/book = ____________

Please send me _____ copies of *A Cow for College* @ $15.00/book

or @ $10.00/book when ordered with *Echoes in the Hallway* = ____________

Total Ordered = __________ **Total Cost = $**____________

Checks Payable to: ***Meadowlark Books*** ***+ $5.00 shipping***

Total Enclosed = $____________

Deliver to: ___________________________________ ***(name)***

___________________________________ ***(address)***

___________________________________ ***(city, state, zip)***

Phone: __________________________ ***Email:*** __________________________

Made in the USA
Monee, IL
12 April 2021